Imitation and Social Learning in Robots, Humans and Animals

Mechanisms of imitation and social matching play a fundamental role in development, communication, interaction, learning and culture. Their investigation in different agents (animals, humans and robots) has significantly influenced our understanding of the nature and origins of social intelligence. Whilst such issues have traditionally been studied in areas such as psychology, biology and ethology, it has become increasingly recognized that a 'constructive approach' towards imitation and social learning via the synthesis of artificial agents can provide important insights into mechanisms and create artifacts that can be instructed and taught by imitation, demonstration and social interaction rather than by explicit programming. This book studies increasingly sophisticated models and mechanisms of social matching behaviour and marks an important step towards the development of an interdisciplinary research field, consolidating and providing a valuable reference for the increasing number of researchers in the field of imitation and social learning in robots, humans and animals.

CHRYSTOPHER L. NEHANIV is Research Professor of Mathematical and Evolutionary Computer Sciences in the School of Computer Science at the University of Hertfordshire, where he works with the Adaptive Systems, Algorithms and BioComputation Research Groups. He is the Director of the UK EPSRC Network on Evolvability in Biological and Software Systems and an Associate Editor of *BioSystems: Journal of Biological and Information Processing Sciences* and *Interaction Studies: Social Behaviour and Communication in Biological and Artificial Systems*.

KERSTIN DAUTENHAHN is Research Professor of Artificial Intelligence in the School of Computer Science at the University of Hertfordshire, where she is a coordinator of the Adaptive Systems Research Group. Her research interests include social learning, human–robot interaction, social robotics, narrative and robotic-assisted therapy for children with autism. She is the Editor-in-Chief of *Interaction Studies: Social Behaviour and Communication in Biological and Artificial Systems* and the general chair of the IEEE International Symposium on Robot and Human Interactive Communication (RO-MAN 2006).

Imitation and Social Learning in Robots, Humans and Animals

Behavioural, Social and Communicative Dimensions

Edited by

Chrystopher L. Nehaniv and Kerstin Dautenhahn

CAMBRIDGE
UNIVERSITY PRESS

CAMBRIDGE UNIVERSITY PRESS
Cambridge, New York, Melbourne, Madrid, Cape Town, Singapore, São Paulo

Cambridge University Press
The Edinburgh Building, Cambridge CB2 8RU, UK

Published in the United States of America by Cambridge University Press, New York

www.cambridge.org
Information on this title: www.cambridge.org/9780521845113

© Cambridge University Press 2007

First published 2007

Printed in the United Kingdom at the University Press, Cambridge

A catalogue record for this publication is available from the British Library

Library of Congress cataloguing in publication data
Imitation and social learning in robots, humans and animals: behavioural, social and
communicative dimensions / edited by Chrystopher L. Nehaniv and Kerstin Dautenhahn.
    p.   cm.
Includes bibliographical references and index.
ISBN-13: 978-0-521-84511-3 (hardback)
1. Robotics.   2. Robots – Control systems.   I. Nehaniv, Chrystopher L., 1963–.
II. Dautenhahn, Kerstin.
TJ211.I38   2006
629.8′92 – dc22
2206023587

ISBN 978-0-521-84511-3 hardback

To our parents,
Chrystyna, Bohdan, Annelie and Claus-Peter

Contents

Contents

Plates

Between pages 332 and 333.

1. **Figure 20.1** Curious keas (*Nestor notabilis*) in Mt Cook National Park, New Zealand.
   (Photos by D. Werdenich and B. Voelkl)
2. **Figure 21.1** Leaf mimicry.
   a. Australian Leaf-wing butterfly, *Dolleschallia bisaltide*;
   b. Cockatoo waspfish, *Ablabys taenianotus*;
   c. Juvenile round batfish, *Platax orbicularis*;
   d. Broadclub cuttlefish, *Sepia latimanus*, 'impersonating' dead mangrove leaf;
   e. Same individual in resting colour pattern.
   (Photos by M. Norman)
3. **Figure 21.2** Camouflage and deceptive resemblance in cephalopods.
   a. *Octopus* sp. 5 (Norman, 2000) active in rock pools;
   b. Same individual moments later in camouflage;
   c. Hairy octopus (*Octopus* sp. 16 (Norman, 2000)) showing branching skin sculpture;
   d. Snail mimic octopus (*Octopus* sp. 6 (Gosliner *et al.*, 1996));
   e. Giant cuttlefish, *Sepia apama* – sneaker male (centre) impersonating female amongst breeding pair (male on right)
   (Photos a, b & e by M. Norman; c by Becca Saunders and d by M. Severns)
4. **Figure 21.3** Mimic octopus (*Octopus* sp. 19 (Norman, 2000)) and models.
   a. Sentinel state in mouth of burrow;
   b. Normal foraging colour pattern;
   c. Flatfish mimicry;
   d. Flatfish model, banded sole (*Zebrias* sp.);
   e. Lionfish mimicry;
   f. Lionfish model (*Pterois* sp.);

x

Figures

Tables

Contributors

ARIS ALISSANDRAKIS University of Hertfordshire, Adaptive Systems Research Group, UK

CHRISTOPHER ATKESON ATR Computational Neuroscience Laboratories, Department of Humanoid Robotics and Computational Neuroscience, Kyoto, Japan and Carnegie Mellon University, Robotics Institute, Pittsburgh, USA

TONY BELPAEME University of Plymouth, School of Computing, Communications and Electronics, UK

DARRIN BENTIVEGNA ATR Computational Neuroscience Laboratories, Department of Humanoid Robotics and Computational Neuroscience, Kyoto, Japan and Computational Brain Project, ICORP, Japan Science and Technology Agency, Kyoto, Japan

AUDE BILLARD Swiss Federal Institute of Technology Lausanne (EPFL), Autonomous Systems Lab, Switzerland

GEOFFREY BIRD Department of Psychology and Institute of Cognitive Neuroscience, University College London, UK

JOSEP CALL Max Planck Institute for Evolutionary Anthropology, Leipzig, Germany

SYLVAIN CALINON Swiss Federal Institute of Technology Lausanne (EPFL), Autonomous Systems Lab, Switzerland

MALINDA CARPENTER Max Planck Institute for Evolutionary Anthropology, Leipzig, Germany

GORDON CHENG ATR Computational Neuroscience Laboratories, Department of Humanoid Robotics and Computational Neuroscience, Kyoto, Japan and Computational Brain Project, ICORP, Japan Science and Technology Agency, Kyoto, Japan

KERSTIN DAUTENHAHN University of Hertfordshire, Adaptive Systems Research Group, UK

BART DE BOER Rijksuniversiteit Groningen, Kunstmatige Intelligentie, the Netherlands

YIANNIS DEMIRIS Imperial College London, Department of Electrical and Electronic Engineering, UK

CECILIA HEYES Department of Psychology and Institute of Cognitive Neuroscience, University College London, UK

LUDWIG HUBER University of Vienna, Institute of Zoology, Austria

MARCO IACOBONI University of California, Department of Psychiatry and Biobehavioral Sciences, Neuropsychiatric Institute and Brain Research Institute, UK

HIROYUKI IIZUKA University of Tokyo, Department of General Systems Sciences, Japan

TAKASHI IKEGAMI University of Tokyo, Department of General Systems Sciences, Japan

BART JANSEN Vrije Universiteit Brussel (VUB), Artificial Intelligence Lab, Belgiam

MATTHEW JOHNSON Imperial College London, Department of Electrical and Electronic Engineering, UK

CHRISTINA KAOURI University of Hertfordshire, Adaptive Systems Research Group, UK

FRÉDÉRIC KAPLAN Sony Computer Science Laboratory, Paris, France

JONAS KAPLAN University of California, FPR-UCLA Center for Culture, Brain and Development, Department of Psychology, USA

MAJA J. MATARIĆ University of Southern California, Computer Science Department, USA

ANDREW N. MELTZOFF University of Washington, Institute for Learning and Brain Sciences, Seattle, USA

ROBERT W. MITCHELL Eastern Kentucky University, Department of Psychology, USA

JACQUELINE NADEL CNRS, Group Development and Psychopathology, France

CHRYSTOPHER L. NEHANIV University of Hertfordshire, Adaptive Systems and Algorithms Research Groups, UK

MONICA N. NICOLESCU University of Nevada, Department of Computer Science and Engineering, USA

MARK NIELSEN University of Queensland, School of Psychology, Early Cognitive Development Unit, Australia

MARK D. NORMAN Museum Victoria, Department of Marine Invertebrates, Australia

PIERRE-YVES OUDEYER Sony Computer Science Laboratory, Paris

IRENE M. PEPPERBERG MIT School of Architecture and Planning and Brandeis University, Department of Psychology, USA

RAJESH P. N. RAO University of Washington, Department of Computer Science and Engineering, USA

ARNAUD REVEL CNRS, Group ETIS, France

DIANE V. SHERMAN New-Found Therapies, Inc., USA

AARON P. SHON University of Washington, Department of Computer Science and Engineering, USA

VIRGINIA SLAUGHTER University of Queensland, School of Psychology, Early Cognitive Development Unit, Australia

TOM TREGENZA University of Exeter, School of Biosciences, Centre for Ecology & Conservation, UK

JUSTIN H. G. WILLIAMS University of Aberdeen Medical School, Department of Child Health, UK

STEPHEN WILSON University of California, Department of Psychiatry and Biobehavioral Sciences, Brain Research Institute, USA

SARAH N. WOODS University of Hertfordshire, Adaptive Systems Research Group, UK

Introduction: the constructive interdisciplinary viewpoint for understanding mechanisms and models of imitation and social learning

Chrystopher L. Nehaniv and Kerstin Dautenhahn

1   Introduction

Social learning, matched behaviour and imitation are important classes of mechanisms whereby knowledge may be transferred between agents (biological, computational or robotic autonomous systems). They comprise key mechanisms necessary for the evolution and development of social intelligence and culture. Researchers from across disciplines have begun coming together to understand these mechanisms with ever more sophisticated models.

While the importance of Social Learning has grown increasingly apparent to psychologists, ethologists, philosophers, linguists, cognitive scientists and computer scientists, biologists, anthropologists and roboticists, the workers in the field are often unaware of relevant research by others in other disciplines. Social learning has lacked a rigorous foundation and only very few major interdisciplinary publications have been available on the subject for researchers in artificial intelligence or psychology interested in realizations of the mechanisms they study. By bringing social learning techniques into computer and robotic systems, the door is being opened for numerous applications that will allow the acquisition of skills, programs and behaviours automatically by observation in human–computer interfaces (e.g. Lieberman, 2001), human–robot interaction important in service robotics and other applications where robot assistants or companions need to learn from humans, and industrial applications such as automated factory floors in which new robots can acquire skills by observing the behaviour of other robots or humans. Models from psychology and biology are being validated and extended

Imitation and Social Learning in Robots, Humans and Animals, ed. Chrystopher L. Nehaniv and Kerstin Dautenhahn. Published by Cambridge University Press.

as scientists from these fields interact with collaborators from sciences of the artificial, while the latter benefit from the insight of their colleagues in the natural and social sciences in the harnessing of social learning in constructed systems.

Increasingly, it has been recognized that such a constructive approach towards imitation and social learning via the synthesis of artificial agents (in software or robots) can (a) yield important insights into mechanisms that can inform biologists and psychologists by fleshing out theory, as well as (b) help in the creation of artifacts that can be instructed and taught by imitation, demonstration and social interaction rather than by explicit programming.

2   Models and mechanisms: a constructivist viewpoint

Rather than develop approaches to imitation and social learning that are discipline-specific, we seek to understand the possible mechanisms that could generate them, independent of whether they may be realized in robots, humans or other animals. Models and proposed mechanisms that result in matching behaviour and social learning are thus the major focus of this book. By unifying the discussion, deep and sometimes abstract theories from psychology, ethology and neuroscience take their place in and are viewed from a *constructivist* perspective.

The constructive perspective must be adopted explicitly in the work of authors from robotics and computer science, while psychologists and experts in the behaviour and biology of animals are primarily concerned with whether the particular mechanisms and models they propose reflect the reality within the organisms they study. Neuroscience, by examining the neural basis realizing particular capacities, bridges the two.

There are benefits to be reaped by extending the constructive viewpoint to all aspects within the field of social learning and imitation, and many more from the resulting questions that generally require an inter-disciplinary approach for answers. Immediately a constructive approach leads one to ask:

Could an explanation proposed in a theory of imitation actually be validated by building an artifact that exhibits the behaviour the theory is supposed to address? Is the theory or model explicit and detailed enough for one to build artificial systems as instances embodying it? Are there multiple, non-equivalent ways to build realizations of the mechanims? Are there any gaps in the theory revealed by attempts at the explicit construction of models?

On the other hand, does a given constructive model constitute a full realization of a proposed explanation, or is it limited in scope, validating only a portion of the theory? Is the constructed artifact realizing a mechanism thought to occur in animals, or does it instead provide an alternative method to realize a given social learning or imitative phenomenon that may be used in applications of artificial intelligence in engineering and technology for their own sake? Is the construction scalable, and to what extent is this limited essentially or only due to the limitations of the current materials available (generally silicon and steel, and unlike biological brians, currently running at best only with limited concurrency of components)? Are the predictions of theory confirmed in a constructed model? Does the model lead to predictions about the behaviour of organisms?

3   The book

In psychology, biology, ethology and other areas, the study of social learning and imitation in humans and other animals is a very lively and growing area of research which has resulted over the past few years in a number of important books, two of which are published by Cambridge University Press within the series Cambridge Studies in Cognitive and Perceptual Development:

- Cecilia M. Heyes and Bennett G. Galef, Jr, eds., *Social Learning in Animals: The Roots of Culture*, Academic Press, 1996.
- Jacqueline Nadel and George Butterworth, eds., *Imitation in Infancy*, Cambridge University Press, 1999.
- Kerstin Dautenhahn and Chrystopher L. Nehaniv, eds., *Imitation in Animals and Artifacts*, MIT Press, 2002.
- Andrew N. Meltzoff and Wolfgang Prinz, eds., *The Imitative Mind*, Cambridge University Press, 2002.
- Susan Hurley and Nick Chater, eds., *Perspectives on Imitation: From Neuroscience to Social Science* (2 volumes), MIT Press, 2005.

In addition, a number of relevant special journal issues have been published, e.g.:

- C. L. Nehaniv and K. Dautenhahn, guest editors, Imitation in natural and artificial systems, special issue of *Cybernetics and Systems*, **32(1–2)**, 2001.
- A. Billard and R. Siegwart, guest editors, Robot learning from demonstration, special issue of *Robotics and Autonomous Systems*, **47(2–3)**, 2004.
- B. G. Galef, Jr and C. M. Heyes, guest editors, Social learning and imitation, special issue of *Learning and Behavior*, **32(1)**, 2004.

Imitation in Animals and Artifacts (Dautenhahn and Nehaniv, 2002) was the first book to bring together research in biology and psychology with research in computer science and robotics on the particular topics of imitation and social learning, whereby many chapters discuss definitions of imitation and social learning, and study which species of animals imitate and in what way. The robotics/artificial intelligence chapters in this previous publication, although mostly biologically inspired, are similarly focused on particular research questions relevant to the domain of robotics and artificial intelligence. While this had helped set the groundwork for an interdisciplinary dialogue, the present volume, *Imitation and Social Learning in Robots, Humans and Animals: Behavioural, Social, and Communicative Dimensions*, reaches beyond single disciplines and reflects the emergence of numerous genuine cross-disciplinary collaborations between psychologists and biologists working together with roboticists and computer scientists. This new development of truly interdisciplinary work marks an important next step towards the advancement of the research field of imitation and social learning.

Unlike most books in the area of social learning and imitation, this particular volume thus emphasizes the interdisciplinary perspective on imitation in the context of human, animal and robotic behaviour. Many chapters are co-authored by experts pioneering collaborations across traditional disciplinary boundaries.[1] Several chapters are co-authored by researchers from different disciplines who have brought cross-disciplinary expertise to bear on models and mechanisms of social learning.[2] This serves both to consolidate and to provide a valuable reference for the increasing number of researchers entering this interdisciplinary field.

4   Organization and themes

Next we overview the major themes, organization and contents of the book. Chapters are grouped into a number (in the cognitively manageable range 7 ± 2) of overarching and overlapping thematic parts, numbered by Roman numerals (I–VIII), while chapters are numbered continuously (from 1 to 21, excluding this introduction).

---

[1] All book chapters have been peer reviewed anonymously.

[2] The first forum that deliberately brought together participants from the natural sciences as well as the sciences of the artificial was the First International Symposium on Imitation in Animals and Artifacts, organized in 1999 by Professors Kerstin Dautenhahn and Chrystopher Nehaniv as part of the AISB'99 convention in Edinburgh, Scotland. The Second International Symposium on Imitation in Animals and Artifacts organized by Dautenhahn and Nehaniv was held in April 2003 in Aberystwyth as part of AISB'03. In 2005, as part of AISB'05, the Third International Symposium on Imitation in Animals and Artifacts was held in April at University of Hertfordshire, Hatfield, organized by Dr Yiannis Demiris and the editors.

4.1 Thematic sections

The book is structured according to themes, reflected in the different book sections.

  I Correspondence problems and mechanisms
 II Mirroring and 'mind-reading'
III What to imitate
 IV Development and embodiment
  V Synchrony and turn-taking as communicative mechanisms
 VI Why imitate? – Motivations
VII Social feedback
VIII Ecological context

Note, these themes are multidisciplinary, so that the work on robots, humans and animals is represented across different themes. Each theme is introduced at the beginning of the corresponding section by a short text written by the editors, setting the stage for the chapters belonging to that theme.

Within each theme, we have sought to bring together the perspectives of authors from radically different areas of scientific inquiry (in some cases within a single chapter).

Across the eight themes of the book, several meta-groupings can be identified, cross-linking themes and chapters. In Parts I, III and IV we find chapters addressing *the embodied nature of behavioural mapping between observer and learner*. Parts II, IV, V and VII investigate *neurobiological and developmental foundations of imitation and understanding others' minds. Social and communicative perspectives of imitation and social learning* are highlighted in sections V, VI and VII. Parts VI and VIII address *motivational and evolutionary aspects of social learning and imitation*.

Note, significant progress has been made over the past ten years in fields of research investigating social learning and imitation in humans, animals and artifacts. However, in none of the key themes as identified in the sections of this book are we close to a complete understanding of the issues involved. Thus, imitation and social learning will pose exciting challenges for many years to come, it will continue to challenge our understanding of the psychology and biology of important aspects of animal (social) minds and behaviour, and it will remain a demanding 'benchmark challenge' for artificial intelligence and robotics researchers concerned with socially intelligent artifacts. Cross-disciplinary approaches whereby robots serve as models and tools for the investigation of social learning and imitation in humans and animals could potentially help to synthesize ideas from different fields, that may ultimately lead to unified frameworks.

4.2   Chapters

To allow readers to quickly acquire an overview of the organization of the book, the contents of the chapters are summarized below based on abstracts or introductions provided to the editors by the authors of the individual chapters. A short editorial essay at the beginning of each section of the book introduces the respective theme and chapters in more detail.

I   Correspondence problems and mechanisms
1   Imitation: thoughts about theories
Geoffrey Bird and Cecilia Heyes
How does perception of an action enable the perceiver to produce a matching movement? This chapter examines three functional theories addressing this 'correspondence problem': active intermodal matching, associative sequence learning and ideomotor theories. Bird and Heyes first review behavioural and neurological evidence which is consistent with all three models. These experiments indicate that imitation involves the combination of perceptual and motor representations of action and that, once combined, these representations will support learning of new motor skills, in addition to activation of pre-existing motor patterns. Attention is then turned to evidence bearing on three foci of disagreement between the theories: effector-dependence of imitation, the extent to which observers are aware of information acquired through imitation and the role of experience in the formation of an imitative ability. In the light of this evidence, the authors identify current strengths and weaknesses of the three models, and discuss priorities for future research addressing the correspondence problem.

2   Nine billion correspondence problems
Chrystopher L. Nehaniv
The character and quality of matching behaviour depend crucially on the granularity and measure of similarity. The author outlines a taxonomy of social learning, imitative and matching behaviour according to these dimensions. This yields 24 classes of correspondence problems, in which the particular specialization of the model and 'imitator' embodiment and of the metric yields myriad particular correspondence problems, problems of learning how to imitate. Nehaniv describes how traditional and more recent taxonomies of social learning and behaviour matching are refined and clarified by this system, applicable to both animals (including humans) and constructed agents such as robots. New classes of matched behaviour are also distinguished and illustrated.

Attempts at matched behaviour according to a selected granularity and harnessing reinforcement using the chosen metrics gives rise to generic, schematic mechanisms for these myriad correspondence problems in model systems. By considering measures of salience, it may be possible to adaptively and dynamically choose between possible correspondence problems, in automatic systems that learn what to imitate.

3 Challenges and issues faced in building a framework for conducting research in learning from observation
Darrin Bentivegna, Christopher Atkeson and Gordon Cheng
This chapter presents a framework that allows an agent to learn from observing a task. The authors describe a memory-based approach to learning how to select and provide sub-goals for behavioral primitives, given that an existing library of primitives is available. The framework, algorithms and test environments are used to highlight the challenges that are faced when building robotic systems that will learn from observation and practice. The details of implementing this framework on robots that operate in an air hockey and a marble maze environment are presented. Challenges involved with using observation data and primitives to increase the learning rate of agents are discussed.

II   *Mirroring and 'mind-reading'*
4 A neural architecture for imitation and intentional relations
Marco Iacoboni, Jonas Kaplan and Stephen Wilson
This chapter discusses the neural architecture that allows imitative behaviour and intentional relations. The discussion is at three levels: neural, computational and theoretical. The architecture comprises superior temporal cortex, the rostral part of the posterior parietal cortex and inferior frontal cortex. These three brain areas are mostly concerned with coding actions of self and others. The neural properties of these areas are mapped onto a computational architecture of paired forward and inverse internal models. From a theoretical perspective, this architecture permits a common framework for third-person knowledge (i.e. the observation of actions of others) and first-person knowledge (i.e. internal motor plans), thus facilitating social understanding. Within this framework, links between imitation and other cognitive domains are discussed.

5 Simulation theory of understanding others: a robotics perspective
Yiannis Demiris and Matthew Johnson
When we observe the behaviour of agents in our social environment, we are usually able to understand their actions, the reasoning behind them, and the goals of these actions. This is known as 'having a theory of mind',

i.e. a 'mind-reading' ability, which has evolved to allow us to be able to efficiently understand, and as a result, collaborate or compete with others.

There is intense debate with respect to the nature of this ability (Carruthers and Smith, 1996). Although there are intermediate positions between them, the two opposing theories that have been advocated are the 'simulation theory' and the 'theory theory' of mind reading (Gallese and Goldman, 1998). In the former, we understand the behaviour of others by simulating it using our own cognitive mechanisms underlying behaviour generation, while in the latter, we understand others' behaviours by using an acquired (or for some researchers, innate) theory about behaviours.

This chapter focuses on the simulation theory of mind, starting by briefly examining related biological data, including neurophysiological experiments with primates, and human brain imaging and psychophysical data. The authors subsequently proceed to review their research designing and implementing computational architectures that embody principles of the simulation theory. Experiments are described that implement this theory onto robots, that observe and imitate simple actions by humans, before outlining important remaining challenges.

6   Mirrors and matchings: imitation from the perspective of mirror-self-recognition, and the parietal region's involvement in both

Robert W. Mitchell

Given that mirror-self-recognition and generalized bodily imitation both require recognition of matching between bodies, it is likely that explanations for mirror-self-recognition would be useful for understanding imitation. In this chapter Mitchell presents two models he developed to explain self-recognition (Mitchell, 1993) which should provide a glimpse at imitation from different vantage points. The models should be of interest to researchers attempting to distinguish potential components of imitation. The first model focuses attention on self-recognition (and by extension generalized bodily imitation) as a form of intermodal matching. In this first model, derived from Guillaume's (1925) analysis, self-recognition occurs for the first time because the organism: (1) understands mirror-correspondence; (2) has kinesthetic-visual matching; and (3) can make inferences, such as that the image is 'the same' as its own body. The ability to match between kinesthetic and visual modalities seems essential for generalized bodily imitation as well as self-recognition. In the second model, self-recognition occurs for the first time because the organism: (1) understands mirror-correspondence (as in the first model); (2) objectifies body parts; and (3) understands (sixth-stage) object permanence, such that it recognizes that parts of things are indicative of the whole and has low-level deductive abilities. From these abilities, the organism recognizes (via understanding mirror-correspondence) that the hand (e.g.) in the mirror is a contingent accurate image of its hand, and then recognizes (via its understanding of object permanence) that what is continuous with the hand in the mirror (i.e. the body-image) must be a contingent accurate image of what is continuous with its own hand (i.e. its body). This same sort of process could lead an organism to recognize similarities between its own actions and those of another, an essential component of generalized bodily imitation. The chapter examines the implications of these models for understanding generalized bodily imitation.

III   What to Imitate
7   The question of 'what to imitate': inferring goals and intentions from demonstrations
Malinda Carpenter and Josep Call

A difficult issue for robotics researchers is the question of what to imitate, that is, which aspects of a demonstration robots should copy. Sometimes it is appropriate to copy others' actions, sometimes it is appropriate to copy others' results and sometimes copying both or even neither of these is the most appropriate response. The chapter discusses the advantages of using an understanding of others' goals and intentions to answer this question, copying what the demonstrator intended to do rather than what he actually did. Whereas some animals focus mainly on demonstrators' results or actions, one-year-old human infants appear to use an understanding of others' goals to decide what to imitate. The authors identify some specific ways in which infants can infer the goal of a demonstrator in imitation situations, using such information as the demonstrators' gaze direction, emotional expressions, actions and the context. This is followed by a brief review of what robots currently can do in this regard, proposing some further challenges for them.

8   Learning of gestures by imitation in a humanoid robot
Sylvain Calinon and Aude Billard

In this chapter, Calinon and Billard explore the issue of encoding, recognizing, generalizing and reproducing gestures. They address one major and generic issue, namely *how to discover the essence of a gesture*, i.e. how to find a representation of the data that encapsulates only the key aspects of the gesture, and discards the intrinsic variability across people's motions.

The model is tested and validated in a humanoid robot, using kinematics data of human motion. In order for the robot to learn new skills by imitation, it must be endowed with the ability to generalize over multiple demonstrations. To achieve this, the robot must encode multivariate time-dependent data in an efficient way. *Principal component analysis* and *hidden Markov models* are used to reduce the dimensionality of the dataset and to extract the primitives of the motion.

The model takes inspiration from a recent trend of research that aims at defining a formal mathematical framework for imitation learning. In particular, it stresses the fact that the observed elements of a demonstration, and the organization of these elements should be stochastically described to have a robust robotic application. It bears similarities with theoretical models of animal imitation, and offers at the same time a probabilistic description of the data, more suitable for a real-world application.

9   The dynamic emergence of categories through imitation
Tony Belpaeme, Bart de Boer and Bart Jansen

The authors propose an extension of the study of imitation in artifacts in which imitation takes place at the population level. Instead of assuming a one-to-one teacher–student relation between agents, agents in their set-up do not take a pre-assigned role and have to build up a repertoire of actions through imitative interaction with all other agents in the population. The action–observation categories used by the agents emerge in the population via a process of self-organization in the course of iterated 'imitation games', in which agents take turns controlling a physical robot arm and observing another agent using it. Successful or unsuccessful recognition of category membership of observed actions drive the autonomous formation and revision of the individual agents' categories without direct communication. Thus interaction via imitation games drives the self-organization of categories in a population, where social learning serves a mechanism for 'cultural' transmission.

IV   *Development and embodiment*
10   Copying strategies by people with autistic spectrum disorder: why only imitation leads to social cognitive development
Justin H. G. Williams

Imitation seems likely to be an important process in the development of social cognition and theory of mind. Imitation and mental state communication both depend upon the development of skills through modification of an existing action repertoire, as well as an ability to represent such modifications as resulting from the influences of inner mental states. Therefore, impairment in forming representations of the cognitions generating others actions, or a difficulty modifying the action repertoire, is likely to lead to poor development of both imitation and the ability to communicate mental states. Patterns of repetitive speech and actions are also likely to arise. This picture is consistent with that of autistic spectrum disorder (ASD). People with ASD appear to have impaired imitative skills perhaps reflecting an impaired ability to modify their existing action repertoire as a result of observing novel actions. An fMRI study involving the copying of finger movements in people with ASD and controls, found that the control, but not the ASD group, activated a number of brain areas that included areas previously associated with social cognition, as well as areas serving movement discrimination. Controls appeared to use imitative processes to perform the task whereas the ASD group used visuomotor associative learning processes. Williams suggests that the brain mechanisms utilised for action-copying in the scanner, may reflect approaches taken to social learning in daily life, and that people with ASD place greater reliance on processes involving visuomotor conditioning for social learning. This cognitive approach does not facilitate the modification of an existing action repertoire through the observation of novel actions, and thus either the communication of mental states or imitation. This will lead to poor social cognitive development and rigid and repetitive patterns of behaviour, characteristic of ASD.

11   A Bayesian model of imitation in infants and robots

Rajesh P. N. Rao, Aaron P. Shon and Andrew N. Meltzoff

Learning through imitation is a powerful and versatile method for acquiring new behaviours. In humans, a wide range of behaviours, from styles of social interaction to tool use, are passed from one generation to another through imitative learning. Although imitation evolved through Darwinian means, it achieves Lamarckian ends: it is a mechanism for the inheritance of acquired characteristics. Unlike trial-and-error-based learning methods such as reinforcement learning, imitation allows rapid learning. The potential for rapid behaviour acquisition through demonstration has made imitation-based learning an increasingly attractive alternative to manually programming robots. In this chapter, recent results are reviewed on how infants learn through imitation and the authors discuss Meltzoff and Moore's four-stage progression of imitative abilities: (1) body babbling, (2) imitation of body movements, (3) imitation of actions on objects and (4) imitation based on inferring the intentions of others. These four stages are formalized within a probabilistic framework for learning and inference. The framework acknowledges the role of internal models in sensorimotor control and draws on recent ideas from the field of machine learning regarding Bayesian inference in graphical models. The approach offers two major advantages: (1) the development of new algorithms for imitation-based learning in robots acting in noisy and uncertain environments and (2) the potential for using Bayesian methodologies (such as manipulation of prior probabilities) and robotic technologies to deepen our understanding of imitative learning in humans.

12   Solving the correspondence problem in robotic imitation across embodiments: synchrony, perception and culture in artifacts

Aris Alissandrakis, Chrystopher L. Nehaniv and Kerstin Dautenhahn

Social robotics opens up the possibility of individualized social intelligence in member robots of a community, and allows the harnessing of not only individual learning by the individual robot, but also the acquisition of new skills by observing other members of the community (robot, human or virtual). The chapter describes ALICE (action learning for imitation via correspondences between embodiments), an implemented generic framework for solving the *correspondence problem* between differently embodied robots. ALICE enables a robotic agent to learn a behavioral repertoire suitable to performing a task by observing a model agent, possibly having a different type of body, joints, different number of degrees of freedom, etc. Previously we demonstrated that the character of imitation achieved will depend on the granularity of sub-goal matching, and on the metrics used to evaluate success.

In this work, ALICE is implemented for simple robotic arm agents in simulation using various metrics for evaluating success according to actions, states or effects of weighted combinations. The authors examine the roles of synchronization, looseness of perceptual match and of proprioceptive matching by a series of experiments. As a complement to the social developmental aspects suggested by developmental psychology, their results show that *synchronization* and *loose perceptual matching* also allow for faster acquisition of behavioural competencies at low error rates.

The chapter further discusses the use of social learning mechanisms like ALICE for transmission of skills between robots, and give some examples of transmission of a skill through a chain of robots, despite differences in embodiment of agents involved. This simple example demonstrates that by using social learning and imitation, *cultural transmission* is possible among robots, even heterogeneous groups of robots. Moreover, robustness of the learning mechanism to changing embodiment is studied.

V   Synchrony and turn-taking as communicative mechanisms

13   How to build an imitator

Arnaud Revel and Jacqueline Nadel

Human newborns and some categories of robots are equipped to interact dynamically with physical and social worlds: they are autonomous, novelty expectant, attracted toward movement and able to couple perception and action. How does this fit being an imitator? To explore this question, the chapter adopts the hypothesis that imitation is not a unitary phenomenon but rather embraces a hierarchy of mechanisms which all have in common the ability to react to the perception of goal-directed movements/actions, by the production of similar behaviours. This framework allows developmental psychologists to account for a continuous development of imitation from birth to preschool, and epigenetic roboticists to adopt a bottom-up perspective and develop imitation through the self-generated evolution of an architecture.

14   Simulated turn-taking and development of styles of motion

Takashi Ikegami and Hiroki Iizuka

Turn-taking is studied as temporal and spontaneous role-splitting and switching between turn-giver and taker. Two mobile agents coupled through sensor inputs compute their motor outputs using internal recurrent neural networks. They chase each other on a two-dimensional arena and form co-operative turn-taking. Turn-taking allows a variety of styles of motion, showing regular and irregular spatiotemporal trail patterns. Some chaotic patterns are robust in the presence of noise and create a new style of turn-taking with new agents. Possible interpretations of these findings are given by reference to psychological experiments.

15   Bullying behaviour, empathy and imitation:
an attempted synthesis

Kerstin Dautenhahn, Sarah Woods and Christina Kaouri

This chapter speculates about a possible connection between empathy and imitation in the context of bullying behaviour, autism and psychopathy. The primary aim of this work is to provide a clearer understanding of bullying behaviour, by focusing on cognitive and emotional states that might cause bullies to show anti-social behaviour. A review of relevant research about bullying behaviour is presented followed by a brief discussion of empathy and imitation. Finally, the authors try to bring together these different lines of research and present the hypothesis that bullies possess well-developed automatic as well as cognitive empathy, and that bullying behaviour is caused by an overemphasis of goal-directed processes of controlled empathy that work towards non-empathy. Some speculations on a possible role of imitation in bullying intervention programmes conclude the chapter.

VI   *Why imitate? – Motivations*
16   Multiple motivations for imitation in infancy
Mark Nielsen and Virginia Slaughter

A significant corpus of research has documented how infants use imitation as a particularly powerful means of learning, allowing them to rapidly acquire new skills and promote their understanding about events in the world. However, as I. Č. Užgiris (1981) and other classic authors have argued, infants also imitate in order to initiate and maintain shared experience with others. These important social functions of imitation have been largely neglected in the recent literature on imitation. This chapter reviews a range of studies that highlight imitation as a highly flexible behaviour that serves a host of cognitive (e.g. learning) and social (e.g. communicative, interpersonal, emotional) functions. The authors also show that infants' tendencies to imitate, and their motivations for doing so, develop and change in the first few years of life. This chapter emphasises the multi-faceted nature of imitation, in order to expand our view of this complex and critical ability.

17   The progress drive hypothesis: an interpretation of early imitation
Frédéric Kaplan and Pierre-Yves Oudeyer

Children seem to have a natural tendency to imitate and their interest for particular kinds of imitative behaviour varies greatly with the infant's age. The authors argue that different forms of children's early imitation may be the result of an intrinsic motivation system driving the infant into situations of maximal learning progress. They present a computational model showing how an agent can learn to focus on 'progress niches', situations neither completely predictable nor too difficult to predict given its anticipation capabilities. The existence of such a drive could explain why certain types of imitative behaviour are produced by children at a certain age, and how discriminations between self, others and objects gradually appear.

VII   *Social feedback*
18   Training behaviour by imitation: from parrots to people . . . to robots?
Irene M. Pepperberg and Diane V. Sherman

Imitation occurs at many levels and likely involves several different types of learning. Parrots are well-known for reproducing sounds of human speech, but such behaviour is often considered 'mere' mimicry because these vocalizations rarely are meaningful. For over 25 years, however, the model/rival (M/R) procedure has been used to train Grey parrots (*Psittacus erithacus*) to use elements of human speech referentially (Pepperberg, 1999); that is, not only to imitate the form but also to reproduce appropriate use of various utterances. The parrots' resultant imitative behavior patterns are complex, involving replication at several different levels. Interestingly, this training technique has, somewhat surprisingly, also been shown to be effective in establishing two-way communication and life-style skills in children with various communicative and social dysfunctions, particularly in children for whom standard training interventions have failed. The authors discuss elements of training that appear necessary for such learning, hypothesize a connection with mirror neurons and suggest how studies with animals may provide models for engendering imitation in various subjects, including machines.

19   Task learning through imitation and human–robot interaction
Monica N. Nicolescu and Maja J. Matarić
Human skill and task teaching is a complex process that relies on multiple means of interaction and learning on the part of the teacher and of the learner. In robotics, however, task teaching has largely been addressed by using a single modality. The chapter presents a framework that uses an action-embedded representation to unify interaction and imitation in human–robot domains, thereby providing a natural means for robots to interact with and learn from humans. The representation links perception and action in a unique architecture that represents the robot's skills. The action component allows the use of implicit communication and endows the robot with the ability to convey its intentions through its actions on the environment. The perceptual component enables the robot to create a mapping between its observations and its actions and capabilities, allowing it to imitate a task learned from experiences of interacting with humans. This chapter describes a system that implements these capabilities and presents validation experiments performed with a Pioneer 2DX mobile robot learning various tasks.

VIII   The ecological context
20   Emulation learning: the integration of technical and social cognition
Ludwig Huber
Over the last decades, imitation was regarded as the cognitively most advanced and functionally most important mechanism of social learning.

Recent findings have shown that this claim is not warranted. Among numerous other important modes of social learning, emulation has been found to be particularly useful for the spread of technical innovations. Although emulation still has different meanings to different researchers, it is commonly agreed that by attending to the results of the model's actions, the information processed by the observer has to do with the objects manipulated by the model rather than with the details of the model's behaviour. Such information can include physical or functional properties of, or causal relationships among, objects. Thus, emulation might be considered as a learning mechanism in which social and technical intelligence converge. Animals that are known for both high levels of sociality and of exploratory behaviour, like the kea, are particularly useful models in this respect. In an experiment with captive keas, the success rate of individuals that were allowed to observe a trained conspecific was significantly higher than that of naive control subjects. The observers improved efficiency in dismantling three locking devices of an artificial fruit, which seemed to reflect the acquisition of some functional understanding of the task through observation. Perhaps the keas found the quick solution by the adaptive reorganization of experience with similar problems. Subsequent testing of keas in a number of difficult technical tasks revealed that these birds are able to produce a new adaptive response by the apprehension of a cause–effect relation between two or more physical objects.

21   Mimicry as deceptive resemblance: beyond the one-trick ponies

Mark D. Norman and Tom Tregenza

Octopuses, squid, cuttlefish and nautiluses belong in a strange divergent group of molluscs known as 'cephalopods'. These diverse and complex animals have evolved from clumsy shelled ancestors that survived the explosive radiation of the fishes by taking on four main strategies: hiding in deeper water (nautilus and deep-sea cephalopods), getting fast (squid), getting camouflaged (cuttlefish) or being malleable and cryptic (octopuses). A combination of four aspects of the form of these animals makes them unique: (1) a complex well-developed brain; (2) a plastic/elastic body; (3) polymimetic skin; (4) autonomy of body parts. All may provide lessons for studies of robotics, artificial intelligence and cognition in machines. Equipped with these tools cephalopods are capable of complex behaviours, displays and communications, the ultimate of which is mimicry. Compared with other animal mimics (that can only impersonate a single model), the plastic nature of cephalopods enables some species to mimic multiple models, a phenomenon known as 'dynamic mimicry'.

Examples of mimicry are discussed across different cephalopod groups, illustrating the wide range of behaviours found in these marine creatures. The Mimic Octopus from the Indo-Malayan Archipelago has an extensive repertoire, capable of mimicking sea snakes, flatfish, lionfish, anemones and other dangerous or toxic models. These behaviours are discussed along with their potential origins. Where is most mimicry found in nature? Does context drive the adoption or success of imitation? (In exposed habitats, is mimicry more prevalent? In a sea of poisonous animals, is there accelerated evolution towards mimicry of poisonous models?) Do specific co-inhabitants enable the mimicry to evolve? (Hermit crabs on exposed rubble; Sea snakes and Lionfish on mud substrates). Does heavy selective pressure accelerate development of mimicry? (Nature of predators or exposure). Evolutionary factors that may have led to dynamic mimicry in cephalopods are discussed.

Acknowledgements

The editors would like to thank the Society for the Study of Artificial Intelligence and the Simulation of Behaviour (SSAISB) for running the annual AISB conventions that have hosted thus far three International Symposia on Imitation in Animals and Artifacts, whereby the 1999 and 2003 symposia were supported by grants of the UK Engineering and Physical Sciences Research Council (EPSRC). We are also grateful to the reviewers and authors for their time and dedication to improving the contributions in this volume, and to the kind and dedicated folks at Cambridge University Press.

Reviewers

Andrew Anderson, Aris Alissandrakis, Arnaud Revel, Aude Billard, Bob Mitchell, Cecilia Heyes, Christian Balkenius, Christopher Prince, Colwyn Trevarthen, Cynthia Breazeal, Daniel Osorio, Georgi Stojanov, Giorgio Metta, Hideki Kozima, Iain Werry, Irene Pepperberg, Jessica Meyer, Joe Saunders, Jonas Kaplan, Jun Tani, Justin Williams, Kim Bard, Luc Berthouze, Luciano Fadiga, Malinda Carpenter, Mark Gardner, Michael Arbib, Monica Nicolescu, Peter McOwan, Pierre Andry, René te Boekhorst, Susan Hurley, Takashi Ikegami, Tony Belpaeme, Yiannis Demiris, Yuval Marom and other anonymous reviewers.

REFERENCES

Billard, A. and Siegwart, R., eds. (2004). Robot learning from demonstration, special issue of *Robotics and Autonomous Learning*, **47(2–3)**.

Carruthers, P. and Smith, P. K. (1996). *Theories of Theories of Mind*. Cambridge University Press.

Dautenhahn, K. and Nehaniv, C. L., eds. (2002). *Imitation in Animals and Artifacts*. MIT Press.

Galef, B. G., Jr and Heyes, E. M., eds. (2004). Social learning and imitation, special issue of *Learning and Behavior*, **32(1)**.

Gallese, V. and Goldman, A. (1998). Mirror neurons and the simulation theory of mind-reading. *Trends in Cognitive Sciences*, **2(12)**, 493–501.

Guillaume, P. (1925). *L'imitation Chez L'enfant* [Imitation in Children]. Paris: Alcan.

Heyes, C. M. and Galef, Jr, B. G., eds. (1996). *Social Learning in Animals: The Roots of Culture*. Academic Press.

Hurley, S. and Chater, N., eds. (2005). *Perspectives on Imitation: From Neuroscience to Social Science*. MIT Press. 2 volumes.

Lieberman, H. (ed.) (2001). *Your Wish is My Command: Programming by Example*. Morgan Kaufmann Publishers.

Meltzoff, A. N. and Prinz, W., eds. (2002). *The Imitative Mind: Development, Evolution and Brain Bases*. Cambridge University Press.

Mitchell, R. W. (1993). Mental models of mirror-self-recognition: two theories. *New Ideas in Psychology*, **11**, 295–325; Recognizing one's self in a mirror? A reply to Gallop and Povinelli, De Lannoy, Anderson and Byrne, *New Ideas in Psychology*, **11**, 351–77.

Nadel, J. and Butterworth, G., eds. (1999). *Imitation in Infancy*. Cambridge University Press.

Nehaniv, C. L. and Dautenhahn, K., eds. (2001). Imitation in natural and artificial systems, special issue of *Cybernetics and Systems*, **32(1–2)**.

Pepperberg, I. M. (1999). *The Alex Studies*. Harvard University Press, Cambridge, MA.

Užgiris, I. (1981). Two functions of imitation during infancy. *International Journal of Behavioral Development*, **4**, 1–12.

Part I

Correspondence problems and mechanisms

The problem for one individual of producing behaviour that *matches*, in some aspect, with behaviour it observes in another comprises an instance of the *correspondence problem* (compare Part IV, Development and embodiment, this volume; Nehaniv and Dautenhahn, 2002). The particular nature of the kind of similarity that is matched determines different classes of correspondence problems. The bodies and affordances available to the two individuals are in general not the same, so the problem is non-trivial – even ignoring the complexities of perception in registering the observed behaviour. Mechanisms for solving these correspondence problems are numerous, and, while generally occurring in a social context, they may or may not involve learning. On the other hand, every social learning mechanism solves a particular class of correspondence problems.

Geoffrey Bird and Cecilia Heyes discuss several alternative mechanisms for solving correspondence problems in which the observer must generate motor commands to match visual input. Of particular interest due to the complexity of mechanism they appear to require for their solution are cases in which the perceptual discrepancies cannot be used as simple feedback to guide mismatch reduction and achieve matching behaviour. Various levels of such perceptual opacity occur when the visual experience in observing another[1] individual and the experience which occurs when carrying out the 'same' actions are dissimilar, as in a curtsy bow or in playing tennis. In such cases, not only the proprioceptive feedback experienced in performing actions, but also the visual feedback itself, are very different from what is seen when observing another individual do these things. How can observation of action lead to matching movements? Three theories are assessed in regard to their capability to account for solutions

---

[1] Or one's own behaviour in a mirror, compare Part II, Mirroring and 'mind-reading', this volume.

Imitation and Social Learning in Robots, Humans and Animals, ed. Chrystopher L. Nehaniv and Kerstin Dautenhahn. Published by Cambridge University Press.

of such correspondence problems in humans: active intermodal mapping (AIM) (Meltzoff and Moore, 1994), associative sequence learning (ASL) (Heyes and Ray, 2000), and the theory of goal-directed imitation (GOADI) (Wohlschläger *et al.*, 2003).

The chapter by Chrystopher L. Nehaniv discusses how numerous types of social learning and other social phenomena that involve matching can be formulated as instances of the correspondence problem in a unified framework. Emulation, affordance learning, 'true imitation', so-called simple mimicry or copying, immediate communicative imitation and turn-taking, and interactive synchronization, as well as teaching and other types of social matching may be aligned within or further broken down into a systematic taxonomy of correspondence problems at different levels of granularity and according to which subset of states, actions and effects are matched. Different mechanisms such as social facilitation, stimulus or location enhancement, Hebbian learning of sensorimotor mapping combined with sequence learning (as in Heyes and Ray's ASL), or mirror neuron models, as well as mechanisms for artifacts, have been proposed as solutions to some of these mapping problems.

Darrin Bentivegna, Christopher Atkeson and Gordon Cheng illustrate the constructive solution of skill acquisition correspondence problems for humanoid robots or other agents that learn by observing human behaviour.[2] Their framework is illustrated in experiments in learning how to play competitive air-hockey and how to guide a steel ball through a labyrinthine maze with balance controls. The authors employ a novel set of mechanisms in robotic social learning based on a memory of previous experiences, task-level selection of primitives and autonomous sub-goal generation. The role of primitive units of behaviour and their re-use and adaptation in making learning tractable is discussed. Moreover, through individual learning from practice based on socially acquired behaviours, robotic systems using this framework are able to further refine and improve their skills so that their performance may actually surpass that of human demonstrators.

REFERENCES

Heyes, C. M. and Ray, E. D. (2000). What is the significance of imitation in animals? *Advances in the Study of Behavior*, **29**, 215–45.
Meltzoff, A. N. and Moore, M. K. (1994). Imitation, memory and the representation of Persons. *Infant Behavior and Development*, **17(1)**, 83–99.

---

[2] See also chapter 12 by Aris Alissandrakis and his collaborators in Part IV, Development and Embodiment, this volume, for different constructive approaches to solving correspondence problems by individuals whose bodies may grow and change over time.

Nehaniv, C. L. and Dautenhahn, K. (2002). The correspondence problem. In
  K. Dautenhahn and C. L. Nehaniv (eds.), *Imitation in Animals and Artifacts*,
  Cambridge, MA: MIT Press, 41–61.
Wohlschläger, A., Gattis, M. and Bekkering, H. (2003). Action generation and
  action perception in imitation: an instance of the ideomotor principle. *Philosophical Transactions of the Royal Society of London Series B-Biological Sciences*,
  358, 501–15.

1   Imitation: thoughts about theories

Geoffrey Bird and Cecilia Heyes

Many behavioural features and psychological states can be transmitted between natural systems. A person or animal can acquire through observation of another a tendency to go to the same place, effect the same transformation of an object, perform the same body movements, make the same sounds, feel similar emotions or think similar thoughts. In our discussion of imitation we will focus on cases in which body movements are transmitted or 'copied' between model and observer, because these cases present a distinctive explanatory challenge.

The problem of producing a movement that matches one observed is made difficult due to the nature of the codes representing the observed and executed movements. The observer must formulate *motor* commands to match *visual* input. This is a special case of what has become known as the 'correspondence problem' (Alissandrakis *et al.*, 2002; Nehaniv and Dautenhahn, 2001), and it is made particularly difficult when simple perceptual matching cannot be used to produce imitative movements, as in the following example. A tennis coach demonstrates a serve to a novice, which the novice then attempts to imitate. If the novice successfully imitates the coach's action[1] the two actions will not 'match' from the novice's perspective. The novice will perceive the coach's actions as a whole body movement, in which the back arches and one arm moves in an overhead arc. In contrast, the novice's own actions will be perceived as a movement of their arm and hand from an unseen position behind their head, to a position in front of their body. Similarly, the coach may be able to detect that the novice's action matched the movement they had demonstrated, even though the visual information they received from their own

---

[1] The term 'action' is sometimes used to refer specifically to goal-directed or intentional body movements. We have not adopted this usage here; 'action' and 'movement' are used synonymously.

Imitation and Social Learning in Robots, Humans and Animals, ed. Chrystopher L. Nehaniv and Kerstin Dautenhahn. Published by Cambridge University Press.

movement and that of the novice differed greatly. Thus, an important challenge for theories of imitation is to explain *how* observation of action facilitates production of matching movements. This chapter reviews three theories of imitation which approach this problem in very different ways.

1.1   Three theories

The three theories to be examined in greater detail in this chapter are: active intermodal mapping (e.g. Meltzoff and Moore, 1983, 1994, 1997); associative sequence learning (Heyes, 2001; Heyes, 2005; Heyes and Ray, 2000), and the theory of goal-directed imitation (Wohlschläger *et al.*, 2003). These theories can be divided into two camps based on the information-processing thought to occur during imitation. Both the active intermodal mapping (AIM) and goal-directed (GOADI) theories of imitation suggest that intermediate recoding occurs between observation and execution of an imitative body movement. They imply that, in addition to a visual representation of the observed movement and a motor representation that drives muscle movement, imitation involves a third kind of movement representation, which is neither sensory nor motor. In contrast, the associative sequence learning (ASL) theory of imitation argues that observation of a body movement can prompt the preparation of a matching action directly, without the need for intermediate recoding. We will now give a brief overview of the theories, before discussing their success in explaining imitative phenomena.

1.1.1   Active Intermodal Mapping

The AIM model of imitation introduces three theoretical concepts. The first, 'organ identification', is the process by which infants come to identify parts of their body with parts of the bodies of others. Meltzoff and Moore argue that this is the first step in the imitative process. The second concept 'organ relations', refers to the capacity of the infant to parse an observed action into a series of relationships between organs (parts) of the body. The same capacity allows the infant to identify the organ relations of her own body using proprioceptive feedback, and through organ identification, to actively compare the organ relations of the model with her own organ relations. Organ relations provide a common content for the percept of an action to be compared to the action of the perceiver. The third concept, 'body babbling', refers to the process of learning the relationship between muscle movements and the organ relations which result. It is argued that this process leads to the formation of a 'directory' of muscle movements and associated organ relations. After such experience-dependent learning, the infant will have the ability to produce muscle movements leading to specified organ relations.

Thus far, AIM does not address the correspondence problem. Although the infant can identify the organ relations of her own body, and can identify the organ relations of the model's body, the two representations are still in incommensurate coding systems. Visually coded organ relations must still be compared to proprioceptively coded organ relations in order for a mismatch to be detected. According to AIM, the problem is solved by the use of a supramodal representational system. This system encodes organ relations in a modality-general fashion. Visual and proprioceptive organ relations are translated into this common representational framework allowing them to be compared directly. Meltzoff and Moore suggest that AIM explains infant imitation and forms the basis of adult imitative competency. The major developmental change in imitation occurs after a few weeks of life when perceived actions are no longer coded as organ relations, but rather as goal-directed actions (organ relation transformations; Meltzoff and Moore, 1997). Subsequently, imitation is not of perceived movements, but of inferred goals.

1.1.2   Goal Directed Imitation

The GOADI theory of imitation also denies a direct link between the perception and production of body movements. It suggests that perceived actions are decomposed into a series of 'aspects' (most grossly the goal of a movement and the means to achieve it). Capacity limitations mean that only some goal aspects are imitated; movement end-points and the manipulation of objects are more likely to be imitated than either the effector or the movement path. When the goal of the movement has been selected, the movement most commonly associated with this goal will be performed. Thus, there is no special relationship between matching movements under GOADI. If the observer's most commonly associated movement is the same as that performed by the model, then imitation of the perceived movement will occur. Alternatively, if the movement most commonly associated with the perceived goal is different from the movement of the model, then goal, but not movement, imitation will occur.

GOADI focuses attention on cases of imitation in which an observer's behaviour has the same outcome as that of the model, and it has inspired a series of very interesting studies suggesting that, when they are given non-specific instructions such as 'Do this', observers are more likely to reproduce action outcomes than to reproduce the body movements used to achieve these outcomes (see Wohlschläger et al., 2003). However,

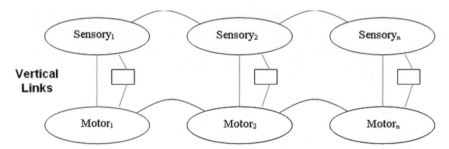

Figure 1.1 Schematic representation of the associative sequence learning theory of imitation learning (see text for details).

GOADI does not deny that people sometimes imitate body movements. It allows that during dance instruction, for example, it may be the goal of the model to produce a certain body movement, and the goal of the imitator is to produce exactly the same body movement. Cases like this pose the correspondence problem, and yet GOADI is silent about how this problem may be solved.

Both AIM and GOADI suggest that the processes mediating imitation involve intermediate action representations which are neither sensory nor motoric. According to AIM, perceived actions are actively processed in order to infer the model's goals. These goals are then translated into supramodal representations which are used to produce motor commands. Under GOADI, goals are also extracted from perceived movements. The goal representation then activates its most commonly associated motor program, irrespective of whether this matches the movement performed by the model. In contrast to these theories, the ASL model argues that the perception of action typically prompts the performance of that action directly, without the need for intermediate representation.

1.1.3   Associative Sequence Learning

The ASL theory suggests that the correspondence problem is solved through the operation of bidirectional excitatory links, or 'vertical associations', between sensory and motor representations of action (see Figure 1.1). Sensory representations are activated when actions are perceived, and they contain information received through the distal senses (vision and audition). Motor representations contain motor commands needed to perform the action, and somatosensory (kinaesthetic and proprioceptive) information received when the movement is performed. Thus, roughly speaking, the sensory representation codes what the action 'looks like' and the motor representation codes what it 'feels like' to perform the action. When a sensory and a motor representation are linked by a vertical association, activation of the sensory representation is propagated to the motor representation. If the sensory and motor components represent the same action (a 'matching vertical association'), this activation of the motor representation makes imitation possible.

According to the ASL model, whereas a few vertical associations may be innate, the majority are formed in a Hebbian fashion, through experience that provokes concurrent activation of sensory and motor representations of the same movement. This experience may consist of concurrent observation and execution of the same movement, leading to a 'direct' vertical association, or it may involve exposure to a common stimulus in conjunction with, on some occasions, observation of the movement, and on other occasions with its execution[2]. For example, a child may hear the sound of a word such as 'frown', sometimes when she is frowning and, at other times, when she sees another person frowning. As a consequence of this 'acquired equivalence' experience (Hall, 1996), sensory and motor representations of frowning will each become linked to a representation of the word. This 'indirect vertical association' enables activation of the sensory representation to be propagated to the motor representation via the word representation, and, to the extent that it allows the sound of the word concurrently to activate sensory and motor representations of frowning, to the formation of a direct vertical association between them.

The ASL model does not specify a system which compares sensory and motor representations of movements. To generate imitative behaviour, the system does not have to 'decide' whether there is a match between the associated sensory and motor representations. Indeed, it is possible for associative links to be formed between sensory and motor representations of actions that do not match from a third-person perspective. The reason why associations are more likely to be formed between matching rather than non-matching movements is due to the environment. Heyes (2005) argues that natural systems develop in environments where matching sensory and motor action representations are more likely to be contiguously activated than non-matching representations, but that this is merely a contingent fact. If, in a wholly unethical experiment, a child was reared in an environment where, for example, every smile was greeted

---

[2] Although concurrent activation or 'contiguity' is emphasised here for clarity of exposition, the ASL model assumes, in line with contemporary theories of associative learning (see Hall, 1994 for a review), that the formation of vertical associations depends on contingency in addition to contiguity.

with a frown, and mirrors were replaced with time-delay video feedback devices, whenever other children imitated, this unfortunate child would show a systematic tendency to counter-imitate. This intuitively implausible suggestion becomes more plausible when one realises that, to support imitation, it is the sensory and motor action representations which must match, rather than the actions of two individuals. Hence, matching sensory and motor representations are activated during unaided and mirror self-observation; the sensory representation of a hand movement will always be activated concurrently with the motor representation of the same hand movement in normal development. Although it is more likely that non-matching movements will be performed at any time between two individuals, the range of possible non-imitative actions is so much larger than that of imitative actions. Thus, associations between specific non-matching actions are unlikely to be formed.

1.2   Contrasting the theories

The theories outlined above present differing views on whether imitation necessarily involves intermediate representation, i.e. representation of action that is neither sensory nor motoric. These views are empirically testable because they lead to different predictions concerning at least two questions. The first of these is whether observation can support effector-dependent learning, and the second is whether imitation learning can occur without awareness.

1.2.1   *Effector-dependent observational learning*

Learning is said to be effector-dependent to the extent that training of one set of muscles (e.g. those of the right hand) does not generalize to another (e.g. those of the left hand). Effector-dependence of practice-based learning has been demonstrated in both monkeys (Rand *et al.*, 1998) and humans (Bapi *et al.*, 2000; Marcovitch and Flanagan, submitted). For example, Marcovitch and Flanagan allowed human participants to learn a sequence of movements to spatial targets with one hand, and then tested performance of the other hand on the training sequence or a novel sequence.

The three theories reviewed make different predictions regarding effector-dependent observational learning. Active intermodel mapping suggests that observational learning will always be effector-independent – that the effects of observational learning will *not* be confined to the effector observed during training. This is because, according to AIM, the perceptual representations formed during action observation are transformed into 'supramodal' representations, and these can be translated into a variety of motor outputs. Goal-directed imitation suggests that observers preferentially encode and imitate more global or distal aspects of observed behaviour. For example, given a choice, they will imitate action effects rather than the body movements used to achieve these effects. Consequently, GOADI predicts that effector-dependent observational learning will be very rare. It will occur only when the observed action could not be encoded at a more global level.

In contrast with AIM and GOADI, ASL suggests that the formation of effector-dependent representations of observed action occurs, and is not unusual. More specifically, it proposes that observation-activated motor representations will be effector-dependent to the extent that prior visual experience of each movement component has been paired with activation of a distinct and constant muscle set. This condition is likely to be met by finger movements. When a person looks at their hands while performing finger movements, the sight of, for example, the left index finger lifting will be paired more reliably with activation of muscles in the left index finger than with activation of muscles in the left ring finger or the right index finger.

Effector-dependent learning by observation has been demonstrated in our laboratory (e.g. Bird and Heyes, 2005; Heyes and Foster, 2002; Osman *et al.*, 2005). In the learning phase of these experiments, observers watch a model performing finger movements on a keyboard. The keys are pressed repeatedly in the same sequence. Observers are then asked to perform a series of tests in which it is an advantage to know the sequence demonstrated by the model. The results of these tests show that observers are better able than controls to perform the finger movement sequence demonstrated by the model, but that they are no better than controls when the task requires expression of the same sequence knowledge using different effectors. For example, if the model used the fingers of her right hand, the observers can perform the sequence with the fingers of their right hands, but not with the fingers of their left hands, or using their thumbs.

These results are consistent with the ASL theory, but not with AIM, which suggests that observational learning should always be effector-independent, or even with GOADI. The GOADI theory would predict that, instead of engaging in effector-dependent observational learning, the observers in our experiments could have encoded the model's actions in terms of their (more distal) effects on the response keys. Thus, evidence of effector-dependent learning by observation provides support for a direct link between the perception and production of action.

1.2.2   Awareness and imitation

Let us now turn to the second question which impacts upon the debate over whether imitation is direct, or mediated by flexible, higher-order goals. This relates to the role of awareness in imitation.

Both AIM and GOADI suggest that imitation occurs via intentional, rather than automatic, processes (Neumann, 1984). AIM makes this explicit when it states that imitation is 'active' rather than passive. In the case of GOADI, intentional processing is implied by the very name of the theory: 'goal-directed imitation'. In contrast, ASL suggests that the intention to imitate is not necessary for imitative performance, that imitation can occur automatically.

Evidence of automatic imitation has been provided recently by electrophysiological studies of motor facilitation by action observation (e.g. Aziz-Zadeh *et al.*, 2002; Maeda *et al.*, 2002; Strafella and Paus, 2000). In these studies, passive participants observed body movements while transcranial magnetic stimulation (TMS)-induced motor evoked potentials (MEPs) were recorded from a range of muscles. It was found that MEPs recorded from muscles involved in execution of the observed movement were greater than those recorded at other muscle sites.

Further evidence of unintentional imitation comes from research examining the 'chameleon effect' in relatively unconstrained social interaction (e.g. Chartrand and Bargh, 1999; Lakin and Chartrand, 2003). Participants in these studies were asked to interact freely with another individual whom they believed was a participant, but who was actually a confederate of the researchers. The confederate exhibited a target behaviour during the interaction (such as tapping their foot), and the tendency of the participant to perform the target behaviour during the interaction was compared to a baseline period when the participant was alone. Results consistently showed an increase in performance of the target behaviour by the participant during the interaction. However, during post-test debriefing, participants reported that they did not notice the target behaviour being demonstrated, that they had no intention to imitate the behaviour, and that they were unaware of doing so.

Research using stimulus-response compatibility (SRC) paradigms implies that movement observation can induce the observer to prepare to perform a matching movement even when performance of such a movement is counter-intentional (Brass *et al.*, 2000; Craighero *et al.*, 1998; Heyes *et al.*, 2005; Stürmer *et al.*, 2000). For example, Brass *et al.* (2000) asked participants to lift (in one test block), or lower (in another test block) their index finger as soon as they saw movement of a stimulus hand. Irrespective of the stimulus movement, participants were always required to perform the same movement throughout a block. Stimulus movements were either compatible (matching), or incompatible (non-matching), with respect to the response movement. Participants were faster to respond on compatible than incompatible trials suggesting that perception of an action primes production of that action even when the identity of observed movements is task-irrelevant.

The foregoing studies demonstrate unintentional activation and/or production of observed body movements that are already part of the observer's behavioural repertoire. It could be argued, therefore, that they are not the kind of phenomenon that AIM and GOADI are seeking to explain. Perhaps these theories are concerned exclusively with imitation *learning*, with cases in which an observer expands their behavioural repertoire by copying the actions of a model. However, the results of some of our recent experiments suggest that imitation learning can be automatic or unintentional. These studies indicate that healthy adults can learn to perform a sequence of finger movements fluently through imitation, without being able subsequently to recognise the sequence (Bird et al., 2005). Participants who had observed the sequence performed by a model executed it faster than controls, but when they were shown sequence segments and asked to rate their familiarity, observers were no better than controls at distinguishing segments of the observed sequence from segments of an unfamiliar sequence with the same, complex structure. This result suggests that participants were not aware of the information they had learned through imitation and, by inference, that imitation had occurred without intention.

1.3   Intentional and incidental imitation

Associative sequence learning does not specify that imitation must involve a representation of the model's action goals, or assign a role to intermediate or amodal (non-sensory, non-motor) representations of action. And yet, introspection suggests that sometimes we *do* focus on goals during imitation, and form amodal representations of what we have observed. Returning to the example presented at the beginning of the chapter, as our novice tennis player watches his coach he may focus entirely on the angle the racquet makes with the ball, ignoring the position of the coach's head, trunk and arms. Furthermore, the novice may formulate a linguistic description of the observed action in his mind, such as, 'The racquet head is at 90 degrees to the ball and is rotated on contact'. He may then re-run this verbal script as he tries to imitate the coach's serve, trying to use it to control his movements. The introspective plausibility of this kind of scenario implies that the ASL model does not capture some important features of our experience of imitation – features that *are* captured by AIM and GOADI. One day, ASL may be extended so that it makes better contact with introspective and experimental evidence relating to goal-directed imitation. For now, we simply offer some thoughts about the relationship between goal-directed or intentional processing and the vertical associations which, according to ASL, mediate imitation.

We suggest that, regardless of whether the observer intends to imitate, movement observation gives rise to motor activation in the manner described by ASL. Provided that the observer's past experience has been such as to provide them with vertical associations relevant to the currently observed movement, its perception will result in activation of the central and peripheral neural mechanisms that mediate performance of the same action. However, at least in humans, this activation is normally inhibited so that it does not result automatically in overt imitative performance. When the observer's intention is to be passive, or to perform a non-imitative movement, this inhibition allows the observer to discharge their intention with minimal interference from observation-induced motor activation. A healthy adult human may perform an echoing twitch when they intend to be still, or may be slower to perform an intended non-imitative movement than they would be in the absence of observation-induced activation (Stürmer *et al.*, 2000), but, unlike some frontal patients (Brass *et al.*, 2003) whose inhibition mechanisms are impaired, a healthy adult does not automatically perform the movements they see.

When movement observation occurs with the intention to imitate, one or both of two processes may occur. First, there may be disinhibition of the motor activation generated via vertical associations. That is, the inhibition which normally prevents matching motor activation from leading to overt performance of an imitative movement may be cancelled, 'releasing' imitative behaviour. Second, the observer may formulate a goal-related verbal description of the observed action, and try to achieve imitation by willing their body to move in a way that conforms to this description. To the extent that what the observer intends to imitate is an effect of a movement on an object (known as 'emulation' in the comparative and developmental literature) this strategy may be effective. However, if the observer's intention is to copy details of the model's body movements, vocabulary limitations are likely to thwart their efforts. Groups with special expertise, such as dancers and gymnasts, have vocabularies that distinguish subtly different body movements, but most of us lack such a facility. Furthermore, insofar as the strategy is effective, it may be due to indirect vertical associations, to bidirectional excitatory links between, on the one hand, acoustic representations of words, and, on the other, visual and motor representations of actions to which they relate.

In sum, it seems that representation of a model's goals may be important in explaining *what* is imitated, but that vertical associations are needed to explain *how* imitation is achieved.

Acknowledgments

This research was supported by the Economic and Social Research Council (ESRC) research centre for Economic Learning and Social Evolution (ELSE), and by a PhD studentship awarded to Geoffrey Bird by the Biotechnology and Biological Sciences Research Council (BBSRC).

REFERENCES

Alissandrakis, A., Nehaniv, C. L. and Dautenhahn, K. (2002). Imitation with ALICE: learning to imitate corresponding actions across dissimilar embodiments. *IEEE Transactions on Systems, Man and Cybernetics: Part A – Systems and Humans*, **32(4)**, 482–96.
Aziz-Zadeh, L., Maeda, F., Zaidel, E., Mazziotta, J. and Iacoboni, M. (2002). Lateralization in motor facilitation during action observation: a TMS study. *Experimental Brain Research*, **144(1)**, 127–31.
Bapi, R. S., Doya, K. and Harner, A. M. (2000). Evidence for effector independent and dependent representations and their differential time course of acquisition during Motor Sequence Learning. *Experimental Brain Research*, **132**, 149–62.
Bird, G. and Heyes, C. M. (2005). Effector-dependent learning by observation of a finger movement sequence. *Journal of Experimental Psychology: Human Perception and Performance*, **31(2)**, 262–75.
Bird, G., Osman, M., Saggerson, A. and Heyes, C. M. (2005). *British Journal of Psychology*, **96(3)**, 371–88.
Brass, M., Bekkering, H., Wohlschläger, A. and Prinz, W. (2000). Compatibility between observed and executed finger movements: comparing symbolic, spatial, and imitative cues. *Brain and Cognition*, **44(2)**, 124–43.
Brass, M., Derrfuss, J., Matthes-von Cramon, G. and von Cramon, D. Y. (2003). Imitative response tendencies in patients with frontal brain lesions. *Neuropsychology*, **17(2)**, 265–71.
Chartrand, T. L. and Bargh, J. A. (1999). The chameleon effect: the perception-behavior link and social interaction. *Journal of Personality and Social Psychology*, **76(6)**, 893–910.
Craighero, L., Fadiga, L., Rizzolatti, G. and Umilta, C. (1998). Visuomotor priming. *Visual Cognition*, **5(1–2)**, 109–25.
Hall, G. (1994). Pavlovian conditioning: laws of association. In N. J. Mackintosh, (ed.), *Animal Learning and Cognition*. San Diego: Academic Press, 15–43.
Hall, G. (1996). Learning about associatively activated stimulus representations: implications for acquired equivalence and perceptual learning. *Animal Learning and Behavior*, **24**, 233–55.
Heyes, C. M. (2001). Causes and consequences of imitation. *Trends in Cognitive Sciences*, **5(6)**, 253–61.

Heyes, C. M. (2005). Imitation by association. In N. Chater and S. Hurley (eds.), *Perspectives on Imitation: from Cognitive Neuroscience to Social Science.* Cambridge, MA: MIT Press.

Heyes, C. M., Bird, G., Johnson, H. L. and Haggard, P. (2005). Experience Modulates Automatic Imitation. *Cognitive Brain Research*, **22(2)**, 233–40.

Heyes, C. M. and Foster, C. L. (2002). Motor learning by observation: evidence from a serial reaction time task. *Quarterly Journal of Experimental Psychology Section A – Human Experimental Psychology*, **55(2)**, 593–607.

Heyes, C. M. and Ray, E. D. (2000). What is the significance of imitation in animals? In *Advances in the Study of Behavior*, Vol. 29, 215–45.

Lakin, J. L. and Chartrand, T. L. (2003). Using nonconscious behavioral mimicry to create affiliation and rapport. *Psychological Science*, **14(4)**, 334–9.

Maeda, F., Kleiner-Fisman, G. and Pascual-Leone, A. (2002). Motor facilitation while observing hand actions: specificity of the effect and role of observer's orientation. *Journal of Neurophysiology*, **87(3)**, 1329–35.

Marcovitch, S. and Flanagan, J. R. (submitted). Effector-specific learning of hand target sequences. *Experimental Brain Research*.

Meltzoff, A. N. and Moore, M. K. (1983). Newborn-infants imitate adult facial gestures. *Child Development*, **54(3)**, 702–9.

Meltzoff, A. N. and Moore, M. K. (1994). Imitation, memory, and the representation of persons. *Infant Behavior and Development*, **17(1)**, 83–99.

Meltzoff, A. N. and Moore, M. K. (1997). Explaining facial imitation: a theoretical model. *Early Development and Parenting*, **6(3–4)**, 179–92.

Nehaniv, C. L. and Dautenhahn, K. (2001). Like me? – Measures of correspondence and imitation. *Cybernetics and Systems*, **32(1–2)**, 11–51.

Neumann, O. (1984). Automatic processing: a review of recent findings and a plea for an old theory. In W. Prinz and A. F. Sanders (eds.), *Cognition and Motor Processes*. Berlin: Springer-Verlag, 255–93.

Osman, M., Bird, G. and Heyes, C. M. (2005) Action observation supports effector-dependent learning of finger movement sequences. *Experimental Brain Research*, **165(1)**, 19–27.

Rand, M. K., Hikosaka, O., Miyachi, S., Lu, X. Miyashita, K. (1998). Characteristics of a long-term procedural skill in the monkey. *Experimental Brain Research*, **118(3)**, 293–7.

Strafella, A. P. and Paus, T. (2000). Modulation of cortical excitability during action observation: a transcranial magnetic stimulation study. *Neuroreport*, **11(10)**, 2289–92.

Stürmer, B., Aschersleben, G. and Prinz, W. (2000). Correspondence effects with manual gestures and postures: a study of imitation. *Journal of Experimental Psychology – Human Perception and Performance*, **26(6)**, 1746–59.

Wohlschläger, A., Gattis, M. and Bekkering, H. (2003). Action generation and action perception in imitation: an instance of the ideomotor principle. *Philosophical Transactions of the Royal Society of London Series B – Biological Sciences*, **358**, 501–15.

2 Nine billion correspondence problems[1]

Chrystopher L. Nehaniv

2.1 Matching behaviours

Numerous insightful descriptions of mechanisms that could be responsible for generating particular examples of social learning and related phenomena in ethology and psychology have been described (see e.g. Zentall and B. G. Galef, 1988; Heyes and Galef, 1996; Tomasello and Call, 1997; Byrne and Russon, 1998; Byrne, 1999; Heyes and Ray, 2000; Dautenhahn and Nehaniv, 2002). For robotics and software, particular *general* methods for solving such problems have been proposed by Nehaniv and Dautenhahn (2001) and Alissandrakis *et al.* (2002).[2] Despite variations in embodiments and what they afford agents (biological, software or robots), this raises the possibility for harnessing sociality and of an artificial basis for cultural transmission of skills in societies of artifacts, which might also learn from and interact with humans (Dautenhahn, 1995; Billard and Dautenhahn, 1998; Alissandrakis *et al.*, 2003a, b; Chapter 12, this volume).

To formulate problems of matched behaviour in general, we use the following variant of Mitchell's (1987) definition of *imitation* for what we will call *matching behaviour*:
1. A behaviour C is produced by an organism and/or machine, where
2. C is similar to another behaviour M,
3. Registration of M is necessary for the production of C, and
4. C is designed to be similar to M.

---

[1] This chapter is based on and substantially extends, C. L. Nehaniv, Nine billion correspondence problems and some methods for solving them, *Proceedings of the Second International Symposium on Imitation in Animals and Artifacts – Abersytwyth, Wales*. The Society for the Study of Artificial Intelligence and Simulation of Behaviour, 93–5, 2003. –Ed.

[2] For an algebraic machine theoretic approach to emulating behaviour, see also (Nehaniv, 1996).

Imitation and Social Learning in Robots, Humans and Animals, ed. Chrystopher L. Nehaniv and Kerstin Dautenhahn. Published by Cambridge University Press.

Note that *novelty* and *learning* are not explicitly required here, and whether or not the entire behaviour, or its application, or its components or some combination of them is novel or being learned is left open (see Whiten, 2002b; Dautenhahn and Nehaniv, 2002).

2.2   Correspondence problems

A *correspondence problem* for one agent – who is *trying to imitate* (compare Dautenhahn, 1994) another – possibly dissimilarly embodied agent is the problem of generating a 'suitable' matching behaviour:

Given an observed behavior of the model, which from a given starting state leads the model through a sequence (or hierarchy) of subgoals – in states, action, and/or effects, while possibly responding to sensory stimuli and external events, find and execute a sequence of actions using one's own (possibly dissimilar) embodiment, which from a corresponding starting state, lead through corresponding subgoals – in corresponding states, actions, and/or effects, while possibly responding to corresponding events. (Nehaniv and Dautenhahn, 2002)

We also consider below methods for solving correspondence problems that use reinforcement and result in learning.

2.3   Granularity and metrics

Notice that to fully specify a correspondence problem one needs a notion of *similarity* of action/events, states, and/or effects. Moreover, *granularity* serves to help specify the goal, or sequence, program or hierarchy of subgoals to be matched.

We consider metrics of dissimilarity that can take into account any matching in aspects of any subset of action/events, states and effects. By '*state*' we refer to aspects of the body state such as posture, by '*effect*' we refer to changes to the external state of the environment including objects external to the body or changes to the body–world relationship (e.g. position relative to certain external items, their states, positions, location and orientations) and by '*action/events*' to the induction of change by the agent's own motor activity ('*action*') or due to the action of external agents or phenomena ('*events*'). That is, an *action* is a self-initiated motor event, while an *event* is any other stimulus such as perception of other-initiated motor events.

We broadly classify granularity into *end* (considering only the overall cumulative changes), *coarse* (considering the overall and also some intermediate changes) and *fine* (considering the course of change at a fine-grained level).

The profound consequences of varying these parameters (metric and granularity) for the character of resulting attempted matched behaviour have been illustrated by computational results of Alissandrakis *et al.* (2002), wherein dissimilarly embodied agents employ different metrics and granularities to match the behaviour of a model.

2.4   Classification of correspondence problems

Depending on which subset of {*actions, states, effects*} is reflected in the measure of similarity of behaviours and depending on the type of granularity {*end, coarse, fine*} defining the sequence, hierarchy, or program of subgoals to be matched, correspondence problems naturally fall into 24 classes as shown in Table 2.1. Most of these classes comprise or refine well-known types of social learning and related phenomena. There are many particular metrics that fall into one of these 24 classes resulting in myriad correspondence problems.

This develops the classification presented by Nehaniv and Dautenhahn (2002), and is related to identification of sources of salient information also discussed by Call and Carpenter (2002) – see below.

2.4.1   *What is matched*

In describing any particular social learning or matching phenomena, it is important to make it clear exactly what is being matched, or at least to articulate hypotheses concerning what is being matched. Within each of the categories of actions, states and effects, there are numerous possibilities. The different ways these various aspects can be matched certainly number more than nine billion![3] Metrics are a way formalizing this (see e.g. Chapter 12, this volume; Nehaniv and Dautenhahn, 2001).

It is already very useful to state what is being matched informally. For example, a seated test subject facing a standing experimenter lifts and then lowers his right arm. This behaviour occurred after the subject had seen the experimenter lift and lower her left arm. We can hypothesize that *actions* are being matched *with mirror symmetry*.

If the subject had lifted his right arm, this would be indicative of matching actions with identical (rather than mirror) symmetry. The fact that the subject matched both raising and lowering of the arm shows us that granularity is not *end* (matching only the overall accumulated action), but must be *coarse* or *fine*. It might also be that the subject is matching

---

[3] Indeed, when formalized by metrics and (e.g. linear) combinations thereof, there are infinitely many.

Table 2.1 *Classes of Correspondence Problems Arising from Particular Combinations of Granularities and Metrics.*

+ or − denotes whether or not the metric measures similarity in the given aspect (action/events, states, or effects) of the model's behaviour

Class	Actions	States	Effects	Granularity
0	−	−	−	end
1	−	−	−	coarse
2	−	−	−	fine
3	−	−	+	end
4	−	−	+	coarse
5	−	−	+	fine
6	−	+	−	end
7	−	+	−	coarse
8	−	+	−	fine
9	+	−	−	end
10	+	−	−	coarse
11	+	−	−	fine
12	−	+	+	end
13	−	+	+	coarse
14	−	+	+	fine
15	+	−	+	end
16	+	−	+	coarse
17	+	−	+	fine
18	+	+	−	end
19	+	+	−	coarse
20	+	+	−	fine
21	+	+	+	end
22	+	+	+	coarse
23	+	+	+	fine

states (body postures, again with mirror symmetry), but if that is the case then he is not matching the overall posture but only the relative state of the arm. This is evidenced by the fact that he remains seated.

Whether or not any learning occurred in this case of social matching, we do not know, but this is unlikely since the matched actions are not novel for an adult human. Notice that no judgment is made concerning whether the subject 'imitated correctly' or 'incorrectly' – we merely describe the type of matching. The kind of behaviour matching in this particular example has often been described as 'just copying' or 'mere mimicry' without being any more specific. A description as *action*-matching with either *coarse* or *fine* granularity using mirror symmetry is much more informative.

2.4.2   Goals

Call and Carpenter (2002) identify sources of information regarding 'goal', 'action' and 'result' in their classification of types of social learning. Their notion of 'result' is a particular, end-granularity case of what we refer to as 'effect'. Their notion of 'goal' matching reflects sensitivity to the model's intentions. Certainly sensitivity to goals is important in numerous cases of social matching and social learning. Carpenter and Call discuss a number of potential sources of information on intentions that cannot be observed directly (see Chapter 7, this volume; cf. Tomasello and Call, 1997).[4]

Unfortunately, it seems problematic for their classification of social learning and related phenomena that one's *goal* may well lie in the particular manner in which *actions* are carried out, as for example in a dance performance, or it may be to achieve particular *results* (e.g. neatly opening an Easter egg which contains chocolate in one of their examples), or it may be a less specific type of result or goal (e.g. getting to the chocolate *somehow* (perhaps by breaking open the egg); or obtaining nourishment somehow. So matching goals might include matching actions, or matching results.

The insights of Call, Carpenter and Tomasello on the importance of goals for social learning are deep. Nevertheless, uses of the term 'goal' in the literature on social learning and imitation can often be factored into the matching of an *effect*, which is also the 'result' according to the intention of the model (as attributed to the model by the experimenter or observer) and the notion that that effect is 'right'.

We prefer therefore to treat as important the issue of determining the goal of a behaviour as integral to the issue of *what to match*. Determining a goal for social matching thus comprises determining the level of granularity and the aspects of *state, actions, effect* to match.

2.4.3   Learning

Separating what is matched from the question of what is learned by social observation or of whether any learning has occurred at all, is recommended in applying the classification of matching behaviour. It is then useful to discuss whether learning is occurring and what form it takes and what mechanisms might be involved.

For example, by observation of a piano teacher and *fine action* matching of her finger movements and timing, a piano student forms a

---

[4] See also Part III, What to Imitate, in this volume for an overview of the problem of determining what aspects of a behaviour should be matched.

sensorimotor association of the sound of a chord progression and control of his/her own finger movements.

Note that the definition of Mitchell (1987) given above for imitation perhaps serves better to describe *social matching*, without mentioning learning. Thus learning and social matching aspects can be examined separately and their conflation avoided.

2.4.4   *Types of social matching*

Types of behaviour-matching that may involve learning such as matched-dependent behaviour, action-level vs. program-level imitation, string parsing, stimulus enhancement, goal emulation, emulation, copying, tool/action affordance learning and other forms of social learning and related phenomena can be analyzed using this scheme (compare Nehaniv and Dautenhahn, 2002). In many cases, these types of behaviour matching will be seen to be further decomposable via application of the classification proposed here.

2.5   Analysis of some cases of social matching

2.5.1   *'Copying'/'mimicry'*

This term is generally used for *action* matching, but sometimes for other types of matching at an unspecified granularity. It is sometimes used to insinuate that the matcher does not understand the purpose (result or 'goal') of the behaviour.

2.5.2   *Stimulus/local enhancement*

Stimulus or *local enhancement* comprises observing the activity of others (usually conspecifics) at a particular kind of locale or in relation to a particular kind of object, combined with individual learning of some benefit that can be derived in this situation. The activity of the model at the locale or stimulus draws attention to the place or stimulus and thus increases its salience to the observer, allowing individual learning to be targeted at the locale or stimulus. A famous example is the social learning by certain British tits that the foil on milk bottles can be opened and nourishment obtained (see Zentall, 2001 for a survey of types of social learning).

Thus it involves the matching of an *effect* in the body–world relationship – in particular the matching of position of the body[5] with respect

---

[5] Or body-part, in which case at least some aspect of postural *state* is matched in addition, so that both *effect* and *state* are factors in matching.

to the locale or object. The granularity is (generally) *end* level since the social learner need only attain a cumulative result of putting itself in a particular relation with the rest of the world. Individual learning then takes over.

2.5.3   Program-level imitation

Program-level imitation involves the matching of a more complex generally sequential procedure involving the checking of conditions, iterations in behaviour considered as a behavioural program for achieving certain results, e.g. peeling and preparing a fruit for consumption (Byrne, 1999; Whiten, 2002a). The granularity here is *coarse* since many particular intermediate states are not necessarily matched, but many sub-goals are matched in the overall organization of the behaviour and *effects* on external objects are matched. Whether or not particular *actions* achieving them are matched is left open and can be studied. Whether the structure of a behavioural program is matched or whether the observer acquires a different program that achieves similar effects can also be investigated (compare studies of primates and human children, Whiten, 2002b).

Learning, if it occurs, concerns the overall program structure (the organization of *effects*, and possibly *actions* achieving them, at a *coarse* level, and the structure of a program).

2.5.4   Emulation and affordance learning

Emulation has been used to describe matching of 'results', and sometimes 'goals' (*goal emulation*) – (see Tomasello and Call, 1997). *Affordance learning* involves learning of *effects* that some objects have. A particularly interesting case is the matching of an *effect* that one object may produce when it is used to act upon another object (*tool affordances*). Granularity of matching is often *end*, focusing on the overall *effect* of the object or tool, but may be *coarse* if the affordance involves passing through several stages.

2.6   Synchrony and turn-taking

2.6.1   Rhythm, interaction and communicative kinesics

There are interesting classes at the head of the table corresponding to the empty subset of *states*, *actions*, *effects* at *fine*, *coarse* and cumulative (*end*) granularity. What could this mean in terms of social matching? A suggestion is that, in the case of immediate synchronic imitation, one might at the coarsest granular level match by making any response at all, as in acknowledgment. At *fine* or intermediate *coarse* granularity, this would reflect matching of timing as in interaction kinesics (aspects of interactive movement such as rhythm and timing in turn-taking, especially non-verbal ones). In these cases, particular aspects of state, action or effects are not matched, but the overall temporal organization of behaviour is matched.

Matching of movement and turn-taking in interaction (*kinesics*) occurs below the level of awareness in human–human interaction and involves subtle adjustments and synchronizations of timing of movement of which we are often unaware (Kendon, 1970; Condon and Ogston, 1967). Interaction kinesics is the study of the role and timing of non-verbal behaviour, including body movements, in communicative and interactional dynamics. Effector movements (hands, limbs, nodding, prosodic aspects of speech – such as coordinated rhythmic timing of vowels in first syllables of words, gaze direction change, etc.) and mirroring are subtly used to regulate human interaction: entering or breaking a rhythm serves in human–human dyads, and also groups, to regulate interactions, such as turn-taking, topic shift and entering or leaving a conversation (Kendon, 1970). Temporal scales of some of this behavioural coordination can be on the order of a few tens of milliseconds. Significant cultural differences in such timing (at this and other scales) and mismatches between cultures can lead to significant difficulties for human interaction (Hall, 1983).

Deferred matching in these classes is certainly conceivable, but perhaps generally without communicative aspects.

2.6.2   *Relation to human–robot interaction*

Robots, unlike humans, do not presently have a natural 'internal clock' and do not adjust the timing of the interaction to that of a human interaction partner, but the timing of robotic interaction could be designed to adaptively help regulate interaction. Some pioneering work of Japanese researchers has recently begun to touch on issues of using adaptive entrainment in human interaction with the artificial interaction partners, e.g. as an aid to walking rehabilitation (Miyake, 2003) or as an attentional, educational and persuasive aid (Ogawa and Watanabe, 2001; Watanabe, 2004). Nevertheless, this is just a foreshadowing of the expected development of this area of robot–human interaction kinesics (Robins *et al.*, 2005).

As examples from non-verbal synchronization and timing show, these types of matching are characteristically employed in communicative interactions as means to initiate, disengage, repair, maintain or regulate human–human interaction (e.g. Condon and Ogston, 1967; Kendon,

1970). Use of such synchronic matching has strong influences on the regulation and 'naturalness' in human–human interaction (Kendon, 1970; Hall, 1983). This suggests that interacting with robots with no sense of human time and timing is also likely to be unnatural or uncomfortable.

Traditionally kinesics has focused on human–human interaction in anthropological and psychological studies, but we propose here a more general view of kinesics motivated by the fact that interactive robots present us with the need to study and understand human–robot kinesics (see Robins *et al.*, 2005). Robot–human temporal interaction kinesics will eventually need to be studied deeply in order to put this dimension within the purview of human–robot interaction designers.

2.7   Solving correspondence problems

To solve correspondence problems one may use reinforcement learning mechanisms that reward actions or sequences of actions yielding a low dissimilarity measure according to the metric used. The result is social learning. A partial correspondence can be re-used in situations presenting new or variant instances of the original correspondence problem. Application of partial correspondences already found to new or somewhat new contexts constitutes generalization of socially learned behaviours. One such generic mechanism is action learning for imitation via correspondences between embodiments (ALICE) (see Alissandrakis *et al.*, 2002, 2003a). This has even been shown in examples to be robust to changes in the learner's embodiment, such as growth or damage (Chapter 12, this volume).

Social transmission of skills (horizontally and vertically) through a homogeneous or heterogeneous community is *cultural transmission*. The type of cultural transmission might by classified according to which of the 24 classes of correspondence problems is being solved, and on whether individual learning is also involved, but might alternatively involve other methods of social transmission that encode information in stories, formulae, and/or language (see Goodenough, 2002).

2.8   Learning what to imitate using measures of salience

The classification of correspondence problems presented here does not directly address the source of the choices of metrics or granularity (which describe the goal of a behaviour). In animal and psychological cases, *salience* of the particular subset of {*action/events, states, effects*} is expected to play a crucial role, as are the capacities of the animal to employ mechanisms that could solve the particular problem.

Calinon and Billard (Chapter 8, this volume) suggest to use invariants of repeated demonstrations to determine what is relevant to imitate. Carpenter and Call (Chapter 7, this volume) survey a number of goal-marking cues in interaction that may serve to allow another agent to determine the goal of a behaviour. Belpaeme, de Boer, and Jansen (Chapter 9, this volume) consider emergent categories of characteristic behaviours in a population of imitating agents, whereby behaviours classified by individual members of the population into a particular category allow the observer to select exhibiting another, possibly different, behaviour from that same category as a goal. Over time, the population's categories for 'what to imitate' emerge in a self-organized way.

In robotics, software and agent implementations, choice of metric and granularity could be similarly driven by salience (e.g. as measured by another metric to guide the agent in choosing between the classes of correspondence problem). Thus a notion of value, meaningfulness or relevance (see Nehaniv, 1999) to the agent could be employed to select and tune metrics – in effect, to allow the agent itself to decide what to imitate (see Dautenhahn and Nehaniv, 2002). This paradigm is suggested here for use in autonomously approaching and solving problems of matched behaviour and social learning.

Acknowledgments

The author is grateful to Kerstin Dautenhahn and Aris Alissandrakis for useful discussions.

REFERENCES

Alissandrakis, A., Nehaniv, C. L. and Dautenhahn, K. (2002). Imitation with ALICE: learning to imitate corresponding actions across dissimilar embodiments. *IEEE Transactions on Systems, Man and Cybernetics: Part A*, **32(4)**, 482–96.
Alissandrakis, A., Nehaniv, C. L. and Dautenhahn, K. (2003a). Solving the correspondence problem between dissimilarly embodied robotic arms using the ALICE imitation mechanism. In *Proceedings of the Second International Symposium on Imitation in Animals and Artifacts* (K. Dautenhahn and C. L. Nehaniv, Programme Chairs). Society for the Study of Artificial Intelligence and Simulation of Behaviour (AISB).
Alissandrakis, A., Nehaniv, C. L. and Dautenhahn, K. (2003b). Synchrony and perception in robotic imitation across embodiments. In *IEEE International Symposium on Computational Intelligence in Robotics and Automation (CIRA'03)*, 923–30.

Billard, A. and Dautenhahn, K. (1998). Grounding communication in autonomous robots: an experimental study. *Robotics and Autonomous Systems*, **24(1–2)**, 71–81.

Byrne, R. W. (1999). Imitation without intentionality: using string parsing to copy the organization of behaviour. *Animal Cognition*, 2, 63–72.

Byrne, R. W. and Russon, A. E. (1998). Learning by imitation: a hierarchical approach. *Behavioral and Brain Sciences*, 21, 667–709.

Call, J. and Carpenter, M. (2002). Three sources of information in social learning. In Dautenhahn, K. and Nehaniv, C. L. (eds.), *Imitation in Animals and Artifacts*. Cambridge, MA: MIT Press, 211–28.

Condon, W. S. and Ogston, W. D. (1967). A segmentation of behavior. *Journal of Psychiatric Research*, 5, 221–35.

Dautenhahn, K. (1994). Trying to imitate – a step towards releasing robots from social isolation. In Gaussier, P. and Nicoud, J.-D. (eds.), *Proceedings of From Perception to Action Conference, Lausanne, Switzerland*. Los Alamitos, CA: IEEE Computer Society Press, 290–301.

Dautenhahn, K. (1995). Getting to know each other – artificial social intelligence for autonomous robots. *Robotics and Autonomous Systems*, 16, 333–56.

Dautenhahn, K. and Nehaniv, C. L. (2002). An agent-based perspective on imitation. In Dautenhahn, K. and Nehaniv, C. L. (eds.), *Imitation in Animals and Artifacts*. Cambridge, MA: MIT Press.

Goodenough, O. (2002). Information and replication in culture: three modes for the transmission of culture through observed action. In Dautenhahn, K. and Nehaniv, C. L. (eds.), *Imitation in Animals and Artifacts*. Cambridge, MA: MIT Press, 573–585.

Hall, E. T. (1983). *The Dance of Life: The Other Dimension of Time*. New York, NY: Anchor Press/Doubleday.

Heyes, C. M. and Galef, B. G. (1996). *Social Learning in Animals: The Roots of Culture*. Academic Press.

Heyes, C. M. and Ray, E. D. (2000). What is the significance of imitation in animals? *Advances in the Study of Behavior*, 29, 215–45.

Kendon, A. (1970). Movement coordination in social interaction: some examples described. *Acta Psychologica*, 32, 100–25.

Mitchell, R. W. (1987). A comparative-developmental approach to understanding imitation. In Bateson, P. P. G. and Klopfer, P. H. (eds.), *Perspectives in Ethology 7: Alternatives*. New York, NY: Plenum Press, 183–215.

Miyake, Y. (2003). Co-creation in man–machine interaction. In *12th IEEE International Workshop on Robot and Human Interactive Communication (ROMAN 2003)*, 321–4.

Nehaniv, C. L. (1996). From relation to emulation: the covering lemma for transformation semigroups. *Journal of Pure and Applied Algebra*, **107(1)**, 75–87.

Nehaniv, C. L. (1999). Meaning for observers and agents. In *IEEE International Symposium on Intelligent Control/Intelligent Systems and Semiotics, ISIC/ISAS'99 – September 15–17, 1999 Cambridge, Massachusetts, USA*, 435–440.

Nehaniv, C. L. and Dautenhahn, K. (2001). Like me? – measures of correspondence and imitation. *Cybernetics and Systems*, **32(1–2)**, 11–51.

Nehaniv, C. L. and Dautenhahn, K. (2002). The correspondence problem. In Dautenhahn, K. and Nehaniv, C. L. (ed.), *Imitation in Animals and Artifacts.* Cambridge, MA: MIT Press.

Ogawa, H. and Watanabe, T. (2001). Interrobot: speech-driven embodied interaction robot. *Advanced Robotics,* **15(3),** 371–7.

Robins, B., Dautenhahn, K., Nehaniv, C. L., Mirza, N. A., Francois, D., and Olsson, L. (2005). Sustaining interaction dynamics and engagement in dyadic child–robot interaction kinesics: lessons learnt from an exploratory study. In *14th IEEE International Workshop on Robot and Human Interactive Communication (ROMAN 2005),* 716–22.

Tomasello, M. and Call, J. (1997). *Primate Cognition.* Oxford: Oxford University Press.

Watanabe, T. (2004). E-cosmic: embodied communication system for mind connection. In *13th IEEE International Workshop on Robot and Human Interactive Communication (ROMAN 2004),* 1–6.

Whiten, A. (2002a). Imitation of sequential and hierarchical structure in action: experimental studies with children and chimpanzees. In Dautenhahn, K. and Nehaniv, C. L. (eds.), *Imitation in Animals and Artifacts.* Cambridge, MA: MIT Press, 191–209.

Whiten, A. (2002b). Selective imitation in ape and child: A window on the construal of others' actions. Presentation at *Perspectives on Imitation: From Cognitive Neuroscience to Social Science (Royaumont Abbey – France, 24–26 May 2002, Organizer: Susan Hurley).*

Zentall, T. and B. G. Galef, J. (eds.) (1988). *Social Learning: Psychological and Biological Perspectives.* Hillsdale, NJ: Lawrence Erlbaum Associates.

Zentall, T. R. (2001). Imitation and other forms of social learning in animals: evidence, function, and mechanisms. *Cybernetics and Systems,* **32(1–2),** 5396.

3   Challenges and issues faced in building a
     framework for conducting research in
     learning from observation

*Darrin Bentivegna, Christopher Atkeson
and Gordon Cheng*

3.1   Introduction

We are exploring how primitives, small units of behavior, can speed up
robot learning and enable robots to learn difficult dynamic tasks in reasonable amounts of time. In this chapter we describe work on learning
from observation and learning from practice on air hockey and marble
maze tasks. We discuss our research strategy, results, and open issues and
challenges.

Primitives are units of behavior above the level of motor or muscle commands. There have been many proposals for such units of behavior in neuroscience, psychology, robotics, artificial intelligence and machine learning (Arkin, 1998; Schmidt, 1988; Schmidt, 1975; Russell and Norvig,
1995; Barto and Mahadevan, 2003). There is a great deal of evidence
that biological systems have units of behavior above the level of activating individual motor neurons, and that the organization of the brain
reflects those units of behavior (Loeb, 1989). We know that in human eye
movement, for example, there are only a few types of movements including saccades, smooth pursuit, vestibular ocular reflex (VOR), optoki-
netic nystagmus (OKN) and vergence, that general eye movements are
generated as sequences of these behavioral units, and that there are distinct brain regions dedicated to generating and controlling each type
of eye movement (Carpenter, 1988). We know that there are discrete
locomotion patterns, or gaits, for animals with legs (McMahon, 1984).
Whether there are corresponding units of behavior for upper limb movement in humans and other primates is not yet clear. There is evidence
from neuroscience and brain imaging that there are distinct areas of the

Imitation and Social Learning in Robots, Humans and Animals, ed. Chrystopher L. Nehaniv
and Kerstin Dautenhahn. Published by Cambridge University Press.

brain for different types of movements (Kandel *et al.*, 1984). Developing a computational theory that explains the roles of primitives in generating behavior and learning is an important step towards understanding how biological systems generate behavior and learn.

The primitives being explored in this research can be referred to as task-level primitives; behavioral actions that are specific to a single task or a related group of tasks. The performance of a primitive leads to an intermediate goal, or sub-goal, and the performance of a sequence of primitives leads to the completion of the task. The primitives are described in terms of the task elements. An example of a primitive in the marble maze is *roll to corner*. A player performs this primitive to maneuver the marble along a wall into a corner. This primitive can be performed many times during the task to maneuver the marble into various corners in the maze. Notice that the primitive is described in terms that are appropriate to the marble maze task such as marble, walls, and corners.

Modularity is key to good design. Behavioral units or primitives are a way to support modularity in the design of behaviors. Primitives are an important step towards reasoning about behavior, abstraction and applying general knowledge across a wide range of behaviors. We believe that restricting behavioral options by adopting a set of primitives is a good way to handle high dimensional tasks. Consider the everyday task of putting on or taking off clothes. Because of the large number of degrees of freedom of the cloth, it is difficult to imagine current planners could plan appropriate motions from scratch or at the level of a sequence of task states. The large number of possible actions and states also make learning difficult, if not impossible. What is the sword that cuts this Gordian knot? If the set of possible actions is restricted to a small set, it becomes possible to explore the space of possible actions and find a sequence that works well. However, the Achilles heel of such an approach is that the set of possible actions must match the task. We need to understand the role of primitives in generating behavior and learning to better understand these challenges, and build more effective learning robots.

3.2   Challenges with using primitives

This section outlines some of the challenges involved with using primitives and provides examples of the methods by which these challenges are being addressed.

A task that is to be performed using primitives must first be decomposed into a set of primitives that include all the actions needed to perform the task. This challenge can be dealt with by having a human task expert define the set of primitives (Ryan and Reid, 2000) or have the robot discover primitives automatically after observing a performance of the task (Fod *et al.*, 2000) or operating in the task environment (McGovern and Barto, 2001). Once a set of primitives is defined, the robot must have a way to learn how to perform them. Some research deals with this by explicitly programming the primitive performance policy into the agent (Brooks, 1986) or having the robot learn the policy using learning techniques (Aboaf *et al.*, 1989). Given a set of primitives and a task, the robot must decide on which primitive to perform at any given time. This has been accomplished by a human specifying the sequence of primitive types to be performed (Mataric *et al.*, 1998), using a planning system (Tung and Kak, 1995), or having the robot learn the sequence from observed data (Kuniyoshi *et al.*, 1994).

At first thought, choosing a primitive from among a small set sounds like a simple procedure. But almost all primitives have parameters such as speed of execution and desired ending state (Wooten and Hodgins, 2000). These parameters can have continuous values and therefore can be difficult to select or learn through trial and error (Likhachev and Arkin, 2001).

The advantages of using primitives includes the ability for them to be used multiple times while performing a task and to also use primitives learned in one task in the performance of similar tasks (Dieterich, 1998). Learning can occur at many levels when learning through practice using primitives. Among the items that can be learned while operating in the task environment are the primitive type which should be performed (Balch, 1997), the parameters to use with the chosen primitive (Pearce, Arkin and Ram, 1992), and the primitive execution policy (Lin, 1993). Many methods can be used to learn each of these items and an open issue is how to choose a method that works best for a given environment.

When using observed data to learn a task other challenges are introduced. From all the information that the robot is presented with, it must decide on what is relevant for learning the task (Kaiser and Dillmann, 1996). The observed data must also be segmented into primitives if it is to learn such things as primitive sequence performance, needed parameters or primitive execution policy from the observed data. Segmenting and learning relevant features to observe can be accomplished in many ways. Explicitly providing only the pre-segmented information (Delson and West, 1996), specifying conditions that represent segmentation points (Mori *et al.*, 2001; Kang and Ikeuchi, 1993), and using hidden Markov models (Hovland *et al.*, 1996) are some of the methods that have been explored.

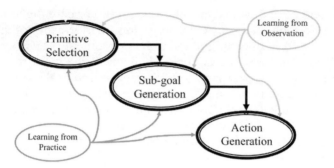

Figure 3.1 Three-part framework for learning using primitives that work best for a given environment.

3.3   Research strategy

Our current research strategy is to focus on the selection of primitives and generation of sub-goals and control policies during learning. Therefore, we use existing libraries of manually generated primitives. We are deferring the question of how to invent new primitives until we better understand how primitives are best used. We are exploring a three-part framework for using primitives as the robot performs the task (Figure 3.1). A classifier selects the type of primitive to use in a given context (*Primitive Selection*). A function approximator produces the appropriate arguments or parameters for the selected primitive (*Sub-goal Generation*). Another function approximator computes the necessary commands to achieve the sub-goal specified by the parameters for the primitive (*Action Generation*). The *Learning from Observation* module segments and formats the observed data.

This framework supports learning from practice. If a single function approximator directly predicted commands, there would be no representation of the desired outcome in that situation, and thus no way to correct the commands for context specific desired outcomes. The Learning from Practice module monitors the robot's progress towards completion of the task and provides feedback to the framework algorithms so they can improve their performance.

In the following sections we describe our approach to learning from observation and practice using primitives. Appendix A describes the details of the method used to choose primitives and compute sub-goals from observing others and Appendix B shows how primitive selection and sub-goal generation are improved through practice. In this presentation we assume the learner already knows how to execute a selected primitive. Our robots have either been programmed to be able to perform each of

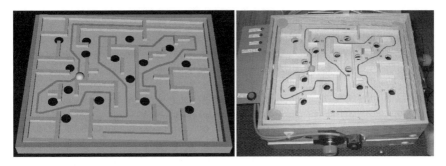

Figure 3.2 Software and hardware Marble Maze environments. The hardware version has motors to move the board and a vision system to observe the position of the marble. The human can play the game by using two knobs connected to encoders.

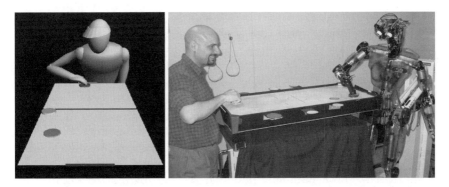

Figure 3.3 (Plate 5) The software air hockey game on the left and air hockey playing with a humanoid robot on the right.

the primitives in our manually designed primitive library or have learned a policy from observing others. The details of how our robots acquire the primitive performance skills are presented in Bentivegna *et al.* (2003) and Bentivegna (2004).

3.3.1   *Testing environments*

We have used two tasks to develop our thinking, marble maze and air hockey (Figures 3.2 and 3.3 (Plate 5)). We selected these tasks because (1) they are challenging dynamic tasks with different characteristics and (2) robots have been programmed to do both tasks (Spong, 1999), so they are doable, and to the extent there are published descriptions, there are other implementations to compare to. The marble maze task is

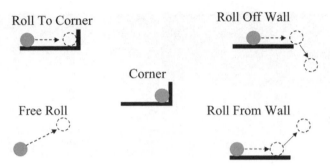

Figure 3.4 Primitives being explored in the marble maze.

similar to parts orientation using tray tilting (Erdmann and Mason, 1988). The marble maze task allows us to explore generalization across different board layouts, while air hockey allows us to explore generalization across different opponents. We have developed versions of these games to be played by simulated agents and by robots. Although hardware implementations necessarily include real world effects, we can collect useful training data from the simulations without the cost of running the full robot setups, and can perform more repeatable and controllable experiments in simulation. We believe that our approach to these tasks can generalize to a wide range of intermittent dynamic tasks.

In the marble maze game (Figure 3.2) a player controls a marble through a maze by tilting the board that the marble is rolling on. The primitives we have manually designed for the marble maze game are based on our observations of human players. The following primitives are currently being explored and are shown in Figure 3.4:

- Roll To Corner: The ball rolls along a wall and stops when it hits another wall.
- Corner: The ball is in a corner and the board is being positioned to move the marble from the corner.
- Roll Off Wall: The ball rolls along a wall and then rolls off the end of the wall.
- Roll From Wall: The ball hits, or is on, a wall and then is maneuvered off it.
- Free Roll: The ball is rolled from one location to another without touching a wall.

The hardware air hockey task has been created using a humanoid robot (Figure 3.3). The humanoid robot has 30 degrees of freedom and is 190 cm tall. It is hydraulically actuated and attached to a stable pedestal at the hips. The robot is placed at one end of the table and plays the

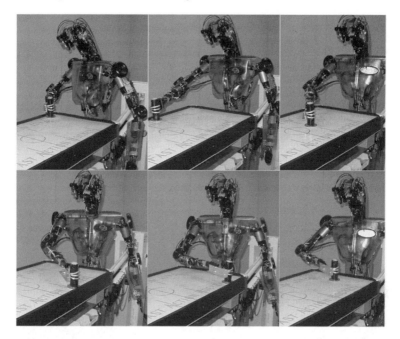

Figure 3.5 (Plate 6) Six manually defined configurations are used to interpolate the body configuration needed to place the paddle at a specific location.

game using one arm. It views the position of the objects using cameras that are on pan-tilt mechanisms on the humanoid's head. The robot uses a simple interpolation scheme to locate the puck and paddles with respect to additional visual markers in the plane of the playing area.

An interpolation scheme is also used to solve the redundant inverse kinematics problem to position the paddle on the playing surface. Figure 3.5 (Plate 6) shows six manually generated body configurations that correspond to a paddle placement location. To position the paddle at any location within these configurations, the closest four configurations are combined using a bilinear interpolation method. While this approach is simple and allows us to solve the redundant inverse kinematics problem, we have found that the accuracy of positioning the paddle is affected by many things such as the initial position of the board, the paddle's movement speed, and the friction between the paddle and the board. More information on the vision system and paddle positioning method can be found in Bentivegna *et al.* (2002).

The manually defined primitives that we are exploring for this task are:

- Straight Shot: A player hits the puck and it goes toward the opponent's goal without hitting a wall.
- Bank Shot: A player hits the puck and the puck hits a wall and then goes toward the opponent's goal.
- Defend Goal: A player moves to a position to prevent the puck from entering their goal area.
- Slow Puck: A player hits a slow moving puck that is within their reach.
- Idle: A player rests their paddle while the puck is on the opponent's side.

3.4   Learning from observation

In learning from observation the robot observes a human or another robot performing a task, and uses that information to do the task. In learning from observation without primitives, the robot learns desired states or state trajectories and corresponding low-level actions or action sequences (Schaal, 1997). It is difficult to generalize much beyond the state trajectories or reuse information across tasks. It is also difficult to reason about what the demonstrator was trying to do at any time during the demonstration. We propose that primitives provide a way to generalize more aggressively, and to reuse information more effectively. Furthermore, selecting the appropriate primitive can be interpreted as selecting a sub-goal in that point of the task, a simple form of reasoning.

The example tasks, marble maze and air hockey, have been chosen to some extent because it is relatively easy to *segment* an observation into distinct primitives. We propose a strategy based on *critical events*. Examples of critical events for air hockey include puck collisions with a wall or paddle, in which the puck speed and direction are rapidly changed. In the marble maze, initiating and terminating contact with a wall are examples of critical events (Figure 3.6). In this preliminary research, algorithms have been manually created that automatically segment the observed data into the predefined primitives by searching for sequences of critical events. Parameters or sub-goals are estimated by observing the state of the task at the transition to the next observed primitive.

In learning from observation using primitives the learner learns a policy of which primitive type and sub-goal to use in each task state. The segmented observation data can be used to train this mechanism. We have taken a memory-based approach, using a k-nearest neighbor scheme for the classifier that selects primitives, and kernel-based regression for the function approximator that provides sub-goals. These methods use a distance function to compute a numerical value that represents how similar a query is to each experience stored in memory. This numerical value is

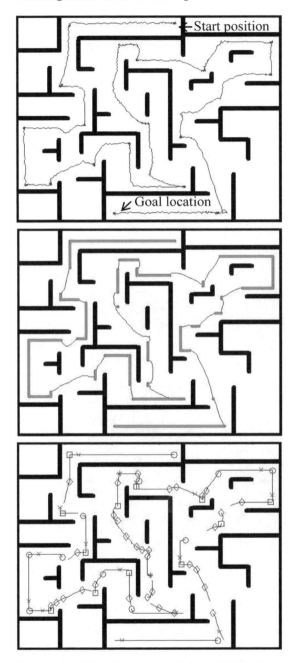

Figure 3.6 Top: Raw observed data. Middle: Wall contact identified by thicker line. Bottom: Symbols show the start of recognized primitives.

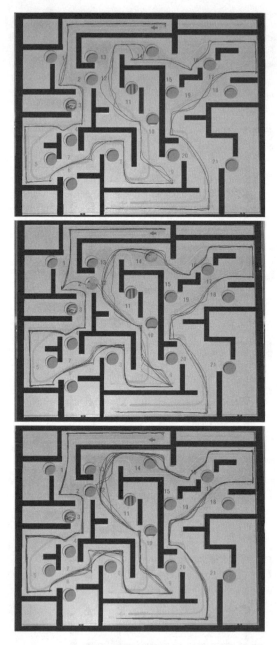

Figure 3.7 Top: The three observed games played by the human teacher. Middle: Performance on ten games based on learning from observation using the three training games. The maze was successfully completed five times, and the small circles mark where the ball fell into the holes. Bottom: Performance on 10 games based on learning from practice after 30 practice games. There were no failures.

then used as a weight to compute an output. Memory-based approaches have a number of other benefits, such as rapid learning, low interference and control over forgetting (Atkeson *et al.*, 1997). Appendix A presents the details of the algorithm used to select a primitive type and compute a sub-goal using the observation data. Chapter 12 (Alissandrakis, Nehaniv and Dautenhahn, this volume) presents the ALICE framework that uses a similar memory-based approach to imitate arm movements.

We first tested our robots to learn from observation only; the Learning from Practice module (Figure 3.1) is not used and the robots do not learn, or change their behavior, as they perform the task. In this situation the robot does not have explicit knowledge of the higher objective of the task and the robot tries to perform the same primitives as the teacher to obtain the observed sub-goals. Figure 3.7 shows the observation data (top) and performance of using that data (middle) on the hardware marble maze task. The humanoid robot playing air hockey provides a fun and challenging opponent and a video of the robot in action can be downloaded from (Bentivegna, 2004).

3.5   Improving performance through practice

It was clear from our preliminary research that learning from demonstration alone has several deficits. Even under ideal conditions the learner learns to imitate the performance of the teacher, not to do better than the teacher. We observe that the same mistakes tend to be made over and over. To improve further additional learning mechanisms are necessary, such as the ability to learn from practice in addition to learning from watching others perform. The *Learning from Practice* module (Figure 3.1) contains the information needed to evaluate the performance of each primitive towards obtaining the task objectives. This information is used to update primitive selection, and sub-goal and action generation. A tough question is where the task objective comes from. Ideally, it should be learned from observation. The learner should infer the intent of the teacher. This is very difficult, and we defer addressing this question by manually specifying a task criterion.

Using the framework, the robots have the ability to increase performance at various levels. Our research focuses on learning at two levels: (1) primitive selection and sub-goal generation and (2) action generation. Our primitive selection and sub-goal generation method provides us with one mechanism, the distance function, that can be used to improve performance in both primitive selection and sub-goal generation. Our system learns by modifying the calculated distances between a query and the stored experiences in memory. Appendix B describes the algorithm

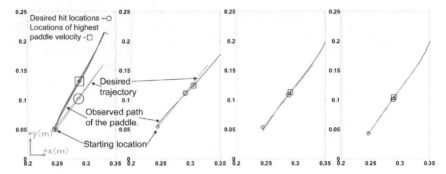

Figure 3.8 The lines with the boxes on them in these graphs show the path of the paddle during shot maneuvers. The lines with the circles on them are the desired trajectories. The graph on the left shows three similar shot attempts overlaid. The errors are due to board placement errors and the robot's variance in making shots at different velocities. The three right graphs show the same shot maneuver being made after practicing.

that combines a locally weighted learning technique (Atkeson *et al.*, 1997) with a Q learning (Watkins and Dayan, 1992) technique to give the robots the ability to increase their performance at selecting primitives and computing sub-goals. Figure 3.7 (bottom) shows that the robot improved its performance at the marble maze task using this learning technique.

In the air hockey task we found that quickly adapting to small changes in the task was very important for acceptable performance by the humanoid robot. More generally, for humanoid robots to be accepted as partners with humans they will be expected to learn quickly and adapt to changes in ways similar to humans. Within a single task there may be many things that can change as humans interact with the robot. The placement of items within the workspace, the physics of the task, and the reaction of the human to the robot's movements are some examples of the things which can vary during the interaction. This type of adaptation and learning can take place at the action generation level. The humanoid robot has the ability to learn models of the environment and its own movements while practicing. Figure 3.8 shows the robot improved its ability to place the paddle at the proper hit position after practicing hit movements. The three graphs on the right show the results of using a trained model to make the same maneuver as the one shown in the graph on the left. Each graph shows one hit maneuver and the robot starts in approximately the same initial state. The graphs show that the robot has learned to more accurately place the paddle at the desired hit location with the velocity vector pointing in the correct direction and the location at which the highest paddle velocity is seen is now much closer to the desired hit position. The action level learning and adaptation methods are more fully presented in Bentivegna *et al.* (2003).

3.6   Discussion

It is a common belief that the most important research issue in primitives is how they are invented for a new task. This is not necessarily correct. It is believed that we are born with an existing library of biological eye movement primitives and gaits (Carpenter, 1988; McMahon, 1984). It may be the case that biological systems utilize a fixed library of motor primitives during their lifetime. It may be the case that we can manually create a library of primitives for robots that cover a wide range of everyday tasks, and that invention of new primitives is simply not necessary; hence the emphasis in this work on exploring how to make effective use of existing primitives. It is our hope that this exploration will inform the design of a general set of primitives.

Several issues have become clearer through this work. We have identified some of the knowledge whose acquisition will have to be automated for fully automatic learning: defining the primitives, determining how to execute the primitives, determining how to recognize primitives, learning a reward function, determining the features, states and actions available in the task, and recognizing special properties of the domain, such as the role of walls and the progressive nature of the marble maze task.

We found that the distance function in a memory-based approach in the marble maze task needed to handle stiff discontinuities, such as not generalizing across walls. We need to develop automatic learning of the range of generalization. There are numerous opportunities to take advantage of symmetry in the marble maze task, and we are exploring alternate features to represent the task and the current context. We need to take into account time and the progressive nature of the task to avoid endlessly repeating cycles of primitives and not making progress. We need to explore learning what to forget, as learned information loses validity.

What properties should a set of primitives have? In order to learn from observation, primitives need to be recognizable from observable data. Good primitives divide learning problems up, so that each individual learning problem is simplified. For example, primitives that break input/output relationships up at discontinuities may lead to a set of simple learning problems with smooth input/output relationships.

An example of the robot learning a new strategy is shown in Figure 3.7. In the three observed games the human maneuvers the marble below hole 14. During practice the agent falls into hole 14 and learns that it can more easily maneuver the marble around the top of hole 14. We did not even know this action was possible until we observed the action discovered by the agent.

3.6.1   Framework considerations

This section discusses some of the design decisions that went into creating the framework sketched in Figure 3.1. While a framework offers structure and can help modularize the problem, it also limits what can be done to only things provided for by the framework. Many decisions have gone into creating our framework that supports an appropriate trade-off between modularization and flexibility. The ability to use observed data in a systematic way and to learn while practicing were two of the main concerns while creating the framework. The ability to generalize within the environment and to other environments was also considered.

Combining primitive type and parameter selection

The framework first selects the primitive type to perform for the observed environment state. The selected primitive type then narrows down the search for the parameters needed. What if we do away with the primitive selection module and just have the sub-goal generation module provide the next sub-goal? To use that sub-goal information there must be a higher level process that can select the primitive policy that needs to be performed to obtain that sub-goal from the agent's current state. We are now back to the original problem of selecting a primitive type to use, but have different information with which to select it. For this situation it would be good if a primitive policy could tell us if it is capable of taking the system from the current state to the goal state. The research of Faloutsos *et al.* provides an example of a method to find the set of preconditions under which a policy will operate correctly and also shows how difficult this is (Faloutsos *et al.*, 2001). It is our belief that by first committing to a primitive type we are simplifying the learning problem by only having to learn the set of parameters appropriate to that primitive type. By separating these modules the method used to provide the needed information can be unique for each decision providing extra flexibility.

Combining parameter selection and primitive execution

Once a primitive type is selected the primitive execution policy can choose the needed parameters thereby eliminating the sub-goal module. This method leads to a loss in generality and flexibility. The primitive execution module contains the policy to bring the system from the current state to a new state within the constraints of the primitive type. The primitive execution policy is designed to be used in different parts of the environment state space. Combining these modules prevents reuse of the execution policies. Also, the sub-goal can be generated using any method and any information needed. By separating these modules the sub-goals can be generated using a coarse discretization of the environment state space and the policy can then use any method appropriate to control the system (for example Morimoto and Doya, 1998).

3.7 Conclusions

Choosing actions to perform when operating in a dynamic environment, such as the marble maze and air hockey environments described in this chapter, is a difficult task. Because the state space is large and continuous, expecting to learn entirely from random actions is not realistic. An initial policy can be created using knowledge of primitive actions performed in the environment and information obtained from observing others. Within our research we find that the performance of the initial policy is quite high but there is still room for improvement. This initial policy provides a very good starting point from which to practice to further increase competence at the task.

Our learning from observation framework described in Section 3.3 provides flexibility in conducting research in learning from observing others. The framework uses the observed data in a systematic way and the organization of the data supports a memory-based approach to learning. The framework also supports continued learning from practicing the task.

Acknowledgments

Support for all authors was provided by ATR Computational Neuroscience Laboratories, Department of Humanoid Robotics and Computational Neuroscience, and the National Institute of Information and Communications Technology (NiCT). It was also supported in part by National Science Foundation Award ECS-0325383, and the Japan Science and Technology Agency, ICORP, Computational Brain Project.

Appendix

A.   Selecting a primitive type and generating a sub-goal

Each time a primitive is observed in the training data a corresponding data point is stored in a database that is indexed by the state of the task at the time the primitive was performed. During execution, the current state is used to look up in the database the most common primitive type near that state, which determines which kind of primitive to use. In the marble maze task, for example, the query consists of the marble's position and velocity, and board tilt angles $(Mx, My, \dot{M}x, \dot{M}y, Bx, By)$. The closest data point can be used to decide which type of primitive to use. The sub-goal of the primitives are also specified by the database of prior observations. The closest N stored experiences that involved the same primitive type are used to compute the sub-goal for the primitive to be performed. We compute the parameters using kernel regression:

$$\hat{\theta}(\mathbf{q}) = \frac{\sum_{i=1}^{N} \theta_i \cdot K(d(\mathbf{x}_i, \mathbf{q}))}{\sum_{i=1}^{N} K(d(\mathbf{x}_i, \mathbf{q}))} \tag{3.1}$$

where $\hat{\theta}(\mathbf{q})$ is the computed sub-goal to be used for query point $\mathbf{q}$, θ_i is the sub-goal specified by a single data point, $d(\mathbf{x}_i, \mathbf{q})$ is the Euclidean distance between the data point $\mathbf{x}_i$ and the query point $\mathbf{q}$ and $K(d)$ is the kernel function and is typically $e^{-d^2/\alpha}$. As can be seen, the estimate for $\hat{\theta}$ depends on the location of the query point, $\mathbf{q}$. We are also exploring using locally weighted regression to perform this interpolation/extrapolation (Atkeson *et al.*, 1997).

B.   *Improving primitive selection and sub-goal generation from practice*

Our system learns from practice by changing the distance function used in the nearest neighbor lookup done in both selecting primitives and generating sub-goals. Let's consider the simplest case, where a nearest neighbor classifier is used to select the primitive used in the experience most similar to the current context. If the closest primitive actually leads to bad consequences, we want to increase the apparent distance, so that a different experience becomes the "closest" and a different primitive is tried. If the closest primitive leads to good consequences, we want to decrease the apparent distance. In the nearest neighbor case, decreasing the distance to the closest point has no effect, but in the k-nearest neighbor and kernel regression cases it increases the likelihood that that primitive type is selected and increases the weighting of its sub-goal.

Let us continue to consider the simplest case, a nearest neighbor approach. We use an estimate of the value function, or actually a Q function, to represent the consequences, numerically represented reward (cost or benefit), of choosing a particular primitive in the current task state (Watkins and Dayan, 1992). A Q function takes as arguments the current task state and an action. In our case, the task state is the query

$\mathbf{q}$ to the database, and the action is choosing the point $\mathbf{x}_i$, so we have $Q(\mathbf{x}_i, \mathbf{q})$ as the consequence. Choosing the point $\mathbf{x}_i$ directly effects the action that is taken in the real world. In the case that we are maximizing the reward, we use this Q value as a scale factor on the distance, where C is a normalizing constant. The distance function $d(\mathbf{x}_i, \mathbf{q})$ in Equation (3.1) is replaced with the new distance function:

$$\hat{d}(\mathbf{x}_i, \mathbf{q}) = d(\mathbf{x}_i, \mathbf{q}) * \frac{C}{Q(\mathbf{x}_i, \mathbf{q})} \qquad (3.2)$$

The scale factor will have the effect of moving a stored experience in relationship to the query point. Scale factors C/Q greater than 1.0 will have the effect of moving the data point farther away from the query point and scale factors less then 1.0 have the effect of moving the data point closer to the query point. For example, if the marble falls into a hole after a selected primitive is performed, the scale factors associated with the set of data points that voted for that primitive selection or contributed to the sub-goal generation can be increased. The next time the agent finds itself in the same state, those data points will appear further away and will therefore have less effect on the chosen action.

In our memory-based approach, we associate the Q values with our experiences, $Q_i(\mathbf{x}_i, \mathbf{q})$. In order to support indexing the Q values with the query $\mathbf{q}$, we actually associate a table of Q values with each stored experience, and use that table to approximate $Q_i(\mathbf{x}_i, \mathbf{q})$. This also solves the problem that from one query point state the chosen experiences may be appropriate, but from a different query point, these experiences may not work very well. With a table associated with each stored experience, we can handle this effect. In the marble maze environment the state space is six dimensional. Each dimension is quantized into five cells. Each stored experience in the database has a table of size 5^6. For any query point in the state space, its position relative to the data point is used to find the cell that is associated with that query point. Since we expect only a small fraction of the cells to be used, the tables are stored as sparse arrays and only when the value in a cell is initially updated is the cell actually created.

Q learning lends itself very well to updating values by taking into account the result of actions taken in the future. The Q values are initialized with a constant and then updated using a modified version of the Q-learning function. For each of the data points chosen, the Q-values are updated as follows:

$$Q(\mathbf{q}_t, \mathbf{x}_m) = Q(\mathbf{q}_t, \mathbf{x}_m) + \alpha \cdot [r + Q(\hat{\mathbf{q}}, \hat{\mathbf{x}}) - Q(\mathbf{q}_t, \mathbf{x}_m)] \qquad (3.3)$$

where:

- α is the learning rate. Since multiple points are used, the weighting given by $K(d(\mathbf{x}_i, \mathbf{q}_t))/\sum_{j=1}^{N} K(d(\mathbf{x}_j, \mathbf{q}_t))$ is used as the learning rate. This weighting has the effect of having points that contributed the most toward selecting the primitive having the highest learning rate.
- r is the reward observed after the primitive has been performed.
- $Q(\hat{\mathbf{q}}, \hat{\mathbf{x}})$ is the future reward that can be expected from the new state $\hat{\mathbf{q}}$ and selecting the data points $\hat{\mathbf{x}}$ at the next time step. This value is given by:

$$\sum_{i=1}^{N} \left[Q(\hat{\mathbf{q}}, \hat{\mathbf{x}}_i) \cdot \frac{K(d(\hat{\mathbf{x}}_i, \hat{\mathbf{q}}))}{\sum_{j=1}^{N} K(d(\hat{\mathbf{x}}_j, \hat{\mathbf{q}}))} \right]$$

Figure 3.7 shows the improved performance at the marble maze task with practice using this Q-like learning algorithm. When a primitive ends a reward is calculated and an update occurs. A more detailed analysis of this algorithm is presented in Bentivegna (2004).

REFERENCES

Aboaf, E., Drucker, S. and Atkeson, C. (1989). Task-level robot learning: juggling a tennis ball more accurately. In *IEEE International Conference on Robotics and Automation, Scottsdale, AZ*, 1290–5.

Arkin, R. C. (1998). *Behavior-Based Robotics*. Cambridge, MA: MIT Press.

Atkeson, C. G., Moore, A. W. and Schaal, S. (1997). Locally weighted learning. *Artificial Intelligence Review*, **11**, 11–73.

Balch, T. (1997). Clay: integrating motor schemas and reinforcement learning. Technical Report GIT-CC-97-11, College of Computing, Georgia Institute of Technology, Atlanta, Georgia.

Barto, A. and Mahadevan, S. (2003). Recent advances in hierarchical reinforcement learning. *Discrete Event Systems*, **13**, 41–77.

Bentivegna, D. C. (2004). *Learning from Observation using Primitives*. PhD thesis, Georgia Institute of Technology, Atlanta, GA, USA. http://etd.gatech.edu/theses/available/etd-06202004-213721/.

Bentivegna, D. C., Atkeson, C. G., and Cheng, G. (2003). Learning from observation and practice at the action generation level. In *IEEE-RAS International Conference on Humanoid Robotics (Humanoids 2003), Karlsruhe, Germany*.

Bentivegna, D. C., Ude, A., Atkeson, C. G., and Cheng, G. (2002). Humanoid robot learning and game playing using PC-based vision. In *Proceedings of the 2002 IEEE/RSJ International Conference on Intelligent Robots and Systems, Switzerland*, Vol. 3, 2449–54.

Brooks, R. A. (1986). A robust layered control system for a mobile robot. *IEEE Journal of Robotics and Automation*, **RA-2(1)**, 14–23.

Carpenter, R. (1988). *Movements of the Eyes*. Pion Press, London, 2nd edn.

Delson, N. and West, H. (1996). Robot programming by human demonstration: adaptation and inconsistency in constrained motion. In *IEEE International Conference on Robotics and Automation*, Vol. 1, 30–6.

Dietterich, T. G. (1998). The MAXQ method for hierarchical reinforcement learning. In *Proceedings of the 15th International Conference on Machine Learning*. San Francisco, CA: Morgan Kaufmann, 118–26.

Erdmann, M. A. and Mason, M. T. (1988). An exploration of sensorless manipulation. *IEEE Journal of Robotics and Automation*, **4**, 369–79.

Faloutsos, P., van de Panne, M. and Terzopoulos, D. (2001). Composable controllers for physics-based character animation. In *Proceedings of SIGGRAPH 2001, Los Angeles, CA*, 251–60.

Fod, A., Mataric, M. and Jenkins, O. (2000). Automated derivation of primitives for movement classification. In *First IEEE-RAS International Conference on Humanoid Robotics (Humanoids-2000), MIT, Cambridge, MA*.

Hovland, G., Sikka, P. and McCarragher, B. (1996). Skill acquisition from human demonstration using a hidden Markov model. In *Proceedings of IEEE International Conference on Robotics and Automation, Minneapolis, MN*, 2706–11.

Kaiser, M. and Dillmann, R. (1996). Building elementary skills from human demonstration. In *Proceedings of the IEE International Conference on Robotics and Automation*, 2700–5.

Kandel, E. R., Schwartz, J. H., and Jessell, T. M. (1984). *Principles of Neural Science*. Norwalle, CT: McGraw-Hill/Appleton and Lange, 4th edn.

Kang, S. B. and Ikeuchi, K. (1993). Toward automatic robot instruction from perception: recognizing a grasp from observation. *IEEE International Journal of Robotics and Automation*, **9(4)**, 432–43.

Kuniyoshi, Y., Inaba, M., and Inoue, H. (1994). Learning by watching: extracting reusable task knowledge from visual observation of human performance. *IEEE Transactions on Robotics and Automation*, **10(6)**, 799–822.

Likhachev, M. and Arkin, R. C. (2001). Spatio-temporal case-based reasoning for behavioral selection. In *Proceedings of the 2001 IEEE International Conference on Robotics and Automation, Seoul, Korea*, 1627–34.

Lin, L. J. (1993). Hierarchical learning of robot skills by reinforcement. In *Proceedings of the 1993 International Joint Conference on Neural Networks*, 181–6.

Loeb, G. E. (1989). The functional organization of muscles, motor units, and tasks. In *The Segmental Motor System*. New York: Oxford University Press, 22–35.

Mataric, M. J., Williamson, M., Demiris, J. and Mohan, A. (1998). Behavior-based primitives for articulated control. In *5th International Conference on Simulation of Adaptive Behavior (SAB-98)*. Cambridge, MA: MIT Press, 165–70.

McGovern, A. and Barto, A. G. (2001). Automatic discovery of sub-goals in reinforcement learning using diverse density. In *Proceedings of the 18th International Conference on Machine Learning*. San Francisco, CA: Morgan Kaufmann, 361–68.

McMahon, T. A. (1984). *Muscles, Reflexes, and Locomotion*. Princeton, NJ: Princeton University Press.

Mori, T., Tsujioka, K. and Sato, T. (2001). Human-like action recognition system on whole body motion-captured file. In *Proceedings of the 2001 IEEE/RSJ International Conference on Intelligent Robots and Systems, Maui, Hawaii,* Vol. 2, 1214–20.

Morimoto, J. and Doya, K. (1998). Hierarchical reinforcement learning of low-dimensional sub-goals and high-dimensional trajectories. In *Proceedings of the 5th International Conference on Neural Information Processing,* Vol. 2, 850–3.

Pearce, M., Arkin, R. C. and Ram, A. (1992). The learning of reactive control parameters through genetic algorithms. In *Proceedings of the 1992 IEEE/RSJ International Conference on Intelligent Robots and Systems, Raleigh, NC,* 130–7.

Russell, S. J. and Norvig, P. (1995). *Artificial Intelligence: A Modern Approach.* Englewood Cliffs, NJ: Prentice Hall.

Ryan, M. and Reid, M. (2000). Learning to fly: an application of hierarchical reinforcement learning. In *Proceedings of the 17th International Conference on Machine Learning.* San Francisco, CA: Morgan Kaufmann, 807–14.

Schaal, S. (1997). Learning from demonstration. In Mozer, M. C., Jordan, M. I., and Petsche, T. (eds.), *Advances in Neural Information Processing Systems,* Vol. 9. Cambridge, MA: MIT Press. 1040.

Schmidt, R. A. (1975). A schema theory of discrete motor skill learning. *Psychological Review,* **83**, 225–60.

Schmidt, R. A. (1988). *Motor Learning and Control.* Champaign, IL: Human Kinetics Publishers.

Spong, M. W. (1999). Robotic air hockey. http://cyclops.csl.uiuc.edu.

Tung, C. and Kak, A. (1995). Automatic learning of assembly tasks using a dataglove system. In *Proceedings of the IEEE/RSJ International Conference on Intelligent Robots and Systems,* Vol. 1.

Watkins, C. and Dayan, P. (1992). Q learning. *Machine Learning,* Vol. **8**, 279–92.

Wooten, W. L. and Hodgins, J. K. (2000). Simulating leaping, tumbling, landing and balancing humans. In *IEEE International Conference on Robotics and Automation,* Vol. 1, 656–62.

Part II

Mirroring and 'mind-reading'

Mirrors, mirror neurons and mirroring the behaviour of others all clearly relate to different types of *matching*. Could mirror-like mechanisms allow us to understand and to generate imitative behaviour? If so, how?

The phrase, 'Monkey see, monkey do' is still being used in public terms to dismiss any behaviour where an animal copies or mirrors what another animal is doing, despite the fact that the research fields of social learning and imitation in humans, animals and, more recently, robotics, have been flourishing, providing rich evidence for the importance of imitation and social learning in social development, skills learning, culture, etc. Similarly, in computer science and robotics the term 'imitation' can be misunderstood easily as simply copying computer programmes e.g. from one machine/robot to another. However, imitation in biological systems is not realized as copying 'behaviour programmes' from one animal to another: even in the hypothetical situation that brain waves could be directly transmitted and exchanged between, for example, humans, they would still have to be perceived and interpreted, they could not be 'loaded' directly into the neural structure of another organism, very different from a particular piece of software where numerous copies can be produced and installed on various computers. Metaphors borrowed from computer science often fail in the realm of biological systems, and 'copying' or 'imitation' is a good example. The embodied nature of living biological systems, the way they are situated and embedded in the environment via perception and action, requiring an 'interpretation' and 'reconstruction' of sensor data that depends on the organism's current situation, internal states, interaction histories, knowledge about the environment (learnt and innate), etc., is a constructive and highly dynamical process. The same applies to how motor commands generate actions to enable an organism to 'behave' in an environment: imitation provides an

Imitation and Social Learning in Robots, Humans and Animals, ed. Chrystopher L. Nehaniv and Kerstin Dautenhahn. Published by Cambridge University Press.
© Cambridge University Press 2007.

excellent example where the generation of action commands is tightly linked to perception and predictions of the outcomes of actions.

The three chapters in this section address different aspects of these issues, highlighting the intricate connection of perception and action in imitation.

Marco Iacoboni, Jonas Kaplan and Stephen Wilson present a neural architecture that supports imitation and intentional relations, i.e. linking others' actions with own internal motor plans. They argue that the central role of imitation in social development is due to the functional properties of this architecture. Starting with neurobiological evidence from macaques, they identify brain areas concerned with coding actions of self and others. Human homologues of these areas are then discussed in the context of their role in imitation and skill learning as well as understanding others. Here, mirror neurons (activated by observed as well as self-generated actions) play an important part in linking perception and generation of actions. Iacoboni *et al.* then map the neurobiological data onto a particular computational architecture, including pairs of forward and inverse internal models, an approach that has also been adopted by roboticists (see Chapter 5). According to the authors the architecture should be viewed as a dynamical system, a network model of complex cognitive functions, with an emphasis on the processes that transform information. Due to the functional properties of the architecture we may attribute the same meaning to actions performed by oneself or another individual, allowing the attributing of mental states to others ('*mind-reading*') and empathy (understanding the emotional states of others). Note, this 'mind-reading' results from the dynamic, active nature of computation in biological systems, which is different from a view of brain functions focusing on representations.

Developmentally, it is argued that dyadic mother–infant interactions play an important role in the formation of the neural architecture underlying imitation, mind-reading and understanding others' emotional states (empathy), compare Part V, Synchrony and turn-taking as communicative mechanisms, in this volume.

The next chapter by Yiannis Demiris and Matthew Johnson presents a robotics approach to the issue of 'mind-reading', focusing on the *simulation theory of mind*, a particular theory proposed in the literature trying to explain the mechanisms underlying mind-reading. The simulation theory of mind assumes that 'one puts oneself into the shoes of another person', trying to simulate another person's behaviour by using one's own cognitive mechanisms underlying behaviour generation. In this way, using our own mind as a model of others' minds, other people's intentions and future actions can be inferred in an off-line mode (simulating behaviour mentally without executing it). This explanation differs from the *'theory theory' of mind-reading*, which assumes that we apply a theory of behaviour (including, for example, axioms and rules of inferences operating on mental states such as beliefs and desires as theoretical entities). The simulation theory of mind has recently gained additional support by the discovery of 'mirror neurons' and is attractive from a robotics point of view since it entails that the same computational systems are used for both behaviour generation and behaviour recognition. Motivated by neurobiological findings, a robotics control architecture is presented, implemented and tested in robotics experiments. The architectures allow a robot to infer the goal of a demonstrated behaviour in a specific experimental context, and subsequently imitate it (see Part III, What to imitate). The central ingredient of the architecture is a pairing of forward and inverse models so that a robot's motor system is directly involved in the recognition process of demonstrated behaviour. Abstraction processes are used to deal with situations where the imitator is not able to perform the demonstrated actions in exactly the same way (see Part I, Correspondence problems and mechanisms). An important part of work linking neurobiologically inspired control architectures with robotics implementations is that the results allow one to test models and theories derived from biological data. Moreover, results from using computational models can lead to predictions that can motivate further research.

The gap between mind-reading in biological systems and robots is still huge. We are far from having robots around that can be claimed to 'truly understand' mental states or emotions of humans (or other robots), if ever possible. However, doing experiments on specific aspects of mind-reading, such as the inference of goals, is, scientifically speaking, within our grasp.

While the first two chapters in this section discuss the issue of understanding others, Robert W. Mitchell is concerned with the relationship between bodily imitation and mirror self-recognition: human children recognize themselves in a mirror around 18 months of age, a time when they show generalized bodily imitation. Children less than 15 months old and animals such as monkeys can use mirrors e.g. in order to obtain objects, but are not able to recognize themselves in the mirror. Two models are presented to explain initial self-recognition: as a main difference between these models, the *kinesthetic-visual matching model* views self-recognition (and generalized bodily imitation) deriving from intermodal matching between kinesthesis and vision, while according to the *object-generalization model*, self-recognition results from a general understanding of objects (including body parts) and similarities between them. The chapter analyzes the biological, psychological and developmental literature in detail in search for support for components of either theory, including examples of clinical syndromes where recognition of oneself, own body parts or other objects in a mirror is impaired. In kinesthetic-visual matching, children realize that what they see in a mirror (e.g. a movement, gesture or posture) looks like what it feels like. Note, since the body of a child is developing, kinesthesis must match a moving target.[1] Components of both theories also play a relevant role in generalized bodily imitation. Neurobiologically, the parietal region as well as adjacent regions including 'mirror neurons', are candidates for the neurobiological substrate of kinesthetic-visual matching. The precise identification of relevant components and relations between them involved in self-recognition, kinesthetic-visual matching and generalized bodily imitation is still ongoing research that can serve as a source of inspiration e.g. to roboticists trying to implement robots that imitate and are able to understand the behaviour of others, as well as robots that recognize their own behaviour as a contingent expression of 'self'.

---

[1] See Part IV, Development and embodiment, this volume.

4 A neural architecture for imitation and intentional relations

Marco Iacoboni, Jonas Kaplan and Stephen Wilson

Imitation is an important form of learning, facilitating the acquisition of many skills without the time-consuming process of trial-and-error learning. Imitation is also associated with the ability to develop social skills and understand the goals, the intentions and the feelings of other people (Meltzoff and Prinz, 2002). The neural underpinnings of imitation and their possible evolutionary precursors have been recently investigated with different approaches, including neurological investigations, brain imaging, single cell recordings and computational models. This chapter discusses a neural architecture for imitation comprising superior temporal cortex, the rostral part of the posterior parietal cortex and inferior frontal cortex. The main thesis of the chapter is that the central role of imitation in the development of social skills is due to the functional properties of this neural architecture. These properties allow a common framework for third person knowledge (i.e. the observation of actions of others) and first person knowledge (i.e. internal motor plans).

4.1 Neurophysiology

Neurons in the superior temporal sulcus (STS) respond to moving biological stimuli, such as hands, faces and bodies (Jellema *et al.*, 2002). The responses of some of these neurons occur only when the body or body part is engaged in goal-oriented actions, for instance when a hand reaches and grasps an object. The sight of a hand reaching toward the object but not grasping it will not activate these STS neurons. Point-light versions of the complete action, i.e. a hand reaching and grasping an object, however, do activate STS cells. This evidence suggests that STS responses to biological stimuli are not driven by low-level visual aspects of the observed action, but rather by the sight of an agent interacting intentionally with the environment (Jellema *et al.*, 2002).

Imitation and Social Learning in Robots, Humans and Animals, ed. Chrystopher L. Nehaniv and Kerstin Dautenhahn. Published by Cambridge University Press.
© Cambridge University Press 2007.

Some premotor neurons have visual responses similar to the ones observed in STS. In area F5 of the macaque inferior frontal cortex there are neurons that fire when the monkey executes goal-directed actions, such as grasping, holding and manipulating an object (Rizzolatti *et al.*, 1988). Some of these neurons, called mirror neurons, will also fire at the sight of somebody else's goal oriented actions (Gallese *et al.*, 1996). Mirror neurons do not fire at the sight of the object alone or at the sight of a pantomime of a goal-oriented action. The functional properties of these neurons make them plausible evolutionary precursors of human neural systems relevant to imitation (Rizzolatti *et al.*, 2001).

Given the extremely similar visual properties of STS neurons and F5 mirror neurons, it is reasonable to assume that F5 mirror neurons receive visual information from STS. F5 and STS, however, are not directly connected. A rostral inferior parietal area of the macaque brain, area PF, is connected with both F5 and STS (Seltzer and Pandya, 1994). This area seems a likely candidate to relay visual information concerning the actions of others from STS to F5. This pattern of cortico-cortical connectivity suggests that F5, PF and STS belong to an integrated circuit for action coding. Indeed, PF contains mirror neurons with functional properties similar to the ones described in F5 (Fogassi and Gallese, 2002). In addition, some of these neurons respond to the observation of a grasping hand and the execution of a biting action with the mouth (Fogassi and Gallese, 2002). These properties suggest that some mirror neurons may be involved in coding sequential actions involving multiple effectors, such as the (seen) hand grasping food and bringing it to the mouth that bites it.

Taken altogether, these three cortical regions of the macaque brain – STS in the superior temporal cortex, area F5 in the inferior frontal cortex and area PF in the posterior parietal cortex – have functional properties and connectivity patterns that may instantiate a whole circuit for coding actions in a form that abstracts across self and other. Brain imaging evidence summarized in the next section suggests that the human homologues of these areas form a core neural architecture for imitation.

4.2   Brain imaging

The properties of superior temporal, posterior parietal and inferior frontal neurons in the macaque brain that are concerned with action coding provide a framework for interpreting signal changes in brain imaging studies of imitation in humans. Imitation includes both observation and execution of an action. Human brain areas endowed with mirror properties should show a pattern of activity such that the sum of the activity during

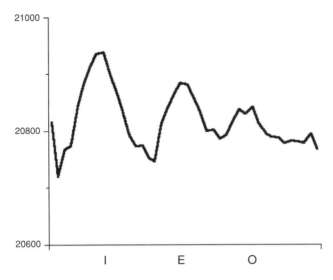

Figure 4.1 Time series in a human premotor area showing the predicted pattern of activity during imitation (I), a control motor execution task with the same motor output of the imitation task (E), and action observation (O). Signal is raw BOLD fMRI signal rescaled by the smoothing process.

observation and during execution of an action roughly corresponds to the total activity during imitation, which combines both observation and execution. Single cell recordings of mirror neurons typically demonstrate a weaker neural response during observation than execution (Gallese *et al.*, 1996). Thus, one might predict that human mirror areas should have an activity profile during observation, execution and imitation of action as depicted in Figure 4.1. Studies on imitation of finger movements using functional magnetic resonance imaging (fMRI), have described two human neural systems with this activity profile (Iacoboni *et al.*, 1999). One is located in inferior frontal cortex, and the other one is located rostrally in posterior parietal cortex. These two systems correspond well anatomically to the areas identified in the macaque brain as having mirror properties.

When evidence from single cell recordings in monkeys and brain imaging and transcranial magnetic stimulation (TMS) studies in humans is taken together, a division of labour between the two human mirror systems described above seems to emerge. The inferior frontal mirror areas code the goal of the imitated action and the posterior parietal mirror areas code the somatosensory, kinesthetic and maybe kinematic aspects of the imitated action. The coding of action goals in inferior frontal mirror areas is suggested by fMRI evidence showing higher activity in pars opercularis of the inferior frontal gyrus for imitation of actions with visible goals, compared to actions with no visible goals (Koski *et al.*, 2002). Further, repetitive TMS on pars opercularis of the inferior frontal gyrus selectively disrupts the imitation of action goals (Heiser *et al.*, 2003). Single cell recordings in macaque areas (Kalaska *et al.*, 1983; Kalaska *et al.*, 1990) anatomically corresponding to the posterior parietal activated areas observed in the human imitation experiments suggest that these areas are concerned with kinesthetics and kinematics. Note that, even though responses of similar nature have also been described in premotor regions, human TMS data seem to suggest that frontal areas are less concerned with this aspect of the imitation process. In fact, Heiser *et al.* (2003) have shown a selective deficit in imitating the goal of the action but no deficits in detailed motor aspects of the imitative action when rTMS was applied to the human ventral premotor cortex.

With regard to STS, several labs have published reports of STS responses to observed actions (Allison *et al.*, 2000). The initial role of STS during imitation would then be to provide a higher order visual description of the action. Recent fMRI data on imitation of finger movements, however, suggest that STS activity follows closely the activity observed in fronto-parietal mirror areas during different kinds of imitation (Iacoboni *et al.*, 2001; Koski *et al.*, 2003). This suggests that STS also receives efferent copies of imitative motor plans from fronto-parietal mirror areas.

To summarize, the information flow within the three areas (superior temporal, posterior parietal, inferior frontal) that form the *neural architecture* for imitation would be as follows (see also Figures 4.2 and 4.3):

• STS provides a higher order visual description of the observed action to be imitated to mirror neurons located in the rostral part of the posterior parietal cortex (the human homologue of monkey PF and PEc).
• Rostral posterior parietal mirror neurons code the somatosensory, kinesthetic and maybe kinematic aspects of the action to be imitated; this information is sent to inferior frontal mirror neurons (the human homologue of monkey F5).
• Human mirror neurons located in inferior frontal cortex (in pars opercularis of the inferior frontal gyrus for distal finger movements and mouth movements, more dorsally in ventral premotor cortex for more proximal arm movements) code the goal of the action to be imitated.
• From a ventral sector of pars opercularis originate efferent copies of motor commands that are sent back to STS (Molnar-Szakacs *et al.*, 2005); this signal provides the predicted sensory consequences of the planned imitative actions.

- The visual description of the action and the predicted sensory consequences of the planned imitative action are matched in STS; if there is a good match, the imitative action is initiated; if there is a large error signal, the imitative motor plan is corrected.

4.3   Computational properties

The information flow outlined above within the neural architecture for imitation is reminiscent of the functional architecture of modular pairs of forward and inverse internal models (Wolpert and Kawato, 1998) recently called MOSAIC (Haruno et al., 2001). This kind of model has been successfully employed in robotic models of imitation (Demiris and Hayes, 2002). Although MOSAIC has been typically associated with cerebellar activity (Imamizu et al., 2000; Miall et al., 2001), functional connectivity between the cerebellum and the inferior frontal cortex has been reported in tool use learning (Imamizu et al., 2003; Tamada et al., 1999) and a role for the posterior parietal cortex in forward modelling during reaching has been proposed (Desmurget and Grafton, 2000).

The role of the inverse model is to retrieve the motor plan necessary to reach a desired sensory state. This is critical for motor control. The desired sensory state is the input of the inverse model and the motor plan necessary to reach that desired sensory state is the output of the inverse model. When an imitator wants to imitate the action of somebody else, the input of the inverse model is created by STS by transmitting the visual description of the observed action into fronto-parietal mirror areas. The inferior frontal cortex produces the motor command necessary to imitate the observed action, which is the output of the inverse model (Figures 4.2 and 4.3).

When an action is planned, it is desirable to predict its consequences. The role of the forward model is to predict the sensory consequences of planned actions. In the neural architecture for imitation, the inferior frontal cortex provides the input of the forward model by means of an efferent copy of the motor command. This signal is sent to STS, which provides the output of the forward model by means of a match between the visual description of the action and of the predicted sensory consequences of the planned imitative action.

When the prediction is confirmed by re-afferent feedback, then a 'responsibility signal' (Haruno et al., 2001) originating in the rostral posterior parietal mirror areas assigns high responsibility for imitating that given action to that specific forward–inverse model pair.

How does the pairing of internal models more precisely occur within the neural architecture for imitation? Here, it is useful to recall the

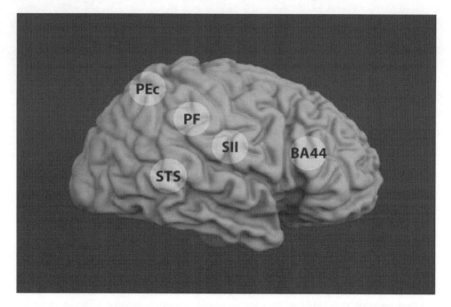

Figure 4.2 Anatomical locations of brain regions implicated in the neural architecture for imitation. Here the posterior parietal cortex is divided into a superior sector (PEc) and an inferior sector (PF). SII: secondary somatosensory cortex. STS: superior temporal sulcus. BA44: Brodmann area 44 in the inferior frontal gyrus.

properties of STS-PF-F5 cells. STS neurons show visual invariance, that is, under widely different visual circumstances STS neurons fire at the sight of the same kind of action (Jellema *et al.*, 2002). PF and F5 neurons also respond to a relatively large class of observed actions under different visual conditions. With regard to their motor properties, however, mirror neurons in PF and F5 often code a specific action (Gallese *et al.*, 1996). Thus, a large variety of visual stimuli in the form of observed actions may activate non-selectively a large number of neurons in superior temporal, posterior parietal and inferior frontal cortex. This non-selective visual activation, however, can be mapped efficiently only onto a few specific motor outputs coded in inferior frontal cortex. When a less efficient motor output is selected, the forward model generates a large error signal, and 'low responsibility' is assigned. When an efficient motor output is selected, a small error signal is generated. When the prediction of the forward model is also confirmed by re-afferent feedback, the pair of forward and inverse model is given 'high responsibility' for that action.

4.4   Intentional relations

The neural architecture for imitation allows a common framework for first-person knowledge about internal motor plans and third-person knowledge about the actions of other people provided by action observation. This framework may allow attributing the same meaning to actions of other individuals that we attribute to our own actions, even though the first-person information that we have of our own actions differs substantially from the third-person information that we have of the actions of others. This common framework for first-person and third-person knowledge is a key mechanism for social understanding (Barresi and Moore, 1996) and makes it possible to have second-order intentional relations, that is, the ability to have a mental state about the mental state of other people (what is commonly known in the neurosciences and in psychology as mind-reading or theory of mind). This is because we can assign the same meaning to actions of self and other. Barresi and Moore (1996) have called this common framework an intentional schema. The intentional schema integrates first and third person sources of knowledge and allows correspondences to be drawn between self and other. In the domain of behavioral sciences, Barresi and Moore have developed an intentional relations theory in which the key functional elements map fairly well onto the components of the neural architecture for imitation, as shown in Figure 4.3.

The intentional relations theory defines an intentional relation as a state of mind directed at an object in the world. This includes overt, purposive actions, as well as more complex states of mind like beliefs and desires. For example, 'Mary hits John' and 'Mary is angry at John' are both intentional relations. Thus the intentional relations theory provides a common framework for conceptualizing how we understand each others' actions and state of mind. In later sections we will discuss how the neural architecture for imitation can be linked to empathic resonance, that is, the ability to understand the emotional states of others, and language, the medium *par excellence* for epistemic relations. First, however, we consider possible ontogenetic mechanisms that may favor the formation of neural systems with properties such as the ones described in the neural architecture for imitation.

4.5   Ontogenesis

Reciprocal imitation between mother and infant is a well-documented phenomenon (Meltzoff and Prinz, 2002; Nadel and Butterworth, 1999) and has inspired some developmental accounts of how imitation is made

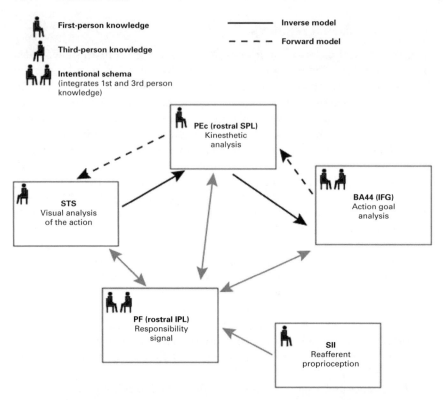

Figure 4.3 The neural architecture for imitation mapped onto the functional elements of intentional relations theory. Each box has three types of descriptions: an anatomical description, a functional description, and an icon representing intentional relations theory. The flow of information from STS to BA44 forms the inverse model (dashed lines), the reentrant signal from BA5 and BA44 to STS represents the forward model (solid black lines), the bidirectional arrows originating from area PF represent 'responsibility signal' that pairs appropriately forward and inverse models. In this schema, the rostral posterior parietal cortex is divided in two sectors. The superior sector is concerned with kinesthetics and kinematics, the inferior sector is concerned with somatosensory information and provides the 'responsibility signal'. STS: superior temporal sulcus. SPL: superior parietal lobule. IPL: inferior parietal lobule. BA44: Brodmann area 44. IFG: inferior frontal gyrus.

possible. According to the associative sequence learning model (Heyes, 2005), imitation is made possible by an excitatory link between a sensory representation of the observed movement (encoding properties of the movement detected via the distal senses) and a motor representation (encoding somatosensory properties and motor commands). Intentional relations theory (Barresi and Moore, 1996) also assumes that co-action and imitation are initial triggers of a cascade that leads to social understanding. To provide a simple example, a sequence of this sort occurs when the baby smiles, the mother smiles back and the baby is able to associate the motor plans she used and the re-afferent proprioception she experienced with the visual description of a smile. This sequence is reminiscent of some form of unsupervised Hebbian-like learning in which temporal correlation of input plays a major role, as also associative sequence learning (Heyes, 2005) and intentional relations theory (Barresi and Moore, 1996) suggest. However, we know that the motor system engages in supervised learning, actively evaluating its output with respect to a desired goal. The interesting computational issue is how a supervised-type learning of internal models emerges from an unsupervised Hebbian-like learning. While this issue is beyond the scope of the present chapter, there are models that successfully combine the two forms of learning and are neurophysiologically plausible (see for instance Fregnac and Shulz, 1999; Hogan and Diederich, 2001; Pennartz, 1997). The combination of Hebbian, supervised and reinforcement learning in this model maps well onto the dyadic mother–baby interactions in which co-occurrence of acts (Hebbian), reciprocal imitation (supervised – when the mother demonstrates an action that the baby has just failed to execute properly), explicit teaching (supervised) and reinforcement (when the mother praises the baby for a well-executed act) all play critical roles. From a neural systems perspective, this means that the neural architecture for imitation described here must interact also with neural systems concerned with reinforcement learning, such as the basal ganglia (Doya, 2000).

4.6   Empathy

How does the neural architecture for imitation support second order intentional relations of affective and motivational type? Mirror neurons and simulation processes have been implicated in the understanding of other minds (Demiris and Johnson, Chapter 5 this volume; Gallese and Goldman, 1998), and there is plenty of evidence in the behavioral sciences that imitation and empathy go together (Hatfield et al., 1994). Empathic individuals tend to automatically mimic the postures and mannerisms of people they interact with socially (the so-called chameleon effect) more so than non-empathic individuals (Chartrand and Bargh, 1999). The neural architecture for imitation and the limbic system may cooperate to support our ability to understand the emotional states of others.

From a neural standpoint, the limbic system and superior temporal, rostral posterior parietal and inferior frontal cortices are well-differentiated systems. The connectivity pattern of the primate brain, however, suggests that a sector of the insular lobe, the dys-granular sector, actually connects the three major components of the neural architecture for imitation with the limbic system (Augustine, 1996). Indeed, recent imaging evidence is in line with the hypothesis that the anterior insula plays a critical role in functionally connecting the amygdala with the inferior frontal and superior temporal cortex during imitation of emotional facial expressions (Carr *et al.*, 2003).

From a computational standpoint, the insula and amygdala might be included in the system at a different hierarchical level. Different levels in the system would have different kinds of paired internal forward/inverse models, ranging from action-specific internal models to increasingly abstract ones, as in a recent hierarchical extension of MOSAIC (Wolpert *et al.*, 2003). In fact, the neural architecture for imitation described here may already represent a higher level of action coding when compared, for instance, to the action level described in the cerebellum.

4.7   A link to language

Language is the most common medium of epistemic second order intentional relations (e.g. 'Marco thinks that the readers will enjoy this chapter'), although these kinds of intentional relations need not be linked necessarily to language. This section discusses homologies between language areas and the neural architecture for imitation, and how the functional properties of the neural architecture for imitation are compatible with some language disorders seen after brain lesions, and some imaging studies on language.

Broca's area, a crucial area for language, is located in the inferior frontal cortex, an area endowed with mirror properties and belonging to the neural architecture for imitation. The superior temporal cortex also has a well-known role in language, with Wernicke's aphasia resulting from lesions in this vicinity, as do parietal areas, with the supramarginal gyrus often implicated in conduction aphasia (Green and Howes, 1978). These correspondences raise the possibility that the neural architecture for imitation discussed in this chapter also provides a substrate for linguistic processing.

Broca's area is mostly involved in speech production. Lesions to Broca's area generally result in articulatory deficits (Mohr, 1976), which is what one would predict if Broca's area codes the output of the inverse model (necessary for control) and the input of the forward model (necessary for prediction, important when planning articulatory sequences), as described above in the case of imitation.

Within the neural architecture for imitation, STS is the site of perceptual representations, and provides the input of the inverse model and the output of the forward model. The posterior superior temporal gyrus is included in all definitions of Wernicke's area, including Wernicke's original monograph (Wernicke, 1874). Recent lesion (Bates *et al.*, 2003) and neuroimaging (Scott *et al.*, 2000) studies have shown that areas important for language extend inferior to the posterior superior temporal gyrus and include the superior temporal sulcus. Further, imaging evidence also suggests that STS is a multi-sensory integration area responding to both visual and auditory stimuli, and integrating them when necessary (as when we see the lips of somebody else moving and simultaneously hear their speech) (Calvert *et al.*, 2000). The anatomical overlap between Wernicke's area and STS suggests that Wernicke's area performs in language an analogous function to STS in imitation. The comprehension deficits of Wernicke's aphasia result from a deficit in perceptual representations. Although patients with Wernicke's aphasia are fluent, they do have severe production problems, ranging from paraphasias in which phonemes are incorrectly selected, to semantic errors in which words are incorrectly selected, to neologisms and jargon (Goodglass, 1993). These deficits can be accounted for by a disorder of the input to the inverse model: no longer can a motor plan be appropriately recovered to achieve a desired perceptual outcome. Furthermore, imaging evidence suggests that the superior temporal cortex receives efferent copies of articulatory motor plans (Paus *et al.*, 1996). This is consistent with the notion of Wernicke's area as the site of the output of the forward model in speech. There appear to be compelling similarities between the role of posterior superior temporal areas in language, and STS in imitation.

Broca's area and Wernicke's area are traditionally held to be connected via the arcuate fasciculus (Geschwind, 1965). However, as noted above, inferior frontal cortex is most densely interconnected with posterior parietal cortex, which in turn is interconnected with superior temporal cortex (Seltzer and Pandya, 1994). Recent diffusion tensor imaging data in humans confirm the existence of such indirect route, parallel to the arcuate fasciculus (Catani *et al.*, 2005). The posterior parietal cortex may serve here as an intermediary in the communication between the classical anterior and posterior language areas. Lesions to the supramarginal gyrus are often associated with conduction aphasia (Green and Howes, 1978), characterized by relatively preserved comprehension, impaired repetition, and paraphasic and otherwise disordered speech. The relatively preserved comprehension in conduction aphasia might be a consequence of the sparing of superior temporal areas. The deficits in repetition and production can be readily understood in terms of the functional properties of the neural architecture for imitation. An inappropriate pairing of forward and inverse model due to deficit in 'responsibility signal', should result in jumbled speech and failed repetition arising from the inability to update the inverse model, on the basis of the forward model. Indeed, a typical symptom of these patients is the so-called *conduite d'approche*, that is, the patient gets closer and closer to the target word through repeated attempts. If the inverse model cannot be updated by the forward model, the only way these patients can correct themselves and finally say a word correctly is by receiving a sensory feedback of their speech output.

In sum, there are strong links between language and the neural architecture for imitation discussed here. These links are both anatomical and functional, and reveal the sensory-motor base on which language is grounded. This sensory-motor grounding of language may provide clues to the evolutionary origins of language in the motor system (Arbib, 2002; Fadiga *et al.*, 2002; Rizzolatti and Arbib, 1998).

4.8   Process vs. representation

The mapping of neural activity onto a computational model can expose some of the theoretical assumptions implicit in that model and challenge its biological plausibility. For example, a debate has been emerging recently on whether the prefrontal cortex is best characterized by the kind of representations it contains or by the kind of processing that it performs (Wood and Grafman, 2003). The distinction between *process* and *representation* is a general issue facing theoretical neuroscience. Here, we address this distinction in the context of the neural architecture of imitation.

The computational framework described here invokes internal models to explain imitation. The term 'model' implies a representation; a forward model is a representation of the future sensory consequences of our action. This model is a stand-in for the actual sensory afferents that will result from our action. There is some debate with regard to the specific definition of a representation, but in general a representation is an entity with informational content about the world that is used as such by the system (Haugeland, 1991). This is precisely what a 'model' does. For example, before we build a full-scale building, we might construct a cardboard model that resembles the final building in terms of its structural relationships but is not the real thing in size or material. In fact, according to Grush (2001), a forward model is the hallmark of a true representation, since the model can be invoked off-line, in the absence of any real stimulus in the world. You don't need to have the real Empire State Building to have a model of one.

However, the metaphor of a model, and a description of brain function in terms of representations does not capture the dynamic, active nature of biological computation. For instance, the forward model is instantiated by information flow between the inferior frontal lobe and STS. It is the process of interaction between these two brain regions that allows the comparison of predicted and actual sensory consequences. In fact the loop we have described with information flowing from STS to a fronto-parietal motor network and back to STS may ultimately be best described as a dynamical system (Beer, 2000). This position does not necessarily imply antirepresentationalism (Haselager *et al.*, 2003), but it does blur the classical notion of what kinds of information are represented by various neural structures.

Traditional computational models have described cognition as consisting of computations operating upon representations (Newell, 1991). Applying this conceptualization to the brain, it is tempting to treat each functional brain region as providing a representation, with transformations of representations occurring via connections between distal regions. For example, we could say that STS represents visual biological motion, and this information is transformed into a motor representation via projections to posterior parietal cortex and then on to frontal premotor cortex. However, in connectionist and dynamical models it may be harder to separate representations from the processes that operate on them. In this view, information is in a constant state of transformation, and therefore it is artificial to separate representations from the processes that transform them.

The circuitry we have described is so interactive that it is difficult to assign 'sensory' or 'motor' properties to particular parts of the circuit. Even STS, which is classically thought to represent visual properties of the world, responds to motor acts (Iacoboni *et al.*, 2001). Rather than specify what kind of information each brain area encodes, it seems more appropriate to describe the processing contribution each region makes to the overall functioning of the network. We see the move from examining cortical regions in isolation to network models of complex cognitive functions like imitation as entailing a shift in focus from representation to process.

4.9   Conclusion

The neural architecture for imitation described here includes superior temporal cortex, the rostral part of posterior parietal cortex and inferior frontal cortex. The functions of these regions can be mapped onto a computational framework of paired forward and inverse internal models and allow a common framework for first-person and third-person knowledge, thus facilitating second order intentional relations and social understanding. Obviously, this architecture does not work in isolation. Future studies will determine the level and type of interactions between this architecture and other large-scale neural systems, such as the cerebellum with regard to specific aspects of actions, the basal ganglia with regard to motivation and reward, and presumably prefrontal cortex with regard to modulatory control of imitative behavior.

Acknowledgments

Supported, in part, by Brain Mapping Medical Research Organization, Brain Mapping Support Foundation, Pierson-Lovelace Foundation, The Ahmanson Foundation, Tamkin Foundation, Jennifer Jones-Simon Foundation, Capital Group Companies Charitable Foundation, Robson Family, Northstar Fund and grants from National Center for Research Resources (RR12169 and RR08655), National Science Foundation (REC-0107077) and National Institute of Mental Health (MH63680).

REFERENCES

Allison, T., Puce, A. and McCarthy, G. (2000). Social perception from visual cues: role of the STS region. *Trends Cogn. Sci.*, **4**, 267–78.
Arbib, M. A. (2002). The mirror system, imitation, and the evolution of language. In *Imitation in Animals and Artifacts*, Dautenhahn, K. and Nehaniv, C. (eds.). Cambridge, MA: MIT Press, 229–80.
Augustine, J. R. (1996). Circuitry and functional aspects of the insular lobes in primates including humans. *Brain Res. Rev.*, **2**, 229–94.
Barresi, J. and Moore, C. (1996). Intentional relations and social understanding. *Behav. Brain Sci.*, **19**, 107–54.
Bates, E., Wilson, S. M., Saygin, A. P., Dick, F., Sereno, M. I., Knight, R. T. and Dronkers, N. F. (2003). Voxel-based lesion-symptom mapping. *Nat. Neurosci.*, **6**, 448–50.
Beer, R. D. (2000). Dynamical approaches to cognitive science. *Trends Cogn. Sci.*, **4**, 91–9.
Calvert, G. A., Campbell, R. and Brammer, M. J. (2000). Evidence from functional magnetic resonance imaging of crossmodal binding in the human heteromodal cortex. *Curr. Biol.*, **10**, 649–57.
Carr, L., Iacoboni, M., Dubeau, M. C., Mazziotta, J. C. and Lenzi, G. L. (2003). Neural mechanisms of empathy in humans: a relay from neural systems for imitation to limbic areas. *Proc. Natl. Acad. Sci. USA*, **100**, 5497–5502.
Catani, M., Jones, D. K. and Ffytche, D. H. (2005). Perisylvian language networks of the human brain. *Ann. Neurol.*, **57**, 8–16.
Chartrand, T. L. and Bargh, J. A. (1999). The chameleon effect: the perception-behavior link and social interaction. *J. Pers. Soc. Psychol.*, **76**, 893–910.

Demiris, J. and Hayes, G. (2002). Imitation as a dual-route process featuring predictive and learning components: a biologically plausible computational model. In *Imitation in Animals and Artifacts*, Dautenhahn, K. and Nehaniv, C. (eds.). Cambridge, MA: MIT Press, 327–61.

Desmurget, M. and Grafton, S. (2000). Forward modeling allows feedback control for fast reaching movements. *Trends Cogn. Sci.*, **4**, 423–31.

Doya, K. (2000). Complementary roles of basal ganglia and cerebellum in learning and motor control. *Curr. Opin. Neurobiol.*, **10**, 732–9.

Fadiga, L., Craighero, L., Buccino, G. and Rizzolatti, G. (2002). Speech listening specifically modulates the excitability of tongue muscles: a TMS study. *Eur. J. Neurosci.*, **15**, 399–402.

Fogassi, L. and Gallese, V. (2002). The neural correlates of action understanding in non-human primates. In *Mirror Neurons and the Evolution of Brain and Language*, Stamenov, M. and Gallese, V. (eds.), Amsterdam: John Benjamins, 13–36.

Fregnac, Y. and Shulz, D. E. (1999). Activity-dependent regulation of receptive field properties of cat area 17 by supervised Hebbian learning. *J. Neurobiol.*, **41**, 69–82.

Gallese, V., Fadiga, L., Fogassi, L. and Rizzolatti, G. (1996). Action recognition in the premotor cortex. *Brain*, **119**, 593–609.

Gallese, V. and Goldman, A. (1998). Mirror neurons and the simulation theory of mind-reading. *Trends Cogn. Sci.*, **2**, 493–501.

Geschwind, N. (1965). Disconnexion syndromes in animals and man. I. *Brain*, **88**, 237–94.

Goodglass, H. (1993) *Understanding Aphasia*. San Diego, CA: Academic Press.

Green, E. and Howes, D. H. (1978). The nature of conduction aphasia: a study of anatomic and clinical features and of underlying mechanisms. In *Studies in Neurolinguistics*, Whitaker, A. and Whitaker, H. A. (eds.). San Diego, CA: Academic Press, 123–56.

Grush, R. (2001). The architecture of representation. In *Philosophy and the Neurosciences*, Bechtel, W., Mundale, J. and Stufflebeam, R. S. (eds.). Malden, MA: Blackwell.

Haruno, M., Wolpert, D. M. and Kawato, M. (2001). Mosaic model for sensorimotor learning and control. *Neural Comput.*, **13**, 2201–20.

Haselager, P., deGroot, A. and vanRappard, H. (2003). Representationalism vs. anti-representationalism: a debate for the sake of appearance. *Philos. Psychol.*, **16**, 5–23.

Hatfield, E., Cacioppo, J. T. and Rapson, R. L. (1994). *Emotional Contagion*. Paris: Cambridge University Press.

Haugeland, J. (1991). Representational genera. In *Philosophy and Connectionist Theory*, Ramsey, W. M., Stich, S. P. and Rumelhart, D. E. (eds.). Hillsdale, NJ: Lawrence Erlbaum.

Heiser, M., Iacoboni, M., Maeda, F., Marcus, J. and Mazziotta, J. C. (2003). The essential role of Broca's area in imitation. *Eur. J. Neurosci.*, **17**, 1123–8.

Heyes, C. (2005). Imitation by association. In *Perspectives on Imitation: From Mirror Neurons to Memes*, Hurley, S. and Chater, N. (eds.). Cambridge, MA: MIT Press.

Hogan, J. M. and Diederich, J. (2001). Recruitment learning of Boolean functions in sparse random networks. *Int. J. Neural Syst.*, **11**, 537–59.

Iacoboni, M., Koski, L. M., Brass, M., Bekkering, H., Woods, R. P., Dubeau, M. C., Mazziotta, J. C. and Rizzolatti, G. (2001). Reafferent copies of imitated actions in the right superior temporal cortex. *Proc. Natl. Acad. Sci. USA*, **98**, 13995–9.

Iacoboni, M., Woods, R. P., Brass, M., Bekkering, H., Mazziotta, J. C. and Rizzolatti, G. (1999). Cortical mechanisms of human imitation. *Science*, **286**, 2526–8.

Imamizu, H., Kuroda, T., Miyauchi, S., Yoshioka, T. and Kawato, M. (2003). Modular organization of internal models of tools in the human cerebellum. *Proc. Natl. Acad. Sci. USA*, **100**, 5461–6.

Imamizu, H., Miyauchi, S., Tamada, T., Sasaki, Y., Takino, R., Putz, B., Yoshioka, T. and Kawato, M. (2000). Human cerebellar activity reflecting an acquired internal model of a new tool. *Nature*, **403**, 192–5.

Jellema, T., Baker, C. I., Oram, M. W. and Perrett, D. I. (2002). Cell populations in the banks of the superior temporal sulcus of the macaque and imitation. In *The Imitative Mind: Development, Evolution and Brain Bases*, Meltzoff, A. N. and Prinz, W. (eds.). New York, NY, US: Cambridge University Press, 267–290.

Kalaska, J. F., Caminiti, R. and Georgopoulos, A. P. (1983). Cortical mechanisms related to the direction of two-dimensional arm movements: relations in parietal area 5 and comparison with motor cortex. *Exp. Brain Res.*, **51**, 247–60.

Kalaska, J. F., Cohen, D. A., Prud'homme, M. and Hyde, M. L. (1990). Parietal area 5 neuronal activity encodes movement kinematics, not movement dynamics. *Exp. Brain Res.*, **80**, 351–64.

Koski, L., Iacoboni, M., Dubeau, M. C., Woods, R. P. and Mazziotta, J. C. (2003). Modulation of cortical activity during different imitative behaviors. *J. Neurophysiol.*, **89**, 460–71.

Koski, L., Wohlschlager, A., Bekkering, H., Woods, R. P., Dubeau, M. C., Mazziotta, J. C. and Iacoboni, M. (2002). Modulation of motor and premotor activity during imitation of target-directed actions. *Cereb. Cortex*, **12**, 847–55.

Meltzoff, A. N. and Prinz, W. (2002). *The Imitative Mind: Development, Evolution and Brain Bases*. Cambridge, UK: Cambridge University Press.

Miall, R. C., Reckess, G. Z. and Imamizu, H. (2001). The cerebellum coordinates eye and hand tracking movements. *Nat. Neurosci.*, **4**, 638–44.

Mohr, J. P. (1976). Broca's area and Broca's aphasia. In *Studies in Neurolinguistics*, Whitaker, A., Whitaker, H. A. (eds.). San Diego, CA: Academic Press, 201–35.

Molnar-Szakacs, I., Iacoboni, M., Koski, L. and Maziotta, J. C. (2005). Functional segregation within pars opercularis of the inferior frontal gyrus: evidence from fMRI studies of imitation and action observation. *Cerebral Cortex*, **15**, 986–94.

Nadel, J. and Butterworth, G. (1999). *Imitation in Infancy*. New York, NY: Cambridge University Press.

Newell, A. (1991). *Unified Theories of Cognition*. Cambridge, MA: Harvard University Press.

Paus, T., Perry, D., Zatorre, R., Worsley, K. and Evans, A. (1996). Modulation of cerebral blood flow in the human auditory cortex during speech: role of motor-to-sensory discharges. *Eur. J. Neurosci.*, **8**, 2236–46.

Pennartz, C. M. (1997). Reinforcement learning by Hebbian synapses with adaptive thresholds. *Neuroscience*, **81**, 303–19.

Rizzolatti, G. and Arbib, M. (1998). Language within our grasp. *Trends Neurosci*, **21**, 188–94.

Rizzolatti, G., Camarda, R., Fogassi, M., Gentilucci, M., Luppino, G., Matelli, M. (1988). Functional organization of inferior area 6 in the macaque monkey. II. Area F5 and the control of distal movements. *Exp. Brain. Res.*, **71**, 491–507.

Rizzolatti, G., Fogassi, L., Gallese, V. (2001). Neurophysiological mechanisms underlying action understanding and imitation. *Nat. Rev. Neurosci.*, **2**, 661–70.

Scott, S. K., Blank, C. C., Rosen, S. and Wise, R. J. (2000). Identification of a pathway for intelligible speech in the left temporal lobe. *Brain*, **123(12)**, 2400–6.

Seltzer, B. and Pandya, D. N. (1994). Parietal, temporal, and occipital projections to cortex of the superior temporal sulcus in the rhesus monkey: a retrograde tracer study. *J. Comp. Neurol.*, **343**, 445–63.

Tamada, T., Miyauchi, S., Imamizu, H., Yoshioka, T. and Kawato, M. (1999). Cerebro-cerebellar functional connectivity revealed by the laterality index in tool-use learning. *Neuroreport*, **10**, 325–31.

Wernicke, C. (1874). *Der Aphasiche Symptomenkomplex*. Breslau, Poland: Cohen & Weigert.

Wolpert, D. M., Doya, K. and Kawato, M. (2003). A unifying computational framework for motor control and social interaction. *Philos. Trans. R. Soc. Lond. B. Biol. Sci.*, **358**, 593–602.

Wolpert, D. M. and Kawato, M. (1998). Multiple paired forward and inverse models for motor control. *Neural Networks*, **11**, 1317–29.

Wood, J. N. and Grafman, J. (2003). Human prefrontal cortex: processing and representational perspectives. *Nat. Rev. Neurosci.*, **4**, 139–47.

5   Simulation theory of understanding others: a robotics perspective

Yiannis Demiris and Matthew Johnson

5.1   Introduction

5.1.1   *Simulation theory*

According to the simulation theory, 'human beings are able to use the resources of their own minds to simulate the psychological etiology of the behaviour of others', typically by making decisions within a 'pretend context' (Gordon, 1999). During observation of another agent's behaviour, the execution apparatus of the observer is taken 'off-line' and is used as a manipulable model of the observed behaviour.

From a roboticist's point of view, the fundamental characteristics of the simulation theory are:

- Utilization of the same computational systems for a dual purpose; both behaviour generation as well as recognition.
- Taking systems off-line (suspending their normal input/output) which necessitates a redirection and suppression of input (feeding 'pretend states' following a perspective taking process, suppressing the current ones that are coming from the visual sensors while this is performed) and output from/to the system to achieve this dual use.

Simulation theory is often set as a rival to the 'theory-theory', where a separate theoretical reasoning system is used; the observer perceives and reasons about the observed behaviour not by simulating it, but by utilizing a set of causal laws about behaviours.

It is important to note that in the experiments we describe here, 'understanding' the demonstrated behaviour equates to inferring its goal in terms of sensorimotor states, and does not imply inference of the emotional, motivational and intentional components of mental states. Although the mechanisms we will describe can be adapted to cover such inferences, utilizing the same generation-prediction principle, this

Imitation and Social Learning in Robots, Humans and Animals, ed. Chrystopher L. Nehaniv and Kerstin Dautenhahn. Published by Cambridge University Press.
© Cambridge University Press 2007.

is beyond the scope of the experiments we describe here, which focus specifically on the goal component of mental states.

5.1.2   *Biological evidence*

Simulation theory attracted a lot of interest following multi-disciplinary evidence of activation of motor areas of the brain even during *perception of actions done by others*. Neurons in area F5 of the premotor cortex of macaque monkeys have been termed 'mirror' neurons (Gallese *et al.*, 1996; Rizzolatti *et al.*, 1996; Fogassi and Gallese, 2002), following the discovery of a fascinating property they have: they are active when the monkey performs a certain action (for example, grasping), as well as when the monkey acts as an observer and sees a demonstrator performing the same task. This 'mirror system' has been proposed (Gallese and Goldman, 1998) to be the mechanism underlying a 'mind-reading' process in primates, following the simulation theory approach. Evidence from human experiments has lent further support to this view: brain imaging data (Decety *et al.*, 1997; Meltzoff and Decety, 2003) have shown clear activation of the human brain motor areas during the execution of actions, as well as their observation when performed by others. These data, along with motor evoked potential (MEP) data from human muscles during action observation experiments (Fadiga *et al.*, 1995), support the simulation theory, since there is a clear involvement of the motor systems even during the observation of actions done by others. These data (further reviews can be found in Buccino *et al.*, 2004; Fadiga and Craighero, 2003; Rizzolatti and Gallese, 2001) are not easily explainable by the rival theory-theory.

Experiments on the interplay between memory and movement imitation are also of interest here, and provide supporting evidence that imitation and observation of an action recruit similar brain areas. Zimmer and Engelkamp (1996) reported that the performance of subjects on free recall of a set of movements was not different in two of the experimental conditions which involved either perceiving the movement or perceiving the movements and subsequently (after the presentation of each of them) imitating them[1]. Related results were reported by Abravanel (1991) who experimented with the effects on memory of immediate vs. deferred imitation of demonstrated actions in infants, and did not find any difference between the two conditions, especially in older infants (17–20 months old). The subjects were able to encode and retain as much from perceiving the modelled acts as from imitating them. This effect was not

---

[1] Other experimental conditions included verbal recall and combinations of the above.

so clear in younger infants (13–16 months old) who performed slightly better when they imitated the actions.

Of relevance to the simulation theory are also psychophysical experiments investigating the differences between observing an action, imagining an action and executing that action. Vogt (1995) performed a series of studies where subjects learned to reproduce a sequence of cyclical arm movements, either through repeatedly observing the sequence on a monitor, or through mentally or physically rehearsing the sequence. The results were very interesting since they demonstrated that observation of mental or physical rehearsal led to similar improvement in temporal consistency when the subject was later asked to reproduce the observations. Some further experiments (Vogt, 1996) with a short-term memory paradigm where subjects were allowed to observe the model movement (more specifically, different patterns of relative timing) only once, showed that timing imitation did not benefit from any further intermediate imitation (imaginary or physical) in the interval between the presentation of the model movement and the point where the subjects were asked to reproduce it. Related results were obtained in 'mental chronometry' experiments by Decety (1996). Subjects were asked to perform a task[2] either mentally or physically. The movement times required to execute the task were very similar irrespective of the modality of execution (mental or physical). In related sets of experiments (Decety *et al.*, 1991; Wang and Morgan, 1992; Wuyam *et al.*, 1995), subjects were asked to mentally perform tasks that would require different physical effort[3] and found that autonomic responses (cardiac and respiratory activity) during motor imagery paralleled the autonomic responses to physically performing the task.

Having reviewed some of the related biological evidence, in the next section we will describe our research towards a robotic implementation of the simulation theory for use in learning by imitation tasks.

5.2 Modelling

5.2.1 Fundamentals

Well-established elements of control theory are used to design and implement systems for our research into the simulation theory. A state space is defined, to describe an embodied entity in a physical environment. A

---

[2] Tasks included drawing a cube, writing a sentence with either hand and walking to targets at various distances.

[3] Tasks included walking, running, walking on a treadmill and lifting dumbbells.

state may be internal to an entity, to describe the entity's *proprioception*, or it may relate to some quality or quantity of the environment as the entity perceives it through *exteroception*. Activations of the entity's *motor units* will cause a movement through the state space, since the entity moves in, and interacts with, the environment. Through learning, or through design, the entity can relate changes in motor unit activation to changes in proprioceptive and exteroceptive state. This results in the entity possessing *internal models* of itself and its environment. The two kinds of internal model used here are *forward models* and *inverse models*. Internal forward and inverse models have been hypothesized to exist in the human cerebellum (Wolpert *et al.*, 1998), where they can be used for motor control and learning (Wolpert and Kawato, 1998; Haruno *et al.*, 2001) and sensorimotor integration (Wolpert *et al.*, 1995).

Forward Models

A forward model uses the current state of the entity and the environment, and the motor activations within the entity, to generate a *prediction* of the environmental and entity states that would result from the entity acting according to its motor activations. In a complex system it is difficult to learn or design a generic forward model that encompasses the entire state space and its dynamics, so *multiple* forward models may be produced, each one specific to a certain sector of the state space.

Inverse Models

In common with the forward model, an inverse model uses the current state of the entity and the environment. However, as the name suggests, its purpose is the inverse of that of the forward model. The inverse model will take as input a *desired goal state*, and generate motor unit activations, with the purpose of making the entity act so as to cause the goal state. In the control literature, the inverse model is often referred to as a *controller* and its outputs are control signals; when applied to the robotics field, the current state is the state of the robot and its environment, and the outputs are motor commands. Inverse models are also known in the robotics field as *behaviours*.

5.2.2   Architectures

Forward and inverse models may be paired, to allow an observer to recognize the actions of other entities (Figure 5.1) in a simulation theory approach by directly involving the motor system in the recognition process.

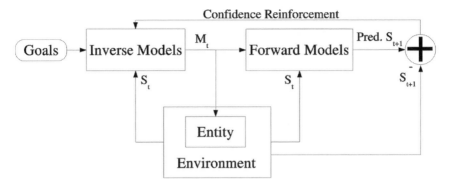

Figure 5.1 Inverse and forward models paired for action recognition; several of these structures operate in parallel.

The core feature of the active recognition system is the pairing of *multiple* inverse models operating in parallel with corresponding forward models to create an execution–prediction sequence. The inverse models give rise to motor activations (Mt), based on their goal state and the current system state as observed (St). We can feed in either the state of the observer or the demonstrator; when we feed in the state of the demonstrator, the observer is essentially *simulating* the actions of the demonstrator. The resulting motor activations are *inhibited* from reaching the observer's motor units, and the forward models provide the predicted results of the actions that would be caused by the motor activations (*Pred. S_{t+1}*). By performing this process with every inverse model, in parallel, and then matching the results of the predictions from the forward models with what is observed from watching an action performed (S_{t+1}), it is possible to determine which inverse models correspond to generating the observed action.

Because recognition is achieved in terms of the observer's own inverse models, the observer can immediately execute those inverse models for himself, and thereby *imitate* the actions he has recognized.

Design and Use of Inverse Models

An action, with its associated goal, can often be subdivided into lower-level actions with corresponding subgoals. To reflect this, inverse models are constructed hierarchically, with the lowest level of inverse model being a *primitive* (Matarić *et al.*, 1998; Bentivegna and Atkeson, 2002). To create a higher-level inverse model to achieve a sophisticated goal, primitive inverse models may be arranged in sequence and in parallel. The resulting high-level inverse model may then be used as part of another inverse model in the same way, creating a *recursive* arrangement (Demiris and Johnson, 2003; Johnson and Demiris, 2004, 2005).

Solving the correspondence problem

The correspondence problem (Nehaniv and Dautenhahn, 2002; Alissandrakis *et al.*, 2002) refers to the need for an agent to go through a process that matches an observed behaviour to the agent's corresponding behaviour, given the agent's potential differences in morphology and sensorimotor capabilities as compared to the demonstrator. With inverse models subdivided as we described earlier, it is possible to use *abstraction* to enhance the ability of the observer to recognize actions and solve this problem (Johnson and Demiris, 2004, 2005). This is important as there are many situations where a demonstrator may not perform a particular action in the same way as the observer already understands it. The demonstrator may be a conspecific, but may have found a more efficient motor program that achieves the action. Or, the morphology of demonstrator and observer may be different. The inverse model that the demonstrator uses to perform the action may then result in completely different movements compared to the movements produced by the inverse model the observer would use to accomplish the same action. Abstraction is then used to concentrate on the parts of a single inverse model that correspond well, while attributing less importance to parts of the inverse model that do not correspond well (Johnson and Demiris, 2004, 2005).

5.3   Robotic implementation

5.3.1   *Implementation of inverse models*

As mentioned earlier, inverse models are implemented as graphs, in a hierarchical fashion where nodes can be arranged in series or in parallel to achieve complex behaviours. At the lowest level, primitives of the form 'open grippers', 'close grippers', 'move forward' etc., are used. An example of graph structure showing a complex behaviour composed of a sequence of primitives is shown in Figure 5.3.

Associated with each inverse model is a *goal state*, which is a single instance of the imitator's state vector, and which represents the point at which the inverse model can consider itself to be complete in terms of execution of its motor program. A graph will execute each of its constituent nodes in turn, until the node indicates it is complete, at which point the node will have its confidence reset and the graph continues execution at the subsequent node. In Johnson and Demiris (2004, 2005), this

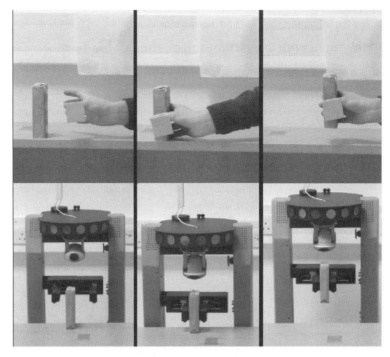

Figure 5.2 The robot imitating picking up an object.

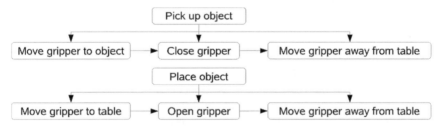

Figure 5.3 Arrangement of primitives in a graphed inverse model: (A) 'Pick up object' (B) 'Place object' (from Johnson and Demiris (2004)).

execution process was extended to introduce an abstraction mechanism, which allows a graph to execute its nodes in a less rigid and predetermined manner to that described here. The mechanism allows the graph to selectively disregard irrelevant nodes, and instead concentrate on nodes relevant to a demonstration in progress. Irrelevant nodes are the nodes that do not contribute in the accurate prediction of the demonstrated state.

5.3.2   *Implementation of forward models*

In this framework it is assumed that primitive inverse models are tightly coupled with associated forward models specific to their function. In the experiments below, higher-level inverse models do not have higher-level forward models associated with them; instead if the framework encounters a primitive during execution of a graph, it will execute the resultant motor command on the primitive's associated forward model. The forward models for the primitives were hand-coded based on experiment, according to the process used in Demiris and Johnson (2003).

5.3.3   *Calculation of confidences*

The confidence level of each inverse model is continuously updated, so as to determine which inverse model best matches with the demonstration in progress. Depending on how well the inverse model matches, its confidence level is adjusted by a reward or penalty factor. In these experiments, constant reward and penalty factors are used for every inverse model in the system. Adaptive versions of the reward functions have also been used in other experiments (Demiris and Hayes, 2002). There is no comparison threshold value, meaning that the predicted state from the internal forward model must match the observed state exactly to generate a reward for the inverse model under consideration. This condition of exact matching is possible as the states are defined qualitatively, rather than on absolute metric information that may be subject to noise in the visual signal.

At every time step, the confidence for each inverse model is calculated according to the following rule:

$$C_t = \begin{cases} C_{t-1} + Kr & \text{if } s_t = \hat{s}_t \\ C_{t-1} - Kp & \text{otherwise} \end{cases} \tag{5.1}$$

where C_t is the confidence of the inverse model at time t, and Kr and Kp are the constant reward and penalty factors; s_t is the perceived value of the demonstrator's state at time t, and $\hat{s}_t$ is the predicted value that was given by the forward model at time $t - 1$ for time t.

Since the perceived state must match exactly with the predicted state for confidence reinforcement to occur, there is far greater opportunity for the penalty to be applied rather than the reward. To correct this bias, Kr was generally chosen to be greater than Kp. In the following experiments, $Kr = 100$ and $Kp = 1$.

5.4   Experiments

The forward–inverse model paired architecture described above has been implemented in a range of different experimental platforms (Demiris and Hayes, 2002; Demiris and Johnson, 2003; Johnson and Demiris, 2004), for a variety of demonstrated tasks involving gestural and object-directed actions. Using the implementation described in the previous section we will show experiments done on a mobile robotic platform (ActivMedia Peoplebot), equipped with cameras and a gripper, with the aim of having the robot learn high-level inverse models through imitation. Examples include picking up an object and putting an object on a table. The robot starts with a set of sensorimotor primitives and assembles hierarchical combinations of these into more complex behaviours that are subsequently added in its repertoire. Figure 5.2 shows the robot imitating the action of picking up an object. In these experiments, visual tracking is performed by marking all relevant objects (including the demonstrator's hand) with colour markers, and calculating all states (e.g. the robot's or the demonstrator's arm) in relative rather than absolute terms (i.e. distance of demonstrator's arm from object, rather than absolute positions in 3-D space) (Johnson and Demiris, 2004). A combination of proprioception based values (position and velocity) and visual tracking of the gripper contributes to the calculation of the robot's state vector.

Figure 5.4 shows the evolution of confidence over time for the inverse models in the imitation system, during learning of a 'pick up object' behaviour. Figures 5.4(A) and 5.4(B) show the robot learning the 'pick up object' behaviour. The first demonstration, shown in Figure 5.4(B), is a teaching demonstration; the 'pick up object' behaviour is unknown to the robot, and the action is recognized only as being a sequence of primitives. When the demonstration is complete, the learning is initiated and a new inverse model is created to describe the behaviour. This is done by assembling the primitives recognized during the teaching demonstration. During the subsequent repeat demonstration of picking up an object, the newly created inverse model acquires confidence while simulating the demonstrated action, and the robot recognizes the demonstrator performing the behaviour it has just learned. The build-up of confidence of the learnt behaviour is shown in Figure 5.4(A), which is ongoing at the same time as the change in confidence of its constituent primitive inverse models in Figure 5.4(B). The learnt 'pick up object' behaviour achieves a confidence level higher than that of any primitive.

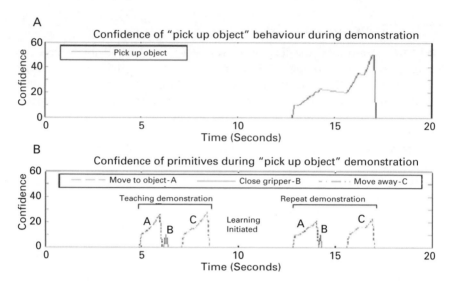

Figure 5.4 Graphs (A) and (B) are concurrent in time, and show the confidences of inverse models while the robot learns to pick up an object. The changes in confidence of the learnt behaviours in graph (A) are separate from those of the primitive inverse models in graph (B), to better show the learning process.

5.5 Discussion

In this chapter, we have described our particular implementation of the simulation theory approach to understanding demonstrated behaviours. In order to achieve what is advocated by this approach, we adopted a distributed network of inverse and forward models which relies primarily on competition, mutual inhibition and quality-of-prediction-based selection of a winner (Demiris and Hayes, 2002; Demiris and Johnson, 2003).

The architecture understands an action by internally generating it. The observer imitates the demonstrated action internally, even when it does not do so externally. This feature of the architecture explains why physically imitating a set of demonstrated movements does not significantly aid their later recall (Zimmer and Engelkamp, 1996), as well as why physical rehearsal of a demonstrated behaviour does not lead to any significant differences in the levels of performance improvement (in terms of temporal consistency) from mental rehearsal or mere observation (Vogt, 1995). Since observation, imagery and imitation are performed using mostly the same structures (inverse and forward models), the same laws should govern their operation. This also hints at an explanation of the mental chronometry data by Decety (1996), indicating that it takes roughly the same time to perform a task mentally or physically. In fact, we have performed experiments using simulated humanoids where we utilized this principle to form predictions about the behaviour of mirror neurons (Demiris and Hayes, 2002) when the demonstrated behaviour was performed at speeds unattainable for the imitator. Limitations in the execution machinery were translated to limitations in what could be perceived: if the monkey observes an action performed at speeds that he cannot match, the corresponding mirror neuron will show little or no activation, despite the fact that the action is in its repertoire.

In our system, the demonstrated action is imitated internally, and the motor commands are suppressed from being sent to the low-level motor systems. If the suppression system is damaged, the demonstrated action would be performed even if that is not required. Evidence from patients with frontal lobe damage indicate that they display a pathological behaviour that has been termed 'imitation behaviour' (Lhermitte *et al.*, 1986) (also similar to a condition known as echolalia). These patients imitate the demonstrator's gesture although they were not instructed to do so, and some times even when told *not* to do so (de Renzi *et al.*, 1996). An explicit, direct command from the doctor to the patient would stop the imitation behaviour but a simple distraction to a different subject was sufficient to see imitation reappearing, despite the patient remembering what (s)he had been told. The inhibition of imitation response tendencies has also recently been investigated using fMRI scanning in non-clinical subjects (Brass *et al.*, 2001), and in patients with frontal brain lesions (Brass *et al.*, 2003). Evidence for the need for active supression of output is also given by Schwoebel *et al.* (2002), who describes the case of a patient with bilateral parietal lesions, who unwillingly executed imagined hand movements.

We have already indicated in Section 2.1 that although several action execution and understanding systems can be made to overlap there are several processes that cannot. For example, a perspective taking process is necessary in order to be able to feed the appropriate demonstrator state information into the imitator's inverse and forward models. This is far from trivial, since it can range from a simple visual transformation to adopting the visual perspective of the demonstrator, to modifying the inverse and forward models to explicitly take into account any known morphological and other differences between the demonstrator and the imitator. There are also differences between the nature of prediction during observation and during planning of actions, since in the case of planning the goal is known, but during observation it is not. Although the simulation theory presents an attractive and efficient account of understanding others, recent evidence from brain scanning raises doubts as to whether it tells the whole story, and in particular whether it can be used for all types of observed behaviour. The study of Ramnanin and Miall (2004) did find evidence of human motor area activation during observation of an associative visuomotor task, but found differences between the sub-areas activated during observation and during execution.

Further neurophysiological, brain imaging and modelling experiments will be necessary in order to determine the extent of use of simulation processes in the mechanisms underlying human understanding of the behaviour of others. Our on-going work is attempting to also bring elements from the theory-theory approach (learning by demonstration without explicit invocation of the motor systems) in attempt to utilize the best aspects of both theories.

Acknowledgments

Research presented here was funded by UK's Engineering and Physical Sciences Research Council (EPSRC) project GR/S11305/01, and the Royal Society. We would also like to thank all members of the Biologically inspired Autonomous Robots Team (BioART) at Imperial for their assistance and comments.

REFERENCES

Abravanel, E. (1991). Does immediate imitation influence long-term memory for observed actions? *Journal of Experimental Child Psychology*, **51**, 235–44.

Alissandrakis, A., Nehaniv, C. L. and Dautenhahn, K. (2002). Imitating with ALICE: learning to imitate corresponding actions across dissimilar embodiments. *IEEE Transactions on Systems, Man, and Cybernetics, Part A: Systems and Humans*, **32(4)**, 482–96.

Bentivegna, D. and Atkeson, C. (2002). A framework for learning from observation using primitives. Presented at the *Symposium of Robocup 2002, Fukuoka, Japan*.

Brass, M., Derrfuss, J., von Cramon, G. M. and von Cramon, D. Y. (2003). Imitative response tendencies in patients with frontal brain lesions. *Neuropsychology*, **17(2)**, 265–71.

Brass, M., Zysset, S. and von Cramon, D. (2001). The inhibition of imitative response tendencies. *NeuroImage*, **14**, 1416–23.

Buccino, G., Binkofski, F. and Riggio, L. (2004). The mirror neuron system and action recognition. *Brain and Language*, **89**, 370–6.

de Renzi, E., Cavalleri, F. and Facchini, S. (1996). Imitation and utilisation behaviour. *Journal of Neurology, Neurosurgery and Psychiatry*, **61**, 396–400.

Decety, J. (1996). Do imagined and executed actions share the same neural substrate? *Cognitive Brain Research*, **3**, 87–93.

Decety, J., Grezes, J., Costes, N., Perani, D., Jeannerod, M., Procyk, E., Grassi, F. and Fazio, F. (1997). Brain activity during observation of actions: influence of action content and subject's strategy. *Brain*, **120**, 1763–77.

Decety, J., Jeannerod, M., Germain, M. and Pastene, J. (1991). Vegetative response during imagined movement is proportional to mental effort. *Behavioural Brain Research*, **42**, 1–5.

Demiris, Y. and Hayes, G. (2002). Imitation as a dual route process featuring predictive and learning components: a biologically plausible computational model. In Dautenhahn, K. and Nehaniv, C. (eds.), *Imitation in Animals and Artifacts*. Cambridge, MA: MIT Press.

Demiris, Y. and Johnson, M. (2003). Distributed, prediction perception of actions: a biologically inspired architecture for imitation and learning. *Connection Science*, **15(4)**, 231–43.

Fadiga, L. and Craighero, L. (2003). New insights on sensorimotor integration: from hand action to speech perception. *Brain and Cognition*, **53**, 514–24.

Fadiga, L., Fogassi, L., Pavesi, G. and Rizzolatti, G. (1995). Motor facilitation during action observation: a magnetic stimulation study. *Journal of Neurophysiology*, **73(6)**, 2608–11.

Fogassi, L. and Gallese, V. (2002). The neural correlates of action understanding. In *Mirror Neurons and the Evolution of Brain and Language*, Amsterdam: John Benjamins Publishing Company, 13–36.

Gallese, V., Fadiga, L., Fogassi, L. and Rizzolatti, G. (1996). Action recognition in the premotor cortex. *Brain*, **119**, 593–609.

Gallese, V. and Goldman, A. (1998). Mirror neurons and the simulation theory of mind-reading. *Trends in Cognitive Sciences*, **2(12)**, 493–501.

Gordon, R. (1999). Simulation vs theory-theory. In Wilson, R. A. and Keil, F. (eds.), *The MIT Encyclopaedia of the Cognitive Sciences*. Cambridge, MA: MIT Press, 765–6.

Haruno, M., Wolpert, D. M. and Kawato, M. (2001). Mosaic model for sensorimotor learning and control. *Neural Computation*, **13**, 2201–20.

Johnson, M. and Demiris, Y. (2004). Abstraction in recognition to solve the correspondence problem for robot imitation. In *Proceedings of TAROS-04*, University of Essex, UK, 63–70.

Johnson, M. and Demiris, Y. (2005). Hierarchies of coupled inverse and forward models for abstraction in robot action planning, recognition and imitation. In *Proceedings of the AISB 2005 Symposium on Imitation in Animals and Artifacts*. AISB.

Lhermitte, F., Pillon, B. and Serdaru, M. (1986). Human autonomy and the frontal lobes – Part I: imitation and utilization behavior: a neuropsychological study of 75 patients. *Annals of Neurology*, **19(4)**, 326–34.

Matarić, M., Williamson, M., Demiris, J. and Mohan, A. (1998). Behaviour-based primitives for articulated control. In *From Animals to Animats 5*, Zurich, Switzerland: MIT Press.

Meltzoff, A. N. and Decety, J. (2003). What imitation tells us about social cognition: a rapprochement between developmental psychology and cognitive neuroscience. *Philosophical Transaction of the Royal Society of London B*, **358**, 491–500.

Nehaniv, C. and Dautenhahn, K. (2002). The correspondence problem. In Dautenhahn, K. and Nehaniv, C. (eds.), *Imitation in Animals and Artifacts*. Cambridge, MA: MIT Press, Chapter 2, pages 41–61.

Ramnanin, N. and Miall, R. C. (2004). A system in the human brain for predicting the actions of others. *Nature Neuroscience*, **7(1)**, 85–90.

Rizzolatti, G., Fadiga, L., Gallese, V. and Fogassi, L. (1996). Premotor cortex and the recognition of motor actions. *Cognitive Brain Research*, **3**, 131–41.

Rizzolatti, G., Fogassi, L. and Gallese, V. (2001). Neurophysiological mechanisms underlying the understanding and imitation of action. *Nature Reviews Neuroscience*, **2**, 661–70.

Schwoebel, J., Boronat, C. B. and Coslett, H. B. (2002). The man who executed imagined movements: evidence for dissociable components of the body schema. *Brain and cognition*, **50**, 1–16.

Vogt, S. (1995). On relations between perceiving, imagining and performing in the learning of cyclical movement sequences. *British Journal of Psychology*, **86**, 191–216.

Vogt, S. (1996). Imagery and perception-action mediation in imitative actions. *Cognitive Brain Research*, **3**, 79–86.

Wang, Y. and Morgan, W. P. (1992). The effect of imagery perspectives on the psychophysical responses to imagined exercise. *Behaviour Brain Research*, **52**, 167–74.

Wolpert, D., Ghahramani, Z. and Jordan, M. (1995). An internal model for sensorimotor integration. *Science*, **269**, 1880–2.

Wolpert, D. M. and Kawato, M. (1998). Multiple paired forward and inverse models for motor control. *Neural Networks*, **11**, 1317–29.

Wolpert, D. M., Miall, R. C. and Kawato, M. (1998). Internal models in the cerebellum. *Trends in Cognitive Sciences*, **2(9)**, 338–47.

Wuyam, B., Moosavi, S., Decety, J., Adams, L., Lansing, R. and Guz, A. (1995). Imagination of dynamic exercise produced ventilatory responses which were more apparent in competitive sportsmen. *Journal of Physiology*, **482**, 713–24.

Zimmer, H. D. and Engelkamp, J. (1996). Routes to actions and their efficacy for remembering. *Memory*, **4(1)**, 59–78.

6 Mirrors and matchings: imitation from the perspective of mirror-self-recognition, and the parietal region's involvement in both

Robert W. Mitchell

6.1 Introduction

In the movie *Duck Soup*, the Marx Brothers Harpo and Groucho come upon each other, face to face. There would have been a mirror between them, but Harpo, in his attempt to avoid being seen by Groucho whom he had been impersonating, ran into it and broke it. The two men look alike; to avoid detection, Harpo imitates Groucho's movements to make it appear that Groucho is seeing himself in a mirror. Testing the "mirror" image, Groucho performs a series of bizarre actions that Harpo imitates simultaneously, thereby supporting the ridiculous conclusion that Groucho is indeed looking in a mirror. The sequence nicely illustrates the similarities between bodily imitation and mirror images. In both, actions of one entity closely mimic the actions of another, such that a resemblance is apparent. Consequently, it seems reasonable to expect that the same processes that allow someone to imitate another person's actions (or to recognize that one's actions are being imitated) might also be useful in determining that the image in the mirror is oneself.

Remarkably, the first explicit recognition of the similarity between bodily imitation and mirror-self-recognition was quite recent, in 1925 by French psychologist Paul Guillaume, in his book about the imitative development of his daughters. Guillaume (1926/1971, p. 152) argued "We must not hesitate to connect this exceptional mirror experiment [i.e., the child's infrequent interactions with mirrors] with the experience of normal imitation. Other adults and also other children in the society in which he lives are for the infant the natural mirror that reflects for him his own image when he proceeds to imitate." (See similar idea in Piaget, 1945/1962, p. 56.) While differences between bodily imitation and self-recognition are, of course, apparent as well, in this chapter I propose that

Imitation and Social Learning in Robots, Humans and Animals, ed. Chrystopher L. Nehaniv and Kerstin Dautenhahn. Published by Cambridge University Press.
© Cambridge University Press 2007.

the similarities are significant enough that theories purporting to explain self-recognition are helpful in understanding bodily imitation. If correct, components of self-recognition are likely to be components of bodily imitation as well. The fact that several developmental psychologists, beginning with Guillaume (1926/1971) and including Piaget (1945/1962), also found the similarities between self-recognition and bodily imitation suggestive of identical processes explaining both (Mitchell, 1997b; 2002b), suggests that I am not, like Groucho, looking for an identity where only similarity exists.

6.2   Two models

I begin by presenting two models I developed to explain initial self-recognition (Mitchell, 1993a,b) which should provide glimpses at imitation from different vantage points. Both models are attempts to solve the problem as to how an organism could recognize, for the first or first few times, that the image of itself in the mirror is just that. Both models distinguish potential components of self-recognition that seem relevant as potential components of imitation. The first model focuses attention on self-recognition (and by extension generalized bodily imitation) as a form of intermodal matching between kinesthesis and vision (the kinesthetic-visual matching model); the second model views self-recognition as deriving from general understanding of objects and similarities between them (the object-generalization model). Note that both models are concerned with explaining *initial* self-recognition in a mirror (or concurrent video). I imagine that, once one's external visual image in a mirror is recognized, knowledge of one's own facial and bodily features may begin to assist in self-recognition, and an understanding of mirror correspondence becomes more developed to include knowledge that when one is looking in a mirror, one sees oneself. However, neither bit of knowledge is available prior to recognizing oneself in a mirror and both may take time to develop (see, for example, Miles, 1994), such that self-recognition will initially depend upon the processes proposed in the models.

In the first model, self-recognition occurs initially because the organism:
(1) understands mirror correspondence, that is, understands that mirrors reflect accurate and contingent images of objects (other than the perceiver) in front of them;
(2) has kinesthetic-visual matching (as evinced at least in generalized bodily imitation), which allows it to recognize that the visual image in the mirror looks like what it feels like and vice versa (and which may, by itself, be enough for some evidence of self-recognition); and

(3) can make inferences, such as that the image is "the same" as its own body.

The ability to match (i.e. recognize, create and test the similarity) between kinesthetic and visual modalities seems essential for generalized bodily imitation as well as self-recognition. (Note that matching between kinesthesis and vision means more than simply coordinating the two as infants do in secondary circular reactions.)

In the second model, self-recognition occurs initially because the organism:

(1) understands mirror correspondence (as in the first model);
(2) objectifies body parts, such that it perceives appendages (its own and others') as distinct yet continuous parts of bodies and also recognizes that these appendages (e.g. its own and others' hands) are similar looking (abilities usually developed and exhibited by naming, or understanding the names of, body parts); and
(3) understands (sixth-stage) object permanence, such that it recognizes that parts of things are indicative of the whole and has low-level deductive abilities.

From these abilities, the organism recognizes (via understanding mirror correspondence) that the hand (for example) in the mirror is a contingent accurate image of its hand, and then recognizes (via its understanding of object permanence) that what is continuous with the hand in the mirror (i.e. the body-image) must be a contingent accurate image of what is continuous with its own hand (i.e. its body). The abilities for body-part objectification and object-permanence understanding do not seem immediately necessary for imitation, but note that they function to do what kinesthetic-visual matching does in the first model, and may be necessary parts of kinesthetic-visual matching.

Although not perfect, some evidence supports the first model. Among animals, some members of great ape (chimpanzee, gorilla, orangutan) and bottlenose dolphin (*Tursiops*) species offer evidence of both generalized bodily imitation and mirror-self-recognition (for overview, see Mitchell, 2002b; Parker *et al.*, 1994). (Some members of other species, such as gibbons, bonobos, and killer whales, exhibit self-recognition, but none have been tested for generalized imitation.) Members of most animal species appear to show neither self-recognition nor generalized bodily imitation. In addition, human children recognize themselves in mirrors at about the time that they start to show generalized bodily imitation (especially synchronic imitation – see Nielsen and Slaughter, Chapter 16 this volume) and soon after they recognize that another is imitating them (Meltzoff, 1990) – another indicator of developing kinesthetic-visual matching (see Mitchell, 1993a; 2002b for chronology). Only one animal has been tested on imitation recognition: a 31-year-old chimpanzee who recognized that his actions and movements were being imitated by a human (Nielsen *et al.*, 2005). Evidence gathering is still in progress, of course, and support for the theory would be helped by more evidence of the developmental congruence of generalized bodily imitation and self-recognition in individual nonhuman animals, which so far only sign-using animals show (see Miles *et al.*, 1996; Mitchell, 2002c). (Obviously blind people develop self-recognition and imitation via non-visual perceptions.)

Almost all of the components of both models were presented in 1906 by David Major, an obscure American developmental psychologist who published a discussion of his sons' understandings of mirror images. Major found it puzzling that his one-year-old child could "seem so naïve [i.e. not recognize himself] when looking at his own image," yet could "prove himself so sophisticated with reference to the [mirror-]images" of objects that Major showed him, as evinced by the child reaching toward the real objects, not their mirror-images (p. 274). In attempting to explain "the agencies and correlations within the child's experience which enable him . . . to realize that the [mirror-]image is related in some way to himself, and, in some cases, cause the child to look upon his image as another self, or double" (pp. 275–276), Major proposed the following:

We may suppose that the child first learns through visual sensations and certain sensations of movement that the movements of parts of his body – his feet, arms, hands and so on – are parts of the same group of experiences which he gradually comes to think of as himself; that is, he sees some of these movements and he "feels" them, at the same time, as belonging to himself. Now, when he looks in a mirror and at the same time moves parts of his body, e.g., his head, or his arms when he tries to grasp the image, or when he opens his mouth – he observes that the changes in the image and the changes which he sees and "feels" his own body making occur at the same time, and so thinks the former changes are in some way related to the latter. He sees and feels his hand move, and he sees a similar movement in the mirror at the same time; he feels his head move and he sees a change in the image and so comes to think of the two in the relation of cause and effect. It seems reasonable to suppose, to use the more technical terms, that the child learns that the image is related to himself partly through the blending of his visual sensations, and partly by the blending of his visual and kinæsthetic sensations. (pp. 276–7)

Major offers here several components to discerning oneself in a mirror: understanding the reflective properties of mirrors toward objects other than oneself; matching between visually similar body parts; and matching (i.e. recognition of similarity, or "blending") between the "feel" of a body part's movement (the "kinæsthetic sensations") and its visual appearance (which includes recognition of the simultaneity of this feeling and visual appearance of a body part). Although he does not make an explicit comparison between these components and those needed for bodily imitation, Major (pp. 131–2) posits a process similar to that for self-recognition when the child "begins to imitate movements of parts of the body, like shaking the hand or nodding the head": such imitation "probably marks an advance in the child's perception of points of similarity between himself and other persons [as well as] in control over separate parts of his own body."

In another analysis of imitation based on extensive ontogenetic observations of the researcher's own children, Guillaume (1925) posited that the human infant's recognition of the similarity between its own actions and those of others (which would lead to flexible bodily imitation) derives from an infant's initially attempting to recreate the objective (visually observed) effects of another's actions on objects, and only later trying to reproduce the movements that led to the effects. Gradually, through reproduction of effects, in which the visually experienced act of the model becomes a cue for the production of the same visually experienced act by the child, the kinesthetic subjective feeling of the child's act is associated with the model's act (which is experienced visually); the ability to imitate others' bodily actions results. In Guillaume's model, visual–visual matching leads to the kinesthetic–visual matching present in generalized imitation – the ability to duplicate to some degree myriad actions of another. Guillaume recognized that the same kinesthetic–visual matching that allowed the child to imitate another's actions also allowed the child to recognize his or her own image in a mirror and to pretend.

Whereas Guillaume derived kinesthetic–visual matching from repeated association and contiguity between visual and kinesthetic experiences, Piaget (1945/1961, p. 44) argued that the child is already organized to match vision and kinesthesis analogically: "the model is assimilated to an analogous schema susceptible of translating the visual into the kinesthetic." Note, however, that these "analogous" schemas, in Piaget's view, are very general: it is not that the child matches the vision of a hand to kinesthetic feelings of his or her own hand, but rather that the child matches aspects of vision (e.g. opening and closing) to similar aspects of kinesthesis (and consequently may make mistakes, such as the child's opening and closing his or her hand when watching someone opening and closing his or her mouth). Piaget's view is that the child tries out various hypotheses in imitation, making errors along the way until the match is best for the child's purposes (resulting in the kinesthetic–visual matching between bodies that appears at the endpoint of the development described by Guillaume). Both Guillaume and Piaget borrow somewhat from Baldwin's (1898/1902, pp. 20, 28) account of imitation (see his notion of imitation as based on having a "kinæsthetic equivalent" – a "thought or mental picture in mind which is equivalent to the feeling of the movement we desire to make").

The ideas of Major, Guillaume and Piaget provoke a variety of responses from the modern reader who is conversant with current conceptions about abilities of infants (e.g. neonatal imitation) that have been described as at conflict with these early ideas. I discuss infant abilities at the end of this chapter, and begin by delineating the pieces of the puzzle present in my models.

6.2.1   Matching

Matching requires that the subject understand or experience a spatial similarity (or identity) between perceptions, and not merely coordinate perceptions. So visual–visual matching occurs when a monkey recognizes that two red circles are the same, or that its hand and my hand are similar, and kinesthetic–kinesthetic matching can occur when an animal intentionally reproduces the same action, as in primary circular reactions and some deception by primates (see Mitchell, 1994a). In generalized kinesthetic–visual matching, the kinesthetic feelings the subject experiences must be his or her own, but these can be matched with the visual perception of the subject's own body, or another's body, or a virtual reality image representing the subject's body. On a more abstract level, two conceptual systems may match via analogy, but here I'm concerned with perceptual matchings. Matching between perceptions need not require absolute identity in experience: I can match one image to similar images even when the two are presented from difference vantage points, or when one is smaller than the other (as in a photograph of myself); the idea is that some essential aspects of spatial arrangement (gestalt properties) are maintained. Which aspects are essential and therefore matched is, of course, the "correspondence problem" (Nehaniv and Dautenhahn, 2002), a problem that seems effortlessly solved by within-modality perception of similarity and identity by organisms, but becomes more complicated when between-modality perception of similarity and identity must be relied upon.

6.2.2   Visual–visual matching

Visual–visual matching (sometimes between visual perception and visual memory) is obviously present as a basic skill for most of the components of the two models, including object-permanence understanding,

understanding of mirror correspondence, and body-part objectification, and it may be a developmental requirement for kinesthetic–visual matching. For body images in the mirror and in imitation by others, often the body parts that are simultaneously present do not appear in the same orientation visually: if you are facing me and I ask you to imitate my putting my right hand's palm out from my body, what you see from your own body is (usually) the back of your hand (but you see the palm of my hand); the same thing happens if you show your palm to the mirror. Although there are some body positions in which an almost identical visual experience is present in both my body and your body (and some normal people and many autistic people seem to try to match visual aspects of their own body with another's body in imitation – Ohta, 1987; Smith, 1995; Smith and Bryson, 1994), visual identity of image and reality is not usually present in either imitation or mirror-images. The visual–visual matching requires, in some sense, knowledge of an object from multiple perspectives to make a match to its image (or vice versa) in the mirror or in imitation. Visual–visual matching seems unlikely to serve as the entire basis for either imitation or self-recognition: most mammals can see parts of their own body in the mirror and outside it, and likely recognize the visual similarity, but still fail to recognize themselves or imitate others (see Anderson, 1994; Mitchell, 1993a,b).

6.2.3   Mirror-correspondence understanding

Understanding mirror correspondence – that mirrors reflect accurate and contingent images of objects (other than the perceiver) in front of them – is a tricky conception. This understanding does not require that an organism have a sophisticated understanding of mirrors or reflective surfaces, just that it recognize visual similarities between objects and images in mirrors, and also recognize that the image in the mirror is related to a similar-looking object outside the mirror (and that the image in the mirror is *not* the object). Visual–visual matching between object and image is thus part of understanding mirror correspondence. Some animals who apparently do not recognize themselves in a mirror, such as monkeys (Anderson, 1994) and infants less than 15 months of age (Robinson *et al.*, 1990), can recognize objects in the mirror, and recognize how to obtain those objects (as Major, 1906, noted). Such findings are why I describe an organism as understanding mirror correspondence when the organism does not apply its understanding to itself. Obviously if an organism completely understands mirrors, it will recognize its image – but such complete understanding of mirrors seems to come after the initial self-recognition usually present in humans at around 18 months of age.

Understanding mirror correspondence seems an important initial component of self-recognition. If the reflective properties of mirrors – that they produce accurate and contingent images of (some) objects outside the mirror – are unknown to an organism, the organism could have various attitudes toward mirror images and even make predictions from these, but could not recognize that its image or even part of its image was of itself, for the organism would have no means of relating any image in the mirror to any object outside the mirror. Conversely, if the organism could use the mirror *only* to see its own image, it would be quite bizarre: "I look like that image in the mirror, but I don't see any similarity to anything else around me" is an anomalous idea (though possible with brain damage; see next paragraph). Understanding mirror correspondence (as a part of understanding mirrors) seems a necessary understanding for initial mirror-self-recognition.

There are, however, conditions in which adult people who already know what they look like in a mirror and even have a conceptual understanding of mirrors completely fail to understand mirror correspondence – at least for anything on the left side of their body. In the neurologically based clinical syndrome of left visual neglect ("hemi-neglect"), people completely ignore their left visual field, including the entire left side of their body, sometimes even believing that it belongs to another person. Apparently this syndrome is common for people following strokes affecting the right brain, especially the right parietal lobe (Ramachandran and Blakesee, 1998, p. 114). Yet these people recognize themselves in a mirror, but see (or at least respond) only to the right side (as, for example, in a man's using a mirror to shave his face – but only the right side). However, if a mirror is positioned at a 60° angle to the person's face, and a pencil is in the person's left visual field (where they apparently do not see it) such that its image appears in the mirror in the person's right visual field (where they can see it), people will try to retrieve the pencil (when asked) from "inside" the space of the mirror. They try repeatedly to obtain the pencil that is "beyond" the mirror, hitting the mirror and saying that the mirror is in the way of the pencil or that the pencil is inside the mirror (Ramachandran and Blakesee, 1998, p. 123). For these people, there is no corresponding object outside the mirror, because it is not available to perception, so visual–visual matching is not possible.

6.2.4   *Object-permanence understanding*

The idea of understanding of object-permanence was inaugurated by Piaget's (1954) analysis of how children come to develop an idea of objects as physical entities that continue to exist even when they are not perceived.

Although controversial, Piaget's well-known view is that children develop through a series of stages of sensorimotor understanding about objects. At the third stage, the child can detect that an object is present upon seeing only a part of it (as when the rest is hidden under a blanket). By the fifth stage, the child can find an object when it has been hidden behind a series of obstacles the child sees it move behind, an ability which was not present at the fourth stage. Given the child's ability to reason about the location of the object at the fifth stage, Piaget attributes to the child primitive deductive abilities. At the sixth stage, the child can figure out where an object, hidden inside another object, will be, based on the trajectory of the hiding object. Piaget believes the child at this stage understands that objects exist independently of his or her perception of them, and thus the child can represent objects mentally – he or she knows that objects exist as relatively permanent structures, and recognizes them from diverse perspectives. But in addition object-permanence understanding, even at the third stage, requires abilities to match between visual experiences of objects and memories of these objects. In relation to self-recognition, these abilities become important not only in relation to understanding mirrors' reflections of objects (see below), but also in thinking about one's own body – an object the child has become quite familiar with through self-exploration. If, at the third stage, children can "reconstruct an invisible whole from a visible fraction" (Doré, 1986, p. 340), they can, from knowledge of what others look like and the visible similarities between their own body and those of others, reconstruct at least an outline of what the rest of their body looks like from the "visible fraction" of it which they can see (see Guillaume, 1926/1971, pp. 152–3). (Tactile experiences can also play a role in understanding object permanence, and certainly do for blind people.) In part Piaget views the idea of objects and other things in the world as based on consolidations of perceptual (visual, tactile) and motor (including kinesthetic) experiences, such that understanding object permanence derives from matchings within and between available perceptual experiences and memories (see Piaget, 1945/1962).

Some understanding of objects seems to be an aspect of normal experience assumed to be present in many studies of imitation: if I am to reach for, grasp, or toss the same object, or the same kind of object, as you do, I have to have some understanding of objects. Clearly a multitude of processes are required at the neurological, sensational and perceptual levels to develop a coherent understanding of objects (Treisman, 1986) and their location relative to one's body (Redding and Wallace, 1997). To some degree, understanding object permanence as described by Piaget seems to be localized in the parietal region, an area of the brain that, as I shall show, is of fundamental importance for some of the other components of self-recognition. According to Buccino *et al.* (2001, p. 400), "When an individual acts upon an object, a specific, pragmatic analysis of the object is carried out in the parietal lobe," an analysis distinct from any semantic analysis. Piaget (1954) provides an overview of the kinds of pragmatic understandings of objects that may develop as perceptual-motor skills mature and become better coordinated. His view concerns the development of the coordination between perception of and action upon objects, a coordination that seems essential for understanding mirror correspondence and imitation of others' actions upon objects.

6.2.5   *Body-part objectification*

Body-part objectification is the recognition of elements of the body as distinct objects, and seems to be dependent upon two components: matching visual experiences and objectification.

Visual–visual matching

The early literature on child psychological development focuses a great deal on children's growing recognition of their body parts as their own (see, for example, Tracy, 1901, pp. 66–7). This recognition is presumed to develop from infants' staring at their body parts, which at times appear to be objects of fascination, and children come to recognize similarities in body parts on their own and others' bodies (e.g., see Guillaume, 1926/1971). In addition, other people's bodies are also objects of fascination, particularly faces. As noted, the visual–visual matching assumed here includes matching the same (or relationally similar) body parts in diverse orientations.

Objectification

If an organism is to know objects, it must view them as separable items. Thus, if a child recognizes that wheels on a car can also be independent objects, and recognizes that they are the same thing whether on the car or off, then the child has objectified wheels. By objectification of body-parts is meant both that: (1) the organism recognizes the similarity between any particular body-part of its own and the same body-part of another (a recognition presupposed by understanding object permanence), and that (2) the organism recognizes a body-part, and recognizes it as part of the body, even when the body-part is decontextualized – that is, separated visually from the body (Mitchell, 1993a). Typically the evidence available for body-part objectification is that a child (or ape) can name the body part and point to it when named by another. Surprisingly, these two abilities are separately represented in the brain: a man who had a tumor in the left parietal region had difficulty pointing to human body parts on others and, to a lesser degree, on himself, but had no difficulty naming these body parts, finding body parts of non-human animals or parts of non-living things (Ogden, 1985). Other sorts of evidence are available for body-part objectification; for example, training animals to select images and three-dimensional representations of "hands" for reward should lead to objectification of hands (Mitchell, 1993a,b).

One relatively common activity for primates looking at themselves in mirrors is to look back and forth between the image of a body part in the mirror and their actual body part. This activity has been observed in talapoin monkeys (Posada and Colell, 2005), a gorilla (Riopelle et al., 1971) and bonobos (S. Macintosh and R. W. Mitchell, personal observation). It may be that seeing one's image in the mirror, even if it is not recognized as such, assists in body-part objectification, as the animal recognizes the part it can see of its own body as the same as part of the image-body it can see in the mirror. Chimpanzees can use an image of their arm to obtain objects when arm and objects are seen only on a video-image (Menzel et al., 1985), so it seems likely that they develop body-part objectification. Monkeys show similar skills, and appear to recognize that the video-image of their body part represents their own body parts; interestingly, this skill seems to develop only after using tools (i.e. objects) to achieve their aims via video-images, and shows extensive involvement of intraparietal neurons (Iriki et al., 2001). The earliest ages at which children and other primates can perform such skills is unknown.

Once body-part objectification is present, object-permanence understanding should be applied to these parts, though whether body parts are interpreted differently than other objects by growing organisms is unknown. Apparently adult people respond differently psychologically to images of objects that are and are not body parts (Kosslyn et al., 1998), which suggests that different "rules" may apply when organisms represent body parts rather than other objects. For example, when engaged in mental rotation of images to see whether or not they match another image, for most objects people tend to imagine rotation of the objects themselves, but for body parts they imagine rotating their own body or body parts to match the stimulus (Parsons, 1987, p. 188). Recognizing which of one's own hands (left or right) matches an image of a hand in various orientations seems to require that this body part is represented via a "visual–kinesthetic image" (Sekiyama, 1982, p. 94; 1983), a representation obviously distinctive to the body. Apparently, in some cases, observation of actual hands performing actions on objects assisted people's abilities to perform similar actions on objects, whereas observation of robotic hands which look like actual hands performing the same actions on objects did not (Castiello *et al.*, 2002). And the movement of body parts on a visible body appears to influence different brain areas than movements of objects (or movements of body parts on an upside down body) (Shiffrar and Pinto, 2002). In fact, body parts may be specifically represented in brain areas: specific cortical neurons stimulated electrically can produce feelings of particular body parts (Penfield, 1950).

6.2.6   *Kinesthetic–visual matching*

Kinesthetic–visual matching is the recognition and/or creation of spatial similarity (or identity) between kinesthetic and visual experiences. Whereas "vision" is obviously the sense of sight, "kinesthesis," with its alternate spellings (kinaesthesis, kinesthesia), alternate namings (somesthesis, proprioception) and their alternate spellings (somasthesis, somaesthesis), has been used to name a variety of sensory phenomena (Corso, 1967; Craig and Rollman, 1999; Geldard, 1953; Schiffman, 1976; Stein, 1992). Proprioception and somesthesis both seem to be the more inclusive terms (perhaps identical in meaning), with tactile, haptic, painful, pressure and temperature sensations included, though sometimes kinesthesis is used to refer similarly (e.g. Dearborn, 1916, p. 194). For my purposes there are two relevant perceptual experiences subsumed under these terms, which I will mean by kinesthesis. One is the feeling of the spatial outline of one's body, one's sense of "the *somatic periphery*, . . . the peripheral body surface" (von Fieandt, 1966, p. 327). (Sometimes this perception is distinguished as "somesthesis" [Funk and Brugger, 2002].) The other is the feeling of the movement of one's body and awareness of the spatial arrangement of the body parts (also called "motor senses" – Stout, 1901). Under normal circumstances, these two perceptual experiences are not differentiated in experience, and are usually experienced as one. However, the somatic periphery can be experienced when muscles are static, but the feeling of movement usually requires movement. Illusions of movement can be produced by applying vibrations to tendons of body parts you aren't looking at: the appendage remains stable but the kinesthetic feelings produced in one arm can make it appear to be in a different location, which can be exhibited through imitation of those feelings by the other arm (Lackner, 1988; Redon *et al.*, 1994). The "perception" of the somatic periphery is present even when there is no soma, as in the phantom limbs experienced by people who were born without limbs or had body parts amputated: they feel their limb or other body part as present, often in the (felt) shape of a normal limb (von Fieandt, 1966). Apparently the experience of the body's outline is pre-programmed to some degree, at least in primates (Melzack, 1989), even if based on reorganization of sensory afferents and musculature following amputation (Wu and Kass, 2002).

Kinesthesis, vision and kinesthetic-visual matching in perception of one's own body

Kinesthesis is a peculiar perception the experience of which seems to be strongly influenced by other perceptual modalities. One can experience changes in kinesthesis that propose preposterous perceptions. For example, if an illusion of your arm's movement away from your nose is created through vibration (as described in the previous paragraph) while your hand touches your nose and your eyes are closed, you will experience your nose as extended toward the transformed location where you experience your hand kinesthetically (Lackner, 1988). The same feeling of extension can occur when, with eyes closed, you repeatedly tap someone else's nose while they simultaneously tap yours in the same pattern (Ramachandran, 1998). Note that both illusions occur when vision is not available, and can be abolished simply by looking (Gandevia and Burke, 1992, p. 620). People with a phantom limb immediately lose the experienced kinesthesis in their missing limb when they see themselves in a mirror (Brugger *et al.*, 2000) – thereby gaining an immediate kinesthetic–visual match between what they see and feel of their body. Both vision and touch appear to be dominant over kinesthesis in most people, though kinesthesis is apparently dominant over vision in most autistic people (see Mitchell, 1997a; 2002a).

Apparently, normal reaching in monkeys and humans may require coordination between "proprioceptive" (i.e. kinesthetic) and visual maps (Jeannerod, 1986; 1994). The relation between Jeannerod's notion of this coordination and the idea of kinesthetic–visual matching is unclear (Mitchell, 1994b; see discussion below). However, following parietal lesions in humans, dissociation is postulated between the proprioceptive and visual maps (Jeannerod, 1986), suggesting that the parietal region may be a locus for kinesthetic-visual matching (Mitchell, 1997a; see below).

There are many fascinating instances of kinesthetic–visual matching in relation to the perception of one's own body. For example, kinesthetic–visual matching is present for people who experience their kinesthetic feelings in misplaced appendages: when someone's arm is placed just below a platform, out of sight, and a rubber arm is visibly placed on the platform above the real arm, if the rubber arm and the person's arm are lightly touched at the same time and on the same area of the arm, people will feel that the touch occurs where they see the rubber arm being touched (Botvinick and Cohen, 1998; Graziano and Botvinick, 2002);

the same effect with a shoe or a table can make people feel that their arm has become the shoe or table (Ramachandran, 1998, p. 1622). (It would be interesting to discover what people experienced if the experiment with the rubber arm were performed with it aligned 180° away from the actual arm, with the rubber hand above where the real elbow would be, and vice versa.) Similar experiences occur when people wear prisms that distort their vision, such that they have kinesthetic experiences of their arm where they see it, rather than where it is (Cohen, 1967; Harris, 1965; Kornheiser, 1976). Even more remarkable are the experiences of people with one amputated arm who, upon seeing through a mirror the reflection of their real arm in the place where their amputated arm would be, are able to experience the movements of both arms (real and phantom) when asked to move both arms simultaneously (Ramachandran, 1998, p. 1621; Ramachandran and Blakesee, 1998, p. 47). Researchers describe these re-placements of kinesthetic sensations into the visually observed (and tactually felt, in the case of the rubber arm) location as an attempt to maintain consistency among perceptual modalities, in which more dominant perceptual modalities hold sway (see discussion in Graziano and Botvinick, 2002; Mitchell, 2002a; Ramachandran and Blakesee, 1998). What is normally experienced as a correspondence or match between "similar" phenomena (seen and felt body parts) becomes lost – when two perceptual modalities are factored in, the correspondence problem (Nehaniv and Dautenhahn, 2002) is even more complicated than it first appears. What is interesting is that kinesthesis is set up to solve the correspondence problem by matching itself to the visual body. This built-in directedness to match kinesthesis to the visual body may be malleable because the visual body changes developmentally, so that kinesthesis must be capable of matching what is a moving target – the developing body (Melzack, 1989; see discussion in Mitchell, 2002b). Kinesthesis is a normal part of mammalian experience (Sheets-Johnstone, 1999), and the spontaneous matching between kinesthesis and vision in relation to one's own body seems likely a constant among mammals.

Kinesthetic–visual matching between bodies (or body-images)
But kinesthetic–visual matching in humans (and some other animals) extends beyond perception of the body. In the Exploratorium in San Francisco, California, there is an installation by artist Ed Tannenbaum that allows people to see, as they move, a silhouette of their body move across a screen in front of them – like a mirror with only two dimensions and without details. As the person moves, the silhouette moves in phases across the screen, changing color as it moves. The person sees what appear to be a series of snapshots of his or her body silhouette. (Online, see

cams.exploratorium.edu/CAM1/index.html.) Although the images created through your body's movement are interesting by themselves, recognizing that you look like the image derives in part from kinesthetic–visual matching. Kinesthetic–visual matching occurs in experiences such as recognizing oneself in a mirror, imitating someone's body movements, recognizing that you are being imitated by someone's body movements, and recognizing your own movement through space when only your joints are illuminated in an otherwise pitch-black room (see Mitchell, 1993a). If kinesthetic–visual matching is to be part of the explanation of any one of these phenomena, it must be present in behavior that is independent of it. Thus, I used the evidence of generalized bodily imitation in children at 18 months, and of a generalized ability to recognize that they are being imitated in children at 14 months, as evidence of kinesthetic–visual matching, and argued that part (or all) of the reason 18-month-old children typically recognize themselves in mirrors is their ability for mature (global and generalizable) kinesthetic–visual matching. It would be nice if there were a single test for kinesthetic–visual matching that could determine if it is present, but there is a difficulty: kinesthetic–visual matching is a skill that develops throughout the early life of (some) organisms (Mitchell, 1993a). Some evidence for it (e.g. recognition of being imitated) occurs earlier than other evidence (e.g. generalized bodily imitation). If Guillaume (1926/1971) is correct, kinesthetic–visual matching between bodies begins with matching between another's and one's own object-related actions, and leads to the ability to match another's actions even without objects present. What I have suggested is that mature kinesthetic–visual matching may be evident in a particular form of imitation: generalized matching of another's gestural and facial actions independent of objects. (Note, of course, that the gestural and facial actions intended here are not extensively sequenced actions, such as dance steps, which require more than kinesthetic–visual matching; rather, they are the kinds of actions that children perform in games like "Simon says.") Synchronic imitation, which certainly incorporates kinesthetic–visual matching and seems, of all imitations, most like mirror-self-recognition, is another contender as evidence of the mature kinesthetic–visual matching needed for mirror-self-recognition.

   Given that both models of self-recognition utilize understanding mirror correspondence, and both lead to the same result, it may be that kinesthetic–visual matching is an amalgam or result of body-part objectification and object-permanence understanding. Indeed, given Guillaume's developmental trajectory for imitation of others, it would seem that objects and body-parts are essential to its beginnings. When a young child sees another obtain an object the child desires, he or she will often attempt to obtain that object (or one like it) usually using the same body part (the hand) independent of any desire to imitate, but eventually the similarity, for whatever reason, will be detected. Add to this developmental account an evolutionary one positing that elaboration of the parietal cortex in primates and especially in humans derives from species-typical uses of the hand for increasingly complex interaction with objects, with a consequent ramification of connections between perceptual modalities and understanding of bodily possibilities for action (Krubitzer and Disbrow, in press). Even in monkeys, experiences with tools extend the responsiveness of neurons in the parietal cortex that are normally responsive only to hands to include the action possibilities of the hand-tool combination (Iriki, in press). Thus, body-part objectification (especially of the hand) and object-permanence understanding may themselves be components of or prerequisites for kinesthetic–visual matching. (If Guillaume's account is not correct, kinesthetic–visual matching may be necessary for body-part objectification – see Mitchell, 1993b.) The fact that body-part objectification, understanding object permanence and kinesthetic–visual matching all appear dependent upon the parietal region (as noted above, and see below) further supports the idea that the two models are identical.

Things like goals can interfere with or assist in active kinesthetic–visual matching (Bekkering and Wohlschläger, 2002; Brass *et al.*, 2000; Stürmer *et al.*, 2000), but that need not, as these authors suggest, indicate the absence or unimportance of kinesthetic–visual matching. Rather, it indicates that kinesthetic–visual matching is integrated into a well-functioning individual whose purposes are, and should be, overriding of any tendency toward spontaneous imitation regardless of a goal. Failure to subserve imitative tendencies to purposes is a sign of brain damage in mature humans (Lhermitte *et al.*, 1986). Indeed, most imitation in humans is goal-relevant, even in games like "Simon says" where one goal is to reproduce the other's actions when told "Simon says, 'Do this'" and another goal is to avoid reproduction of the other's actions when told only "Do this."

6.3   Motor imagery, kinesthetic–visual matching and the parietal region

If people are shown a disembodied hand in diverse orientations and are asked to decide if the hand is a right or left hand, they can imagine moving their appendage and/or body until it matches the hand in order to make or confirm their decision. This imagined appendage or imagined body movement is called "motor imagery." (With images of objects that are not body parts, people usually visually imagine transforming the image of the object to align – or not – with another image, rather than imagining their body moving. But of course either method, or variants of them, can be used with images of body parts or non-body parts.) When people engage in motor imagery, they can experience kinesthesis in the body part they imagine moving (Parsons and Fox, 1998; Sekiyama, 1982). Just as visual imagery depends on vision, and auditory imagery depends on audition, motor imagery depends on motor movements, in that the time required to make the imagined and real movements are correlated (Parsons, 1994). Although some argue that motor imagery and motor preparation (or the intention to move) are identical and that motor imagery is kinesthetic imagery (Jeannerod, 1994), in fact much of what is called motor imagery seems more like visual imagery – one imagines a visual image, or something that is vaguely like a visual image, of one's body or body part moving through space to match the image of the body part (Mitchell, 1994b). This "visual" imagery seems tied to possible kinesthetic experiences (i.e. actions), such that one knows how to (and can) do what is visually imagined.

There is a similarity between motor imagery and kinesthetic–visual matching (Mitchell, 1994b) and thus between motor imagery and bodily imitation (Demiris and Hayes, 2002; Parsons and Fox, 1998, p. 584), but whether or not the similarity is an identity is unclear. If I am to decide whether a left or right hand (for example) is in an image, I can imagine a virtual copy of my body or body part moving as if leaving my physical body until it coheres (or doesn't cohere) with the image. But to imitate, recognize being imitated or recognize myself in a mirror, such a method would not result in a match unless the actions of both parties were bilaterally symmetrical (with the axis of symmetry from head to toe). By contrast, imagine if I were trying to match, through motor imagery, my mirror image when my right arm was pointing up and my left was pointing down – I would not recognize a match through motor imagery because the motor image of my body, as it "moves" from my body and "turns" to fit the mirror-image, would never cohere with the mirrored body position. Motor imagery seems to be centered on one's own body and the image "moves" from it, whereas kinesthetic–visual matching seems to be translatable from one body to another without necessarily showing a similar transformation. My thought experiment might raise doubts about any identity between motor imagery and kinesthetic–visual matching. (In motor imagery studies where subjects must decide whether it is the right or left hand which is presented in various orientations, I wonder what most subjects would experience if experimenters tell them to "imagine that this image is a mirror image of your actual hand [which you cannot see] – which hand is it?" I suspect that people would experience a point-by-point comparison between a visual-like mental image of the felt fingers of their unseen hand and the image shown to them.) I am uncertain as to the exact relation between the two phenomena, but at least the initial "phantom" of the body in motor imagery, before it "leaves" the body, can be used to imitate: some imitations are not mirror-images (e.g. Miles *et al.*, 1996; Mitchell, 2002a) and some seem to be comparable to motor imagery transforms. Other imaginary transformations of the entire body suggest that subjects may be able to move themselves rapidly in imagination to a new location, unhindered by any felt movement of the motor image (Creem *et al.*, 2001).

I suspect that the psychological (and neurological) abilities necessary for kinesthetic–visual matching and motor imagery overlap extensively. However, I also suspect that some of the abilities for motor imagery may be present to a limited extent in monkeys (Rumiati, 2002), who never (or exceedingly rarely) exhibit anything resembling kinesthetic–visual matching, at least in the forms of self-recognition and generalized bodily imitation (see Anderson, 1994; Mitchell and Anderson, 1993; for potential examples of kinesthetic–visual matching in monkeys, see Mitchell, 1993a; 2002b, c; 2006). Monkeys have yet to be tested for recognition of being imitated, which in human infants occurs earlier than more mature kinesthetic–visual matching.

The parietal region as the site for kinesthetic–visual matching
Based on evidence from neurological syndromes in which people with damaged parietal areas exhibit impaired bodily imitation of meaningless or pantomimic gestures (Goldenberg, 1995; Heilman *et al.*, 1982), I hypothesized that kinesthetic–visual matching was localized in the parietal region (Mitchell, 1997a). Indeed, Heilman *et al.* (1982, p. 342) had earlier posited "visuokinesthetic motor engrams, where motor acts may be programmed" in the parietal region. These predictions appear to be confirmed by recent evidence. Use of motor imagery and mental rotation of body parts to match body-part images (Bonda *et al.*, 1996; Crammond, 1997; Creem *et al.*, 2001; Creem-Regehr, in press; Decety *et al.*, 1994; Graziano and Botvinick, 2002; Kosslyn *et al.*, 1998; Parsons *et al.*, 1995; Sirigu and Duhamel, 2001), imitation (Chaminade *et al.*, 2002; Decety *et al.*, 2002), and intent to imitate (Decety *et al.*, 1997) exhibit extensive parietal involvement (for motor imagery, even in a person born without limbs – Brugger *et al.*, 2000), as do people's observations of others engaging in mouth, hand or foot actions toward objects (Buccino *et al.*, 2001). Not only does the parietal region have neurons which respond to kinesthetic, tactile and visual perceptions, but those in area 5 of the parietal region "encode the position of the arm in a supramodal fashion, using

both somesthesis and vision" (Graziano and Botvinick, 2002, p. 143). The posterial parietal cortex is a crossroads where "visual, somaesthetic, proprioceptive, auditory, vestibular, oculomotor, limb motor, and motivation signals can potentially all combine with one another," which coordination may allow us to coordinate diverse frames of reference for purposive actions toward objects (Stein, 1992, pp. 693, 697). In the cat superior colliculus, a brain area homologous with the parietal cortex in primates (Ventre et al., 1984), neurons that are initially responsive only to one modality become responsive to multiple modalities as cats develop (Stein et al., 1999); so far research on primates has focused on adult animals, such that whether or not neurons are polyperceptual at birth is unknown. Diverse areas of the parietal region are responsive during motor imagery, imagined rotation of non-body-part objects, action-oriented visual information, and "motor attention during the mental simulation of hand and limb movements" (Parsons and Fox, 1998, p. 606). Perhaps different purposes of kinesthetic–visual matching may be localized differentially in the parietal regions in the two hemispheres, with recognition of another's imitation of oneself represented in the right parietal cortex and imitation of another's actions by the self in the left parietal region (Decety et al., 2002; see Funk and Brugger, 2002, for intriguing comparison). Whether the parietal region encodes body space topographically (Buccino et al., 2001) or is an attentional center which allows for algorithmic translation between visual and motor information (Stein, 1992; also Klingberg et al., 2002, p. 6) is unclear at present.

While the parietal region plays a leading role in kinesthetic–visual matching, it is not, of course, the only brain area involved (see Crammond, 1997). Motor and premotor cortices (adjacent to the parietal region) are implicated in some apparent matchings (or, perhaps, only coordinations) between vision and kinesthesis at the neural level in "mirror neurons" (Gallese et al., 1996; Shiffrar and Pinto, 2002). Perhaps, as Decety et al. (1997, p. 1775) suggest, "Joint action of areas 40 [in the parietal cortex] and 6 [in the premotor cortex] during preparation for imitation would thus account for transferring the processing of novel movements into a motor code." In addition, the parietal region has direct neural outputs to the F5 region in the premotor cortex in monkeys (homologous to Broca's area in humans), and some F5 neurons of a macaque monkey responded to both visual observation and kinesthetic feelings of particular actions toward objects by the monkey (and, perhaps, by visual observation of an experimenter's similar actions toward the objects) (see Gallese et al., 1996; 2002).

Surprisingly, almost all studies of parietal involvement in kinesthetic–visual matching involve imitation of action *toward objects*, or recognition of imitation in action *toward objects*. (The same appears to be true of mirror neurons – they are always responsive to actions toward objects, and are not responsive to pantomimes of actions toward (nonexistent) objects [Gallese *et al.*, 2002].) What happens when gestures are imitated without objects – what I am suggesting as evidence of mature kinesthetic–visual matching? Apparently the parietal region is also activated: when people attended to non-object-oriented actions that they knew they had to imitate later, the parietal region responded when the actions were meaningless movements and when they were pantomimes of actions toward imagined objects, though more so toward meaningless actions (Decety *et al.*, 1997). More research is needed here, but it is interesting that when a person born without limbs complied with requests to "rotate" her phantom limbs to have them align with images of her missing appendages, her brain showed extensive activation in the parietal region; the same is true for normal individuals who imagined rotating their limbs for similar alignments (Brugger *et al.*, 2000).

6.4   Imitation and other activities in early infancy as objections to the models

The two models require that the different components must develop such that all the components are normally mature at about 18 months in humans – the time when children usually recognize themselves in mirrors. Thus, although some components can come to maturity prior to 18 months, at least one of the components of either model (it would seem) must come to maturity at 18 months and not before (unless, of course, it is the coordination among components that comes to maturity at 18 months).

One apparent problem for the first model is neonatal imitation (e.g. Meltzoff and Moore, 1989). If mature kinesthetic–visual matching is already present in the imitation of neonates, and if understanding of mirror correspondence is present prior to 18 months, it suggests that the first model is false. However, no-one who studies neonatal imitation suggests that it is identical to mature kinesthetic–visual matching (see Nadel and Butterworth, 1999). The evidence for neonatal imitation is different from the evidence for mature generalized bodily imitation in relation to such factors as generalizability, consistency of ability, production of novel behaviors and cause (Anisfeld, 1991; Mitchell, 1993a,b; 1997a,b; 2002d; Užgiris, 1999). Yet, oddly, some researchers persist in erroneously describing neonatal imitation and generalized bodily imitation as identical (see discussion in Mitchell, 1993b, p. 357; Mitchell, 1997b, Footnote 3). As Užgiris (1999) notes, if neonates are skilled at bodily and facial imitation, their skill is more limited than that exhibited in later imitations. Indeed, some researchers have argued that the evidence for neonatal imitation of actions other than tongue protrusion is inadequate (Anisfeld et al., 2001; Poulson, et al., 1989), and even those who characterize neonatal imitation as a relatively generalizable ability for bodily matching argue that it is based on amodal matching skills, not kinesthetic–visual matching ones that develop later (Meltzoff, 1990). In addition, after years in which infants were believed to show extraordinary cross-modal matching abilities, recent more controlled studies are suggesting that these findings may be the result of confounding influences (e.g. see Anisfeld et al., 2001; Maurer et al., 1999). Indeed, some purported evidence of cross-modal matchings by infants disappears when more appropriate statistics are used (see, for example, Streri and Gentaz, 2003, p. 17, where two goodness of fit chi-square tests were used instead of a single – and more appropriate – chi-square test of independence).

A similar apparent problem for the second model is the evidence of understanding of object permanence early in human infancy (e.g. Baillargeon et al., 1985). But again, once confounding influences are removed, infants' early understanding is no longer evident (Rivera et al., 1999).

The point here is not to indicate that neonatal imitation and early understanding of object permanence are necessarily false. They may or may not be accurate portrayals of infant cognition. My point is that what we know about them indicates that they cannot be used as evidence against either of the two models I present. Both models describe mature components that develop from earlier forms, and equating early and later forms (as some critics have) can only create confusion. Mature kinesthetic–visual matching may develop from neonatal imitation, and mature understanding of object permanence may derive from earlier conceptions of objects. Similarly, the scientific evaluation of the evidence for or against the two models is itself a developmental process, which requires more time for maturity.

6.5   Summary

My brief discussion of the likely components of mirror-self-recognition and of potentially similar components in generalized bodily imitation offers suggestions to roboticists, neuropsychologists and comparative-developmental psychologists who wish to imagine ways of explaining both phenomena. The relations among the different components are complicated, and the components themselves may comprise more elementary components, some of which are shared across components.

The types of matchings so essential for generalized bodily imitation are clearly present in mirror-self-recognition, such that what is learned about one area helps us to understand the other. My hope is that this chapter will influence researchers in diverse areas to direct their attention to the perceptual-motor and cross-modal aspects of both imitation and mirror-self-recognition, in order to solve the intricate puzzle that they present.

Acknowledgments

I greatly appreciate the criticisms, suggestions and encouragement of Teresa Bejaranos, Fran Dolins, Atsushi Iriki, two anonymous reviewers and the editors.

REFERENCES

Anderson, J. R. (1994). The monkey in the mirror: a strange conspecific. In S. T. Parker, R. W. Mitchell and M. L. Boccia (eds.), *Self-awareness in Animals and Humans*. New York: Cambridge University Press, 315–29.

Anisfeld, M. (1991). Neonatal imitation. *Developmental Review*, **11**, 60–97.

Anisfeld, M., Turkewitz, G., Rose, S. A., Rosenberg, F. R., Sheiber, F. J., Couturier-Fagan, D. A., Ger, J. S. and Sommer, I. (2001). No compelling evidence that neonates imitate oral gestures. *Infancy*, **2**, 111–22.

Baillargeon, R., Spelke, E. S. and Wasserman, S. (1985). Object permanence in five-month-old infants. *Cognition*, **20**, 191–208.

Baldwin, J. M. (1898/1902). *The Story of the Mind*. New York: D. Appleton and Co.

Bekkering, H. and Wohlschläger, A. (2002). Action perception and imitation: a tutorial. In W. Prinz and B. Hommel (eds.), *Common Mechanisms in Perception and Action: Attention and Performance XIX*. Oxford: Oxford University Press, 294–314.

Bonda, E., Frey, S. and Petrides, M. (1996). Evidence for a dorso-medial parietal system involved in mental transformations of the body. *Journal of Neurophysiology*, **76**, 2042–8.

Botvinick, M. and Cohen, J. (1998). Rubber hands "feel" touch that eyes see. *Nature*, **39**, 756.

Brass, M., Bekkering, H., Wohlschläger., A. and Prinz, W. (2000). Compatibility between observed and executed finger movements: comparing symbolic, spatial, and imitative cues. *Brain and Cognition*, **44**, 124–43.

Brugger, P., Kollias, S. S., Müri, R. M., Crelier, G., Hepp-Reymond, M.-C. and Regard, M. (2000). Beyond re-membering: phantom sensations of congenitally absent limbs. *Proceedings of the National Academy of Sciences USA*, **97**, 6167–72.

Buccino, G., Binkofski, F., Fink, G. R., Fadiga, L., Fogassi, L., Gallese, V., Seitz, R. J., Zilles, K., Rizzolatti, G. and Freund, H. J. (2001). Action observation activates premotor and parietal areas in a somatotopic manner: an fMRI study. *European Journal of Neuroscience*, **13**, 400–4.

Castiello, U., Lusher, D., Mari, M., Edwards, M. and Humphreys, G. W. (2002). Observing a human or a robotic hand grasping an object: Differential motor priming effects. In W. Prinz and B. Hommel (eds.), *Common Mechanisms in Perception and Action: Attention and Performance XIX.* Oxford: Oxford University Press, 315–33.

Chaminade, T., Meltzoff, A. N. and Decety, J. (2002). Does the end justify the means? A PET exploration of the mechanisms involved in human imitation. *NeuroImage*, **15**, 318–28.

Cohen, M. M. (1967). Continuous versus terminal visual feedback in prism aftereffects. *Perceptual and Motor Skills*, **24**, 1295–1302.

Corso, J. F. (1967). *The Experimental Psychology of Sensory Behavior.* New York: Holt, Rinehart and Winston.

Craig, J. C. and Rollman, G. B. (1999). Somesthesis. *Annual Review of Psychology*, **50**, 305–31.

Crammond, D. J. (1997). Motor imagery: never in your wildest dream. *Trends in Neuroscience*, **20**, 54–7.

Creem, S. H., Downs, T. H., Wraga, M., Harrington, G. S., Proffitt, D. R. and Downs, J. H., III. (2001). An fMRI study of imagined self-rotation. *Cognitive, Affective and Behavioral Neurosciences*, **1**, 239–49.

Creem-Regehr, S. H. (in press). Body mapping and spatial transformations. In F. Dolins and R. W. Mitchell (eds.), *Spatial Perception, Spatial Cognition.* Cambridge, UK: Cambridge University Press.

Dearborn, G. V. N. (1916). Movement, cenesthesia, and the mind. *Psychological Review*, **23**, 190–207.

Decety, J., Chaminade, T., Grèzes, J. and Meltzoff, A. N. (2002). A PET exploration of the neural mechanisms involved in reciprocal imitation. *NeuroImage*, **15**, 265–72.

Decety, J., Grèzes, J., Costes, N., Perani, D., Jeannerod, M., Procyk, E., Grassi, F. and Fazio, F. (1997). Brain activity during observation of actions: influence of action content and subject's strategy. *Brain*, **120**, 1763–77.

Decety, J., Perani, D., Jeannerod, M., Bettinardi, V., Tadary, B., Woods, R., Mazzlotta, J. C. and Fazio, F. (1994). Mapping motor representations with positron emission tomography. *Nature*, **371**, 600–2.

Demiris, J. and Hayes, G. (2002). Imitation as a dual-route process featuring predictive and learning components: a biologically plausible computational model. In K. Dautenhahn and C. L. Nehaniv (eds.), *Imitation in Animals and Artifacts.* Cambridge, MA: MIT Press, 327–61.

Doré, F. Y. (1986). Object permanence in adult cats (*Felis catus*). *Journal of Comparative Psychology*, **100**, 340–7.

Funk, M. and Brugger, P. (2002). Visual recognition of hands by persons born with only one hand. *Cortex*, **38**, 860–3.

Gallese, V., Fadiga, L., Fogassi, L. and Rizzolatti, G. (1996). Action recognition in the premotor cortex. *Brain*, **119**, 593–609.

Gallese, V., Fadiga, L., Fogassi, L. and Rizzolatti, G. (2002). Action representation and the inferior parietal lobule. In W. Prinz and B. Hommel (eds.),

Common Mechanisms in Perception and Action: Attention and Performance XIX. Oxford: Oxford University Press, 334–55.

Gandevia, S. C. and Burke, D. (1992). Does the nervous system depend on kinesthetic information to control natural limb movements? *Behavioral and Brain Sciences,* **15,** 614–32.

Geldard, F. A. (1953). *The Human Senses*. New York: John Wiley and Sons.

Goldenberg, G. (1995). Imitating gestures and manipulating a mannikin – the representation of the human body in ideomotor apraxia. *Neuropsychologia,* **33,** 63–72.

Graziano, M. and Botvinick, M. (2002). How the brain represents the body: insights from neurophysiology and psychology. In W. Prinz and B. Hommel (eds.), *Common Mechanisms in Perception and Action: Attention and Performance XIX*. Oxford: Oxford University Press, 136–57.

Guillaume, P. (1925). *L'imitation Chez L'Enfant* [Imitation in Children]. Paris: Alcan.

Guillaume, P. (1926/1971). *Imitation in Children* (trans. E. P. Halperin). Chicago: University of Chicago.

Harris, C. S. (1965). Perceptual adaptation to inverted, reversed, and displaced vision. *Psychological Review,* **72,** 419–44.

Heilman, K. M., Rothi, L. J. and Valenstein, E. (1982). Two forms of ideomotor apraxia. *Neurology,* **32,** 342–6.

Iriki, A. (in press). "Understanding" of external space generated by bodily remapping: an insight from the neurophysiology of tool-using monkeys. In F. Dolins and R. W. Mitchell (eds.), *Spatial Perception, Spatial Cognition*. Cambridge, UK: Cambridge University Press.

Iriki, A., Tanaka, M., Obayashi, S. and Iwamura, Y. (2001). Self-images in the video monitor coded by monkey intraparietal neurons. *Neuroscience Research,* **40,** 163–73.

Jeannerod, M. (1986). Mechanisms of visuomotor coordination: a study in normal and brain-damaged subjects. *Neuropsychologia,* **24,** 41–78.

Jeannerod, M. (1994). The representing brain: neural correlates of motor intention and imagery. *Behavioral and Brain Sciences,* **17,** 187–246.

Klingberg, T., Forssberg, H. and Westerberg, H. (2002). Increased brain activity in frontal and parietal cortex underlies the development of visuospatial working memory capacity during childhood. *Journal of Cognitive Neuroscience,* **14,** 1–10.

Kornheiser, A. S. (1976). Adaptation for laterally displaced vision: a review. *Psychological Bulletin,* **83,** 783–816.

Kosslyn, S. M., Digirolamo, G. J., Thompson, W. L. and Alpert, N. M. (1998). Mental rotation of objects versus hands: neural mechanisms revealed by positron emission tomography. *Psychophysiology,* **35,** 151–61.

Krubitzer, L. and Disbrow, E. (in press). The evolution of the parietal areas involved in hand use in primates. In F. Dolins and R. W. Mitchell (eds.), *Spatial Perception, Spatial Cognition*. Cambridge, UK: Cambridge University Press.

Lackner, J. R. (1988). Some proprioceptive influences on the perceptual representation of body shape and orientation. *Brain,* **111,** 281–97.

Lhermitte, F., Pillon, B. and Serdaru, M. (1986). Human autonomy and the frontal lobes, II: imitation and utilization behavior: a neuropsychological study of 75 patients. *Annals of Neurology*, **19**, 335–43.

Major, D. R. (1906). *First Steps in Mental Growth*. New York: The Macmillan Co.

Maurer, D., Stager, C. L. and Mondloch, C. J. (1999). Cross-modal transfer of shape is difficult to demonstrate in one-month-olds. *Child Development*, **70**, 1047–57.

Meltzoff, A. N. (1990). Foundations for developing a concept of self: the role of imitation in relating self to other and the value of social mirroring, social modeling, and self practice in infancy. In D. Cicchetti and M. Beeghly (eds.), *The Self in Transition: Infancy to Childhood*. Chicago: University of Chicago Press, 139–64.

Meltzoff, A. N. and Moore, M. K. (1989). Imitation in newborn infants: exploring the range of gestures imitated and the underlying mechanisms. *Developmental Psychology*, **25**, 954–62.

Melzack, R. (1989). Phantom limbs, the self, and the brain. *Canadian Psychology*, **30**, 1–16.

Menzel, E. W., Jr., Savage-Rumbaugh, E. S. and Lawson, J. (1985). Chimpanzee (*Pan troglodytes*) spatial problem solving with the use of mirrors and televised equivalents of mirrors. *Journal of Comparative Psychology*, **99**, 211–17.

Miles, H. L. (1994). ME CHANTEK: The development of self-awareness in a signing orangutan. In S. T. Parker, R. W. Mitchell and M. L. Boccia (eds.), *Self-awareness in Animals and Humans*. New York: Cambridge University Press, 254–72.

Miles, H. L., Mitchell, R. W. and Harper, S. (1996). Simon says: the development of imitation in an enculturated orangutan. In A. Russon, K. Bard and S. T. Parker (eds.), *Reaching into Thought: The Minds of the Great Apes*. New York: Cambridge University Press, 278–99.

Mitchell, R. W. (1993a). Mental models of mirror-self-recognition: two theories. *New Ideas in Psychology*, **11**, 295–325.

Mitchell, R. W. (1993b). Recognizing one's self in a mirror? A reply to Gallup and Povinelli, De Lannoy, Anderson, and Byrne. *New Ideas in Psychology*, **11**, 351–77.

Mitchell, R. W. (1994a). The evolution of primate cognition: simulation, self-knowledge, and knowledge of other minds. In D. Quiatt and J. Itani (eds.), *Hominid Culture in Primate Perspective*. Boulder: University Press of Colorado, 177–232.

Mitchell, R. W. (1994b). Are motor images based on kinesthetic–visual matching? *Behavioral and Brain Sciences*, **17**, 214–15.

Mitchell, R. W. (1997a). A comparison of the self-awareness and kinesthetic–visual matching theories of self-recognition: autistic children and others. *Annals of the New York Academy of Sciences*, **818**, 39–62.

Mitchell, R. W. (1997b). Kinesthetic–visual matching and the self-concept as explanations of mirror-self-recognition. *Journal for the Theory of Social Behavior*, **27**, 101–23.

Mitchell, R. W. (2002a). Imitation as a perceptual process. In K. Dautenhahn and C. L. Nehaniv (eds.), *Imitation in Animals and Artifacts*. Cambridge, MA: MIT Press, 441–69.

Mitchell, R. W. (2002b). Subjectivity and self-recognition in animals. In M. R. Leary and J. Tangney (eds.), *Handbook of Self and Identity*. New York: Guilford Press, 567–93.

Mitchell, R. W. (2002c). Kinesthetic–visual matching, imitation, and self-recognition. In M. Bekoff, C. Allen and G. Burghardt (eds.), *The Cognitive Animal*. Cambridge, MA: MIT Press, 345–51.

Mitchell, R. W. (2002d). Review of *Imitation in Infancy*, ed. J. Nadel and G. Butterworth. *British Journal of Developmental Psychology*, **20**, 150–1.

Mitchell, R. W. (2006). Pretense in Animals: the continuing relevance of children's pretense. In A. Göncü and S. Gaskins (eds.), *Play and Development: Evolutionary, Sociocultural and Functional Perspectives*. Hillsdale, NJ: Lawrence Erlbaum, 51–76.

Mitchell, R. W. and Anderson, J. R. (1993). Discrimination learning of scratching, but failure to obtain imitation and self-recognition in a long-tailed macaque. *Primates*, **34**, 301–9.

Nadel, J. and Butterworth, G. (eds.) (1999). *Imitation in Infancy*. Cambridge, UK: Cambridge University Press.

Nehaniv, C. L. and Dautenhahn, K. (2002). The correspondence problem. In K. Dautenhahn and C. L. Nehaniv (eds.), *Imitation in Animals and Artifacts*. Cambridge, MA: MIT Press, 41–61.

Nielsen, M., Collier-Baker, E., Davis, J. and Suddendorf, T. (2005). Imitation recognition in a captive chimpanzee (*Pan troglodytes*). *Animal Cognition*, **8**, 31–6.

Ogden, J. A. (1985). Autotopagnosia: occurrence in a patient without nominal aphasia and with an intact ability to point to parts of animals and objects. *Brain*, **108**, 1009–22.

Ohta, M. (1987). Cognitive disorders of infantile autism: a study employing the WISC, spatial relationship conceptualization, and gesture imitations. *Journal of Autism and Developmental Disorders*, **17**, 45–62.

Parker, S. T., Mitchell, R. W. and Boccia, M. L. (eds.) (1994). *Self-awareness in Animals and Humans*. New York: Cambridge University Press.

Parsons, L. M. (1987). Imagined spatial transformations of one's body. *Journal of Experimental Psychology: General*, **116**, 172–91.

Parsons, L. M. (1994). Temporal and kinematic properties of motor behavior reflected in mentally simulated action. *Journal of Experimental Psychology: Human Perception and Performance*, **20**, 709–30.

Parsons, L. M. and Fox, P. T. (1998). The neural basis of implicit movements used in recognising hand shape. *Cognitive Neuropsychology*, **15**, 583–615.

Parsons, L. M., Fox, P. T., Downs, J. H., Glass, T., Hirsch, T. B., Martin, C. C., Jerabek, P. A. and Lancaster, J. L. (1995). Use of implicit motor imagery for visual shape discrimination as revealed by PET. *Nature*, **375**, 54–8.

Penfield, W. (1950). *The Cerebral Cortex of Man: A Clinical Study of Localization of Function*. New York: Hafner Publishing Co.

Piaget, J. (1945/1962). *Play, Dreams, and Imitation in Childhood*. New York: W. W. Norton.

Piaget, J. (1954). *The Construction of Reality in the Child.* New York: Basic Books.

Posada, S. and Colell, M. (2005). Mirror responses in a group of *Mitopithecus talopoin. Primates,* **46,** 165–72.

Poulson, C. L., Nunes, L. R. de P. and Warren, S. F. (1989). Imitation in infancy: a critical review. *Advances in Child Development and Behavior,* **22,** 271–98.

Ramachandran, V. S. (1998). The perception of phantom limbs. *Brain,* **121,** 1603–30.

Ramachandran, V. S. and Blakesee, S. (1998). *Phantoms in the Brain.* New York: Morrow.

Redding, G. M. and Wallace, B. (1997). *Adaptive Spatial Alignment.* Mahwah, NJ: Lawrence Erlbaum.

Redon, C., Hay, L., Rigal, R. and Roll, J. P. (1994). Contribution of the proprio-muscular channel to movement coding in children: a study involving the use of vibration-induced kinaesthetic illusion. *Human Movement Science,* **13,** 95–108.

Riopelle, A. J., Nos, R. and Jonch, A. (1971). Situational determinants of dominance in captive young gorillas. *Proceedings of the 3rd International Congress of Primatology,* **3,** 86–91.

Rivera, S. M., Wakeley, A. and Langer, J. (1999). The *drawbridge* phenomenon: representational reasoning or perceptual preference? *Developmental Psychology,* **35,** 427–35.

Robinson, J. A., Connell, S., McKenzie, B. E. and Day, R. H. (1990). Do infants use their own images to locate objects reflected in a mirror? *Child Development,* **61,** 1558–68.

Rumiati, R. I. (2002). Processing mechanisms and neural structures involved in the recognition and production of actions: introduction to Section III. In W. Prinz and B. Hommel (eds.), *Common Mechanisms in Perception and Action: Attention and Performance XIX.* Oxford: Oxford University Press, 289–93.

Schiffman, H. R. (1976). *Sensation and Perception.* New York: John Wiley and Sons.

Sekiyama, K. (1982). Kinesthetic aspects of mental representations in the identification of left and right hands. *Perception and Psychophysics,* **32,** 89–95.

Sekiyama, K. (1983). Mental and physical movements of hands: kinesthetic information preserved in representational systems. *Japanese Psychological Research,* **25,** 95–102.

Sheets-Johnstone, M. (1999). *The Primacy of Movement.* Amsterdam: John Benjamins Publishing Company.

Shiffrar, M. and Pinto, J. (2002). The visual analysis of bodily movement. In W. Prinz and B. Hommel (eds.), *Common Mechanisms in Perception and Action: Attention and Performance XIX.* Oxford: Oxford University Press, 381–99.

Sirigu, A. and Duhamel, J. R. (2001). Motor and visual imagery as two complementary but neurally dissociable mental processes. *Journal of Cognitive Neuroscience,* **13,** 910–19.

Smith, I. M. (1995). *Imitation and Gestural Representation in Autism.* Poster presented at meeting of the Society for Research in Child Development, Indianapolis, Indiana.

Smith, I. M. and Bryson, S. E. (1994). Imitation and action in autism: a critical review. *Psychological Bulletin,* **116**, 259–73.

Stein, B. E., Wallace, M. T. and Stanford, T. R. (1999). Development of multi-sensory integration: transforming sensory input into motor output. *Mental Retardation and Developmental Disabilities Research Reviews,* **5**, 72–85.

Stein, J. F. (1992). The representation of egocentric space in the posterior parietal cortex. *Behavioral and Brain Sciences,* **15**, 691–700.

Stout, G. F. (1901). *A Manual of Psychology.* London: University Tutorial Press.

Streri, A. and Gentaz, E. (2003). Cross-modal recognition of shape from hand to eyes in human newborns. *Somatosensory and Motor Research,* **20**, 13–18.

Stürmer, B., Aschersleben, G. and Prinz, W. (2000). Correspondence effects with manual gestures and postures: a study of imitation. *Journal of Experimental Psychology: Human Perception and Performance,* **26**, 1746–59.

Tracy, F. (1901). *The Psychology of Childhood,* 5th edn. Boston: D. C. Heath and Co.

Treisman, A. (1986). Properties, parts, and objects. In K. R. Boff, L. Kaufman and J. P. Thomas (eds.), *Handbook of Perception and Human Performance, Vol. II: Cognitive Processes and Performance.* New York: Wiley, Chap. **35**, 1–70.

Užgiris, I. Č. (1999). Imitation as activity: its developmental aspects. In J. Nadel and G. Butterworth (eds.), *Imitation in Infancy.* Cambridge, UK: Cambridge University Press.

Ventre, J., Flandrin, J. M. and Jeannerod, M. (1984). In search for the egocentric reference: a neurophysiological hypothesis. *Neuropsychologia,* **22**, 797–806.

von Fieandt, K. (1966). *The World of Perception.* Homewood, IL: Dorsey Press.

Wu, C. W.-H. and Kaas, J. H. (2002). The effects of long-standing limb loss on anatomical reorganization of the somatosensory afferents in the brainstem and spinal cord. *Somatosensory and Motor Research,* **19**, 153–63.

Part III

What to imitate?

Social learning and behaviour matching are prevalent and important in learning by animals and humans. But as we saw in the section on correspondence problems and mechanisms, there are many possibilities for what aspects of an observed behaviour an individual may attempt to match. This is the problem of 'what to imitate?'[1] and has been identified as amongst the big five problems for the study of social learning (Dautenhahn and Nehaniv, 2002). This is of course closely linked to the question 'why imitate?' as it potentially requires discussion of the internal motivational states that cannot be directly observed by the social learner (see Part VI, Why imitate? – Motivations, this volume).

In this section, three very different constructive approaches toward solving this problem are put forth by ethologists Malinda Carpenter and Josep Call, roboticists Sylvain Calinon and Aude Billard, and artificial intelligence researchers Tony Belpaeme, Bart de Boer and Bart Jansen.

Malinda Carpenter and Josep Call approach the problem of what to imitate in artificial constructed systems from an ethologist's viewpoint. With reference to studies of primates, especially human children, and other animals including birds and dolphins, they present an illuminating survey of several different ways in which an observer might infer the goals or sub-goals of an observed behaviour. These include explicit goal-marking by the model, e.g. via the use of joint attention, deixis, vocal or other types of feedback, the observation of impairment of effectors (e.g. a limb) that could otherwise be used in performance of behaviour or of cues suggesting a failed attempt (e.g. signs of dissatisfaction, repeated attempts), previous observation of similar behaviour by the model or another individual or applied to other objects, as well as salience of the

---

[1] In the discussion here, 'imitation' is broadly construed to include any form of social matching behaviour.

Imitation and Social Learning in Robots, Humans and Animals, ed. Chrystopher L. Nehaniv and Kerstin Dautenhahn. Published by Cambridge University Press.

results or other aspects of the behaviour (see Part VII, Social feedback, this volume). Based on this, they propose an architecture for solving this problem iteratively, employing both observed action/result information and goal-relevant information in parallel, and using this together with previous experience or features of the currently observed situation, to generate a behavioural plan (which they call an *intention*) to achieve the 'inferred' goal. Here the attributed goal plays a dual role in guiding the imitator's behavioural plans and in evaluating whether or not the attempted matched behaviour is successful. Rather than simply matching movements via some simple perceptual rule that reduces discrepancies in visuomotor matching, such more complex processing allows for the 'reading' of goals and intentions enabling social learning that goes beyond merely what is 'seen' toward matching internal states that cannot be directly observed. The constructive use of such methods in artificial systems taking advantage of goal-relevant information such as gaze direction, emotional expression, context and teacher feedback suggests rich directions for the current vibrant research into the problem of goal attribution in artificial intelligence and robotics.

Sylvain Calinon and Aude Billard describe goal extraction in robotic imitation of gesture via probabilistic machine learning techniques. Their system is based on detecting *invariants* of multiple demonstrations of the task. Those aspects of the behaviour that vary little from one demonstration to the next are assumed to reflect important features of the behaviour and are given more weight in attempts to imitate. Those aspects which are inconstant between demonstrations are considered non-essential, and therefore are not treated as (sub-)goals for the attempted matched behaviour. The authors also review and discuss the relationship of their constructive algorithmic techniques to models of imitation from psychology and ethology: R. W. Byrne's string-parsing model (Byrne, 1999), and Heyes and Ray's associative sequence learning theory (ASL) (Heyes and Ray, 2000), as well as in the framework of the correspondence problem (Nehaniv and Dautenhahn, 1998) – see Part I, Correspondence problems and mechanisms, and see Part IV, Development and embodiment, in this volume).

The third chapter by Tony Belpaeme and his collaborators describes a model in which social interaction leads to a community of individuals sharing a growing set of goals in an 'imitation game'. Imitation is studied at the population level for its self-organizing role as a cultural transmission mechanism. The shared goal categories concern relationships between entities in the agents' world and they are determined via a self-organizing process of interaction via imitation. Such an imitation game is implemented using a physical robotic arm by the authors, and similar games have been used to model the self-organized emergence of vowel categories in natural languages (de Boer, 2000). Successful imitation is used to reinforce existing categories and failed imitation to revise them. Thus, the social context of the successful or unsuccessful use of imitated behaviours leads to the self-organization of categories, which describe 'what to imitate' for members of the population (compare Part IV, Development and embodiment).

REFERENCES

de Boer, B., (2000). Self-organisation of vowel systems, *Journal of Phonetics*, **28(4)**, 441–65.
Byrne, R. W. (1999). Imitation without intentionality: using string parsing to copy the organization of behaviour. *Animal Cognition*, **2**, 63–72.
Dautenhahn, K. and Nehaniv, C. L. (2002). The agent-based perspective on imitation. In K. Dautenhahn and C. L. Nehaniv (eds.), *Imitation in Animals and Artifacts*. Cambridge, MA: MIT Press, 1–40.
Heyes, C. and Ray, E. D. (2000). What is the significance of imitation in animals? *Advances in the Study of Behavior*, **29**, 215–45.
Nehaniv, C. L. and Dautenhahn, K. (1998). Mapping between dissimilar bodies: affordances and the algebraic foundations of imitation. In J. Demiris and A. Birk, (eds.), *Proceedings of the European Workshop on Learning Robots 1998 (EWLR-7)*, (Edinburgh, Scotland – 20 July 1998).

7   The question of 'what to imitate': infε goals and intentions from demonstrat

Malinda Carpenter and Josep Call

Getting a robot to imitate is a difficult task. Currently, researchers are tackling difficult issues such as the 'correspondence problem' (Nehaniv and Dautenhahn, 2002) of how to map different aspects of a demonstration to one's own imitative response, how to decide whom, when and what to imitate, and how to evaluate success (Dautenhahn and Nehaniv, 2002a, b). From our perspective, the most interesting of these issues is the question of *what* to imitate, that is, which aspects of a demonstration robots should copy. This is because in many situations, instead of copying others' actions and their results on the environment exactly, it is often more useful to extract and adopt the goal of the demonstrator's actions, and only copy the actions and results of the demonstrator if they are intended and relevant or essential to the task.

To illustrate, imagine the following scenarios. A robot is presented with the following demonstration and then told to imitate.

(1) *An actor approaches a lever and pushes it with his foot.*
Here, copying the actor's action and its result might be appropriate: the robot should also push the lever with its foot (assuming it has one).

(2) *An actor whose arms are broken pushes the lever with his foot.*
Now it might be more appropriate for the robot to use a different action to achieve the same result: it could push the lever with its hands (assuming it has them), as the constraint of not having usable hands – the normal thing to use to push things – does not apply to it.

(3) *While approaching a nearby dial, an actor bumps into the lever and knocks it over with his foot.*
In this case, the robot should copy neither the actor's action nor his result on the lever because both were produced accidentally.

(4) *An actor pushes and pushes against the lever but it does not move. He scratches his head and walks away.*

Imitation and Social Learning in Robots, Humans and Animals, ed. Chrystopher L. Nehaniv and Kerstin Dautenhahn. Published by Cambridge University Press.

135

Here the robot does not even see the result on the lever. It needs to work out what the intended result might be and choose an action to achieve that result. The action the robot chooses might be the same general action of pushing (perhaps with more force or a different body part) or some other action (e.g. ramming into it). In any case, the robot should ignore the action of scratching the head because it was irrelevant to the task of pushing the lever.

The overall point here is that the robot should copy the demonstrator's actions and results selectively, in some circumstances, but not others. It should do this as a function of the demonstrator's goals and intentions in the task. Instead of reproducing the demonstrator's 'surface behavior' and all the effects on the environment that result, the robot needs to infer the underlying goal of the demonstrator and use this to decide: (1) whether to reproduce the demonstrator's actions (and if so at what level of precision), and (2) whether to reproduce the results of those actions or else try to achieve some other result.

The question of 'what to imitate' is an important one for robotics researchers for several reasons. First, whenever the imitator and the demonstrator have different embodiments, as, for example, when a robot imitates a human, then at some level imitation cannot be achieved by copying actions. To use Nehaniv and Dautenhahn's (2001) example, a smaller imitator watching a larger demonstrator paint a wall would not succeed in painting the entire wall if it copied the demonstrator's actions exactly. Instead, it would need to extend its arms more, use larger brush strokes or climb a ladder to cover the entire wall. Second, whenever a demonstration is not 'perfect,' that is, whenever irrelevant actions, accidents or failed attempts are involved, an ability to infer what the demonstrator is trying to do and to only copy elements relevant to his goal would result in more flexible, efficient imitation. Finally, sometimes the exact same two demonstrations can have different goals underlying them (e.g. see Behne *et al.*, 2006b, below), and conversely two very different demonstrations can have the same goal underlying them (e.g. see Meltzoff, 1995, below). This means that relying on surface aspects of the demonstration and copying all actions and results can be misleading and result in imitation either of superfluous or insufficient elements of the demonstration. Thus, a robot who could evaluate what a demonstrator is trying to achieve and then decide whether to use the demonstrator's means or its own means to achieve the same result or a different one – and do this flexibly across different demonstrators, situations and constraints – would be able to achieve the same goal in the most efficient manner possible.

Many robotics researchers have already focused on the question of 'what to imitate,' and have, in various ways, noted the importance of reproducing the goal or 'purpose' or 'effect' of the demonstrator instead of his actions. For example, Nehaniv and Dautenhahn (e.g. 1998; 2001), Breazeal and Scassellati (2002), Billard and colleagues (e.g. Billard *et al.*, 2003), and Demiris and colleagues (e.g. Johnson and Demiris, 2004) (see also Gergely, 2003) all have discussed the advantages of building robots that can do something like inferring a demonstrator's goal, and indeed much progress already has been made in actually designing artificial systems that can perform some steps along the way to inferring others' goals (see review below). In this chapter, we show how some living beings (in particular some non-human animals and human infants) answer the question of 'what to imitate,' and we identify specific ways in which a learner can infer the goal of a demonstrator. Then we very briefly review what robots currently can do in this regard and propose some further challenges for them.

But before we begin, let us be clear what we mean by goal and by intention. These terms are often used as synonyms but we think that it is important to distinguish them. By goal we mean an internal representation of the desired state of affairs, that is, a mental goal, not an external one. A goal is thus different from a result, in that in some cases there may be a mismatch between an actor's goal (the desired result) and the result he actually achieves. Translated into robotic terms, a goal could be something like a reference value. By intention, we mean the action plan (the means) chosen to achieve the goal (the end) (see Tomasello *et al.*, 2005, for more discussion of both of these).

7.1 How animals and infants answer the question of 'what to imitate'

At a general level, there are two factors that influence what learners might copy from a demonstration: (1) the function of imitation at that particular moment and (2) the components of the demonstration the learners are able or motivated to pay attention to and copy.

7.1.1 *The functions of imitation*

Evolutionarily speaking, one of the main functions of social learning was to produce solutions to problems that individuals faced in their environment such as the efficient harvest of food resources. For instance, chimpanzee infants probably use various social learning mechanisms to learn from adults that certain nuts are edible and can be cracked open with stones or wooden tools (Boesch and Boesch, 2000). This instrumental function of social learning has been the focus of the vast majority of studies on non-human animals (see, e.g. Galef and Zentall, 1988; Heyes and Galef, 1996). A second function that has been proposed in humans, but that has received far less attention from a comparative perspective, is the social function of imitation (Užgiris, 1981). Here individuals copy the actions of others as a way to relate socially with each other: instead of being a means of obtaining a tangible resource, imitation is a means toward the social end of engaging in interaction. It is likely that in some situations the degree to which an imitator will copy a demonstrator exactly will depend on whether the imitator is trying to solve some instrumental problem (then he might ignore the demonstrator's means and use the most efficient means possible) or whether the imitator's goal is to engage socially with the demonstrator (in which case he might be more likely to copy the demonstrator's actions more exactly). One could think about designing a robot that possesses both the instrumental and the social functions. In this chapter, however, we will focus mainly on the instrumental function (see Carpenter, 2006, for more on the social function).

7.1.2   *The components of a demonstration*

An imitator can gather several different sources of information from a demonstration (Call and Carpenter, 2002; Carpenter and Call, 2002). Some of these sources of information, actions and results, are observable but one, the goal, is only inferable. That is, one can observe the demonstrator's body movements (actions) and the changes in the environment that those body movements bring about (results). From these and other sources of information (see below), it is often possible to infer the goal of the demonstrator, the internal representation of the result that he wants to achieve.

Different species appear to have different predispositions for which of these components they reproduce. Apes, for instance, focus more on results than actions (see, e.g. Call and Carpenter, 2003, and Tomasello, 1996, for reviews). Even when they are trained to reproduce actions upon request until they do so reliably, apes still make numerous mistakes such as confusing body parts or choosing incorrect body-part configurations – a vivid reminder that other animals also struggle with the correspondence problem. Some of the mistakes apes make are very telling because they are reminiscent of their preference for reproducing results. For instance, apes perform better when there is contact between the body part that executes the action and another body part or an object (presumably because this contact clearly marks the end state), they improve if there is an observable outcome, and actions on objects are easier than actions alone (Call, 2001; Custance *et al.*, 1995; Myowa-Yamakoshi and Matsuzawa, 1999). (Note that these same sorts of distinctions are found in the mirror neuron system in macaques, when certain neurons fire when the subject sees someone else grasp an object but do not fire if the same grasping action is observed in the absence of an object; Rizzolatti *et al.*, 2001). Apes may understand something about others' goals (e.g. Call *et al.*, 2004; Call and Tomasello, 1998), but as yet there is only very limited evidence that perhaps they use this understanding in imitation situations (Tomasello and Carpenter, 2005; see also Call *et al.*, 2005; Myowa-Yamakoshi and Matsuzawa, 2000).

In contrast, other species such as dolphins are very skilful at reproducing the actions of others, even when they have to copy the actions of a human experimenter whose body *Bauplan* is quite different from their own (Herman, 2002). Some birds also copy the actions that demonstrator birds use, for example using the same body part (foot or beak) the demonstrator has used to operate a treadmill (Zentall *et al.*, 1996; see also Atkins and Zentall, 1996, Atkins *et al.*, 2002; Campbell *et al.*, 1999; Mottley and Heyes, 2003; and Klein and Zentall, 2003). Whether or not dolphins and birds can also reproduce results using actions different from those used by a demonstrator, whether they have a greater predisposition to reproduce actions over results, and whether they have and use an understanding of others' goals all are unresolved questions that await further research.

Finally, other species such as humans can use results, actions and goals, but which of these three components they focus on changes with development. Although little research has been done on young infants to tease apart whether they primarily copy actions or results, beginning around their first birthday infants can use information about others' goals to work out what others are trying to do (e.g. Carpenter *et al.*, 1998, 2005; Meltzoff, 1995; see below). After this, throughout childhood and adulthood, whether humans copy actions or results depends on a complex interplay of the demonstrator's goal (and whether this includes his action), the social motivational state of the imitator and task difficulty.

As discussed above, there are many advantages to using goals as opposed to actions or results as the component of a demonstration to copy. Sometimes an efficient or 'correct' response to a demonstration is to copy the demonstrator's actions, and sometimes it is to copy only the results. Sometimes it is both of these, and sometimes it is neither (for example, if an adult demonstrates a failed attempt to separate a small dumbbell into two parts and then gives a child a giant dumbbell, then the child should use a different action to achieve a result they never saw; Meltzoff *et al.*, 1999). In all cases, the correct answer can be found by inferring the goal of the demonstrator and adopting it.

7.1.3   *Inferring goals*

Goals are unobservable and must be inferred using observable information. This information can include the demonstrator's actions and result but also additional information from the situation or context and other aspects of the demonstrator's behavior. Next we review some ways in which human infants infer the goal of a demonstrator.

Sometimes it is 'easy' and the demonstrator gives explicit feedback communicatively to the imitator (e.g. 'Watch how I put this here,' or 'No, do it *this* way'). Other times the demonstrator is less actively helpful – she may even perform the action without knowing the imitator is observing – and the imitator must pick up goal-relevant information on his own, exploiting other behavior such as gaze direction and facial expressions. For example, infants as young as 14 months of age can use verbal or emotional markers of intentionality to determine what an adult is trying to do. For instance, when shown the same sequences of two actions, each marked in different ways (i.e. as accidents vs. intended actions: 'Whoops, there!' vs. 'There, whoops!'), 14- to 18-month-olds copy actions marked with 'There' more often than actions marked with 'Whoops' (Carpenter *et al.*, 1998). Similarly, when shown the exact same action (e.g. moving the fingers along the furry end of a dumbbell), 18-month-olds respond differently when the action is accompanied by satisfied vs. dissatisfied emotional expressions and vocalizations (Behne *et al.*, 2006b). After seeing it accompanied by satisfied expressions, infants correctly perform actions similar to the demonstrated action (e.g. stroke the fur). But after seeing it accompanied by dissatisfied expressions, infants instead complete the action (e.g. open the dumbbell). (See also Rakoczy *et al.*, 2004, and Meltzoff *et al.*, 1999, for similar findings with older children). Infants can thus use adults' explicit markers of satisfaction and dissatisfaction to infer which of their actions were intended and what, in particular, they were trying to do. And it is striking that from an adult observer's perspective, we simply 'see' such identical actions differently depending on such markers (see Figure 7.1, Plate 7).

In other cases the information imitators use to infer others' goals is less explicit but still observable in various aspects of the demonstrator's surface behavior. For example, the direction of a demonstrator's gaze can provide information about directedness or intentionality. Behne *et al.* (2006a) showed that if 18-month-olds see an adult performing an unusual

Figure 7.1 (Plate 7) The demonstrator performing the action (a) in a happy, satisfied manner and (b) in a frustrated, dissatisfied manner in Behne and colleagues' (2006b) study.

 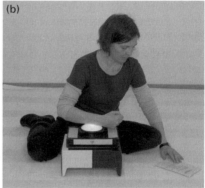

Figure 7.2 (Plate 8) The demonstrator (a) attending and (b) not attending to her action in Behne and colleagues' (2006a) study.

action (switching on a light with her forearm) while looking at her action, they copy this unusual action. However, if they see her perform the exact same action but while bending down and looking at something on the floor, they do not copy the unusual action, instead turning on the light themselves with their hand (see Figure 7.2, Plate 8). The timing of gaze shifts can also inform observers about the intentionality of an action: if the demonstrator looks first and then acts, the action is probably intentional; if she acts first and then looks, it may be accidental (Baldwin and Baird, 2001). Finally, more socially, if the demonstrator looks pointedly to the imitator during parts of the demonstration, this might also mark those parts of the demonstration as *for* the imitator and thus worthy of imitation.

Observation of the demonstrator's patterns of behaviour across time can also provide information about the goal of the action. For example, if 18-month-olds are shown a partial action done in three slightly different ways, they take this as a failed attempt and complete the action themselves when given a chance to interact with the object (whereas presumably if they had seen the action done three times identically they would copy it exactly; Meltzoff, 1995). Two-year-old children can even use the demonstrator's prior actions on *different* objects to work out exactly what she is trying to do on the demonstration object. For example, if they see an adult open three different boxes in turn, each in a different way, then they know that when the adult approaches a fourth box she is about to open it as well (Carpenter et al., 2002). This can be done at a more general level too, by observing the behaviour of others and detecting statistical regularities in their behavior. For example, Byrne (1999) has noted that when gorillas process food, although the exact actions that produce an outcome may be different for each individual, all individuals follow the same basic steps, for instance, they all fold certain leaves to avoid thorns before ingesting the plants, but the way they do it or the hand they use may vary across individuals. Noting which of these steps are invariant can provide clues about the demonstrator's goal. Conversely, noting behaviours that are not the 'usual' way to do things (such as turning on a lamp with one's head; see below) may also provide information about a demonstrator's goal because these types of behaviours can trigger a search for the relevance of that particular choice of action – why is he doing *that*? – and so highlight the rationality of (i.e. the reason for) that choice (Tomasello, personal communication).

Finally, in some cases imitators can go beyond behaviour and also use various types of information in the context or situation to determine whether the particular way of doing something is essential to the demonstration, that is, to gain information about the demonstrator's sub-goals or intentions. For example, if 14-month-olds see an adult performing an unusual action (turning on a light with her head), they copy this unusual action if the adult's hands were free, but do not copy it (instead using their hand) if there are constraints on the adult that do not apply to the infant (the adult's hands are occupied holding a blanket around her shoulders; Gergely et al., 2002). Twelve-month-old infants also copy adults' actions differentially depending on the objects present in the physical environment. For example, if they see an adult perform an action in a certain way, for example make a toy mouse move toward a location with a hopping vs. a sliding motion, infants do not copy the particular action the adult used if there is a little house in that location but they do copy it if there is no house. Presumably in this study even though infants see the exact same actions, they interpret the adult's goal as putting the mouse in the house in the first case and as hopping or sliding the mouse in the second (Carpenter *et al.*, 2005; see also Bekkering *et al.*, 2000, for a similar study with older children). Note that in this case the information about the demonstrator's goal does not involve the demonstrator at all, only the physical context.

Several types of observable behavioural information can thus be used to infer others' goals and intentions: explicit markers and gaze direction can be used to determine whether actions were intended or not, facial expressions and repeated attempts can be used to determine whether goals have been achieved or not, and previous actions on other objects can be used to infer the specific goal. Finally, constraints and situational factors can be used to decide how closely to copy demonstrators' actions, that is whether to achieve the end result in the most efficient manner for oneself or whether the particular action the demonstrator used is an essential part of the demonstration. These are all important types of information that robots could use to infer demonstrators' goals and intentions and become more flexible and efficient imitators. (See also Baldwin and Baird, 2001, for further discussion of ways to read intentions from behaviour and situations.)

7.1.4   Implementing goals

Inferring goals from a demonstration is important but of course that is only the first step in being able to then adopt and achieve the goal oneself. Once an imitator has inferred the goal of the demonstrator and adopted it, he must decide how to reproduce it. If it is not important for him to copy the demonstrator's actions exactly, or if the demonstrator's actions were not successful in achieving the desired result, then to achieve the goal himself, the imitator must evaluate different possible means and then choose one of these, thus forming an intention or plan (see Tomasello *et al.*, 2005). Then he must enact this intention, producing an action aimed at achieving the goal, and then observe any result of this action. If this result matches his goal (and that of the demonstrator), he is done; if not, he must re-evaluate his choice of means or the inferred goal and try again.

In order to evaluate and choose the best means and enact his intention, the imitator must have some prior knowledge of causality and an awareness of his own skills and body, and any constraints. He thus must have had some experience acting himself, to learn about the effects that his behaviour has on the environment. Play is one of the main ways in which children and animals may accomplish this. By engaging in motor activity directed at the environment they learn about the consequences of their actions and this information can be later applied to problem-solving situations (see also Chapter 11 in this volume).

7.1.5   Stepwise chain of events in imitation

Here are thus the main steps involved in inferring and reproducing the goal of a demonstrator's action. Figure 7.3 presents these steps in the form of a simple flowchart.

- *Perceive relevant aspects of the demonstration.* First, imitators must parse the continuous streams of behaviour they see into meaningful, goal-directed sequences of actions (Baldwin *et al.*, 2001). Relevant aspects of the demonstration then include the demonstrator's actions, the results of these actions on the environment (if any) and information about other aspects of the demonstration and demonstrator that could be useful for inferring the goal, for example facial expressions, direction of gaze, prior actions, other objects or constraints present, etc., before, during and after the demonstrator's action and the result ('goal-relevant information' in Figure 7.3).
- *Infer the goal of the demonstrator.* This involves processing the perceived information about the actions and results, and the goal-relevant information, using observable information to make inferences about the goal of the demonstrator. It may involve a hierarchical processing of goal-relevant information, for example, if the demonstrator is looking at what she is doing (normally this is associated with intentional behaviour) but says 'Whoops!', then this latter explicit marker of accidental action would override the looking to make the imitator discount the action performed immediately before it as unintentional.
- *If needed, evaluate different actions that could be used to achieve the goal and choose one of these as an intention.* If using the same means as the demonstrator is not part of the goal, then an imitator needs to consider which is the best way to achieve the goal. He can use two types of stored knowledge to do this. One type of stored knowledge is more general or 'long-term' knowledge, including information about objects and actions and their relations, for both self and other. This includes what the imitator already has learned about causality (what actions typically lead to what results), other individuals' typical actions (e.g. using one's hand to press things is typical, but using one's head is not), and what he himself is capable of doing. The second type of stored knowledge is more situation-specific, 'short-term' information gathered from the current demonstration situation. This includes things like differences in constraints or body size or skills between the demonstrator and the imitator and whether the situation is a social or an instrumental one. Both of these types of stored information are used to consider all the various means that might be appropriate (including the one the demonstrator

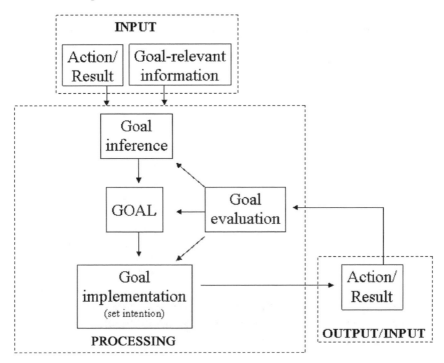

Figure 7.3 Components and processes of a flexible imitation system.

used) and to choose one of them. This one is then set as the plan or intention.

- *Enact the chosen intention.*
- *Perceive the action and the results of the action on the environment.*
- *Evaluate whether the results match the goal (and the demonstrator's goal) and repeat needed steps if not.* If the results do not match the goal because the produced action was ineffective, then the imitator must go back to the goal implementation step and seek an alternative means to achieve the goal. If they do match but the demonstrator is not satisfied, the imitator must go back to the goal inference step (a second demonstration might help here) to re-evaluate the goal of the demonstrator.

It is thus interesting to note that 'goal' is a two-sided coin in that it both guides the imitator's choice of the plan for action (forward flow in Figure 7.3) and constitutes the reference value that is used to evaluate whether the imitator's action and result matched the demonstrator's goal (backward flow in Figure 7.3).

7.2   How artificial systems currently answer the question of 'what to imitate'

Artificial systems research has focused on some of the above steps more than others. Here we review (only very superficially) some progress that has been made at each of the steps involving perceiving and inferring goals and choosing intentions.

- *Perceive relevant aspects of the demonstration.* Many artificial systems can perceive others' actions and the results they achieve on the environment. More interestingly in this context, some can also perceive some types of goal-relevant information. For example, several robots can detect human faces and eyes, and can even follow others' gaze direction (see, for example, Breazeal and Scassellati, 2002; Kozima and Yano, 2001). Progress is also being made in the area of recognizing human facial expressions and affective vocalizations (see, e.g. Breazeal and Scassellati, 2002). Furthermore, some systems can use a demonstrator's previous actions to extract invariants across multiple, different demonstrations (Billard *et al.*, 2003). They can also filter out insignificant movements and segment actions to detect the beginning and end of voluntary movements (Billard and Schaal, 2001). Finally, Johnson and Demiris's (2004) abstraction mechanism may also help robots focus on relevant aspects of a demonstration and match them with the robots' own capabilities. Demiris and Hayes (2002) also discuss how a robot could use a forward model to predict the demonstrator's next step. This could be helpful when there is a mismatch between the predicted next step and the actual one, leading to something like surprise and a search for a reason for that unexpected action.
- *Infer the goal of the demonstrator.* Currently, in most systems the goal is given to the system by researchers. For example, Alissandrakis *et al.* (2002) describe how a system could be told to imitate at the 'path' level, the 'trajectory' level or the 'end-point' level (i.e. corresponding to something like action, subgoal and goal or result, respectively, in our terms), and they show how their system can successfully imitate at the trajectory level when set to do so. One system that can itself infer the goal of the demonstrator in some situations is that of Billard *et al.* (2003). Their robot can observe a demonstrator, for example, moving several boxes using the same action (e.g. using the left hand) each time or moving just one of the boxes using several different types of actions. The robot extracts the invariants across each series of demonstrations and copies them appropriately, that is, copying the demonstrator's action in the first case and moving just that one box in the second case. (See also Nehaniv and Dautenhahn, 2001, for a suggestion for

an algorithm that artificial systems could use to extract goals from a demonstration.)

- *If needed, evaluate different actions that could be used to achieve the goal and choose one of these as an intention.* Alissandrakis *et al.* (2002) have developed a system that builds up a 'correspondence library' that stores actions and their related effects on the environment. This type of system can thus select among different actions to achieve the same effects as the demonstrator.

Much progress has clearly been made at each step. Some combination of these systems might someday yield a robot that can perceive various different types of goal-relevant information from a demonstration, process this information to infer the demonstrator's goal, and then decide what it must do to achieve the same goal in the most efficient or relevant manner in a wide variety of contexts. Along with: (1) increasing the different types of goal-relevant information that can be picked up and processed, (2) getting robots to infer the goal themselves, and (3) making them able to come up with more possible different solutions to a problem, another future challenge for this field would be to design a robot that can reproduce a demonstrator's goal even when this goal is not fulfilled, that is, when the intended result is never achieved (as in Meltzoff's, 1995, study). Thinking about 'goals' rather than 'effects' would help solve this problem.

7.3   Conclusion and further challenges

Developing the ability to read and reproduce others' goals and intentions was an important step in human evolution (Tomasello *et al.*, 1993). We predict that it will be an important step in robot evolution as well. As discussed in this chapter, it will enable flexible, efficient imitation. But the ability to infer others' goals and intentions is also important in non-imitative contexts, in that it could also open up the possibility of what was another important step in human evolution: the ability to engage in collaborative interactions (see Tomasello *et al.*, 2005). If robots can infer other robots' goals and intentions, then they can work together in new ways to solve problems that would not be possible to solve individually, especially if more research attention can also be paid to providing robots with social motivations, along the lines of Dautenhahn's (1994; 1995), Breazeal and Scassellati's (2002), and Kozima and Yano's (2001) work.

Acknowledgments

We thank Chrystopher Nehaniv and Kerstin Dautenhahn, two anonymous reviewers and Steffen Grünewälder for helpful comments on a previous draft.

REFERENCES

Alissandrakis, A., Nehaniv, D. and Dautenhahn, K. (2002). Imitation with ALICE: learning to imitate corresponding actions across dissimilar embodiments. *IEEE Transactions on Systems, Man and Cybernetics – Part A: Systems and Humans*, **32**, 482–96.

Atkins, C. K., Klein, E. D. and Zentall, T. R. (2002). Imitative learning in Japanese quail (*Coturnix japonica*) using the bidirectional control procedure. *Animal Learning & Behavior*, **30**, 275–81.

Atkins, C. K. and Zentall, T. R. (1996). Imitative learning in male Japanese quail (*Coturnix japonica*) using the two-action method. *Journal of Comparative Psychology*, **110**, 316–20.

Baldwin, D. A. and Baird, J. A. (2001). Discerning intentions in dynamic human action. *Trends in Cognitive Sciences*, **5**, 171–8.

Baldwin, D. A., Baird, J. A., Saylor, M. M. and Clark, M. A. (2001). Infants parse dynamic action. *Child Development*, **72**, 708–17.

Behne, T., Carpenter, M. and Tomasello, M. (2006a). From attention to intention: 18-month-olds use others' focus of attention for action interpretation. Poster presented at the meetings of the International Conference on Infancy Studies, Kyoto, Japan.

Behne, T., Carpenter, M., van Veen, A. and Tomasello, M. (2006b). Infants use attention and reaction information to infer others' goals. Unpublished data.

Bekkering, H., Wohlschläger, A. and Gattis, M. (2000). Imitation of gestures in children is goal-directed. *Quarterly Journal of Experimental Psychology*, **53A**, 153–64.

Bellagamba, F. and Tomasello, M. (1999). Re-enacting intended acts: comparing 12- and 18-month-olds. *Infant Behavior and Development*, **22**, 277–82.

Billard, A., Epars, Y., Cheng, G. and Schaal, S. (2003). Discovering imitation strategies through categorization of multi-dimensional data. *Proceedings of the 2003 IEEE/RSJ International Conference on Intelligent Robots and Systems*, Las Vegas, Nevada.

Billard, A. and Schaal, S. (2001). Robust learning of arm trajectories through human demonstration. In *Proceedings of the 2001 IEEE/RSJ International Conference on Intelligent Robots and Systems*, Maui, Hawaii.

Boesch, C. and Boesch, H. (2000). *The Chimpanzees of the Tai Forest*. Oxford: Oxford University Press.

Breazeal, C. and Scassellati, B. (2002). Challenges in building robots that imitate people. In K. Dautenhahn and C. L. Nehaniv (eds.), *Imitation in Animals and Artifacts*. Cambridge, MA: MIT Press, 363–90.

Byrne, R. W. (1999). Imitation without intentionality. Using string parsing to copy the organization of behaviour. *Animal Cognition*, **2**, 63–72.

Call, J. (2001). Body imitation in an enculturated orangutan. *Cybernetics and Systems*, **32**, 97–119.

Call, J. and Carpenter, M. (2002). Three sources of information in social learning. In K. Dautenhahn and C. L. Nehaniv (eds.), *Imitation in Animals and Artifacts*. Cambridge, MA: MIT Press, 211–28.

Call, J. and Carpenter, M. (2003). On imitation in apes and children. *Infancia y Aprendizaje*, **26**, 325–49.

Call, J., Carpenter, M. and Tomasello, M. (2005). Copying results and copying actions in the process of social learning: chimpanzees (*Pan troglodytes*) and human children (*Homo sapiens*). *Animal Cognition*, **8**, 151–63.

Call, J., Hare, B., Carpenter, M. and Tomasello, M. (2004). Unwilling or unable: Chimpanzees' understanding of human intentional action. *Developmental Science*, 7, 488–98.

Call, J. and Tomasello, M. (1998). Distinguishing intentional from accidental actions in orangutans (*Pongo pygmaeus*), chimpanzees (*Pan troglodytes*) and human children (*Homo sapiens*). *Journal of Comparative Psychology*, **112**, 192–206.

Campbell, F. M., Heyes, C. M. and Goldsmith, A. R. (1999). Stimulus learning and response learning by observation in the European starling in a two-object/two-action test. *Animal Behaviour*, **58**, 151–8.

Carpenter, M. (2006). Instrumental, social, and shared goals and intentions in imitation. In S. Rogers and J. Williams (eds.), *Imitation and the Development of the Social Mind*: Lessons from Typical Development and Autism. New York: Guilford, 48–70.

Carpenter, M., Akhtar, N. and Tomasello, M. (1998). Fourteen through 18-month-old infants differentially imitate intentional and accidental actions. *Infant Behavior and Development*, **21**, 315–30.

Carpenter, M. and Call, J. (2002). The chemistry of social learning. *Developmental Science*, 5, 22–4.

Carpenter, M., Call, J. and Tomasello, M. (2002). Understanding 'prior intentions' enables 2-year-olds to imitatively learn a complex task. *Child Development*, **73**, 1431–41.

Carpenter, M., Call, J. and Tomasello, M. (2005). Twelve- and 18-month-olds imitate actions in terms of goals. *Developmental Science*, **8**, F13–20.

Custance, D., Whiten, A. and Bard, K. (1995). Can young chimpanzees imitate arbitrary actions? *Behaviour*, **132**, 839–58.

Dautenhahn, K. (1994). Trying to imitate – a step towards releasing robots from social isolation. In P. Gaussier and J.-D. Nicoud (eds.), *Proceedings from Perception to Action Conference*. Lausanne, Switzerland: IEEE Computer Society Press.

Dautenhahn, K. (1995). Getting to know each other – artificial social intelligence for autonomous robots. *Robotics and Autonomous Systems*, **16**, 333–56.

Dautenhahn, K. and Nehaniv, C. L. (2002a). The agent-based perspective on imitation. In K. Dautenhahn and C. Nehaniv (eds.), *Imitation in Animals and Artifacts*. Cambridge, MA: MIT Press, 1–40.

Dautenhahn, K. and Nehaniv, C. L. (eds.) (2002b). *Imitation in Animals and Artifacts*. Cambridge, MA: MIT Press.

Demiris, J. and Hayes, G. (2002). Imitation as a dual-route process featuring predictive and learning components: a biologically plausible computational model. In K. Dautenhahn and C. Nehaniv (eds.), *Imitation in Animals and Artifacts*. Cambridge, MA: MIT Press, 327–61.

Galef, B. and Zentall, T. (1988). *Social learning: Psychological and biological perspectives*. Hillsdale, NJ: LEA.

Gergely, G. (2003). What should a robot learn from an infant? Mechanisms of action interpretation and observational learning in infancy. *Connection Science,* **15,** 191–209.

Gergely, G., Bekkering, H. and Király, I. (2002). Rational imitation in preverbal infants. *Nature,* **415,** 755.

Herman, L. M. (2002). Vocal, social, and self-imitation by bottlenosed dolphins. In K. Dautenhahn and C. L. Nehaniv (eds.), *Imitation in Animals and Artifacts* Cambridge, MA: MIT Press, 63–108.

Heyes, C. and Galef, B. G. (1996). *Social Learning in Animals.* San Diego: Academic Press.

Johnson, M. and Demiris, Y. (2004). Abstraction in recognition to solve the correspondence problem for robot imitation. In *Proceedings of TAROS,* Essex.

Klein, E. D. and Zentall, T. R. (2003). Imitation and affordance learning by pigeons (*Columba livia*). *Journal of Comparative Psychology,* **117,** 414–19.

Kozima, H. and Yano, H. (2001). A robot that learns to communicate with human caregivers. In *Proceedings of the 1st International Workshop on Epigenetic Robotics: Modeling Cognitive Development in Robotic Systems.* Lund University Cognitive Studies, 47–52.

Meltzoff, A. N. (1995). Understanding the intentions of others: re-enactment of intended acts by 18-month-old children. *Developmental Psychology,* **31,** 1–16.

Meltzoff, A. N., Gopnik, A. and Repacholi, B. M. (1999). Toddlers' understanding of intentions, desires, and emotions: explorations of the dark ages. In P. D. Zelazo, J. W. Astington and D. R. Olson (eds.), *Developing Theories of Intention: Social Understanding and Self-control.* Mahwah, NJ: Lawrence Erlbaum, 17–41.

Mottley, K. and Heyes, C. (2003). Budgerigars (*Melopsittacus undulatus*) copy virtual demonstrators in a two-action test. *Journal of Comparative Psychology,* **117,** 363–70.

Myowa-Yamakoshi, M. and Matsuzawa, T. (1999). Factors influencing imitation of manipulatory actions in chimpanzees (*Pan troglodytes*). *Journal of Comparative Psychology,* **113,** 128–36.

Myowa-Yamakoshi, M. and Matsuzawa, T. (2000) Imitation of intentional manipulatory actions in chimpanzees. *Journal of Comparative Psychology,* **114,** 381–91.

Nehaniv, C. L. and Dautenhahn, K. (1998). Mapping between dissimilar bodies: affordances and the algebraic foundations of imitation. In J. Demiris and A. Birk (eds.), *Proceedings of the European Workshop on Learning Robots (EWLR-7),* (Edinburgh, Scotland, 20 July 1998).

Nehaniv, C. L. and Dautenhahn, K. (2001). Like me? – Measures of correspondence and imitation. *Cybernetics and Systems: An International Journal,* **32,** 11–51.

Nehaniv, C. L. and Dautenhahn, K. (2002). The correspondence problem. In K. Dautenhahn and C. L. Nehaniv (eds.), *Imitation in Animals and Artifacts.* Cambridge, MA: MIT Press, 41–61.

Rakoczy, H., Tomasello, M. and Striano, T. (2004). Young children know that trying is not pretending – a test of the "behaving-as-if" construal of children's early concept of "pretense." *Developmental Psychology,* **40,** 388–99.

Rizzolatti, G., Fogassi, L. and Gallesse, V. (2001). Neurophysiological mechanisms underlying the understanding and imitation of action. *Nature Reviews Neuroscience*, **2**, 661–9.

Tomasello, M. (1996). Do apes ape? In C. M. Heyes and B. G. Galef, Jr. (eds.). *Social Learning in Animals: The Roots of Culture*. New York: Academic Press, 319–46.

Tomasello, M. and Carpenter, M. (2005). The emergence of social cognition in three young chimpanzees. *Monographs of the Society for Research in Child Development*, **70**(1, Serial No. 279).

Tomasello, M., Carpenter, M., Call, J., Behne, T. and Moll, H. (2005). Understanding and sharing intentions: the origins of cultural cognition. *Behavioral and Brain Sciences*, **28**, 675–735.

Tomasello, M., Kruger, A. C. and Ratner, H. (1993). Cultural learning. *Behavioral and Brain Sciences*, **16**, 495–552.

Užgiris, I. Č. (1981). Two functions of imitation during infancy. *International Journal of Behavioral Development*, **4**, 1–12.

Zentall, T. R., Sutton, J. E. and Sherburne, L. M. (1996). True imitative learning in pigeons. *Psychological Science*, **7**, 343–6.

8 Learning of gestures by imitation in a humanoid robot

Sylvain Calinon and Aude Billard

8.1   Introduction

Traditionally, robotics developed highly specific controllers for the robot to perform a specific set of tasks in highly constrained and deterministic environments. This required the embedding of the controller with an extensive knowledge of the robot's architecture and of its environment. It was soon clear that such an approach would not scale up for controlling robots with multiple degrees of freedom, working in highly variable environments, such as humanoid robots required to interact with humans in their daily environment. The field has now moved to developing more flexible and adaptive control systems, so that the robot would no longer be dedicated to a single task, and could be re-programmed in a fast and efficient manner, to match the end-user needs.

Robot learning by imitation, also referred to as robot programming by demonstration, explores novel means of implicitly teaching a robot new motor skills (Billard and Siegwart, 2004; Dillmann, 2004; Schaal *et al.*, 2003). This field of research takes inspiration in a large and interdisciplinary body of literature on imitation learning, drawing from studies in psychology, ethology and the neurosciences (Demiris and Hayes, 2001; Billard and Hayes, 1999; Alissandrakis *et al.*, 2002). To provide a robot with the ability to imitate is advantageous for at least two reasons: it provides a natural, user-friendly means of implicitly programming the robot; it constrains the search space of motor learning by showing possible and/or optimal solutions.

In this chapter, we explore the issue of recognizing, generalizing and reproducing arbitrary gesture (Billard *et al.*, 2004). In order to take a general stance toward gesture recognition and reproduction, we address one major and generic issue, namely how to discover the essence of a

Imitation and Social Learning in Robots, Humans and Animals, ed. Chrystopher L. Nehaniv and Kerstin Dautenhahn. Published by Cambridge University Press.

gesture, i.e. how to find a representation of the data that encapsulates only the key aspects of the gesture, and discards the intrinsic variability across people motion.

To illustrate the idea, consider the following examples: when asked to imitate someone writing letters of the alphabet on a board, you will find it sufficient to only track the trajectory followed by the demonstrator's hand on the board. In contrast, when learning to play tennis, you will find it more important to follow the trajectories of the demonstrator's arm joint angles, rather than the position of the hand (the ball's position varying importantly over the trials). Choosing, in advance, the optimal representation of the data (whether hand path or joint angles) would greatly simplify the analysis and speed up learning.

In the application presented in this chapter, the robot is endowed with numerous sensors enabling it to track faithfully the demonstrator's motions. Some of the data gathered by the sensors are redundant and correlated. The first stage of processing performed on our data consists of applying principal component analysis (PCA) in order to determine a space in which the data are decorrelated, and, consequently, to reduce the dimensionality of the dataset, so as to make the analysis more tractable.

In order for the robot to learn new skills by imitation, it must be endowed with the ability to generalize over multiple demonstrations. To achieve this, the robot must encode multivariate time-dependent datasets in an efficient way. One of the major difficulties in learning, recognizing and reproducing sequential patterns of motion is to deal simultaneously with the variations in the data and with the variations in the sequential structure of these data. The second stage of processing of our model uses hidden Markov models (HMMs) to encode the sequential patterns of motion in stochastic finite state automata. The motion is then represented as a sequence of states, where each state has an underlying description of multi-dimensional data (see Figure 8.4). The system takes inspiration from a recent trend of research that aims at defining a formal mathematical framework for imitation learning (Schaal, 1999; Nehaniv and Dautenhahn, 2000; Billard *et al.*, 2004). We present an implementation of these approaches in a noisy real-world application.

The remainder of this chapter is divided as follows: Section 8.2 presents the experimental set-up; Section 8.3 describes in detail the model; results are presented in Section 8.4, and discussed in Section 8.5, stressing the parallels existing between our robotic model and theoretical models of imitation learning in animals.

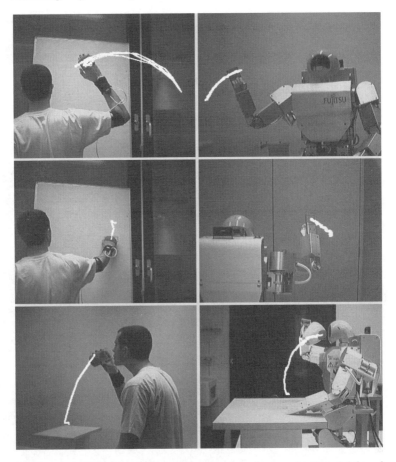

Figure 8.1 Demonstration (*left column*) and reproduction (*right column*) of different tasks: waving goodbye (*1st line*), knocking on a door (*2nd line*), and drinking (*3rd line*). Three gyroscopic motion tracking sensors are attached on the upper arm, lower arm and torso of the demonstrator. The trajectories of the demonstrator's hand, reconstructed by the stereoscopic vision system, are superimposed to the image.

8.2   Experimental set-up

Data used for training the robot have been generated by eight healthy volunteers (students at the EPFL School of Engineering). Subjects have been asked to imitate a set of six motions performed by a human demonstrator in a video. The motions are represented in Figures 8.1 and 8.2, and consist of:

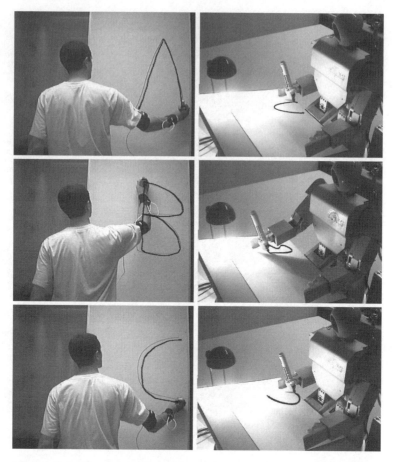

Figure 8.2 Demonstration (*left column*) and reproduction (*right column*) of drawing the three stylized alphabet letters A, B and C. The motion reproduced by the robot follows a trajectory generalized across the different demonstrations. As the trajectory is projected by PCA in two dimensions, the letters can be written on a different plane.

- Knocking on a door.
- Raising a glass, drinking and putting it back on a table.
- Waving goodbye.
- Drawing the stylized alphabet letters A, B and C.

The subject's gestures have been recorded by three x-sens motion sensors, attached to the torso and the right upper and lower arm. Each sensor provides the 3-D absolute orientation of each limb segment, by integrating the 3-D rate-of-turn, acceleration and Earth magnetic field, at a rate of 100Hz. The joint angle trajectories of the shoulder joint (three degrees of freedom (DOFs)) and of the elbow (one DOF) are reconstructed with a precision of 1.5 degrees, taking the torso as reference. These sensors provide a motor representation of the gesture, that can be used without major modification to control the robot.

A color-based stereoscopic vision system tracks the 3-D position of a marker placed on the demonstrator's hand, at a rate of 15Hz, with a precision of 10 mm. The system uses two Phillips webcams with a resolution of 320 × 240 pixels. The tracking is based on color segmentation in the YCbCr color space (Y is dismissed to be robust to changes in luminosity).

The robot is a Fujitsu humanoid robot HOAP-2 with 25 DOFs. In the experiments reported here, only the robot's right arm (four DOFs) is used for the task. The torso and legs are set to a constant and stable position, in order to support the robot standing up.

8.3   Data processing

The complete dataset consists of the trajectories of four joint angles and the 3-D trajectory of the hand in Cartesian space. Figure 8.3 shows a schematic of the sensory-motor flow. The data are first projected onto an uncorrelated, low-dimensional subspace, using PCA. The resulting signals are then encoded in a set of hidden Markov models (HMMs). A generalized form of the signals is then reconstructed by interpolating across the time series output by the HMMs and reprojecting onto the original space of the data using the PCA eigenvectors.

For each experiment, the dataset is split in two. The first half is used to train the model, and the second half to test the model.

Let $\{X_1, X_2, X_3\}$ be the hand path in Cartesian space, and $\{\vec{\Theta}_1, \vec{\Theta}_2, \vec{\Theta}_3, \vec{\Theta}_4\}$ the joint angle trajectories of the right arm, after interpolation, normalization in time (same number of data points for each time series) and shifting such that the first data points coincide.

8.3.1   Preprocessing by principal component analysis (PCA)

Principal component analysis (PCA) is a technique used extensively to discover and reduce the dimensionality of a dataset. In this work, we use it to find a suitable representation of our multivariate dataset (Jolliffe, 1986). PCA consists of determining the directions (eigenvectors) along

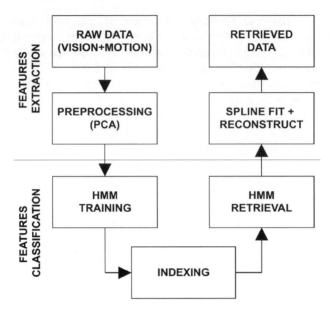

Figure 8.3 Schematic of the sensory-motor flow: the data are first projected onto an uncorrelated, low-dimensional subspace, using PCA. The resulting signals are, then, encoded in a set of HMMs. A generalized form of the signals is then reconstructed by interpolating across the time series output by the HMMs and reprojecting onto the original space of the data using the PCA eigenvectors.

which the variability of the data is maximal. It assumes that the data are linear and normally distributed.

By projecting the data onto the referential defined by the eigenvectors, one obtains a representation of the dataset that minimizes the statistical dependence across the data. Consecutively, dimensionality reduction can be achieved by discarding the dimensions along which the variance of the data is smaller than a criterion. This provides a way of compressing the data without losing much information and simplifying the representation.

Principal component analysis is applied separately to $\{X_1, X_2, X_3\}$ and $\{\Theta_1, \Theta_2, \Theta_3, \Theta_4\}$ to determine if a better representation in each dataset can be used. The means $\{\vec{m}_1^X, \vec{m}_2^X, \vec{m}_3^X\}$ and $\{\vec{m}_1^\Theta, \vec{m}_2^\Theta, \vec{m}_3^\Theta, \vec{m}_4^\Theta\}$ are subtracted for each dimension. Then, the three eigenvectors $\{\vec{v}_1^X, \vec{v}_2^X, \vec{v}_3^X\}$ and associated eigenvalues $\{e_1^X, e_2^X, e_3^X\}$ are calculated for the hand path. The four eigenvectors $\{\vec{v}_1^\Theta, \vec{v}_2^\Theta, \vec{v}_3^\Theta, \vec{v}_4^\Theta\}$ and associated eigenvalues $\{e_1^\Theta, e_2^\Theta, e_3^\Theta, e_4^\Theta\}$ are calculated for the joint angle dataset. An indication of the relative importance of each direction is given by its eigenvalue. Let I and $\mathcal{J}$ be the number of eigenvectors required to obtain a satisfying representation of $\{X_1, X_2, X_3\}$ and $\{\vec{\Theta}_1, \vec{\Theta}_2, \vec{\Theta}_3, \vec{\Theta}_4\}$, such that the information lost by projecting the data onto these eigenvectors is small. By expressing these datasets in their new basis, given respectively by I and $\mathcal{J}$ eigenvectors, the time series become $\{S_1^X, S_2^X, \ldots, S_I^X\}$ with $I \leq 3$ to represent the hand path, and $\{S_1^\Theta, S_2^\Theta, \ldots, S_{\mathcal{J}}^\Theta\}$ with $\mathcal{J} \leq 4$ to represent the joint angle trajectories. The selection criterion is to retain the first K components that cover over 80 % of the data's spread, i.e. to have $\sum_{i=1}^{K} e_i > 0.8$.

Applying PCA before encoding the data in an HMM has the following advantages:

- It helps to reduce noise, as the noise is now encapsulated in the lower dimensions.
- It reduces the dimensionality of the dataset, which reduces the number of parameters in the hidden Markov models, and makes the training process faster.
- It produces a representation of the dataset that is easier to handle and that can be used under different conditions, for the reproduction of the task (e.g. learning to write an alphabet letter on a plane, and writing it on another plane).

For example, while drawing an alphabet letter, the dimensionality of the 3-D Cartesian path can be reduced to a 2-D trajectory. By projecting the dataset on the drawing plane defined by the two eigenvectors, the trajectory is then described by two signals (the 3rd eigenvector is not used to reconstruct the dataset). Similarly, when reaching for an object, the joint angle trajectory of the shoulder is correlated with the joint angle trajectory of the elbow and, thus, the shoulder and elbow trajectories can usually be expressed by only one signal.

8.3.2   Encoding in hidden Markov models (HMMs)

For each gesture, a set of time series $\{S_1^X, S_2^X, \ldots, S_I^X, S_1^\Theta, S_2^\Theta, \ldots, S_{\mathcal{J}}^\Theta\}$ is used to train a hidden Markov model with $I + \mathcal{J}$ output variables. The parameters are expressed as a set of parameters $\{\vec{\pi}, \mathbf{A}, \vec{\mu}, \vec{\sigma}\}$, representing respectively the initial state distribution, the state transition probabilities, the means of the output variables and the standard deviations of the output variables.[1]

Continuous HMMs are used to encode the data with a parametric description of the distributions. A single Gaussian is assumed to

---

[1] Readers unfamiliar with HMMs should refer to Rabiner (1989) –Ed.

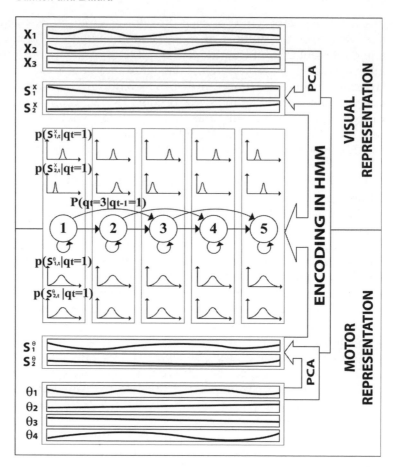

Figure 8.4 Encoding of the hand path in Cartesian space $\{\mathbf{X}_1, \mathbf{X}_2, \mathbf{X}_3\}$ and joint angles trajectories $\{\vec{\Theta}_1, \vec{\Theta}_2, \vec{\Theta}_3, \vec{\Theta}_4\}$ in an HMM. The data are pre-processed by PCA, and the resulting signals $\{\mathbf{S}_1^X, \mathbf{S}_2^X, \ldots, \mathbf{S}_I^X\}$ and $\{\mathbf{S}_1^\Theta, \mathbf{S}_2^\Theta, \ldots, \mathbf{S}_J^\Theta\}$ are learned by the HMM. The data are represented as sequences of states, with transition probabilities between the states (not all the transitions are depicted). Each state in the HMM outputs multivariate data, represented by Gaussian functions.

approximate sufficiently each output variable (see Figure 8.4). A mixture of Gaussians could approximate any shape of distribution. However, it is not useful in our system, since the training is performed with too few training data to generate an accurate model of distribution with more than one Gaussian.

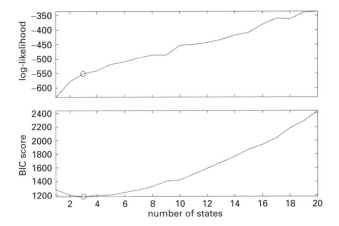

Figure 8.5 A BIC criterion is used to determine the optimal number of states of the HMM, required to encode the data. *Top*: log-likelihood of the HMM according to the number of states used to represent the data. *Bottom*: the minimum BIC score gives a criterion to select the minimal number of states required to represent the data. It finds a trade-off between maximizing the likelihood of the model and minimizing the number of parameters used to model the data. Here, the gesture *waving goodbye* is modeled optimally with only three states.

The transition probabilities $P(q_t = j | q_{t-1} = i)$ and the observation distributions $p(S_t | q_t = i)$ are estimated by Baum–Welch, an expectation maximization (EM) algorithm that maximizes the likelihood that the training dataset can be generated by the corresponding model. The optimal number of states in the HMM may not be known beforehand. The number of states can be selected by using a criterion that weights the model fit (i.e. how well the model fits the data) with the economy of parameters (i.e. the number of states used to encode the data). In our system, the Bayesian information criterion (BIC) (Schwarz, 1978) is used to select an optimal number of states for the model:

$$BIC = -2 \, \log L + n_p \, \log T \qquad (8.1)$$

The first term is used for the model fit, with L the likelihood of the fitted model; the second term is a penalty term, with n_p the number of independent parameters in the HMM and T the number of observation data used in fitting the model. Data are encoded in different HMMs from 1 to 20 states, and the model with the minimum score is retained (see Figure 8.5).

8.3.3   Recognition

Once trained, the HMM can be used to recognize whether a new gesture is similar to the ones encoded in the model. For each of the HMMs, we run the forward algorithm to estimate the likelihood that the new signals could have been generated by one of the models. A measure of distance across two model's predictions is compared to a model-dependent threshold, to guarantee that the gesture is close to a model, but far enough from the others to be considered as recognized (see Calinon and Billard, 2004 for details).

8.3.4   Data retrieval

When a gesture is recognized by an HMM, a generalization of the gesture is reproduced. Given the observation of the gesture and the parameters $\{\vec{\pi}, \mathbf{A}, \vec{\mu}, \vec{\sigma}\}$ of the HMM, a sequence of states is reconstructed by the Viterbi algorithm. Given this sequence of states, the output variables $\{S_1'''^X, S_2'''^X, \ldots, S_I'''^X, S_1'''^\Theta, S_2'''^\Theta, \ldots, S_{\bar{\jmath}}'''^\Theta\}$ are retrieved, by taking the mean value $\vec{\mu}$ of the Gaussian distribution for each output variable.

Keypoints $\{S_1''^X, S_2''^X, \ldots, S_I''^X, S_1''^\Theta, S_2''^\Theta, \ldots, S_{\bar{\jmath}}''^\Theta\}$ are then extracted from these time series. If there is a transition to a state n at time t_1 and if there is a transition to another state at time t_2, a keypoint is created at the mean time $t_1 + t_2/2$. By interpolating between these key points and normalizing in time, the output variables $\{S_1'^X, S_2'^X, \ldots, S_I'^X, S_1'^\Theta, S_2'^\Theta, \ldots, S_{\bar{\jmath}}'^\Theta\}$ are reconstructed (see Figure 8.6). Finally, by using the eigenvectors found by PCA, the whole hand path $\{X_1', X_2', X_3'\}$ and joint angle trajectories $\{\vec{\Theta}_1', \vec{\Theta}_2', \vec{\Theta}_3', \vec{\Theta}_4'\}$ are reconstructed.

8.3.5   Imitation metrics

In Billard *et al.* (2004), Calinon and Billard (2004) and Calinon *et al.* (2005), we have developed a general formalism for determining a metric of imitation performance. The metric measures the quality of the reproduction and, as such, drives the selection of an appropriate controller for the reproduction of the task.

One way to compare the relative importance of each set of variables (i.e. joint angles, hand path) in our experiment is to look at their variability. Here, we take the perspective that the relevant features of the movement, i.e. those to imitate, are the features that appear most frequently, i.e. the invariants in time, and apply the metric to determine the relevance of the Cartesian and joint angle representation to reproduce a gesture.

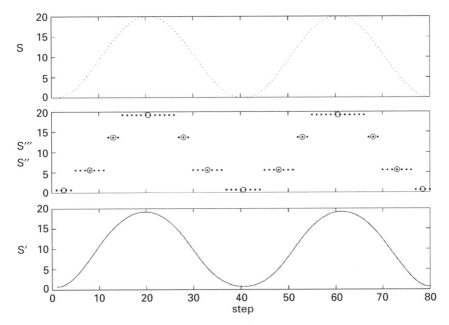

Figure 8.6 Example of the retrieval process. The original signal S (*dotted line*) is encoded in an HMM with four states. A sequence of states and corresponding output variables S''' are retrieved by the Viterbi algorithm (*points*). Keypoints S'' are defined from this sequence of output variables (*circles*). The retrieved signal S' (*straight-line*) is then computed by interpolating between the keypoints and normalizing in time.

Following this framework, we model the task's cost function as a weighted linear combination of metrics applied to the joint angle trajectories and the hand path.

Unidimensional case

Let $D = \{x_1, x_2, \ldots, x_T\}$ and $D' = \{x'_1, x'_2, \ldots, x'_T\}$ be the demonstration and the reproduction datasets of a variable x. The cost function $\mathcal{J}$ is defined by:

$$\mathcal{J}(D, D') = 1 - f(e) \tag{8.2}$$

$\mathcal{J} \in [0, 1]$ calculates an estimation of the quality of the reproduction, using two different metrics. Optimizing the imitation consists of minimizing $\mathcal{J}$ ($\mathcal{J} = 0$ corresponds to a perfect reproduction). e is the mean error of the observed data D' compared to the dataset D. A transformation

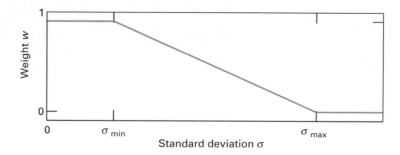

Figure 8.7 Function used to transform a standard deviation σ to a weight factor $w \in [0, 1]$. σ_{min} corresponds to the accuracy of the sensors. σ_{max} represents the maximal standard deviation measured during a set of demonstrations generated by moving randomly the arms during one minute.

function $f(e)$ normalizes and bounds each variable within minimal and maximal values (see Figure 8.7). This results in the elimination of the effect of the noise, intrinsic to each variable, so that the relative importance of each variable can be compared.

The metric uses the HMM representation of the data to compute an error value e, robust to distortion in time. The Viterbi algorithm is first used to retrieve the best sequence of states $\{q_1, q_2, \ldots, q_T\}$, given the observation data $D' = \{x'_1, x'_2, \ldots, x'_T\}$ of length T. If $\{\mu_1, \mu_2, \ldots, \mu_T\}$ is the sequence of means associated with the sequence of states, we define:

$$e = \frac{1}{T} \sum_{t=1}^{T} |x'_t - \mu_t| \qquad (8.3)$$

We have compared this error measure to the commonly used root mean square (RMS) error, calculated with signals rescaled in time, using the demonstration data (see examples in Figure 8.8). The RMS error is computed as:

$$e' = \frac{1}{T} \sum_{t=1}^{T} |x'_t - x_t| \qquad (8.4)$$

The results of the metric calculated using e or e' are presented in Figure 8.9. Each dataset has been tested with the two models, and should produce, respectively, a low value of $\mathcal{J}$ if they belong to the corresponding model and a high value if they do not. The metric using the HMM representation of the time series gives better results than the one using

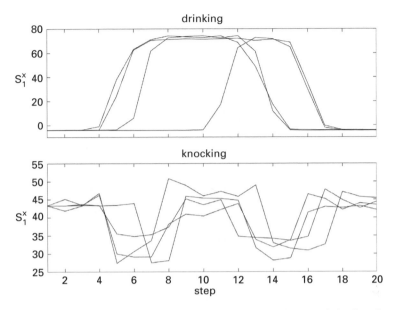

Figure 8.8 Four demonstrations of the *drinking* gesture and the *knocking* gesture (only one variable from the visual information is represented). Even if the trajectories are rescaled in time, data do not overlap, because they present non-homogeneous distortions in time. By encoding the data in HMMs, it is still possible to distinguish very well the two datasets.

the static error computed on rescaled signals (see Figure 8.9). Indeed, HMMs can deal with the distortions in time in the two datasets.

Multidimensional case

When data have K dimensions, the metric $\mathcal{J}_{tot}$ is expressed as

$$\mathcal{J}_{tot} = \frac{1}{K} \sum_{i=1}^{K} w_i \mathcal{J}(D_i, D_i') \tag{8.5}$$

where $w_i \in [0, 1]$ weights the importance of variable i. These factors are extracted from the demonstrations and reflect the variance of the data during the demonstration. To evaluate this variability, we use the statistical representation provided by the HMM. The Viterbi algorithm is used to retrieve the best sequence of states $\{q_1, q_2, \ldots, q_T\}$, given the observation data D'. If $\{\sigma_1^i, \sigma_2^i, \ldots, \sigma_T^i\}$ is the sequence of standard

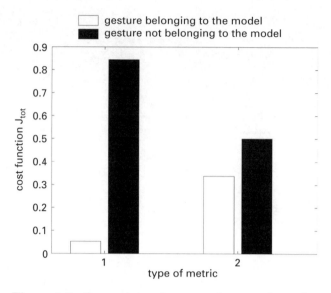

Figure 8.9 Comparison of two metrics to evaluate the quality of a reproduced trajectory. *Left:* using the error measure e based on HMM encoding of the dataset. *Right:* using the RMS error e' with the trajectories rescaled in time. The white and black bar corresponds respectively to the data belonging to the model, and not belonging to the model. The error based on HMM encoding discriminates better the two datasets.

deviations of variable i, associated with the sequence of states, we define:

$$w_i = f\left(\frac{1}{T}\sum_{t=1}^{T}\sigma_t^i\right) \tag{8.6}$$

If the variance of a given variable is high, i.e. showing no consistency across demonstrations, then, satisfying some particular instance of this variable will have little bearing on the task. The factors w_i in the cost function equation reflect this assumption: if the standard deviation of a given variable is low, the value taken by the corresponding w_i is close to one. This way, the corresponding variable will have a strong influence in the reproduction of the task.

A mean standard deviation is thus calculated over the whole path, and is transformed by a normalization function (see Figure 8.7) to give a weight $w_i \in [0, 1]$, estimating the relevance of variable i. w_i can then motivate the use of either a direct joint angles controller or an inverse kinematics controller. In order to use both controllers simultaneously, one can extend the inverse kinematics solution to encapsulate constraints on the joint angles, as in Calinon *et al.* (2005).

Since the demonstrator and the robot do not share the same embodiment (they differ in the length of their arms and in the range of motion of each DOF), there is a correspondence problem (Nehaniv and Dautenhahn, 2000).[2] Here, this problem is solved by hand. The joint angle trajectories of the demonstrator are automatically shifted and scaled, when required, to ensure that these fit within the range of motion of the robot.

8.4   Results and performance of the system

The training set consists of the joint angle trajectories and hand path of four subjects performing the six different motions. The test set consists of four other subjects performing the same six motions, using only the hand path trajectories as observation variables in order to demonstrate the recognition ability of the model even in the face of missing data. Once a gesture has been recognized by the model based on the hand path only, the complete joint angle trajectories can be retrieved.

Twenty-three motions have been recognized correctly (recognition rate of 96 %). The only error occurred for one instance of the *knocking on a door* motion, which was confused with the *waving goodbye* motion. This is not surprising. Indeed, when projecting these two motions on the first principal component of their respective model, one observes that the resulting trajectories are quite similar (both motions involve a principal oscillatory component). Thus, it can be difficult to classify them correctly using exclusively the time series after projection. The robustness of the system could be improved by comparing the principal components extracted from the test set with the ones extracted from the training set, in combination with HMM classification. The drawback is that the system would not be able to recognize a similar gesture performed in a different situation. For example, the principal components of an alphabet letter are not the same if the user writes it on a table or on a blackboard. After projection, the resulting signals are, however, similar and can be recognized by HMM.

Figures 8.1, 8.2 and 8.10 show the encoding and decoding of the six motions. As expected, two principal components are sufficient to represent the hand path when drawing each of the three letters, as well as when performing the knocking gesture. For waving and drinking, a single component is sufficient. Consistently, two principal components are sufficient to represent the joint trajectories when drawing the three

---

[2] See also Part I, Correspondence problems and mechanisms of this volume. –Ed.

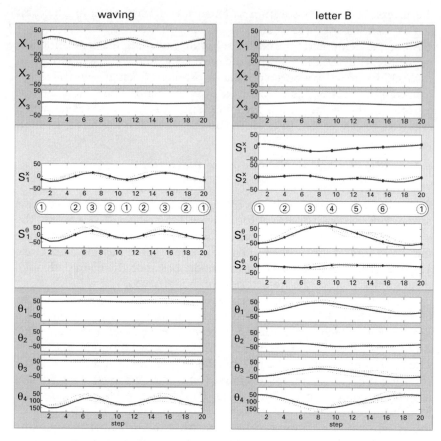

Figure 8.10 Demonstration, transformation by PCA, encoding in HMM and retrieval of the two different motions *waving goodbye* and *drawing letter B*. The five demonstrations in visual coordinates $\{\mathbf{X}_1, \mathbf{X}_2, \mathbf{X}_3\}$ and motor coordinates $\{\vec{\Theta}_1, \vec{\Theta}_2, \vec{\Theta}_3, \vec{\Theta}_4\}$ are represented by dotted lines. The retrieved generalized trajectory is in bold line.

letters of the alphabet, while only a single component is required to represent the gestures of waving, knocking and drinking.

The resulting signals for letter A, waving, knocking and drinking are modeled by HMMs of three states. Letter B is modeled with six states, and letter C with four states. The keypoints in the trajectories correspond roughly to inflexion points or relevant points describing the motion. The number of states found by the BIC criterion grows with the complexity of the signals modeled.

Figure 8.11 represents the values of the cost function $\mathcal{J}$, when testing the gestures of the test set with the different HMM models. The weights w_i

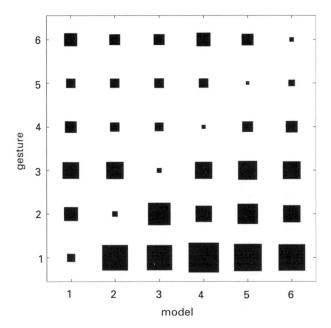

Figure 8.11 Cost function $\mathcal{J}_{tot}$, when testing the gestures of the test set with the different HMMs (the size of the square is proportional to $\mathcal{J}_{tot}$). Each row corresponds to a specific gesture: (1) drawing letter A, (2) drawing letter B, (3) drawing letter C, (4) waving goodbye, (5) knocking on a door, (6) drinking. These gestures are tested with the six corresponding models. For each row, the column with lowest value indicates what is the best model corresponding to the gesture.

found by the system are always quite similar for the motor and visual representations, which means that both representations could be used to reproduce the motion, with a slight preference for the visual representation. Indeed, we see in Figure 8.10 that there is not much difference between the variations of the signals in both representations. This could be due to the experimental setup, where the motions of the users are recorded in only one situation. In future experiments, different situations or environments should be used to provide more variations in one or the other dataset.

8.5   Discussion of the model

The combination of PCA and HMM is used successfully in our application to reduce the dimensionality of a dataset and to extract the primitives of a motion. Pre-processing of the data using PCA removes the noise and reduces the dimensionality of the dataset, making the HMM encoding more robust. The parameters of the whole model are then $\{\vec{v}^X, \vec{v}^\Theta, \vec{m}^X, \vec{m}^\Theta, \vec{\pi}, \mathbf{A}, \vec{\mu}, \vec{\sigma}\}$. This requires less parameters than HMM encoding of the raw data (see Inamura *et al.*, 2003; Calinon and Billard, 2004), as the number of output values and number of states are optimally reduced.

The advantage of encoding the signals in HMMs, instead of using a static clustering technique to recognize the signals retrieved by PCA, is that it provides a better generalization of the data, with an efficient representation robust to distortion in time. As an example, let us consider a situation where two demonstrators A and B raise a glass at the same time, but A drinks faster than B. The gesture is similar but the timing is different. In HMM, the differences in amplitude are fitted by a Gaussian, for each state and each variable. Using an HMM, the distortions in time are handled by using a probabilistic description of the transitions between the states, while a simple normalization in time would not have generalized correctly over the two demonstrations.

The model is general in the sense that no information concerning the data is encapsulated in the PCA preprocessing or in the HMM classification, which makes no assumption on the form of the dataset. However, extracting the statistical regularities is not the only means of identifying the relevant features in a task, and the statistical framework alone would probably require a large training set to learn a more complicated task. In further work, we will exploit the use of other machine-learning techniques to extract the optimal representation. In addition, we will consider the use of explicit pointers (e.g. speech) in combination with statistics, in order to extract the key features more robustly and more efficiently.

Finally, it would be interesting to extend the model to using asynchronous HMMs. Such models have been exploited successfully in speech processing to model the joint probability of pairs of asynchronous sequences describing the same sequence of events (e.g. visual lip reading and audio signals) (Bengio, 2004). It could be used in our application to learn and retrieve the best alignment between two sequences in visual and motor representations. This could be useful since the datasets are not always synchronized, but still needs to have correspondence between the different representations.

8.5.1   *Similarity with work in psychology and ethology*

Some of the features of our model bear similarities with those of theoretical models of animal imitation. These models often assume that data are correctly discretized, segmented and classified. By using PCA and HMM to encode the information, it is still possible to keep the elements of these frameworks that are relevant to a robotic system, offering at the same time a probabilistic description of the data, more suitable for a real-world application with robots.

Imitation using string parsing

R. W. Byrne has suggested the study of the cognitive processes underlying animal imitation by using string parsing to segment a continuous task into basic elements (Byrne, 1999). Imitating a task with a sequential or hierarchical organization of basic actions has been observed in species as diverse as rats and apes, to learn complex feeding skills. The process requires an effective segmentation of the elements, so that imitation learning becomes a practical method to acquire more complex skills from basic elements. Such a segmentation allows the reuse of known features, and the extraction of the underlying structure in the observed behavior (see Figure 8.12). If the whole task is perceived as a discrete sequence of items, the statistical regularities can be extracted, and the hierarchical structure is discovered by observing the same task several times.

Similarly, in a robotic system using PCA and HMM, the structure that underlies a sequence of elements can be acquired statistically by observing regularities across multiple demonstrations. Moreover, in the HMM learning algorithm, a discrete set of key features is extracted from a continuous flow of motion data, and the sequential organization of the key features is learned by the model. The structure of the observed behavior is described probabilistically by transition probabilities between the key features. By using a fully connected model, it is thus possible to extract statistically the sequential structure of a task, with recurring elements and optional parts that are not always needed. In our implementation, HMMs are used to find the key features in the trajectories, and learn gestures by extracting the regularities in the sequences. Two concurrent stochastic processes are involved, one modeling the sequential structure of the data, and one modeling the local properties of the data.

Associative sequence learning (ASL)

C. M. Heyes and E. D. Ray's associative sequence learning (ASL) mechanism (Heyes and Ray, 2000; Heyes, 2001) suggests that imitation requires an association between a model's action, as viewed from the imitator's point of view, and the corresponding imitator's action (see Figure 8.13). The vertical links between the sensory representation of the observed task and the motor representation are part of a repertoire, where elements can be added or refined. Associative sequence learning suggests

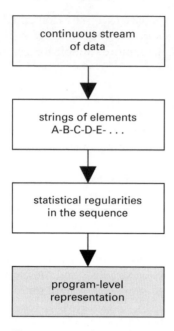

Figure 8.12 R. W. Byrne's string parsing imitation model (schema inspired from Byrne, 1999).

that the links are created essentially by experience, with a concurrent activation of sensory and motor representations. A few of them can also be innate, as biological data seem to indicate. The model pictures that the mapping between the sensory and motor representation can be associated with a higher level representation (boxes depicted in Figure 8.13).

The horizontal links model the successive activation of sensory inputs to learn the new task, which at the same time, activate the corresponding motor representation to copy the observed behavior. Repetitive activation of the same sequence strengthens the links to help motor learning. Depending on the complexity of task organization, numerous demonstrations may be needed to provide sufficient data to extract the regularities. The more data available, the more evident is the underlying structure of the task, i.e. to clarify which elements are essential, which are optional and which are variations in response to changing circumstances.

This stresses the need of a probabilistic framework in a robotic application that can extract invariants across multiple demonstrations. Such a model is in agreement with an HMM decomposition of the task, where

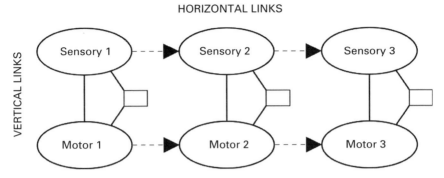

Figure 8.13 C. M. Heyes and E. D. Ray's associative sequence learning (ASL) model (schema inspired from Heyes, 2001).

the underlying structure is learned by using multiple demonstrations. If a given pattern appears frequently, its corresponding transition links are strengthened. If each action perceived by the imitator is also coded as an action that it can execute, the reproduction of a task can be considered. Any action that the imitator is able to perform can then also be recognized by observation of a model demonstrating the task.

Each hidden state in an HMM can output multimodal data. It can thus model multiple variables in different frames of reference. Its role is to make a link between the different datasets, and can be considered as a label or as a higher level representation common to the visual and motor data (see Figure 8.4). Indeed, in HMM, the sequence of states is not observed directly, but generates the visual or motor representation.

Thus, the architecture of a multivariate HMM has a horizontal process to associate the elements in a sequential order, by learning transition probabilities between the hidden states, and a vertical process that associates each sensory representation to appropriate motor representation, which is done through the hidden state. If data are missing from one part or the other (visual or motor representation), it is still possible to recognize a task and retrieve a generalization of the task in the other representation, if required.

By using a similar representation of the ASL model in Figure 8.13, our system focuses on learning the horizontal links. The vertical associations represented through the hidden states are still hard-coded, i.e. created by observing multiple demonstrations and specifying prior knowledge in the robot architecture (rescaling of the joint angles to fit the range of motion of the robot).

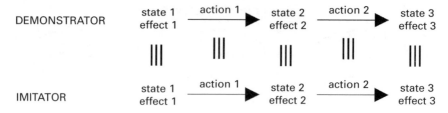

Figure 8.14 C. L. Nehaniv and K. Dautenhahn's algebraic framework to map states, effects and/or actions of the demonstrator and the imitator (schema inspired from Nehaniv and Dautenhahn, 2002).

Algebraic framework for the correspondence problem
The correspondence problem refers to the problem of creating an appropriate mapping between what is performed by the demonstrator and what is reproduced by the imitator. The two agents may not share the same embodiments (e.g. difference in limb lengths, sensors or actuators). Such correspondences can be constructed at various levels of granularity, reflecting the choice of a sequence of subgoals. C. L. Nehaniv and K. Dautenhahn have suggested a general algebraic framework (Nehaniv and Dautenhahn, 2001, 2002), to address the matching problem in both natural and artificial systems, and interpret the ASL model in this framework. It consists of representing the behavior performed by the demonstrator and imitator as two automata structures, with states and transitions. The *states* are the basic elements segmented from the whole task, that can produce *effects*, i.e. responses in the environment (e.g. object displaced), while an *action* is the transition from one state to another state.

An imitation process is defined as a partial mapping process (relational homomorphism) between the demonstrator and imitator states, effects, and actions. An observer (e.g. external observer, demonstrator or imitator) decides which of the states, actions or effects are the most important ones to imitate, by fixing an imitation metric. Different metrics are used to yield solutions to different correspondence problems. These metrics also allow the formal quantification of the success of an imitation.

This notation is closely related to the one used in our system. An HMM is an extension of the automata depicted in this algebraic framework. The difference is that these automata are described stochastically, and are thus more suitable to be used with noisy data in a real-world application. Each hidden state outputs probabilistically distributed values that can be seen as effects, and the equivalent of actions are the transitions between hidden states, also probabilistically defined. Note that encoding the data in HMM does not resolve the correspondence problem, but gives a suitable framework for its representation, to treat the *what to imitate* and *correspondence* problems in a common framework.

In further research, our work will address the correspondence problem paradigm (Nehaniv and Dautenhahn, 2000; 2001; 2002; Alissandrakis *et al.*, 2002). The contribution in our system would be to ensure a robust mapping between the two agents. In Alissandrakis *et al.*'s work, an external observer decides which mappings are relevant to the imitation, i.e. decides which of the states, the actions or the effects should be mapped. The similarity is measured by observer-dependent metrics.[3] The contribution of our work would be to extract the relevant features of a task from the statistical regularities across multiple demonstrations, instead of specifying them in advance.

8.6   Conclusion

This chapter has presented an implementation of an HMM-based system to encode, generalize, recognize and reproduce gestures, with representation of the data in visual and motor coordinates. The model has been tested and validated in a humanoid robot, using kinematics data of human motion.

The framework offers a stochastic method to model the process underlying gesture imitation. It makes a link between theoretical concepts and practical applications. In particular, it stresses the fact that the observed elements of a demonstration, and the organization of these elements, should be stochastically described to have a robust robot application that takes account of the high variability and the discrepancies across demonstrator and imitator points of view.

Acknowledgments

Thanks to the undergraduate students C. Dubach and V. Hentsch who helped to develop the motion tracking with x-sens and vision. This work was supported in part by the Swiss National Science Foundation, through grant 620-066127 of the SNF Professorships program, and by the European Commission Division FP6-IST Future and Emerging Technologies under Contract FP6-002020, Integrated Project COGNIRON.

---

[3] The algebraic framework for addressing the correspondence problem mentioned here can also be used with internally generated and internally assessed metrics. Indeed, the formulation of this framework explicitly takes into account "the observer (who may perhaps be the agent itself)" (Nehaniv and Dautenhahn, 2001, p. 21), so that the framework may also be applied for an internal observer (e.g. within an autonomous robot learning to solve a correspondence problem), as well as an external one. –Ed.

REFERENCES

Alissandrakis, A., Nehaniv, C. L. and Dautenhahn, K. (2002). Imitating with ALICE: learning to imitate corresponding actions across dissimilar embodiments. *IEEE Transactions on Systems, Man and Cybernetics, Part A: Systems and Humans*, **32(4)**, 482–96.

Bengio, S. (2004). Multimodal speech processing using asynchronous hidden Markov models. *Information Fusion*, **5(2)**, 81–9.

Billard, A., Epars, Y., Calinon, S., Cheng, G. and Schaal, S. (2004). Discovering optimal imitation strategies. *Robotics and Autonomous Systems*, **47(2–3)**, 69–77.

Billard, A. and Hayes, G. (1999). Drama, a connectionist architecture for control and learning in autonomous robots. *Adaptive Behavior*, **7(1)**, 35–64.

Billard, A. and Siegwart, R. (2004). Robot learning from demonstration. *Robotics and Autonomous Systems*, **47(2–3)**, 65–7.

Byrne, R. (1999). Imitation without intentionality: using string parsing to copy the organization of behaviour. *Animal Cognition*, **2**, 63–72.

Calinon, S. and Billard, A. (2004). Stochastic gesture production and recognition model for a humanoid robot. In *Proceedings of the IEEE/RSJ Intl Conference on Intelligent Robots and Systems (IROS), Sendai, Japan*, 2769–74.

Calinon, S., Guenter, F. and Billard, A. (2005). Goal-directed imitation in a humanoid robot. In *Proceedings of the IEEE Intl Conference on Robotics and Automation (ICRA), Barcelona, Spain*.

Demiris, J. and Hayes, G. (2001). Imitation as a Dual-Route Process Featuring Predictive and Learning Components: A Biologically Plausible Computational Model. In C. L. Nehaniv and K. Dautenhahn (eds.), *Imitation in Animals and Artifacts*, MIT Press, 327–61.

Dillmann, R. (2004). Teaching and learning of robot tasks via observation of human performance. *Robotics and Autonomous Systems*, **47(2–3)**, 109–16.

Heyes, C. (2001). Causes and consequences of imitation. *Trends in Cognitive Sciences*, **5**, 253–61.

Heyes, C. and Ray, E. (2000). What is the significance of imitation in animals? *Advances in the Study of Behavior*, **29**, 215–45.

Inamura, T., Toshima, I. and Nakamura, Y. (2003). Acquiring Motion Elements for Bidirectional Computation of Motion Recognition and Generation. In B. Siciliano and P. Dario (eds.), *Experimental Robotics VIII*, Springer-Verlag, 372–81.

Jolliffe, I. (1986). *Principal Component Analysis*. Springer-Verlag.

Nehaniv, C. L. and Dautenhahn, K. (2000). Of Hummingbirds and Helicopters: An Algebraic Framework for Interdisciplinary Studies of Imitation and Its Applications. In J. Demiris and A. Birk (eds.), *Interdisciplinary Approaches to Robot Learning*. World Scientific Press, 136–61.

Nehaniv, C. L. and Dautenhahn, K. (2001). Like me? – measures of correspondence and imitation. *Cybernetics and Systems: An International Journal*, **32(1–2)**, 11–51.

Nehaniv, C. L. and Dautenhahn, K. (2002). The Correspondence Problem. In C. L. Nehaniv and K. Dautenhahn (eds.), *Imitation in Animals and Artifacts*. Cambridge, MA: MIT Press, 41–61.

Rabiner, L. (1989). A tutorial on hidden Markov models and selected applications in speech recognition. *Proceedings of the IEEE*, **77(2)**, 257–85.

Schaal, S. (1999). Is imitation learning the route to humanoid robots? *Trends in Cognitive Sciences*, **3(6)**, 233–42.

Schaal, S., Ijspeert, A. and Billard, A. (2003). Computational approaches to motor learning by imitation. *Philosophical Transactions of the Royal Society of London: Series B, Biological Sciences*, **358(1431)**, 537–47.

Schwarz, G. (1978). Estimating the dimension of a model. *Annals of Statistics*, **6**, 461–4.

9 The dynamic emergence of categories through imitation

Tony Belpaeme, Bart de Boer and Bart Jansen

9.1 Introduction

Imitation is a powerful mechanism to culturally propagate and maintain knowledge and abilities. Not only humans rely heavily on imitation and social learning in general, but also animals such as dolphins, some bird species and some primates rely on imitation to acquire gestures and articulations (see e.g. Dautenhahn and Nehaniv, 2002b; Whiten and Ham, 1992). Studies on social learning in cognitive science have concentrated on mimicry, joint attention, the relationship between imitator and imitated, theory of mind, intentionality, speech (Kuhl and Meltzoff, 1996) and learning affordances of objects and tools (Tomasello, 1999). All these issues have been considered by artificial intelligence in constructing artefacts that learn from imitation, either in simulation (e.g. Alissandrakis *et al.*, 2001) or on robotic platforms (e.g. Kuniyoshi *et al.*, 1994; Gaussier *et al.*, 1998; Billard and Hayes, 1997; Schaal, 1999). In this chapter however we wish to pay attention to the role of the social medium in which imitation takes place. Often, imitation is considered to take place only between two agents: one acts as teacher and the other as student. The teacher is in possession of a full repertoire of gestures, actions or articulations, which the student has to acquire through imitation learning. This is of course a valid approach when one is interested in the paradigm of imitation to program artefacts by demonstration (Bakker and Kuniyoshi, 1996). However, when studying imitation from a broader perspective, including aspects such as the propagation of learned behaviour, it is also necessary to take into account the social setting, or rather the population, in which imitation occurs. This chapter attempts to lay bare the issues that are concerned with imitation in agent populations, presents the theoretical framework of our experiments and results from experiments on robots.

Imitation and Social Learning in Robots, Humans and Animals, ed. Chrystopher L. Nehaniv and Kerstin Dautenhahn. Published by Cambridge University Press.
© Cambridge University Press 2007.

9.2   Towards imitation in populations

Often imitation in artefacts is studied as a one-way relationship between teacher and student. The teacher, be it a human or an artificial system, possesses a repertoire of behaviour which the student has to acquire (e.g. Kuniyoshi *et al.*, 1994; Billard and Matarić, 2001). However, imitation in a teacher–student relationship addresses only a sub-set of the issues surrounding imitation. Teacher–student imitation is a powerful approach for building intelligent systems, and occurs in humans (in learning social behaviour, tool use, language, etc.) and animals such as higher primates (learning tool affordances in chimpanzees for example). However, it does not tackle some issues that are fundamental to more basic imitation, such as the emergence of roles, the transition from non-imitative behaviour to imitative behaviour, the construction of a repertoire of behaviours through imitation, the propagation of imitated behaviour in a population, and the stability of imitated behaviour over time. In this chapter we will re-evaluate these issues related to imitation between two agents and extend them to study imitation on a population level.

Alissandrakis *et al.* (2003, 2004, Chapter 12, this volume) in a similar manner study the social transmission of behaviours in a chain of imitating agents. However, the focus in Alissandrakis' work lies on the transmission of behaviours across dissimilar embodiments, and not on studying what behaviour could emerge in a group of agents that culturally transmit behaviours.

Dautenhahn and Nehaniv (2002a) summarized the issues for imitating agents in five central questions: *Whom* to imitate? *When* to imitate? *What* to imitate? *How to map* observed behaviour onto an internal representation and eventually onto imitated behaviour. And, *how to evaluate* the quality of the imitation. In the simplest teacher–student scenarios, often only the question of *how* to map observed behaviour onto an internal representation and onto imitated behaviour is addressed. The other questions are then resolved by carefully defining the roles of the agents and the rules of their interactions. When one studies imitation without any prior assumptions, all the above questions have to be addressed. The only situation in which all five questions can be attended to is in a multi-agent setting. For this reason we study imitation in a population of agents – i.e. artificial individuals – where no roles or target repertoires of behaviours are pre-defined. In order to facilitate the work, some rules of interaction are pre-defined, but one of the aims of the research is to determine which rules have to be defined beforehand, and which can be emergent.

9.2.1   Agents

In our studies, a population consists of agents with each agent having the following seven properties:

(1) An agent needs to be able to solve the correspondence problem: perceived behaviour should be mapped appropriately onto the imitator's body coordinates. The correspondence problem might be a challenge when the population is heterogeneous. If agents have different embodiments, for example when the population consists of both robots and humans, the mapping between robot behaviour and human behaviour, and vice versa, is far from trivial. The correspondence problem can be viewed at different levels: states could be imitated, or action sequences, or goals or a combination of these three (see Nehaniv and Dautenhahn, 2000).

(2) Each agent has to implement a category membership function: when behaviour is observed it should be matched to representations of previously observed behaviour.

(3) The agents should engage in imitative interactions, i.e. the agent should have some behaviour which facilitates imitation. This might be very minimal. In our work we do not wish to elaborate on the origins of imitative behaviour, therefore our agents are already endowed with mechanisms for observing actions, categorizing actions (using techniques such as dynamic time warping[1]), and producing actions (see Section 9.2.1).

(4) The action space in which actions are observed and performed is a continuous action space. Though this is not a requirement to study imitation in artificial systems (Alissandrakis et al., 2001), a continuous action space is interesting as actions are temporal sequences with noise on the perception and execution. The noise level will influence the successful acquisition of new actions. An important problem that has to be solved in a system with a continuous space of possible actions is how to make the transition from the continuous space of possibilities to a discrete number of action categories (see e.g. Oudeyer, 2002).

(5) The agents have no specific role in the population. Each agent can be either the initiator or the imitator; instead turn taking – not necessarily between the same agents – is used.

---

[1] Dynamic time warping is a technique for warping the time axes of two time series in such a way that corresponding events appear at the same moment on a common time axis. This alignment procedure allows the two time series to be more easily compared. For an introduction to this and other techniques for sequence comparison, see Sankoff and Kruskal (1983). –Ed.

(6) All agents start out as *tabulae rasae*. The action repertoire is com-
    pletely bootstrapped through interactions with other agents.
(7) A source of innovation is needed for the agents to explore new actions.
    Agents explore the action space by performing a random action. If
    other agents pick up such an action, it might propagate through the
    population. This implies that other agents need to assess whether an
    action is to be learned or not. If a game fails and the action used was
    successful in the past, a new action is created, rather than modifying
    the existing action.

Implementation of an agent

Each agent has a way to perceive actions of others and has a way to
express stored representations of actions. In order to store representations
an agent has two 'memories', one memory serves to store observations
of actions, the other stores representations for expressing actions. The
agent can translate observations to action representations by using inverse
kinematics; when an agent is, for example, using a robot arm, the inverse
kinematics translate a trajectory of observed 3-D coordinates to a series
of motor commands for the arm. An association between an observation
and an action is called a category in our framework. Each category c is
the combination of one observation o and one action a: $c = \{o, a\}$ (see
Figure 9.1). Together with the action and the observation, usage and
success counters are maintained as well.

Actions are executed with a commercially available robot arm which has
six degrees of freedom of which four are used in the experiments. Actions
are represented as a start position and an end position. These actions are
observed as a time series of arm positions using a vision system. The vision
system uses colour templates to find the gripper of the arm and stereo
vision to obtain depth information. As observations are time series of
points in 3-D space, they can be compared using dynamic time warping
(DTW). This way, observations can be categorized by comparing the
observation of every category in the repertoire with the new observation
using DTW. The category with the best matching observation will be the
category of the new observation.

9.2.2   Imitation games

As agents need to engage in imitative interactions, we impose a simple interaction on the agents; this interaction is dubbed the 'imitation
game'. An imitation game is played between two agents: one acting as
the initiator, the other as the imitator. The initiator executes an action
that is observed by the imitator. The imitator maps this onto an internal

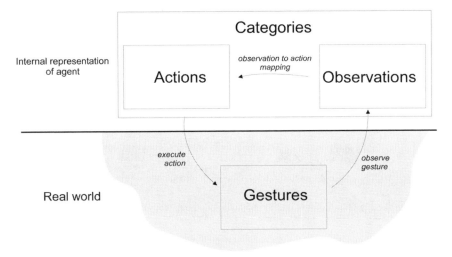

Figure 9.1 An agent has categories; each category is made up of an action and an observation. Actions can be expressed as gestures in the real world, and observing these gestures results in observations. An observation in turn can be mapped onto categories using inverse kinematics (Jansen *et al.*, 2004b).

representation and tries to repeat the observed action, not by mimicking the observed action, but by executing the action through mapping its internal representation onto motor actions. The initiator then gives feedback on how well the imitation succeeded. The feedback is then used by the imitator to refine its internal representation so that later imitations are expected to be more successful.

The imitation game is played between two agents, one initiator and one imitator, randomly picked from the population. The game follows five steps (see Figure 9.2):

(1) At the beginning of every game both agents can add a new random category to their repertoire. This is done with a very small probability. The initiator starts the actual game by demonstrating an action randomly picked from its repertoire of already learned categories. If the repertoire is empty, a new random category is added first.

(2) This action is observed by the imitator, and the observation is matched to the observations of the categories in its repertoire. The observed action is categorized as the category with best matching observation.

(3) The action of this category is then executed by the imitator using the robot arm.

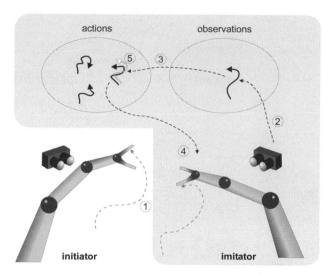

Figure 9.2 Schematic outline of the imitation game.

(4) The initiator observes this imitation and categorizes it as the category with best matching observation from its own repertoire. The imitation is successful if the category initially selected is the same as the category of the observed behaviour. The initiator provides feedback to the imitator on whether the imitation matches the demonstrated action or not.

(5) Depending on this feedback, both agents adapt their internal representation of the action to be more successful in the future. This adaptation consists of shifting the action representation to better resemble what was observed during phase 1. Moreover, categories that have proven not to be successful in past interactions are removed from the repertoire and categories that are very similar are merged into a single category.

9.2.3   *Embodiment*

It is important that experiments on imitation in artefacts be implemented on robots and not just in simulation. Theories of learning and imitation, especially when imitation takes place in a population, are typically very complex. Testing these theories is therefore not always possible with traditional 'pen-and-paper' analysis. This is where computer simulations prove to be extremely useful. However, in computer simulations it is often possible to ignore detail that is considered irrelevant for the problem at hand, and to implement a much-simplified model. Because of the

Figure 9.3 Agents use a robot arm to execute actions and a stereo camera to observe actions.

complex dynamics of learning and imitation, this might result in throwing out the baby with the bath water. Therefore we argue for also doing experiments with robots that operate in the real world. In a real-world situation it is harder to, inadvertently or not, cut corners (for a defense of robot modelling see Webb, 2001). Both methods, simulations and robot experiments, complement each other in important ways. However, eventually it should be shown that models of learning and imitation work in the real world. Especially with the recent availability of off-the-shelf actuators and perception systems this has become feasible, as researchers can now concentrate on the cognitive aspects rather than on the details of robotics. Figure 9.3 shows the robotic setup used in our experiments; as there is only one camera and one robot arm, the equipment is alternately shared by the agents.

9.2.4   Self-organization

Through the population dynamics the emerging action repertoire will become shared throughout the population. Yet, the repertoire will only consist of actions that are well-imitated. Actions that are not transferred to other agents will, under influence of the imitation game, die out. This is a self-organizing system, and just like any other self-organizing system it has two components: random fluctuation (implemented in the exploration of agents creating random actions) and positive feedback (the success of the imitation game given by the initiator to the imitator) (Steels, 2000). This feedback causes pressure on the action repertoire to be imitable. This self-organizing effect eventually yields a coherent and shared repertoire of actions throughout the population.

9.3   Imitation and communication

Experience with imitation in a different domain, namely the emergence of vowel systems, has led us to believe that cultural learning of repertoires of actions through imitation is feasible. The aim of the experiments in de Boer (2000) was to investigate the role of self-organization in determining the universal tendencies of sound systems as used by human languages. For this, a computer model was used in which a repertoire of vowel signals emerged in a population of agents. The main behaviour responsible was imitation, coupled with a drive to imitate the other agents as well as possible with a repertoire of sounds that was as large as possible. This emergence was caused by imitation. Agents in the population tried to imitate (the sounds of) the other agents as accurately as possible. At the same time they tried to increase the size of their repertoires of sounds. As vowel sounds are both easiest to implement in a computer model and best investigated by linguists, these were the speech signals of choice. Each agent in the population was a priori able to produce and perceive vowel sounds in a human-like way, but each agent also started out *tabula rasa*. As all agents were identical, the same inverse (kinematic) mapping between perception and action could be used. Through repeated interactions aimed at imitation and occasional random insertions, shared vowel systems emerged. An agent could extend its repertoire of vowels when imitation failed (this was therefore used as a means of novelty detection). It was found that the emerging vowel systems were realistic in the sense that they were very much like the vowel systems that are found in human languages.

Individual agents discover vowel categories through learning of articulatory and acoustic prototypes. Acoustic as well as articulatory prototypes are represented by low-dimensional vectors, and with each vowel category, both an acoustic and an articulatory prototype are associated. In response to either success or failure of imitation, prototypes can be moved, merged, removed or added. It must be stressed that the learning procedure is not biologically inspired, but was specifically designed for this task (the imitation game).

These experiments showed that it is indeed possible to have a repertoire of shared actions (in this case, vowel articulations) emerge in a population of agents that imitate each other. No roles or action repertoires were predefined in the population. This shows that successful imitation can emerge without explicit teacher–student relations defined beforehand. The fact that not just random systems emerged, but systems that showed remarkable similarities to human vowel systems demonstrates that even though action categories are not defined beforehand, only a limited set of possible sets of categories can stably emerge. The stability of potential sets is determined by the constraints of perception and production, but also by how well the learned systems conform to what is already present in the population, and by the relative positions of the action categories within a system. Such constraints cannot necessarily be determined beforehand and sometimes the constraints that do emerge are unexpected. It is therefore quite possible that given a certain experimental set-up, behaviours that have been defined a priori by a human operator are not stably transferable from a teacher to a student. In the case of emergent action categories, this problem is avoided.

The experiments with vowels showed that imitation is a feasible way of learning a shared repertoire of action categories in a population. A number of corners have been cut in these experiments in order to make them work. Most notably, production and perception were rather simplified with respect to the real thing. The experiments on robots, described here, implement a very similar imitation game, with gestures rather than vowels, on a real robot arm.

9.4   Experimental results

9.4.1   Monitoring performance

While monitoring an experimental run, several measures are used. One measure is the imitative success, the average number of successful imitation games over the last $n = 100$ games. Initially, the imitative success will be high. This is due to the nature of the imitation game: if an agent has only one category, any observation will match that category and the imitation game will be a success. However, for the experiment to succeed, the imitative success has to stay high during the entire run. A second measure is the number of categories, which tracks the running average ($n = 100$) of the number of categories in a population. Another very informative measure is the category variance, which gives an idea of how similar the categories of agents are. It is defined in Eq. (9.1) and measures the distance between the categories of two agents A and B. a and b are the respective categories of agent A and B, while $|A|$ and $|B|$ are the number of categories of agents A and B. The distance function $d(a, b)$ used here is dynamic time warping on the observations associated with the categories.

$$CV(A, B) = \frac{\sum\limits_{a \in A} \min\limits_{b \in B} d(a, b) + \sum\limits_{b \in B} \min\limits_{a \in A} d(a, b)}{|A| + |B|} \qquad (9.1)$$

The average category variance $\overline{CV}$ for an entire population P consisting of N agents is given in Eq. (9.2):

$$\overline{CV}(P) = \frac{2}{N(N-1)} \sum_{i=1}^{N-1} \sum_{j=i+1}^{N} CV(A_i, A_j) \qquad (9.2)$$

A fourth measure, the information flow, gives an idea of the complexity of the categorical repertoire that is successfully transmitted. For this we take an information theoretical viewpoint and consider the initiator to be a source of information, the perception and production of actions is the noisy channel and the imitator is the destination. The communication can succeed or fail, depending on the success of the imitation game. The information flow for a single game is defined as:

$$I = \begin{cases} \log_2(|A|) & \text{if the game succeeds} \\ 0 & \text{if the game fails} \end{cases} \qquad (9.3)$$

The information flow is the running average of I, averaged over the entire population. It is expressed in bits. The more behaviours a population successfully imitates, the higher the information flow will be.

9.4.2   Results

The following figures show results from imitation games on robotic agents. In de Boer (2000, 2001), Jansen (2003) and Jansen *et al.* (2003) it is shown how the imitation game performs in populations of simulated agents, but the imitation game also translates well to actual robots. Figure 9.4 shows results from a run on two robots (only two robotic agents are considered in this experiment, as more agents would make the experiment prohibitively slow), where both take turns at being the initiator and imitator. The agents play a total of 50 000 imitation games. Figure 9.4(a) shows the imitative success, which is stable over the duration of run, meaning that the agents build a repertoire of actions that is properly imitable. Figure 9.4(b) shows the number of categories created.

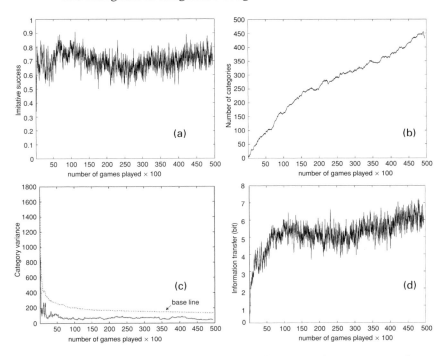

Figure 9.4 Results for 50 000 imitation games between two robots; (a) the imitative success, (b) the number of categories created, (c) the variance between categories of the agents and (d) the amount of information transferred between agents expressed in bits.

Note that the number of categories appears to increase linearly with time. In fact the increase slows over time and approaches a maximum number, limited by the accuracy with which categories can be distinguished. As categories could be distinguished very accurately in the simulation, the maximum number was not reached in the time the robot setup was run (the experiment lasted for several weeks). In simulations it was shown that this limit is reached (see Figure 9.5) just as a finite number of vowels emerged from de Boer's simulations (de Boer, 2000). Figure 9.4(c) shows the category variance, indicating how the categories of both agents over time adapt to be similar; this occurred without the agents resorting to any explicit exchange of their representations.[2] The coherence of their internal representations is merely caused by imitating each other. Finally, Figure 9.4(d) shows the information transfer: this is an information theoretic measure, expressed in bits, for the amount of information

---

[2] A baseline category variance is shown as well. The baseline is the category variance which is to be expected if the agents had random categories instead of the ones they have learnt.

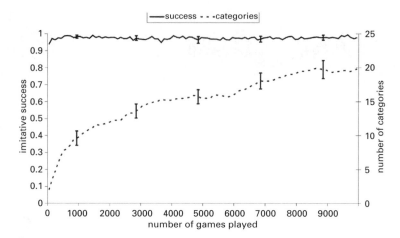

Figure 9.5 Imitative success and number of actions learnt in a simulation of the imitation game.

the agents can transfer with their actions. The increasing information flow shows that the agents arrive at a complex and functional repertoire of actions.

9.5   Discussion

We have argued for experiments that take a broader perspective on imitation than is generally assumed in experiments on imitation in artefacts, or even in much research on imitation in animals and humans. Often fixed roles of student and teacher are assumed, as well as a fixed repertoire that has to be transferred. Although many cases of social learning occurring in humans, apes and monkeys are of this kind, it is just a subset of the whole problem of imitation. When imitating other agents, in general an agent also has to decide what to imitate and when to imitate, and possibly also which other agents to imitate. When doing this, it has to solve the problems of the correspondence between observed actions and actions it can perform itself, of the identity between different actions, of role taking, and when imitation fails, of how to invent a new action itself. Having a repertoire of actions emerge in a population of agents circumvents the problem of implementing behaviours in a teaching agent that cannot be learned reliably by a student agent. It is very hard to determine beforehand, given the actuators, sensors and learning mechanism of an agent, what behaviours it can and cannot learn. It is therefore quite possible to design a teacher-and-student experiment that is bound to fail. When behaviours are emergent, only imitable action repertoires will emerge. These can always be used later in a teacher–student setting. In this respect emergence of behaviours in a population through imitation is not just a super-set of teacher–student imitation, but might be a necessary precursor.

The difficulty however, which was not addressed here, is the emergence of 'useful' behaviour instead of mere gestures. Our mechanism does not guarantee that the behaviour that propagates in the population is useful according to any criterion. In order for behaviour to be useful, semantics and goals should be attributed to behaviours and their propagation should depend not only on their ease of being imitated, but also on their success in transmitting information or their success in accomplishing goals (Jansen *et al.*, 2004a).

The scenario that was introduced for investigating this is the imitation game in a population of agents. All agents in the population start without a repertoire of actions (*tabula rasa*) and have to develop a repertoire of actions that they can imitate from each other (it has been shown in simulation that such a set-up works for agents that have to develop a set of shared speech sounds).

In order to avoid inadvertently cutting corners, it is necessary to show that the set-up also works with a population of robots. Simulations are definitely useful for developing the theory, but eventually one has to show that the theory also works in the real world. For this, we have worked on experiments that employ off-the-shelf robotic components to implement an imitation game for gestures. In such a robotic setting, problems of noise, calibration, handling time-series data, detecting novelty and measuring category membership make the problem of imitation much more challenging. But such a setting also confronts the researcher with a better assessment of where the real difficulties are with imitation. Also, the constraints of perception and articulation limit what repertoires of actions can successfully be learned and transferred. Thus robotic work automatically takes into account that an agent's abilities are not only limited by its cognitive system, but also by its embodiment.

We hope that the views expressed here and the accompanying experiments have provided material for discussing the issues surrounding imitation in populations, and the use of robots and simulations for investigating them.

Acknowledgments

The authors wish to thank Bart De Vylder for his valuable input. Tony Belpaeme is a postdoctoral fellow of the Flemish Fund for Scientific

Research (FWO – Vlaanderen). Bart Jansen is sponsored by a grant from the Institute for the Promotion of Innovation by Science and Technology in Flanders (IWT). This work was in part conducted within the EU Integrated Project COGNIRON (FP6-IST-002020).

REFERENCES

Alissandrakis, A., Nehaniv, C. L. and Dautenhahn, K. (2001). Through the looking-glass with ALICE – trying to imitate using correspondences. In Balkenius, C., Zlatev, J., Kozima, H., Dautenhahn, K. and Breazeal, C. (eds.), *Proceedings of the First International Workshop on Epigenetic Robotics: Modeling Cognitive Development in Robotic Systems, Lund University Cognitive Studies. September 17–18, 2001, Lund, Sweden*, Vol. 85.

Alissandrakis, A., Nehaniv, C. L. and Dautenhahn, K. (2003). Synchrony and perception in robotic imitation across embodiments. In *IEEE International Symposium on computational intelligence in robotics and automation (CIRA '03)*, 923–30.

Alissandrakis, A., Nehaniv, C. L. and Dautenhahn, K. (2004). Towards robot cultures? Learning to imitate in a robotic arm test-bed with dissimilar embodied agents. *Interaction studies: Social behaviour and communication in biological and artificial systems*, 5, 3–44.

Bakker, P. and Kuniyoshi, Y. (1996). Robot see, robot do: an overview of robot imitation. In *Proceedings of the AISB Workshop on Learning in Robots and Animals, Brighton, UK, April 1996*, 3–11.

Billard, A. and Hayes, G. (1997). Transmitting communication skills through imitation in autonomous robots. In Birk, A. and Demiris, Y. (eds.), *Proceedings of EWLR97, Sixth European Workshop on Learning Robots*. Brighton, UK, July 1997.

Billard, A. and Matarić, M. J. (2001). Learning human arm movements by imitation: evaluation of a biologically inspired connectionist architecture. *Robotics and Autonomous Systems*, 37(2–3), 145–60.

Dautenhahn, K. and Nehaniv, C. L. (2002a). The agent-based perspective on imitation. In Dautenhahn, K. and Nehaniv, C. L. (eds.), *Imitation in Animals and Artifacts*. Cambridge, MA: MIT Press, 1–40.

Dautenhahn, K. and Nehaniv, C. L. (eds.) (2002b). *Imitation in Animals and Artifacts*. Cambridge, MA: MIT Press.

de Boer, B. (2000). Self-organisation in vowel systems. *Journal of Phonetics*, 28(4), 441–65.

de Boer, B. (2001). *The Origins of Vowel Systems*. Oxford, UK: Oxford University Press.

Gaussier, P., Moga, S., Quoy, M. and Banquet, J.-P. (1998). From perception-action loops to imitation processes: a bottom-up approach of learning by imitation. *Applied Artificial Intelligence*, 12(7–8), 701–27.

Jansen, B. (2003). An imitation game for emerging action categories. In Banzhaf, W., Christaller, T., Dittrich, P., Kim, J. T. and Ziegler, J. (eds.), *Advances in Artificial Life, 7th European Conference on Artificial Life (ECAL 2003)*,

Dortmund, Germany, Vol. 2801 of *Lecture Notes in Computer Science*. Berlin: Springer, 800–9.

Jansen, B., de Boer, B. and Belpaeme, T. (2004a). You did it on purpose! Towards intentional embodied agents. In Iida, F., Pfeifer, R., Steels, L. and Kuniyoshi, Y. (eds.), *Embodied Artificial Intelligence*. Berlin: Springer, 271–7.

Jansen, B., De Vylder, B., Belpaeme, T. and de Boer, B. (2003). Emerging shared action categories in robotic agents through imitation. In Dautenhahn, K. and Nehaniv, C. L. (eds.), *Second International Symposium on Imitation in Animals and Artifacts 2003*. The Society for the Study of Artificial Intelligence and the Simulation of Behavior, 145–52.

Jansen, B., ten Thij, T., Belpaeme, T., De Vylder, B. and de Boer, B. (2004b). Imitation in embodied agents results in self-organization of behavior. In Schaal, S., Ijspeert, A. J., Billard, A. and Vijayakumar, S. (eds.), *From Animals to Animats: Proceedings of the 8th Conference on the Simulation of Adaptive Behavior*. Cambridge, MA: The MIT Press.

Kuhl, P. K. and Meltzoff, A. N. (1996). Infant vocalizations in response to speech: vocal imitation and developmental change. *The Journal of the Acoustical Society of America*, **100(4)**, 2425–38.

Kuniyoshi, Y., Inaba, M. and Inoue, H. (1994). Learning by watching: extracting reusable task knowledge from visual observation of human performance. *IEEE Transactions on Robotics and Automation*, **10(6)**, 799–822.

Nehaniv, C. L. and Dautenhahn, K. (2000). The correspondence problem. In Dautenhahn, K. and Nehaniv, C. (eds.), *Imitation in Animals and Artifacts*. Cambridge, MA: MIT Press, 41–61.

Oudeyer, P.-Y. (2002). Phonemic coding might be a result of sensory-motor coupling dynamics. In Hallam, J. (ed.), *Proceedings of the 7th International Conference on the Simulation of Adaptive Behavior*. Cambridge, MA: MIT Press, 406–16.

Sanleoff, D. and Kruskal, J. B. (1983). Time Warps, String Edits, and Macromolecules: The Theory and Practice of Sequence Comparison, Reading, MA: Addison-Wesley.

Schaal, S. (1999). Is imitation learning the route to humanoid robots? *Trends in Cognitive Sciences*, **3(6)**, 233–42.

Steels, L. (2000). Language as a complex adaptive system. In Schoenauer, M., Deb, K., Rudolph, G., Yao, X., Lutton, E., Merelo, J. J. and Schwefel, H.-P. (eds.), *Proceedings of Parallel Problem Solving from Nature VI*, Lecture Notes in Computer Science. Berlin, Germany: Springer.

Tomasello, M. (1999). *The cultural origins of human cognition*. Cambridge, MA: Harvard University Press.

Webb, B. (2001). Can robots make good models of biological behavior? *Behavioral and Brain Sciences*, **24(6)**, 1033–50.

Whiten, A. and Ham, R. (1992). On the nature and evolution of imitation in the animal kingdom: reappraisal of a century of research. In Slater, P., Rosenblatt, J., Beer, C. and Milinski, M. (eds.), *Advances in the Study of Behavior*, Vol. 21. San Diego, CA: Academic Press, 239–83.

Part IV

Development and embodiment

Imitation plays an important part in social and cognitive development of humans and possibly could also do so for artifacts (Dautenhahn, 1995). This section is concerned with issues of embodiment and development of imitative capabilities in infants, people with autistic spectrum disorder and robots. The first chapter links, in a developmental sense, the imitation of body movements to learning about the meaning of actions and mental states of others, a prerequisite for the transmission and communication of mental states ('mind-reading'). Studying imitation skills in people with autistic spectrum disorders, who show impairments in social understanding and imitation, is hoped to shed light on the role of imitation in social cognition. The second chapter discusses a four-stage model of imitative abilities in infants in the context of a formal framework aimed at implementing robotic imitators. The stages range through learning about controlling one's own body, to imitation of body movements and actions on objects, to learning about inferring others' intentions and goals. The final chapter addresses the correspondence problem that robotic imitators need to solve when mapping observed behaviour (of possibly dissimilarly embodied models) to their own behaviours. In simulation studies conditions of synchrony, perceptual and proprioceptive matching, as well as cultural transmission of skills are investigated. Moreover, the bodies of the imitators may also grow and change, and the effect of this is studied. The three chapters range from developmental studies with humans to interdisciplinary work on robotic imitators inspired by developmental models and approaches. The latter is related to the area of robot 'programming by demonstration' that has attracted much attention in the machine-learning and robotics community. Robots that learn by imitation flexibly, efficiently and (last but not least) socially, open up the possibility of a new generation of adaptive intelligent robots, which at the same time could serve as interesting tools for the study of

Imitation and Social Learning in Robots, Humans and Animals, ed. Chrystopher L. Nehaniv and Kerstin Dautenhahn. Published by Cambridge University Press.
© Cambridge University Press 2007.

imitative capabilities in animals and artifacts (cf. Part VII, Social feed-back, this volume).

Justin H. G. Williams discusses the role of imitation in social cognitive development in the context of fMRI brain imaging studies involving people with autistic spectrum disorder (ASD) and controls. Williams argues that in order to successfully imitate, one must have a set of motor skills in common with the model. This pre-existing action repertoire must be sufficiently developed in order to be receptive to a new skill being observed. During imitation the pre-existing actions are modified and further developed influenced by observed actions. According to Williams the same applies to the communication of mental states that are viewed as a skill that develops through imitation. Importantly, a mind-reader needs to represent a perceived action as a modification of an action category, e.g. to represent a broad smile as a member of the categories of smiles rather than a completely novel action unrelated to what is known.[1] In order to appreciate the meaning and mental state associated with a broad smile it must be related to a 'generic' smile. An inability to form such secondary representations can severely limit the scope of grasping the underlying 'meaning' of actions and might thus lead to symptoms we find in ASD. Results from neuroimaging studies provide support for this argument showing that for ASD subjects, differently from controls, brains areas are activated that, in control subjects, are involved in conditioned visuo-motor learning tasks. Thus, copying in ASD subjects seems to occur on the level of behavioural transmission, rather than the transmission of mental states. This distinction raises interesting issues regarding possible studies in developmental robotics: how robots can grasp the 'meaning' of what they perceive, let alone the meaning of social interactions, still remains a hard problem where brain imaging and neurobiological studies might bridge the gap between levels of sensory processing on the one hand, and a 'theory of mind' on the other (see Part II, Mirroring and 'mind-reading', in this volume).

In the second chapter of this section Rajesh P. N. Rao, Aaron P. Shon and Andrew N. Meltzoff try to bridge the gap between models of imitative abilities in children and implementations in robots. In the first part of the chapter the four-stage model of imitative abilities, as proposed by Meltzoff and Moore (see Meltzoff, 2002), is revisited in light of experimental results on imitative learning abilities in infants. The first stage, body babbling, that can begin in utero, allows the infant to map out an internally represented 'act space'. Mapping body

---

[1] It is interesting to compare the work by T. Belpaeme *et al.* (Chapter 9 of this volume) describing mechanisms for the emergence of categories via imitation in robotic imitators.

movements to goal states is a precursor of stage two where infants demonstrate body movement imitation whereby body states observed in the model are mapped to the imitator's own body. Newborns show imitation of facial acts that they have not seen before, they are able to correct their actions without feedback, and demonstrate not only immediate but also delayed imitation. Once infants, at around 1–1.5 years old, are able to imitate actions on objects (stage three), a new realm of possible interactions and learning scenarios are enabled, including learning and cultural transmission of tool use. The fourth stage considers imitation involving the inference of other's intentions. Eighteen-month olds have been shown to infer a model's intention and attribute goals. When observing a 'failed demonstration' they are thus able to respond with the 'correct answer' although they haven't seen it themselves. Goals and intentions are attributed to people, but interestingly, not to inanimate devices (as already demonstrated 10 years ago with a simple robot serving as a model). The second part of the chapter discusses a formalization of this four-stage model in light of a probabilistic framework for learning and inference. Such a framework would allow the programming of robots to show imitative abilities similar to infants. To illustrate the framework, a simple maze navigation problem is simulated in a 2-D environment.

The final chapter in this section by Aris Alissandrakis and his collaborators picks up on three issues relevant to imitation that were touched upon in the previous chapter: the correspondence problem, cultural transmission of skills acquired by imitation and the role of embodiment. The problem of how an imitator maps (sequences of) states, actions or effects observed in a model to its own body is known as the correspondence problem (Nehaniv and Dautenhahn, 2002); see Part I, Correspondence problem and mechanisms, this volume. An implemented generic framework called ALICE is used and studied in two different testbeds: 'Chessworld' and 'Rabit'. In the latter, simulated robotic arms can learn by imitation from a model that can have a different type of body with different numbers of joints, etc. Different metrics are used to evaluate the similarity between the behaviours of imitator and model. Such work is motivated by the challenge of robots trying to imitate humans (where necessarily the embodiment will differ – along a spectrum of some similarities in the case of humanoid robots or very few similarities e.g. when using mobile mechanistic robot platforms). Similar problems are being faced e.g. in studies where dolphins imitate humans (e.g. Herman, 2002) or where Grey parrots learn by imitation from humans (see Part VII, Social feedback, this volume). Animals such as dolphins and Grey parrots seemingly bridge the 'species gap' of dissimilar bodies, thus solving the correspondence problem naturally. Formalizing this problem and testing a computational framework is the target of this chapter. Results also show the impact of the following parameters on the imitation success: synchronization of imitator and model behaviour, including the imitator's proprioceptive information (information about its own states during observation of the model), and varying the degree of perceptual match between observed behaviour and previously encountered behaviour. Note that these parameters can be viewed as varying an agent's degree of embodiment (Dautenhahn *et al.*, 2002) with respect to the (social) environment which is relatively straightforward to manipulate, compared to studies with biological systems. The authors' framework also provides robustness of learning to changes in the imitator's embodiment, which may grow or otherwise change in the course of learning – an issue naturally faced in their course of ontogeny for biological social learners. Future work could test hypotheses gained from such studies with humans or other animals, and vice versa.

REFERENCES

Dautenhahn, K. (1995). Getting to know each other – artificial social intelligence for autonomous robots. *Robotics and Autonomous Systems*, **16**, 333–56.
Dautenhahn, K., Ogden, B. and Quick, T. (2002). From embodied to socially embedded agents – implications for interaction-aware robots. *Cognitive Systems Research*, **3(3)**, 397–428.
Herman, L. M. (2002). Vocal, social, and self-imitation by bottlenosed dolphins. In K. Dautenhahn and C. L. Nehaniv (eds.), *Imitation in Animals and Artifacts*. Cambridge, MA: MIT Press, 63–108.
Meltzoff, A. N. (2002). Elements of a developmental theory of imitation. In A. N. Meltzoff and W. Prinz (eds.), *The Imitative Mind: Development, Evolution, and Brain Bases*. Cambridge, UK: Cambridge University Press, 19–41.
Nehaniv, C. L. and Dautenhahn, K. (2002). The correspondence problem. In K. Dautenhahn and C. L. Nehaniv (eds.), *Imitation in Animals and Artifacts*. Cambridge, MA: MIT Press, 41–61.

10 Copying strategies by people with autistic spectrum disorder: why only imitation leads to social cognitive development

Justin H. G. Williams

10.1 Introduction

In neuroscience, if we wish to identify the brain areas that serve particular functions, a common approach is to study behaviour when part of the brain has been rendered inoperative as a result of injury or illness. By identifying the functional loss of a particular brain area, we can learn something about the role of that brain area in normal conditions. One problem with this approach is that it treats the brain as if its functional specialization was static rather than a dynamic and developing process. A brain area may feasibly serve a role in the development of a function, but lose that later in life. Therefore, we need to understand the processes that are necessary for the development of function and ask about the brain mechanisms that serve them. Then, if we can examine a condition in which those processes are impaired, and we can find the brain bases for that impairment, this might be a better way to appreciate the role of that brain area in serving the function in question. The way that we understand other people's thoughts may be a good case in point. It may be profitable to study the processes that contribute to the development of social understanding, if we are to understand its neural substrate in adulthood. Imitation seems likely to be one important developmental process, necessary for the acquisition of culture, language, knowledge and social cognitive abilities (Whiten *et al.*, 2003; Meltzoff and Moore, 1999). Also, Russon (1998) argues that in being necessary for the development of expertise, the ability to imitate is a crucial component of Machiavellian intelligence – those cognitive abilities required to co-operate and compete successfully with other human beings in a hierarchical struggle.

Autistic spectrum disorder (ASD) is associated with poor social understanding and an imitative deficit (Williams *et al.*, 2004; Rogers, 1999;

Imitation and Social Learning in Robots, Humans and Animals, ed. Chrystopher L. Nehaniv and Kerstin Dautenhahn. Published by Cambridge University Press.
© Cambridge University Press 2007.

Smith and Bryson, 1994) and so by studying imitation in autism, we hope to learn more about the role of imitation in the development of social cognition and the brain bases for these processes. Autistic spectrom disorder is now defined by a constellation of features characterized by pervasive and persistent impairments in social communication and reciprocity, and patterns of stereotyped and repetitive behaviours, from before the age of three years. This includes poor development of communicative processes that depend on actions such as voice, facial expression, gesture and eye contact to communicate mental states such as feelings. Actions and speech are often repetitive, stereotyped or ritualized and interests can also be very limited.

In this chapter, I will seek to present a synthesis of some of our recent research, along with some fresh analysis, that started with a theoretical consideration of the role of imitative psychopathology in the development of autistic spectrum disorder (Williams *et al.*, 2001). This was further considered in a systematic review of the literature investigating action-imitation in autism (Williams *et al.*, 2004) and then by an empirical study of action imitation using functional magnetic resonance neuroimaging (fMRI) in individuals with ASD (Williams *et al.*, 2006).

10.2   The imitative origins of mind-reading

In recent years, much interest has been shown in the possibility that specific neural mechanisms might exist that serve to relate perceptions of other individuals' actions and behaviours to those coding for the same actions and perceptions by the self, and that these mechanisms may be important for imitation (e.g. Hurley and Chater, 2004; Nehaniv & Dautenhahn, 2002). Others have argued that imitation is developmentally linked to 'theory of mind'. Meltzoff and Moore (1997) suggest that neonatal facial imitation depends upon the formation of representation through an 'active intermodal mapping' process, because the stimulus and response are not temporally coupled or compulsorily linked. Melzoff and Gopnik (1993) and Meltzoff and Decety (2003) consider how this connectivity between action and perception forms the bedrock of a 'like-me' equivalence system that is central in the development of theory of mind. Furthermore, such cross-modal matching of representations, may be necessary for the development of inter-subjective understanding and social communication (e.g. Meltzoff and Prinz, 2002). Rogers and Pennington (1991) suggested that problems with these self–other matching mechanisms at an early age may lie at the core of autism. Hobson (1990) also argued that inter-subjective impairment and an ability to identify with others was of primary importance in explaining the failure of children with autism to derive concepts of mind. More recently, Hobson and colleagues (Hobson and Lee, 1999; Hobson *et al.*, 2003), demonstrated the inability of children to imitate the force and speed of actions (what they term 'style') and therefore the potential importance of this aspect of action processing in the development of social cognition. They consider this to reflect an impairment in 'identification' processes between self and other.

Williams *et al.* (2001) noted the close relationships between 'theory of mind' and imitation. 'Theory of mind' is concerned with the ability to attribute mental states to others and is dependent on the ability to generate a mental representation of another person's mental state. Imitation may also be dependent upon generating representations of another's mental state if it is defined as the ability to incorporate the novel aspects of an observed action into the behavioural repertoire. This requires that the form of the action be copied but also that its purpose (goal) and context is understood. In this way it may depend upon the attribution of a mental state (intention) to the model.

'Theory of mind' and imitation may also be interdependent at higher cognitive levels. It has been argued that we understand the mental states of others through a process of mental simulation (Gordon, 1996). That is, when we observe the behaviour of others, which might include them providing a description of their experiences, we imagine that it was us that were behaving in that manner. We put ourselves in their shoes. In doing this, we imitate the other individual but through a process of simulation, with no overt behaviour. The following example was taken from the work of Jerry Fodor and was cited by Gordon (1996, p. 11).

In Shakespeare's 'A Midsummer Night's Dream', Lysander, cast under a magic spell abandons Hermia while she is asleep in the forest. When Hermia wakes up and doesn't find her lover beside her, she concludes that his rival Demetrius murdered Lysander. How do we understand her thinking in her coming to this conclusion? How does Hermia come to believe that Demetrius desired to kill Lysander to the point of committing the act? There are two ways that she could have reached such a conclusion. One is through logical reasoning: Lysander has to be murdered to be removed, Demetrius wants him removed and can murder him. The second is through placing herself in Demetrius's shoes and imagining herself in his position. She might imagine herself loving someone and having a rival for that love, even to the extent of imagining him loving herself and having Lysander for a rival. According to Gordon, "she would simulate Demetrius, using her own motivational and emotional resources, and her own capacity for practical reasoning, adjusted or calibrated as necessary."

So how do these joint processes develop? For an individual to successfully imitate behaviour, they must first have a set of common motor skills with the model, such that they have the capacity to make the change from their existing behavioural repertoire to incorporate the novel behaviour. For example, flint knapping is a skill that is slow to acquire and requires extensive training (Stout, 2002). Each stage of skill development cannot occur until the previous level is achieved. This means that for a model possessing a skill to be imitated, that skill is embedded as a modification of a pre-existing action repertoire. In order for it to be transmitted from model to student, the student must possess a pre-existing action repertoire that is sufficiently developed to be receptive to the new skill. Then, any cognitive representation that is transmitted through imitation has to be as a modification of a similar action repertoire, at least in respect of the action to be learnt, possessed by both teacher and student. If the student has not developed the requisite abilities when observing the novel action, it will not be possible to learn from it what the teacher intended. I would like to suggest that learning about mental state transmission is essentially the same process. Human beings communicate the patterns of neural activity that make up their thoughts by transmitting them as modifications of a commonly held action repertoire. I suggest that through developing a system that can process the language and actions of others, it is a natural consequence to develop the means to process the non-verbal cognitions such as intentions, desires and emotions, which are communicated as modifications of simpler actions. I will attempt to clarify this further in the following discussion of this developmental process.

The newborn infant tunes in to the communications going on all around it, some directed towards it and some directed elsewhere. When an infant imitates a motor act, for example a raising or lowering of the eyebrows, it utilizes a motor program to perform the action. This motor program corresponds to that in the brain of the model who executed the action the infant observed, in that model and infant both use the occipitofrontalis muscle innervated by the 7th cranial nerve. Therefore, if the infant can link the perception of the eyebrow movement to its motor programme for executing an eyebrow movement, the imitating infant has the rudiments of a system to know what neural processes are going on in the model's brain, by knowing the neural processes it has to perform to achieve imitation. By recreating even a very simple observed action (how it does this is considered further below), it generates a cognitive representation that corresponds to that operating in the mind of another individual. At this point two representations exist in the infant's brain as separate cognitive representations of perceived and executed actions that can become linked. Consequently, the infant can relate the representation of a perceived action to that required to execute the same action. The infant's motor abilities then develop, not in isolation of observing other's actions, but in tune with them, and so the action–perception matching system develops along with the motor skills. As the motor skills develop, so the ability to relate to behaviour shown by others becomes increasingly sophisticated.

This developmental process can lay down the foundations for self–other understanding and communication, whereby cognitive representations for action in two individuals can be connected through a language of action. Thoughts and feelings can then be transmitted as cognitive representations that modify more basic functional actions. The mental state of an individual affects the tone of the voice, the speed and force of body movements, the facial expression and tones of expression in language. In this example, surprise or concern affects the raising or lowering of the eyebrows. Through the course of development the communication of a mental state through eyebrow movement can then become increasingly sophisticated and subtle depending on the amount, the context and the concomitant use of other facial features. The point is that the communication of mental states is a skill that, like others, is developed through imitation and as such depends upon the progressive development of motor skills that are receptive to modification through the influence of observed actions. Development of this communication process can sometimes progress to highly complex levels, mired in ambiguity, but which if successfully utilized, probably plays an important role in maintaining social relationships.

In summary, I suggest that for actions to convey mental states there are a number of developmental steps:

(1) Infants form self–other matching mechanisms that represent relationships between perceived and executed actions. These are probably present in some form at birth.
(2) They perform actions, and then modify them as a result of experiencing mental states such as feelings.
(3) They represent the relationships between underlying actions, modified actions and the mental states such as feelings that cause the modification.
(4) They are able to incorporate these representations of action–mental state relationships into their perceptions of other's actions to perform 'true imitation', as well as forming an ability to represent others' mental states.
(5) They become increasingly sensitive to fine differences in the way others modify underlying actions, when these correspond to a manner by which they might modify that action in their own repertoire as the result of a mental state.

(6) This influences the way that they modify their own actions in an increasingly sophisticated fashion, which feeds back into the previous stage.

(7) More sophisticated mental state attribution abilities develop.

10.3   The correspondence problem

Whilst I have laid down a suggestion as to how the growth of the action–perception matching system may be associated with the development of 'theory of mind', I have not solved the 'correspondence problem' (Nehaniv and Dautenhahn, 2002; Heyes, 2001), which is concerned with how the matching forms in the first place. It has been suggested that this function may be served by 'mirror neurons'. These neurons fire both in response to an observed action, and when that same action is performed (di Pellegrino *et al.*, 1992; Rizzolatti *et al.*, 1996; Gallese *et al.*, 1996). Could impairment in the function of these neurones lie at the core of autism? Williams *et al.* (2001) suggested that neurons with action–perception matching properties, like those of 'mirror neurons', might lie at the base of a developmental cascade. If this cascade failed, this might result in autism.

10.4   Imitation and mind-reading in ASD

From this discussion, it appears that a number of factors are required in addition to correspondence, for mind-reading and imitation to develop. The successful mind-reader (Whiten, 1996) needs to be able to discriminate between two actions that might differ in subtle ways, and needs to be able to appreciate the relationships between underlying actions and those modified by higher mental states. That is, the mind-reader needs to be able to represent a perceived action as a modification of an underlying action, as a secondary representation (Suddendorf and Whiten, 2001) to the primary representation of the core action, rather than simply as another novel action to be imitated. If a smile is broad, it needs to be distinguished from a narrow smile if the mental state underlying it is to be appreciated. That means a broad smile must be perceived as a member of the category of smiles, if its meaning is to be appreciated. Here I suggest that imitation and mind-reading may take a qualitatively different form in autism, reflecting the inability of the person with autism to secondarily represent the perceived action (e.g. the broad smile), as the modification by a mental state, of an underlying action (a 'generic' smile). Thus a smile is not categorized as a type of smile, and so its meaning is lost. As shown by Weeks and Hobson (1987), children with autism don't tend to categorize faces by their emotional expression. I suggest that this could be a function of the fusiform area (in connection with anterior cortical areas), so well known to function poorly in ASD (Schultz *et al.*, 2000, 2003).

We considered the case of a boy with Asperger's syndrome who does an excellent impression of Cliff Richard and performs very well in drama classes. Unfortunately he stumbles when he is asked to improvize. This seems to reflect a strong ability for imitation, but the failure to represent the actions as functional actions modified by higher-level cognitive representations. For example, he may be very good at displaying the motor behaviour required to recite the song with appropriate changes in pitch and tone, but he does not necessarily associate those changes in pitch and tone with any emotional emphasis or meaning attached to them by the original singer. Therefore, he does not recreate in his mind, the mental state of the individual he is copying and he is unable to 'place himself in someone else's shoes'.

Children with ASD are well recognized to have motor-learning difficulties and do poorly on standard tests of motor ability (Green *et al.*, 2002), tests of motor planning (Hughes, 1996) and executive function tests requiring planning (Hughes *et al.*, 1994). There are a number of possible reasons for this (see Williams *et al.*, 2004). One reason suggested by Williams *et al.* (2001), is that imitative processes may have an important role in the development of motor-learning skills and executive function. As motor learning develops in tune with others, so does motor-planning ability, and the observation of other's motor and planning skills may facilitate development. Furthermore, the possession of motor skills may facilitate observing them in others. We also suggested that shared attention, well recognized to be impaired in ASD, could be conceptualized as a form of imitation. It is also concerned with forming representations of another's mental state (their attentional direction) by observing their behaviour (eye and head movement) and matching the way these actions are performed, to one's own motor representations utilized for regulating one's own attentional direction (also see Williams *et al.*, in press).

Therefore, impairment in the ability to develop correspondences between perceived and executed actions, to represent relationships between actions and mental states and difficulty distinguishing between similar actions that differ in force and speed is likely to lead to poor development of communicative processes that depend on actions such as voice, facial expression and gesture to communicate mental states. And if the action repertoire is resistant to modification, whether because novel actions are not perceived as novel, or because they are resistant to change by mental states or other factors, patterns of repetitive speech and actions are also likely to arise. This picture is consistent with that of autistic spectrum disorder (ASD) as described earlier.

10.5   Imitation in autism

Williams *et al.* (2004) carried out a detailed study of the imitation literature to look for further clues as to how the imitation process might be disrupted in autism. Twenty-one studies were identified that were concerned with action imitation, and which were also controlled. These studies involved examining a total of 268 children with autism across a range of abilities, from severely learning disabled to high functioning, and from toddlerhood to adulthood. We found an apparent delay in the development of imitative skills that was specific to autism. This effect seemed to be most robust in studies of gestural imitation where the gesture was meaningless (e.g. Smith and Bryson, 1998; Stone *et al.*, 1990; Rogers *et al.*, 1996). In imitative tasks involving actions upon objects or meaningful gestures, findings were more negative (Roeyers *et al.*, 1998). An exception to this was when the action performed by the subject was novel such as pressing a button with the forehead instead of the hand (Charman and Baron-Cohen, 1994). In addition, children engaged well with the experiments and did well on the simpler tasks, suggesting that the deficit was unlikely to be the result of a core deficit in social attention or motivation. We concluded that the imitative deficit in autism was most likely to be the result of a deficit in self–other mapping neural systems, rather than core deficits associated with motivation or executive function. Object re-enactment is the re-creation of the changes created by actions on objects, without necessarily requiring any attention to be paid to the action itself, if previously learnt actions can be utilized to perform these changes on the object (Whiten *et al.*, 2004). Therefore, we considered that mechanical changes to objects could be observed and recreated without being dependent upon actual imitation. Similarly, knowledge of meaning could be used to scaffold gestures, thereby reducing the need for true imitation in the sense of matching the form of action to that of perception. We hypothesized that autistic disorders are characterized by the development of neurocognitive mechanisms that apply 'folk physics' and knowledge to copy actions, at the expense of developing 'true imitation' using self–other mapping. This is consistent with the studies by Hobson and colleagues cited above, that imitation of force and speed are particularly impaired in ASD, where such compensatory mechanisms cannot operate. In addition, recent evidence has come from a study by Avikainen *et al.* (2003). They found that whilst normal participants made less imitation errors when imitating in the mirroring condition as opposed to crossed-over condition, those with ASD made no such improvement. This suggests that they used the same cognitive processes when imitating an act whether it was crossed over or mirrored, whereas the control subjects were able to use an alternate, more efficient strategy when mirroring, which they couldn't use for the crossing-over task. This then seems to be evidence for some sort of action–perception matching mechanism informing action planning that is absent in the ASD group.

So, in summary, behavioural studies and clinical observation show that individuals with autism make more errors during imitation, but this doesn't occur across the board and seems to affect gesture alone more than actions involving objects, and particularly situations where imitation is dependent upon self–other matching of bodily action. At the same time they show qualitatively different imitation, particularly in the area of speech where echolalia is a very common symptom. Therefore, people with autism appear to be using their brain differently when they copy the actions of others. In some areas they seem to lack the ability to map actions to perception that may be necessary for the development of social communication and reciprocity. Rather they seem to be more dependent upon other forms of action copying, such as stimulus-enhanced learning or result emulation, which involves recreating the changes on environments, observed to be created by the actions of others. To investigate this, we carried out a study of imitation by individuals with and without autistic spectrum disorder using fMRI. This was reported by Williams *et al.* (2006). Here I report a summary of the methods and some additional analysis.

10.6   Neuroimaging of imitation in autism

Iacoboni *et al.* (1999, 2001) carried out a study of imitation using fMRI to test the hypothesis that 'mirror neurons' exist in humans and play a role in imitation. Their task involved the observation of a finger movement shown to participants lying in a scanner as an animation of a series of five photographs presented in a three second period (either the index or middle finger being extended). There were six conditions. In the imitation condition, the participant was asked to execute the same action they observed. In the other execution conditions, they were asked to make the same movements but in response to the observation of a cross marking either finger on a still photograph of the hand (symbolic cue condition) or in response to a cross on one side of the screen (spatial cue condition). In addition there were three observation conditions that entailed observing the animation, the spatial cue and the symbolic cue. Brain activity during imitation could then be compared to observation only, and also to the two execution conditions. These conditions provided corollaries to alternative means by which actions can be imitated. That means that in this experiment, one can perform the imitation task either by action–perception matching (what one might call 'true' imitation), or by lifting the left or right finger, depending on whether the left or right finger is seen to be extended using simple rules learnt through associative learning processes (what one calls visuomotor learning). It seems likely that this visuomotor learning process will utilize a similar neural substrate to the spatial cue and symbolic cue execution processes (Toni and Passingham, 1999). We therefore sought to utilize this protocol to compare brain activity during imitation in participants with ASD to normal controls.

Participants with autistic spectrum disorder were all right-handed males aged 13–20 yrs with normal IQ, recruited from our clinical population and through voluntary agencies. All had an unequivocal clinical diagnosis of ASD and all met full diagnostic criteria for autism on the Autism Diagnostic Interview – Revised (2000) (Lord *et al.*, 1994). All but one met diagnostic criteria for autistic spectrum disorder on the Autism Diagnostic Observation Schedule (Lord *et al.*, 2000). He was still included as his diagnosis was judged to be unequivocal on the ADI-R and through clinical judgement. All had IQ assessed on the Wechsler Adult Intelligence Scale – IV or Wechsler Intelligence Scale for Children. Participants were then matched to controls of similar age and IQ. They all then underwent fMRI scanning using the paradigm described by Iacoboni *et al.* (1999, 2001), using the same stimuli kindly provided by these authors. There were two differences. We presented visual cues at the beginning of blocks to remind participants whether they were required to just observe or execute in response to the cue. This was to minimize the use of internal speech and it also meant that minimal pre-scan training was required. Also, our scanner was less powerful, being 1.5T as opposed to 3T as used by them. Analyses presented have all been carried out using statistical parametric mapping (SPM2), random effects approach.

10.7   Results

Task performance during scans was very close to 100 %, with just two subjects making minor errors on two occasions. Of 124 scan blocks processed (4 per subject), 54 from controls and 52 from ASD subjects were free from movement artefact and therefore suitable for analysis. This means that group differences were not due to performance differences, but rather because the two groups used different brain mechanisms to perform the same tasks.

(a) Controls
(thresholded at p <= 0.001)

(b) ASD group
(thresholded at p <= 0.001)

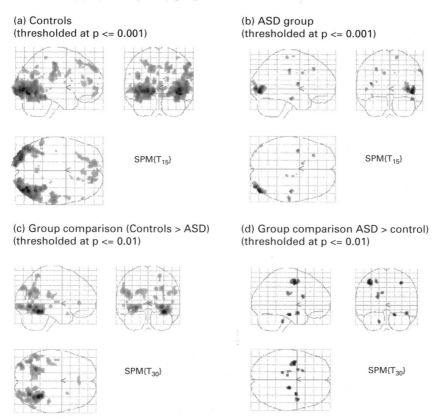

(c) Group comparison (Controls > ASD)
(thresholded at p <= 0.01)

(d) Group comparison ASD > control)
(thresholded at p <= 0.01)

Figure 10.1 Glass brains showing areas of brain activation during fMRI that were greater during the imitation condition than the spatial cue-execution condition. The first two analyses show how these contrasts appeared for the groups separately. The second two contrasts show the voxels where this difference was significantly greater for one group or the other. See tables for anatomical localization of clusters.

We compared the spatial cue execute condition to imitation. As can be seen (Figure 10.1, b) the ASD group showed additional activation of the posterior superior temporal sulcus in an area that has been associated with observation of hand actions (Hermsdorfer *et al.*, 2001). There is very little other additional activity, suggesting that among the individuals with ASD, activation associated with imitation consists of that required for spatial cue execution (the visuomotor learning condition), plus that associated with observing finger movement. Further support for this notion comes from the group comparison of ASD to controls, on the imitation vs.

spatial cue comparison, which identifies a cluster of activation in the dorsal premotor cortex. This is consistent with associative visuomotor learning (Toni and Passingham, 1999).

Among the control subjects on the other hand, imitation is associated with considerable additional activation. This is in the hand-processing region where it seemingly occupies a much larger area than the ASD group. Inferior aspects of visual cortex and ventral aspects of temporal cortex are also affected bilaterally. Finally there are areas of medial frontal cortex and superior frontal gyrus activated in the frontal regions.

The control subjects appear to imitate by activating a network of visual regions that have been related to a social cognitive function including the right posterior temporal region (Vogeley *et al.*, 2001; Castelli *et al.*, 2000), the ventral temporal cortical regions (Vogeley *et al.*, 2001; Schultz *et al.*, 2003; Schultz *et al.*, 2000), and the medial frontal cortex (Fletcher *et al.*, 1995; Happe *et al.*, 1996; Gallagher *et al.*, 2000; Frith and Frith, 2000; Frith and Frith, 1999). In contrast, when individuals with autism are asked to imitate an action, they do not engage those processes concerned with understanding and analyzing the action. They use the mechanisms used by controls to serve action recognition and spatial cue execution. They recreate the movement that they observe, not by copying its form but by associating an action to a stimulus – that which Whiten *et al.* (2004), would term stimulus-enhanced learning. I would like to suggest that whilst the task utilized in the scanner may be considered very simple, these differences reflect the differences that these two groups would take to more complex and truly imitative tasks carried out, outside the scanner. This task does not appear to have a goal or any intention underlying it, but I suggest that when control participants decide 'to imitate' they activate (as a result of executive function – see Grezes *et al.*, 1998), a network of structures that they would normally use for imitation. In contrast, participants with ASD, simply took a visuomotor-learning approach to the task.

According to our discussion above, imitation has to be done in a certain way for social cognition to develop. The approach taken by the ASD group did not depend upon action–perception matching as the stimulus was not perceived as a moving finger, but as a change in the spatial configuration of a stimulus that is conditionally related to a previously learnt movement. This mechanism allowed actions to be copied with fidelity, but cognitive development remained at the level of behavioural as opposed to thought transmission. I would suggest that only the mechanism of imitation allows for the development of social cognition according to the processes outlined in the introduction, because only this process can represent relationships between underlying actions and those same actions modified by other mental states.

Therefore, people with ASD may copy actions through processes of visuomotor learning other than imitation. This may mean that they can do well when tasks only involve copying the visible properties of actions. However, performance will deteriorate when the task requires drawing out elements of the action to incorporate and modify their behavioural repertoire. fMRI supports this idea, finding that people with autism use similar processes to a conditioned visuomotor learning task, whereas controls use many other brain areas that are also used for social cognition. It is difficult to see how imitation of a finger movement could draw on mechanisms dedicated to 'mind-reading'. It is more likely that the areas serving imitation are consequently utilized as mind-reading skills develop, because both processes depend upon similar learning processes. I suggest that mind-reading is the inevitable consequence of action–perception matching mechanisms that can represent complex relationships between actions and modifications of those actions by mental states such as emotions. People with ASD fail to develop social cognitive abilities because conditional visuomotor mapping systems do not have these capacities.

Acknowledgments

The fMRI study was funded by the Chief Scientist's Office of the Scottish Executive. I am much indebted to my colleagues, Andy Whiten, David Perrett, Alison Murray, Gordon Waiter, Anne Gilchrist and Emma Hepburn who were my collaborators on the fMRI project. I am also very grateful to the participants who volunteered to participate in this project and to the editors and two anonymous reviewers who helped me to considerably improve this manuscript.

REFERENCES

Avikainen, S., Wohlschlager, A., Liuhanen, S., Hanninen, R., Hari, R. *et al.* (2003). Impaired mirror-image imitation in Asperger and high-functioning autistic subjects. *Current Biology*, **13**, 339–41.

Castelli, F., Happe, F., Frith, U. and Frith, C. (2000). Movement and mind: a functional imaging study of perception and interpretation of complex intentional movement patterns. *NeuroImage*, **12**, 314–25.

Charman, T. and Baron-Cohen, S. (1994). Another look at imitation in autism. *Development and Psychopathology*, **6**, 403–13.

di Pellegrino, G., Fadiga, L., Fogassi, L., Gallese, V. and Rizzolatti, G. (1992). Understanding motor events: a neurophysiological study. *Experimental Brain Research*, **91**, 176–80.

Fletcher, P. C., Happe, F., Frith, U., Baker, S. C., Dolan, R. J., Frackowiak, R. S. *et al.* (1995). Other minds in the brain: a functional imaging study of 'theory of mind' in story comprehension. *Cognition*, **57**, 109–28.

Frith, C. D. and Frith, U. (1999). Interacting minds – a biological basis. *Science*, **286**, 1692–5.

Frith, C. D. and Frith, U. (2000). The physiological basis of theory of mind: functional neuroimaging studies. In S. Baron-Cohen, H. Tager-Flusberg and D. J. Cohen (eds.), *Understanding Other Minds – Perspectives from Developmental Cognitive Neuroscience*. Oxford, UK: Oxford University Press, 334–56.

Gallagher, H. L., Happe, F., Brunswick, N., Fletcher, P. C., Frith, U. and Frith, C. D. (2000). Reading the mind in cartoons and stories: an fMRI study of 'theory of mind' in verbal and nonverbal tasks. *Neuropsychologia*, **38**, 11–21.

Gallese, V., Fadiga, L., Fogassi, L. and Rizzolatti, G. (1996). Action recognition in the premotor cortex. *Brain*, **119**, 593–609.

Gallese, V. and Goldman, A. (1998). Mirror neurons and the simulation theory of mind-reading. *Trends in Cognitive Sciences*, **2**, 493–501.

Gordon, R. M. (1996). 'Radical' simulationism. In P. Carruthers and P. K. Smith (eds.), *Theories of Theories of Mind*. Cambridge, UK: Cambridge University Press, 11–21.

Green, D., Baird, G., Barnett, A. L., Huber, J. and Henderson, S. E. (2002). The severity and nature of motor impairment in Asperger's Syndrome: a comparison with Specific Developmental Disorder of Motor Function. *Journal of Child Psychology and Psychiatry*, **43**, 655–68.

Grezes, J., Costes, N. and Decety, J. (1998). Top-down effect of strategy on the perception of human biological motion: a PET investigation. *Cognitive Neuropsychology*, **15**, 553–82.

Happe, F., Ehlers, S., Fletcher, P., Frith, U., Johansson, M., Gillberg, C. *et al.* (1996). 'Theory of mind' in the brain. Evidence from a PET scan study of Asperger syndrome. *Neuroreport*, **8**, 197–201.

Hermsdorfer, J., Goldenberg, G., Wachsmuth, C., Conrad, B., Ceballos-Baumann, A. O. *et al.* (2001). Cortical correlates of gesture processing: clues to the cerebral mechanisms underlying apraxia during the imitation of meaningless gestures. *Neuroimage*, **14**, 149–61.

Heyes, C. (2001). Causes and consequences of imitation. *Trends in Cognitive Sciences*, **5**, 253–61.

Hobson, R. P. (1990). On the origins of self and the case of autism. *Development and Psychopathology*, **2**, 163–81.

Hobson, R. P. and Lee, A. (1999). Imitation and identification in autism. *Journal of Child Psychology and Psychiatry*, **40**, 649–59.

Hobson, R. P., Lee, A. and Meyer, J. (2003). Identification in autism. Presentation at the biennial meeting of the Society for Research in Child Development, Tampa, Florida.

Hughes, C. (1996). Brief report: planning problems in autism at the level of motor control. *Journal of Autism and Developmental Disorders*, **26**, 99–107.

Hughes, C., Russell, J. and Robbins, T. W. (1994). Evidence for executive dysfunction in autism. *Neuropsychologia*, **32**, 477–92.

Hurley, S. and Chater, N. (eds.) (2004). *Perspectives on Imitation: from Cognitive Neuroscience to Social Science*, Vols. 1 and 2. Cambridge, MA: MIT Press.

Hurley, S. and Chater, N. (2004). *Perspectives on Imitation*. Cambridge, MA: MIT Press.

Iacoboni, M., Koski, L. M., Brass, M., Bekkering, H., Woods, R. P., Dubeau, M. C. *et al.* (2001). Reafferent copies of imitated actions in the right superior temporal cortex. *Proceedings of the National Academy of Sciences USA*, **98**, 13995–9.

Iacoboni, M., Woods, R. P., Brass, M., Bekkering, H., Mazziotta, J. C. and Rizzolatti, G. (1999). Cortical mechanisms of human imitation. *Science*, **286**, 2526–8.

Lord, C., Rutter, M. and Le Couteur, A. (1994). Autism Diagnostic Interview – Revised: a revised version of a diagnostic interview for caregivers of individuals with possible pervasive developmental disorders. *Journal of Autism and Developmental Disorders*, **24**, 659–85.

Lord, C., Risi, S., Lambrecht, L., Cook, E. H., Jr., Leventhal, B. L., DiLavore, P. C., Pickles, A. and Rutter, M. (2000). The autism diagnostic observation schedule – generic: a standard measure of social and communication deficits associated with the spectrum of autism. *Journal of Autism and Developmental Disorders*, **30**, 205–23.

Meltzoff, A. N. and Decety, J. (2003). What imitation tells us about social cognition: a rapprochement between developmental psychology and cognitive neuroscience. *Philosophical Transactions of the Royal Society of London, Biological Sciences*, **358**, 491–500.

Meltzoff, A. and Gopnik, A. (1993). The role of imitation in understanding persons and developing a theory of mind. In S. Baron-Cohen, H. Tager-Flusberg and D. J. Cohen (eds.), *Understanding other minds: perspectives from autism*, 1st edn. Oxford, UK: Oxford University Press, 335–66.

Meltzoff, A. N. and Moore, M. K. (1997). Explaining facial imitation: a theoretical model. *Early Development and Parenting*, **6**, 179–92.

Meltzoff, A. N. and Moore, M. K. (1999). Persons and representation: why infant imitation is important for theories of human development. In J. Nadel and G. Butterworth (eds.), *Imitation in Infancy*. Cambridge, UK: Cambridge University Press, 7–35.

Meltzoff, A. N. & Prinz, W. (2002). The Imitative Mind: Development, Evolution and Brain Bases. Cambridge, UK: Cambridge University Press.

Nehaniv, C. L. and Dautenhahn, K. (2002). The correspondence problem. In K. Dautenhahn and C. L. Nehaniv (eds.), *Imitation in Animals and Artifacts*. Cambridge, MA: MIT Press, 41–61.

Rizzolatti, G., Fadiga, L., Gallese, V. and Fogassi, L. (1996). Premotor cortex and the recognition of motor actions. *Brain Research and Cognitive Brain Research*, **3**, 131–41.

Roeyers, H., Van Oost, P. and Bothuyne, S. (1998). Immediate imitation and joint attention in young children with autism. *Developmental Psychopathology*, **10**, 441–50.

Rogers, S. J. (1999). An examination of the imitation deficit in autism. In J. Nadel and G. Butterworth (eds.), *Imitation in Infancy*. Cambridge: Cambridge University Press, 254–83.

Rogers, S. J. and Pennington, B. F. (1991). A theoretical approach to the deficits in infantile autism. *Developmental Psychopathology*, **3**, 137–62.

Rogers, S. J., Bennetto, L., McEvoy, R. and Pennington, B. F. (1996). Imitation and pantomime in high-functioning adolescents with autism spectrum disorders. *Child Development*, **67**, 2060–73.

Russon, A. E. (1998). Exploiting the expertise of others. In A. Whiten and R. W. Byrne (eds.), *Machiavellian Intelligence II – extensions and evaluations*. Cambridge, UK: Cambridge University Press, 174–206.

Schultz, R. T., Gauthier, I., Klin, A., Fulbright, R. K., Anderson, A. W., Volkmar F. *et al.* (2000). Abnormal ventral temporal cortical activity during face discrimination among individuals with autism and Asperger syndrome. *Archives of General Psychiatry*, **57**, 331–40.

Schultz, R. T., Grelotti, D. J., Klin, A., Kleinman, J., Van der G. C., Marois, R. *et al.* (2003). The role of the fusiform face area in social cognition: implications for the pathobiology of autism. *Philosophical Transactions of Royal Society of London: Biological Sciences*, **358**, 415–27.

Smith, I. M. and Bryson, S. E. (1994). Imitation and action in autism: a critical review. *Psychological Bulletin*, **116**, 259–73.

Smith, I. M. and Bryson, S. E. (1998). Gesture imitation in autism I: nonsymbolic postures and sequences. *Cognitive Neuropsychology*, **15**, 747–70.

Stone, W. L., Lemanek, K. L., Fishel, P. T., Fernandez, M. C. and Altemeier, W. A. (1990). Play and imitation skills in the diagnosis of autism in young children. *Pediatrics*, **86**, 267–72.

Stout, D. (2002). Skill and cognition in stone tool production. An ethnographic case study from Irian Jaya. *Current Anthropology*, **43**, 693–722.

Suddendorf, T. and Whiten, A. (2001). Mental evolution and development: evidence for secondary representation in children, great apes, and other animals. *Psychological Bulletin*, **127**, 629–50.

Toni, I. and Passingham, R. E. (1999). Prefrontal-basal ganglia pathways are involved in the learning of arbitrary visuomotor associations: a PET study. *Experimental Brain Research*, **127**, 19–32.

Vogeley, K., Bussfeld, P., Newen, A., Herrmann, S., Happe, F., Falkai, P. *et al.* (2001). Mind reading: neural mechanisms of theory of mind and self-perspective. *Neuroimage*, **14**, 170–81.

Weeks, S. J. and Hobson, R. P. (1987). The salience of facial expression for autistic children. *Journal of Child Psychology and Psychiatry*, **28**, 137–52.

Whiten, A. (1996). When does smart behaviour-reading become mind-reading? In P. Carruthers and P. K. Smith (eds.), *Theories of Theories of Mind*. Cambridge, UK: Cambridge University Press, 277–92.

Whiten, A., Horner, V., Litchfield, C. and Marshall-Pescini, S. (2004). How do apes ape? *Learning and Behaviour*, **32**, 36–52.

Whiten, A., Horner, V. and Marshall-Pescini, S. (2003). Cultural Panthropology. *Evolutionary Anthropology*, **12**, 92–105.

Williams, J. H., Whiten, A., Suddendorf, T. and Perrett, D. I. (2001). Imitation, mirror neurons and autism. *Neuroscience and Biobehavioral Reviews*, **25**, 287–95.

Williams, J. H. G., Whiten, A. and Singh, T. (2004). A systematic review of action imitation in autistic spectrum disorder. *Journal of Autism and Developmental Disorders*, **34**, 285–99.

Williams, J. H. G., Waiter, G. D., Perra, O., Perrett, D. I. and Whiten, A. (in press). An fMRI study of joint attention experience. *NeuroImage*.

TABLES

Tables show details of clusters of brain activation illustrated in Figure 10.1. For each cluster, anatomical location, Talairach coordinates of the peak voxel, size of the cluster and statistical significance is shown.

Table 10.1 *Imitation vs. spatial cue execution (thresholded at z = 3.25, p < = 0.0006, extent > 20 voxels), maximum cluster co-ordinate and z-score quoted).*

Site	Brodmann's Area	Controls			ASD		
		Co-ordinates	z	Cluster size (voxels)	Co-ordinates	z	Cluster size (voxels)
LEFT							
Lingual Gyrus	17	−22,−87,1	5.17	2041			
Middle Temporal Gyrus	22	−51,−49,1	4.17	95			
Middle Temporal Gyrus	39	−40,−63,25	4.09	91			
Middle Temporal Gyrus	39	−42,−60,9	3.71	27			
Superior Frontal Gyrus	9	−16,56,30	4.05	220			
Medial Frontal Gyrus	10	−10,47,11	3.9	53			
Medial Frontal Gyrus	10	−2,60,−5	3.7	137			
Cingulate Gyrus	31	−4,−55,29	3.25	20			
RIGHT							
Inferior Occipital Gyrus	19	40,−72,−6	5.41	3192	46,−78,1	4.42	355
Postcentral Gyrus	2	59,−21,47	4.34	477	61,−20,36	3.67	27
Superior Frontal Gyrus	9	22,52,36	4.06	101			
Inferior Frontal Gyrus	9	51,1,24	3.56	47			
Precuneus	19	30,−78,37	3.55	34			
Medial Frontal Gyrus	9	16,43,14	3.49	10			
Anterior Cingulate	24	4,33,6	3.39	68			
Precuneus	7	2,−54,41	3.36	18			
Superior Temporal Gyrus	39	51,−59,32	3.33	31			
Sub-Gyral	20				44,−18,−16	3.87	28

Table 10.2 *Imitation vs. spatial cue execution (Group differences –
control >ASD) execute (thresholded at z = 3.25 (p< = 0.0006,
extent > 20 voxels), maximum cluster co-ordinate and z-score
quoted).*

Site	Co-ordinates	Brodmann's Area	Z-score	Number of voxels
LEFT				
Parahippocampal Gyrus	−26,−55,−2	19	4.22	439
Middle Occipital Gyrus	−32,−84,−1	18	3.64	144
Middle Temporal Gyrus	−40,−65,24	39	3.63	379
Inferior Occipital Gyrus	−42,−72,−5	19	3.41	66
Insula	−44,−26,20	13	3.00	124
RIGHT				
Fusiform Gyrus	34,−49,−11	37	5.20	1447
Precuneus	30,−78,37	19	3.25	146

Table 10.3 *Imitation vs. spatial cue execution (Group differences –
ASD >control) execute (thresholded at z = 3.25 (p < = 0.0006,
extent >20 voxels), maximum cluster co-ordinate and z-score
quoted).*

Site	Co-ordinates	Brodmann's Area	Z-score	Number of voxels
LEFT				
Middle Frontal Gyrus	−36,−4,44	6	3.23	151
RIGHT				
Parahippocampal Gyrus	18,−16,−16	28	3.27	35

11 A Bayesian model of imitation in infants and robots

Rajesh P. N. Rao, Aaron P. Shon and Andrew N. Meltzoff

11.1 Introduction

Humans are often characterized as the most behaviourally flexible of all animals. Evolution has stumbled upon an unlikely but very effective trick for achieving this state. Relative to most other animals, we are born 'immature' and helpless. Our extended period of infantile immaturity, however, confers us with benefits. It allows us to learn and adapt to the specific physical and cultural environment into which we are born. Instead of relying on fixed reflexes adapted for specific environments, our learning capacities allow us to adapt to a wide range of ecological niches, from Alaska to Africa, modifying our shelter, skills, dress and customs accordingly. A crucial component of evolution's design for human beings is imitative learning, the ability to learn behaviours by observing the actions of others.

Human adults effortlessly learn new behaviours from watching others. Parents provide their young with an apprenticeship in how to behave as a member of the culture long before verbal instruction is possible. In Western culture, toddlers hold telephones to their ears and babble into thin air. There is no innate proclivity to treat hunks of plastic in this manner, nor is it due to trial-and-error learning. Imitation is chiefly responsible.

Over the past decade, imitative learning has received considerable attention from cognitive scientists, evolutionary biologists, neuroscientists and robotics researchers. Discoveries in developmental psychology have altered theories about the origins of imitation and its place in human nature. We used to think that humans gradually learned to imitate over the first several years of life. We now know that newborns can imitate body movements at birth (Meltzoff and Moore, 1983, 1997). Such imitation reveals an innate link between observed and executed acts, with important

Imitation and Social Learning in Robots, Humans and Animals, ed. Chrystopher L. Nehaniv and Kerstin Dautenhahn. Published by Cambridge University Press.
© Cambridge University Press 2007.

implications for neuroscience. Evolutionary biologists are using imitation in humans and non-human animals as a tool for examining continuities and discontinuities in the evolution of mind.

Darwin inquired about imitation in non-human animals, but the last 10 years have seen a greater number of controlled studies of imitation in monkeys and great apes than in the previous 100 years. The results indicate that monkey imitation is hard to come by in controlled experiments, belying the common wisdom of 'monkey see monkey do' (Tomasello and Call, 1997; Visalberghi and Fragaszy, 2002; Whiten, 2002). Non-human primates and other animals (e.g. songbirds) imitate, but their imitative prowess is more restricted than that of humans (Meltzoff, 1996). Meanwhile, neuroscientists and experimental psychologists have started investigating the neural and psychological mechanisms underlying imitation, including the exploration of 'mirror neurons' and 'shared neural representations' (e.g. Decety, 2002; Prinz, 2002; Rizzolatti *et al.*, 2002; Meltzoff and Decety, 2003; Jackson *et al.*, 2006).

The robotics community is becoming increasingly interested in robots that can learn by observing movements of a human or another robot. Such an approach, also called 'learning by watching' or 'learning by example', promises to revolutionize the way we interact with robots by offering a new, extremely flexible, fast and easy way of programming robots (Berthouze and Kuniyoshi, 1998; Mataric and Pomplun, 1998; Billard and Dautenhahn, 1999; Breazeal and Scassellati, 2002; Dautenhahn and Nehaniv, 2002; see also *Robotics and Autonomous Systems* (special issue), 2004). This effort is also prompting an increased cross-fertilization between the fields of robotics and human psychology (Demiris *et al.*, 1997; Schaal, 1999; Demiris and Meltzoff, in press).

In this chapter, we set the stage for re-examining robotic learning by discussing Meltzoff and Moore's theory about how infants learn through imitation (Meltzoff, 2005, 2006; Meltzoff and Moore, 1997). They suggest a four-stage progression of imitative abilities: (1) body babbling, (2) imitation of body movements, (3) imitation of actions on objects and (4) imitation based on inferring intentions of others. We formalize these four stages within a probabilistic framework that is inspired by recent ideas from machine learning and statistical inference. In particular, we suggest a Bayesian approach to the problem of learning actions through observation and imitation, and explore its connections to recently proposed ideas regarding the importance of internal models in sensorimotor control. We conclude by discussing two main advantages of a probabilistic approach: (1) the development of robust algorithms for robotic imitation learning in noisy and uncertain environments and (2) the potential for applying Bayesian methodologies (such as manipulation of prior probabilities) and robotic technologies to obtain a deeper understanding of imitative learning in human beings. Some of the ideas presented in this chapter appeared in a preliminary form in Rao and Meltzoff (2003).

11.2   Imitative learning in human infants

Experimental results obtained by one of the authors (Meltzoff) and his colleagues over the past two decades suggest a progression of imitative learning abilities in infants, building up from 'body babbling' (random experimentation with body movements) in neonates to sophisticated forms of imitation in 18-month-old infants based on inferring the demonstrator's intended goals. We discuss these results below.

11.2.1   Body babbling

An important precursor to the ability to learn via imitation is to learn how specific muscle movements achieve various elementary body configurations. This helps the child learn a set of 'motor primitives' that could be used as a basis for imitation learning. Experiments suggest that infants do not innately know what muscle movements achieve a particular goal state, such as tongue protrusion, mouth opening or lip protrusion. It is posited that such movements are learned through an early experiential process involving random trial-and-error learning. Meltzoff and Moore (1997) call this process 'body babbling'.

In body babbling, infants move their limbs and facial parts in repetitive body play analogous to vocal babbling. In the more familiar notion of vocal babbling, the muscle movements are mapped to the resulting auditory consequence; infants are learning an articulatory–auditory relation (Kuhl and Meltzoff, 1996). Body babbling works in the same way, a principal difference being that the process can begin in utero. What is acquired through body babbling is a mapping between movements and a resulting body part configuration such as: tongue-to-lips, tongue-between-lips, tongue-beyond-lips. Because both the dynamic patterns of movement and the resulting endstates achieved can be monitored proprioceptively, body babbling can build up a 'directory' (an 'internal model') mapping movements to goal states (Meltzoff and Moore, 1997). Studies of fetal and neonatal behaviour have documented self-generated activity that could serve this hypothesized body babbling function (Patrick et al., 1982). Neonates can acquire a rich store of information through such body babbling. With sufficient practice, they can map out an 'act space' enabling new body configurations to be interpolated within this space. Such an interpretation is consistent with the probabilistic notion of forward models and internal models discussed in Section 11.3.1.

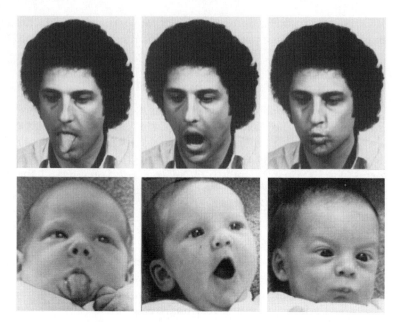

Figure 11.1 Imitative responses in 2- to 3-week-old infants (from Meltzoff and Moore, 1977).

11.2.2 *Imitating body movements*

In addition to body babbling, infants have been shown to demonstrate imitative learning. Meltzoff and Moore (1983, 1989) discovered that newborns can imitate facial acts. The mean age of these infants was 36 hours old, the youngest being 42 minutes old at the time of testing. Facial imitation in human infants thus suggests an innate mapping between observation and execution. Moreover, the studies provide information about the nature of the machinery infants use to connect observation and execution, as will be illustrated in the following brief review.

In Meltzoff and Moore (1977), 12- to 21-day-olds were shown to imitate four different gestures, including facial and manual movements. Infants didn't confuse either actions or body parts. They differentially responded to tongue protrusion with lip protrusion and without lip protrusion (Figure 11.1), showing that the specific *body part* can be identified. They also differentially responded to lip protrusion versus lip opening, showing that differential *action patterns* can be imitated with the same body part. This is confirmed by research showing that infants differentially imitate two different kinds of movements with the tongue (Meltzoff and Moore, 1994, 1997). In all, there are more than 24 studies of early imitation from 13 independent laboratories, establishing imitation for an impressive set of elementary body acts (for a review, see Meltzoff, 2005). This does not deny further development of imitative abilities. Young infants are not as capable as older children in terms of motor skills and the neonate is certainly less self-conscious about imitating than the toddler (Meltzoff and Moore, 1997). The chief question for theory, however, concerns the neural and psychological processes linking the observation and execution of matching acts. How do infants crack the correspondence problem:[1] how can observed body states of a teacher be converted to 'my own body states'? Two discoveries bear on this issue.

First, early imitation is not restricted to direct perceptual-motor resonances. Meltzoff and Moore (1977) put a pacifier in infants' mouths so they couldn't imitate during the demonstration. After the demonstration was complete, the pacifier was withdrawn, and the adult assumed a passive face. The results showed that infants imitated during the subsequent 2.5-minute response period while looking at a passive face. More dramatically, 6-week-olds have been shown to perform deferred imitation across a 24-hour delay (Meltzoff and Moore, 1994). Infants saw a gesture on one day and returned the next day to see the adult with a passive-face pose. Infants stared at the face and then imitated from long-term memory.

Second, infants correct their imitative response (Meltzoff and Moore, 1994, 1997). They converge on the accurate match without feedback from the experimenter. The infant's first response to seeing a facial gesture is activation of the corresponding body part. For example, when infants see tongue protrusion, there is a dampening of movements of other body parts and a stimulation of the tongue. They do not necessarily protrude the tongue at first, but may elevate it or move it slightly in the oral cavity. The important point is that the tongue, rather than the lips or fingers, is energized before the precise imitative movement pattern is isolated. It is as if young infants isolate what part of their body to move before how to move it. Meltzoff and Moore (1997) call this 'organ identification'. Neurophysiological data show that visual displays of parts of the face and hands activate specific brain sites in monkeys and humans (Buccino *et al.*, 2001; Gross, 1992). Specific body parts could be neurally represented at birth and serve as a foundation for infant imitation.

In summary, the results suggest that: (1) newborns imitate facial acts that they have never seen themselves perform, (2) there is an innate observation–execution pathway in humans and (3) this pathway is

---

[1] For more on the issue of correspondence problems, see Part I, 'Correspondence Problem and Mechanisms' of this volume. –Ed.

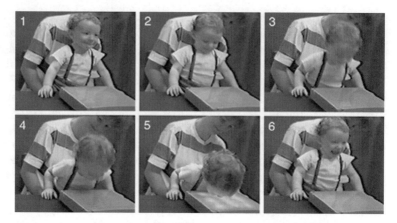

Figure 11.2 A 14-month-old infant imitating the novel action of touching a panel with the forehead (from Meltzoff, 1999).

mediated by a representational structure that allows infants to defer imitation and to correct their responses without any feedback from the experimenter.

11.2.3 Imitating actions on objects

More sophisticated forms of imitation than facial or manual imitation can be observed in infants who are several months older. In particular, the ability to imitate in these infants begins to encompass actions on objects that are external to the infant's body parts. In one study, toddlers were shown the act of an adult leaning forward and using the forehead to touch a yellow panel (Meltzoff, 1988b). This activated a microswitch, and the panel lit up. Infants were not given a chance for immediate imitation or even a chance to explore the panel during the demonstration session; therefore, learning by reinforcement and shaping was excluded. A one-week delay was imposed. At that point, infants returned to the laboratory and the panel was put out on the table. The results showed that 67 % of the infants imitated the head-touch behaviour when they saw the panel. Such novel use of the forehead was exhibited by 0 % of the controls who had not seen this act on their first visit. An example of the head-touch response is shown in Figure 11.2

Successful imitation in this case must be based on observation of the adult's act because perception of the panel itself did not elicit the target behaviour in the naive infants. Moreover, the findings tell us something about what is represented. If the only thing they remembered is that 'the panel lit up' (an object property), they would have returned and used their hands to press it. Instead, they re-enacted the same unusual act as used by the adult. The absent act had to have been represented and used to generate the behaviour a week later.

The utility of deferred imitation with 'real world' objects has also been demonstrated. Researchers have found deferred imitation of peer behaviour. In one study, 16-month-olds at a day-care centre watched peers play with toys in unique ways. The next day, an adult went to the infants' house (thereby introducing a change of context) and put the toys on the floor. The results showed that infants played with the toys in the particular ways that they had seen peers play 24 hours earlier (Hanna and Meltzoff, 1993). In another study, 14-month-olds saw a person on television demonstrate target acts toys (Figure 11.3). When they returned to the laboratory the next day, they were handed the toys for the first time. Infants re-enacted the events they saw on TV the previous day (Meltzoff, 1988a).

Taken together, these results indicate that infants who are between 1 and 1.5 years old are adept at imitating not only body movements but also actions on objects in a variety of contexts. For imitation to be useful in cultural learning, it would have to function with just such flexibility. The ability to imitate the actions of others on external objects undoubtedly played a crucial role in human evolution by facilitating the transfer of knowledge of tool use and other important skills from one generation to the next.

11.2.4 Inferring intentions

A sophisticated form of imitative learning is that requiring an ability to read below the perceived behaviour to infer the underlying goals and intentions of the actor. This brings the human infant to the threshold of 'theory of mind', in which they not only attribute visible behaviours to others, but develop the idea that others have internal mental states (intentions, perceptions, emotions) that underlie, predict and generate these visible behaviours.

One study involved showing 18-month-old infants an unsuccessful act (Meltzoff, 1995). For example, an adult actor 'accidentally' under- or overshot his target, or he tried to perform a behaviour but his hand slipped several times; thus the goal-state was not achieved (Figure 11.4, top row). To an adult, it was easy to read the actor's intention although he did not fulfill it. The experimental question was whether infants also read through the literal body movements to the underlying goal of the act. The measure of how they interpreted the event was what they chose to re-enact. In this

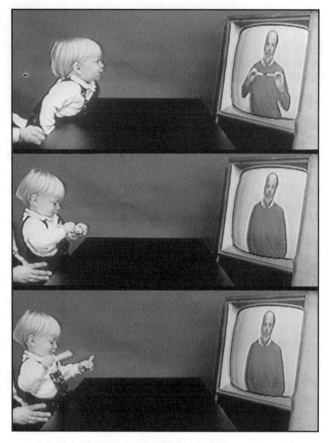

Figure 11.3 Infants as young as 14-months-old can imitate actions on objects as seen on TV (from Meltzoff, 1988a). Experiments have shown infants can also perform deferred imitation based on actions observed on TV the previous day (Meltzoff, 1988a).

case, the correct answer was not to imitate the movement that was actually seen, but the actor's goal, which remained unfulfilled.

The study compared infants' tendency to perform the target act in several situations: (1) after they saw the full target act demonstrated, (2) after they saw the unsuccessful attempt to perform the act, and (3) after it was neither shown nor attempted. The results showed that 18-month-olds can infer the unseen goals implied by unsuccessful attempts. Infants who saw the unsuccessful attempt and infants who saw the full target act both produced target acts at a significantly higher rate than controls. Evidently, toddlers can understand our goals even if we fail to fulfill them.

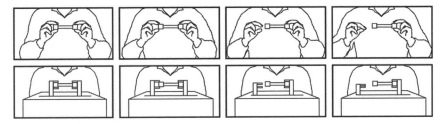

Figure 11.4 Human actor demonstrating an unsuccessful act (top panel) and an inanimate device mimicking the same movements (bottom). Infants attributed goals and intentions to the human but not to the inanimate device (from Meltzoff, 1995).

If infants can pick up the underlying goal or intention of the human act, they should be able to achieve the act using a variety of means. This was tested by Meltzoff (2006) in a study of 18-month-olds using a dumbbell-shaped object that was too big for the infants' hands. The adult grasped the ends of the dumbbell and attempted to yank it apart, but his hands slid off so he was unsuccessful in carrying out his intention. The dumbbell was then presented to the child. Interestingly, infants did not attempt to imitate the surface behaviour of the adult. Instead, they used novel ways to struggle to get the gigantic toy apart. They might put one end of the dumbbell between their knees and use both hands to pull it upwards, or put their hands on inside faces of the cubes and push outwards, and so on. They used different means than the demonstrator in order to achieve the same end. This fits with Meltzoff's (1995) hypothesis that infants had inferred the goal of the act, differentiating it from the surface behaviour that was observed.

People's acts can be goal-directed and intentional but the motions of inanimate devices are not – they are typically understood within the framework of physics, not psychology. In order to begin to assess whether young children distinguish between a psychological vs. purely physical framework, Meltzoff (1995) designed an inanimate device made of plastic, metal and wood. The device had poles for arms and mechanical pincers for hands. It did not look human, but it traced the same spatiotemporal path that the human actor traced and manipulated the object much as the human actor did (see Figure 11.4). The results showed that infants did not attribute a goal or intention to the movements of the inanimate device. Infants were no more (or less) likely to pull the toy apart after seeing the unsuccessful attempt of the inanimate device as in the baseline condition. This was the case despite the fact that infants pulled the dumbbell apart if the inanimate device successfully completed this act.

Evidently, infants can pick up certain information from the inanimate device, but not other information: they can understand successes, but not failures. In the case of the unsuccessful attempts, it is as if they see the motions of the machine's mechanical arms as 'physical slippage' but not as an 'effort' or 'intention' to pull the object apart. They appear to make attributions of intentionality to humans but not to this mechanical device. One goal of our current research program is to examine just how 'human' a model must look (and act) in order to evoke this attribution. We plan to test infants' interpretations of the 'intentional' acts of robots.

11.3   A probabilistic model of imitation

In recent years, probabilistic models have provided elegant explanations for a variety of neurobiological phenomena and perceptual illusions (for reviews, see Knill and Richards, 1996; Rao *et al.*, 2002). There is growing evidence that the brain utilizes principles such as probability matching and Bayes theorem for solving a wide range of tasks in sensory processing, sensorimotor control and decision-making. Bayes theorem in particular has been shown to be especially useful in explaining how the brain combines prior knowledge about a task with current sensory information and how information from different sensory channels is combined based on the noise statistics in these channels (see chapters in Rao *et al.*, 2002).

At the same time, probabilistic approaches are becoming increasingly popular in robotics and in artificial intelligence (AI). Traditional approaches to AI and robotics have been unsuccessful in scaling to noisy and realistic environments due to their inability to store, process and reason about uncertainties in the real world. The stochastic nature of most real-world environments makes the ability to handle uncertainties almost indispensable in intelligent autonomous systems. This realization has sparked a tremendous surge of interest in probabilistic methods for inference and learning in AI and robotics in recent years. Powerful new tools known as *graphical models* and *Bayesian networks* (Pearl, 1988; Jensen, 2001; Glymour, 2001) have found wide applicability in areas ranging from data mining and computer vision to bioinformatics, psychology and mobile robotics. These networks allow the probabilities of various events and outcomes to be inferred directly from input data based on the laws of probability and a representation based on graphs.

Given the recent success of probabilistic methods in AI/robotics and in modelling the brain, we believe that a probabilistic framework for imitation could not only enhance our understanding of human imitation but also provide new methods for imitative learning in robots. In this section, we explore a formalization of Meltzoff and Moore's stages of imitative learning in infants within the context of a probabilistic model.

11.3.1 Body babbling: learning internal models of one's own body

Meltzoff and Moore's theory about body babbling can be related to the task of learning an 'internal model' of an external physical system (also known as 'system identification' in the engineering literature). The physical system could be the infant's own body, a passive physical object such as a book or toy, or an active agent such as an animal or another human. In each of these cases, the underlying goal is to learn a model of the behaviour of the system being observed, i.e. to model the 'physics' of the system. Certain aspects of the internal model, such as the structure of the model and representation of specific body parts (such as the tongue), could be innately encoded and refined prior to birth (see Section 11.2.2) but the attainment of fine-grained control of movements most likely requires body babbling and interactions with the environment after birth.

A prominent type of internal model is a forward model, which maps actions to consequences of actions. For example, a forward model can be used to predict the next state(s) of an observed system, given its current state and an action to be executed on the system. Thus, if the physical system being modelled is one's own arm, the forward model could be used to predict the sensory (visual, tactile and proprioceptive) consequences of a motor command that moves the arm in a particular direction.

The counterpart of a forward model is an inverse model, which maps desired perceptual states to appropriate actions that achieve those states, given the current state. The inverse model is typically harder to estimate and is often ill-defined, due to many possible actions leading to the same goal state. A more tractable approach, which has received much attention in recent years (Jordan and Rumelhart, 1992; Wolpert and Kawato, 1998), is to estimate the inverse model using a forward model and appropriate constraints on actions (priors), as discussed below.

Our hypothesis is that the progression of imitative stages in infants as discussed in Section 11.2 reflects a concomitant increase in the sophistication of internal models in infants as they grow older. Intra-uterine and early post-natal body babbling could allow an infant to learn an internal model of its own body parts. This internal model facilitates elementary forms of imitation in Stage 2 involving movement of body parts such as tongue or lip protrusion. Experience with real-world objects after birth allows internal models of the physics of objects to be learned, allowing imitation of actions on such objects as seen in Stage 3. By the time infants are about 1.5 years old, they have interacted extensively with other humans, allowing them to acquire internal models (both forward and inverse) of active agents with intentions (Meltzoff, 2006). Such learned forward models could be used to infer the possible goals of agents despite witnessing only unsuccessful demonstrations while the inverse models could be used to select the motor commands necessary to achieve the undemonstrated but inferred goals. These ideas are illustrated with a concrete example in a subsequent section.

11.3.2 Bayesian imitative learning

Consider an imitation learning task where the observations can be characterized as a sequence of discrete states $s_1, s_2, \ldots, s_N$ of an observed object.[2] A first problem that the imitator has to solve is to estimate these states from the raw perceptual inputs $I_1, I_2, \ldots, I_N$. This can be handled using state estimation techniques such as the forward–backward algorithm for hidden Markov models (Rabiner and Juang, 1986) and belief propagation for arbitrary graphical models (Pearl, 1988; Jensen, 2001). These algorithms assume an underlying generative model that specifies how specific states are related to the observed inputs and other states through conditional probability matrices. We refer the interested reader to Jensen (2001) for more details. We assume the estimated states inferred from the observed input sequence are in object-centred coordinates.

The next problem that the imitator has to solve is the mechanism problem (Meltzoff and Moore, 1983, 1997) or correspondence problem (Nehaniv and Dautenhahn, 1998; Alissandrakis *et al.*, 2002; Nehaniv and Dautenhahn, 2002): how can the observed states be converted to 'my own body states' or states of an object from 'my own viewpoint'? Solving the correspondence problem involves mapping the estimated object-centred representation to an egocentric representation. In this chapter, for simplicity, we use an identity mapping for this correspondence function but the methods below also apply to the case of non-trivial correspondences (e.g. Nehaniv and Dautenhahn, 2001; Alissandrakis *et al.*, 2002a).

In the simplest form of imitation-based learning, the goal is to compute a set of actions that will lead to the goal state s_N, given a set of observed and remembered states $s_1, s_2, \ldots, s_N$. We will treat s_t as the random variable for the state at time t. For the rest of the chapter, we assume discrete state and action spaces. Thus, the state s_t of the observed object could be one of M different values $S_1, S_2, \ldots, S_M$ while the current action a_t could be one of $A_1, A_2, \ldots, A_P$.

---

[2] We have chosen to focus here on discrete state spaces but Bayesian techniques can also be applied to inference and learning in continuous state spaces (e.g. Bryson and Ho, 1975).

Consider now a simple imitation learning task where the imitator has observed and remembered a sequence of states (for example, $S_7 \to S_1 \to \ldots \to S_{12}$). These states can also be regarded as the sequence of sub-goals that need to be achieved in order to reach the goal state S_{12}. The objective then is to pick the action a_t that will maximize the probability of taking us from a current state $s_t = S_i$ to a remembered next state $s_{t+1} = S_j$, given that the goal state $g = S_k$ (starting from $s_0 = S_7$ for our example). In other words, we would like to select the action a_t that maximizes:

$$P(a_t = A_i | s_t = S_i, s_{t+1} = S_j, g = S_k) \tag{11.1}$$

This set of probabilities constitutes the inverse model of the observed system: it tells us what action to choose, given the current state, the desired next state and the desired goal state.

The action selection problem becomes tractable if a forward model has been learned through body babbling and through experience with objects and agents in the world. The forward model is given by the set of probabilities:

$$P(s_{t+1} = S_j | s_t = S_i, a_t = A_i) \tag{11.2}$$

Note that the forward model is determined by the environment and is therefore assumed to be independent of the goal state g, i.e.:

$$\begin{aligned}
P(s_{t+1} = S_j | s_t &= S_i, a_t = A_i, g = S_k) \\
&= P(s_{t+1} = S_j | s_t = S_i, a_t = A_i)
\end{aligned} \tag{11.3}$$

These probabilities can be learned through experience in a supervised manner because values for all three variables become known at time step $t + 1$. Similarly, a set of prior probabilities on actions

$$P(a_t = A_i | s_t = S_i, g = S_k) \tag{11.4}$$

can also be learned through experience with the world, for example, by tracking the frequencies of each action for each current state and goal state.

Given these two sets of probabilities, it is easy to compute probabilities for the inverse model using Bayes' theorem. Given random variables A and B, Bayes' theorem states that:

$$P(B|A) = P(A|B)P(B)/P(A) \tag{11.5}$$

This equation follows directly from the laws of conditional probability:

$$P(B|A)P(A) = P(B, A) = P(A, B) = P(A|B)P(B) \tag{11.6}$$

Given any system that stores information about variables of interest in terms of conditional probabilities, Bayes' theorem provides a way to invert the known conditional probabilities $P(A|B)$ to obtain the unknown conditionals $P(B|A)$ (in our case, the action probabilities conditioned on states). Our choice for a Bayesian approach is motivated by the growing body of evidence from cognitive and psychophysical studies suggesting that the brain utilizes Bayesian principles for inference and decision-making (Knill and Richards, 1996; Rao *et al.*, 2002; Gopnik *et al.*, 2004).

Applying Bayes' theorem to the forward model and the prior probabilities given above, we obtain the inverse model:

$$P(a_t = A_i | s_t = S_i, s_{t+1} = S_j, g = S_k)$$
$$= cP(s_{t+1} = S_j | s_t = S_i, a_t = A_i)P(a_t = A_i | s_t = S_i, g = S_k)$$

$$(11.7)$$

where $c = 1/P(s_{t+1} = S_j | s_t = S_i, g = S_k)$ is the normalization constant that can be computed by marginalizing over the actions:

$$P(s_{t+1} = S_j | s_t = S_i, g = S_k)$$
$$= \Sigma_m P(s_{t+1} = S_j | s_t = S_i, a_t = A_m)$$
$$\times P(a_t = A_m | s_t = S_i, g = S_k)$$

$$(11.8)$$

Thus, at each time step, an action A_i can either be chosen stochastically according to the probability $P(a_t = A_i | s_t = S_i, s_{t+1} = S_j, g = S_k)$ or deterministically as the one that maximizes:

$$P(a_t = A_i | s_t = S_i, s_{t+1} = S_j, g = S_k)$$

$$(11.9)$$

The former action selection strategy is known as probability matching while the latter is known as maximum a posteriori (MAP) selection. In both cases, the probabilities are computed based on the current state, the next sub-goal state and the final goal state using the learned forward model and priors on actions (Eq. 11.7). This contrasts with reinforcement learning methods where goal states are associated with rewards and the algorithms pick actions that maximize the total expected future reward. Learning the 'value function' that estimates the total expected reward for each state typically requires a large number of trials for exploring the state space. In contrast, the imitation-based approach as sketched above utilizes the remembered sequence of sub-goal states to guide the action-selection process, thereby significantly reducing the number of trials needed to achieve the goal state. The actual number of trials depends on the fidelity of the learned forward model, which can be fine-tuned during body babbling and 'play' with objects as well as during attempts to imitate the teacher.

A final observation is that the probabilistic framework introduced above involving forward and inverse models can also be used to infer the intent of the teacher, i.e. to estimate the probability distribution over the goal state g, given a sequence of observed states $s_1, s_2, \ldots, s_N$ and a sequence of estimated actions $a_1, a_2, \ldots, a_{N-1}$:

$$
\begin{aligned}
P(g &= S_k | a_t = A_i, s_t = S_i, s_{t+1} = S_j) \\
&= k_1 P(s_{t+1} = S_j | s_t = S_i, a_t = A_i, g = S_k) \\
&\quad \times P(g = S_k | s_t = S_i, a_t = A_i) \\
&= k_2 P(s_{t+1} = S_j | s_t = S_i, a_t = A_i, g = S_k) \\
&\quad \times P(a_t = A_i | s_t = S_i, g = S_k) P(g = S_k | s_t = S_i) \\
&= k_3 P(s_{t+1} = S_j | s_t = S_i, a_t = A_i) P(a_t = A_i | s_t = S_i, g = S_k) \\
&\quad \times P(s_t = S_i | g = S_k) P(g = S_k)
\end{aligned}
\tag{11.10}
$$

where the k_i are normalization constants. The above equations were obtained by repeatedly applying Bayes' rule. The first probability on the right hand side in Eq. (11.10) is the learned forward model and the second is the learned prior over actions. The last two probabilities capture the frequency of a state given a goal state and the overall probability of the goal state itself. These would need to be learned from experience during interactions with the teacher and the environment. It should be noted that the derivation of Eq. (11.10) above uses the remembered state s_t of the teacher in lieu of the actual state s_t (as in Equation 11.7) and is based on the assumption that the teacher's forward model is similar to the imitator's model – such an assumption may sometimes lead to inaccurate inferences, especially if the forward model is not sufficiently well-learned or well-matched with the teacher's, or if the observed state estimate itself is not accurate.

11.3.3 Example: learning to solve a maze task through imitation

We illustrate the application of the probabilistic approach sketched above to the problem of navigating to specific goal locations within a maze, a classic problem in the field of reinforcement learning. However, rather than learning through rewards delivered at the goal locations (as in reinforcement learning), we illustrate how an 'agent' can learn to navigate to specific locations by combining in a Bayesian manner a learned internal model with observed trajectories from a teacher (see also Hayes and Demiris, 1994). To make the task more realistic, we assume the presence of noise in the environment leading to uncertainty in the execution of actions.

11.3.3.1   Learning a forward model for the maze task

Figure 11.5(a) depicts the maze environment consisting of a 20 × 20 grid of squares partitioned into several rooms and corridors by walls, which are depicted as thick black lines. The starting location is indicated by an asterisk (*) and the three possible goal locations (Goals 1, 2 and 3) are indicated by circles of different shades. The goal of the imitator is to observe the teacher's trajectory from the start location to one of the goals and then to select appropriate actions to imitate the teacher.

The states s_t in this example are the grid locations in the maze. The five actions available to the imitator are shown in Figure 11.5(b): North (N), East (E), South (S), West (W) or remain in place (X). The noisy 'forward dynamics' of the environment for each of these actions is shown in Figure 11.5(c) (left panel). The figure depicts the probability of each possible next state s_{t+1} that could result from executing one of the five actions in a given location, assuming that there are no walls surrounding the location. The states s_{t+1} are given relative to the current state i.e. N, E, S, W, or X relative to s_t. The brighter a square, the higher the probability (between 0 and 1), with each row summing to 1. Note that the execution of actions is noisy: when the imitator executes an action, for example $a_t =$ E, there is a high probability the imitator will move to the grid location to the east ($s_{t+1} =$ E) of the current location but there is also a non-zero probability of ending up in the location west ($s_{t+1} =$ W) of the current location. The probabilities in Figure 11.5(c) (left panel) were chosen in an arbitrary manner; in a robotic system, these probabilities would be determined by the noise inherent in the hardware of the robot as well as environmental noise. When implementing the model, we assume that the constraints given by the walls are enforced by the environment (i.e. it overrides, when necessary, the states predicted by the forward model in Figure 11.5(c)). One could alternately define a location-dependent, global model of forward dynamics but this would result in inordinately large numbers of states for larger maze environments and would not scale well. For the current purposes, we focus on the locally defined forward model described above that is independent of the agent's current state in the maze.

We examined the ability of the imitator to learn the given forward model through 'body babbling' which in this case amounts to 'maze wandering'. The imitator randomly executes actions and counts the frequencies of outcomes (the next states s_{t+1}) for each executed action. The resulting learned forward model, obtained by normalizing the frequency counts to

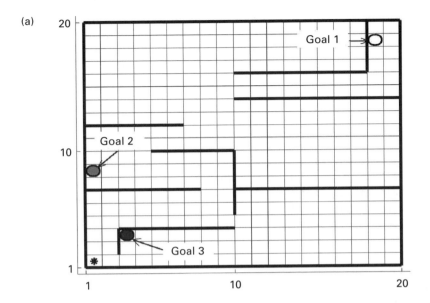

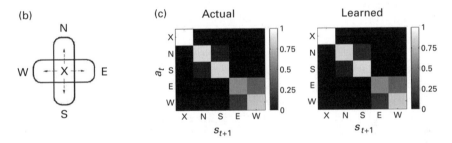

Figure 11.5 Simulated maze environment and learned forward model. (a) Simulated maze environment. Thick lines represent walls. Shaded ovals represent goal states. The instructor and the observer begin each simulated path through the maze at location (1,1), marked by the dark asterisk in the lower left corner of the maze. (b) Five possible actions at a maze location: agents can move north (N), south (S), east (E), west (W), or remain in place (X). (c) Actual and learned probabilistic forward models. The matrix on the left represents the true environmental transition function. The matrix on the right represents an estimated environmental transition function learned through interaction with the environment. Given a current location, each action a_t (rows) indexes a probability distribution over next states s_{t+1} (columns). For the states, the labels X, N, S, E, W are used to denote the current location and locations immediately to the north, south, east, and west of the current location respectively. The learned matrix closely approximated the true transition matrix. These matrices assume the agent is not attempting to move through a wall.

yield probabilities, is shown in Figure 11.5(c) (right panel). By comparing the learned model with the actual forward model, it is clear that the imitator has succeeded in learning the appropriate probabilities $P(s_{t+1}|s_t, a_t)$ for each value of a_t and s_{t+1} (s_t is any arbitrary location not adjacent to a wall). The 'body babbling' in this simple case, while not directly comparable to the multi-stage developmental process seen in infants, still serves to illustrate the general concept of learning a forward model through experimentation and interactions with the environment.

11.3.3.2   *Imitation using the learned forward model and learned priors*

Given a learned forward model, the imitator can use Eq. (11.7) to select appropriate actions to imitate the teacher and reach the goal state. The learned prior model $P(a_t = A_i|s_t = S_i, g = S_k)$, which is required by Eq. (11.7), can be learned through experience, for example, during earlier attempts to imitate the teacher or during other goal-directed behaviours. The learned prior model provides estimates of how often a particular action is executed at a particular state, given a fixed goal state. For the maze task, this can be achieved by keeping a count of the number of times each action (N, E, S, W, X) is executed at each location, given a fixed goal location.

Figure 11.6(a) shows the learned prior model:

$$P(a_t = A_i|s_t = S_i, g = S_k) \tag{11.11}$$

for an arbitrary location S_i in the maze for four actions $A_i = $ N, S, E, and W when the goal state g is the location $(1,8)$ (Goal 2 in Figure 11.5(a)). The probability for a given action at any maze location (given Goal 2) is encoded by the brightness of the square in that location in the maze-shaped graph for that action in Figure 11.6(a). The probability values across all actions (including X) sum to one for each maze location.

It is clear from Figure 11.6(a) that the learned prior distribution over actions given the goal location points in the correct direction for the maze locations near the explored trajectories. For example, for the maze locations along the bottom-left corridor (from $(2,5)$ to $(7,5)$), the action with the highest probability is E while for locations along the middle corridor (from $(2,8)$ to $(8,8)$), the action with the highest probability is W. Similar observations hold for sections of the maze where executing N and S will lead the imitator closer to the given goal location. The priors for unexplored regions of the maze were set to uniform distributions for these simulations (dark regions in Figure 11.6(a)).

The learned forward model in Figure 11.5(c) can be combined with the learned prior model in Figure 11.6(a) to obtain a posterior distribution over actions as specified by Eq. (11.7). Figure 11.6(c) shows an example

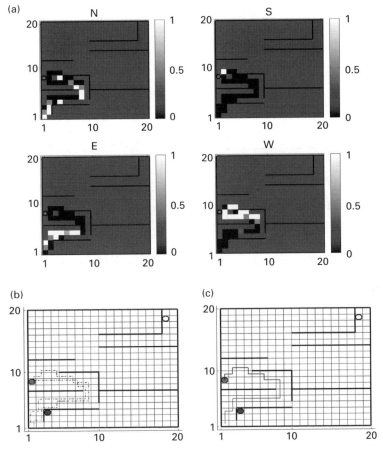

Figure 11.6 Learned priors and example of successful imitation: (a) Learned prior distributions $P(a_t | s_t, s_G)$ for the four directional actions (north, south, east, and west) for Goal 2 (map location $(1,8)$) in our simulated maze environment. Each location in the maze indexes a distribution over actions (the brighter the square, the higher the probability), so that the values across all actions (including X – not shown) sum to one for each maze location. (b) Trajectories (dashed lines) demonstrated by the instructor during training. The goal location here is Goal 2 depicted by the grey circle at map location $(1,8)$. Trajectories are offset within each map cell for clarity; in actuality, the observer perceives the map cell occupied by the instructor at each time step in the trajectory. So, for example, both trajectories start at map cell $(1,1)$. Time is encoded using greyscale values, from light grey (early in each trajectory) to black (late in each trajectory). (c) Example of successful imitation. The observer's trajectory during imitation is shown as a solid line, with greyscale values as in (b). Imitation is performed by combining the learned forward and prior models, as described in the text, to select an action at each step.

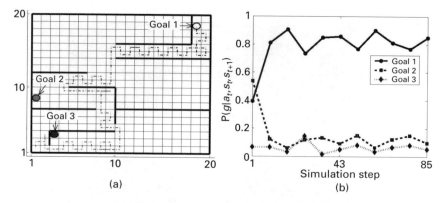

Figure 11.7 Inferring the intent of the teacher. (a) Dashed line plots a testing trajectory for intent inference. Greyscale values show the progression of time, from light grey (early in the trajectory) to black (late in the trajectory). The intended goal of the instructor was Goal 1 (the white circle at the top right). (b) Inferred intent, shown as a distribution over goal states. Each point in the graph represents the output of the intent inference algorithm, averaged over eight individual simulation steps (the final data point is an *average* over five simulation steps). Note that the instructor's desired goal, Goal 1, is correctly inferred as the objective for all points on the graph except the first. Potential ambiguities at different locations are not obvious in this graph due to averaging and unequal priors for the three goals (see text for details).

of the trajectory followed by the imitator after observing the two teacher trajectories shown in Figure 11.6(b). Due to the noisy forward model as well as limited training data, the imitator needs more steps to reach the goal than does the instructor on either of the training trajectories for this goal, typically involving backtracking over a previous step or remaining in place. Nevertheless, it eventually achieves the goal location as can be seen in Figure 11.6(c).

11.3.3.3 *Inferring the intent of the teacher*
After training on a set of trajectories for each goal (one to two trajectories per goal for the simple example illustrated here), the imitator can attempt to infer the intent of the teacher based on observing some or all of the teacher's actions. Figure 11.7(a) depicts an example trajectory of the teacher navigating to the goal location in the top right corner of the maze (Goal 1 in Figure 11.5(a)). Based on this observed trajectory of 85 total steps, the task of the imitator in this simple maze environment is to infer the probability distribution over the three possible goal states given

the current state, the next state and the action executed at the current state. The trajectory in Figure 11.7(a) was not used to train the observer; instead, this out-of-sample trajectory was used to test the intent inference algorithm described in the text. Note that the desired goal with respect to the prior distributions learned during training is ambiguous at many of the states in this trajectory.

The intent inference algorithm provides an estimate of the distribution over the instructor's possible goals for each time step in the testing trajectory. The evolution of this distribution over time is shown in Figure 11.7(b) for the teacher trajectory in (a). Note that the imitator in this case converges to a relatively high value for Goal 1, leading to a high certainty that the teacher intends to go to the goal location in the top right corner. Note also that the probabilities for the other two goals remain non-zero, suggesting that the imitator cannot completely rule out the possibility that the teacher may in fact be navigating to one of these other goal locations. In this graph, the probabilities for these other goals are not very high even at potentially ambiguous locations (such as location (9,9)) because: (1) the plotted points represent averages over five simulation steps and (2) Eq. (11.10) depends on $P(g = S_k)$, the prior probabilities of goals, which in this case involved higher values for Goal 1 compared to the other goals. Other choices for the prior distribution of goals (such as a uniform distribution) can be expected to lead to higher degrees of ambiguity about the intended goal at different locations. The ability of the imitator to estimate an entire probability distribution over goal states allows it to ascribe degrees of confidence to its inference of the teacher's intent, thereby allowing richer modes of interaction with the teacher than would be possible with purely deterministic methods for inferring intent (see Verma and Rao, 2006).

11.3.3.4 Summary
Although the maze task above is decidedly simplistic, it serves as a useful first example in understanding how the abstract probabilistic framework proposed in this chapter can be used to solve a concrete sensorimotor problem. In addition, the maze problem can be regarded as a simple 2-D example of the general sensorimotor task of selecting actions that will take an agent from an initial state to a desired goal state, where the states are typically high-dimensional variables encoding configurations of the body or a physical object rather than a 2-D maze location. However, because the states are assumed to be completely observable, the maze example by itself does not provide an explanation for the results obtained by Meltzoff (1995) showing that an infant is able to infer intent from an unsuccessful human demonstration but not an unsuccessful mechanical demonstration

Figure 11.8 Robotic platforms for testing Bayesian imitation models. (a) A binocular pan-tilt camera platform ('Biclops') from Metrica, Inc. (b) A miniature humanoid robot (HOAP-2) from Fujitsu Automation, Japan. Both robotic platforms are currently being used to test the Bayesian framework sketched in this chapter.

(Figure 11.4). An explanation for such a phenomenon would require the correspondence problem to be addressed as well as a sophisticated forward model of finger and hand movements, topics that we intend to address in future modelling studies.

11.3.4 *Further applications in robotic learning*

We are currently investigating the applicability of the probabilistic framework described above to the problem of programming robots through demonstration of actions by human teachers (Demiris *et al.*, 1997; Berthouze and Kuniyoshi, 1998; Mataric and Pomplun, 1998; Schaal, 1999; Billard and Dautenhahn, 1999; Breazeal and Scassellati, 2002; Dautenhahn and Nehaniv, 2002). Two robotic platforms are being used: a binocular robotic head from Metrica, Inc. (Fig 11.8(a)), and a recently acquired Fujitsu HOAP-2 humanoid robot (Fig 11.8(b)).

In the case of the robotic head, we have investigated the use of 'oculomotor babbling' (random camera movements) to learn the forward model probabilities $P(s_{t+1} = S_j | s_t = S_i, a_t = A_i)$. The states S_i in this case are the feedback from the motors ('proprioception') and visual information (for example, positions of object features). The learned forward model for the robotic head can be used in the manner described in Section 11.3.2 to solve head movement imitation tasks (Demiris *et al.*, 1997). In particular, we intend to study the task of robotic gaze following. Gaze following is an important component of language acquisition: to learn words, a first step is to determine what the speaker is looking at, a problem solved by the human infant by about one year of age (Brooks and Meltzoff, 2002, 2005). We hope to design robots with a similar capability (see Hoffman *et al.*, 2006, for progress).

Other work will focus on more complex imitation tasks using the HOAP-2 humanoid robot, which has 25 degrees of freedom, including articulated limbs, hands and a binocular head (Fig 11.8 (b)). Using the humanoid, we expect to be able to rigorously test the strengths and weaknesses of our probabilistic models in the context of a battery of tasks modeled after the progressive stages in imitative abilities seen in infants (see Section 11.2). Preliminary results can be found in Grimes *et al.*, 2006.

11.3.5   Towards a probabilistic model for imitation in infants

The probabilistic framework sketched above can also be applied to better understand the stages of infant imitation learning described by Meltzoff and Moore. For example, in the case of facial imitation, the states could encode proprioceptive information resulting from facial actions such as tongue protrusion or at a more abstract level, 'supramodal' information about facial acts that is not modality-specific (visual, tactile, motor, etc.). Observed facial acts would then be transformed to goal states through a correspondence function, which has been hypothesized to be innate (Meltzoff, 1999). Such an approach is consistent with the proposal of Meltzoff and Moore that early facial imitation is based on active intermodal mapping (AIM) (Meltzoff and Moore, 1977, 1994, 1997). Figure 11.9 provides a conceptual schematic of the AIM hypothesis. The key claim is that imitation is a matching-to-target process. The active nature of the matching process is captured by the proprioceptive feedback loop. The loop allows infants' motor performance to be evaluated against the seen target and serves as a basis for correction. One implementation of such a match-and-correction process is the Bayesian action selection method described above with both visual and proprioceptive information being converted to supramodal states. The selection of actions according to Eq. (11.7) followed by subsequent matching of remembered and actual states could implement the closed-loop matching process in the AIM model.

As a second example of the application of the probabilistic framework, consider imitation learning of actions of objects. In this case, the

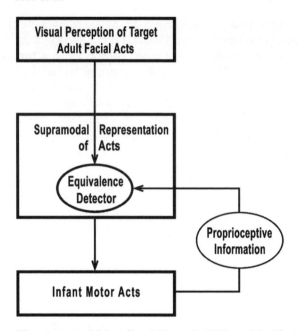

Figure 11.9 Meltzoff and Moore's AIM model of facial imitation (from Meltzoff and Moore, 1997).

states to be encoded are the states of the object ('joined together', 'pulled apart', etc. for the dumbbell-shaped object mentioned above). The forward model to be used would presumably be one that has been learned from experience with similar objects ('objects that can be pulled apart'). This, along with the learned priors for various actions, would allow appropriate actions to be selected based on the observed sequence of object states.

Finally, consider the case where an infant learns from unsuccessful demonstrations by inferring the intention of a human demonstrator. In this case, forward models could be put to good use to infer intention. By using a forward model of a human manipulating an object, the consequences of attempted actions by the human demonstrator can be predicted. For example, in the case of the dumbbell-shaped object used by Meltzoff (1995), the forward model, presumably learned through prior experience with pulling apart objects, would predict that when a person is applying forces at the two ends in opposite directions (away from the centre), there is a high probability for the state where the object has been pulled apart into two halves. This state could in turn be adopted as the desired goal state and the appropriate action that maximizes the probability of achieving this state could be selected in the Bayesian manner described above. On the other hand, in the case of an inanimate device demonstrating a failed action (Figure 11.4), the infant presumably does not apply its forward model to predict the consequences of the attempted action, perhaps because the inanimate device is not deemed to be human enough to use the infant's forward model (cf. the 'like me' hypothesis of Meltzoff, 2006, 2007). The important question of what type of forward model is chosen for predicting outcomes and intentions under specific circumstances remains a topic for further study.

The Bayesian model sketched in this chapter is only a first step towards more sophisticated probabilistic models of imitation. For example, it does not explain why human infants are superior in their imitation abilities when compared to apes and other animals that could potentially possess many of the same components of the Bayesian model as an infant might possess. Addressing such distinctions between imitative abilities will likely require a more in-depth study of the types of internal models used by infants and animals, and an examination of their ability to generalize to novel circumstances when using these internal models for imitation.

11.4   Prospects for developmental robotics

Humans at birth do not have the full set of skills and behaviours exhibited by adults. Human beings are not 'turn key' systems that function perfectly out of the box. There are at least four sources of behavioural change in human development: (1) maturational changes in the sensory, motor and cognitive system, (2) reinforcement learning, (3) independent invention and discovery, often called 'insight' and (4) imitative learning. The first three have been widely celebrated: maturation has been studied by neuroscientists; reinforcement learning by Skinner (1953) and generations of learning theorists; and independent invention and solitary discovery by Piaget (1954) and others. The imitative competence of young infants has only recently been discovered, and its enormous impact on human development and learning only recently sketched (e.g. see Meltzoff, 2005, 2006, 2007).

Imitative learning is more flexible and responsive to cultural norms than maturation; it is safer for the child than Skinnerian trial-and-error learning; and it is faster than relying on Piagetian solitary discoveries. These advantages of imitation learning apply equally well to robots and other autonomous agents. In particular, learning through imitation offers substantial benefits over other leading robotic learning methods (such as reinforcement learning) by: (1) overcoming the need for a huge number of learning trials and (2) avoiding the need for risky and dangerous experimentation during learning. At the same time, unlike supervised learning methods, imitative learning does not require a human to provide the exact motor signals needed to accomplish each task – the robot deduces these based only on observing a human or robotic demonstrator.

In this chapter, we discussed some of the main results obtained from studies of imitative learning in infants. These results suggest a four-stage progression of imitative learning abilities: (1) body babbling, (2) imitation of body movements, (3) imitation of actions on objects and (4) imitation based on inferring intentions of others. We took a first step towards formalizing these stages within a probabilistic framework inspired by recent ideas from machine learning, and provided an example demonstrating the application of the framework to the imitation learning problem.

The probabilistic approach is well-suited to imitation learning in real-world robotic environments which are noisy and uncertain. The success of recent approaches to robotic navigation and control can be attributed to the use of probabilistic techniques such as Kalman filtering and particle filtering for handling uncertainty (Blake and Yuille, 1992; Fox *et al.*, 2001). Similarly, techniques based on statistical learning form the backbone of several recent successful computer vision systems for tracking and recognizing persons (for example, see Jojic and Frey, 2001). We are optimistic that a probabilistic approach to robotic imitation learning will offer many of the advantages of these preceding systems, including the ability to handle missing data, robustness to noise, ability to make predictions based on learned models, etc. We are currently testing our ideas on a binocular robotic head and a humanoid robot. An important issue we intend to explore is the scalability of the proposed approach. The Bayesian model requires both a forward model as well as a prior model to be learned. In the case of the maze example, the forward and prior models were learned using a relatively small number of trials due to the small size of the state space. A more realistic scenario involving, for example, a humanoid robot would presumably require a larger number of trials due to the greater degrees of freedom available; however, the problem may be alleviated to some extent by learning forward and prior models only for the parts of the state space that are selectively utilized in imitative sessions (e.g., Grimes *et al.*, 2006). Hierarchical state-space models may also help in this regard. We hope to explore the issue of scalability in future studies involving the humanoid robot.

The probabilistic approach also opens up the possibility of applying Bayesian methodologies such as manipulation of prior probabilities of task alternatives to obtain a deeper understanding of imitation in humans. For example, one could explore the effects of biasing a human subject towards particular classes of actions (e.g. through repetition) under particular sets of conditions, a manipulation that would in effect test the contributions of the prior model in Eq. (11.7). One could also manipulate the forward model used by subjects with the help of virtual reality environments. Such manipulations have yielded valuable information regarding the type of priors and internal models that the adult human brain uses in perception (see chapters in Rao *et al.*, 2002) and in motor learning (Wolpert *et al.*, 1995).

We believe that the application of such methodology to imitation could shed new light on the problem of how infants acquire internal models of the people and things they encounter in the world. Conversely, we believe that biologically inspired models will help shape the architecture and algorithms used to solve imitative learning problems in robots (see Demiris *et al.*, 1997; Schaal, 1999; Demiris and Hayes, 2002). For example, Meltzoff and Moore's four stages of imitation in infants suggests a hierarchical approach to robotic imitation, starting from learning internal models of self motion to more sophisticated models of interactions with active behaving agents.

Imitation is an especially fruitful domain for interdisciplinary collaboration between robotics and developmental science. It is a perceptual-motor activity of great adaptive value and a channel for learning that lends itself to computational modelling. Additionally, it presents an interesting challenge to robotics and offers an extremely versatile and flexible way to program robots. Such interdisciplinary collaborations could eventually allow us to investigate interactions between young children and robots. Do young children, prior to developing the prejudices and philosophies of adults, think that robots have subjective beliefs, desires, emotions and intentions? Experiments addressing such questions will not only provide new insights into how humans develop a 'theory of other minds', but at the same time, will allow us to use unprejudiced humans (children) as judges of robots in a new form of the celebrated 'Turing test' for autonomous machines. We therefore look forward to rich bi-directional benefits emerging from collaborations between developmental science and robotics in the coming years.

Acknowledgments

We would like to thank the reviewers for their constructive comments and suggestions. This work is supported by grants to RPNR from ONR (grant no. N00014-03-1-0457), NSF (AICS-0413335) and the Packard Foundation, and grants to ANM from NIH (HD-22514) and NSF (SBE-0354453).

REFERENCES

Alissandrakis, A., Nehaniv, C. L. and Dautenhahn, K. (2002). Do as I do: correspondences across different robotic embodiments. In D. Polani, J. Kim, and T. Martinetz (eds.), *Proceedings of the 5th German Workshop on Artificial Life*, 143–52.

Alissandrakis, A., Nehaniv, C. L. and Dautenhahn, K. (2002a). Imitation with ALICE: learning to imitate corresponding actions across dissimilar embodiments, *IEEE Transactions on Systems, Man, and Cybernetics*, Part A, **32(4)**, 482–96.

Berthouze, L. and Kuniyoshi, Y. (1998). Emergence and categorization of coordinated visual behaviour through embodied interaction. *Machine Learning*, **31**, 187–200.

Billard, A. and Dautenhahn, K. (1999). Experiments in learning by imitation – grounding and use of communication in robotic agents. *Adaptive Behaviour*, **7**, 415–38.

Blake, A. and Yuille, A. (eds.) (1992). *Active Vision*. Cambridge, MA: MIT Press.

Breazeal, C. and Scassellati, B. (2002). Challenges in building robots that imitate people. In K. Dautenhahn and C. L. Nehaniv (eds.), *Imitation in Animals and Artifacts*. Cambridge, MA: MIT Press, 363–90.

Brooks, R. and Meltzoff, A. N. (2002). The importance of eyes: how infants interpret adult looking behavior. *Developmental Psychology*, **38**, 958–66.

Brooks, R. and Meltzoff, A. N. (2005). The development of gaze following and its relation to language. *Developmental Science*, **8**, 535–43.

Bryson, A. E. and Ho, Y. C. (1975). *Applied Optimal Control*. Bristol, PA: Taylor and Francis.

Buccino, G., Binkofski, F., Fink, G. R., Fadiga, L., Fogassi, L., Gallese, V., Seitz, R. J., Zilles, K., Rizzolatti, G. and Freund, H.-J. (2001). Action observation activates premotor and parietal areas in a somatotopic manner: an fMRI study. *European Journal of Neuroscience*, **13**, 400–4.

Dautenhahn, K. and Nehaniv, C. L. (2002). *Imitation in Animals and Artifacts*. Cambridge, MA: MIT Press.

Decety, J. (2002). Is there such a thing as functional equivalence between imagined, observed, and executed action? In A. N. Meltzoff and W. Prinz (eds.), *The Imitative Mind: Development, Evolution, and Brain Bases*. Cambridge, UK: Cambridge University Press, 291–310.

Demiris, J. and Hayes, G. (2002). Imitation as a dual-route process featuring predictive and learning components: A biologically plausible computational model. In K. Dautenhahn and C. Nehaniv (eds.), *Imitation in animals and artifacts*. Cambridge, MA: MIT Press, 327–61.

Demiris, Y. and Meltzoff, A. N. (in press). The robot in the crib: A developmental analysis of imitation skills in infants and robots. *Infant and Child Development*.

Demiris, J., Rougeaux, S., Hayes, G. M., Berthouze, L. and Kuniyoshi, Y. (1997). Deferred imitation of human head movements by an active stereo vision head. *Proceedings of the 6th IEEE International Workshop on Robot and Human Communication (Sept 29–Oct 1, Sendai, Japan)*, 88–93.

Fox, D., Thrun, S., Dellaert, F. and Burgard, W. (2001). Particle filters for mobile robot localization. In A. Doucet, N. de Freitas and N. Gordon (eds.), *Sequential Monte Carlo Methods in Practice*. New York: Springer Verlag, 401–28.

Glymour, C. (2001). *The Mind's Arrows: Bayes Nets and Graphical Causal Models in Psychology*. Cambridge, MA: MIT Press.

Gopnik, A., Glymour, C., Sobel, D. M., Schulz, L. E., Kushnir, T. and Danks, D. (2004). A theory of causal learning in children: causal maps and Bayes nets. *Psychological Review*, **111**, 1–30.

Grimes, D. B., Chalodhorn, R. and Rao, R. P. N. (2006). Dynamic imitation in a humanoid robot through nonparametric probabilistic inference. *Proceedings of the 2006 Robotics Science and Systems Conference* (Aug. 16–19, University of Pennsylvania, Philadelphia, PA).

Gross, C. G. (1992). Representation of visual stimuli in inferior temporal cortex. In V. Bruce, A. Cowey and A. W. Ellis (eds.), *Processing the Facial Image*. New York: Oxford University Press, 3–10.

Hanna, E. and Meltzoff, A. N. (1993). Peer imitation by toddlers in laboratory, home, and day-care contexts: implications for social learning and memory. *Developmental Psychology*, **29**, 701–10.

Hayes, G. and Demiris, J. (1994). A robot controller using learning by imitation. *Proceedings of the 2nd International Symposium on Intelligent Robotic Systems, Grenoble, France*, 198–204.

Hoffman, M., Grimes, D. B., Shon, A. P. and Rao, R. P. N. (2006). A probabilistic model of gaze imitation and shared attention. *Neural Networks*, **19**, 299–310.

Jackson, P. L., Meltzoff, A. N. and Decety, J. (2006). Neural circuits involved in imitation and perspective-taking. *NeuroImage*, **31**, 429–39.

Jensen, F. V. (2001). *Bayesian Networks and Decision Graphs*. New York: Springer-Verlag.

Jojic, N. and Frey, B. (2001). Learning flexible sprites in video layers. *IEEE Conference on Computer Vision and Pattern Recognition (CVPR)*.

Jordan, M. I. and Rumelhart, D. E. (1992). Forward models: supervised learning with a distal teacher. *Cognitive Science*, **16**, 307–54.

Knill, D. C. and Richards, W. (eds.) (1996). *Perception as Bayesian Inference*. Cambridge, UK: Cambridge University Press.

Kuhl, P. K. and Meltzoff, A. N. (1996). Infant vocalizations in response to speech: vocal imitation and developmental change. *Journal of the Acoustical Society of America*, **100**, 2425–38.

Mataric, M. J. and Pomplun, M. (1998). Fixation behaviour in observation and imitation of human movement. *Cognitive Brain Research*, 7, 191–202.

Meltzoff, A. N. (1988a). Imitation of televised models by infants. *Child Development*, **59**, 1221–9.

Meltzoff, A. N. (1988b). Infant imitation after a 1-week delay: long-term memory for novel acts and multiple stimuli. *Developmental Psychology*, **24**, 470–6.

Meltzoff, A. N. (1995). Understanding the intentions of others: re-enactment of intended acts by 18-month-old children. *Developmental Psychology*, **31**, 838–50.

Meltzoff, A. N. (1996). The human infant as imitative generalist: a 20-year progress report on infant imitation with implications for comparative psychology. In C. M. Heyes and B. G. Galef (eds.), *Social Learning in Animals: The Roots of Culture*. New York: Academic Press, 347–70.

Meltzoff, A. N. (1999). Origins of theory of mind, cognition, and communication. *Journal of Communication Disorders*, **32**, 251–69.

Meltzoff, A. N. (2005). Imitation and other minds: the 'Like Me' hypothesis. In S. Hurley and N. Chater (eds.), *Perspectives on Imitation: From Cognitive Neuroscience to Social Science*: Vol. 2. Cambridge, MA: MIT Press, 55–77.

Meltzoff, A. N. (2006). The 'like me' framework for recognizing and becoming an intentional agent. *Acta Psychologica*, doi:10.1016/j.actpsy.2006.09.005.

Meltzoff, A. N. (2007). 'Like me': a foundation for social cognition. *Developmental Science*, **10**, 126–34.

Meltzoff, A. N. and Decety, J. (2003). What imitation tells us about social cognition: a rapprochement between developmental psychology and cognitive neuroscience. *Philosophical Transactions of the Royal Society B*, **358**, 491–500.

Meltzoff, A. N. and Moore, M. K. (1977). Imitation of facial and manual gestures by human neonates. *Science*, **198**, 75–8.

Meltzoff, A. N. and Moore, M. K. (1983). Newborn infants imitate adult facial gestures. *Child Development*, **54**, 702–9.

Meltzoff, A. N. and Moore, M. K. (1989). Imitation in newborn infants: exploring the range of gestures imitated and the underlying mechanisms. *Developmental Psychology*, **25**, 954–62.

Meltzoff, A. N. and Moore, M. K. (1994). Imitation, memory, and the representation of persons. *Infant Behaviour and Development*, **17**, 83–99.

Meltzoff, A. N. and Moore, M. K. (1997). Explaining facial imitation: a theoretical model. *Early Development and Parenting*, **6**, 179–92.

Nehaniv, C. L. and Dautenhahn, K. (1998). Mapping between dissimilar bodies: affordances and the algebraic foundations of imitation. In J. Demiris and A. Birk (eds.), *Proceedings of the European Workshop on Learning Robots*.

Nehaniv, C. L. and Dautenhahn, K. (2001). Like me? – measures of correspondence and imitation. *Cybernetics and Systems*, **32(1–2)**, 11–51.

Nehaniv, C. L. and Dautenhahn, K. (2002). The correspondence problem. In K. Dautenhahn and C. L. Nehaniv (eds.), *Imitation in Animals and Artifacts*. Cambridge, MA: MIT Press, 41–61.

Patrick, J., Campbell, K., Carmichael, L., Natale, R. and Richardson, B. (1982). Patterns of gross fetal body movement over 24-hour observation intervals during the last 10 weeks of pregnancy. *American Journal of Obstetrics and Gynecology*, **142**, 363–71.

Pearl, J. (1988). *Probabilistic Reasoning in Intelligent Systems*. San Francisco, CA: Morgan Kaufman.

Piaget, J. (1954). *The Construction of Reality in the Child*. New York: Basic Books.

Prinz, W. (2002). Experimental approaches to imitation. In A. N. Meltzoff and W. Prinz (eds.), *The Imitative Mind: Development, Evolution, and Brain Bases*. Cambridge, UK: Cambridge University Press, 143–62.

Rabiner, L. R. and Juang, B. H. (1986). An introduction to hidden Markov models. *IEEE ASSP Magazine*, **3(1)**, 4–16.

Rao, R. P. N. and Meltzoff, A. N. (2003). Imitation learning in infants and robots: towards probabilistic computational models. *Proceedings of the 2003 Artificial Intelligence and Simulation of Behaviour (AISB) Convention: Cognition in Machines and Animals, UK.*

Rao, R. P. N., Olshausen, B. A. and Lewicki, M. S. (eds.) (2002). *Probabilistic Models of the Brain: Perception and Neural Function.* Cambridge, MA: MIT Press.

Rizzolatti, G., Fadiga, L., Fogassi, L. and Gallese, V. (2002). From mirror neurons to imitation, facts, and speculations. In A. N. Meltzoff and W. Prinz (eds.), *The Imitative Mind: Development, Evolution, and Brain Bases.* Cambridge, UK: Cambridge University Press, 247–66.

Robotics and Autonomous Systems (2004). Special Issue: Robot Learning from Demonstration, **47(2–3)**.

Schaal, S. (1999). Is imitation learning the route to humanoid robots? *Trends in Cognitive Sciences*, **3**, 233–42.

Skinner, B. F. (1953). *Science and Human Behaviour.* New York: The Macmillan Company.

Tomasello, M. and Call, J. (1997). *Primate Cognition.* New York: Oxford University Press.

Verma, D. and Rao, R. P. N. (2006). Goal-based imitation as a probabilistic inference over graphical models. In Y. Weiss, B. Schölkopf and J. Platt (eds.), *Advances in Neural Information Processing Systems 18.* Cambridge, MA: MIT Press, 1393–400.

Visalberghi, E. and Fragaszy, D. (2002). 'Do monkeys ape?' Ten years after. In K. Dautenhahn and C. L. Nehaniv (eds.), *Imitation in Animals and Artifacts.* Cambridge, MA: MIT Press, 471–99.

Whiten, A. (2002). The imitator's representation of the imitated: ape and child. In A. N. Meltzoff and W. Prinz (eds.), *The Imitative Mind: Development, Evolution, and Brain Bases.* Cambridge, UK: Cambridge University Press, 98–121.

Wolpert, D. M., Ghahramani, Z. and Jordan, M. I. (1995). An internal model for sensorimotor integration. *Science*, **269**, 1880–2.

Wolpert, D. M. and Kawato, M. (1998). Multiple paired forward and inverse models for motor control, *Neural Networks* **11(7–8)**, 1317–29.

12   Solving the correspondence problem in robotic imitation across embodiments: synchrony, perception and culture in artifacts

Aris Alissandrakis, Chrystopher L. Nehaniv and Kerstin Dautenhahn

12.1   The Agent-based perspective

Imitation is a powerful learning mechanism and a general agent-based approach must be used in order to identify the most interesting and significant problems, rather than the prominent ad hoc approaches in imitation robotics research so far. The traditional approach concentrates in finding an appropriate mechanism for imitation and developing a robot control architecture that identifies salient features in the movements of an (often visually observed) model, and maps them appropriately (via a built-in and usually static method) to motor outputs of the imitator (Kuniyoshi *et al.*, 1994, 1990). Model and imitator are usually not interacting with each other, neither do they share and perceive a common context. Effectively this kind of approach limits itself to answering the question of how to imitate for a particular robotic system and its particular imitation task. This has led to many diverse approaches to robot controllers for imitative learning that are difficult to generalize across different contexts and to different robot platforms. In contrast to the above, the agent-based approach for imitation considers the behaviour of an autonomous agent in relation to its environment, including other autonomous agents. The mechanisms underlying imitation are not divorced from the behaviour-in-context, including the social and non-social environments, motivations, relationships among the agents, the agents individual and learning history etc. (Dautenhahn and Nehaniv, 2002).

Such a perspective helps unfold the full potential of research on imitation and helps in identifying challenging and important research issues. The agent-based perspective has a broader view and includes five

Imitation and Social Learning in Robots, Humans and Animals, ed. Chrystopher L. Nehaniv and Kerstin Dautenhahn. Published by Cambridge University Press.

central questions in designing experiments on research on imitation: who to imitate, when to imitate, what to imitate, how to imitate and how to evaluate a successful imitation. A systematic investigation of these research questions can show the full potential of imitation from an agent-based perspective. In addition to deciding who, when and what to imitate, an agent must employ the appropriate mechanisms to learn and carry out the necessary imitative actions. The embodiment of the agent and its affordances will play a crucial role, as stated in the correspondence problem (Nehaniv and Dautenhahn, 2002):

> Given an observed behaviour of the model, which from a given starting state leads the model through a sequence (or hierarchy [or program]) of sub-goals in states, action and/or effects, one must find and execute a sequence of actions using ones own (possibly dissimilar) embodiment, which from a corresponding starting state, leads through corresponding sub-goals – in corresponding states, actions, and/or effects, while possibly responding to corresponding events.

This informal statement[1] of the correspondence problem draws attention to the fact that the agents may not necessarily share the same morphology or may not share access to the same affordances even among members of the same 'species'. This is true for both biological agents (e.g. differences in height among humans) and artificial agents (e.g. differences in motor and actuator properties). Having similar embodiments and/or affordances is just a special case of the more general problem. In order to study the correspondence problem we developed the ALICE (**A**ction **L**earning via **I**mitation between **C**orresponding **E**mbodiments) generic imitation framework, and implemented it in different simple software testbeds.[2]

12.2   ALICE overview

The imitative performance of an agent with a dissimilar embodiment to the model will not be successful unless the correspondence problem between the model and the imitator is (at least partially) solved.

To address this in an easy to generalize way, we developed ALICE as a generic framework for building up correspondences based on *any* generating method for attempts at imitation. This framework is related to

---

[1] For a formal statement of the correspondence problem relating to the use of different error metrics and for other applications, see also Nehaniv and Dautenhahn, 1998, 2000, 2001.

[2] These testbeds were implemented using the Swarm agent simulation system (http: \\wiki.swarm.org).

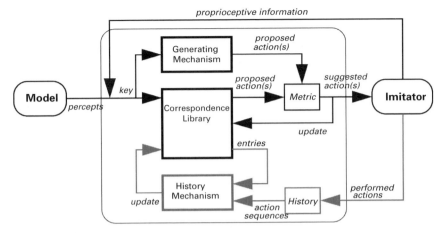

Figure 12.1 The ALICE framework. The *percepts* of the imitator arising from the model's behaviour (actions, states and effects) and *proprioceptive information* (state) of the imitator form a *key* that is used by the *correspondence library* (if it matches any of the existing entry keys at that stage of the library's growth) and the *generating mechanism* to produce a sequence of one or more *proposed action(s)*. These are evaluated using a *metric*, and the correspondence library is updated accordingly with the resulting *suggested action(s)* for the imitator. In parallel (shown in the figure using a grey colour), the *history mechanism* can be used to discover any *action sequences* from the *history*, that can improve any of the existing library entries. The history is composed by the sequence of all the actions performed so far by the imitator.

statistical string parsing models of social learning from ethology (Byrne, 1999) and also the associative sequence learning (ASL) theory from psychology (Heyes and Ray, 2000).

The ALICE framework (shown in Figure 12.1) creates a *correspondence library* that relates the actions, states and effects of the model (that the imitator is being exposed to) to actions (or sequences of actions) that the imitator agent is capable of, depending on its embodiment and/or affordances. These corresponding actions are evaluated according to a *metric* and can be looked up in the library as a partial solution to the correspondence problem when the imitator is next exposed to the same model action, state or effect. It is very important to note that the choice of metric can have extreme qualitative effects on the imitators resulting behaviour (Alissandrakis *et al.*, 2002), and on whether it should be characterized as 'imitation', 'emulation', 'goal emulation', etc. (Nehaniv and Dautenhahn, 2002).

12.2.1   The generating mechanism

The *generating mechanism* is used in the ALICE framework to produce the contents of the correspondence library; it can be *any* algorithm or mechanism that generates actions (or sequences of actions) that are valid (i.e. within the agent's repertoire) and possible in the context of the imitator. Sophisticated applications of ALICE can benefit by replacing, in a modular way, this action-generating mechanism with a more sophisticated one, appropriate to the given application. In the ALICE framework, no direct feedback from the model is used, instead the metrics are used to evaluate the imitation attempts.

12.2.2   The history mechanism

If only the actions found by the generating mechanism are used to build-up the correspondence library, the performance of the imitator would be directly limited by the choice of the algorithm. Moreover, some of the stored actions, although valid solutions to the correspondence problem, may become invalid in certain contexts. The *history mechanism* helps to overcome these difficulties: the imitator can examine its own history to discover further correspondences without having to modify or improve the generating algorithm used. These correspondences will be sequences of actions since, no matter how simplistic, the generating mechanism is required to be able to explore the entire search-space of single actions. An agent's history is defined as the list of actions that were performed so far by the agent while imitating the model together with their resulting state and effects. This kind of history provides valuable experience data that can then be used to extract useful mappings to improve and add to the correspondence library created up to that point. This approach can be useful to overcome possible limitations of the generating mechanism (Alissandrakis *et al.*, 2002).

12.2.3   Building up the correspondence library

When the imitating agent is exposed to each action, state and effect that comprises the model behaviour, the generating mechanism produces a candidate corresponding action. If there is no entry in the correspondence library related to the current action, state and effect of the model, a new entry is created, using these as entry keys with the generated action as the (initial) solution.[3]

---

[3] More precisely, the contents of the perceptual key depend on the metric the agent is using, for example, each of the keys will only contain state(s) and action(s) if a composite state–action metric is used.

If instead an entry already exists, the new action is compared to the stored action.[4] If the generated action is worse, according to the metric used, then it is discarded and the existing action from the correspondence library is performed. If on the other hand the new action is better, then it is performed by the agent and the library entry is updated. This could mean that the new action simply replaces the already existing one, or is added as an alternative solution.

Over time as the imitating agent is being exposed to the model agent, the correspondence library will reflect a partial solution to the correspondence problem that can be used to achieve a satisfactory imitation performance. Effectively ALICE provides a combination of learning and memory to help solve the correspondence problem. There is generalization in that the learned corresponding actions (or sequence of actions) can be reused by the imitator in new situations and contexts.

A more detailed description of the ALICE framework can be found in Alissandrakis (2003).

12.3   The CHESSWORLD testbed

The creation of CHESSWORLD was inspired by the need to implement a shared environment for interacting agents of different embodiments affording different relationships to the world. In the rules of the game of chess, each player controls an army of chess pieces consisting of a variety of different types with different movement rules. We borrow the notion of having different types of chess pieces able to move according to different movement rules, and we treat them as agents with dissimilar embodiments moving on the chequered board. Note that the actual game of chess is not studied. We simply make use of the familiar context of chess in a generic way, to illustrate the correspondence problem in imitation (Figure 12.2).

The range of possible behaviours by the chess agents is limited to movement-related ones. As a model agent performs a random walk on the board, an imitator observes the sequence of moves used and the relevant displacements achieved and then tries to imitate them, starting from the same starting point. Considering the moves sequentially the agent will try to match them, eventually performing a similar walk on the board. This imitative behaviour is performed after exposure to a complete model behaviour with no obstacles present, neither static (e.g. walls)

---

[4] There is generally more than one stored corresponding action (or sequence of actions) for each entry, reflecting alternative ways to achieve the same result.

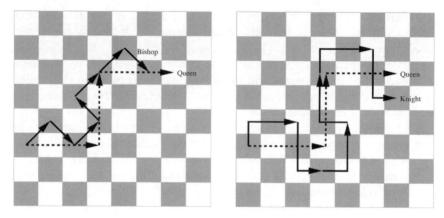

Figure 12.2 Two CHESSWORLD examples. Two imitator agents (solid paths), a bishop (left) and a knight (right) attempt to imitate the movements of the model queen agent (dotted path).

nor dynamic (e.g. other moving chess pieces), besides the edges of the board which can obstruct movement.

An action for a given agent is defined as a move from its repertoire, resulting in a relative displacement on the board. For example, a Knight agent can perform move $E2N1$ (hop two squares east and one square north) resulting in a displacement of $(-2, +1)$ relative to its current square.

Addressing what to imitate, the model random walk is segmented into relative displacements on the board by using different granularities. For example, *end-point level granularity* ignores all the intermediate squares visited and emulates the overall goal (i.e. cumulative displacement) of the model agent. In contrast, *path level granularity* not only considers all the squares visited by the model but also the intermediate ones that the chess piece 'slides across' on the chessboard while moving. Between these two extremes, *trajectory level granularity* considers the sequence of relative displacements achieved by the moves of the model during the random walk.

Depending on the embodiment as a particular chess piece, the imitator agent must find a sequence of actions from its repertoire to sequentially achieve each of those displacements. The assessment of how successful a sequence is in achieving a displacement and moving the agent as close as possible to the target square can be evaluated using different simple geometric metrics (Hamming norm, Euclidean distance and infinity norm) that measure the difference between displacements on the chessboard.

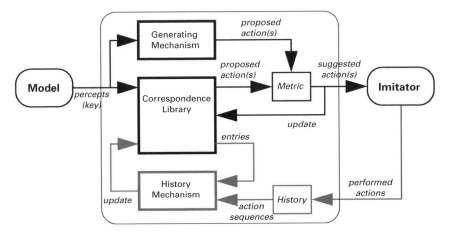

Figure 12.3 The ALICE framework as realized in the CHESSWORLD testbed. Note that compared to the generic version of the framework (shown in Figure 12.1), *proprioceptive information* from the imitator is not used here, as the realization of the ALICE framework in Chessworld only considers the *action* aspects of the agent's behavior and not the *state* or the *effects*. Other components are as explained in Figure 12.1.

12.3.1 *ALICE in CHESSWORLD*

The ALICE realization in Chessworld (seen in Figure 12.3) corresponds model actions (moves that result in a relative displacement of the chess piece on the board) to actions (or more probably sequences of actions) that can be performed by the imitator. The generating mechanism is a simple greedy algorithm, returning sequences of actions from the imitator agent's repertoire. The list of past moves performed by the imitator is defined as the history, from which the agent's history mechanism is looking for sequences of actions that can achieve the same relative displacement as model action entries in the correspondence library. The history mechanism is used in parallel to take advantage of this experiential data, compensating for the generating mechanism not allowing moves that locally might increase the distance, but globally reduce the error, within the generated sequences. The success and character of the imitation observed can be greatly affected by agent embodiment, together with the use of different metrics and sub-goal granularities.

For a more detailed description of CHESSWORLD and the ALICE implementation in this testbed, see Alissandrakis *et al.* (2002).

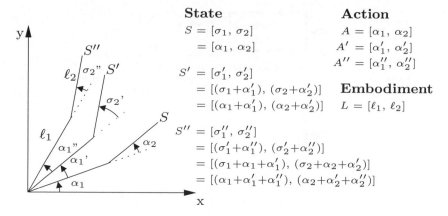

Figure 12.4 Example embodiment of a RABIT agent. A two-joint robotic arm, with arms of length ℓ_1 and ℓ_2, moving from state S to state S' to state S'', as it sequentially performs actions A, A', and A''. Note that the effects are not shown in this figure.

12.4   The RABIT testbed

The RABIT (**R**obotic **A**rm em**B**odiment for **I**mitation **T**estbed) environment was created as simple, yet 'rich enough' to allow for several dissimilarly embodied model and imitator agents to be considered. A RABIT agent (see Figure 12.4) occupies a 2-D workspace and is embodied as a robotic arm that can have any number of rotary joints, each of varying length. Each agent embodiment is described by the vector $L = [\ell_1, \ell_2, \ell_3, \cdots, \ell_n]$, where ℓ_i is the length of the ith joint. There are no complex physics in the workspace and the movement of the arms is simulated using simple forward kinematics but without collision detection or any static restraints (in other words, the arms can bend into each other). Our intention is to demonstrate the features of the imitative mechanism and not to build a faithful simulator.

An *action* of a given agent is defined as a vector describing the change of angle for each of the joints, $A = [\alpha_1, \alpha_2, \alpha_3, \ldots, \alpha_n]$, where n is the number of its joints. These angles are relative to the previous state of the arm and can only have three possible values, $+10°$ (anti-clockwise), $0°$ or $-10°$ (clockwise).

A *state* of an agent is defined as the absolute angle for each of the joints, $S = [\sigma_1, \sigma_2, \sigma_3, \ldots, \sigma_n]$, where n is the number of its joints. A distinction can be made between the *previous state* and the *current state* (the state of the arm after the current action was executed). As a result of the possible

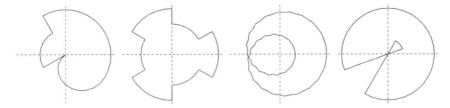

Figure 12.5 Different examples of RABIT behaviours. Shown are four different effect trails (the agent embodiment is not shown), drawn by the end tip of the each agent manipulator arm. All agents shown have the same embodiment $L = [20, 20, 20]$.

actions, the absolute angle at each joint can be anywhere in the range of $0°$ to $360°$ (modulo $360°$) but only in multiples of $10°$.

The end tip of the arm can leave a trail of 'paint' on the workspace, as it moves along the workspace. The *effect* is defined as a directed straight line segment connecting the end tip of the previous and the current states of the arm (approximating the paint trail). The effect is internally implemented as a vector of displacement $E = (x_c - x_p, y_c - y_p)$, where (x_p, y_p) and (x_c, y_c) are the end tip coordinates for the previous and current state respectively.

The model behaviour is broken down as a sequence of actions that move the robotic arm of the agent from the previous state to the current state, while leaving behind a trail of paint as the effect. The nature of the experimental testbed with the fixed base rotary robotic arms favours circular looping effects and the model behaviours used in the experiments were designed as such (see Figure 12.5).

Each complete behaviour (or 'pattern') that returns the arm to its initial state observed by the imitator is called an exposure, and the imitator is exposed to repeated instances of the same behavioural pattern. At the beginning of each new exposure it is possible to reset the imitating agent to the initial state. This resetting is called *synchronization* in our experiments.

12.4.1 Metrics

The imitating agents can perceive the actions, states and effects of the model agents, and also their own actions, states and effects, and therefore we define several metrics to evaluate the similarity between them. Ideally the metric value should be zero, indicating a perfect match. An example of using the different metrics described below is shown in Figure 12.6.

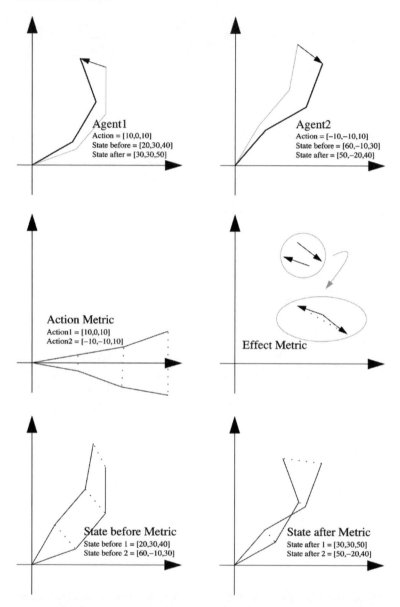

Figure 12.6 An example of using the metrics to compare actions, states (before and after) and effects between two RABIT agents, *Agent1* (top, left) and *Agent2* (top, right). The figure visualizes the vectors used (depending on the metric) and the distances that are summed and then averaged to give each metric value. Both agents have the same embodiment $L = [20, 20, 20]$.

State metric
The state metric calculates the average distance between the various joints
of an agent (posed in a particular state) and the corresponding joints of
another agent[5] (posed in a different state) as if they were occupying the
same workspace. Ideally this distance should be zero when the arms take
corresponding poses, but this may not be possible due to embodiment
differences. Using forward kinematics, the coordinates of the ends for
each joint are found.

$$x_i = \sum_{j=1}^{i-1} x_j + \ell_i \cos \left(\sum_{j=1}^{i} \sigma_j \right) \qquad (12.1a)$$

$$y_i = \sum_{j=1}^{i-1} y_j + \ell_i \sin \left(\sum_{j=1}^{i} \sigma_j \right) \qquad (12.1b)$$

If both agents have the same number of joints the correspondence
between them is straightforward; the Euclidean distance for each pair is
calculated, the distances are then all summed and divided by the number
of joints to give the metric value.

$$d_i = \sqrt{\left(x_i^{model} - x_i^{imitator} \right)^2 + \left(y_i^{model} - y_i^{imitator} \right)^2} \qquad (12.2)$$

$$\mu^{state} = \frac{1}{n} \sum_{i=1}^{n} d_i \qquad (12.3)$$

If the agents have a different number of joints, then some of the
joints of the agent with more are ignored. To find which joint corresponds with which, the ratio of the larger over the smaller number of
joints is calculated, and if not integer, is rounded to the nearest one. The
ith joint of the agent with the smaller number of joints, will correspond
to the (ratio $\times$ i)th joint of the agent with the larger number of joints. For
example if one of the agents has twice the number of joints, only every
second joint will be considered.

Action metric
For the action metric, the same algorithm as the one described above for
the state metric is used, but considering the action vectors instead of the

---

[5] The state metric can be used not only between different agents, but also to evaluate the
  similarity between two states of the same agent. This is true for the action and the effect
  metric as well.

state vectors. The value in the case of the state metric represents an absolute position error; for the action metric, it represents the relative error between the changes of the state angles, due to the compared actions.

Effect metric

The effect metric is defined as the Euclidean length of the vector difference between two effects (x_1, y_1) and (x_2, y_2).

$$\mu^{\text{effect}} = \sqrt{(x_1 - x_2)^2 + (y_1 - y_2)^2} \tag{12.4}$$

12.4.2 ALICE implementation

In the RABIT implementation of ALICE, each entry in the correspondence library can use as a key the action/state/effect of the observed model agent and the current state of the imitator, as perceptual and proprioceptive components, respectively. The key can be composed of just a single of these aspects (e.g. action only), or a combination (e.g. action, state and the imitator's state for proprioception).

For the generating mechanism, an algorithm that returns single, random (yet valid) actions is used. It is possible to replace it with a more complex generating mechanism (i.e. inverse kinematics), but the idea is to have a mechanism that simply returns valid actions from the search space. In order to speed up the learning, it is possible to generate more than one random action and choose a best one.

It is possible not to require an exact match for the perceptual and/or the proprioceptive components of the trigger key, but a loose one that is 'close enough', controlled by a threshold. We call this *loose perceptual matching* and we hypothesized that it should support learning and generalization.

In the current implementation, each entry can store up to three possible corresponding actions that can be seen as possible alternatives.[6]

For a more detailed description of RABIT and the ALICE implementation in this testbed, see Alissandrakis (2003).

12.5 Experiments on aspects of imitation

Using the robotic arm testbed we conducted various experiments to study the possibility of social transmission of behaviours through heterogeneous

---

[6] Note that the history mechanism which also considers sequences of past imitative attempts when updating the correspondence library entries is not implemented in the RABIT testbed since simple action to action correspondence suffices here. In contrast, corresponding sequences of actions are necessary in CHESSWORLD as most chess pieces are unable to move as far as their model using only a single action.

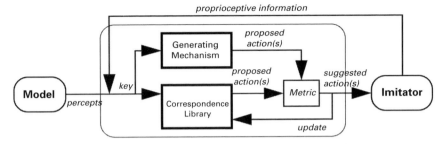

Figure 12.7 The ALICE framework as realized in the RABIT testbed. Note that compared to the generic version of the framework (shown in Figure 12.1), the *history mechanism* is not used in parallel to update the correspondence library, as the realization of the ALICE framework in RABIT testbed considers only single actions and not sequences. Other components are as explained in Figure 12.1.

agents, the effect of proprioception, loose perceptual matching and synchronization on the imitation learning performance, and also the robustness of the ALICE mechanism when the imitator embodiment changes during the learning process, and also after achieving a successful imitative performance.

12.5.1 Cultural transmission of behaviours and emergence of 'proto-culture'

Besides being a powerful learning mechanism, imitation broadly construed is required for cultural transmission (e.g. Dawkins, 1976). Transmission of behavioural skills by social learning mechanisms like imitation may also be fundamental in non-human cultures, e.g. in chimpanzees (Whiten *et al.*, 1999), whales and dolphins (Rendell and Whitehead, 2001). The robotic arm testbed makes it possible to study examples of behavioural transmission via imitation, with an imitator agent acting as a model for another imitator. If the original model and the final imitator have the same embodiment but the intermediate imitator a different one, we can look at how the different embodiment and the choice of metrics for the evaluation of a successful imitation attempt can affect the quality of the transmitted behaviour.

The example shown in Figure 12.8 shows such a transmission of the original model behaviour via an intermediate agent. Although the intermediary has a different embodiment, the original model and final imitator have the same embodiment, and the model behavioural pattern is transmitted perfectly. This is partially helped by the use of the action metric for evaluation to overcome the dissimilar embodiment of the transmitting

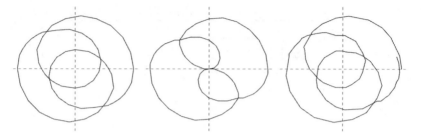

Figure 12.8 An example of social transmission. The original model ($L = [20, 20, 20]$) is shown to the left. In the middle, an imitator ($L = [30, 30]$) acts also as a model for the imitator on the right ($L = [20, 20, 20]$). Both imitators use the action metric.

agent. This example serves as proof of the concept that by using social learning and imitation, rudimentary cultural transmission with variability is possible among robots, even heterogeneous ones.

The choice of metrics and the particular embodiment of the agents greatly affect the qualitative aspects of imitation, making not every combination suitable for passing on model behaviours, besides crucial aspects of the model behaviours themselves. Note that in Figure 12.8, the intermediate agent imitates qualitatively differently, due to its dissimilar embodiment. If the particular embodiment of the intermediate agent greatly distorts the model pattern, then such a transmission might be impossible.

The examples shown in Figures 12.9 and 12.10 illustrate the emergence of 'proto-culture' in a cyclically ordered chain of three and eight imitators with no overall model. The agents imitate only the agent clockwise from them, using the action metric. Initially they move randomly, as the generating mechanism is trying to discover correspondences for the (also random) actions of their model. Over time, they are able to imitate each other's actions and a stable behavioral pattern emerges.

Different runs yield different emergent culturally sustained behaviours. The location and orientation of the emergent pattern is different in each agent's workspace, since the location and orientation are irrelevant to the action metric; they will depend on the state of the agent at the moment that it has solved its correspondence problem. Each agent's state will vary as a result of the agents not synchronizing.

The cultural transmission of skills through a heterogeneous population of robots using the ALICE framework could potentially be applied to the acquisition and transmission of skills in more complex populations of robots, involved in carrying out useful tasks, e.g. on the shop-floor

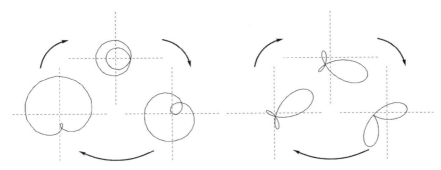

Figure 12.9 Examples of emerging 'proto-culture'. Two groups of three RABIT agents. All the agents on the left have $L = [20, 20, 20]$ and all the agents on the right have $L = [15, 15, 15, 15]$. Each agent imitates the agent on its left (anti-clockwise) and acts as a model for the agent on its right (clockwise). The emergent behaviour is composed of a single action. $[10, 10, 0]$ left, $[10, -10, -10, -10]$ right.

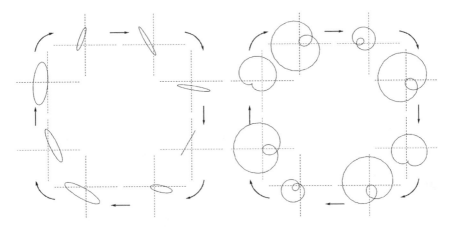

Figure 12.10 More examples of emerging 'proto-culture'. Two groups of eight RABIT agents. All the agents on the left have $L = [15, 15, 15, 15]$. The agents on the right have alternating embodiments $L = [30, 30]$ and $L = [15, 15, 15, 15]$. Each agent imitates the agent on its left (anti-clockwise) and acts as a model for the agent on its right (clockwise). The emergent behaviour is composed of a single action. $[10, -10, -10, 0]$ left, $[10, 10]$ and $[0, 10, 0, 10]$ right.

of a factory, with new robots coming and going acquiring behaviours by observation without having to be explicitly programmed and without humans having to develop different control programs for different types of robots that need to perform the same task. Instead, the robots would autonomously create their own programs (using social learning) and correspondence libraries, even as new types of robots with different embodiments come and go from the population.

12.5.2 Synchronization

At the end of each exposure of the imitating agent to the model, it is possible to reset the imitator arm to the same initial position, as a result synchronizing the imitation attempt to the model behaviour. We conducted ten experimental runs, each with two imitating agents trying to imitate a model agent, one of them synchronizing with the model by resetting to the outstretched initial state after the completion of each exposure, and the other starting each attempt from the final reached state of the previous attempt (ideally the same as the initial state, as all the model patterns are designed as closed loops). Both model and imitator agents had the same embodiment ($L = [20, 20, 20]$) and the metric used was a weighted half-half combination of the action and state metrics. Both imitating agents used proprioception and allowed for a 10% margin of looseness for matching the trigger keys (see section 12.5.4 below). The generating mechanism created five random actions to choose from. Each run lasted 20 exposures and the maximum metric value for each exposure was logged. The ratio of the maximum error of the imitating agent using synchronization over the maximum error of the agent not resetting back to the start position at the end of each exposure can be seen in the bottom panel of Figure 12.11, constantly decreasing and below one. This indicates that the numerator is minimized faster than the denominator, indicating that it is very difficult for an imitating agent that does not synchronize to reach again states relevant to the model pattern if the initial imitation attempts are not successful. This reduces the chance to update and improve the relevant correspondence library entries as the agent wanders with no point of reference. If the state space is large enough, it is possible for the agent to get completely lost.

12.5.3 Proprioceptive matching

The correspondence library entry keys can contain both perceptive (the action, state and effect of the model agent) and proprioceptive (the imitators own state at the time of the observation) data. It is possible to ignore the proprioception and trigger the keys based only on the perception.

We conducted ten experimental runs, each with two imitating agents trying to imitate a model agent, one of them using proprioception, the other not. Both model and imitator agents had the same embodiment ($L = [20, 20, 20]$) and the metric used was a weighted half-half

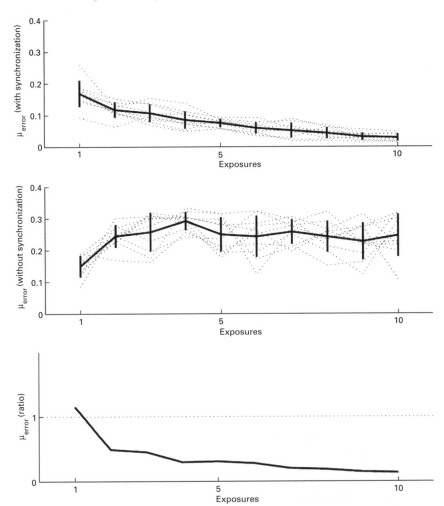

Figure 12.11 Experiments comparing the use of synchronization. The average maximum error metric value of robotic agents over ten exposures using synchronization (top panel) vs not using synchronization (middle panel). The ratio of the maximum error per exposure of the imitating agent using synchronization over the maximum error of the imitating agent that does not use synchronization (bottom panel) indicates a comparative many-fold reduction of error with use of synchronization. In each panel, the thicker line shows the average values of all the ten experiments, with the bars indicating the standard deviation. Both model and imitator agents have the same embodiment $L =$ [20, 20, 20] and the imitator agents use a half-half composite of the action and state metrics. Both imitators use proprioception and allow for 10% loose perceptual matching.

combination of the action and state metrics. Both imitating agents used a loose perceptual matching of 10% (see section 12.5.4 below) and the generating mechanism created five random actions to choose from. Each run lasted 20 exposures and the maximum error metric value for each exposure was logged.

The ratio of the maximum error per exposure of the imitating agent not using proprioceptive matching over the maximum error of the imitating agent that does can be seen in Figure 12.12 (bottom panel), constantly decreasing and below one. This indicates that the numerator is minimized faster than the denominator. This indicates that ignoring the proprioceptive component improves the performance rate. Ignoring the proprioceptive component of the entry keys will confine the number of entries only to the number of different actions, states and effects that define each model pattern, resulting in a much smaller search space. This reduced number of entries in the correspondence library will have the opportunity to update and improve more often, and explains the performance rate improvement. However given enough time, it is expected that proprioception would allow the imitator to eventually learn much finer control in distinguishing appropriate choices of matching actions depending on its own body state.[7]

12.5.4   *Loose perceptual matching*

When the ALICE mechanism looks in the correspondence library to find the relevant entry to the currently perceived model actions, states and effects, it is possible not to require an exact match of the entry keys, but one that is close enough, depending on a threshold. We conducted ten experimental runs under the same conditions. Each run consisted of 20 exposures to the model behaviour for two imitating agents, one of them accepting a 10% margin of looseness for the trigger keys and the other one requiring an exact match, both using proprioception. Model and imitator agents had the same embodiment ($L = [20, 20, 20]$) and the metric used was a weighted half-half combination of the action and state metrics. The generating mechanism for the imitating agents created five random actions to choose from. The maximum metric value for each exposure was logged and is shown in Figure 12.13, using loose matching (top panel) and exact matching (middle panel).

The ratio of the maximum error of the agent using loose over the agent using exact matching can be seen in the bottom panel of Figure 12.13,

---

[7] In this implementation, using proprioception increases the size of the search space by a factor of 36 to the *n*th power, where *n* is the number of joints in the imitator.

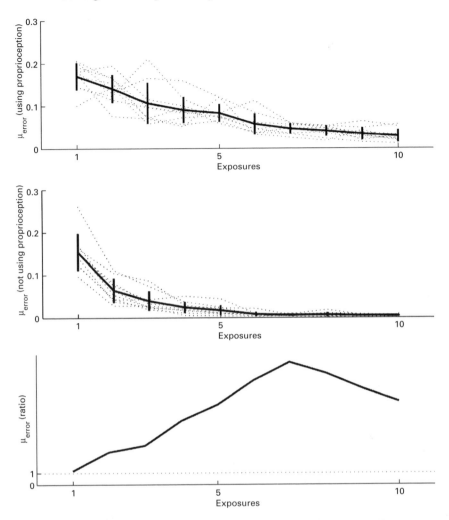

Figure 12.12 Experiments comparing using and not using proprioception. The maximum error metric value of robotic agents over ten exposures not using proprioception (top panel) vs using proprioception (middle panel) when searching through the correspondence library entry keys. The ratio of the maximum error per exposure of the imitating agent not employing proprioception over the maximum error of the imitating agent that does (bottom panel) indicates some comparative reduction of error when not using proprioception. In each panel, the thicker line shows the average values of all the ten experiments, with the bars indicating the standard deviation. Both model and imitator agents have the same embodiment $L = [20, 20, 20]$ and the imitator agents use a half-half composite of the action and state metrics. Both imitators synchronize and allow for 10% loose perceptual matching.

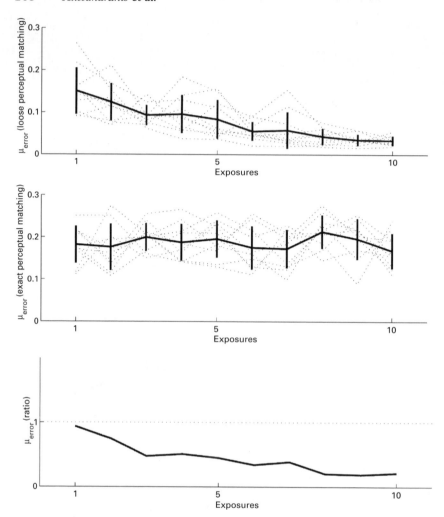

Figure 12.13 Experiments comparing the use of loose perceptual matching. The average maximum error metric value of robotic agents over ten exposures using loose matching (top panel) vs. using exact matching (middle panel). The ratio of the maximum error per exposure of the imitating agent using loose matching over the maximum error of the imitating agent that uses exact matching (bottom panel) indicates a comparative many-fold reduction of error with use of loose matching. In each panel, the thicker line shows the average values of all the ten experiments, with the bars indicating the standard deviation. Both model and imitator agents have the same embodiment $L = [20, 20, 20]$ and the imitator agents use a half-half composite of the action and state metrics. Both imitators synchronize and use proprioception.

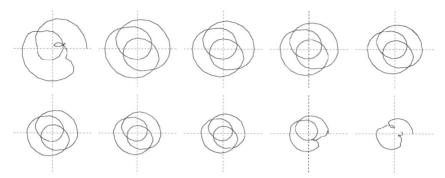

Figure 12.14 Example of an agent imitating with a changing embodiment. The initial embodiment of the imitator is $L = [20, 20, 20]$ (top left). Shown are the effect trails of the imitator (left to right, top to bottom) for ten consecutive imitation attempts. A growth vector $G = [-1, -1, -1]$ is used. The final embodiment is $L = [10, 10, 10]$ (bottom right).

constantly decreasing and below one. This indicates that the numerator is minimized faster than the denominator, showing a faster improvement of performance for the imitator agent using loose matching. Examining the middle panel of Figure 12.13, there is no obvious performance improvement in this early stage of learning, although the same amount of time is enough to minimize the error for the agent using a loose matching in the top panel. This is mostly due to the large number of entries created in the correspondence library due to the different proprioceptive states that the agent visits during the imitation attempts. The exact match requirement will create a large number with the same perceptive but different proprioceptive part of the keys.

12.5.5 Changes in the agent embodiment

For each agent, vector L defines its embodiment, the number of arm segments and their lengths. We can define a growth vector G, of the same size as L. By adding (or subtracting) these two vectors we get L, a new embodiment with modified joint lengths, simulating the development of the agent. The growth vector can either increase or reduce the length for each of the joints. The number of joints must remain constant because such a change makes the existing contents so far of the correspondence library invalid.[8] The growth vector can be used to simulate the body development of the imitator agent during the learning process.

---

[8] A robotic arm with a different number of joints would not be able to perform the stored actions, as they describe the angle changes for each of the existing arm joints when those actions were created.

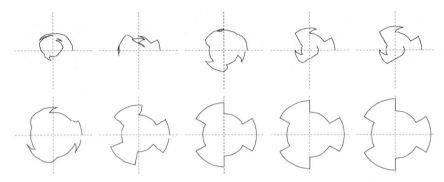

Figure 12.15 Example of an agent imitating with a changing embodiment. The initial embodiment of the imitator is $L = [10, 10, 10]$ (top left). A growth vector $G = [1, 1, 1]$ is used. The final embodiment is $L = [20, 20, 20]$ (bottom right).

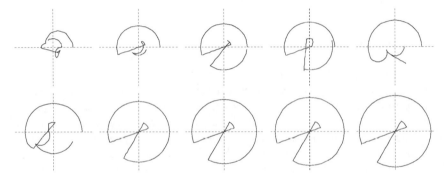

Figure 12.16 Example of an agent imitating with a changing embodiment. The initial embodiment of the imitator is $L = [10, 10, 10]$ (top left). A growth vector $G = [1, 1, 1]$ is used. The final embodiment is $L = [20, 20, 20]$ (bottom right).

Figures 12.14 to 12.16 show examples of imitator agents that try to imitate a model while a growth vector is used after each imitation attempt, modifying their embodiment.[9] In these examples, the growth vectors equally expand or shorten the length of the imitator's arm segments. Although the imitator constantly changes embodiment, the learning process is relatively unaffected, resulting in a robust imitation performance.

The metric used in these examples is the action metric, compensating for the large range of dissimilar embodiments, and the difference in what

[9] The model agents preserve a constant embodiment.

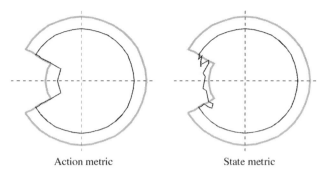

Action metric   State metric

Figure 12.17   Qualitative effect of the metric used by an imitating agent that changes embodiment. Both imitator agents have the same initial embodiment as the model ($L = [20, 20, 20]$). The figure showns the imitators after ten imitation attempts, having used a growth vector $G = [0, -1, 0]$ after each exposure, with modified embodiments $L = [20, 10, 20]$. The imitator on the left used the action metric, while the imitator on the right used the state metric. The superimposed grey trail shows the model effect pattern for qualitative comparison.

they afford. The choice of metrics greatly affects the character and quality of the imitation, especially between dissimilar embodiments. For example if the effect metric is used instead of the action metric, very poor results are observed, as the paint strokes created by the shorter joints cannot successfully compensate for the longer strokes achieved by the longer arms of the reference model. Figure 12.17 shows an example of the qualitative effect if the state metric is used, instead of the action metric. The growth vector used is $G = [0, -1, 0]$, shortening the imitator's middle arm segment. The action metric is less affected by the embodiment modification, resulting in a 'smaller' version of the model's effect trail (shown in grey). In contrast, the imitator using the state metric effectively tries to conserve the shape of the pattern by performing actions that achieve similar states.

These examples show that the ALICE mechanism can be robust enough (with a certain tolerance) to compensate for embodiment changes during the initial learning stage (or even later, if the imitator can again be exposed to the model).

12.6   Conclusions and discussion

In nature, many organisms' bodies grow and change in the course of their lives. Still, the ones that learn socially are able to retain and adapt socially transmitted capabilities despite these changes, whether injurious or natural, to their embodiment. Robots too and other artificial agents that learn socially could benefit from such robustness to embodiment changes. Such a capacity to adapt social learning despite embodiment change has been demonstrated here via an artificial intelligence learning mechanism framework (ALICE), where the learning is guided by previous experience and evaluation according to given metrics to solve a correspondence problem.

We also showed that loose perceptual matching and synchronization with the demonstrator each resulted in faster learning with lower error rates. Counter-intuitively, in the experiments here use of proprioception in building up a correspondence slowed learning. This is most likely due to the larger state space – there is more to learn if proprioception is employed; however, we hypothesize that further work will show that its employment is ultimately beneficial for longer term learning in more complex scenarios.

The work here demonstrates the principle that artificial social learning mechanisms, such as implementations of ALICE, for solving the correspondence problem can be used in populations of robots or agents, to achieve cultural transmission in such populations, even heterogeneous ones consisting of individuals whose embodiments are dissimilar. This may in the future prove useful in the autonomous social learning and adaptation of groups of robots, on factory shop floor or elsewhere, and in social learning interactions in which heterogeneous agents are involved, e.g. in human–robot interaction. For example, a human might demonstrate a task to a factory robot, which then carries it out, adapting its actions even when its embodiment is perturbed (e.g. by wear-and-tear). Later, when new model robots with different kinds of actuators, degrees of freedom, and so on, come to work in the factory, they acquire skills and task capabilities by learning socially from the robots that are already there. Over generations of robots, cultural knowledge is transmitted, with the robots adapting it to their own changing embodiments.

Acknowledgments

The work described in this paper was partially conducted within the EU Integrated COGNIRON ('The Cognitive Robot Companion') and funded by the European Commission Division FP6-IST Future and Emerging Technologies under Contract FP6-002020.

REFERENCES

Alissandrakis, A. (2003). *Imitation and Solving the Correspondence Problem for Dissimilar Embodiments – A Generic Framework*. PhD thesis, University of Hertfordshire.

Alissandrakis, A., Nehaniv, C. L. and Dautenhahn, K. (2002). Imitation with ALICE: learning to imitate corresponding actions across dissimilar embodiments. *IEEE Transactions on Systems, Man and Cybernetics: Part A*, **32(4)**, 482–96.

Byrne, R. W. (1999). Imitation without intentionality. Using string parsing to copy the organization of behaviour. *Animal Cognition*, **2**, 63–72.

Dautenhahn, K. and Nehaniv, C. L. (2002). An agent-based perspective on imitation. In Dautenhahn, K. and Nehaniv, C. L. (eds.), *Imitation in Animals and Artifacts*. Cambridge, MA: MIT Press, 1–40.

Dawkins, R. (1976). *The Selfish Gene*. Oxford, UK: Oxford University Press.

Heyes, C. M. and Ray, E. D. (2000). What is the significance of imitation in animals? *Advances in the Study of Behavior*, **29**, 215–45.

Kuniyoshi, Y., Inaba, M. and Inoue, H. (1994). Learning by watching: extracting reusable task knowledge from visual observations of human performance. *IEEE Transactions on Robotics and Automation*, **10**, 799–822.

Kuniyoshi, Y., Inoue, H. and Inaba, M. (1990). Design and implementation of a system that generates assembly programs from visual recognition of human action sequences. In *Proceedings of the IEEE International Workshop on Intelligent Robots and Systems IROS '90*, 567–74.

Nehaniv, C. L. and Dautenhahn, K. (1998). Mapping between dissimilar bodies: affordances and the algebraic foundations of imitation. In Demiris, J. and Birk, A. (eds.), *Proceedings of the European Workshop on Learning Robots 1998 (EWLR-7), Edinburgh, 20 July 1998*, 64–72.

Nehaniv, C. L. and Dautenhahn, K. (2000). Of hummingbirds and helicopters: an algebraic framework for interdisciplinary studies of imitation and its applications. In Demiris, J. and Birk, A. (eds.), *Interdisciplinary Approaches to Robot Learning*. World Scientific Series in Robotics and Intelligent Systems, 136–61.

Nehaniv, C. L. and Dautenhahn, K. (2001). Like me? – measures of correspondence and imitation. *Cybernetics and Systems*, **32(1–2)**, 11–51.

Nehaniv, C. L. and Dautenhahn, K. (2002). The correspondence problem. In Dautenhahn, K. and Nehaniv, C. L. (eds.), *Imitation in Animals and Artifacts*. Cambridge, MA: MIT Press, 41–61.

Rendell, L. and Whitehead, H. (2001). Culture in whales and dolphins. *Behavioral and Brain Sciences*, **24(2)**, 309–82.

Whiten, A., Goodall, J., McGrew, W., Nishida, T., Reynolds, V., Sugiyama, Y., Tutin, C., Wrangham, R. and Boesch, C. (1999). Cultures in chimpanzees. *Nature*, **399**, 682–5.

Part V

Synchrony and turn-taking as communicative mechanisms

The following three chapters highlight the important role of synchrony and turn-taking in imitative interactions. Two particular aspects are emphasized in this section: firstly, the *communicative* role and function of imitation which, in particular in research involving robots or other artifacts, has often been neglected in favour of the skill acquisition aspect of imitation, and secondly, the *dynamical* nature of imitative interactions where synchrony and turn-taking facilitate inter-subjectivity, sharing of experience, communication and empathy.

The first two chapters in this section provide excellent examples of Braitenberg's synthetic psychology approach (Braitenberg, 1984) where the synthesis and study of artifacts (simulated agents or robots) can shed light on psychological phenomena that have been observed in humans and other animals. In experiments with artifacts the systems' design parameters as well as input/output characteristics can be accessed directly, which can give rise to studies and types of analysis otherwise impossible with biological systems. Both chapters demonstrate how psychological experiments have led to robotic experiments and computer simulations, whose results in turn can be compared to work in psychology and inform further studies and the development of theoretical frameworks that apply across biological and artificial systems.

Arnaud Revel and Jacqueline Nadel present inter-disciplinary work that compares imitation in human infants and autonomous robots, providing concrete examples from both research areas that are underpinning their framework. The chapter highlights the communicative function of synchronization and turn-taking. Imitation is seen as a continuous phenomenon throughout development whereby learning and communication are intrinsically linked, grounded in and resulting from the dynamics of synchrony and turn-taking in perception–action couplings. Many approaches on imitation in animals and artifacts have focused on

Imitation and Social Learning in Robots, Humans and Animals, ed. Chrystopher L. Nehaniv and Kerstin Dautenhahn. Published by Cambridge University Press.
© Cambridge University Press 2007.

situations whereby a learner benefits from observations of or interactions with a knowledgeable teacher (see Part VII, Social feedback, in this volume), whereby the individual (or the group/species) can benefit from imitation and social learning by learning new skills, e.g. skills of how to cope with or more efficiently exploit environmental resources. In contrast, communicative imitation leads to benefits in both interaction partners, generating changes in both in a dynamical process coupling the imitator and the imitatee, who reverse roles. This 'two-body' psychology, applied to robots or other artifacts, can potentially open new research avenues where sharing of experience is seen as an important prerequisite that might lead to sophisticated forms of interaction and communication that are truly grounded in the dynamics and the experience of the two partners involved in the dyad.

In the second chapter of this section, Takashi Ikegami and Hiroyuki Iizuka study dynamical properties of interaction and turn-taking whereby turn-taking is considered a realization of inter-subjectivity. Ikegami and Iizuka take the view that turn-taking emerges from body synchrony but requires cooperative and co-creative activity as well as mutual adaptation among the participants, involving temporal and spontaneous role splitting and role switching. These issues are investigated in a simulation study involving dynamically coupled agents chasing each other in a 2-D world whereby turn-taking behaviour is being evolved in two separate populations for both agents using a genetic algorithm. Alternate turn-taking and the ability to predict each other's behaviour increase the agents' fitness. Results, including a variety of spatio-temporal movement patterns emerging, are discussed in the context of infant–caretaker or child–child interaction. The objective of their work is to understand key mechanisms of coupled dynamics that elicit turn-taking behaviour with the ultimate aim to develop a theoretical framework of turn-taking behaviour, derived from studies with robots and computer simulations.

The third chapter by Kerstin Dautenhahn, Sarah Woods and Christina Kaouri is a speculative position paper fleshing out possible connections between bullying behaviour on the one hand and autism and psychopathy on the other hand, discussed in light of mechanisms of imitation and empathy. Evidence in the literature suggests that bullies as well as psychopaths possess a well-developed theory-of-mind and are very able to manipulate and 'read' others' minds. In bullies, processes of automatic and controlled empathy might still be intact: anti-social behaviour could arise from an overemphasis on goal-directed processes of controlled empathy. In contrast, psychopaths might have impairments in processing emotional information which could prevent them from genuinely experiencing empathy with another person on an emotional, rather than

cognitive level. Intervention programmes for bullies (as well as psychopaths) focusing on the cognitive level of empathy and social understanding have yet to demonstrate any long-term success. According to the
argument presented in this chapter, intervention programmes focusing on
the emotional level involved in automatic empathy could be exploited, e.g.
by building upon immediate imitation and imitative turn-taking games
that might facilitate intersubjectivity and empathy. It is an open issue how
exactly this might be achieved – however, this proposed direction might
inspire new research.

The three chapters in this section highlight the many facets of imitation in a social context, where inter-subjectivity and the ability to
'connect' with others via a dynamic process of mutual coupling of bodies
and minds in interaction is a core element. The dynamics of social interaction, and turn-taking in particular, are often viewed as 'easy', after all,
we all 'know' how to do it already from birth. Only when trying to design
socially intelligent robots, where turn-taking and synchronization with
the social environment are usually absent e.g. due to 'rule-based' control
mechanisms, does it become apparent what is lacking, namely important building blocks for social cognition, empathy and inter-subjectivity
which cannot be 'taught', but are grounded in the dynamics of interaction
with the social and non-social environment, and need to be 'experienced'
by an agent (see Part IV, Development and embodiment, and Part II,
Mirroring and 'mind-reading', in this volume).

REFERENCE

Braitenberg, V. (1984). *Vehicles: Experiments in Synthetic Psychology*. Cambridge,
MA: MIT Press.

13   How to build an imitator

Arnaud Revel and Jacqueline Nadel

13.1   Introduction

The aim of this chapter is to parallel the development of imitation in a human infant and in an autonomous robot. To draw a valid comparison between the two systems – namely the infant and the robot – it is necessary to insure that their respective architectures present sufficient basic similarities. The present chapter will thus start with a description of the main features that enable a human neonate and the autonomous robot designed by the ETIS group to develop a capacity to imitate. Note that the robot is not implemented to imitate and that imitation will develop spontaneously as a result of the capacity of the robot to couple perception and action together with an imprecision in its visual perception.

Within the framework of a bottom-up perspective, we propose in the second part of the chapter to consider the development of imitation as a continuous phenomenon throughout development. Consequently, we will devote the third part of the chapter to show how basic perception–action coupling may not only account for the development of learning but also for the development of the communicative function of imitation. Exploring the communicative function of imitation is a new topic for roboticists, who classically consider imitation as a way to learn more rapidly relevant interactions within a novel environment. A model of synchronization of rhythm between two systems describes the first steps toward a communicative use of imitation. To conclude, we emphasize the benefit of drawing parallels between different autonomous entities to understand the basic conditions for building a self-developing imitator.

Imitation and Social Learning in Robots, Humans and Animals, ed. Chrystopher L. Nehaniv and Kerstin Dautenhahn. Published by Cambridge University Press.
© Cambridge University Press 2007.

13.2   Human neonates and the ETIS robot share sensory equipment and perceptual competence, motor equipment and autonomy. Is it enough to share the ability to imitate?

13.2.1   Vision

The ETIS robot captures visual information via a CCD camera. Vision includes the processing of several basic perceptual features such as edge detection, Gabor filtering, optical flow, etc., and possibly the analysis of "what is interesting in a visual scene." This attention mechanism is highlighted by "pop-out" behaviors (Treisman, 1988). It follows that our robot is not visually naive but rather is "encouraged" to focus "attention" on visual points emphasized by the pop-out: corners, highly contrasted zones, moving areas and so on. In this respect the robot, like the human newborn, has pre-organized vision. Indeed, though visually naive, human neonates are able to show consistent, preferential looking for patterned, 3-D, highly contrasted and face-like stimuli (Slater, 1998). Their behavior demonstrates that organizing features of perception, such as visual constancies, are present at birth. Newborns do not only react selectively to visual stimuli, they also actively explore their visual world according to a few simple rules such as the search for edges (Haith, 1980).

13.2.2   Sensitivity to movement

When coupled with a "pop-out" mechanism, the optical flow allows the ETIS robot to be visually sensitive to movement (attention is focused on moving objects). Similarly, the basic visual preference of the human newborn for dynamic vs. static patterns is well established. This sensitivity to movement is an important condition for a system to generate dynamics such as the development of imitation. Human newborns do not pay much attention to stationary stimuli, and consequently neonatal imitation cannot be elicited with static models (Vinter, 1986).

13.2.3   Kinesthesis

The ETIS robot gets kinesthetic information thanks to internal feedback in actuators, and a kind of tactile sense through infrared (IR) sensors. Initially, the robot has never experienced the use of its actuators and thus has no kinesthetic background. In contrast, human neonates are born kinesthetically experienced, although visual–kinesthetic matching is not mature at birth (see Mitchell, Chapter 6, this volume).

Figure 13.1 Simple sensorimotor connections allow the building of "reflex" behaviours.

Figure 13.2 Any low-level processing allows the building of "perceptive" information.

13.2.4 Motor equipment

Human newborns are equipped with prewired sensorimotor coupling (a repertoire of more than 15 different motor patterns at birth) set off in response to classes of stimuli. Robot's effectors (wheels, grabbers, etc.) are designed so as to play the same role as the infant's limbs. Like a neonate, the robot has motor patterns that it can use from scratch to interact with its environment. Reflexes such as phototaxy, obstacle avoidance (Braitenberg, 1984) have been embedded in the robot architecture. At the very beginning, simple "reflex" behaviors can be obtained by directly connecting the sensors to the effectors (see Figure 13.1).

A slightly more complex alternative consists in adding a low-level process of sensing that can be interpreted as leading to perception (see Figure 13.2).

For instance, coupling the detection of the optical flow to the robot's own movement can allow the robot to follow moving things.

13.2.5 Autonomy

Human infants are not only responsive to the stimuli of their environment, they are also stimulus-expectant. In other words, they actively seek for selected classes of stimuli such as moving stimuli, face-like stimuli, voice-like sounds and so on. They have their own goals that are not dictated by the necessity to respond to prepotent stimuli. Rather they create and modify their environment via the dynamics of their search for given stimuli, and bidirectionally they evolve, thanks to the processing of the stimuli they seek for. They therefore constitute a dynamic system with their environment (Thelen *et al.*, 2001). The ETIS robot is also an autonomous system insofar as it develops selective interaction with its environment according to goals that have not been implemented as such. In a way, its designers cannot predict precisely how it will develop.

13.2.6   Attraction toward novelty

Human newborns and the ETIS robot share attraction toward novelty. It has been demonstrated that newborns habituate to a repeated stimulus and finally ignore it (Sokolov, 1963), and that they prefer novel stimuli compared to familiar ones (Fantz, 1964). Put together, these two findings lead to "the habituation paradigm," a basic protocol testing the infant's ability to differentiate between two stimuli. The way in which newborns expect new experiences is largely dependent on neural activity induced by species-typical aspects of the pre-natal and post-natal environments. However, environmental features are not defined once and for all; they change throughout development under the bidirectional influences of maturational processes – which open new avenues for exploration – and of previous experience – which provides new definitions of what is novel. Probabilistic epigenesis (Gottlieb, 1992) sustains the idea that infants select their own necessary input for subsequent development. Preference for human patterns orients toward social stimuli. Attraction toward novelty filters novel patterns as prepotent stimuli and prepares the field for the learning of appropriate responses to new situations. The changes influence subsequent structure of the brain via a rich epigenetic interaction between mind and environment (Karmiloff-Smith, 1992). Similarly, neural connections in the robot can locally change over time, thus simulating the role of experience in brain maturation. Additionally, the constraints of immaturity guide the infant's developmental pathways. Let us take the example of the newborn's vision. Newborn vision is poor (approximately a factor of five less than a normal adult's), but infants cannot see better than their basic neural structures allow. Higher visual functioning would generate more problems than it would provide solutions for the developing infant. The infant would need to filter more visual "noise" to attend to relevant information during a period when s/he does not know what relevant information is (Hainline, 1998). While it might appear that the infant's visual functioning is rather erratic, the search for visual information actually benefits from a level of immaturity. Within the framework of a probabilistic epigenesis, immaturity can be seen, at least to some extent, as guiding the infant's experience, directing and simplifying the search and processing of information in the same way as the

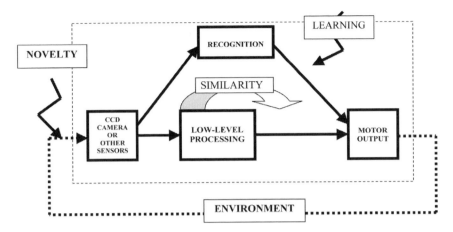

Figure 13.3 Complete PerAc architecture. Sensors can either be connected directly to motor commands in order to perform "reflexes," or be integrated in a perceptual system of recognition which could learn a novel behavior.

robot's explorations benefit from the architectural constraints given by the designer.

13.2.7 Perception–action coupling

The choice to elaborate only upon architectures in which perception and action are intrinsically coupled leads to considering the whole dynamics of the system formed by the robot and the environment. In this case an invariant is defined as a given perception–action configuration that *emerges* from the dynamical interaction with the environment and is able to self-maintain through time. As a consequence of these dynamics, the architectures we use are all based on a generic unsupervised neural network control architecture called PerAc (Perception–Action architecture – see Figure 13.3 – (Gaussier and Zrehen, 1995) inspired by Albus (1991), Brooks (1986), and Hecht-Nielsen (1987)). This architecture allows on-line learning of sensory–motor associations. Depending on the learning procedure used to associate the recognition system and the system of selection of action, different behaviors can be obtained.

If the learning process is an associative rule (Hebbian rule), the robot learns to associate the perceptual recognition of a situation with an action (Pavlovian conditioning). Via the use of neurons the activities of which are linked with the recognition of a given place as sensory input, the PerAc architecture allows the robot to learn a basin of attraction. This basin of attraction defines dynamically the recognition of the location of a goal insofar as only locations in the vicinity of the goal are learned (Gaussier and Zrehen, 1995). The use of reinforcement learning as an adaptive rule allows for an even more flexible system. For instance, a robot was trained to reach the exit of a maze using only local visual cues (Gaussier *et al.*, 1997).

That the human infant is born capable of primitive perception–action coupling is still a matter of debate. Pre-wired fetal sensorimotor patterns can be modulated and adapted to visual perception of external models, as attested by neonatal imitation. This can be considered as an example of perception–action coupling.

13.3   Anything else needed to be an imitator?

Perceptually and motorally equipped as they are, attracted toward novel and moving stimuli, and able to couple perception and action, will our two autonomous systems show an immediate ability to imitate? The response, of course, depends on how we define imitation. Psychologists are not unanimous on this. Imitation may be defined in a variety of ways. The broadest definition of imitation is that of a matching behavior. Such a definition fits perfectly well our hypothesis of an underlying basic mechanism of perception–action coupling from which emerges cognitively higher classes of imitations. It is not however the main stance held. Many attempts have been undertaken to reduce the ambiguity linked to such a broad definition. Intentionality on one hand (Whiten and Ham, 1992) and novelty on the other hand (Tomasello, 1998), have been esteemed by major psychologists to be two decisive features of imitation which contribute to disambiguate the link between imitation and other matching behaviors. The wide range of matching behaviors, which are either enhanced by object properties or suggested by social observation, do not require an intention to imitate. Indeed, producing a behavior which is similar to another does not necessarily stem from the intention to imitate. Several observers facing the same stimulus may simultaneously produce the same action just because object A suggests action A'. Instead of reflecting imitation, such a behavioral similarity is considered to be driven by *stimulus enhancement*, since it is the stimulus which affords the action. The neonate is not supposed to have acquired such knowledge about affordances between actions and objects. Similarly, at the start, our autonomous robot has not experienced object–action relationships.

Another category of matching, labeled by Bandura (1971) as *social facilitation*, originates from social influence and concerns the cases when behavior by agent A appears to be prepotent among all potential behaviors and suggests the display of the same behavior to B. This again does not require the intention to imitate, although social facilitation may be handled as an intentional social signal. In all cases, the behavior matched is familiar to B, and not necessarily explicitly intentional. In contrast, those behaviors which were called "true imitations" in the 30s (Guillaume, 1926; Piaget, 1945; Wallon, 1942) were characterized as intentional reproductions of an action that has never been previously performed by the imitator. Paradoxically, the core imitative process is not considered as resulting in similar behavior, but rather in similar goals that may be achieved via different procedures. Similarly, "genuine imitation" is the label presently used mainly for reproductions of novel patterns of actions, or programs of actions. Such a restrictive definition of imitation solves some important problems. It clearly assumes, for instance, that imitation is intentional, and involves planning as well as encoding of new procedures. It stresses the evolutionary links between intelligence and imitation (Byrne and Russon, 1998). It rehabilitates the cognitive status of imitation. This exclusive position however reactivates the debate about neonatal imitation among developmental psychologists (Heyes, 2001).

A number of psychologists consider that neonatal imitation depends on a process of active intermodal mapping by which infants' self-produced movements provide proprioceptive feedback that can be compared to the visually specified target, via a common supramodal framework (Meltzoff and Moore, 1999). This renders authors like Mitchell (Mitchell, 2002; see also Chapter 6, this volume) sceptical about the very existence of neonatal imitation since kinesthetic–visual matching is not mature at birth. There is an alternative, however, to the idea that neonatal imitation originates from intermodal matching. Another explanation, from Jeannerod (1997) is that imitation is a perception–action coupling which simply requires the respond to the perception of movement by similar movement. As Meltzoff put it, neonatal imitation reveals an innate link between observed and executed acts (Meltzoff, 2002). The concept of shared motor representations accounts for the fact that doing something, seeing something being done and doing what we see being done share the same cerebral activations (Decety and Grèzes, 1999, Decety, 2002). When facing adults protruding their tongue, neonates do not open their mouth (Meltzoff and Moore, 1983), or blink their eyes (Kugiumutzakis, 1999), and three-month-olds are able to imitate a motor trajectory like touching their cheek with their hand (Nadel et al., 2004). Using a preference looking paradigm, Rochat (1998) has shown that three-month-olds prefer looking at their own legs moving than at other legs, thus suggesting a close link between self-perception and action. Recent neuroimaging studies support the idea that perception and action share the same biological finality (Decety, 2002). Perrett and colleagues have discovered in the superior temporal sulcus (STS) neurons that are selectively activated for recognition of action, and that respond specifically to interactions between hand and object (Perrett *et al.*, 1990). Another area involved in observation of action is the discovery by Rizzolatti and colleagues in the monkey (Di Pellegrino *et al.*, 1992) and then in the human premotor cortex (Fadiga *et al.*, 1995) of a class of premotor neurons that they called "mirror neurons" because they discharge both when a movement or an action is performed or observed. This does not necessarily lead to the production of the movement or the action observed, rather it is a motor representation of the observed movement or action which may be used to imitate immediately or later. According to Rizzolatti *et al.* (2002), two mechanisms may account for the involvement of mirror neurons: a low-level resonance mechanism in play when they discharge while performing or observing simple movements, and a high-level resonance mechanism in play when mirror neurons discharge for the representation of the neural activity generated by the effective production of the action observed. This is an interesting proposal which could lead to the adoption of a broad definition of imitation, including neonatal capacity to reproduce movements. Indeed, producing a behavior which is similar to another does not necessarily require a semantic representation of the action to be performed, nor does it stem from an intention to imitate.

A century ago, the possibility that newborns can imitate was already debated in relation to the definition of imitation itself. Piaget (1945), inspired by Baldwin (1894), denied any imitative capacity in the newborn, originating imitation (perception–action loop) from circular reactions (action–perception loop) that take place during the first months of life. Against this view, Zazzo (1957) reported imitation of tongue protrusion in newborns aged 7 to 15 days. Maratos (1973), Meltzoff and Moore (1983), Kugiumutzakis (1999) and other authors confirmed his observations. According to Rizzolatti *et al.* (2002), mirror neurons' discharges for simple movements may explain low-level matchings such as social facilitation, stimulus enhancement and neonatal imitation. By contrast, mirror neurons' discharges for actions may be involved in high-level imitations insofar as high-level imitations imply the understanding of the model's goal. The speculations held by Rizzolatti *et al.* (2002) would lead us to draw a continuum between primitive uncontrolled matching behaviors and those matching behaviors that concern familiar actions and are not informed by the intention to imitate. The recent perspective held by Byrne and Russon (1998) also avoids a clear-cut distinction. They do not deny the label of imitation to certain behaviors such as social facilitations but rather distinguish between two levels of imitation: a low-level

imitation regrouping primary matching behaviors and a high-level imitation regrouping creative insights about interesting goals. Following this
path, we will propose that human newborns and the ETIS robot, because
they are able to couple perception and action, are capable of reacting to
a movement by re-enacting the movement.

13.4   What is needed to be a self-developing imitator?

In order to be a self-developing imitator, neonates and the ETIS robot
do not only need to present the relevant features described above. They
also need to have motives to imitate, since imitation grows when used.
The adoption of a functionalist perspective is not widespread among
specialists of imitation development. Nonetheless it is a crucial question.

13.4.1   The two adaptive functions of imitation: learning
and communication

A clear motive to imitate novel actions or movements is the attraction toward novelty that neonates and the ETIS robot demonstrate.
This attraction accounts for the learning function of imitation, a crucial
adaptive function allowing cultural knowledge and transfer of abilities
(Tomasello, 1998). Imitation has long been viewed by behaviorists as
prompted by purposes of learning: the "look-at-me and do-like-me" procedure is a key for elementary academic and other kinds of acquisitions.

In the 80s however, a few voices started to propose that imitation has
two functions, a cognitive and a social function according to Užgiris
(1981), a function of learning and a function of communication according
to Nadel and colleagues (Nadel, 1986, Nadel-Brulfert and Baudonnière,
1982). The demonstration of a communicative function of imitation is
given when we take account of the fact that imitation has two facets:
imitating and being imitated. The recognition of being imitated changes
the social position of the imitatee: it is a way to take the floor. Nadel
(1986) discovered years ago that around 18 months non-verbal children
start taking an explicit advantage of these two facets of imitation to take
turns. The co-ordination of imitating and being imitated takes the form
of a communicative system without words but with shared motor actions
related to shared motor representations.

The imitations concern familiar or novel actions or movements. The
motive of this use of imitation was shown to be exploring the behavior
of others, sometimes monitoring their behavior and sometimes following
their monitoring: it was sharing (Nadel, 2002).

What adds the description of a communicative function to the
description of imitation as a social behavior? Social behaviors are those

behaviors that are socially embedded. This, however, does not mean that they lead to inter-subjective sharing. Learning via imitation benefits the individual, the group or species, but does not imply sharing anything with the model. The model may be absent, unrelated, unknown, dead or an abstract structure of thinking or doing. By contrast, communicating via imitation requires the presence of a partner, shared attention (each partner's attention focused on the other), synchronized tempo (Trevarthen, 1999) and turn-taking between the initiator and the responder. When one communicates with a partner via imitation, it benefits the two partners in as much as imitation generates changes in the imitator as well as in the model. Model and imitator form a new dynamic system, an evolving system of similarities built on the basis of two different individual epigeneses from the interaction of which emerges new possibilities for both.

How can we state that imitation serves a communicative function and not simply a social function? Because it presents the key features of a communicative system where young human beings interact dynamically in a way which changes the states of mind of each partner (Nadel, 2002). Among these features, two are of particular interest for a comparison with ETIS autonomous robots because they are observed very early in development. These two main features are: turn-taking and synchrony.

13.4.1.1   Turn-taking

Meeting without an adult present in an experimental setting composed of two identical sets of attractive toys, dyads or triads of two-year-olds take advantage of the fact that imitation involves two roles: imitator and model. They use these two roles alternately and share the monitoring of role switching. The monitoring is efficient since we found a strong positive correlation per children between the number of times they were an imitator and the number of times they were a model (Nadel, 1986). This is a sophisticatedly intentional use of imitation. Nine-month-olds with their mother simply alternate matching the same action, thus achieving turn-taking in imitations, in a way described by Pawlby (1977) as imitative rounds. Eckerman (1993) comments on this phenomenon as "imitation begets imitation." This phenomenon seems to appear far earlier than nine months. We have found it already in dyads of two-month-olds interacting with their mother via our TV system. This TV system allows us to present alternately to the infants an on-line or a replayed image of their mother (Nadel *et al.*, 1999). During on-line interaction, mothers often imitate their infants. By contrast, mother's imitations cannot occur during the replayed situation. Comparing the number of times infants imitate their mother during on-line maternal communication and during the similar maternal episode replayed, we found a highly significant difference

Figure 13.4 1. The infant raises his arm. 2. Mother imitates and then raises her fingers and turns her wrist. 3. The infant starts turning his wrist and raising his finger.

between the two situations: the mean number of imitations was 3.3 for a 30 second on-line episode and 0.3 for the same episode replayed (Nadel *et al.*, 2004). This suggests an influence of mother's imitation on infant imitation. Reciprocal imitations observed in five out of the ten infants (see an example depicted in Figure 13.4) confirms the idea of an early sensitivity to being imitated.

The rounds of reciprocal imitations that Pawlby (1977) and Užgiris and colleagues (1989) found at 12 weeks in naturalistic situations gives a convergent picture in favor of an early influence of being imitated on imitative performance.

13.4.1.2 *Synchrony*
Once roles are momentarily distributed, partners coordinate their tempo in order to achieve synchrony between the model and the imitator's activity (Nadel *et al.*, 1999): before starting an action, the model waits until the imitator is ready and the imitator rushes to perform simultaneously.

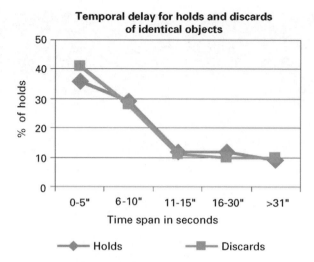

Figure 13.5   Temporal delay for holds and discards.

They are also able to plan temporal coordination of action between model and imitator so as to achieve almost perfect contingency: the model waits while the imitator rushes. This co-ordination results in a very short delay between the starts and ends of similar actions.

To sum up, the distinction between two functional uses of imitation in human development is a decisive one. But there is no hierarchy of importance between the two functions. Rather, the development of each has a positive effect on the development of the other. For instance, seeing her own actions repeated by another (as is the case in the communicative use of imitation) contributes to intermodal calibration of the body (I see what I do) and to the building of motor representations of actions. These developmental pieces are building blocks for the development of learning by imitation, that requires the recombination of stored actions and representations into new schemas of action. Conversely, learning new actions enriches the motor repertoire and allows the infant to imitate the partner more readily and more frequently, thus facilitating the development of imitation for communicative purpose – a dynamical process reorganizing the system composed by the imitator and the imitatee.

13.4.2   Robot

We can assume that in the not so far future, humans will have to share their environment with robots: at home (think of AIBO or tamagochi), in the streets (washing robots, etc.) or in a business context (handler robots etc.). If we want everybody to be able to interact with those robots, they should be easy to use and adaptive. To simplify relationships between robots and humans, a natural way to give them orders could be to "show" the robot what to do instead of programming it. This is typically what is called "imitating" by roboticists, that is, learning to reproduce a task demonstrated by a human.

The main approach in robotics has first been based on a definition of imitation as observational learning. This definition fits well with Turing's paradigm: imitation is tackled from a point of view that consists of an analytical top-down decomposition of the process into several abstract symbolic problems as, for instance, in Kuniyoshi (1994). Kuniyoshi proposes a system allowing the imitation of the movement of a teacher's hand by a kind of observational learning. Decomposing the problem this way makes the control of the robot very simple since it consists of memorizing a series of symbols in order to reproduce them. However key problems remain unsolved, such as how to categorize the perceived movement properly according to the repertoire of actions and how to code the control of atomic actions in a proper way. Although individual, the interest of imitation in its learning function also has a social effect since it allows the transfer of knowledge from one individual to another. At another level, roboticists often neglect the fact that imitation can boost the speed of learning in a population of robots. Indeed, if a robot is alone in an environment, it has to learn to solve by its self all the tasks which are linked to this environment. In fact, the complexity of the possible sensory–motor associations is so huge that the task cannot be solved by an individual alone in a reasonable time (or even cannot be solved at all). On the contrary, if different members of a population of robots can learn by themselves, but also from each other, this drastically reduces the complexity of the learning task by allowing the spread of a given knowledge over the entire population. This is a case of observational learning, which can in turn speed up the learning of subsequent tasks by the individual. It has been underlined that in this case, imitation has not merely a learning function but also a social function which benefits everyone. Yet, although a "social" function directly involves interaction, it does not lead inevitably to a "communicative" function.

Our claim is that roboticists should take seriously the communicative function of imitation when designing a robot. In a sense, this looks like a little "Copernican" revolution since every aspect of the robot development must be seen as a dynamical process involving both learning and communication intrinsically interacting. The new focus of interest for roboticists is no longer the robot alone, but the system involving the robot and the other agent with which the robot interacts. While it is a rather original idea in robotics, this concept is already depicted in psychology as "two-body" psychology (Nadel et al., 2004).

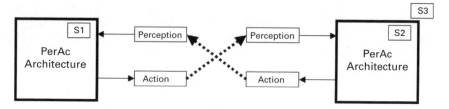

Figure 13.6 Two PerAc systems S1 and S2 in interaction (the perception of one system is linked to the action of the other system and vice versa) create a new dynamical system S3. First of all and apart from any consideration, the fact that S1 and S2 interact forces each one to stay coupled with the other and thus create a kind of "social filter" that guides the behavior of each of them.

The next question which is interesting to solve now is "what are the minimal communicative abilities which are necessary for a system to develop in a two-body psychology context?"

If we define communication as a means for two entities S1 and S2 to create something new while interacting with each other and from which each one can benefit, we can formalize this approach considering three inter-meshed dynamical systems (see Figure 13.6). According to a "one-body psychology" point of view, S1 and S2 are two dynamical systems interacting with their environment. Besides, S3, which is the result of the interaction of S1 with S2 is also a dynamical system that can be studied as such: this dynamical system S3 is more than the sum of S1 + S2. The attractor formed by the interaction of S1 and S2 is a shared attractor in the field of interest of "two-body psychology." Yet, either S1 or S2 have also converged to a dynamical attractor in their own perspective (one-body psychology). The result is that the dynamical attractor formed by the interaction produces two sensory-motor attractors, entity centered. Then, several scenarios can occur according to the "role" and "history" of S1 and S2.

One of the pioneers of an approach introducing an interactional perspective is Dautenhahn (1995) who has proposed an architecture in which one robot follows another via the use of a simple rule that consists in maintaining a homeostatic sensory–motor state in order to minimize the energetic loss. Practically, this rule simply consists of the robot maintaining contact with a moving object. By acting this way, the robot and its teacher perform similar movements and the follower "looks as if" it is imitating. Yet, in this experiment, nothing is learned by the "student" robot which therefore cannot take advantage of its experience in the long term. In fact, the main effect is that the interaction creates a dynamical

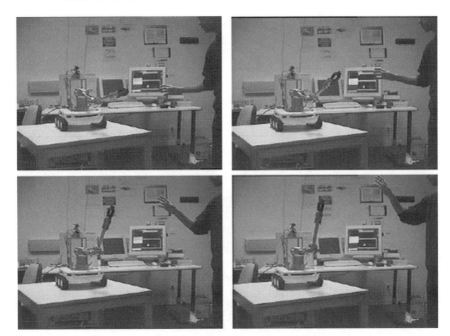

Figure 13.7 First, a neural controller learns the visuo-motor associations. To obtain a low-level imitation, we simply shift the head's position
with the body and the arm. The perceived movement is interpreted as an
error, inducing corrective movements of the arm: an imitating behavior
emerges.

attractor. The same principle has been developed with a robot doll called
Robota which mirrors classes of gestures performed by children, thus
looking as if interacting via imitation (Billard and Dautenhahn, 1998).

Following Dautenhahn, but without holding a clear distinction
between "teacher" and "student", Andry and Gaussier (Andry *et al.*,
2001) have proposed the use of the "reflex link" of their PerAc architecture as a bootstrap for interaction and imitation. The key idea is that
a perceptual "misunderstanding" can serve the function of communication between systems instead of perturbing the system seen as a whole.
In Andry and Gaussier's view, the PerAc architecture is first used to learn
visuo-motor coordination, thanks to the homeostatic principle. Second,
the very same architecture can look as if it is imitating by simply shifting
attention from self-movement to others' movement (see Figure 13.7).

An interesting point in this experiment is that a very "poor" a priori is
needed to allow imitation capabilities: here the robot does not know that
it imitates but instead tries to stay in a sensory–motor attractor which

constrains it to follow every moving object. In a framework concerning two robots following each other, Moga has shown that a robot can "learn" a sequence of actions from another (Moga and Gaussier, 1999). Limits concern how far the interactions between two autonomous robots can go. The problem rises from the fact that robot 1, acting as a model, is controlled by an open loop that does not integrate the imitator. In fact, the dynamics of interaction, as intrinsically taken into account by a human teacher, is a unique way for the imitator to learn something. There is thus a need of synchrony, which is itself linked with the ability to produce or recognize a rhythm.

13.4.2.1   *Synchrony*

To interact with another, it is necessary to be temporarily accorded with him. A second need is to share a minimal behavioral base on which each one can construct new behaviors, but also find a common repertoire for interaction.

Recently, Ito and Tani (2004) have proposed an architecture based on a recurrent neural network (RNN) which allows a humanoid robot to learn several patterns of actions from a human. They have shown that the dynamics of the learning system can adapt to the human rhythm and synchronicity. In addition, after several patterns have been learned they can be recalled by interacting with the human and novel patterns are either identified with previously learned patterns (the pattern is assimilated with an action of the repertoire), leading to a dynamical attractor being a "merging" of the learned patterns, or lead to a chaotic behavior.

As an illustration of the concept of synchronicity, Andry and Gaussier (Andry *et al.*, 2000) designed an architecture embedding the sensitivity to rhythm and the ability to use synchrony as information to generate self-reinforcement and, consequently, to learn. This approach is very interesting to interface machine communication since although no "explicit" reinforcement has been given, and no explicit time-unit has been imposed, the system has been able to learn an arbitrary rule: synchronize rhythms. Note that the goal remains to learn rather than to interact, even if interaction is the condition that allows learning to occur. Andry and Gaussier (Andry *et al.*, 2000) modified the architecture so that the goal would be to produce a given rhythm enabling the robots to remain engaged in an interaction. Detection of the frequency of the production of robot 1 can allow acceleration in the rate of production of robot 2 in order to stay in phase with robot 1. Conversely, detection of the frequency of the production of robot 1 can induce deceleration in robot 2. No distinction between the "learner" and the "teacher" exists anymore since each can self-synchronize with the rhythm of the other.

Another obstacle must be (but has not yet been) overcome: the information about the interaction itself must be taken into account for one system to act either as an "imitator" or as an "imitatee."

13.4.2.2   *Turn-taking*

The simple set-up presented above naturally leads to "turn-taking". Indeed, if one is the imitatee and the other the imitator, the former produces a behavior while the imitator tries to reduce the discrepancy between what it knows and what it perceives, thanks to learning. This continues until what the imitator does is exactly what the imitatee does: the system has thus come to an equilibrium. The gain for the imitatee is not learning, but rather a self-reinforcement linked to the achievement of equilibrium. This dynamical equilibrium state is necessarily linked with the actions of the other and thus introduces interaction into the loop. The achievement of a dynamical equilibrium leads the imitatee to stop its activity. The previous imitator performs other actions on its own, and in particular can exhibit behaviors that the previous imitatee does not know. The previous imitatee can then imitate these behaviors: the roles have thus switched.

13.5   Concluding comments

We have proposed that the two functions of imitation: learning and communication feed one another. We have started to build a system able to maintain an interaction with another system of similar architecture via a kind of "seeking for synchrony."

Our aim now is to explore when it is really important to introduce explicitly this seeking for synchrony in the system and what the effects are of this seeking on the functional use of imitation.

The architectures of the ETIS robots are mainly based on the ambiguity of perception. Within this framework, the interactive "other" is perceived as ones' own production or as a "mirror" of it. Similarly, early in human development, imitating and being imitated do not imply distinguishing between self and other. Even older human infants, when imitated, can temporarily take the behavior of their imitator as being theirs (see Figure 13.8).

We now need to explore how far we can distort the dynamical perception–action loop while staying in interaction. For that purpose, we have designed several experiments whose goal is to explore some perturbation of the dynamics along two main axes: perception and rhythm or synchrony.

Figure 13.8 Child A's hat has slipped behind his back. Child B seeks for his hat behind his back although his hat is still on his head.

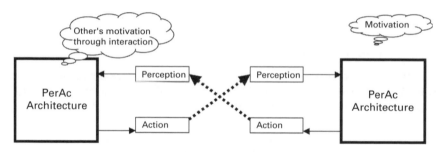

Figure 13.9 Each system has its own motivations which are only accessible to the other system via the interaction.

In particular, what happens if robot S1 is already able to perform the behavior demonstrated by robot S2? In this case, the goal of the imitator cannot be learning anymore. Which benefits may result if both keep on imitating each other? In fact, we can guess that both get the pure benefit of communication (see Figure 13.9). By imitating, each one can perceive the other's goal through interacting with the other. In human dyads, the pride to experience efficient self-agency in monitoring the other's behavior, and the interest in discovering the other's goal via imitation both derive from and result in shared motor representations where the perception of one is coupled with the action of the other.

REFERENCES

Albus, J. S. (1991). Outline for a Theory of Intelligence. *IEEE Transactions on Man Systems and Cybernetics*, **21(3)**, 473–509.

Andry, P., Moga, S., Gaussier, P., Revel, A. and Nadel, J. (2000). Imitation: learning and communication. In J. A. Meyer, A. Berthoz, D. Floreano, H. Roitblat, and S. Wilson (eds.), *Proceedings of the Sixth International Conference on Simulation of Adaptive Behavior*. Cambridge, MA: MIT Press, 353–62.

Andry, P., Gaussier, P., Moga, S., Banquet, J. P. and Nadel, J. (2001). Learning and communication in imitation: an autonomous robot perspective. *IEEE Transaction on Systems, Man and Cybernetics. Part A: Systems and Humans*, **31(5)**, 431–44.

Baldwin, W. (1894). Imitation, a chapter in the natural history of consciousness. *Mind*, **3**, 26–55.

Bandura, A. (1971). *Psychological Modelling Conflicting Theories*. Chicago: Aldine.

Billard, A., Dautenhahn, K. and Hayes, G. (1998). Experiments on human/robot communication with Robota, an imitative learning and communicating robot. *Proceedings of Socially Situated Intelligence Workshop*, part of the Fifth International Conference of The Society for Adaptive Behaviour 98, SAB 98.

Braitenberg, V. (1984). *Vehicles: Experiments in Synthetic Psychology*. Cambridge, UK: Bradford Books.

Brooks, R. A. (1986). A robust layered control system for a mobile robot. *IEEE Journal of Robotics and Automation*, **2(1)**, 14–23.

Byrne, R. W. and Russon, A. E. (1998). Learning by imitation: a hierarchical approach. *Behavioral and Brain Sciences*, **21**, 667–721.

Dautenhahn, K. (1995). Getting to know each other – artificial social intelligence for autonomous robots. Robotics and Autonomous Systems, **16(2–4)**, 333–56.

Decety, J. (2002). Is there such a thing as functional equivalence between imagined, observed, and executed action? In A. Meltzoff and W. Prinz (eds.), *The imitative mind*. Cambridge, UK: Cambridge University Press, 291–310.

Decety, J. and Grezes, J. (1999). Neural mechanisms subserving the perception of human actions. *Trends in Cognitive Sciences*, **3**, 172–8.

Di Pellegrino, G., Fadiga, L., Fogassi, L., Gallese, V. and Rizzolatti, G. (1992). Understanding motor events: a neurophysiological study. *Experimental Brain Research*, **91**, 176–80.

Eckerman, C. O. (1993). Imitation and toddler's achievement of coordinated action with others. In J. Nadel and L. Camaioni (eds.), *New Perspectives in Early Communicative Development*. New York: Routledge, 116–38.

Fadiga, L., Fogassi, L., Pavesi, G. and Rizzolatti, G. (1995). Motor facilitation during action observation: a magnetic stimulation study. *Journal of Neurophysiology*, **73**, 2608–11.

Fantz, R. (1964). Visual experience in infants: decreased attention to familiar patterns relative to novel ones. *Science*, **164**, 668–70.

Gaussier, P., Revel, A., Joulain, C. and Zrehen, S. (1997). Living in a partially structured environment: how to bypass the limitations of classical reinforcement techniques. *Robotics and Autonomous Systems*, **20(2–4)**, 225–50.

Gaussier, P. and Zrehen, S. (1995). PerAc: a neural architecture to control artificial animals. *Robotics and Autonomous System*, **16(2–4)**, 291–320.

Gottlieb, G. (1992). *Individual Development and Evolution: The Genesis of Novel Behavior*. New York: Oxford University Press.

Guillaume, T (1926). *L'imitation Chez L'enfant*. Paris: Alcan.

Hainline, L. (1998). The development of basic visual abilities. In A. Slater (ed.), *Perceptual Development*. Hove: Psychology Press, 5–50.

Haith, M. (1980). *Rules that Babies Look by*. Hillsdale, NJ: Erlbaum.

Hecht-Nielsen, R. (1987). Counterpropagation Networks. *Applied Optics*, **26(23)**, 4979–84.

Heyes, C. (2001). Causes and consequences of imitation. *Trends in Cognitive Sciences*, **5(6)**, 253–61.

Ito, M. and Tani, J. (2004). On-line imitative interaction with a humanoid robot using a dynamic neural network model of a mirror system. *Adaptive Behavior*, in press.

Jeannerod M. (1997), *The Cognitive Neuroscience of Action*, New York: Blackwell.

Karmiloff-Smith, A. (1992). *Beyond Modularity*. Cambridge, Ma: The MIT Press.

Kugiumutzakis, J. (1999). Development of imitation during the first six months of life. *Uppsala Psychological Reports, no 377*, Uppsala, Sweden, Uppsala University.

Kuniyoshi, Y. (1994). The science of imitation – towards physically and socially grounded intelligence. Special Issue, RWC Technical Report, TR-94001, *Real World Computing Project Joint Symposium*, Tsukuba-shi, Ibaraki-ken.

Maratos, O. (1973). The origin and development of imitation in the first six months of life. Paper presented at the British Psychological Society Annual Meeting, Liverpool.

Meltzoff, A. N. (2002). Elements of a developmental theory of imitation. In A. N. Meltzoff and W. Prinz (eds.), *The Imitative Mind: Development, Evolution and Brain Bases*. Cambridge: Cambridge University Press, 19–41.

Meltzoff, A. and Moore, M. (1983). Newborn infants imitate adult facial gestures. *Child Development*, **54**, 704–9.

Meltzoff, A. and Moore, M. (1999). Persons and representations: why infant imitation is important for theories of human development. In J. Nadel and G. Butterworth (eds.), *Imitation in Infancy*. Cambridge, UK: Cambridge University Press, 9–35.

Mitchell, R. (2002). Kinesthetic–visual matching, imitation, and self-recognition. In M. Bekoff, C. Allen and G. Bughardt (eds.), *The Cognitive Animal*. Cambridge, MA: MIT Press, 345–51.

Moga, S. and Gaussier, P. (1999). A neuronal structure for learning by imitation. In D. Floreano, J-D. Nicoud, and F. Mondada (eds.), *Lecture Notes in Artificial Intelligence – European Conference on Artificial Life ECAL99*. Berlin: Springer, 314–18.

Nadel, J. (1986). *Imitation et Communication Entre Jeunes Enfants*. Paris: PUF.

Nadel, J. (2002). Imitation and imitation recognition: their functional role in preverbal infants and nonverbal children with autism. In A. Meltzoff and

W. Prinz (eds.), *The Imitative Mind: Development, Evolution and Brain Bases.* Cambridge, UK: Cambridge University Press, 42–62.

Nadel-Brulfert, J. and Baudonnière, P. M. (1982).The social function of reciprocal imitation in 2-year-old peers, *International Journal of Behavioral Development*, **5**, 95–109.

Nadel, J., Guérini, C., Pezé, A. and Rivet, C. (1999). The evolving nature of imitation as a transitory means of communication. In J. Nadel and G. Butterworth (eds.), *Imitation in Infancy.* Cambridge, UK: Cambridge University Press, 209–34.

Nadel, J., Revel, A., Andry, P. and Gaussier, P. (2004). Toward communication: first imitations in infants, low-functioning children with autism and robots. *Interaction Studies*, **5(1)**, 45–73.

Pawlby, S. (1977). Imitative interaction. In H. Schaffer (ed.), *Studies in Mother–Infant Interaction.* London: Academic Press, 203–23.

Perrett, D., Mistlin, A., Harries, M. and Chitty, A. (1990). Understanding the visual appearance and consequence of actions. In M. A. Goodale (ed.), *Vision and Action.* Norwood, NJ: Ablex, 163–80.

Piaget, J. (1945). *La Formation du Symbole Chez L'enfant*, Neuchâtel/Paris: Delachaux and Niestlé.

Rizzolatti, G., Fadiga, L., Fogassi, L. and Gallese, V. (2002). From mirror neurons to imitation: facts and speculations. In A. Meltzoff and W. Prinz (eds.), *The Imitative Mind: Development, Evolution and Brain Bases.* Cambridge, UK: Cambridge University Press, 247–66.

Rochat, P. (1998). Self-perception and action in infancy. *Experimental Brain Research*, **123**, 102–9.

Slater, A. (1998). The competent infant: innate organization and early learning in infant visual perception. In A. Slater (ed.), *Perceptual Development.* Hove: Psychology Press, 105–30.

Sokolov, E. (1963). *Perception and the conditioned Reflex.* New York: Macmillan.

Thelen, E., Schöner, G., Scheier, C. and Smith, L. (2001). The dynamics of embodiment: a field theory of infant perseverative reaching. *Behavioral and Brain Sciences*, **24(1)**, 1–86.

Tomasello, M.(1998). Emulation, learning and cultural learning. *Behavioral and Brain Sciences*, **21**, 703–4.

Treisman, A. (1988). Features and objects: the fourteenth Bartlett memorial lecture. *The Quarterly Journal of Experimental Psychology*, **40.A(2)**, 201–37.

Trevarthen, C. (1999). Musicality and the intrinsic music pulse: evidence from human psychobiology and infant communication. *Musicae Scientiae: Rhythms, Musical Narrative, and the Origins of Human Communication.* Liége: European Society for the Cognitive Sciences of Music, 157–213.

Užgiris, I.Č. (1981). Two functions of imitation during infancy. *International Journal of Behavioral Development*, **4**, 1–12.

Užgiris, I.Č., Broome, S. and Kruper, J, (1989). Imitation in mother–child conversations: a focus on the mother. In G. E. Speidel and K. E. Nelson (eds.), *The Many Faces of Imitation in Language Learning.* New York: Springer-Verlag, 91–120.

Vinter, C. (1986). *L'imitation Chez Le Nouveau-né*. Lausanne: Delachaux and Niestlé.

Wallon, H. (1942). *De L'acte à la Pensée*. Paris: Flammarion.

Whiten, A. and Ham, R. (1992). On the nature and evolution of imitation in the animal kingdom. In P. J. B. Slater, J. S. Rosenblatt, C. Beer, and M. Milinski (eds.), *Advances in the Study of Behavior*. San Diego: Academic Press, 239–83.

Zazzo, R. (1957). Le problème de l'imitation chez le nouveau-né. *Enfance*, **10**, 135–42.

14 Simulated turn-taking and development of styles of motion

Takashi Ikegami and Hiroyuki Iizuka

14.1 Intersubjectivity and turn-taking

We introduce a simulation study designed to develop a "synthetic psychology" (Braitenberg, 1984). Instead of studying real human/animal behavior, we study autonomous behavior of mobile agents that have virtual sensors to "see" the world and move around with virtual "wheels." The autonomous behavior is synthesized by the agent's internal dynamics, which evolve using a genetic algorithm. A purpose of synthetic psychology is to create a new concept in order to understand an essential psychological phenomenon. Therefore, the simulation framework has to use models sufficiently simple to analyze the behavior, but sufficiently complex to provide a theory to understand the psychological experiments.

As an example of synthetic psychology, we describe a simulation study of turn-taking using coupled dynamical recognizers. Studying turn-taking phenomena in robot experiments (e.g. Brooks *et al.*, 1999; Dautenhahn, 1999; Steels and Kaplan, 2001; Miyake *et al.*, in press) stresses the importance of embodiment and situatedness. In particular, MIT AI Lab's well-designed face robot, Kismet (Kismet project, 2000), can make use of human social protocols to stimulate natural emotions and social responses in humans. Even conversational turn-taking is established with a human subject. To do this, Kismet relies on subtle cues of human expression and interaction dynamics. Dautenhahn *et al.* used a mobile robot and a small humanoid robot to investigate the use of robotic toys in therapy and education of children with autism (Dautenhahn *et al.*, 2002; AuRoRA project, 2005). These robots engage in playing a game with autistic children to elicit turn-taking and imitation.

We are now at the stage of constructing a phenomenological theory of turn-taking behavior from computer simulation and robotic experiments. In particular, we need to understand the key mechanisms of coupled

Imitation and Social Learning in Robots, Humans and Animals, ed. Chrystopher L. Nehaniv and Kerstin Dautenhahn. Published by Cambridge University Press.

301

dynamics that elicit turn-taking behavior. Fortunately, there are many fascinating concepts and psychological experiments (e.g. Trevarthen, 1993; Nadel, 2002, among others) that stimulate theoretical modeling. There, bodily synchrony and shared intentionality provide two complementary facets of pre-verbal communication. Bodily synchrony is realized through turn-taking and shared intentionality is realized through intersubjectivity. To bridge the gap between the two, we developed a computer simulation model of turn-taking. Intersubjectivity is an ongoing negotiation process that probes mental states to share intentions with others. Trevarthen (1980), who first noted its importance, classified two types of intersubjectivity. Primary intersubjectivity is found between an infant and a caretaker. Trevarthen suggested that there may exist an unconscious ability to organize intersubjectivity. From approximately the age of seven months, secondary intersubjectivity develops. It starts to involve a third object, or event, as well as person-to-person relationships. Intersubjectivity is a concept closely related to participatory joint attention (Uno and Ikegami, 2003).[1] Joint attention requires coordinated pre-verbal behavior between two or more persons. A simple example is a child pointing to attract the attention of its mother. It is a process of sharing one's experience of observing an object or events with others by following pointing gestures or eye gaze.

However, it is difficult to measure intersubjectivity objectively. Therefore, turn-taking has been studied as an objective realization of intersubjectivity. Turn-taking is a very objective phenomenon and is observed in many situations. It starts with the primitive interaction between mother and child but the mechanism of turn-taking is not fully understood as yet. According to Trevarthen's pioneering work (Trevarthen, 1993, 1999, 1980) and J. Nadel's recent work (Nadel, 2002), turn-taking is a co-operative and co-creative activity of the participants. That is, turn-taking is not a simple entrainment of two coupled non-linear pendulums but it requires mutual adaptation of the participants and has to be maintained intentionally. Mere body synchrony is more like entrainment, but turn-taking is an emergent phenomenon on top of that. Therefore the aim of this study is to reveal the complexity of turn-taking behavior that emerges from simple body synchrony. Computer simulation can only study turn-taking overtly but, by studying a capability of mutual adaptation, we can

---

[1] In the context of verbal communication, we generalize the concept of joint attention and distinguish two types of joint attention. If a person uses joint attention as a tool to achieve a goal (e.g. establishing joint attention to let your dog pick up a ball), we call this instrumental joint attention. However, if a person makes joint attention as a goal in itself, we call this participatory joint attention. For example, when two are looking at the sunset and say "Now the sun sets," it does not require further achievements.

indirectly study the characteristics of intersubjectivity behind the turn-taking.

In the following, we introduce a means of inferring intersubjectivity by simulating turn-taking behavior. By coupling two model cognitive agents, called dynamical recognizers, we analyze three characteristics of simulated turn-taking: (1) the prediction capability of the agents, (2) turn-taking with a non-interactive "virtual" agent that acts in a set manner rather than in response to the partner and (3) the evolution of adaptability. In the discussion section, we compare our findings with psychological data.

14.2 Overview of the model

14.2.1 Dynamical recognizer

We call our agents dynamical recognizers (DR) because they perceive the environment, infer the context and produce the motion using their internal dynamical system. As Pollack (1991) first showed explicitly, a DR as a recurrent neural network system can imitate the behavior of a finite automaton. Dynamical recognizers have been used to imitate human language performance (Elman, 1995), to mimic more complex machine behavior (e.g. context-sensitive grammar, Blair and Pollack, 1997), and to achieve robot navigation (Tani, 1996).

For the first time, we coupled two DRs to study the complex situation when both agents try to learn from, or mimic, the other without fear of infinite regression. For example, we studied various game situations (such as the iterated prisoner's dilemma game (Ikegami, 1998; Taiji and Ikegami, 1999), Dubey's game (Ikegami and Taiji, 1999) and the coalition game (Ikegami and Morimoto, 2003)) and linguistic interactions (Igari, 2000).

In the present study, we implemented a new method of coupling agents; that is, turn-taking organization (Iizuka and Ikegami, 2004, 2003). This differs from previous studies of coupled DRs in that the agents have "loose coupling" in the sense that the agents can attach/detach from each other. We used a standard genetic algorithm to evolve the network structure of the DRs.

14.2.2 Agent's description

We assume agents to be mobile vehicles with a circular body and two wheels. The two agents chase each other on the unlimited 2-D plane.

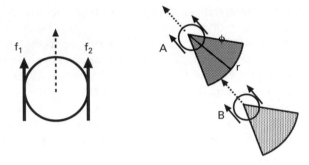

Figure 14.1 Left: a schematic view of the mobile agent with two wheels (actuators). It computes the force vector (f_1, f_2) on each actuator. Right: Two mobile agents interact to perform turn-taking behavior by sensing each other's position, distance and angle. It is A's turn when A positions itself near B's rear scope (RS). The shape of this RS is parameterized by r and ϕ.

They do not bump into each other as we assume that agents have dimensionless bodies.

In order to move around the agents compute the two motor outputs from the outputs of the sensors attached to the body. On the left of Figure 14.1, a schematic view of an agent is illustrated. Each agent can perceive the distance and the direction relative to the heading direction. More precisely, one agent can perceive that the other agent is r units distance away in the direction of θ from its heading direction. Therefore, each agent knows whether the other agent is in the rear or in front.

Each agent then computes two different types of output, motion and prediction. The entire neural architecture of an agent is shown in Figure 14.2. The prediction output is used to predict the other agent's movement one step into the future. However, it is only indirectly influencing the motion behaviour, as it is not fed back into the input layer.

Using the agents, we study the agents' attempts to co-ordinate turn-taking behavior, each trying to get behind the other. An agent's turn is defined when it stays in the rear scope (RS) of the other agent. The RS is illustrated in Figure 14.1. Both agents cannot be in the other's RS simultaneously. Therefore, it is necessary to have spontaneous symmetry breakdown, i.e. role-splitting. One plays the role of chaser (i.e. getting in the RS of the other agent) and the other plays the role of evader (i.e. showing its RS to the other agent). However, mere role-splitting is not sufficient; we require temporal role-switching. Below, we demonstrate that turn-taking behavior is self-organized by the developed coupled DRs.

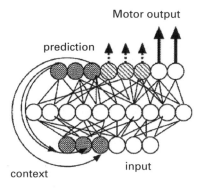

Figure 14.2 An agent has a three-layered recurrent network. The first layer is the input neurons and context neurons. Input neurons receive the other agent's relative position. The second layer is composed of hidden neurons. The third layer consists of three types of neuron: context, prediction and motor. Context nodes feed back to the input layer. Prediction nodes output a prediction of the other's relative position and heading direction at the next time step. The motor nodes provide the driving force vector (f_1 and f_2).

14.2.3 Evolution schema

The internal neural dynamics of each agent organizes the co-ordination of turn-taking behavior. The turn-taking performance is measured by the agents co-operatively switching roles. The agents' neural dynamics are parameterized by the strengths of connections that link neurons (see Figure 14.2). Therefore, we develop the neural connections to evolve turn-taking performance.

In a real developmental process, children would learn eye-gazing, imitation, reciprocal actions and other basic body conditions before achieving turn-taking. However, some of these conditions may be innate. Here in the simulation model, we use an evolutionary technique, a genetic algorithm, to develop[2] turn-taking behavior. We did not use simple learning dynamics, as the system is easily trapped by artificial metastable states. On the other hand, the genetic algorithm (GA) basically exhaustively searches in a state space. Therefore, it avoids being trapped by metastable states, but the developmental stages of genetic algorithm are difficult to interpret. Nevertheless, we sometimes have a good interpretation of

---

[2] More precisely, we demonstrate how turn-taking behavior can be evolved in a population in the Darwinian sense of evolution. Note that individuals here do not directly develop turn-taking behavior in the course of their lifetimes, instead the population evolves such behavior over evolutionary time. -Ed.

developmental stages. As we discuss in detail below, the style of turn-taking progresses from a geometrical regular form to chaotic adaptive forms. The other reason to use GA is that we are interested in investigating different styles of motion in turn-takers. We currently have no other method, or principle of programming, for building turn-taking behaviors into autonomous agents. Therefore, GA provides an interesting boot-strap method for obtaining various different neural connection patterns that exhibit simple turn-taking behavior.

We applied a genetic algorithm (GA) on two separate populations to avoid turn-taking between genetically similar agents. As a result, a player would not have to play against itself, which we wished to avoid. It may be unusual to use two populations instead of one but we expected that turn-taking should be established with a variety of styles of motion. To focus on the variety of styles of motion, we believe that having two populations was advantageous.

The performance of all paired agents from the separate populations was evaluated at each generation. Agents able to exchange turns equally were evaluated as having the greater fitness. The highest value was given when both agents took their turn alternately and the agents could predict each other's behavior. A one-sided (i.e. role-fixed) behavior was associated with lower fitness values. In addition to the turn-taking performance, we also evaluated the agents' prediction capabilities. If an agent could adequately predict the other agent's movement one step ahead, the agent was rewarded. The prediction reward was added to the turn-taking evaluation, which was then used for determining the best agents in each population.

We used the three best agents from each population to create the populations of the next generation with some mutations. We used mutation to cause variations in the connection weights, so that we had a chance to have better agents in the next generation.

By repeating the process, a variety of turn-taking patterns have evolved. In Figure 14.3, we computed the fitness value of the best agent in each population as a function of GA generations. In the following sections, we describe the evolution of the style of turn-taking and the characterization of the styles.

Note the following conditions of the simulation environment:
(1) The turn-taking performance was evaluated for unspecified periods of time, so that agents could not tell when the evaluation time was over.
(2) During the first 100 GA generations, we did not count the prediction capability as a fitness factor as otherwise it was difficult to elevate the fitness of the agents.

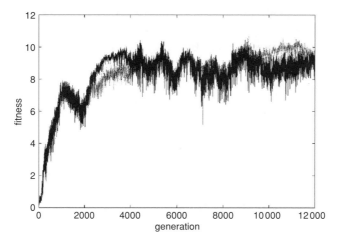

Figure 14.3 The fitness value of the best agent as a function of GA generations. The two lines correspond to the agents of populations A and B, respectively.

(3) There were two timescales: the agent's navigation timescale (ΔT_1), and the neural network computation timescale (ΔT_2). On the assumption that the vehicle navigation motion was faster than the internal neural timescale, we took $100\Delta T_1 = \Delta T_2$. The time evolution of the vehicle navigation was computed using the fourth-order Runge–Kutta method, where ΔT_1 was set to 0.01.

(4) We know that our perception has to deal with noisy inputs. Therefore, we simulated the agents' interacting with each other in a noisy environment. Noise was added to the input neurons at every navigation time step, which was provided by uniform random numbers between zero and almost the maximum distance the agent can move during one step.

Details of this are given in the Appendix.

14.3   Simulation results

We observed a variety of turn-taking patterns based on this simulation frame-work. The basic dynamics of the turn-taking were observed to be as follows. Two agents adjust their velocities and heading directions to take turns, spontaneously switching from the role of evader to chaser and vice versa. A role switches when an agent outruns the other agent. Development of turn-taking spatial trails from one GA run is shown in

Figure 14.4. Usually overtaking occurs when the trails start to bend. We categorized the style of motion of turn-taking corresponding to the organized spatial trails on the 2-D plane. Two agents tend to have similar styles of motion but each agent takes their turn at a different portion of the trail. In the earlier stages (the first three pictures of Figure 14.4), one agent takes its turn at the outgoing lines and the other at the incoming lines. However, in the later stages one agent takes its turn on the curling parts of a trail, whereas the other does so at the straight sections. Although the length of trails for each turn look different, the times for each turn of the agents are almost equal.

We approximately classified the turn-taking behaviors into two types, geometrically regular (the first three generations of Figure 14.4) and chaotic irregular turn-taking styles. Agents take turns at the same locations in the geometric case, but in the chaotic cases they act chaotically with regard to both time and position.

As a GA generation progresses, the early regular pattern is replaced by the chaotic pattern at approximately the 6000th GA generation. Note that the classification includes many different styles within each regular and chaotic case. Apart from the visual pattern of the trails we show that these styles of motion have interesting dynamic characteristics. Below, we characterize the turn-taking process and these styles of motion.

14.3.1   Solo motion style

To develop some intuition as to basic movement of the agents we simulated the agents' motion behavior with random inputs. No coupling between agents was assumed here. When we fixed the input, the agents made circles for both the regular and irregular turn-taking cases. However, the radius of the circles changed, depending on the input pattern. Therefore, when we sequentially gave random inputs for each 100 time steps, agents moved around in space, making both large and small circles (Figure 14.5). However, as can be seen, we found no significant difference between agents from the earlier stages and those from the later stages. Therefore, co-ordinated turn-taking behavior, salient styles of motion, only appears with coupling between agents.

14.3.2   Prediction breakdown

To address novelty preference in the discussion, we analyzed the prediction outputs, which are tuned to predict the other agent's next movement but are not fed back into the input neuron.

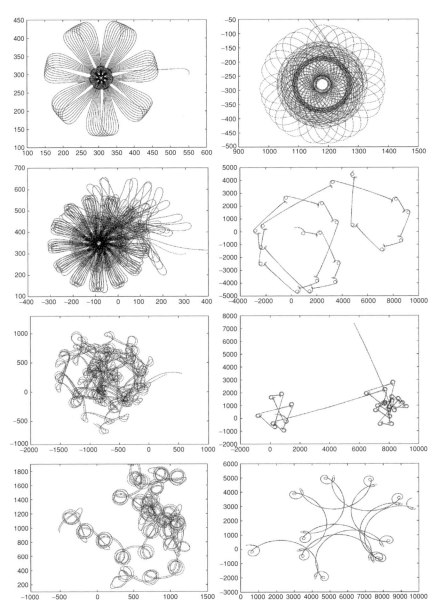

Figure 14.4 Spatial patterns of turn-taking behavior observed in the simulations. Two agents' trails are overlaid in each figure. From the top to the bottom in the left column, they are from the 3000th, 5000th, 8000th and 15 000th GA generations. The right column shows results of another GA run. These are from the 3000th, 7000th, 9000th and 17 000th GA generation.

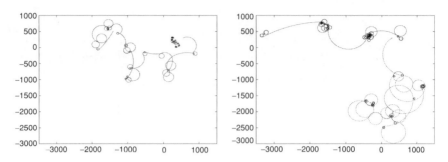

Figure 14.5 Spatial trails of the agents with sequential random inputs for each 100 steps: agents from the 3000th generation (left) and from the 9000th generation (right).

In Figure 14.6, it can be seen that an agent's prediction precision produces a spiky time series. These spiky patterns are synchronous with the timing of the turn-exchange patterns. However, the precision is much higher within either turn-holding phase, because our simulation setting requires agents to develop both good prediction and co-operative turn-taking. In our simulations so far, we have not had turn-taking with perfect prediction capabilities. For example, if two agents chase each other in the same circular pattern, their prediction may improve. As described above, geometrically regular patterns were overtaken by more irregular chaotic patterns. Therefore, the prediction precision did not improve with later evolution.

On the other hand, the adaptability of agents, the capability of turn-taking with new agents, did improve with evolution. The adaptability was measured by the number of possible turn-takers over the whole generation. We believe that the chaotic turn-taking structure, which has a limited prediction precision by definition, increases adaptability by sacrificing predictability. Therefore, prediction does not contribute to the turn-taking organization. It is difficult to develop a good prediction module using the same context neurons as those producing adequate motor output for turn-taking. Prediction is often taken as a basis for cognitive interaction (e.g. to infer the other one's intention) but as shown here turn-taking as a precursor for cognitive interaction can be established without prediction.

14.3.3 *Coupling with a noise and a non-responding agent*

Note that these agents establish turn-taking behavior with sensor noise, but the sensor noise is not always a disturbing factor. Some turn-taking

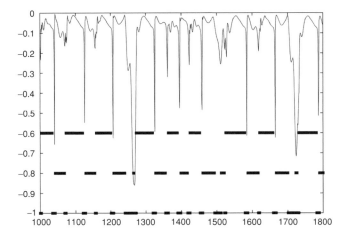

Figure 14.6 Prediction performance (top spiky lines) and turns (line segments) for an agent after 10 000 GA generations. A horizontal line expresses time steps for two agents moving in the 2-D arena. The top two line segments correspond to turns of the coupled agents. The bottom segments correspond to when no one has a turn. This shows that the prediction precision decreases rapidly when turns switch.

can only be established in the presence of noise. For example, there are two attractors where agents' roles are fixed, and the roles of chaser and evader can be exchanged randomly by virtue of noise. On the other hand, chaotic irregular turn-takers can show spatio-temporal irregular trails with and without sensor noise. Depending on the noise pattern, turns will be exchanged at different positions and times; however, the same pairing of agents yields similar spatio-temporal patterns. This robustness of turn-taking was already acquired by the geometrically regular turn-takers.

An important aspect of turn-taking is that it is a mutually co-operative phenomenon rather than coupled altruistic behavior. That is, if one independently generates a pattern and the other tries to synchronize with it, the turn-taking will be difficult. To show this practically, we generated a virtual agent in several ways.

We first studied externally controlled experiments, simulating the turn-taking dynamics for a certain period of time then fixing the motor output of one of the agents (Figure 14.7). The result was that in both cases, regular and chaotic, turn-taking disappeared. The agent tried to cope with the controlled agent but never succeeded. It therefore shows that turn-taking is a product of mutual co-operation.

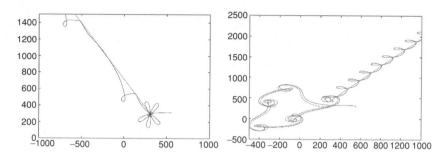

Figure 14.7 Spatial trails of agents from 3000th (left) and 9000th generation (right) in interactions with a controlled agent to constant output.

Next we simulated turn-taking between two agents recording one agent's trail. Calling this trail a virtual agent, we simulated turn-taking between another agent and this virtual agent. The virtual agent cannot react to the other agent; it simply replays the previous action sequence. By adding a little noise to the recorded trail, we studied the the resulting turn-taking pattern. In the case of the geometrical agent, with a few exceptions, turn-taking was possible even with the perturbed virtual agent. However, in the case of a chaotic agent, the small difference was amplified, and turn-taking did not become established.

This difference between the regular and irregular chaotic cases reflects the potential adaptability of the two dynamics. In other words, regular turn-takers are more independent of the other agent's response than the chaotic turn-takers are. Because turn-taking is possible for noisy inputs but not for the virtual agent case, we insist that turn-taking by the agents in the chaotic case distinguishes between noisy inputs and noisy but adaptive inputs generated by the other agent. We therefore think chaotic turn-taking is established by mutually adaptive behavior. To measure this quantitatively, we studied the adaptability of the agents.

14.3.4 *Evolution of adaptability*

We selected two individuals from different generations to create a novel pair. This was to examine whether a novel pair can also perform turn-taking. The novel pairs generally showed far poorer performance than the original pairs. Within a new pair, the responses of one agent to the other were often inappropriately timed compared with the original pairs, which showed complete synchronization of turn-taking. It is worth noting that new pairs sometimes generated new spatial patterns, but that sometimes

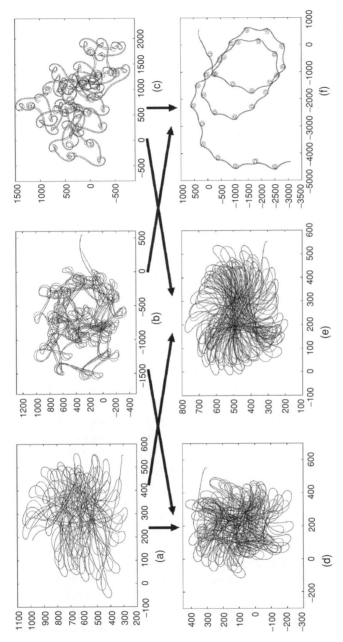

Figure 14.8 Spatial patterns of the original pairs and newly coupled agents at 7000, 8000 and 10000 GA generations. (a), (b), and (c) show the patterns of the original pairs at 7000, 8000 and 10000 generations, respectively. The bottom row shows newly coupled agents' patterns; the arrows indicate pairing of partners from different generations.

the pattern was entrained to either one of the pair's original patterns. For example, in Figure 14.8, the agent from the 7000th GA generation can entrain to the dynamics of the agent from the 10 000th generation. On the other hand, the agent from the 8000th generation with the agent from the 10 000th generation generates a new pattern. Both spatial patterns are chaotic.

To see the generation of new couplings more systematically, we studied a coupling between two agents from different generations. We then examined the performance of the new coupling by detailed testing of all pairings up to 12 000 generations. We defined the adaptability of an agent as its turn-taking performance against the new agents from other GA generations. By summing the performance against every other agent, we computed the adaptability measure for each agent. As shown in Figure 14.9, the agents' adaptability gradually increased as the GA proceeded. In particular, the adaptability increased rapidly after approximately 5000–6000 GA generations. This corresponds to the transition from regular to chaotic turn-taking phase. Therefore, it was verified that agents showing chaotic turn-taking can be more adaptive but that not all chaotic turn-takers are equally adaptive. Some agents are more adaptive than others, but on average, chaotic turn-takers are more adaptive.

14.4   Discussion

It is interesting to see how children develop interaction with other children. An example can be found in the synchronous imitation game (Nadel, 2002). Synchronous imitation is defined as children showing lasting dyadic play through the alternation of imitating and being imitated. From observation of children at approximately 20 months, it has been reported that children perform synchronous imitation of each other (Nadel, 2002; Nielsen and Dissanayake, 2003). Therefore, children not only are capable of imitating one another, but also seem to enjoy the detection of the intention behind the imitation game. For example, a child is happy to mimic another's novel use of objects – e.g. putting a bucket on the head –, but at the next moment may perform another novel action – e.g. using an umbrella as a stick to conduct a concert (Nadel, 2002; Nadel and Revel, 2003). That is, children have to understand a partner's intention to perform a novel action (here the unusual use of objects). The novel action pattern attracts children and therefore interaction is maintained. Therefore, novelty has to be generated constantly to maintain the interaction, but we also think that simply random behavior may not attract children (this has not yet been reported). Therefore, mild novelty is required to sustain the mutual imitation game, including turn-taking.

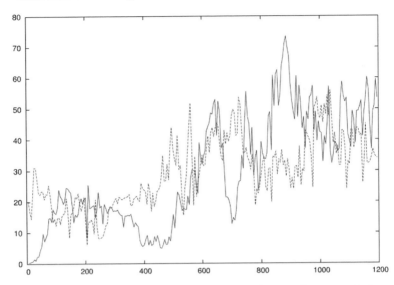

Figure 14.9 Adaptability is computed for each agent from populations A and B. As shown in the figure, adaptability gradually increases with later GA generations.

Such novelty cannot be prepared in advance: it must be the ongoing product of communication or interaction. Co-operative synthesis of novelty may be the prerequisite for turn-taking.

The above observation corresponds closely with our simulation results. Of course, it is still hypothetical, but we can provide some possible mechanisms for turn-taking to form a relationship with intersubjectivity.

The preference of healthy children for unexpected behavior can be compared with our experiments showing prediction breakdown (Section 14.3.2). From our simulation results, prediction capability was not improved significantly. For chaotic turn-taking in particular, amplification of different sensory noise revealed that the chaotic turn-taking pattern is indeed chaotic. Because agents show chaotic turn-taking patterns in later stages, it is difficult for prediction to improve. As above, the prediction and motor outputs share the same context neurons. Therefore, the failure of prediction tells us that the same context state cannot be recruited for both purposes when roles switch. We hypothesize from this that prediction-based turn-taking may be difficult to develop. Indeed, our preliminary studies on the explicit use of the prediction outputs implied that it was not a simple task. A requirement of high prediction accuracy suppresses the evolution of turn-taking. However, it was also shown that agents that synthesize chaotic turn-taking in one generation have a tendency to establish turn-taking with agents from different generations, this being what we call adaptability, an ability to show turn-taking with new agents.

Our simulations showed that turn-taking is established by sacrificing predictability. The point has to be emphasized. Perfect predictability of others is not required for turn-taking. To take turns with others for the first time, we have to develop a readiness for interaction. If we take the bodily turn-taking as proto-communication, this readiness is necessary to start communication with strangers.

The performance for our non-interactive virtual agent in the experiment in Section 14.3.3 is consistent with the microcontingency reported in Nadel's experiment (Nadel *et al.*, 1999); Trevarthen also puts stress on this aspect (Murray and Trevarthen, 1985). It has been reported that a mother's response to a baby should be of the right style and timing, otherwise the infant will withdraw its interaction; for example, if a recorded video of a mother was displayed to a baby, the baby became withdrawn and depressed. We also reported that an agent becomes sensitive to the ongoing dynamics of the other agent from our experiment in Section 14.3.3. If one agent is replaced with a non-reacting record (i.e. a virtual agent), turn-taking fails easily. Although this sounds rather contrary to our previous discussion, predictability is unnecessary to establish turn-taking, but what we mean here is that turn-taking is a co-operative activity between two agents, and preference for imperfect contingency is a sign of the co-creative aspect of interaction. Trevarthen stresses the co-creative aspects of communication in terms of musicality (Trevarthen, 1999).

Our contention is that co-creative activity relies on co-operation. The adaptability of the turn-taking system increases at the regular to chaotic turn-taking phase as is shown in Section 14.3.4. We interpret this as establishing the co-operative activity first and the co-creative activity second, because agents that show chaotic turn-taking can create new turn-taking patterns with other agents as shown in Figure 14.8. Such a potential of style of motion is a characteristic of a developed turn-taking system; that is, a variety of styles of motion is prepared in evolved agents. They are not pre-defined solely in a single agent (as seen in Figure 14.5) but will emerge dynamically when interacting with others. A richness of a style of motion is a product of turn-taking.

Hobson claimed, after studying children's imitative behavior of adults' displays, that healthy infants are sensitive to the style of action, but autistic children are insensitive to it (Hobson, 2002). When an adult played the toy violin either tenderly or aggressively, healthy children could imitate the action and its the style, whereas autistic children could imitate the action but were poor at imitating the style.

We assume that a style of motion of turn-taking reflects the agents' intentions. Shared intentionality requires detecting the intentions of the other agents. Therefore, the insensitivity to the style of motion means lacking the detection of intention, but we are not saying that we need an intention-detection module: rather, we are saying that detection of intention is simply a result of turn-taking. Our claim is that the lack of sensitivity to the style of motion comes from the difficulty of co-ordinating a style of motion with turn-taking behavior. This may provide a means of bridging the gap between turn-taking and intersubjectivity, and also between languages. We think that turn-taking behavior enables us to synthesize and to become sensitive to a variety of styles of motion. These styles are, however, ad hoc and are fine-tuned by the other agent. Therefore, a grammar or rule that governs the style is not static or explicit. It is more like a micro (private) code established between agents (Nadel, 2003). However, once the style is recognized automatically by the other agent via turn-taking, the code is shared and reused to synthesize a new communication. In this way, turn-taking provides a boot-strapping mechanism for intersubjectivity and joint attentions.

Acknowledgments

We would like to thank Philippe Roche for the critical reading of the manuscript. This work was partially supported by Grants-in-Aid (No. 09640454 and No. 13-10950) from the Ministry of Education, Science, Sports and Culture, the 21st Century COE (Center of Excellence) program (Research Center for Integrated Science) of the Ministry of Education, Culture, Sports, Science and Technology, Japan, and the ECAgent project, sponsored by the Future and Emerging Technologies program of the European Community (IST-1940).

Appendix

(1) Navigation of an agent is described by the following equation of motion for an agent's heading angle (θ) and velocity (v) in a given direction.

$$M\dot{v} + D_1 v + f_1 + f_2 = 0 \tag{14.1}$$
$$I\ddot{\theta} + D_2\dot{\theta} + \tau(f_1, f_2) = 0 \tag{14.2}$$

where f_1 and f_2 are the forward driving forces, and τ is the torque. D_1 and D_2 express the resistance coefficients, and the agents have mass (M) and momentum (I). We iterate the equations using the Runge–Kutta integration. At each time step, agents compute the forces from the inputs using the internal DR, as explained below.

(2) The neural dynamics of an agent are represented by the following equations:

$$h_j(t) = g\left(\sum_i w_{ij} y_i(t) + \sum_l w'_{lj} cl(t-1) + b_{j1} \right) \qquad (14.3)$$

$$z_k(t) = g\left(\sum_j u_{jk} h_j(t) + b_{j2} \right) \qquad (14.4)$$

$$c_l(t) = g\left(\sum_l u'_{jl} h_j(t) + b_{j3} \right) \qquad (14.5)$$

$$g(x) = 1/(1 + e^{-x}) \qquad (14.6)$$

where y_i, z_k, h_j and c_l represent values at input, output, hidden and context nodes, respectively. A bias constant for each function is given by b_j. The respective number of nodes in these layers is set to $(I, K, \mathcal{J}, L) = (3, 5, 10, 3)$ throughout this paper. The symbols w_{ij}, u_{jk}, w'_{lj} and u'_{jl} denote the weights from input to hidden, hidden to output, context to hidden and hidden to context neurons, respectively, and parameter b is a bias node.

(3) A genetic algorithm was used to update the synaptic weight linking neurons. In practice, the weight set of the neural networks has a vector representation of the real weight values, which evolve using a genetic algorithm.

There are two populations, each containing P individuals ($P = 15$ throughout this study). The performance of all P^2 paired agents from the separated populations is evaluated at each generation. Agents that can exchange turns equally are evaluated as having greater fitness. At first, individuals in each population are initialized with random weight values. Then we calculate the fitness of each individual, based on its performance.

Practically, the fitness of an agent a from a population (A) against an agent b from another population (B) is calculated as follows. Below, we define a total fitness F as the sum of two fitnesses associated with prediction and turn-taking, respectively. When one agent gets behind the other, by definition the other agent has its turn. Here "getting behind" means entering the region in the other's rear scope (RS), which is parameterized by two parameters, r and ϕ. The agent in this state is said to be having its turn and is rewarded. The spatial position of agent b at time step t is represented as $\text{Pos}_b(t)$. This is compared with agent a's prediction value $\text{Pos}_{a\to b}$ for b's position. Therefore, the squared difference (Eq. 14.11) is a measure of error in agent a's prediction.

$$F_a = \frac{1}{P} \sum^{P} \left(s_1 \times F_a^{\text{turn}} + s_2 \times F_a^{\text{predict}} \right) \tag{14.7}$$

$$F_a^{\text{turn}} = \sum_t^T g_a(t) \times \sum_t^T g_b(t) \tag{14.8}$$

$$g_a(t) = \begin{cases} 1 & \text{Pos}_a(t) \in RS_b(t) \\ 0 & \text{Pos}_a(t) \notin RS_b(t) \end{cases} \tag{14.9}$$

$$F_a^{\text{predict}} = -\sum_t^T P_a(t) \times \sum_t^T P_b(t) \tag{14.10}$$

$$P_a(t) = (\text{Pos}_b(t) - \text{Pos}_{a\to b}(t))^2 \tag{14.11}$$

The turn-taking performance is evaluated for different periods of time ($T = 500$, 1000 and 1500), so that agents cannot know when the evaluation is complete. After evaluating the turn-taking performance at each GA generation, we leave the best E individuals in each population and allow them to reproduce with specified mutation rates. The relative weights s_1 for turn-taking as compared to s_2 for prediction in Eq. (14.7) giving an agent's fitness are given as 5:2 throughout the simulation. However, during the first 100 GA generations, we set $s_2 = 0$.

REFERENCES

AuRoRA project (2005). See http : //www.aurora-project.com/.
Blair, A. D. and Pollack, J. B. (1997). Analysis of dynamical recognizers. *Neural Computation*, **9(5)**, 1127–42.
Braitenberg, V. (1984). *Vehicles: Experiments in Synthetic Psychology*. Cambridge, MA: MIT Press.
Brooks, R. A., Breazeal, C., Marjanovic, M., Scassellati, B. and Williamson, M. M. (1999). The Cog Project: building a humanoid robot. In C. L. Nehaniv (ed.), *Computation for Metaphor, Analogies and Agents*, Lecture Notes in Computer Science, **1562**, 52–87.
Dautenhahn, K. (1999). Embodiment and interaction in socially intelligent life-like agents. In C. L. Nehaniv (ed.), *Computation for Metaphor, Analogies and Agents*, Lecture Notes in Computer Science, **1562**, 102–42.
Elman, J. L. (1995). Language as a dynamical system. In R. Port and T. van Gelder (eds.), *Mind as Motion: Explorations in the Dynamics of Cognition*. Cambridge, MA: MIT Press, 195–223.

Hobson, P. (2002). *The Cradle of Thought*. London: Macmillan.

Igari, I. (2000). *Coevolution of Mind and Language*. PhD thesis, University of Tokyo.

Iizuka, H. and Ikegami, T. (2003). Adaptive coupling and intersubjectivity in simulated turn-taking behaviour. In W. Banzhaf, T. Christaller, P. Dittrich, J. T. Kim and J. Ziegler (eds.), *ECAL*, vol. 2801 of *Lecture Note in Computer Science*. London, UK: Springer, 336–45.

Iizuka, H. and Ikegami, T. (2004). Adaptability and diversity in simulated turn-taking behavior. *Artificial Life*, **10(4)**, 361.

Ikegami, T. and Morimoto, G. (2003). Chaotic itinerancy in coupled dynamical recognizers. *Chaos: An Interdisciplinary Journal of Nonlinear Science*, **13(3)**, 1133–47.

Ikegami, T. and Taiji, M. (1999). Imitation and cooperation in coupled dynamical recognizers. In *ECAL '99: Proceedings of the 5th European Conference on Advances in Artificial Life*. London, UK: Springer Verlag, 545–54.

Ikegami, T. (1998). Structures of possible worlds in a game of players with internal models. *Acta Polytechnica Scandinavica*, **91**, 83–92.

Dautenhahn, K., Werry, I., Rae, J., Dickerson, P., Stribling, P. and Ogden, B. (2002). Robotic playmates: analysing interactive competencies of children with autism playing with a mobile robot. In K. Dautenhahn, A. Bond, L. Cañamero and B. Edmonds (eds.), *Socially Intelligent Agents – Creating Relationships with Computers and Robotics*. Kluwer Academic Publishers.

Kismet project (2000). See e.g. http : //www.ai.mit.edu/projects/humanoid-robotics-group/kismet/kismet.html.

Miyake, Y., Miyagawa, T. and Tamura, Y. (in press). Man–machine interaction as co-creation process. *Transactions of the Society of Instrument and Control Engineers*.

Murray, L. and Trevarthen, C. (1985). Emotional regulation of interaction between two-month-olds and their mothers. In T. Field and N. Fox (eds.), *Social Perception in Infants*. Norwood, NJ: Ablex, 101–25.

Nadel, J. (2002). Imitation and imitation recognition: functional use in preverbal infants and nonverbal children with autism. In A. Meltzoff and W. Prinz (eds.), *The Imitative Mind*. Cambridge, UK: Cambridge University Press, 42–62.

Nadel, J. (2003). Private communication.

Nadel, J. and Revel, A. (2003). How to build an imitator. In K. Dautenhahn, and C. L. Nehaniv (eds.), *Proceedings of the AISB'03 Second International Symposium on Imitation in Animals and Artifacts*. Society for the Study of Artificial Intelligence and Adaptive Behaviour, 120–4.

Nadel, J., Carchon, I., Kervella, C., Marcelli, D. and Rsérbat-Plantey, D. (1999). Expectancies for social contingency in 2-month-olds. *Developmental Science*, **2(2)**, 164–73.

Nielsen, M. and Dissanayake, C. (2003). Synchronic imitation as pre-linguistic social interaction. In K. Dautenhahn and C. L. Nehaniv (eds.), *Proceedings of the AISB'03 Second International Symposium on Imitation in Animals and Artifacts*. Society for the Study of Artificial Intelligence and Adaptive Behaviour, 131–7.

Pollack, J. B. (1991). The induction of dynamical recognizers. *Machine Learning*, 7, 227–52.

Steels, L. and Kaplan, F. (2001). AIBO's first words: the social learning of language and meaning. *Evolution of Communication*, **4(1)**, 3–32.

Taiji, M. and Ikegami, T. (1999). Dynamics of internal models in game players. *Physica D*, **134(2)**, 253–66.

Tani, J. (1996). Model based learning for mobile robot navigation from the dynamical systems perspective. *IEEE Transactions on Systems Man and Cybernetics B*, **26(3)**, 421–36.

Trevarthen, C. (1980). The foundations of intersubjectivity: development of interpersonal and cooperative understanding in infants. In D. Olson (ed.), *The Social Foundation of Language and Thought*. New York: W. W. Norton.

Trevarthen, C. (1993). The self born in intersubjectivity: the psychology of an infant communicating. In U. Neisser (ed.), *The Perceived Self*. Cambridge, UK: Cambridge University Press, 121–73.

Trevarthen, C. (1999). Musicality and the intrinsic motive pulse: evidence from human psychology and infant communication. *Musicae Scientiae: Rhythms, Musical Narrative and the Origins of Human Communication*. Liége: European Society for the Cognitive Sciences of Music, 155–215.

Uno, R. and Ikegami, T. (2003). Joint attention/prediction and language: a mechanism of sharing the internationality. *Studies in Cognitive Linguistics No.2*, 231–74, in Japanese, the English version will be published elsewhere.

15 Bullying behaviour, empathy and imitation: an attempted synthesis

Kerstin Dautenhahn, Sarah N. Woods and Christina Kaouri

15.1 Introduction

15.1.1 Overview

This chapter proposes a possible connection between bullying behaviour, empathy and imitation. The primary aim of our work is to provide a clearer understanding of bullying behaviour, by focusing on cognitive and emotional states that might cause bullies to show anti-social behaviour. We begin by providing a review of relevant research about bullying behaviour including definitions of bullying behaviour, the behavioural characteristics of bullies and victims, precursors of bullying behaviour and several ideas about how bullies become bullies. This is followed by a discussion of empathy and imitation[1] where two contrasting case studies of autism and psychopathy are given to illustrate differences in imitation and empathic skills and deficits. Finally, we try to bring together these different lines of research and present the hypothesis that bullies possess well-developed automatic as well as cognitive empathy, and that bullying behaviour is caused by an overemphasis of goal-directed processes of controlled empathy that work towards non-empathy. The importance of gaining a deeper understanding of empathic and imitation skills/deficits for different bullying roles is highlighted and discussed in relation to implications for anti-bullying intervention initiatives, where empathy and imitative interactive behaviour can be integrated.

---

[1] Since many subject areas are covered in this article, detailed literature reviews are not possible due to space limitations.

Imitation and Social Learning in Robots, Humans and Animals, ed. Chrystopher L. Nehaniv and Kerstin Dautenhahn. Published by Cambridge University Press.
© Cambridge University Press 2007.

15.1.2   *What is bullying?*

The pervasive nature and deleterious consequences of bullying and victimization behaviour has generated a great deal of research interest over
the past decade. Bullying behaviour is distinguishable from aggressive
behaviour per se as it has to be a *repeated action that occurs regularly
over time* (Olweus, 1999), and it *usually involves an imbalance in strength*,
either real or perceived (Whitney and Smith, 1993). Bullying constitutes a diverse array of behaviours which have generally been categorized
under the terms 'direct' physical bullying, verbal bullying and relational
'indirect' bullying (Björkqvist, 1994).[2] Direct physical bullying includes
actions such as being hit, kicked or punched, and taking belongings. Verbal bullying comprises of name calling, cruel teasing, taunting or being
threatened, and relational or 'indirect' bullying refers to behaviours such
as social exclusion, malicious rumour spreading and the withdrawal of
friendships (Wolke *et al.*, 2000). There are different profiles involved in
bullying behaviour namely, 'pure' bullies, 'pure' victims, bully/victims
and neutral. Each profile is distinct in terms of behavioural and personality characteristics (Wolke and Stanford, 1999; Sutton and Smith, 1999).

15.1.3   *'Pure' bully characteristics: mindreading and empathy*

Victims fit the profile of having poor prosocial skills, are unable to employ
adaptive coping mechanisms and are susceptible to internalized psychological problems such as anxiety and depression (Wolke and Stanford,
1999; Bond *et al.*, 2001). There remains uncertainty within the literature
regarding the profile of 'pure' bullies. The traditional stereotype of bullies is that they are male, physically strong, not academically bright and
resort to violence to resolve conflicts as this is the only response mechanism available to them (Sutton *et al.*, 1999). For example, Randall
(1997) claimed that 'pure' bullies 'fail to understand the feelings of others' and 'have little awareness of what other children actually think of
them . . . a symptom of social blindness'. Other studies have reported
that bullies are anxious, depressed, insecure individuals characterized
by low self-esteem (Salmon *et al.*, 1998) who have problem behaviours
(Farrington, 1993). In contrast, Sutton *et al.* (1999) argue that 'pure'
bullies have a superior theory of mind and are actually extremely socially
competent and have termed this 'cool cognition'. It is now believed that
the ability of bullies to understand and manipulate the minds of others

---

[2] We are not describing bullying in a clinical sense but refer to a set of behavioural traits as
defined in the literature.

provides the context and skills for effective and recurrent bullying without getting found out.

Linked into the notion of bullies having a superior theory of mind is the ongoing debate concerning whether 'pure' bullies lack empathic skills and whether this exacerbates the recurrent nature of bullying behaviour due to the bully not feeling any empathy or sympathy towards the victim. In support of this assertion, several studies have suggested that if a victim displays distress, this only serves to reinforce the bullies' behaviour even more (Davis, 1994). Sutton et al. (1999) believe that 'pure' bullies understand the emotions of others but do not share them resulting in a 'theory of nasty minds'. This is backed up by Evans et al. (2002) who examined a sub-set of children who were characterized by those close to them as being inter-personally negative, displaying spiteful and hostile behaviour and general anti-social behaviour. Findings revealed that these children could be described as having *inhibited* empathy rather than a *lack* of empathy.

Social intelligence and empathy are not totally independent of each other. Kaukainen et al. (1999) believe that empathy is characterized by sensitivity toward the feelings of others, whereas social intelligence can be applied without emotions in a cold-hearted manner. Findings revealed that social intelligence highly correlated with indirect forms of bullying but not physical or verbal bullying. These findings are strongly related to the findings by Sutton et al. (1999) that 'pure' bullies have a superior theory of mind.

15.1.4   Precursors of bullying

Controversy surrounds the precursors of becoming a 'pure' bully and the persistent nature of this behaviour. This is likely to be due to the lack of theoretical frameworks and models to examine possible precursors, and the reliance on models explaining anti-social behaviour as opposed to bullying per se. Social information processing models proposed by Crick and Dodge (1996) and later by Arsenio et al. (2000) provide initial attempts to explain the mechanisms of children's social adjustment. Rubin et al. (1990) postulated that the deviant pathway for bullies is linked to dispositional and temperamental traits in the child such as being fussy, difficult to soothe, having insecure-avoidant attachment patterns which ultimately leads to hostility, peer rejection and externalizing behaviour problems. The family background of bullies has also been implicated as a strong precursor for developing bullying traits. Bowers et al. (1994) and Farrington (1993) revealed that there was a concern with power in the families of bullies and a lack of family cohesion resulting in bullies feeling like they have little control at home. Stevens *et al.* (2002) considered the relationship between the family environment and involvement in bully/victim problems at school. Child and parent perceptions of family functioning differed substantially. For example, bullies described their families as 'less cohesive, more conflictual and less organized and controlled'. In contrast, parent perceptions only differed from parents of victims, bully/victims and neutral children by reporting more punishment. Conversely, the family background for victims of bullying indicated maternal over-protectiveness and critical and distant relationships with the father among boys. For girls, victimization was related to maternal hostility. A common pathway for victimization may occur when maternal behaviour hinders both boys' and girls' social and developmental goals (Wolke and Stanford, 1999).

A summary of research findings regarding the profile of 'pure' bullies points towards them as being socially intelligent and manipulative in social situations as opposed to the popular stereotype of bullies being psychopaths and 'strong but dumb and brutal characters' as frequently portrayed in movies and fiction.

15.1.4.1   How do bullies become bullies?

Since bullying behaviour is a relatively new subject in the psychology literature, research to date has mainly focused on building character profiles of bullies based on cross-sectional data. There are no long-term longitudinal studies available that have considered the crucial questions of how bullies become bullies, and why some children become bullies while others develop into victims, bully/victims or neutrals. It is only recently that studies have begun to consider the stability of bullying roles over time but this has not shed light on the developmental trajectories for becoming a 'pure' bully. As discussed above, correlational statistical data can give some hints surrounding the circumstances that bullies are associated with, but such data have little causal explanatory power. Since bullying is such a complex behaviour, it is unlikely that some children are 'naturally born bullies', i.e. it seems unlikely that there is a simple genetic explanation such as a 'bullying gene'. Neither is there convincing evidence that bullies are being 'taught' directly to be bullies (e.g. by family, peers or media such as computer games or television), although there is evidence to suggest that 'pure' bullies may come from families where the father was a bully, indicating links with social learning (Farrington, 1993). Also, it seems that being a bully is not a 'conscious' choice, e.g. a child who previously suffered from being bullied is unlikely to suddenly become a bully by conscious decision.

In the following we explore the possibility that particular events during child development, in particular during critical periods of socialization, might provide predispositions for becoming a bully.

15.2   Imitation

15.2.1   Imitation and inter-subjectivity

Developmental studies have identified important steps in the development of a child as a 'social being'. Early childhood interaction 'games' between infants and their caretakers play an important role in how children first make contact with the social world (cf. neonatal imitation research, e.g. Meltzoff, 1996). It has been suggested that imitation plays an important part in how inter-subjectivity arises (e.g. Nadel *et al.*, 1999). Although imitation is also a powerful means for humans to acquire new skills, the social function of imitation is a stepping stone in the development of humans as *social beings*. Synchronization of behaviour in infant–caretaker (playful) interactions leads to a meaningful 'dance' that allows the co-creation of inter-subjectivity (sharing of experiences and emotions), and meaning in interactions (Trevarthen *et al.*, 1999). Note that such games are dynamically emerging in face-to-face interaction, and they emerge from 'local rules' of co-ordination and synchronization, rather than representing a cognitively planned sequence of actions.

An interesting distinction, for the purpose of this paper, is to separate automatic from controlled empathy (Hodges and Wegner, 1997). A simple and developmentally early example of automatic empathy is automatic emotional empathy that helps infants and babies to share happiness and distress with others. Also, later in life, emotional contagion still plays an important part in our lives, as a means to share emotional expressions or physiological states of others (e.g. we tend to smile when watching others smiling). Automatic empathy is immediate, and not intentional. Even in adults this helps us share feelings, i.e. experiencing emotions that we observe. This process, for example, helps us to experience some pain when we see another person being hurt. We cannot wilfully 'switch off' emotional contagion.

Controlled empathy, as distinguished by Hodges and Wegner, can be produced consciously and intentionally. It usually involves an effortful search for cues in one's own memory that could trigger automatic empathy, a process that we try to control, e.g. by controlling our exposure (actual or imagined) to the stimuli evoking this response. During controlled empathy we gain knowledge that we can use in a variety of ways, i.e. for the purpose of better understanding oneself, for better understanding others in order to help them, or for manipulating others/ gaining a personal advantage. Cognitive empathy refers to the cognitive perspective, and means that an observer tries to understand how a target feels in a given situation. The cues available for the observer are the behaviour of the subject (including bodily and especially the facial expression of emotion) and the situation the target is dealing with. The result of this process of understanding is a cognition, e.g. 'I think the target is feeling sad, because he lost his wallet.' Cognitive empathy can also be automatic, too. For example, when remembering a particular person we might tend to adopt that person's viewpoints or opinions. Similarly, being situated in a particular environment might evoke automatic cognitive empathy that changes our state of mind (Hodges and Wegner, 1997).

Automatic processes of empathy help us to establish inter-subjectivity with other people, and it allows us to share experiences; experiences that can be shared on the emotional basis, on the level of affect rather than physically experiencing exactly the same situations as the person we empathize with. Such 'second-hand' experience can be an indirect source of learning from experience, by sharing the effects and affective qualities of other people's experiences.

15.3   Empathy and imitation

15.3.1 Deficits in empathy and autism

A general deficit in relating to other people and empathy has been discussed in the literature for autism, a life-long developmental disorder. People with autism show impairments in communication, social interaction, and imagination and fantasy. A specific theory of mind (TOM) deficit has been hypothesized as a cognitive explanation of autistic behaviour (Baron-Cohen *et al.*, 1985). Although the TOM explanation of autistic deficits has been accepted by many researchers, it is not uncontroversial. Primary deficits in emotional, interactive or other factors central to the *embodied* and *inter-subjective* nature of social understanding have been suggested as possible causes of autism. Affective theories see a lack of empathy, which in typically developing children develops through co-ordinated interchanges that result in inter-subjectivity and emotional engagement, as central to autism (Hobson, 1993). According to Hobson autistic children do not participate in inter-subjective social experiences from early on in their lives in the same way as typically developing children do. Bruner and Feldman (1993) proposed the *narrative deficit hypothesis of autism*, that hypothesizes a failure of infants to participate in narrative construction through *pre-verbal* transactional formats. Many theories aim at explaining the underlying causes of autism, and we cannot provide a comprehensive review here (but see Jordan, 1999). For the purpose of this paper it suffices that researchers have highlighted two different aspects of empathy in typically developing children, namely a cognitive as well as an emotional side which, as we suggest, can be linked with controlled/automatic empathy as discussed above.

15.3.1.1 *Deficits in imitation and autism*

Discussions of deficits for children with autism with respect to imitation are controversial (e.g. Rogers, 1999; Charman and Baron-Cohen, 1994). Generally children with autism seem to have some impairment in imitation skills, in particular they seem less able to imitate actions and gestures. However, it has been shown by Nadel and Pezé (1993) that even low-functioning children with autism can produce spontaneous imitations when encountering a non-autistic child (see discussions in Nadel *et al.*, 1999; Nadel 2002). Others have suggested a possible link between autism and a neurobiological disorder in the 'mirror system', that is involved in establishing a connection between what actions one sees others perform, and what actions one is able to do (Williams *et al.*, 2001). It has been hypothesized that this mirror system could provide a 'neural substrate' for a simulation theory of empathy (Gallese and Goldman, 1998).

People with autism provide an example of the consequences of having difficulty in possibly both automatic as well as controlled empathy which makes it difficult for them to share experiences with others and to perceive others as *people* with emotions, goals and other mental states. As a consequence, although their behaviour might appear 'rude' or 'cold' to others, it is based on how they perceive the (social) world. People with autism generally do not lie, deceive or manipulate: since they cannot perceive other people as 'mindful' they lack the notion of manipulating minds, and rather tend to believe that other's perceptions and states of mind are identical to their own. This is very different from how psychopaths perceive the social world.

15.3.1.2 *Empathy and psychopathy*

Psychopaths suffer from an anti-social personality disorder. According to Hare's Psychopathy Checklist – Revised (Hare, 1991), psychopaths are described as superficial, egocentric, grandiose, lack remorse or guilt, demonstrate abnormal emotional functioning, lack empathy, are deceitful and are manipulative. Interpersonally, psychopaths on the one hand lack empathy, but on the other hand are very skilful at manipulating and deceiving others. Behaviourally, psychopaths are risk-taking, sensation seekers who act impulsively and get involved in criminal activities. Affectively, they display shallow emotions and are unable to form strong emotional bonds with others. Clinicians have characterized the emotions of psychopaths as 'proto-emotions', i.e. 'primitive responses to immediate needs' (Pitchford, 2001). Blair *et al.* (1996) reported that psychopaths do not have a theory of mind deficit although differences in processing emotional information have been suggested, which might explain why psychopaths have a lack of moral emotions (e.g. feel little guilt or remorse for their actions (Blair, 1997)).

Psychopaths also experience 'semantic dementia'. According to this concept, psychopaths would have an appropriate cognitive representation of the lexical meaning of emotions, but not the affective value normally attached to them (Johns and Quay, 1962; Patrick *et al.*, 1994). According to Cleckley (1984) the psychopath is able to reproduce adequately the 'pantomime' of emotions, without experiencing the emotions itself. Psychopaths have been described as not possessing strong empathic capacities and are expected to be more self-centred, not to be propelled to suppress their aggressive impulses (Saltaris, 2002).

Martens (2000) revealed that a history of rejection, neglect, physical and sexual abuse, parental antisocial behaviour, substance abuse, and divorce, adoption, and a bad and unsafe neighbourhood might be linked to emotional deficits in psychopaths. Also, the emergence of abnormal moral emotions later in life may be linked to temperament and attachment deficiencies in early childhood of the psychopath (Saltaris, 2002).

15.3.1.3   Psychopathic-like traits in children and adolescents
In childhood and adolescence, patterns of psychopathic deviancy can be prospectively predicted to appear in later life (Saltaris, 2002). The most severely anti-social children are more likely to receive an adult diagnosis of psychopathy as well as a sub-group of conduct disordered children characterized by undersocialized aggressive conduct disorder (Johnstone and Cooke, 2004). Lynam (1996, as cited in Johnstone and Cooke, 2004) suggested that the 'fledgling psychopath' is likely to be within the group of children who have both conduct problems and hyperactivity- impulsivity-attention (HIA) problems. This condition is linked with an early onset of behavioural disturbance and a more severe pattern of dysfunction in childhood, such as delinquency and offending.

15.3.1.4   Differences in empathy for autism and psychopathy
Thus, autism and psychopathy illustrate two extreme examples of the consequences of deficits in empathy: autistic people have a fundamental problem with behaving socially and perceiving others as 'persons that can

empathize and can be empathized with'. Their behaviour might at times appear rude, insensitive or inappropriate, but this is not due to a wilful choice but is due to a lack of understanding of what behaviour would be appropriate. On the other hand, psychopaths are very skilful mind-readers and social manipulators, but the consequences of their actions are anti-social because of an extremely egocentric viewpoint that is possibly due to impaired processing of emotional information. Impaired emotion processing is likely to directly impact on automatic empathy by affecting the crucial link that allows us to relate to another person's emotions and experiences. Psychopaths know that others have a mind, and they know how to manipulate minds.

15.3.2   Empathy and bullying behaviour

How could bullying be explained in the context of empathy and imitation? Several explanations are possible:

In contrast to previous suggestions that bullies are 'strong but dumb', i.e. lack social intelligence, are not able to understand and interpret others' emotions and mental states, evidence points towards bullies as possessing well-developed social intelligence and being good mind-readers. It seems bullies are good at manipulating others because they can easily understand and predict the consequences of their actions. This is what makes them 'leaders' who control other children. Research studies examining the profiles of 'pure' bullies, in particular relational bullies highlight some similarities with the profile outlined for psychopaths. For example, Sutton et al. (1999) state 'while it is not suggested that bullies are all budding psychopaths, they have been reported to have higher levels of psychoticism than victims and controls'. Different from the conventional stereotypes, it seems that victims are poor mind-readers, not bullies. Victims appear to have deficits in theory of mind that prevents them from successfully predicting and dealing with a bully's manipulations. Recent research also suggests that victims of relational bullying, but not victims of physical bullying have poor abilities in perceiving the emotions of others, whereas bullies and neutral children do not (Woods and Wolke, 2005).

If bullies are good mind-readers and socially intelligent in terms of manipulating others, can bullies feel empathy at all? Have bullies psychopath-like tendencies with impaired emotion processing? We are not aware of any evidence suggesting a direct link between childhood bullies automatically developing into psychopaths later in life. An alternative view that we suggest is to consider bullies as possessing both automatic as well as controlled empathy (different from both people with autism as

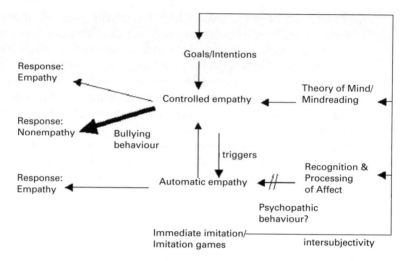

Figure 15.1 Sketching possible connections between imitation, empathy and bullying behaviour. We hypothesize that although bullies possess the capacity of empathy, bullying behaviour is caused by an overemphasis of goal-directed processes of controlled empathy that work towards nonempathy. People with autism seem to have impairments in both automatic and controlled empathy.

well as from psychopaths), but (possibly intentionally) using processes of controlled empathy for the goal of non-empathy. Thus, a bully might be perfectly able to recognize and understand the suffering of his victim (e.g. a child who he just beat), his emotion processing could give him the 'correct' interpretation (e.g. of pain), and via controlled empathy automatic empathic responses might be triggered in his memory (e.g. reminding him of an instance when he felt pain) but the cognitive, goal-directed processes of controlled empathy would work towards non-empathy (see Figure 15.1). (Note, goal-oriented processes play an important role for all of us in empathy. However, in bullies the tendency to display controlled empathy is, according to our hypothesis, more pronounced). Similarly, imagine the news of a famous, conservative politician caught in an embarrassing instance of private exposure. If the same happened to a family member, we would clearly feel and express empathy. In the case of the politician we are more likely to react in an ironic, or otherwise clearly non-empathic way. Thus, the goals we pursue in controlled empathy can shape emotional, automatic responses either towards empathy or non-empathy. In bullies, non-empathy is used deliberately in a context that expresses power over the victims.

Plate 1 (Figure 20.1) Curious keas (*Nestor notabilis*) in Mt. Cook National Park, New Zealand.
(Photos by D. Werdenich and B. Voelkl)

Plate 2 (Figure 21.1) Leaf Mimicry.
a. Australian Leaf-Wing Butterfly, *Dolleschallia bisaltide*;
b. Cockatoo Waspfish, *Ablabys taenianotus*;
c. Juvenile Round Batfish, *Platax orbicularis*;
d. Broadclub Cuttlefish, *Sepia latimanus*, 'impersonating' dead mangrove leaf;
e. same individual in resting colour pattern.
(Photos by M. Norman)

Plate 3 (Figure 21.2) Camouflage and deceptive resemblance in cephalopods.

a. *Octopus* sp. 5 (Norman, 2000) active in rock pools;
b. same individual moments later in camouflage;
c. Hairy Octopus (*Octopus* sp. 16 (Norman, 2000)) showing branching skin sculpture;
d. Snail Mimic Octopus (*Octopus* sp. 6 (Gosliner *et al.*, 1996));
e. Giant Cuttlefish, *Sepia apama* – sneaker male (centre) impersonating female amongst breeding pair (male on right)

(Photos a, b & e by M. Norman; c by Becca Saunders and d by M. Severns)

Plate 4 (Figure 21.3) Mimic Octopus (*Octopus* sp. 19 Norman 2000)
and models.
a. sentinel state in mouth of burrow;
b. normal foraging colour pattern;
c. flatfish mimicry;
d. flatfish model, banded sole (*Zebrias* sp.);
e. lionfish mimicry;
f. lionfish model (*Pterois* sp.);
g. sea snake mimicry;
h. sea snake model, banded sea snake (*Laticauda* sp.).
(Photos a, b, d–f by M. Norman and c, g & h by R. Steene)

Plate 5 (Figure 3.3) The software air hockey game on the left and air hockey playing with a humanoid robot on the right.

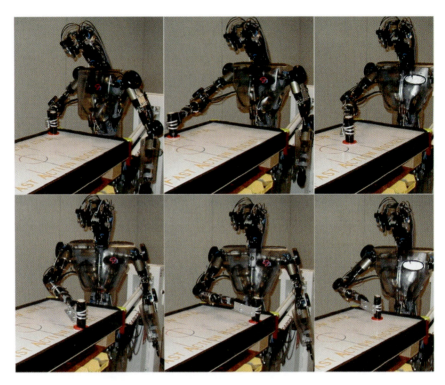

Plate 6 (Figure 3.5) Six manually defined configurations are used to interpolate the body configuration needed to place the paddle at a specific location.

Plate 7 (Figure 7.1a and b) The demonstrator performing the action (a) in a happy, satisfied manner and (b) in a frustrated, dissatisfied manner in Behne and colleagues' (2006b) study.

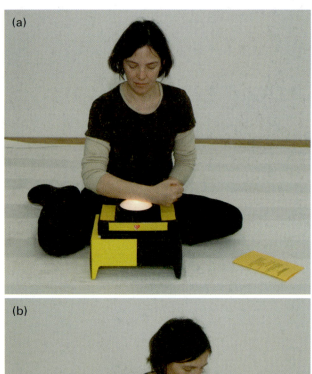

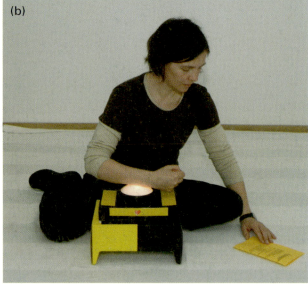

Plate 8 (Figure 7.2a and b) The demonstrator (a) attending and (b) not attending to her action in Behne and colleagues' (2006a) study.

15.3.2.1   The distinction between automatic and controlled empathy in bullies

The hypothesis outlined above suggests that bullies direct controlled empathy in instances of bullying towards non-empathy. What predictions derive from this hypothesis, and how could it be tested?

Based on our hypothesis, bullies have unimpaired empathic skills as far as the processes are involved that trigger automatic empathy. Accordingly, they are able to express empathy, possibly in contexts outside schools. This hypothesis could be disconfirmed by evidence of a substantial impairment of automatic and/or controlled empathy processes, impairments that could prevent bullies from *genuinely* experiencing empathy. Evidence of bullies who only show bullying behaviour in certain contexts, but not in others, would confirm our hypothesis. It would point towards a picture of bullies as children who can strongly control their empathic skills, in the extreme case possibly even switch them on and off depending on the context (i.e. their own social goals). In a longitudinal study following the lives of bullies we would predict that while some bullies might prefer consciously to make a career as a 'bully', others might no longer show any bullying behaviour after a certain period (e.g. due to a change in personal social goals).

If bullies are very much goal-oriented empathizers, we might find more bullies in situations where children are involved in strong competition for resources, e.g. competition for the attention/affection of parents/caregivers, competition with siblings or peers, or competition for elementary resources such as food, in extreme circumstances. We predict that such contexts can facilitate bullying behaviour. Changing family and/or other environmental conditions should therefore influence the behaviour and motivation of bullies. There are no longitudinal studies which have considered the justifications that children provide for bullying others. However, there is some evidence that bullying may be related to critical life experiences, and personal social goals such as moving into a new school when dominance is initially being negotiated for new peer relationships (Pellegrini and Long, 2002). There is also evidence that children who are very aggressive to their siblings are likely to have problems with peers outside the family, namely rejection by peers and that the personality characteristics of bullies appear to be stable across social situations where there is 'forced' formation of the group composition (Dishion, 1990; Bowers *et al.*, 1994).

In terms of bullying intervention, according to our hypothesis, an educational or cultural environment that focuses on problem-solving and goal-oriented behaviour should facilitate the occurrence of bullies since it supports their tendency towards goal-oriented empathic understanding.

An environment that raises awareness of bullying and the plight of victims should, according to our hypothesis, help bullies to refine their bullying skills by: (1) enhancing their understanding of how bad they can make the victim feel and (2) show them strategies and counter-strategies that they might use in further instances of bullying.

15.4   Bullying intervention

15.4.1   *Characteristics of bullying intervention programmes*

There are a wide range of anti-bullying initiatives that have been developed and implemented in the hope of tackling and reducing bullying problems in schools. Farrington (1993) categorized intervention programmes as focusing on the bully, the victim or the environment as a whole. More recent intervention approaches include the use of virtual characters to induce empathy with the user (e.g. Woods *et al.*, 2003a; 2003b).

Intervention programmes which place emphasis on 'bullies' are diverse in nature and researchers have expressed contrary viewpoints in terms of the most favoured techniques. For example, the use of physical punishment to deter bullies was considered to be helpful by some in a study carried out by Stephenson and Smith (1989) whereas others such as Pikas (1989) with the 'method of shared concern' and Maines and Robinson (1991) with the 'no blame approach' believe that physical punishment and reprimands are not effective in reducing bullies behaviour and suggest that bullies should be made to see and understand the viewpoint of victims and make amends for their upsetting behaviour. These methods are usually carried out with the bully and victim individually and subsequently followed by a group discussion with the bully, victim and an adult group mediator.

The success rates of anti-bullying initiatives are difficult to evaluate in real-life situations due to the large differences between schools, school ethos and individual differences between children and adults. However, the overall picture highlights that intervention strategies to date are successful in the short-term but do not have long-term success rates in terms of reducing and eliminating bullying problems (Roland, 2000; Eslea and Smith, 1998).

15.4.1.1   *Empathy as a tool for bullying intervention programmes*
If bullies use empathic skills mainly in a goal-oriented manner, can we change their goals? We believe not, based on evidence that insight-oriented intervention programmes seem not very successful, as discussed above. It is likely that any intervention trying to convince a bully that they

should change their goals will result in a bully who is even more aware of his/her goals. Likewise, any other 'cognitive' approaches towards educating bullies might fail for the same reasons. A similar counter-productive effect of insight-oriented therapy is being discussed for psychopaths: after such therapy psychopaths seem more likely to reoffend (Quinsey and Lalumière, 1995), possibly because it helped them to even further perfect their skills in psychological manipulation (Hare, 1993).

Thus, if not on the cognitive level, then can the emotional levels that are involved in automatic empathy be strengthened in bullies? Any empowerment of this kind would have to be taught on the emotional level, not the cognitive level of, for example, 'explaining emotions' in discussions or writings.

15.4.1.2   The use of imitative interactive behaviour for bullying interventions
As a proposal for a behavioural intervention programme for children with a tendency towards bullying behaviour we suggest to investigate the impact of imitative, interactive behaviour.

As we discussed above, a major achievement in a child's childhood is to 'make emotional contact' with people, to share experiences, to create inter-subjectivity, a crucial stepping stone in becoming a social being. Interestingly, this is not achieved by watching and analyzing interactions from a distance, or by reading about it or being taught explicitly: it is mainly achieved through imitative interaction games. Such inter-subjectivity that one can find in immediate imitation results from being part of an interaction. Immersion in the interaction, as well as a synchronization and sharing of goals makes this interaction socially and emotionally important. Infants playing turn-taking and imitation games with their caretakers, either vocally or involving body movements, share emotional experiences, a key element in automatic empathy that 'just happens'. Later in life a 'theory of mind' and cognitive processes complement this 'immediate link' towards another person's feelings.

Thus, a bully might have to be reminded of what it means to connect to people. He might know how to connect to others in principle, but he might use this skill very selectively, e.g. directed only towards his closest friends, while for other children his cognitive control of empathy dominates. Such children might have to be reminded that the world consists of many other 'sentient beings' whose emotional states deserve attention, not just of bullies and victims (and other bystanders/neutrals that can easily be ignored or recruited). We speculate that behavioural intervention programmes based on imitation and the elicitation of automatic empathic responses (e.g. emotional contagion) might help to strengthen empathic responses in children with a tendency towards bullying behaviour.

An important consideration for bullying intervention programmes concerns the environment and the individuals involved. As previously stated, intervention strategies which have focused upon trying to re-establish amicable relations between bullies and victims have received limited success. The inclusion of the whole family in intervention programmes for bullies could be explored; for example, the parents of bullies may benefit from being involved in imitation and empathy skills training. Evidence for this family involvement in intervention programmes is derived from Stevens *et al.* (2002) who reported that the family backgrounds for bullies had similar characteristics of aggressive children including less pro-social interactions, reinforcement of aggressive behaviour and inconsistent and harsh discipline methods. Therefore, it could be argued that if bullies participate in imitative and empathy skills training in isolation from family members, any new skills learnt are likely to be short-lived as the rest of the family will not support any visible behavioural changes in the bully.

15.5   Conclusion

This paper is very speculative, due to very little information on 'what bullies are' and 'where they come from'. Likewise, the causes and universal characteristics of autism and psychopathy are similarly controversial. Bullying is a growing and quite serious problem in schools (and elsewhere) worldwide. Intervention programmes so far have not been significantly successful, we therefore hope that a fresh perspective can contribute to future research in this area.

REFERENCES

Arsenio, W. F., Cooperman, S. and Lover, A. (2000). Affective predictors of preschoolers' aggression and peer acceptance: direct and indirect effects. *Developmental Psychology*, **36**(4), 438–48.
Baron-Cohen, S., Leslie, A. and Frith, U. (1985). Does the autistic child have a 'theory of mind'? *Cognition*, **21**, 37–46.
Björkqvist, K. (1994). Sex differences in physical, verbal, and indirect aggression: a review of recent research. *Sex Roles*, **30**(3/4), 177–88.
Blair, R. J. R., Sellars, C., Strickland, I., Clark, F., *et al.* (1996). Theory of mind in the psychopath. *Journal of Forensic Psychiatry*, **7**(1), 15–25.
Blair, R. J. R. (1997). Moral reasoning and the child with psychopathic tendencies. *Personality and Individual Differences*, **22**(5), 731–9.
Bond, L., Carlin, J. B., Thomas, L., Kerryn, R. and Patton, G. (2001). Does bullying cause emotional problems? A prospective study of young teenagers. *BMJ*, **323**, 480–4.

Bowers, L., Smith, P. K. and Binney, V. (1994). Perceived family relationships of bullies, victims and bully/victims in middle childhood. *Journal of Social and Personal Relationships*, **11**, 215–32.

Bruner, J. and Feldman, C. (1993). Theories of mind and the problem of autism. In S. Baron-Cohen, H. Tager-Flusberg and D. J. Cohen (eds.), *Understanding other Minds: Perspectives from Autism*. Oxford: Oxford University Press.

Charman, T. S. and Baron-Cohen, S. (1994). Another look at imitation in autism. *Development and Psychopathology*, **1**, 1–4.

Cleckley, H. (1984). *Mask of Insanity*. Mosby: St Louis: C.V.

Crick, N. R. and Dodge, K. A. (1996). Social information-processing mechanisms in reactive and proactive aggression. *Child Development*, **67**, 993–1002.

Davis, M. H. (1994). *Empathy, A Social Psychological Approach*. USA: Wm. C. Brown Communications, Inc.

Dishion, T. J. (1990). The family ecology of boys' peer relations in middle childhood. *Child Development*, **61**, 864–73.

Eslea, M. and Smith, P. K. (1998). The long-term effectiveness of anti-bullying work in primary schools. *Educational Research*, **40(2)**, 1–16.

Evans, I. M., Heriot, S. A. and Friedman, A. G. (2002). A behavioural pattern of irritability, hostility and inhibited empathy in children. *Clinical Child Psychology and Psychiatry*, **7**, 211–24.

Farrington, D. P. (1993). Understanding and preventing bullying. In M. Tonry, (ed.), *Crime and Justice*, Vol. 17. Chicago: University of Chicago, 381–458.

Gallese, V. and Goldman, A. (1998). Mirror neurons and the simulation theory of mind-reading. *Trends in Cognitive Sciences*, **2(12)**, 493–501.

Hare, R. (1991). *The Hare Psychopathy Checklist – Revised*. Toronto: Multi-Health Systems.

Hare, R. (1993). *Without Conscience: The Disturbing World of the Psychopaths Among Us*. New York: Simon and Schuster.

Hobson, P. (1993). Understanding persons: the role of affect. In S. Baron-Cohen, H. Tager-Flusberg and D. J. Cohen (eds.). In *Understanding Other Minds, Perspectives from Autism*. Oxford: Oxford University Press, 204–27.

Hodges, S. D. and Wegner, D. M. (1997). Automatic and controlled empathy. In W. Ickes (ed.), *Empathic Accuracy*. Guildford: The Guildford Press, 311–39.

Johns, J. H. and Quay, H. C. (1962). The effect of social reward on verbal conditioning in psychopathic and neurotic military offenders. *Journal of Consulting Psychology*, **26**, 217–20.

Johnstone, L. and Cooke, D. (2004). Psychopathic-like traits in childhood: conceptual and measurement concerns. *Behavioral Sciences and the Law*, **22**, 103–25.

Jordan, R. (1999) *Autistic Spectrum Disorders – An Introductory Handbook for Practitioners*. London: David Fulton Publishers.

Kaukiainen, A., Bjorkqvist, K., Lagerspetz, K., Osterman, K., Salmivalli, C., Rothberg, S. and Ahlbom, A. (1999). The relationship between social intelligence, empathy and three types of aggression. *Aggressive Behaviour*, **25**, 81–9.

Maines, B. and Robinson, G. (1991). Don't beat the bullies. *Educational Psychology in Practice*, **7(3)**, 168–72.

Martens, W. H. J. (2000). Antisocial and psychopathic personality disorders: causes, course and remission – a review article. *International Journal of Offender Therapy and Comparative Criminology*, **44**, 406–30.

Meltzoff, A. (1996). The human infant as imitative generalist: a 20 year progress report on infant imitation with implications for comparitive psychology. In *Social Learning in Animals: The Roots of Culture*, B. G. Galef and C. M. Heyes (eds.). New York: Academic Press, 347–70.

Nadel, J. (2002). Imitation and imitation recognition: functional use in preverbal infants and nonverbal children with autism. In A. N. Meltzoff and W. Prinz (eds.), *The Imitative Mind: Development, Evolution and Brain Bases*. Cambridge studies in cognitive perceptual development. New York: Cambridge University Press, 42–62.

Nadel, J. and Pezé, A. (1993). What makes immediate imitation communicative in toddlers and autistic children? In J. Nadel and L. Camaioni (eds.), *New Perspectives in Early Communicative Development*. London, New York: Routledge, 139–56.

Nadel, J., Guérini, C. and Pezé, A. (1999). The evolving nature of imitation as a format of communication. In J. Nadel and G. Butterworth (eds.), *Imitation in Infancy*. Cambridge, UK: Cambridge University Press, 209–34.

Olweus, D. (1999). Sweden. In P. K. Smith, Y. Morita, J. Junger-Tas, D. Olweus, R. Catalano and P. Slee (eds.), *The Nature of School Bullying: A Cross-national Perspective*. London: Routledge, 10.

Patrick, C. J., Cuthbert, B. N. and Lang, P. J. (1994). Emotion in the criminal psychopath: fear image processing. *Journal of Abnormal Psychology*, **103**, 523–34.

Pellegrini, A. D. and Long, J. D. (2002). A longitudinal study of bullying, dominance and victimization during the transition from primary school through secondary school. *British Journal of Developmental Psychology*, **20**, 259–80.

Pitchford, I. (2001) The origins of violence: is psychopathy an adaptation? *The Human Nature Review*, **1**, 28–36.

Pikas, A. (1989). A pure concept of mobbing gives the best results for treatment. *School Psychology International*, **10**, 95–104.

Quinsey, V. L. and Lalumière, M. L. (1995) Psychopathy is a nonarbitrary class. *Behavioural and Brain Sciences*, **18**, 571.

Randall, P. (1997). *Adult Bullying: Perpetrators and Victims*. London: Routledge.

Rogers, S. J. (1999). An examination of the imitation deficit in autism. In J. Nadel and G. Butterworth (eds.), *Imitation in Infancy*. Cambridge, UK: Cambridge University Press, 254–83.

Roland, E. (2000). Bullying in school: three national innovations in Norwegian schools in 15 years. *Aggressive Behaviour*, **26**, 135–43.

Rubin, K. H., LeMare, L. J. and Lollis, S. (1990). Social withdrawal in childhood: developmental pathways to peer rejection. In S. R. Asher and J. D. Coie (eds.), *Peer Rejection in Childhood*. Cambridge, UK: Cambridge University Press.

Salmon, G., James, A. and Smith, D. M. (1998). Bullying in schools: self reported anxiety, depression and self esteem in secondary school children. *British Medical Journal*, **317**, 924–5.

Saltaris, C. (2002). Psychopathy in juvenile offenders: Can temperament and attachment be considered as robust developmental precursors? *Clinical Psychology Review*, **22**, 729–52.

Stephenson, P. and Smith, D. (1989). Bullying in the junior school. In D. P. L. Tattum (ed.), *Bullying in Schools*, 1st edn. Stoke-on-Trent: Trentham Books, 45–57.

Stevens, V., De Bourdeaudhuij, I. and van Oost, P. (2002). Relationship of the family environment to children's involvement in bully/victim problems at school. *Journal of Youth and Adolescence*, **31(6)**, 419–28.

Sutton, J. and Smith, P. K. (1999). Bullying as a group process: an adaptation of the participant role approach. *Aggressive Behaviour*, **25**, 97–111.

Sutton, J., Smith, P. K. and Swettenham, J. (1999). Bullying and 'theory of mind': A critique of the 'social skills deficit' view of anti-social behaviour. *Social Development*, **8(1)**, 117–27.

Trevarthen, C., Kokkinaki, T. and Fiamenghi Jr., G. A. (1999). What infants' imitation communicate: with mothers, with fathers and with peers. In J. Nadel and G. Butterworth (eds.), *Imitation in Infancy*. Cambridge, UK: Cambridge University Press, 127–85.

Whitney, I. and Smith, P. K. (1993). A survey of the nature and extent of bullying in junior/middle and secondary schools. *Educational Research*, **35(1)**, 3–25.

Williams, J. H. G., Whiten, A., Suddendorf, T. and Perrett, D. I. (2001). Imitation, mirror neurons and autism. *Neuroscience and Biobehavioral Reviews*, **25(4)**, 287–95.

Wolke, D., Woods, S., Bloomfield, L. and Karstadt, L. (2000). The association between direct and relational bullying and behaviour problems among primary school children. *Journal of Child Psychology and Psychiatry*, **41(8)**, 989–1002.

Wolke, D. and Stanford, K. (1999). Bullying in school children. In D. Messer, and S. Millar (eds.), *Developmental Psychology*. London: Arnold Publishers.

Woods, S., Hall, L., Sobral, D., Dautenhahn, K. and Wolke, D. (2003a). Animated characters in bullying intervention. *Lecture Notes in Computer Science*, **2792**, 310–14.

Woods, S., Hall, L., Sobral, D., Dautenhahn, K. and Wolke, D. (2003b). A study into the believability of animated characters in the context of bullying intervention, presented at *Intelligent Virtual Agents 2003, Kloster, Germany*.

Woods, S. and Wolke, D. (2005). Emotion recognition abilities, and empathy in bullies and victims. Paper presented at the XIIth European Conference on Developmental Psychology, University of Laguna, Faculty of Psychology, Tenerife, 24–28 August.

Part VI

Why imitate? – Motivations

The question of why animals, humans and robots should or do engage in social learning or social matching behaviour has at least two major answers: *learning* and *communicative interaction* (Užgiris, 1981). The link between the motivations for imitative behaviour and development are the common theme of the two chapters in this section of the book. The former, acquisition of new behaviours via *observational learning* (Bandura, 1977), has been better studied, the latter motivation for behaviour matching less so, but it clearly plays a communicative role when turn-taking, role-taking, being imitated and topic-sharing occur in communicative social interactions of pre-verbal young children (Nadel *et al.*, 2002), compare Part V, Synchrony and turn-taking as communicative mechanisms, in this volume.

Psychologists Mark Nielsen and Virginia Slaughter discuss results on the development in human children of different types of imitative capacities including immediate, deferred and synchronic imitation, and the capacity to imitate after having observed incomplete or failed behaviours. Following Užgiris and Nadel, they discuss the development of imitation for interactive and communicative functions, where imitation is 'conceived fundamentally as a social act', as opposed to its role in skill learning. They assess evidence from their own experiments and the studies of others on imitation as a communicative mechanism. Here imitation serves to initiate and maintain social engagement, for example, in turn-taking games. The importance of various factors such as attention to actions or attention to the model, as well as vocal imitation are also discussed.

Artificial intelligence researchers Frédéric Kaplan and Pierre-Yves Oudeyer discuss the role of imitation in the development of children and its relationship to the balance between seeking novelty and being able to anticipate the effects of behaviour. They propose that an intrinsic *progress drive* for the maximization of learning progress could be used to

Imitation and Social Learning in Robots, Humans and Animals, ed. Chrystopher L. Nehaniv and Kerstin Dautenhahn. Published by Cambridge University Press.
© Cambridge University Press 2007.

achieve such a balance between seeking novelty and seeking mastery in natural and artificial systems. The authors then review developmental steps in children's use of imitation and the role of imitation in exploring niches leading to the ontogeny of *self*, *other* and *object* concepts as well as the understanding of *object affordances*. Considering the propensities for different types of imitation at different stages in child development, they suggest that these could be parsimoniously explained by hypothesizing such an innate progress drive in children. Here, selection of forms of imitation and self-imitation serve as an exploration mechanism in a zone of proximal development (Vygotsky 1978) allowing an individual to grow and develop at the boundary of what has already been mastered with the help of social learning.

Imitation, social learning and matching thus can guide learning by making use of social interaction to achieve acquisition of new behaviours and mastery of skills, but can also play a role as mechanisms for supporting social interaction itself. These dual motivations to imitate may either occur in isolation or together, and the dynamic feedback between activity in these two roles could serve to bootstrap processes of development in humans, animals and robots (see Part IV, Development and embodiment, in this volume).

REFERENCES

Bandura, A. (1977). *Social Learning Theory*. Englewood Cliffs, NJ: Prentice-Hall, 1977.
Užgiris, I. Č. (1981). Two functions of imitation during infancy. *International Journal of Behavioral Development*, **4**, 1–12.
Nadel, J., Guérini, C., Pezé, A. and Rivet, C. (2002). The evolving nature of imitation as a format for communication. In J. Nadel and G. Butterworth (eds.). *Imitation in Infancy*, (Cambridge Studies in Cognitive and Perceptual Development). Cambridge, UK: Cambridge University Press, 209–34.
Vygotsky, L. S. (1978). *Mind in Society: The Development of Higher Psychological Processes*. Cambridge, MA: Harvard University Press.

16 Multiple motivations for imitation in infancy

Mark Nielsen and Virginia Slaughter

As the chapters in this book attest, during the last decade the study of imitation has become a topic of central importance through a diverse range of disciplines.[1] There have been a greater number of controlled studies of imitation in non-human animals than ever before. Possible neural foundations of imitation have been identified. Encouraging progress has been made in developing imitation in constructed systems. Our understanding of the processes and mechanisms of imitation has been markedly advanced. Nonetheless, during this period most researchers have primarily focused on how imitation facilitates the acquisition of new skills or behaviours. In so doing, some important aspects of imitation have been neglected. In human development, infants imitate for a wide variety of reasons, both within and across different developmental stages and within and across different contexts. More specifically, for human infants imitation is an important form of pre-verbal communication that provides a means by which they can engage in social interaction. Our aim in this chapter is to provide an overview of the evidence that infants imitate not only to acquire new skills but also to engage socially with others, and this social engagement can itself take a number of different forms, with imitation being used flexibly as a means to various social ends.

Before going further a brief note on definition is warranted. The focus on imitation during the last decade has been accompanied by a proliferation in the number of terms used to define and describe different

---

[1] See also C. M. Heyes and B. G. Galef, Jr. (eds.) *Social Learning in Animals: The Roots of Culture*. New York: Academic Press, 1996; J. Nadel and G. Butterworth (eds.) *Imitation in Infancy*, Cambridge, UK: Cambridge University Press, 1999; K. Dautenhahn and C. L. Nehaniv (eds.) *Imitation in Animals and Artifacts*, Cambridge, MA: MIT Press, 2002; A. N. Meltzoff and W. Prinz (eds.) *The Imitative Mind*, Cambridge, UK: Cambridge University Press, 2002, and other references mentioned in the Introduction of this volume. – Ed.

Imitation and Social Learning in Robots, Humans and Animals, ed. Chrystopher L. Nehaniv and Kerstin Dautenhahn. Published by Cambridge University Press.
© Cambridge University Press 2007.

aspects of social learning (for recent reviews see Call and Carpenter, 2002; Want and Harris, 2002; Zentall, 2001). This terminology has been useful in providing a framework for studies of social learning and for providing a way of characterizing the types of social learning mechanisms of distinct populations, such as different species or children of different ages, tend to use. Unfortunately, the number of definitions now available and the lack of concurrence over what they mean and how to correctly apply them has led to some confusion and disagreement on how particular studies are to be interpreted. Where some see imitation others see alternative mechanisms of social learning, such as mimicry (copying another's behaviour without understanding its functional significance) or goal emulation (where the focus is on reproducing the outcome of another's behaviour but not the process by which it was achieved, Tomasello, Kruger and Ratner, 1993; Whiten and Ham, 1992). In the present chapter we are primarily concerned with how age and specific task demands affect the manner in which infants respond to a model. While acknowledging that other mechanisms of social learning may be at play we thus use the term 'imitation' to broadly refer to instances in which infants reproduce actions or behaviours they have witnessed being produced by another individual.

Over twenty years ago Užgiris (1981) noted that imitation serves two distinct functions in human infants: learning and communication (a perspective recently revived by Nadel and her colleagues, e.g. Nadel *et al.*, 1999; Nadel and Revel, Chapter 13 this volume).[2] Based on her analysis of the imitation literature at the time, Užgiris argued that there are two primary ways in which imitation can be conceived: one that emphasizes the cognitive function of imitation in promoting infants' learning about events in the world, and one that emphasizes the interpersonal function of imitation in promoting infants' sharing of experience with others. To illustrate the reality of these two distinct functions of imitation, she reviewed results of an experiment (Killen and Užgiris, 1981) in which infants of different ages were exposed to models performing a variety of acts: simple actions (e.g. banging a block), complex actions with appropriate toys (e.g. drinking from a cup) and complex actions with inappropriate toys (e.g. drinking from a toy car). The infants' tendencies to imitate these different types of acts changed over the course of the first two years of life, such that imitation of simple acts was high in the youngest, 7-month-old group, decreased in the 10-month-olds, but increased again in the older 16-and 22-month-old infants. The 22-month-olds were also highly

---

[2] Precedents of this idea can be found in Baldwin (1894), Wallon (1934), and Yando *et al.* (1978).

engaged in imitating complex actions with appropriate toys, even though mastery of these acts was already evident in the 16-month-olds. Užgiris thus argued that the 22-month-olds imitated the simple actions and the actions with appropriate toys not so much to learn about how the objects could be used, but more to communicate and share their understanding of those acts with the experimenter. Užgiris also noted that infants did not simply imitate more often, or preferentially imitate the more complex or puzzling acts as they got older, as a pure skill-learning conception of imitation would predict. Instead, she argued, the pattern of results was best interpreted in terms of infants' changing motivations for imitating; young infants may imitate simple acts to satisfy cognitive motivations, while older infants may imitate in the same context in order to satisfy social motivations. Thus the developmental nature of imitation is complex and multi-faceted: infants of different ages may choose to imitate the same model, performing the same act, in the same context, for entirely different reasons.

Užgiris (1981) emphasized that infants' tendencies to imitate change with development as a result of cognitive developmental achievements and also as a result of infants' changing social and communicative needs and motivations. In the next sections we will extend Užgiris' analysis by briefly reviewing various forms of imitation that, although highly diverse in form, are similar in function to the extent that non-cognitive motivations for imitating can be implicated. Our aim is to highlight imitation as a multi-faceted skill that serves multiple purposes (see also Mitchell, 1987, 1990, 1994).

16.1   Neonatal imitation

In traditional developmental theory facial imitation was restricted to infants older than 8 to 12 months of age (J. M. Baldwin, 1897; Guillaume, 1926/1971; Piaget, 1962). Piaget (1962) maintained that infants could not exhibit facial imitation until they had either received adequate mirror exposure in conjunction with specific perceptual–cognitive development or had received sufficient tactual experience of touching the faces of their mothers and comparing it with tactual exploration of their own faces. However, there is now evidence that a capacity for imitating a limited range of facial acts is present at birth. Meltzoff and Moore (1977) presented neonates, some as young as an hour old, with four different gestures in a random order: lip protrusion, mouth opening, tongue protrusion and sequential finger movement (opening and closing the hand by serially moving the fingers). The reaction of the neonates in response to the modelled gestures was videotaped and later presented to naive coders who were required to judge which of the target behaviours the neonates exhibited (the judges were blind to which actions had been modelled in each trial). Meltzoff and Moore reported that the neonates not only imitated actions with several parts of the body, but also did not confuse either actions or bodily organs. That is, the neonates responded to tongue protrusion with tongue protrusion and not lip protrusion, and differentiated between two different actions produced by the same organ (lips protruding vs. lips opening). There have also been reports of imitation of other facial gestures by neonates, including emotional expressions (Field *et al.*, 1982; Legerstee, 1991; for a review see Meltzoff and Moore, 1999).

Although there are those who have questioned the certitude of neonatal imitation (Abravanel and Sigafoos, 1984; Anisfield, 1991; Jones, 1996; McKenzie and Over, 1983) this phenomenon continues to be compelling, not least in part because of its potential importance for early social development. Meltzoff and Moore (1992; 1995) argue for the social relevance of neonatal imitation; they suggest that imitation by newborns is crucial for initial identification of conspecifics and for forging social relationships. They argue that the human tendency to match bodily movements of the self with movements of others provides newborn infants with a powerful early means of social interaction; by imitating others, infants may begin to recognize the similarity between themselves and other people, and in so doing enter into the social world of humans and begin to develop concepts of self and others as animate, intentional agents. Meltzoff and Moore (1992; 1995) further argue that imitation has a recognition function, that infants link specific gestures to individuals, and produce specific imitative acts to indicate their recognition of those individuals. In this context neonatal imitation is conceived as a fundamentally social act.

In fact, it is difficult to conceive of neonatal imitation as a cognitive act, as it is not clear what sort of skill-learning would be implicated. The bodily acts demonstrated by neonates in the imitation studies are already within the newborn behavioural repertoire, indeed this fact is sometimes used as an arguing point against neonatal behavioural copying as a genuine form of imitation. But if we focus on the social implications of neonatal imitation, then the form becomes less important than the function, namely the social function of recognition of and communication with conspecifics (Meltzoff and Moore, 1992; 1995).

16.2   Deferred imitation

Deferred imitation, the capacity of the individual to encode a model's behaviour at the time of demonstration and to re-enact that demonstration following a retention interval, has long been regarded as an important acquisition in children's social and cognitive development (e.g. Piaget, 1962). A large body of research has now mapped out the proclivity of infants to engage in deferred imitation, from infants as young as six to nine months reproducing simple one-step actions (Barr et al., 1996; Heimann and Meltzoff, 1996; Meltzoff, 1988c) to two-year-olds reproducing multi-step sequences that transcend alterations in the test environment from initial exposure to the time of the test (Barnat et al., 1996; Hanna and Meltzoff, 1993; Hayne et al., 2000; Klein and Meltzoff, 1999). To the best of our knowledge though, no controlled study of deferred imitation has explicitly aimed at disentangling infants' cognitive and social motivations for reproducing modelled acts after a delay.

According to Užgiris (1981) the cognitive and inter-personal conceptions of imitation can be distinguished by evaluating the most significant elements of a demonstration that infants attend to. If imitation is fulfilling a cognitive function infants will predominantly attend to the act modelled. If imitation is fulfilling a social function infants will predominantly attend to the model. In this context we can look at whether there is evidence that, in studies of deferred imitation, infants focus more on what the model does (i.e. the act modelled) or on how they do it (i.e. the model). For example, in an influential study of deferred imitation, Meltzoff (1988b) assessed the ability of 14-month-olds to replicate the novel goal-directed actions of an adult. Infants watched as an experimenter leaned forward and touched the top of a plastic box with his head. This action illuminated the box by turning on a light that was hidden inside. A week later the infants were given the opportunity to play with the box, at which point a majority (67 %) produced the novel behaviour of the experimenter: they leaned forward and touched their head to the box. Importantly, the infants didn't activate the switch using their hands. In this case it appears that the infants were focused on copying the model's specific actions at least as much as they were on producing the outcome modelled.

Perhaps, then, the infants in Meltzoff's study were motivated to show mutuality with the experimenter by doing things how he did them (the experimenter who modelled the actions was present when the infants were given the opportunity to act on the objects). However, a recent study suggests this is not so. Gergely et al. (2002) replicated Meltzoff's experiment and included a condition in which the experimenter modelled the target actions after he had wrapped himself in a blanket. In this scenario there was a clear reason for the experimenter to use his head – his hands were occupied. Gergely et al. reported that, like those in Meltzoff's study, a majority of the infants (69 %) who saw the action modelled by an experimenter whose hands were free subsequently copied his behaviour and activated the light by touching the switch with their head. In contrast, of the infants who saw the model when his hands were occupied, only 21 % used their head like the experimenter. The remaining infants turned the light on using their hands. It thus appears that in Meltzoff's study the infants may have copied the actions of the experimenter not so much because they wanted to be 'like' him but because they judged his actions as based on a rational choice about how to proceed, given the situation.

It is notable, however, that in Gergely *et al.*'s (2002) study, one-fifth of infants faithfully copied the model's head action when given the opportunity to engage with the box. Why? Perhaps this minority of infants chose to focus on the model rather than on the outcome. This is a nice example of how, in a given imitative context, infants' behaviour may be influenced by cognitive or social motivations, or both simultaneously. Infants' immediate interests and needs, their perceptions of the situation, the demands of the task and their level of understanding may all affect how infants react when presented with the opportunity to imitate. While we are attempting to draw attention to the social aspects of imitation in this chapter we do not wish to de-emphasize the cognitive aspects. Indeed, any imitative act is likely to involve both cognitive and social-communicative motivations.

Controlled studies of deferred imitation have generally not addressed the notion that infants might see the task as an opportunity for social interaction. Of course this need not mean that deferred imitation does not provide an inter-personal function. Take the classic example of Piaget's (1962) description of his daughter, Jacqueline, reproducing the actions of a temper tantrum she had previously seen thrown by a young friend. Jacqueline could have imitated the tantrum in order to understand the puzzling event she had seen or to accommodate to novel aspects of reality (fulfilling the cognitive function of imitation according to Užgiris). She may have equally imitated the tantrum to evoke her no longer present friend or to re-create a situation that she found amusing (fulfilling the inter-personal function of imitation). Our point here is that although the vast majority of studies of deferred imitation have focused on imitation serving an acquisitive purpose, a greater understanding of this important developmental milestone will come from incorporating an approach that also recognizes the social functions of imitation.

16.3   Synchronic imitation

Towards the middle of the second year infants begin to sustain dyadic play by synchronically imitating one another (for recent reviews see Nadel, 2002; Nadel *et al.*, 1999). In synchronic imitation infants consistently alternate between model and imitator while playing with similar objects, using them in a similar postural, motoric and symbolic way. In controlled studies of synchronic imitation an adult experimenter continuously models actions on an object to infants who have a duplicate of the object available to them (Asendorpf *et al.*, 1996; Nielsen and Dissanayake, 2003, 2004). To show synchronic imitation, infants must not only reproduce the actions of the experimenter, but do so continuously and simultaneously with him or her. In a recent longitudinal study, 86 infants were assessed for immediate, deferred and synchronic imitation at intervals of three months from 12 to 24 months of age (Nielsen and Dissanayake, 2003). Infants sat on a play mat opposite an experimenter who took an object and offered the infant a duplicate of the object. The experimenter continuously modelled an action for 15 seconds and then performed a second action with the same object for a further 15 seconds. This procedure was repeated on an additional three objects. Following Asendorpf *et al.* (1996), infants were considered to have engaged in synchronic imitation if they used the duplicate object to continuously copy the experimenter for a minimum of three seconds. Synchronic imitation was coded for as long as the infant continued to copy the modelled action and continued to look at the experimenter at least once every ten seconds. Hence, for each session toddlers could engage in synchronic imitation from 0 to 120 seconds. Illustrating the argument that there are developmental changes in the way infants respond to different tests of imitation, the majority of infants showed immediate and deferred imitation at 12 months of age but did not show synchronic imitation until 18 months (see Figure 16.1). How might we account for the later emergence of synchronic imitation?

The synchronic imitation task embodies both cognitive and social elements. Because it presents infants with an opportunity to acquire new skills or behaviours it could be that, when they were younger, the infants did not engage in synchronic imitation because the modelled actions were either too difficult for them to reproduce or of too little interest for them to bother trying. Neither of these possible explanations is likely to be correct however, because as early as12 months of age it was not uncommon for the infants to copy the actions of the experimenter during the synchronic imitation task. What they did not do at that stage was copy him continuously and simultaneously; they imitated but did not synchronically imitate. Because the synchronic imitation task also presents infants with a means of engaging in inter-personal interaction, it may be that only the older infants synchronically imitated because they were motivated to demonstrate connectedness and mutuality with the experimenter, more so than learning new skills or behaviours. This pattern of developmental changes in performance on a single imitation task is reminiscent of Killen and Užgiris' (1981) findings; in this developmental study of synchronic

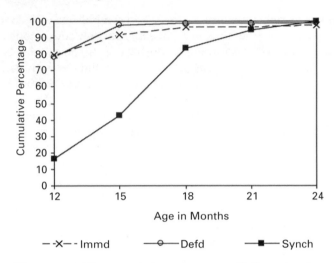

Figure 16.1 The cumulative percentage of infants showing evidence of immediate imitation (Immd), deferred imitation (Defd) and synchronic imitation (Synch) (from Nielsen and Dissanayake, 2003).

imitation, there was evidence for an increasing tendency for infants to imitate for what appear to be purely social reasons, in the second year of life.

16.4   Imitation of intended but incomplete acts

Infants in their second year also produce outcomes that they have seen others attempt but fail to complete. In his behavioural re-enactment study, Meltzoff (1995) showed 18-month-olds a demonstrator trying, but failing, to produce specific actions on a range of novel objects (e.g. pulling apart a dumbbell apparatus). When provided with the opportunity to play with the objects the infants produced the outcomes the experimenter had attempted but failed to produce nearly as frequently as infants who saw the experimenter successfully demonstrate the complete actions. Meltzoff argued that 18-month-olds did this because they were able to 'see through' the physical behaviour of another and discern his or her intention to complete an action (see Huang *et al.*, 2002). This interpretation is in line with a growing body of literature that has identified the middle of the second year as the period when infants develop a capacity for reading intentionality into the behaviour of others (Baldwin and Baird, 2001; Bellagamba and Tomasello, 1999; Carpenter *et al.*, 1998a; Moore and Corkum, 1998; Repacholi and Gopnik, 1997).

Intuitively, the behavioural re-enactment paradigm used by Meltzoff appears to emphasize the cognitive function of imitation to provide for the acquisition of new skills. Having understood what can be done with the novel objects, infants produce the intended but incomplete actions of others in order to learn how to correctly use the objects. Conversely, infants may actually have produced the unconsummated acts because they wished to demonstrate to the model that they understood what he or she was trying to do. In this case, the infants may have imitated to share effect and to demonstrate and communicate a sense of mutuality with the model who failed to successfully perform the act. Indeed, infants do not re-enact the incomplete actions of inanimate objects, even if the demonstration takes the exact same physical form as the intended but incomplete act modelled by a human (Meltzoff, 1995; Slaughter and Corbett, in press). In a study conducted by Slaughter and Corbett (in press), 18-month-old infants saw attempted but incomplete actions demonstrated by one of four models: (1) a fully visible person; (2) a person's disembodied hands; (3) a pair of disembodied mittens and (4) a pair of mechanical robot pincers. The infants produced the target actions above baseline only when the model was a fully visible person. This suggests that imitation in this paradigm is dependent, at least in part, on inter-personal factors, and again highlights the possibility that an individual act of imitation can be simultaneously motivated by both cognitive and social motives.

16.5   Imitation from television

Infants and young children are capable of imitating the novel actions of a human model presented on television (Barr and Hayne, 1999; Hayne et al., 2003; McCall et al., 1977; Meltzoff, 1988a). However, there is some evidence that imitation from television emerges later in development than imitation from a live model (Barr and Hayne, 1999; Hayne et al., 2003; McCall et al., 1977). Hayne and her colleagues reported that 15-month-old infants failed to imitate actions from a televized model (Barr and Hayne, 1999) that 6-month-olds readily imitated from a live model (Barr et al., 1996; Hayne et al., 2000). Thus the television presentation, and not the complexity of the modelled acts, was likely to be responsible for the older infants' failure. Moreover, even in their third year, infants will imitate more actions when the model is live than when he or she is presented on television (Hayne et al., 2003). Hayne et al. (2003) proposed that the developmental lag in infants' ability to imitate from television, relative to live demonstrations, may be due to age-related changes in a fundamental cognitive process. When actions are modelled on television, infants see a 2-D image that they must then match to the 3-D target object presented in the test phase. The overlap in surface features may not be enough for infants or young children to perceive the functional similarity of objects presented via these different modes. Hence, it may not be until they are older that infants can appreciate the similarity between objects presented on television and their real world counterparts.

However, Meltzoff (Meltzoff, 1988a) reported that 65 % of 14-month-old infants successfully replicated an action they saw performed on television by an experimenter. In a previous study (Meltzoff, 1985), a similar proportion (75 %) of 14-month-olds replicated the same action when a live experimenter performed it. Thus there is some evidence that infants can imitate a televized model at similar levels to their imitations of a live model. How might we account for the discrepancy between the results reported by Meltzoff and those reported by Hayne and her colleagues? One potential reason for the discrepancy is that Meltzoff used simple one-step actions whereas Hayne and her colleagues used more complex three-step sequences. Another reason is that in the Hayne studies the televized model was presented on previously recorded video, whereas in Meltzoff's study, the televised model was presented live, via closed-circuit monitors. Although appearing on a television screen, Meltzoff's model was able to respond contingently to the infants, thereby providing a sense of social interactivity even over the television screen. Thus it is possible that apparent differences between imitation from television and imitation from a live model are due, not to the hypothesized cognitive complexity of interpreting actions and objects presented on television screens, but to the lack of opportunity for inter-personal interaction inherent in pre-recorded video (see Troseth *et al.*, 2006). Focused studies to explore this hypothesis are warranted; if the data are supportive, this would further highlight how social motivations may influence the expression of infants' imitative skill.

16.6   Changing motivations to imitate in development

Killen and Užgiris' (1981) study provided an early demonstration that infants' imitative responses to the exact same model change with development. That is, infants imitate for different reasons, at different developmental stages. Recent research in our lab (Nielsen, 2006) provided another demonstration of how infants of varying ages respond differently to a model's invitation to imitate. Infants at ages 12, 18 and 24 months watched as an experimenter demonstrated how a series of three novel boxes could be opened to obtain a desirable toy. Each box required that a switch be manipulated to open it. Half of the infants saw the experimenter operate the switches using her hands. The remaining half saw the experimenter operate the switches using a 'tool'. As expected, the older infants were more likely to open the boxes than younger infants in the 'hand' condition, reflecting the general developmental finding that older infants imitate more consistently than do younger infants. In contrast, when the experimenter used a tool to open the boxes, 24-month-olds were no more likely to successfully open the boxes than 12-month-olds. This surprising finding can be interpreted by examination of the specific actions of the infants. Whereas the 24-month-olds attempted to open the boxes using the tool, as was modelled to them, the 12-month-olds only attempted to open the boxes with their hands. It thus appears that the 12-month-olds focused on the outcome of the model's actions, while the 24-month-olds focused on the specific form of the actions. Eighteen month olds showed reactions that were intermediate between the older and younger age groups. In a further study 12-month-olds watched as a model successfully used an object after first 'attempting but failing' to activate the switches by hand. In this condition 12-month-olds subsequently used the object in an attempt to activate the switches. It is therefore unlikely that 12-month-olds fail to copy the model's object use because they cannot use the object or because they do not focus on this aspect of the demonstration.

It thus appears that 24-month-olds will attempt to bring about the same outcome as that demonstrated by a model by adopting and persisting with the model's behavioural means. Twelve-month-olds, in contrast, are more likely to focus solely on reproducing the outcome. This finding indicates that, as well as changes in general imitative competencies, there is a transition through the second year in infants' attention to, and reproduction of, details of a model's behaviour. Thus, as Užgiris (1981) argued, older infants are not simply more competent imitators than younger infants, they engage in imitation differently.

16.7   Echolalia

The examples of imitation discussed thus far have focused on the reproduction of actions or gestures. Of course infants also engage in vocal imitation. While a full discussion of vocal imitation is beyond the scope of this chapter we would like to comment on a specific type of this behaviour: echolalia. Echolalia refers to the echoing or repetition of vocalizations made by another person. Echolalia is a relatively common behavioural symptom in autism and is also seen in some other disorders of development (e.g. language disorders, blindness, Tourette's syndrome). It has been hypothesized that this form of vocal imitation may serve a communicative function in children whose social-communicative skills are poorly developed (e.g. Prizant and Duchan, 1981; Rhode, 1999). However, in general, echolalia is not well understood and it is not clear why it is common to fairly diverse clinical populations (Wicks-Nelson and Israel, 2000). In fact a conundrum has been noted in that children with autism are poor at many forms of imitation, but they often exhibit echolalia (Williams *et al.*, 2001).

Echolalia is often discussed in the context of clinical populations but it is frequently overlooked as an imitative form in typically developing children. However, echolalia is not uncommon, it meets our minimal definition of imitation as copying the actions of another, and it provides an example of imitative behaviour that, at least in typically developing children, is very often socially motivated. In typically developing children echolalia does not have the automatic character that it has in children with autism, although some children may perform echolalia out of what appears to be habit. It is used as an element of well-practiced game routines and may be used in a deliberate attempt to annoy another person. Thus, in typically developing children echolalia is a form of imitation that is socially motivated, and those motivations can be either positive or negative. It is also worth noting that in typical development, echolalia may evolve into mature forms of mimicry and parody, which are also used for positive (entertaining) and negative (humiliating) social ends (e.g. Mitchell, 1994).

16.8   The multi-faceted nature of imitation

This brief review has explored multiple forms of imitation that, at varying levels, appear to function as distinct from, or in addition to, the acquisition of knowledge about the world or development of a specific skill. These examples highlight the diversity of imitative behaviours that are common in early development, as well as the flexibility of imitative behaviour. Imitation appears in many forms in early human development, and these forms are flexibly used as means to a variety of different ends that may be dictated by developmental stage, social context, immediate motivations or all of these. As Užgiris (1981) pointed out, infants' tendencies to imitate, and their motivations for doing so, develop and change in the first few years of life. Imitation is not a unilateral cognitive achievement, but a rich cognitive and social tool. It is also worth mentioning that the diversity of imitation over development is also influenced by individual differences: a particular infant may, or may not, choose to imitate at any given time, in any given context.

So why do infants imitate? To summarize, there are a host of possible reasons. Infants imitate in order to acquire a new skill or to achieve a desired outcome, as has been amply demonstrated and debated in recent literature. Infants also imitate in order to initiate social interaction and also to maintain social interaction, as evidenced by copying responses like neonatal imitation, complex forms like synchronic imitation, and echolalia. In the course of development, the forms and functions of imitation are likely to interact with the acquisition of other key social-cognitive skills such as the well-documented emergence of joint attention and language at the end of the first year of life (Bakeman and Adamson, 1984; Carpenter *et al.*, 1998b; Mundy and Gomes, 1998; Tomasello, 1988; Tomasello and Todd, 1983) and the capacity for reading intentionality into the behaviour of others in the second year of life (Carpenter *et al.*, 1998a; Meltzoff, 1995; Moore and Corkum, 1998; Repacholi and Gopnik, 1997; Tomasello *et al.*, 2005). Besides initiating and maintaining social interactions, imitation also complements other modes of communication, and can be performed for fun and entertainment (there are a host of imitation games played in infancy and later in childhood imitation between peers taking numerous forms including imitation to annoy). Infants, like older children and adults, may also imitate explicitly in order to 'be like' someone else, and to express this mutuality to the imitative partner.[3]

In conclusion, we wish to emphasize that imitation, like language, meta-representation, mental time-travel and other complex cognitive skills (e.g. Perner, 1991; Suddendorf, 1999; Suddendorf and Busby, 2003), sub-serves a number of different functions, encompassing a range of cognitive (learning) and social (communicative, inter-personal, emotional) functions throughout life. Some types of imitation are evident at birth and recent neuropsychological findings suggest that there may be brain structures that are dedicated for imitative 'mirroring' (Gallese *et al.*, 1996; Iacoboni *et al.*, Chapter 4 this volume), suggesting that imitation may have an innate component. Imitation is also highly flexible (as discussed above), and, to make our point explicit, it is deployed in multiple contexts, for multiple purposes that are determined by any number of personal, inter-personal and situational variables. Imitation serves as a means to a variety of cognitive, social and emotional ends; there are multiple motivations for imitating, and most of these are already evident in the first two years of life.

Acknowledgments

Preparation of this manuscript was supported by a Postdoctoral Research Fellowship to the first author. We thank Gabrielle Simcock for helpful comments on a previous draft.

---

[3] Rochat (2002) has also recently proposed a novel function for imitation that is neither cognitive nor social; he proposes that imitation serves an 'ego function' whereby infants' repetitive self-copying of actions contributes to the development of self-awareness.

REFERENCES

Abravanel, E. and Sigafoos, A. D. (1984). Exploring the presence of imitation during early infancy. *Child Development*, **55**, 381–92.

Anisfield, M. (1991). Neonatal imitation. *Developmental Review*, **11**, 60–97.

Asendorpf, J. B., Warkentin, V. and Baudonnière, P.-M. (1996). Self-awareness and other-awareness II: mirror self-recognition, social contingency awareness, and synchronic imitation. *Developmental Psychology*, **32**, 313–21.

Bakeman, R. and Adamson, L. (1984). Coordinating attention to people and objects in mother infant and peer infant interactions. *Child Development*, **55**, 1278–89.

Baldwin, D. A. and Baird, J. A. (2001). Discerning intentions in dynamic human action. *Trends in Cognitive Sciences*, **5**, 171–8.

Baldwin, J. M. (1894). *Mental Development in the Child and the Race*. New York: MacMillan.

Baldwin, J. M. (1897). *Social and Ethical Interpretations in Mental Development*. New York: MacMillan.

Darnat, S. B., Klein, P. J. and Meltzoff, A. N. (1996). Deferred imitation across changes in context and object: memory and generalisation in 14-month-old infants. *Infant Behaviour and Development*, **19**, 241–51.

Barr, R., Dowden, A. and Hayne, H. (1996). Developmental changes in deferred imitation by 6- to 24-month-old infants. *Infant Behaviour and Development*, **19**, 159–71.

Barr, R. and Hayne, H. (1999). Developmental changes in imitation from television during infancy. *Child Development*, **70**, 1067–81.

Bellagamba, F. and Tomasello, M. (1999). Re-enacting intended acts: comparing 12- and 18-month-olds. *Infant Behaviour and Development*, **22**, 277–82.

Call, J. and Carpenter, M. (2002). Three sources of information in social learning. In K. Dautenhahn and C. L. Nehaniv (eds.), *Imitation in Animals and Artifacts*. Cambridge, MA: MIT Press, 211–28.

Carpenter, M., Akhtar, N. and Tomasello, M. (1998a). Fourteen- through eighteen-month-old infants differentially imitate intentional and accidental actions. *Infant Behaviour and Development*, **21**, 315–30.

Carpenter, M., Nagell, K. and Tomasello, M. (1998b). Social cognition, joint attention, and communicative competence from 9 to 15 months of age. *Monographs of the Society for Research in Child Development*, **63(4)**, Serial No. 255.

Field, T. M., Woodson, R., Greenberg, R. and Cohen, D. (1982). Discrimination and imitation of facial expressions in neonates. *Science*, **218**, 179–81.

Gallese, V., Fadiga, L., Fogassi, L. and Rizzolatti, G. (1996). Action recognition in the premotor cortex. *Brain*, **119**, 593–609.

Gergely, G., Bekkering, H. and Kiraly, I. (2002). Rational imitation in preverbal infants. *Nature*, **415**, 755.

Guillaume, P. ((1926/1971). *Imitation in Children* (2nd edn.). Menlo Park, CA: Benjamin/Cummings.

Hanna, E. and Meltzoff, A. N. (1993). Peer imitation in laboratory, home, and day-care contexts: implications for social learning and memory. *Developmental Psychology*, **29**, 1–12.

Hayne, H., Boniface, J. and Barr, R. (2000). The development of declarative memory in human infants: age-related changes in deferred imitation. *Behavioral Neuroscience*, **114**, 77–83.

Hayne, H., Herbert, J. and Simcock, G. (2003). Imitation from television by 24- and 30-month-olds. *Developmental Science*, **6**, 254–61.

Heimann, M. and Meltzoff, A. N. (1996). Deferred imitation in 9- and 14-month-old infants: a longitudinal study of a Swedish sample. *British Journal of Developmental Psychology*, **14**, 55–64.

Huang, C., Heyes, C. and Charman, T. (2002). Infants' behavioral reenactment of 'failed attempts': exploring the roles of emulation learning, stimulus enhancement, and understanding of intentions. *Developmental Psychology*, **38**, 840–55.

Jones, S. S. (1996). Imitation or exploration? Young infants' matching of adults' oral gestures. *Child Development*, **67**, 1952–69.

Killen, M. and Užgiris, I. (1981). Imitation of actions with objects: the role of social meaning. *Journal of Genetic Psychology*, **138**, 219–29.

Klein, P. J. and Meltzoff, A. N. (1999). Long-term memory, forgetting, and deferred imitation in 12-month-old infants. *Developmental Science*, **2**, 102–13.

Legerstee, M. (1991). The role of person and object in eliciting early imitation. *Journal of Experimental Child Psychology*, **51**, 423–33.

McCall, R. B., Parke, R. D. and Kavanagh, R. D. (1977). Imitation of live and televised models by children one to three years of age. *Monographs of the Society for Research in Child Development*, **425(5)**, Serial No. 173.

McKenzie, B. and Over, R. (1983). Young infants fail to imitate facial and manual gestures. *Infant Behaviour and Development*, **6**, 85–95.

Meltzoff, A. N. (1985). Immediate and deferred imitation in fourteen and twenty-four-month-old infants. *Child Development*, **56**, 62–72.

Meltzoff, A. N. (1988a). Imitation of televised models by infants. *Child Development*, **59**, 1221–9.

Meltzoff, A. N. (1988b). Infant imitation after a 1-week delay: long-term memory for novel acts and multiple stimuli. *Developmental Psychology*, **24**, 470–6.

Meltzoff, A. N. (1988c). Infant imitation and memory: nine-month-olds in immediate and deferred tests. *Child Development*, **59**, 217–25.

Meltzoff, A. N. (1995). Understanding the intentions of others: re-enactment of intended acts by 18-month-old children. *Developmental Psychology*, **31**, 838–50.

Meltzoff, A. N. and Moore, M. K. (1977). Imitation of facial and manual gestures by human neonates. *Science*, **198**, 75–8.

Meltzoff, A. N. and Moore, M. K. (1992). Early imitation within a functional framework: the importance of person identity, movement and development. *Infant Behaviour and Development*, **15**, 83–9.

Meltzoff, A. N. and Moore, M. K. (1995). Infants' understanding of people and things: from body imitation to folk psychology. In J. Bermúdez, A. J. Marcel and N. Eilan (eds.), *The Body and the Self*. Cambridge, MA: MIT Press, 43–69.

Meltzoff, A. N. and Moore, M. K. (1999). Persons and representation: why infant imitation is important for theories of human development. In J. Nadel and G. Butterworth (eds.), *Imitation in Infancy*. Cambridge, UK: Cambridge University Press, 9–35.

Mitchell, R. W. (1987). A comparative developmental approach to understanding imitation. In P. P. G. Bateson and P. H. Klopfer (eds.), *Perspectives in Ethology*. New York: Plenum Press, Vol. 7, 183–215.

Mitchell, R. W. (1990). A theory of play. In M. Bekoff and D. Jamieson (eds.), *Interpretation and Explanation in the Study of Animal Behavior*. Boulder, CO: Westview Press, Vol. 1, 197–227.

Mitchell, R. W. (1994). The evolution of primate cognition: simulation, self-knowledge, and knowledge of other minds. In D. Quiatt and J. Itani (eds.), *Hominid Culture in Primate Perspective*. Boulder: University Press of Colorado, 177–232.

Moore, C. and Corkum, V. (1998). Infant gaze following based on eye direction. *British Journal of Developmental Psychology*, **16**, 495–503.

Mundy, P. and Gomes, A. (1998). Individual differences in joint attention skill development in the second year. *Infant Behavior and Development*, **21**, 469–82.

Nadel, J. (2002). Imitation and imitation recognition: functional use in pre-verbal infants and nonverbal children with autism. In A. Meltzoff and W. Prinz (eds.), *The Imitative Mind: Development, Evolution, and Brain Bases*. Cambridge, UK: Cambridge University Press, 63–73.

Nadel, J., Guérini, C., Pezé, A. and Rivet, C. (1999). The evolving nature of imitation as a format for communication. In J. Nadel and G. Butterworth (eds.), *Imitation in Infancy*. Cambridge, UK: Cambridge University Press, 209–34.

Nielsen, M. (2006). Copying actions and copying outcomes: social learning through the second year. *Developmental Psychology*, **42**, 555–65.

Nielsen, M. and Dissanayake, C. (2003). A longitudinal study of immediate, deferred, and synchronic imitation through the second year. *The Interdisciplinary Journal of Artificial Intelligence and the Simulation of Behaviour*, **1**, 305–18.

Nielsen, M. and Dissanayake, C. (2004). Pretend play, mirror self-recognition and imitation: a longitudinal investigation through the second year. *Infant Behavior and Development*, **27**, 342–65.

Perner, J. (1991). *Understanding the Representational Mind*. Cambridge, MA: MIT Press.

Piaget, J. (1962). *Play, Dreams, and Imitation in Childhood*. New York: Norton.

Prizant, B. M. and Duchan, J. F. (1981). The functions of immediate echolalia in autistic children. *Journal of Speech and Hearing Disorders*, **46**, 241–9.

Repacholi, B. M. and Gopnik, A. (1997). Early reasoning about desires: evidence from 14- and 18-month-olds. *Developmental Psychology*, **33**, 12–21.

Rhode, M. (1999). Echo or answer? The move towards ordinary speech in three children with autistic spectrum disorder. In A. Alvarez and S. Reid (eds.), *Autism and Personality: Findings from the Tavistock Autism Workshop*. Florence, KY: Taylor and Frances/Routledge, 79–92.

Rochat, P. (2002). Ego function of early imitation. In A. N. Meltzoff and W. Prinz (eds.), *The Imitative Mind: Development, Evolution, and Brain Bases*. Cambridge, UK: Cambridge University Press, 85–97.

Slaughter, V. and Corbett, D. (in press). Differential copying of human and non-human models at 12 and 18 months of age. *European Journal of Developmental Psychology, Special Issue on Social Cognition During Infancy.*

Suddendorf, T. (1999). The rise of metamind: beyond the immediately present. In M. C. Corballis and S. Lea (eds.), *Evolution of the Hominid Mind.* Oxford, UK: Oxford University Press, 218–60.

Suddendorf, T., & Busby, J. (2003). Mental time travel in animals? *Trends in Cognitive Sciences,* 7, 391–6.

Tomasello, M. (1988). The role of joint attention in early language development. *Language Sciences,* 11, 69–88.

Tomasello, M., Carpenter, M., Call, J., Behne, T. and Moll, H. (2005). Understanding and sharing intentions: the origins of cultural cognition. *Behavioral and Brain Sciences,* 28, 675–735.

Tomasello, M., Kruger, A. and Ratner, H. (1993). Cultural learning. *Behavioural and Brain Sciences,* 16, 495–552.

Tomasello, M. and Todd, J. (1983). Joint attention and lexical acquisition style. *First Language,* 4, 197–212.

Troseth, G. L., Saylor, M. M. and Archer, A. H. (2006). Young children's use of video as a source of socially relevant information. *Child Development,* 77, 786–99.

Užgiris, I. (1981). Two functions of imitation during infancy. *International Journal of Behavioral Development,* 4, 1–12.

Wallon, H. (1934). *Les origines du charactére chez l'enfant.* Paris: Boivin and Co.

Want, S. C. and Harris, P. L. (2002). How do children ape? Applying concepts from the study of non-human primates to the developmental study of 'imitation' in human children. *Developmental Science,* 5, 1–13.

Whiten, A. and Ham, R. (1992). On the nature and evolution of imitation in the animal kingdom: reappraisal of a century of research. In P. J. B. Slater, J. S. Rosenblatt, G. Beer and M. Milinski (eds.), *Advances in the Study of Behaviour.* New York: Academic Press, Vol. 21, 239–83.

Wicks-Nelson, R. and Israel, A. (2000). *Behaviour Disorders of Childhood,* 4th edn. Upper Saddle River, NJ: Prentice Hall.

Williams, J. H. G., Whiten, A., Suddendorf, T. and Perrett, D. I. (2001). Imitation, mirror neurons and autism. *Neuroscience and Biobehavioral Reviews,* 25, 287–95.

Yando, R., Seitz, V. and Zigler, E. (1978). *Imitation: A Developmental Perspective.* Oxford, England: Lawrence Erlbaum.

Zentall, T. R. (2001). Imitation in animals: evidence, function and mechanisms. *Cybernetics and Systems,* 32, 53–96.

17 The progress drive hypothesis: an interpretation of early imitation

Frédéric Kaplan and Pierre-Yves Oudeyer

17.1 Introduction

The functional role of early imitation has been discussed in a variety of contexts. Its role for the cognitive development of the child has been regularly emphasized since Piaget (1962). Its communicative function and its role for the development of social coordination know-how have also been put forward (Nadel, 2002). Early imitative capabilities could also be important in the process of identification with others helping the very young infant to take a 'like-me stance' (Meltzoff and Gopnick, 1993). Eventually, it has been argued that infants also engage in 'self-imitation' and that this process is crucial for the objectivation of themselves as distinct entities (Rochat, 2002). This multiplicity of approaches points to a consensus that early imitation is a crucial basic mechanism for the development of cognitive, social and communicative aspects of children's behaviour and even more generally for the construction of their awareness about themselves, others and the external environment. Despite its importance, a question regarding early imitation remains only partially answered: what pushes animals and infants to engage in imitative behaviour?

Early imitation seems to appear at an age when children do not discriminate clearly between themselves and others. It is argued that early imitation actually plays a role for identification with and discrimination from others. As a consequence, potential mechanisms for early imitation should not rely on the notions of self and others. In such conditions some authors have partially assimilated early imitation as the result of very general mechanisms such as the 'propensity of young organisms to repeat their own actions' (Rochat, 2002), the homeostatic regulation of sensory-motor couplings (Andry *et al.*, 2001) or a side-effect of particular neuronal dynamics (Oudeyer, 2005). The common idea of all these

Imitation and Social Learning in Robots, Humans and Animals, ed. Chrystopher L. Nehaniv and Kerstin Dautenhahn. Published by Cambridge University Press.
© Cambridge University Press 2007.

approaches is that some general dynamics lead the infant into particular forms of imitative behaviour, explaining a 'natural' tendency to imitate.

Does this mean that early imitation is the result of an automatic process? The existence of imitative reflexes associated with innate mappings between observation and execution is sometimes suggested (Meltzoff and Moore, 1977). However, explanations must also account for certain contextual and 'habituation' effects associated with early imitation:

(1) Early imitation is not an automatic response to a stimulus. 'The infant must be alert, attentive and motivated to engage with another person' (Heimann, 2002). That is to say, that in order to show early imitation the child must 'want' to imitate. Where does such will-to-imitate come from?

(2) The interest in imitation varies greatly with the infant's age: pre-verbal children enjoy imitative games whereas they avoid them once they master language (Nadel, 2002). More generally, most kinds of imitative behaviour are typically transient phenomena: interesting for some time, boring when repeated too often.

Apart from sucking, crying and breathing which can be viewed as having a clear survival function, the explorative behaviour of young infants goes far beyond fixed-action patterns. The way they explore the possibilities of their own body movements and later on their propensity for discovering new aspects of their environment may be linked with a putative 'pleasure' leading to this kind of open-ended development (Rochat, 2002). Psychologists have argued that activities enjoyable for their own sake may be accounted for by the existence of an intrinsic psychobiological human motivation (White, 1959). By contrast with extrinsically motivated types of behaviour directed towards the gain of external rewards, intrinsic motivation drives children and adults to engage in explorative and playful activities. The notion of intrinsic motivation can be historically linked to a long series of related concepts: drives for mastery like Herder's *appetitus noscendi* (Herder, 1772), drives for novelty like Konrad Lorenz's *neophily* (Lorenz, 1968), drives for knowledge like Dennett's epistemic hunger (Dennett, 1996), situations in which skills and challenges are well-balanced such as Csikszenthmihalyi's *flow experiences* (Csikszenthmihalyi, 1990).

The concept of intrinsic motivation has recently received increased attention from several research groups in the fields of artificial intelligence, machine learning and developmental robotics trying to design motivational systems for artificial agents enabling learning in a task-independent manner. Such systems are designed in order to allow autonomous development, a very challenging issue for artificial systems (Weng *et al.*, 2001). As a result of these investigations, operant models of this notion of intrinsic motivation have been proposed. They consist of computational architectures the behaviour of which can be tested through software simulations or robotic experiments. Such kinds of models permit the addressing of the possible role of intrinsic motivation during the developmental processes in a more scientific manner.

The issue considered in this chapter is the following: can we interpret early imitation phenomena, including self-imitation and simple interpersonal co-ordination, as being the result of a *progress drive*, an intrinsic motivation system driving the infant into situations expected to result in maximal learning progress? In order to investigate this hypothesis the next section introduces a computational model of what such a drive could be. A simple experiment illustrates how a progress-driven agent manages to adapt its behaviour in order to progress maximally in prediction. It shows how this agent performs an evaluation of learning progress for different kinds of sensorimotor interactions in order to focus on the most adapted ones at a given time of its development. This leads to an emergent organization of its behaviour based on self-evaluated predictability levels. Taking ground on these preliminary results, a scenario presenting the putative role of the progress drive for the development of imitation is discussed. We argue in particular that progress-driven learning could help to understand why children focus on specific imitative activities at a certain age and how they progressively organize preferential interactions with particular entities present in their environment.

17.2   Progress-driven learning

This section introduces progress-driven learning in a step-by-step manner. We discuss three kinds of architectures: mastery-driven systems, novelty-driven systems and progress-driven systems. All three systems are based on action-selection strategies related to the agent's anticipatory capabilities. In mastery-driven systems, the agents acts in order to be in situations in which its error in prediction is minimal. Conversely, in novelty-driven systems, the agent chooses actions leading to situations in which its error in prediction is maximal. Eventually, with progress-driven systems, it acts in order to be in situations in which its error in prediction *decreases* maximally fast. We will argue with a simple experiment, that among these three closely related architectures only progress-driven systems capture some aspects of the open-ended nature of children's development.

Progress-driven learning can be viewed as a particular form of reinforcement learning. In reinforcement learning models a controller chooses which action a to take in a context s based on rewards provided by a *critic*. Traditional models view the critic as being external to the agent. Such situations correspond to extrinsically motivated forms of learning. But the critic can also be part of the agent itself (as clearly argued by Sutton and Barto (1998) p.51–54). As a consequence reinforcement learning is a well-adapted framework to model intrinsic motivation (Barto *et al.*, 2004).

For our concerns, the main issue is to design a critic capable of producing internal rewards in order to guide the agent towards learning new skills. All the complex issues traditionally encountered in reinforcement learning, like delayed rewards or trade-off between exploration and exploitation, are also important for progress-driven learning. However, we will not address these questions in this chapter and only focus on the issue of designing a source of internal rewards suitable for active and autonomous development.

17.2.1   *Prediction and meta-prediction*

What unifies most of the models of intrinsic motivation proposed so far is that internal rewards are related to capabilities of the agent to anticipate the effects of its own action on the environment. We can formalize this kind of architecture in the following way. Let's call P the prediction system responsible for anticipating the consequences y' of the action a chosen among all the possible actions A and taken in a given state s in the state space S. Once the actual outcome y is known, the error $e = y - y'$ in prediction can be computed and used as a feedback to improve the performances of P. Another prediction system called *metaP* is responsible for predicting e, the error in prediction of P. Taking also s and a as inputs, it makes a prediction e' and compares it to the actual error e. It learns using the feedback signal $\delta = e - e'$ (Figure 17.1). No assumption is made regarding the kind of prediction devices that are used for P and *metaP* (neural networks, prototype-based predictors, support vector machines, etc.). Different techniques can be used for both systems. We consider the choice of a particular implementation as being part of a particular embodiment of the agent.

$$P(s, a) \rightarrow y' \tag{17.1}$$

$$metaP(s, a) \rightarrow e' \tag{17.2}$$

17.2.2   *Mastery-driven systems*

For each state–action pair such a system is capable of predicting the outcome y' as well as the expected error e' of this prediction. This can serve

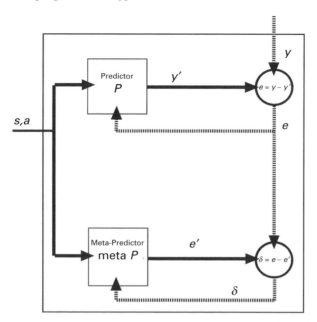

Figure 17.1 The critic uses a predictor P and a metapredictor *metaP* (see text). s is the current state, a a possible action, y the actual consequence of a, y' the predicted consequences of a, e the actual error in prediction, e' the predicted error in prediction, δ the error on error prediction.

as a basis for an internal reward signal. In mastery-driven systems the controller chooses actions corresponding to the minimum expected error. For this reason, mastery-driven systems are related to models which view homeostasis as a major drive for living creatures. Unpredicted situations may be seen as perturbations (Ashby, 1960; Varela *et al.*, 1991) for such a creature and learning as a way to reach again a form of equilibrium state (e.g. Andry *et al.*, 2001).

17.2.3 Novelty-driven systems

Taking an opposite point of view, other authors have suggested that in order to learn efficiently agents should focus on 'novel', 'surprising' or 'unexpected' situations. This would mean that a 'curious' agent should focus on situations for which it does not yet have adequate prediction capabilities (e.g. Huang and Weng, 2002; Thrun, 1995; Marshall *et al.*, 2004; Barto *et al.*, 2004). Such a strategy can be realized by choosing the actions corresponding to the maximum expected error.

17.2.4 The 'screen' problem

In order to compare mastery-driven systems and novelty-driven systems, we will consider a very simple experimental set up. At first glance, this toy problem seems unrelated to issues concerning early imitation. We will show in the next section how it nevertheless captures some important aspects of the problems we are considering in this chapter. The 'screen' problem puts the agent in a situation where three different kinds of sensorimotor relations can be discovered. The first one is very easy to master, the second one is impossible to master and the third one can be learned with experience. The environment consists of a screen and four buttons. The agent must anticipate what it will see on the screen based on the current state of the pixels and the buttons which it presses. In this context, $s(t) = y(t)$ is a 9-D vector corresponding to the nine pixels of the screen. $y'(t)$ is also a 9-D vector corresponding to the prediction of $s(t + 1)$. Each pixel can take the value 0 or 1 and $u(t)$ is a 4-D vector of binary values corresponding to the four buttons. Button 1, called 'Noise' puts white noise on the screen when activated (values of pixels are set randomly to 0 or 1) and does nothing otherwise. Button 2, called 'Reset' puts all the pixels to 0 when activated and does nothing otherwise. Button 3, called 'Move+' increments a hidden variable *pos* when activated and does nothing otherwise. Button 4, called 'Move−' decrements the same hidden variable when activated and does nothing otherwise. If Noise and Reset are both deactivated, the pixel corresponding to the value of *pos* is switched to 1 and all the others are switched to zero (see Figure 17.2).[1]

As we mentioned, three situations are remarkable in terms of predictability. The most unpredictable situations happen when Noise is activated. The most predictable situations are obtained when all pixels are set to zero, that is when Noise is deactivated and Reset is activated. The interesting situation corresponding to the control of the '*pos*' pixel only happens when both Noise and Reset are deactivated. The desirable behaviour of an agent intrinsically motivated for learning should be to quickly discover that pressing the Reset button leads to an easily predictable situation, to avoid pressing the Noise button as no learning can take place in such a context and to focus on the 'interesting' situation corresponding to the prediction of the screen values in the context where Noise and Reset are deactivated.

---

[1] When 'Move+' is activated and *pos* corresponds to the last pixels then *pos* is set to correspond to the first pixel. In the same manner when 'Move−' is activated and *pos* corresponds to the first pixels, *pos* is set to the last pixel. The effects of Reset are applied before the ones of Noise, which means that if both buttons are activated, pixels will take random values. Experiments start with all pixels set to 0 and *pos* equals 4.

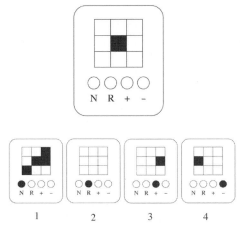

Figure 17.2 The screen problem: (1) Button N (Noise) puts white noise on the screen, (2) Button R (Reset) erases all the pixels, (3) Button + (Move +) moves the cursor to the right (4) Button − (Move −) moves the cursor to the left.

It is clear that neither mastery-driven systems nor novelty-driven systems will perform appropriately in this context. The first ones by trying to minimize the error in prediction will focus only on situations where Reset is pressed. The second ones in maximizing the error will be 'trapped' by the noise channel, pressing constantly the Noise button. Both kinds of systems will miss the interesting thing to learn.

17.2.5 Progress-driven systems

An alternative to maximizing or minimizing the error in prediction consists in *maximizing learning progress*. Learning progress may be defined in various ways. A straightforward definition is to associate progress with error reduction over time. A progress-driven system keeps track of the series of prediction errors $\{e\}$. With this list, it can compute the mean error $\langle e(t) \rangle$ for the last τ time steps. The learning progress $p'(t)$ can be defined by comparing the current average error with the average error θ time steps before. The action selection mechanism can consist of choosing actions that maximize the expected progress $p'(t)$.

$$\text{progress}\,(s\,(t),a) = p'(t) = \langle e(t-\theta) \rangle - \langle e(t) \rangle \qquad (17.3)$$

Several models have been proposed based on this scheme (Herrmann *et al.*, 2000; Kaplan and Oudeyer, 2003, 2004). They have proven to give adapted results in various contexts. However, they will not perform appropriately for the 'screen' problem. In such a context, an oscillatory behaviour consisting of alternating between the easy and difficult situations is observed. By producing alternatively sequences where Noise is pressed followed by sequences where Reset is pressed, the agent experiences successive important decreases of its error in prediction. It is progressing in time but not relative to the different sensorimotor situations present in the environment. In particular it does not focus on the interesting part of the problem, situations where both Noise and Reset are deactivated.

To avoid such oscillatory behaviour, learning progress must be evaluated by comparing the prediction errors corresponding to the *same kind of situations* and not necessarily the most recent situations (Schmidhuber 1991, 2003; Oudeyer and Kaplan 2004, 2006). This can be achieved by a classification process T associating to each state–action pair, a class z corresponding to a particular partition of the state–action space. The progress must then be computed locally to this partition z by a specialized expert. Each expert consists in a predictor P_z, a meta-predictor $metaP_z$ specialized in only the partition z. To compute the local progress, each expert can monitor the evolution of its own error curve. Provided that the partition z groups similar state–action pairs, learning progress is evaluated in respect to prediction errors corresponding to the same kind of situations.

$$T(s, a) \to z \tag{17.4}$$

$$\text{progress}_z(s(t), a) = p'_z(t) = \langle e_z(t - \theta) \rangle - \langle e_z(t) \rangle \tag{17.5}$$

A possible way for constructing incrementally the classification process T and computing the local progress $p'_z(t)$ for each partition is to build a tree of local experts. We designed an algorithm called *intelligent adaptive curiosity* that can perform progress-driven learning using this method (Oudeyer and Kaplan, 2004). In this algorithm, the tree is built by successively splitting the state space S and the action space A into different regions. This leads to a structure in which a single expert E_z is assigned for each non-overlapping partition z created in the state–action space.[2]

---

[2] Different criteria can be used to realize the splitting of the experts and the incremental construction of the tree. We will describe a particular one corresponding to the model used in the experiments presented in this chapter (see Oudeyer and Kaplan (2006) for another possible splitting method). The splitting method used is inspired by the *marginal attribution* mechanism described in (Drescher, 1991). For the sake of simplicity we will describe the system in the case were s and a are vectors of binary values that can be either 'on' or 'off'. Only small changes are necessary for the extension of this model to discrete and continuous values. Each expert E_z computes its average current error in prediction $\langle e_z(t) \rangle$. For each variable v of s and a, it also computes a set of finer statistics of the average

17.2.6 Experimental results for the 'screen problem'

We present results obtained in a typical experimental run.[3] In order to characterize the behaviour of the agent, we measured statistics on the value of the Noise and Reset motor variables (we also measured them for Move+ and Move− but no particular patterns where found). Figure 17.3 shows the evolution of the average values of these variables for a progress-driven agent. Three clearly distinct zones can be spotted. In a first phase, the agent shows no clear preference between activation or deactivation of the two buttons. Around iteration 700, its behaviour switches rapidly to a situation where mostly the case (Noise off Reset on) is explored. After iteration 1500, the agent switches behaviour again in order to explore the case (Noise off Reset off) that corresponds to the learning of the control task with the two other buttons. Self-evaluation of learning progress permits an autonomous progressive scaling of the difficulty in the choice of the learning task. The agent learns first the simplest parts of its environment and focuses later, when the simple zones are well mastered, on more challenging learning situations. Sensorimotor relations too difficult to learn are ignored.

Figure 17.4 shows the structure of the tree of experts built during the experiment, underlying the observed behaviour. The system starts to make a distinction between situations when Noise is activated or deactivated. The noisy situations are then all directed to a specialized expert that does not divide anymore. The unnoisy branch is then rapidly divided into

prediction error in the cases where the variable is 'on' or 'off': $\langle e_z(t)\rangle_{v,\mathrm{on}}$, $\langle e_z(t)\rangle_{v,\mathrm{off}}$. We can define $R_{v,\mathrm{on}}(t)$ and $R_{v,\mathrm{off}}(t)$, respectively the reliability of prediction when v is on or off, and μ the marginal reliability ratio of v as:

$$R_{v,\mathrm{on}}(t) = 1 - \langle e_z(t)\rangle_{v,\mathrm{on}}, \quad R_{v,\mathrm{off}}(t) = 1 - \langle e_z(t)\rangle_{v,\mathrm{off}}, \quad \mu_v(t) = \frac{R_{v,\mathrm{on}}}{R_{v,\mathrm{off}}} \quad (17.6)$$

At each time t, the system checks whether $\mu_v(t)$ (or $1/\mu_v(t)$) is superior to a threshold η significantly different from 1. This means that prediction is much better when the variable is either on or off. In such a case the expert E_z will be divided into two more specialized experts: one will only be applied to situations in which v is 'on' and the other to situations in which v is off. The internal data of the prediction devices (weight of neurons, prototypes, etc.) are copied to both experts. The more general expert is destroyed so that the state–action space is divided into non-overlapping zones. Just after the splitting, one expert is expected to be 'better' than the other. But as both will adapt to their specialized context this situation may change. The system initially starts with a single predictor E_0 that can recursively divide itself into more specialized versions forming a tree of specialized experts.

[3] In this experiment the splitting threshold η was set to 1.3, the parameters for computing the error average and the progress were $\theta = \tau = 150$. The predictors used were Elman recurrent neural networks with $9 + 4 = 13$ input neurons, 9 output neurons and 50 neurons in the hidden layer (Elman, 1990).

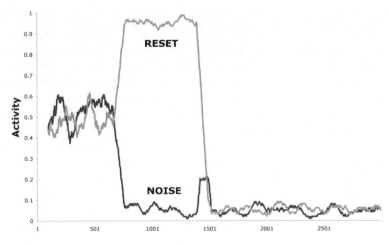

Figure 17.3 Evolution of the average values of the Noise and Reset buttons. After an initial period of indecision, the agent focuses first on the trivial task (NOISE OFF RESET ON) and then on the interesting one (NOISE OFF RESET OFF).

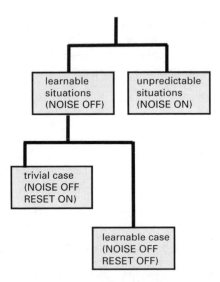

Figure 17.4 Structure of local experts built during the experiments. The state–action space has been divided into three zones of different level of predictability difficulty.

two branches: one for the very predictable case (Noise off Reset on) and another for the remaining cases. No other divisions are then observed, even for much longer runs of these experiments.

17.2.7 'Progress niches'

We can introduce the notion of 'progress niches' to characterize the behaviour of the model. The progress drive pushes the agent to discover and focus on situations which lead to maximal learning progress. These situations, neither too predictable nor too difficult to predict, are 'progress niches'. Progress niches are not intrinsic properties of the environment. They result from a relation between a particular environment, a particular embodiment (sensors, actuators, features detectors and techniques used by the prediction algorithms) and a particular time in the developmental history of the agent. Once discovered, progress niches progressively disappear as they become more predictable.

The concept of progress niches is related to Vygotsky's *zone of proximal development*, where the adult deliberately challenges the child's level of understanding. Adults push children to engage in activities beyond their current mastery level, but not too far beyond so that they remain comprehensible (Vygotsky, 1978). We could interpret the zone of proximal development as a set of potential progress niches organized by the adult in order to help the child learn. But it should be clear that independently of adults' efforts, what is and what is not a progress niche is ultimately defined from the child's point view.

Progress niches also share similarities with Csikszenthmihalyi's *flow experiences* (Csikszenthmihalyi, 1991). Csikszenthmihalyi argues that some activities are *autotelic* when challenges are appropriately balanced with the skills required to cope with them (Luc Steels has suggested a way to operationalize this principle in an autonomous robot – see Steels, 2004). We prefer to use the term *progress niche* by analogy with ecological niches as we refer to a transient state in the evolution of a complex 'ecological' system involving the embodied agent and its environment.[4]

17.3   Possible underlying developmental mechanisms for early imitation

The computational model of progress-driven development presented in this chapter shows how an agent can: (1) separate its sensorimotor space

---

[4] One should note however that the term 'evolution' in this chapter is used in a general dynamical systems sense, rather than in a Darwinian sense. –Ed.

into zones of different predictability levels and (2) choose to focus on the one which leads to maximal learning progress at a given point in time, called a 'progress niche'. This section discusses some speculations about the possible relevance of this motivational principle to explain the different kinds of imitative behaviour that successively appear during the first year of a child's life. It is argued that: (1) the meaningful distinctions necessary for the development of imitation (self, others and objects in the environment) may be the result of discriminations constructed during a progress-driven process and that (2) imitative behaviour can more generally be understood as a way of producing actions in order to experience learning progress.

17.3.1   *Neonate imitation (0 m)*

Simple forms of imitative behaviour have been argued to be present just after birth. They could constitute a process of early identification. Some totally or partially nativist explanations could account for this early 'like-me stance' (Meltzoff and Gopnick, 1993; Moore and Corkum, 1994). This would suggest the possibility of an early distinction between persons and things.

If an inter-modal mapping facilitating the match between what is seen and what is felt exists, the hypothesis of a progress drive would suggest that infants will indeed create a discrimination between such easily predictable couplings (interaction with peers) and unpredictable situations (all the other cases) and that they will focus on the first zone of their sensorimotor space that constitutes a 'progress niche'. Neonate imitation (when it occurs) would be the result of the exploitation of the easiest predictable coupling present just after birth.

17.3.2   *Self-imitation (1–2 m)*

During the first two months of their life, infants perform repeated body motion. They kick their legs repeatedly, they wave their arms. This process is sometimes referred to as 'body babbling'. However, nothing indicates that this exploratory behaviour is randomly organized. Rochat argues that children are in fact performing self-imitation, trying to imitate themselves (Rochat, 2002). This would mean that children are structuring their own behaviour in order to make it more predictable and in this way form 'circular reactions' (Baldwin, 1925; Piaget, 1952).

Such self-imitative behaviours can be well explained by the progress-drive hypothesis. Sensorimotor trajectories directed towards the child's own body can be easily discriminated from trajectories directed towards other people by comparing their relative predictability difficulty. By many

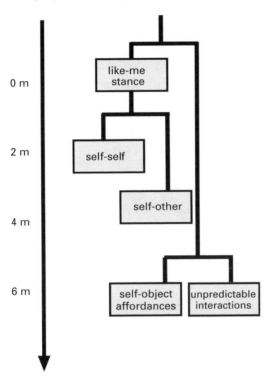

0 m

2 m

4 m

6 m

Figure 17.5 Tree-like structure showing how the child could progressively organize its sensorimotor space into sub-branches corresponding to self-centered interactions, interactions with peers and interactions with objects in the world. It could be argued that such discriminations are the result of significant differences in predictability levels.

respects, making progress in understanding primary circular reactions is easier than in the cases involving other agents: self-centred types of behaviour are 'progress niches'. In such a scenario the 'self' emerges as a meaningful discrimination for achieving better predictability. Once this distinction is made, progress for predicting the effects of self-centred actions can be rapidly made.

17.3.3 Pseudo-imitation (2–4 m)

After two months, infants become more attentive to the external world and particularly to people. Parental scaffolding plays a critical role for making the interaction with the child more predictable (Schaffer, 1977). Parents adapt their own responses so that interactions with the child follow the normal social rules that characterize communicative exchanges (e.g. turn-taking). Moreover, if an adult imitates an infant's own actions, it can trigger continued activity in the infant. This early imitative behaviour is referred to as 'pseudo-imitation' by Piaget (Piaget, 1962).

Pseudo-imitation and focus on scaffolded adult behaviour are predictable effects of the progress drive. As the self-centred trajectories start to be well mastered (and do not constitute 'progress niches' any more), the child's focus shifts to another branch of the discrimination tree, the 'self–other' zone.

17.3.4   *Interaction with objects (5–7 m)*

After five months, attention shifts again from people to objects. Children gain increased control over the manipulation of some objects on which they discover 'affordances' (Gibson, 1986). Parents recognize this shift and initiate interactions about those affordant objects. However, children do not alternate easily their attention between the object and their care-giver.

A progress-driven process can account for this discrimination between affordant objects and unmastered aspects of the environment. Although this stage is typically not seen as imitative, it could be argued that the exploratory process involved in the discovery of the object affordances shares several common features with the one involved for self-imitation: the child structures its world looking for 'progress niches'.

17.3.5   *Summary*

It appears from this brief overview that several aspects of the development of imitative capabilities could be interpreted as a result of a progress-driven process. Figure 17.5 shows a putative tree-like structure, similar to the ones obtained with our computational model, that could account for the progressive discrimination between self, others and other aspects of the environment. In such a context, early imitation can be seen as the result of a process by which an agent looks for 'progress niches' by picking up easy-to-predict aspects of its environment, by engaging in scaffolded social interactions, by performing self-centred circular reactions and by discovering particular affordances of certain objects.

17.4   Conclusion

It has been argued that children are intrinsically motivated to imitate and that, at each stage of their developmental history, they engage in particular forms of imitative behaviour because they are inherently interesting or enjoyable. Our hypothesis states that different forms of children's early imitation may be the result of an intrinsic motivation system driving the infant into situations that are expected to lead to maximal learning progress. The existence of a *progress* drive could explain why certain types of imitative behaviour are produced by children at certain ages and stop being produced later on. It could also explain how discrimination between actions oriented towards the self, towards others and towards the environment may occur.

However, we do not claim that maximizing learning progress is the only motivational principle driving children's development. The complete picture is likely to include a complex set of drives. Developmental dynamics are certainly the result of the inter-play between intrinsic and extrinsic forms of motivation, particular learning biases, as well as embodiment and environmental constraints. We believe that computational and robotic approaches can help specify the contribution of these different components in the overall observed patterns and shed new light on the particular role played by intrinsic motivation in these complex processes.

Acknowledgments

Research funded by Sony CSL Paris with additional support from the ECAGENTS project founded by the Future and Emerging Technologies program (IST-FET) of the European Community under EU R&D contract IST-2003-1940. We would like to thank Luc Steels for his continuous support of the developmental robotics project and Verena Hafner for constructive discussions on these issues.

REFERENCES

Andry, P., Gaussier, P., Moga, S., Banquet, J. and Nadel, J. (2001). Learning and communication in imitation: an autonomous robot perspective. *IEEE Transaction on Systems, Man and Cybernetics, Part A: Systems and Humans*, **31(5)**, 431–44.
Ashby, W. (1960). *Design For a Brain*. London: Chapman and Hall.
Baldwin, J. (1925). *Mental Development in the Child and the Race*. The Macmillan Company, New York.
Barto, A., Singh, S. and Chentanez, N. (2004). Intrinsically motivated learning of hierarchical collections of skills. In *Proceedings of the 3rd International Conference on Development and Learning (ICDL 2004)*.
Csikszenthmihalyi, M. (1990). *Flow: The Psychology of Optimal Experience*. New York: Harper Perennial.
Dennett, D. C. (1996). *Kinds of Minds: Towards an Understanding of Consciousness*. New York: Basic Books.

Drescher, G. L. (1991). *Made-up Minds*. Cambridge, MA: MIT Press.

Elman, J. (1990). Finding structure in time. *Cognitive Science*, 14, 179–211.

Gibson, J. J. (1986). *The Ecological Approach to Visual Perception*. Hillsdale, NJ: Lawrence Erlbaum Associates.

Heimann, M. (2002). Notes on individual differences and the assumed elusiveness of neonatal imitation. In A. N. Meltzoff and W. Prinz (eds.), *The Imitative Mind: Development, Evolution and Brain Bases*. Cambridge, UK: Cambridge University Press, 74–84.

Herder, J. (1772). *Traite sur l'origine de la langue*. Aubier Montaigne: Palimpseste (1992 edn.).

Herrmann, J., Pawelzik, K. and Geisel, T. (2000). Learning predictive representations. *Neurocomputing*, 32–3, 785–91.

Huang, X. and Weng, J. (2002). Novelty and reinforcement learning in the value system of developmental robots. In C. Prince, Y. Demiris, Y. Marom, H. Kozima and C. Balkenius (eds.), *Proceedings of the 2nd International Workshop on Epigenetic Robotics: Modeling Cognitive Development in Robotic Systems*. Lund University Cognitive Studies, 94, 47–55.

Kaplan, F. and Oudeyer, P.-Y. (2003). Motivational principles for visual knowhow development. In C. Prince, L. Berthouze, H. Kozima, D. Bullock, G. Stojanov and C. Balkenius (eds.), *Proceedings of the 3rd International Workshop on Epigenetic Robotics: Modeling Cognitive Development in Robotic Systems*. Lund University Cognitive Studies, 101, 73–80.

Kaplan, F. and Oudeyer, P.-Y. (2004). Maximizing learning progress: an internal reward system for development. In F. Iida, R. Pfeifer, L. Steels and Y. Kuniyoshi (eds.), *Embodied Artificial Intelligence*, LNAI 3139. New York: Springer-Verlag, 259–70.

Lorenz, K. (1968). *Vom Weltbild des Verhaltensforschers*. Munchen: dtv.

Marshall, J., Blank, D. and Meeden, L. (2004). An emergent framework for self-motivation in developmental robotics. In *International Conference on Development and Learning*. San Diego: Salk Institute.

Meltzoff, A. and Gopnick, A. (1993). The role of imitation in understanding persons and developing a theory of mind. In S. Baron-Cohen, H. Tager-Flusberg and D. Cohen (eds.), *Understanding Other Minds*. Oxford, UK: Oxford University Press, 335–66.

Meltzoff, A. and Moore, M. (1977). Imitation of facial and manual gestures by human neonates. *Science*, 198(4312), 74–8.

Moore, C. and Corkum, V. (1994). Social understanding at the end of the first year of life. *Developmental Review*, 14, 349–72.

Nadel, J. (2002). Imitation and imitation recognition: functional use of imitation in preverbal infants and nonverbal children with autism. In A. Meltzoff and W. Prinz (eds.), *The Imitative Mind: Development, Evolution and Brain Bases*. Cambridge, UK: Cambridge University Press, 42–62.

Oudeyer, P.-Y. (2005). The self-organization of speech sounds. *Journal of Theoretical Biology*, 233(3), 435–49.

Oudeyer, P.-Y. and Kaplan, F. (2004). Intelligent adaptive curiosity: a source of self-development. In L. Berthouze, H. Kozima, C. G. Prince, G. Sandini, G. Stojanov, G. Melta and C. Balkenius (eds.) *Proceedings of the 4th International*

Workshop on Epigenetic Robotics, Lund University Cognitive Studies, vol. 117, 127–30.

Oudeyer, P.-Y. and Kaplan, F. (2006). Discovering communication. *Connection Science*, **18(2)**, 189–206.

Piaget, J. (1952). *The Origins of Intelligence in Children.* New York: Norton.

Piaget, J. (1962). *Play, Dreams and Imitation in Childhood.* New York: Norton Press.

Rochat, P. (2002). Ego function of early imitation. In A. Meltzoff and W. Prinz (eds.), *The Imitative Mind: Development, Evolution and Brain Bases.* Cambridge, UK: Cambridge University Press, 85–97.

Schaffer, H. (1977). Early interactive development in studies of mother-infant interaction. In *Proceedings of Loch Lomonds Symposium.* New York: Academic Press, 3–18.

Schmidhuber, J. (1991). Curious model-building control systems. In *Proceedings of the International Joint Conference on Neural Networks.* Singapore: IEEE, Vol. 2, 1458–63.

Schmidhuber, J. (2003). Exploring the predictable. In S. Ghosh and S. Tsutsui (eds.), *Advances in Evolutionary Computing: Theory and Applications.* New York: Springer-Verlag, 579–612.

Steels, L. (2004). The autotelic principle. In I. Fumiya, R. Pfeifer, L. Steels and K. Kunyoshi (eds.), *Embodied Artificial Intelligence*, Vol. 3139 of *Lecture Notes in AI.* New York: Springer Verlag, 231–42.

Sutton, R. and Barto, A. (1998). *Reinforcement Learning: An Introduction.* Cambridge, MA: MIT Press.

Thrun, S. (1995). Exploration in active learning. In M. Arbib (ed.), *Handbook of Brain Science and Neural Networks.* Cambridge, MA: MIT Press.

Varela, F., Thompson, E. and Rosch, E. (1991). *The Embodied Mind: Cognitive Science and Human Experience.* Cambridge, MA: MIT Press.

Vygotsky, L. (1978). *The development of higher psychological processes. Mind in Society.* Cambridge, MA: Harvard University Press.

Weng, J., McClelland, J., Pentland, A., Sporns, O., Stockman, I., Sur, M. and Thelen, E. (2001). Autonomous mental development by robots and animals. *Science*, **291**, 599–600.

White, R. (1959). Motivation reconsidered: the concept of competence. *Psychological review*, **66**, 297–333.

Part VII

Social feedback

The two chapters in this section highlight the important role of social context and feedback provided in experimental teacher–learner setups for social learning and imitation in animals and machines (see Part III, What to imitate, this volume). Moreover, the articles exemplify social learning that occurs across species boundaries, including Grey parrots and a mobile robot, learning from human teachers.

In the first chapter, Irene M. Pepperberg and Diane V. Sherman discuss a particular training procedure called model/rival (M/R) where learning occurs in a triad consisting of the learner, the teacher (principal trainer), and a model/rival who serves as a model for the learner's behaviour and at the same time competes with the learner for the teacher's attention. This procedure comprises role-switch between model/rival and trainer, as well as extensive social interaction including positive and negative effects provided in response to correct or incorrect answers. It has been used very successfully by Pepperberg with Grey parrots, highlighting that the social context and feedback provided during the training sessions are vital for the success of the training. Some aspects of the procedure could be changed without significantly influencing the learning, e.g. adding a bird as another model/rival to the already existing triad. However, birds' abilities to learn decreased when interaction was restricted or removed (e.g. training in audio or video sessions). Interestingly, the same procedure has been used successfully by Sherman to teach children with various disabilities, including children with autism and within the autistic spectrum who have impairments in communication and social interaction. An adaptation of the original M/R procedure, including that children are initially taught via the M/R procedure to imitate responses of the model, allowed the children to learn more effectively when other training paradigms had failed.

Imitation and Social Learning in Robots, Humans and Animals, ed. Chrystopher L. Nehaniv and Kerstin Dautenhahn. Published by Cambridge University Press.
© Cambridge University Press 2007.

In the second chapter of this section on social feedback, Monica N. Nicolescu and Maja J. Matarić present a computational framework that implements action-based representations to unify interaction and imitation in a context where a robot interacts with and learns from a human. The architecture uses perceptual components that allow the robot to map its observations to its own actions, thus learning to perform a particular task while it interacts with a human, as well as active components that allow the robot to express its intentions and convey certain messages by performing specific actions in the environment. The robot can implicitly, non-verbally communicate its 'intentions' to the human. In the robotic experiments, the robot first identifies whether a particular person is helpful, as opposed to uninterested or interested but unhelpful. In the experiment the robot can communicate to the human that it requires help, e.g. when its path is blocked and it needs the human's help to complete the task. In a different set of experiments the human teacher, knowing about the robot's behavioural and sensory capabilities, provided direct feedback using verbal commands and attentional cues, thus helping the robot to learn high level tasks. Here, the teacher 'puts the robot through' the task while the robot follows the teacher. The teacher can intervene and refine the robot's behaviour while the robot demonstrates what it has learnt. This practice-feedback helps the robot to refine its previously learnt task representation while executing the learnt behaviour in a different environment.

With regard to social feedback, both chapters in this section highlight the importance, complexity and potential of social feedback and social context in teaching a learner, whether it be a parrot, a child or a mobile robot. While the first chapter experimentally investigates which specific aspects of the social context contribute to the success or failure of learning by analyzing responses of adept learners with the potential to learn socially, such as Grey parrots, the second chapter faces the challenge of *synthesizing* a robot control architecture for social learning, exploiting general social feedback cues while assuming that the human is able to interpret the robot's 'body language' correctly. Generally, getting a robot to learn anything is already non-trivial, getting it to learn socially requires additional skills such as identifying the teacher and his/her behaviour etc., recognizing social cues, etc. The work by Nicolescu and Matarić demonstrates the need to investigate systematically issues of social feedback and social context in human–robot teaching scenarios.

Pepperberg and Sherman's chapter has interesting implications for possible implementations in robots and other computational agents, where imitation could be seen as a stepping stone towards implementing the M/R technique and thus give rise to powerful means of social learning that have been shown to work successfully in Grey parrots and children with disabilities. However, comparing robots and animals bears a certain risk: children with autism, even with impairments in social interaction and communication, as well as Grey parrots, are sentient beings born into a social context, they develop as social beings, although, in children with autism, their social behaviour and responses might not be 'typical'. In contrast, present-day robots do not possess any 'innate' skills at all that in conjunction with their environment can scaffold their social development. Any drives, motivations or affect in robots are directly or indirectly programmed. Since extensive interaction and affect (requiring the perception and processing of, as well as the ability to express, affect in the learner/teacher) plays an important role in the M/R technique, it is unclear how robots without such skills could benefit from it. On the bright side, the study of motivational and affective regulatory systems in robots is an active area of research (Cañamero and Gaussier, 2005). Long-term progress in this area would still not make robots sentient, but at least provide them with rudimentary pre-requisites that might allow them to participate in complex social learning settings such as the M/R procedure. Research in the area of human–robot interaction (Fong *et al.*, 2003) increasingly investigates social cues and social feedback, verbal and non-verbal communication, the role of affect and personality, etc. In the context of human–machine interaction, attempting to make machines more socially aware and socially competent interaction partners can certainly benefit greatly from interaction studies of humans or other animals.

Thus, social feedback and social context is a challenging domain within the field of social learning and imitation. Investigating these issues systematically as well as in more depth in an inter-disciplinary context are hoped to further our understanding not only of social learning and imitation but also of deep issues regarding the nature of social intelligence in animals and machines.

REFERENCES

Cañamero, L. and Gaussier, P. (2005). Emotion understanding: robots as tools and models. In J. Nadel and D. Muir (eds.), *Emotional Development: Recent Research Advances*. Oxford, UK: Oxford University Press, 235–58.
Fong, T., Nourbakhsh, I. and Dautenhahn, K. (2003). A survey of socially interactive robots. *Robotics and Autonomous Systems*, **42(3–4)**, 143–66.

18 Training behavior by imitation: from parrots to people . . . to robots?

Irene M. Pepperberg and Diane V. Sherman

18.1 Introduction

Learning by imitation is not a unitary task; thus understanding its various levels in order to potentiate imitative learning is daunting, whether subjects are human, animal or inanimate. For some syndromes arising in childhood (e.g. autism), *lack* of imitative ability (i.e. excluding rote, meaningless, often involuntary mimetic behavior, e.g. echolalia) is a defining characteristic (Hobson and Lee, 1999; Williams *et al.*, 2001). What constitutes imitation in animals is still under study (Hurley and Chater, 2005; Nehaniv and Dautenhahn, this volume). And computers (and, by inference, robots using computer intelligence) may be "smart" in terms of brute processing power, but their learning is limited to what is easily programmed. Most computers and robots are presently analogous to living systems trained in relatively simple conditioned stimulus-response paradigms: given specific input parameters (that can, of course, be numerous and diverse), computers quickly and efficiently produce a predetermined, correct output (Pepperberg, 2001); computers can, however, generally solve only those new problems that are similar to ones they have already been programmed to solve. And although connectionist models are making significant advances, allowing generalization beyond training sets for a number of individual problems (e.g. Schlesinger and Parisi, 2004), at present most computational mechanisms – and autistic children – cannot learn in ways normal humans do. No one model, for example, does all the following: form new abstract representations, manipulate these representations to attain concrete goals, transfer information acquired in one domain to manage tasks in another, integrate new and existing disparate forms of knowledge (e.g. linguistic, contextual, emotional) to solve novel problems – nor can any one model achieve these behavior patterns through imitation in ways managed by every normal

Imitation and Social Learning in Robots, Humans and Animals, ed. Chrystopher L. Nehaniv and Kerstin Dautenhahn. Published by Cambridge University Press.
© Cambridge University Press 2007.

young child (see Lieberman, 2001). Even the Grey parrots (*Psittacus erithacus*) we study, with walnut-sized brains,[1] succeed on such tasks (Pepperberg, 1999).

The parrots' success likely arises for two reasons. First, parrots, like normal young children, have a repertoire of desires and purposes that cause them to form and test ideas about the world and how to deal with the world (Pepperberg, 1999);[2] these ideas, unlike conditioned stimulus-responses, may represent outcomes of cognitive processing. Second, because socially interactive procedures are necessary to train them to communicate with humans via English vocalizations, parrots' learning processes likely resemble young children's. (For parallels between parrots and other birds, see, e.g. Pepperberg, 1985.) Moreover, social interaction training techniques used with these parrots have successfully been adapted to assist children with dysfunctions, particularly those within the autistic spectrum disorder, to establish meaningful communication and social functioning with adults and peers in cases where conditioning-style techniques fail (Pepperberg and Sherman, 2000, 2002, 2004); aspects of these children's learning can be classified as imitative. Might imitative learning be expanded to other systems?

We focus on two questions central to this issue: what processes and mechanisms *are* involved in imitative/social learning – for animals and humans? Can these processes be adapted for robotic intelligence? Research provides some answers to the first question; our results are described below, centering on processes involved in acquisition of social and communicative competence (not specifically language). For now, the second question is left for robotics experts; after examining our data, hypotheses and proposals, we hope their response is affirmative.

18.2   Animals, learning and cognitive processing

Previous papers delineated differences between conditioned stimulus response paradigms and forms of advanced learning we *define* as involving

---

[1] The extent to which parrot, songbird and human neural architecture differ is currently being examined (e.g. Jarvis, 2004); for example, brain areas once thought to be analogous are now considered possibly homologous.

[2] Our parrots may, for example, take a label that they have seen used in a very specific context, such as "wool" for a woolen pompom, and pull at a trainer's sweater while uttering that label. The probability of such action happening by chance is slim; at that stage the bird usually has at least three and usually four other labels. The birds – like children (Brown, 1973) – seem to be testing use of the label and recognizing their trainers as sources of information; our responses of high affect, which stimulate them further, show them the power of their utterances and reinforce these early attempts at categorization (Pepperberg, 2001). Behavior of this nature is not seen in most autistic children (Pepperberg and Sherman, 2000, 2002).

cognitive processing and imitation (Pepperberg, 2001, 2005); only a brief review is provided here. Advanced learning is an ethological adaptation whereby social creatures acquire information and actions from one another that improve their fitness and allow flexible responses to changing environments. Such learning involves the ability to choose the set of rules, among many learned possibilities, from which the appropriate response can be made; and creativity to build upon learned information to devise novel solutions to novel problems (Pepperberg, 1990). In contrast, conditioned learning does not create insight that enables immediate transfer across domains, nor the ability to alter behavior quickly based on the immediate past, much less flexibility to respond to changing conditions.

Specifically, the trial-and-error, stimulus-response conditioning that is frequently mathematically modeled for machine learning and often employed in childhood interventions (see Pepperberg and Sherman, 2002) fails at extended generalization: if input is novel and output not already known, such programming does not produce appropriate responses, both in computational mechanisms and similarly "programmed" living systems (Woodard and Bitterman, 1972). The system, animal or computer, may more quickly learn closely related tasks (Rumbaugh and Pate, 1984), but never shows insightful behavior that characterizes normal human or other forms of animal intelligence (Pepperberg and Lynn, 2000). Conditioned learning is likely implicit, unconscious (Damasio, 1999; but see Lovibond and Shanks, 2002) and stimulus driven, even within learning sets (King, 1966). Although simple associations (stimuli-response) may be what are first linked in memory, in nature repeated interactions both sharpen and broaden these connections (Bloom, 2000), resulting in more complex learning involving representation formation. Advanced learning, likely including high-level imitation, derives from manipulation and matching of one's actions to such representations. These representations may be imagery-based and not require language for their formation.

Thus, although anthropocentric biases often lead us to concentrate on human communication, particularly language, both as a descriptor and measure of most forms of cognitive processing, animal models can help us understand how *learning* (and likely motivation) is involved in cognitive processing, imitation *and* communication. Acquisition processes for communication in non-humans and humans demonstrate striking parallels (Pepperberg, 1999; Savage-Rumbaugh *et al.*, 1993), but proceed more slowly in animals, allowing for detailed examination. Too, researchers studying animals can determine if varying input can affect communicative and cognitive competence (Pepperberg, 1999) – something not possible with human infants.

18.2.1   Studies on Grey parrots

Grey parrots (*Psittacus erithacus*) are good subjects for such studies. Parrots, like children and computers, can detect/represent speech segments in terms of phoneme probabilities, chunk speech into syllable-like units, produce phonemes, visually detect items, represent shape, color and number, and attend to and remember co-occurring auditory (speech) and visual representations of items (Pepperberg, 1999). Parrots, like computers and robots, but unlike children, are not predisposed to learn human language, and like children and unlike current computers and robots, have, as noted above, a repertoire of desires and purposes that cause them to form and test ideas about the world and how to deal with the world; these ideas are likely representations of the results of cognitive processing, open to investigation and modeling (Pepperberg, 2001).

For over 25 years, Grey parrots have been trained to communicate with humans via English speech; this two-way communication code is then used to examine their cognitive processing (Pepperberg, 1999). The oldest subject, Alex, labels more than 50 exemplars (e.g. paper, keys, wood, wool, etc.), 7 colors, 5 shapes, quantity to 6, 3 categories (material, color, shape), and uses "no," "come here," "wanna go X" and "want Y" (X, Y are appropriate location or item labels). He combines labels to identify, classify, request or refuse approximately 100 different items (e.g. colored and shaped exemplars) and to alter his environment. He processes queries about concepts of category, relative size, quantity, presence or absence of similarity or difference in attributes, and shows label comprehension; he semantically separates labeling from requesting. He processes conjunctive, recursive queries to state, for example, the material of one object, among seven, having a particular color *and* shape, or the number of green blocks in a collection of green and blue blocks and balls. He understands hierarchical categories – that specific attributes labeled "blue," "green," etc. are subsumed under a category labeled "color," whereas attributes of "3-corner," "4-corner," etc. are subsumed under one labeled "shape." Shown a novel item and told its "color" is "taupe," he correctly categorizes a second novel object of that hue. He forms new categories readily. He transferred knowledge of absence of similarity and difference to respond correctly when, without training, he was given two equal-sized objects and asked to label the bigger item (Pepperberg and Brezinksy, 1991). He thus exhibits capacities once presumed limited to humans or apes (Premack 1978, 1983). He is not unique: other Greys replicate some of his results (Pepperberg, 1999). So: (1) how does a creature with a walnut-sized brain organized differently from that of mammals and even other birds (Striedter, 1994; but see Jarvis, 2004 and Jarvis and

Mello, 2000 for arguments concerning similarities in brain organization) learn elements of human language? and (2) how does he solve complex cognitive tasks requiring generalization and concept formation?

"How" his brain functions remains to be discovered, and we can propose only hypotheses and parallels with children. We do, however, know the input parrots need in order to learn these elements of human language and cognition, that is, the tools that enable them to transition from simple associations to advanced learning.

18.2.2   The model/rival (M/R) technique

Pepperberg was not the first researcher to study avian–human communication (Pepperberg, 1999, 2001): Mowrer (1952, 1954, 1969/1980), using standard conditioning techniques and food rewards unrelated to labels or concepts being trained, failed to teach several psittacids referential English speech. Other researchers, possibly believing Mowrer's social setting caused his failure, themselves failed to train mimetic birds under more rigorous operant conditions, using sound isolation boxes and human audiotapes (Ginsburg, 1960, 1963; Gossette, 1969; Grosslight and Zaynor, 1967; Grosslight et al., 1964; Gramza, 1970). In contrast, Greys that observed two humans interactively model vocal dialogues acquired targeted speech patterns (Todt, 1975). Todt developed the model/rival (M/R) technique in which humans assume roles played by psittacine peers in nature, demonstrating to parrots the interactive vocalizations to be learned.[3] In Todt's procedure, one human is exclusively the principal trainer of each parrot, asking questions and providing increased visual and vocal attention for appropriate responses. Another human is exclusively the *model* for the parrot's behavior and simultaneously the parrot's *rival* for the principal trainer's attention. So, for example, the trainer says "What's your name?"; the human model/rival responds "My name is Lora." Such human interchanges resemble duets observed between parrots in large aviaries (Mebes, 1978). Todt's parrots learned the model/rival's response often in less than a day, unlike the slow, sparse acquisition in operant paradigms. This rapid acquisition was impressive, but the phrases used did not allow Todt to show if a bird understood their meaning (i.e. utterances did not refer to specific

---

[3] At the time Todt performed his studies, little was known about the extent to which songbirds needed live interaction to learn their songs. The few oscine species studied (e.g. white-crowned sparrows, Marler, 1970) seemed to need only tape tutoring to learn their species-specific song and to filter out all allospecific song; only in the 1980s did researchers (reviewed in Pepperberg, 1985, 1999) begin to demonstrate how live interactive models were crucial for some conspecific and most allospecific song acquisition.

objects or actions, such as "tickle," to which experimenters could respond by scratching the bird's head). Thus Todt's birds may have learned a human-imposed form of antiphonal duetting (i.e. a form of contact calling between social peers; Thorpe and North 1965; Thorpe 1974) or a simple conditioned response (e.g. Lenneberg 1971, 1973). Too, Todt's parrots learned only vocalizations spoken by the model/rival, never the principal trainer.[4] Todt's intent, however, had not been to train birds to communicate meaningfully with humans, but only to determine optimal learning conditions.

Pepperberg recognized, however, that the parrots' acquisition, because it was allospecific, involved *exceptional learning*: learning that is unlikely to occur in the normal course of development; such learning had been shown to require special forms of input (see Pepperberg, 1999 for a review). She thus adapted Todt's procedure: adding *reference* so words and phrases referred to specific objects and actions,[5] adding *functionality* so birds saw that learning human sounds enabled them to obtain desired interactions or objects and *exchanging roles* of model/rival and trainer, so birds recognized the process as interactive – that one individual was not always the questioner and another the respondent.[6] The extensive *social interaction* between trainers and among trainers and a bird also involved affect: positive for correct responses, negative for errors. Alex's results are described above (for details, see Pepperberg, 1999).[7] Interestingly, Kanzi (*Pan paniscus*), an ape proficient in symbolic communication, initially learned to use computer keys to label and request objects by watching his mother's sessions (Savage-Rumbaugh *et al.*, 1993), that is, via M/R-like training.[8] But data acquisition on referential speech use was just the beginning: what made our modeling technique so successful? Could it

---

[4] That is, Todt's birds learned that *if X is heard, then the response is Y*, so that when the trainer said "X" to the bird, it learned to say "Y" in response, never "X."

[5] Reference is added in that the model or the bird receives X if and only if it says X in response to "What's this?" or "What's here?"; that is, there exists a 1:1 correlation between the label to be used and the object received. In contrast, in most operant procedures, whatever the task, the reward is a one specific item – generally a food item and the same food whatever the response – likely leading the subject to think that a number of responses and tasks all involve requests for the same food. In M/R training the bird also learns the *function* of the label – that it can be used to request a specific item or action.

[6] Note that M/R procedural use of a "referential square" (two trainers, the object and the subject) compared to the "referential triangle" (one trainer, the object and the subject) of standard training situations (e.g. Baldwin, 1995; Tomasello, 1999) allows the subject to more easily understand how to separate vocal instruction about an action from the replication of the action. This point will be discussed in more detail later in the chapter.

[7] See also Pepperberg (2002) for M/R learning by other birds, and for other M/R variants. – Ed.

[8] Savage-Rumbaugh did not use our exact M/R system, but Kanzi's mother did model both correct and incorrect behavior patterns and their consequences.

Table 18.1 *Effects of Training Method*

Method	Reference?	Functionality?	Interaction?	Model?	Learning?
M/R	Y	Y	Y	Y	Y
No Jt Atten	Y	N	partial	N	N
HAG-dual	Y	Y	Y	Y	Y
HAG-solo	Y	Y	partial	Y	Y-slow
HG-solo	Y	partial	Y	N	latent
Video	Y	partial	N/some	not live	N
Audio	N	N	N	N	N

be the basis for a new learning paradigm? A series of experiments was designed to answer those questions.

18.2.3   How aspects of M/R training affect learning

What if M/R training lacked aspects of input: reference, functionality, social interaction or role reversal? Table 18.1 depicts various training paradigms given Pepperberg's birds, showing the lacking aspect(s) of input in each case. The study "No Jt Atten" tested effects of training that lacked joint attention. Here a student sat with her back to the bird, talking about an object within the bird's reach (Pepperberg and McLaughlin, 1996). She neither attended to the object nor interacted directly with the bird.[9] Normal children in such a situation failed to acquire the object label (Baldwin, 1995), and autistic children may even associate seemingly irrelevant words from such discourse with an action or their emotional response to the situation; for example, saying "leaf-blower" instead of "I'm frustrated" (Sherman, pers. obs.). HAG-dual (HAG = "Human–Alex–Griffin") tested addition of the already-talking conspecific, Alex, to the human pair who performed M/R training with a younger bird, Griffin; the M/R procedure was thus expanded to include a third individual, albeit one without full competence: Alex could act only as another model/rival because he could not at the time question Griffin. In HAG-solo, Alex *replaced* one human in the M/R procedure; now, because Alex did not question Griffin but only modeled responses, some normal interaction (role reversal) was missing (Pepperberg *et al.*, 2000). In HG-solo (HG = "Human–Griffin"), a single student conversed with a bird about targeted objects, maintaining joint attention, but eliminating the model/rival and thus both role reversal and some functionality

---

[9] That is, lacking both the referential square and the referential triangle noted above.

(Pepperberg *et al.*, 2000). In video training, parrots watched a tape of Alex's session for each targeted label, with various levels of interaction with a human: from no human present to one who labeled the item Alex received in the video (Pepperberg *et al.*, 1998; Pepperberg *et al.*, 1999). In audio sessions, birds simply heard audio portions of videos (Pepperberg, 1994). The final column shows that when any aspect of M/R training was missing, birds failed to learn, with the intriguing exception of latent learning in HG-solo: after 50 HG-solo training sessions, Griffin still had not uttered targeted labels, but when labels trained in this manner were immediately switched into M/R format, he began producing the labels after only two or so sessions, unlike the twenty or so M/R sessions generally needed. Therefore, when full functionality was lacking (i.e. because of use of only a single trainer and thus the inability to model an interaction), Griffin apparently learned the label, but not what to *do* with it.

M/R training gave birds tools to learn new labels and concepts, but was not the entire story. First, our parrots' initial label learning, like children's (e.g. Hollich *et al.*, 2000), was still slow and difficult although not stimulus-bound; and, like children, later label acquisition was faster and involved interesting types of transfer and concept formation. Second, considerable learning occurred outside of sessions, and some was initiated by the birds, much like children playing the "naming game" (Brown, 1973). Discussion of these additional learning strategies is in Pepperberg (2001, 2004, 2005); here we focus on parallels with learning by children with various dysfunctions, in the hope that such parallels can be extended to machine learning.

18.3   M/R adaptations for children with dysfunctions

A detailed literature review (Pepperberg and Sherman, 2000, 2002) shows that behavioral intervention programs for children with social disabilities, both in private practice and in school districts, generally achieve limited success. Interestingly, these programs lack some elements of M/R input shown to be crucial for Grey parrot referential learning; that is, protocols fail to demonstrate functionality, role reversal, two-person modeling and/or consequences of errors. We briefly summarize the material and suggest why M/R training is successful.

18.3.1   *Current intervention strategies for children*

Use of modeling and observational learning to help children with disabilities acquire appropriate lifestyle skills is not new (reviews in, e.g. Garfinkle and Schwartz, 2002; Ihrig and Wolchik, 1988; Lanquetot, 1989; Pierce and Schreibman, 1997b). Most studies, however, involve a single model (peer-to-child or adult-to-child; Koegel and Rincover, 1974; Strain *et al.*, 1979) and have limited success, except when successive single-trainer models are used (Pierce and Schreibman, 1995, 1997a)[10] or children work together (e.g. Sherratt, 2002). Interestingly, just like children with disabilities, Grey parrots often fail to learn referential labels during interactions with a single caretaker (Pepperberg *et al.*, 2000), but achieve significant success in labeling and acquisition of concepts via our two-trainer M/R system (see above). Human studies using some form of two-trainer interactions, or groups of interacting children with and without disabilities, also successfully trained receptive labeling (Charlop *et al.*, 1983), expressive language (Ihrig and Wolchik, 1988), learning-readiness skills (Lanquetot, 1989), play skills (Garfinkle and Schwartz, 2002; Pierce and Schreibman, 1997b), and generalizing accomplishments to natural environmental settings.

Sherman's initial adaptation of M/R techniques (Pepperberg and Sherman, 2000) generated considerable success for children with various disabilities. Sherman evaluated each child entering, identified a series of targeted behaviors for the child to acquire and designed an M/R procedure for each behavior. As the child acquired each behavior and generalized it appropriately to other environments (as reported by teachers, parents, aides), instruction for the next level was instituted. In addition to these regular M/R sessions, Sherman also opportunistically used "real" life situations (e.g. an incident not entirely relevant to the planned program) as the basis for M/R training of new behavior; she then intensified and escalated the challenges, changes and types of M/R interactions given the child to facilitate flexibility and adaptive responses. Children with dysfunctions, particularly those with autism and within the autistic spectrum, thereby process and cross-apply their learning with full cognitive integration. They avoid meaningless rote responses; over-focusing on an area, topic or object; or behavioral patterns limited to one environment or situation.[11] A specific example is a four-year-old autistic female whose expressive speech was merely fragmented non-linear phrases from movies accompanied by flat body affect, who had minimal social skills (could use only "hi" and "how are you") and inappropriate play skills

[10] Note that what these researchers call "single-trainer" sessions involved one trainer, but also one other normal individual; their procedure did not match ours exactly but did have certain similarities to the M/R system; for details, see the relevant articles.

[11] Note that parrots trained in operant-like situations utter meaningless rote vocalizations, fail to generalize and in general act in ways that are similar to those of untrained autistic children (Mowrer, 1952, 1954, 1980).

(could only imitate the sound and motion of single windup toy), and who was unable to answer questions but could request various foods, liquids or toys with a full sentence (e.g. "I want milk"). After approximately four and one half months of intervention, she learned to respond to questions concerning the non-immediate past and to request to be taught a skill she perceived as lacking in order to interact better with her peers (e.g. how to climb a play structure without fear), was able to generalize playground skills to situations such as a birthday party, and could initiate and sustain play with a slightly older neighborhood child.

Pollard (2001), based on Sherman's work, directly compared children receiving M/R training to those receiving more standard intervention (e.g. Hadwin *et al.*, 1996). Pollard's conclusion was that the M/R two-trainer method, even when additionally adapted to a clinical laboratory setting, enabled all children to make significantly greater gains than other procedures in all areas evaluated. She examined belief (recognizing other's knowledge), reading emotion, understanding pretense and cross-applying skills in different settings without facilitation.[12]

Subsequently, Sherman (Pepperberg and Sherman, 2002) demonstrated that children diagnosed as autistic who had failed to progress in other training paradigms could learn empathic skills via M/R training. A four-year-old male who, at the beginning of training, was unable to answer questions but could request various items with two-word phrases (e.g. utter "want this" while pointing to the item), who could not use or understand language involved in typical daily social interactions and could not recall information heard on a daily basis because question words still confused him, learned to communicate with appropriate responses and to make eye contact in all settings spontaneously; he began to process, understand and respond to an entire "question" sentence (e.g. "How many more times do you want to swing? 1, 2, 3 more times?," "How are you?," "How old are you?"), learned how to use appropriate greetings including how to approach other children who were not part of the training scenario, and learned how to interact using both questions and answers appropriately in a variety of settings. He also noted peers or adults who were absent from the clinic and spontaneously questioned them about their health upon their return, which could involve even a three-week hiatus. Communication generalized to

---

[12] Details of Pollard's work are in her thesis. As mentioned in Footnote 2, M/R training also facilitates our birds' recognition of others as sources of information and generalization of their behavior; by modeling the association of positive effect with correct answers and negative effect with errors, M/R training facilitates reading of emotion in both birds and humans.

peers in other settings (e.g. pre-school). Another autistic female child, who initially had been non-verbal, had poor eye contact, and had non-purposeful repetitive behaviors and minimal speech, progressed through each stage of M/R training to gain complex imaginary play skills, began to participate in mainstream extra-curricular activities of her choice without adult intervention, started to use and understand joint attention and false-belief, to understand humor and sarcasm and now figures out how to obtain desired responses from others (i.e. can negotiate); most interesting of all, she demonstrates empathy for others as a model in M/R sessions.[13]

Most recently, Sherman (Pepperberg and Sherman, 2004) has begun using M/R training to teach higher level autistic and autistic spectrum children expanded levels of empathy, to self-modulate, to recognize how their behavior impacts on others, to read and regulate voice tone, facial expressions and other non-verbal cues in order to recognize and understand emotions (skills that would be helpful for computer and robotics interfaces) and to train violent children how to express themselves non-violently. These children learned to make concerned queries about others' health, others' thoughts, or whereabouts; to anticipate others' actions and reactions; to anticipate and plan future events such as making queries about a particular period in art history in order to learn more; and expressing when, how and with whom they would like to visit a museum in a foreign country.

Sherman has found that autistic and autistic spectrum children, like Grey parrots, fail to learn from single trainer instruction and from video with a single human model. An older autistic child was to assist in training a younger non-autistic child to perform a physical task, that is, to demonstrate the behavior and "spot" (visually attend to and physically be prepared to catch the younger child if he fell off the equipment). Sherman demonstrated the targeted behavior (giving assistance) and gave verbal instructions to the older autistic child, who had received extensive M/R training on other targeted behaviors he had thereby attained. The autistic child's first attempt failed at this new level of "giving assistance." A video of what had happened during the trial was presented to the autistic child to assess his performance; although the autistic child identified himself in the video, he could not associate the video with his behavior and was not aware of the other child in the video even when prompted by Sherman's queries. A second trial also failed. The video of this attempt was

[13] Although understanding humor and sarcasm might not be of use for parrots or robots (although one could certainly imagine a scenario where such traits would be helpful), these human achievements demonstrate the power of the M/R procedure.

presented but now Sherman pointed out exactly what targeted behavior patterns were missing and explained what was required. The subsequent, third attempt also failed. Sherman then used M/R training to demonstrate the targeted behavior of "giving assistance;" in the fourth attempt, the autistic child now recognized his errors, self-regulated his actions, attended to task, anticipated the younger child's reactions and responded accurately. The interaction with the younger child was repeated over several sessions; the autistic child consistently performed targeted behaviors without intervention from Sherman. Moreover, after the first M/R session on "giving assistance," the autistic child spontaneously said to the younger child, "Good job little buddy," a phrase not used in the autistic child's environment.[14] Unlike his usual pattern of speech and body language, here voice quality was soft and body language was lowered to the younger child's level, as would be used by a non-autistic child in these circumstances and emulated that of Sherman's general style when talking to a younger child. This untrained action is noteworthy because it demonstrates spontaneous emergence of self-modulated emotion and caring.

Similarly, Sherman found that autistic and autistic spectrum children failed to learn from a computer program without M/R training. The program shows human facial emotions; children were required to identify six emotions and imitate one facial emotion seen on the screen. After verbal prompts but no M/R training from Sherman in three to four trials, children identified three of the six emotions, and imitated only one element out of three facial components. Children were then given a mirror to compare their facial expressions with the picture on the computer; their imitations were still distorted, that is, did not reproduce the picture on the screen. After one M/R session, children accurately identified facial emotions and imitated facial expressions for all six emotions.

In all cases, no child reached totally normative (physical-age appropriate) levels, but all significantly improved their empathic social communication skills and use of contextually appropriate behavior after receiving M/R training. So . . . why was M/R training more successful than standard interventions?

18.3.2   What mediates M/R success?

Typically, not all learning is disrupted in autistic children, and stimulus-response training can effect certain behavioral changes (Hadwin *et al.*, 1996); M/R training, however, more effectively enabled children to

---

[14] NB: This utterance also suggested that the child had learned to cross-apply M/R training.

acquire social skills and transfer information across situations (Pollard, 2001). We suggest (Pepperberg and Sherman, 2002) that input elements that facilitate exactly this type of learning in Grey parrots are crucial for children with disabilities or deficits. We thus propose that the typical single-trainer instruction, that is, "do as I do" might – as it did for Griffin in HG solo training, or for some of the autistic children – actually prevent subjects from separating the targeted behavior pattern or target of the command from the command itself and thus inhibit building a representation of the required response (Pepperberg, 2005; Pepperberg and Sherman, 2002);[15] remember, formation of a representation probably enables advanced learning. Quite likely, subjects observing and identifying with a *model* responding to "do X" more easily determine and represent behavior patterns to be learned and connect those patterns with "X". (Think about a single person training two different commands such as "touch your nose" vs. "touch my nose."[16])

Specifically, what Sherman (Pepperberg and Sherman, 2000, 2002, 2004) is initially teaching children to do via the M/R system is to *imitate* responses of the *model* – to attend to and identify with the model, to take the model's point of view so as to recreate that individual's actions in oneself, form a representation of the model's action and compare one's actions with that representation so as to refine one's actions – not simply focusing on results, but on actions leading to the results, and specific cause–effect relationships including social ones (Call and Carpenter, 2002). Such behavior is higher-order or controlled imitation (reviews in Byrne, 2002; Whiten, 2002), behavior also required for success on "mindreading" problems (Baron-Cohen *et al.*, 2001) and empathic responses, and is behavior that most autistic children lack (Smith and Bryson, 1994; Hobson and Lee, 1999; Wolf *et al.*, 2001).

Interestingly, Williams and colleagues (2001) argue that the correlation between autism and lack of imitation may be through a faulty "mirror neuron" (MN) system – MNs being that part of the nervous system that responds to an observed action just as though the action were actively being executed by the observer (Arbib and Rizzolatti, 1996); importantly, the agent of the observed action must attend to the action for

---

[15] Social communication requires that the participants actively take turns; although such behavior is natural to parrots (they engage in duetting; see review in Pepperberg, 1999), an autistic child generally needs to *learn* such behavior. Observation of M/R procedures provides the chance to observe such interaction, which is by definition absent in single-trainer settings.

[16] Such training could be particularly relevant for robots. Billard (2002), for example, could likely train "touch *your* nose" with her imitation program, but would have difficulty training the difference between that command and "touch *my* nose" without adding some kind of inversion of meaning into the system.

the observer's MNs to respond appropriately, suggesting a role for joint attention (Jellema *et al.*, 2000). MNs are also purportedly involved in the evolution and possibly development of human language (Arbib, 2002, 2005; Fadiga *et al.*, 2002). In autistic children, the MN system apparently functions properly at the motor cortex level (i.e. neurons respond appropriately to observed actions, Avikainen *et al.*, 1999), but lacks the ability to integrate such activity into a cognitive system to engender overt imitation – specifically, of novel actions. Apparently, autistic MN systems develop to levels correlated with only low-level imitation (e.g. echolalia, echopraxia). To understand this difference, a monkey model may be useful: monkey MNs respond only to goal-oriented actions already in the repertoire (Buccino *et al.*, 2001; Chaminade *et al.*, 2001, 2002; Fogassi, 2000; Rizzolatti *et al.*, 2001), whereas intact human MNs respond more broadly (Fadiga *et al.*, 1995), for example, to actions that are novel and lacking a clear goal. Monkeys, unlike intact humans, do not exhibit exact imitation (Visalberghi and Fragaszy, 2002); that is, they often attain the goal of a demonstrated action without recreating the action itself (i.e. "emulation", Tomasello, 1999). Some autistic children behave similarly (Hobson and Lee, 1999). Too, autistic behavior and its communicative deficits often appear just when: (1) self-awareness, (2) the need to understand self as separate from others and (3) recognition of others as information sources all become critical for learning (Tager-Flusberg, 2000) – exactly the same requirements needed for controlled imitation. This point might match the time when some executive process, missing in an autistic's mirror neuron system, would normally begin functioning fully. Interestingly, in intact humans, particular brain areas (right inferior parietal, precuneus and somatosensory cortex) are specifically involved in distinguishing self-produced actions from those generated by others (Ruby and Decety, 2001), which suggests a further level of complexity with respect to MNs. And, consistent with our findings that video modeling is less successful than that presented live, Jaervelaeinen and colleagues (2001) found a stronger reactivity of MN-related brain areas during observation of live rather than video motor acts.

How these findings relate to our birds – whether parrots have MNs and how such MNs might function in learning and imitation – is unclear, but suggestive evidence exists from studies on both parrot and songbird brain activation (Jarvis, 2004, Jarvis *et al.*, 2005; Pepperberg, 2005), and parrots seemingly have brain areas that at least *function* in ways similar to primate MN sites – the monkey F5 and human Broca's area (Arbib, 2005; Jarvis, 2004, Jarvis *et al.*, 2005; Pepperberg and Shive, 2001).[17]

---

[17] Space is too limited for a detailed comparison of avian and mammalian/human brains; the information can be found in Jarvis, 2004.

Of course, MNs' role in imitation is not yet clear, nor are the overall relationships and interactions between MNs and other brain areas fully understood; too, MN systems of varying complexity apparently exist. These different systems likely relate to different levels of imitation (Pepperberg, 2004, 2005). High-level, novel imitative patterns, like those found in intact humans, take longer to construct than those involved in low-level imitation (e.g. emulation), require strong levels of reference, functionality and interaction for inception (e.g. Pepperberg, 1985), and, most likely, involve construction of neural pathways that only then are recruited into the intact, adult mirror system (Pepperberg, 2005). These actions might also involve beginnings of "mindreading." Possibly M/R training strengthens or forms additional connections in whatever MN system exists for autistic children helped by Sherman (Pepperberg and Sherman, 2000, 2002, 2004; note Wolf *et al.*, 2001) and in parrots. Specifically, M/R training (with high levels of reference, functionality and interaction), which enables various forms of *exceptional* learning – learning that is unlikely to occur in the normal course of development, whether the reasons involve the need to over-ride innate predispositions (Pepperberg, 1985) or to assist systems that have been damaged in some manner (Pepperberg and Sherman, 2002) – might help develop higher-level MN systems from existent lower level ones.[18] Such an assumption is consistent with Gordon and Barker's (1994) argument that autistic children lack not a theory of behavior, but a skill.[19] If action planning (necessary for high-level imitation) is the ability to select (even if unconsciously) appropriate neurons and combine them into patterns of appropriate temporal activation (Arbib and Rizzolatti, 1996), then this skill indeed could be trained through our modeling system.

The question then arises that ties what might appear a digression back to the central theme of this paper: can robotic or computer MN equivalents be built that M/R procedures can train? Given that monkey brains can control robot arms as shown by Wessberg *et al.* (2000), one might imagine the following: an animate subject's MNs are harnessed to control robot arms (carefully eliminating the "inverted" spinal MNs that prevent overt unintended replication during observation; see Baldissera *et al.*, 2001) while the subject watches/is trained to follow modeled actions;

[18] Too, separation of the observed command and the observed behavior that occurs in M/R training may enable subjects to recognize the difference between the goal (instantiated in the command) and the actions leading to the goal (the observed behavior); might this recognition then help to entrain higher level MNs?

[19] We do not intend, however, to argue for "simulation theory" over "theory theory" with respect to these behavior patterns, although MN data appear to support simulation theory (e.g. Gallese and Goldman, 1988). For a detailed discussion of the two theories of mind-reading, see, for example, Michlmayr, 2002.

might neurobiological and mathematical analyses then allow us to model MN processes computationally for machines? Arbib *et al.* (2000), Billard and Arbib (2002), and Demiris and Hayes (2002) describe mathematical MN models, but their systems seemingly involve automatic replication of what is viewed, and none describe, for example, how a robotic or computational system would recognize the social agent to be imitated, determine what actions should be imitated, or incorporate an understanding of why the action should be imitated (see Dautenhahn and Nehaniv, 2002). One might argue that success of the M/R system is dependent upon the subject already having, for example, both social awareness and motivation, but the former is usually initially lacking in the children seen by Sherman; the latter may also not be particularly strong in these individuals – and social awareness and motivation, interestingly, appear to be outcomes of M/R training. Nevertheless, our point is not that M/R training can necessarily engender such traits in robots or atavars, but rather that the creation of such traits in computational mechanisms (e.g. Billard, 2002; Breazeal and Scassellati, 2002) should not be seen as an end, but rather a beginning that can enable the implementation of M/R training. Such a scenario suggests how understanding the bases for imitation in animals and humans might assist in developing appropriate control programs for mechanical systems.

18.4   Conclusion: the future

Much is still to be determined about learning and imitation – for birds and children – but we again suggest that animal models can help us to understand mechanisms involved both in transitioning between simple and complex (advanced) learning and to develop computational mechanisms for imitation. To understand the transition, we must learn more about emergent processes: how do birds form representations and their syntax of imagery? How important is interaction/guidance? How important is emotional interaction? Will generalization occur without feedback? How closely do their processes parallel those in humans? For imitation, what is the role of M/R training? What is the role of awareness/"mindreading"? How do these issues correlate to MNs? Are MNs truly central to imitative processes? Once we understand these issues, particularly their causal elements, we can proceed further in achieving imitative learning in machines.

Acknowledgments

This paper was written with the support of the many donors to *The Alex Foundation* and the MIT School of Architecture and Planning, and edited with the support of the Radcliffe Institute for Advanced Studies. We thank two anonymous reviewers and Chrystopher Nehaniv for their helpful comments.

REFERENCES

Arbib, M. A. (2002). The mirror system, imitation, and the evolution of language. In K. Dautenhahn and C. L. Nehaniv (eds.), *Imitation in Animals and Artifacts*. Cambridge, MA: MIT Press, 229–79.

Arbib, M. A. (2005). From monkey-like action recognition to human language: an evolutionary framework for neurolinguistics. *Behavioral and Brain Sciences*, **28**, 105–67.

Arbib, M. A., Billard, A., Iacoboni, M. and Oztop, E. (2000). Synthetic brain imaging: grasping, mirror neurons and imitation. *Neural Networks*, **13**, 975–97.

Arbib, M. A. and Rizzolatti, G. (1996). Neural expectations: a possible evolutionary path from manual skills to language. *Communication and Cognition*, **29**, 393–424.

Avikainen, S., Kulomaeki, T. and Hari, R. (1999). Normal movement reading in Asperger subjects. *Neuroreport: For Rapid Communication of Neuroscience Research*, **10**, 3467–70.

Baldissera, F., Cavallari, P., Craighero, L. and Fadiga, L. (2001). Modulation of spinal excitability during observation of hand actions in humans. *European Journal of Neuroscience*, **13(1)**, 190–4.

Baldwin, D. A. (1995). Understanding the link between joint attention and language. In C. Moore and P. J. Dunham (eds.), *Joint Attention: Its Origin and Role in Development*. Hillsdale, NJ: Erlbaum Associates, 131–58.

Baron-Cohen, S., Wheelwright, S., Hill, J., Raste, Y. and Plumb, I. (2001). The "Reading the mind in the eyes" test revised version: a study with normal adults, and adults with Asperger syndrome or high-functioning autism. *Journal of Child Psychology and Psychiatry and Allied Disciplines*, **42(2)**, 241–51.

Billard, A. (2002). Imitation: a means to enhance learning of a synthetic protolanguage in autonomous robots. In K. Dautenhahn and C. L. Nehaniv (eds.), *Imitation in Animals and Artifacts*. Cambridge, MA: MIT Press, 281–310.

Billard, A. and Arbib, M. (2002). Mirror neurons and the neural basis for learning by imitation: computational modeling. In M. I. Stamenov (ed.), *Mirror Neurons and the Evolution of Brain and Language*. Philadelphia, PA: John Benjamins, 343–53.

Bloom, L. (2000). The intentionality model: how to learn a word, any word. In R. M. Golinkoff, K. Hirsh-Pasek, L. Bloom, L. B. Smith, A. L. Woodward, N. Akhtar, M. Tomasello and G. Hollich (eds.), *Becoming a Word Learner: A Debate on Lexical Acquisition*. New York: Oxford University Press, 124–35.

Breazeal, C. and Scassellati, B. (2002). Challenges in building robots that imitate people. In K. Dautenhahn and C. L. Nehaniv (eds.), *Imitation in Animals and Artifacts*. Cambridge, MA: MIT Press, 363–90.

Brown, R. (1973). *A First Language: the Early Stages*. Cambridge, MA: Harvard University Press.

Buccino, G., Binkofski, F., Fink, G. R., Fadiga, L., Fogassi, L., Galese, V., Seitz, R. J., Zilles, K., Rizzolatti, G. and Freund, H.-J. (2001). Action observation activates premotor and parietal areas in somatotopic manner: an fMRI study. *European Journal of Neurosciences*, **13**, 400–4.

Byrne, R. W. (2002). Imitation of novel complex actions: what does evidence from animals mean? In P. J. B. Slater, J. S. Rosenblatt, C. T. Snowdon and T. J. Roper (eds.), *Advances in the Study of Behavior*. San Diego, CA: Academic Press, Vol. 31, 77–105.

Call, J. and Carpenter, M. (2002). Three sources of imitation in social learning. In K. Dautenhahn and C. L. Nehaniv (eds.), *Imitation in Animals and Artifacts*. Cambridge, MA: MIT Press, 211–28.

Chaminade, T., Meary, D., Orliaguet, J.-P. and Decety, J. (2001). Is perceptual anticipation a motor simulation? A PET study. *Brain Imaging*, **12(17)**, 3669–74.

Chaminade, T., Meltzoff, A. N. and Decety, J. (2002). Does the end justify the means? A PET exploration of the mechanisms involved in human imitation. *NeuroImage*, **15**, 318–28.

Charlop, M. H., Schreibman, L. and Tryon, A. S. (1983). Learning through observation: the effects of peer modeling on acquisition and generalization in autistic children. *Journal of Abnormal Child Psychology*, **11(3)**, 355–66.

Damasio, A. (1999). *The Feeling of What Happens*. San Diego, CA: Harcourt, Inc.

Dautenhahn, K. and Nehaniv, C. L. (2002). The agent-based perspective on imitation. In K. Dautenhahn and C. L. Nehaniv (eds.), *Imitation in Animals and Artifacts*. Cambridge, MA: MIT Press, 1–40.

Demiris, J. and Hayes, G. (2002). Imitation as a dual-route process featuring predictive and learning components: a biologically plausible computational model. In K. Dautenhahn and C. L. Nehaniv (eds.), *Imitation in Animals and Artifacts*. Cambridge, MA: MIT Press, 327–62.

Fadiga, L., Craighero, L., Buccino, G. and Rizzolatti, G. (2002). Speech listening specifically modulates the excitability of tongue muscles: a TMS study. *European Journal of Neuroscience*, **15(2)**, 399–402.

Fadiga, L., Fogassi, L., Pavesi, G. and Rizzolatti, G. (1995). Motor facilitation during action observation: a magnetic stimulation study. *Journal of Neurophysiology*, **73**, 2608–11.

Fogassi, L. (2000). *Mirror neurons and language origin*. Paper presented at the International Conference on the Development of Mind, Tokyo, Japan, August.

Gallese, V. and Goldman, A. (1998). Mirror neurons and the simulation theory of mind-reading. *Trends in Cognitive Sciences*, **2**, 493–501.

Garfinkle, A. N. and Schwartz, I. S. (2002). Peer imitation: increasing social interactions in children with autism and other developmental disabilities in inclusive preschool classrooms. *Topics in Early Childhood Special Education*, **22(1)**, 26–38.

Ginsburg, N. (1960). Conditioned vocalization in the budgerigar. *Journal of Comparative and Physiological Psychology*, **53(2)**, 183–6.

Ginsburg, N. (1963). Conditioned vocalization in the mynah bird. *Journal of Comparative and Physiological Psychology*, **56(6)**, 1061–3.

Gordon, R. M. and Barker, J. A. (1994). Autism and the "theory of mind" debate. In G. Graham and G. L. Stephens (eds.), *Philosophical Psychopathology*. Cambridge, MA: MIT Press, 163–81.

Gossette, R. L. (1969/1980). Personal communication to O. H. Mowrer. *Psychology of Language and Learning*. New York: Plenum Press, 105–6.

Gramza, A. F. (1970). Vocal mimicry in captive budgerigars (*Melopsittacus undulatus*). *Zeitschrift für Tierpsychologie*, 27(8), 971–83.

Grosslight, J. H. and Zaynor, W. C. (1967). Vocal behavior of the mynah bird. In K. Salzinger and S. Salzinger (eds.), *Research in Verbal Behavior and Some Neuro-physiological Implications*. New York: Academic Press, 5–9.

Grosslight, J. H., Zaynor, W. C. and Lively, B. L. (1964). Speech as a stimulus for differential vocal behavior in the mynah bird (*Gracula religiosa*). *Psychonomic Science*, 11, 7–8.

Hadwin, J., Baron-Cohen, S., Howlin, P. and Hill, K. (1996). Can we teach children with autism to understand emotions, belief, or pretence? *Development and Psychopathology*, 8(2), 345–65.

Hobson, P. R. and Lee, A. (1999). Imitation and identification in autism. *Journal of Child Psychology and Psychiatry*, 40(4), 649–59.

Hollich, G. J., Hirsh-Pasek, K. and Golinkoff, R. M. (2000). Breaking the language barrier: an emergentist coalition model for the origins of word learning. *Monographs of the Society for Research in Child Development*, 262, 1–138.

Hurley, S. and Chater, N. (eds.) (2005). *Perspectives on Imitation: From Neuroscience to Social Science*. Cambridge, MA: MIT Press.

Ihrig, K. and Wolchik, S. A. (1988). Peer versus adult models and autistic children's learning: acquisition, generalization, and maintenance. *Journal of Autism and Developmental Disorders*, 18(1), 67–79.

Jaervelaeinen, J., Schürmann, M., Avikainen, S., Hari, R. (2001). Stronger reactivity of the human primary motor cortex during observation of live rather than video motor acts. *Neuroreport: For Rapid Communication of Neuroscience Research*, 12(16), 3493–5.

Jarvis, E. D. (2004). Learned birdsong and the neurobiology of human language. *Annals of the New York Academy of Sciences*, 1016, 749–77.

Jarvis, E., Güntürkün, O., Bruce, L., Csillag, A., Karten, H., Kuenzel, W., Medina, L., Paxinos, G., Perkel, D. J., Shimizu, T., Striedter, G., Wild, J. M., Ball, G. F., Dugas-Ford, J., Durand, S. E., Hough, G. E., Husband, S., Kubikova, L., Lee, D. W., Mello, C. V., Powers, A., Siang, C., Smulders, T. V., Wada, K., White, S. A., Yamamoto, K., Yu, J., Reiner, A. and Butler, A. B. (2005). Avian brains and a new understanding of vertebrate evolution. *Nature Reviews Neuroscience*, 6, 151–9.

Jarvis, E. D. and Mello, C. V. (2000). Molecular mapping of brain areas involved in parrot vocal communication. *Journal of Comparative Neurology*, 419, 1–31.

Jellema, T., Baker, C. I., Wicker, B. and Perrett, D. I. (2000). Neural representation for the perception of the intentionality of actions. *Brain and Cognition*, 44, 280–302.

King, J. E. (1966). Transfer relationships between learning set and concept formation in rhesus monkeys. *Journal of Comparative and Physiological Psychology*, 61(3), 414–20.

Koegel, R. L. and Rincover, A. (1974). Treatment of psychotic children in a class-room environment: I. Learning in a large group. *Journal of Applied Behavior Analysis*, **7(1)**, 45–59.

Lanquetot, R. (1989). The effectiveness of peer modeling with autistic children. *Journal of the Multi-handicapped Person*, **2(1)**, 25–34.

Lenneberg, E. H. (1971). Of language, knowledge, apes, and brains. *Journal of Psycholinguistic Research*, **1(1)**, 1–29.

Lenneberg, E. H. (1973). Biological aspects of language. In G. A. Miller (ed.), *Communication, Language, and Meaning*. New York: Basic Books, 49–60.

Lieberman, H. (ed.) (2001). *Your Wish Is My Command: Programming by Example*. San Francisco, CA: Morgan Kaufmann/Academic Press.

Lovibond, P. F. and Shanks, D. R. (2002). The role of awareness in Pavlovian conditioning: empirical evidence and theoretical implications. *Journal of Experimental Psychology: Animal Behavior Processes*, **28(1)**, 3–26.

Marler, P. (1970). A comparative approach to vocal learning: song development in white-crowned sparrows. *Journal of Comparative and Physiological Psychology*, **71**, 1–25.

Mebes, H.-D. (1978). Pair-specific duetting in the Peach-faced Lovebird *Naturwissenschaften*, **65**, 66–7.

Michlmayr, M. (2002). Simulation theory versus theory theory: theories concerning the ability to read minds. *Diplomarbeit zur Erlangung des akademischen Grades eines Magisters an der Geisteswissenschaftl -ichen Fakultät der Leopold-Franzens-Universität Innsbruck*.

Mowrer, O. H. (1952). The autism theory of speech development and some clinical applications. *Journal of Speech and Hearing Disorders*, **17**, 263–8.

Mowrer, O. H. (1954). A psychologist looks at language. *American Psychologist*, **9**, 660–9.

Mowrer, O. H. (1969/1980). *Theory and Research – A Review*. Urbana: University of Illinois. Mimeographed, cited in O. Hobart Mowrer, *Psychology of Language and Learning*. New York: Plenum Press.

Pepperberg, I. M. (1985). Social modeling theory: a possible framework for understanding avian vocal learning. *Auk*, **102(4)**, 854–64.

Pepperberg, I. M. (1990). Cognition in an African Grey parrot (*Psittacus erithacus*): further evidence for comprehension of categories and labels. *Journal of Comparative Psychology*, **104(1)**, 41–52.

Pepperberg, I. M. (1994). Vocal learning in African Grey parrots: effects of social interaction. *Auk*, **111(2)**, 300–13.

Pepperberg, I. M. (1999). *The Alex Studies*. Cambridge, MA: Harvard University Press.

Pepperberg, I. M. (2001). Lessons from cognitive ethology: animals models for ethological computing. *Proceedings of Epigenetic Robots, Lund, Sweden*, September, 5–12.

Pepperberg, I. M. (2002) Allospecific referential speech acquisition in Grey parrots (*Psittacus erithacus*): evidence for multiple levels of avian vocal imitation. In K. Dautenhahn and C. L. Nehaniv (eds.), *Imitation in Animals and Artifacts*. Cambridge, MA: MIT Press, 109–31.

Pepperberg, I. M. (2004). Evolution of communication from an avian perspective. In K. Oller and U. Grieble (eds.), *Evolution of Communication*. Cambridge, MA: MIT Press, 171–92.

Pepperberg, I. M. (2005). Insights into vocal imitation in Grey Parrots (*Psittacus erithacus*). In S. L. Hurley, N. Chater (eds.), *Perspectives on Imitation*. Cambridge, MA: MIT Press, Vol. 1, 243–62.

Pepperberg, I. M. and Brezinsky, M. V. (1991). Relational learning by an African Grey parrot (*Psittacus erithacus*): discriminations based on relative size. *Journal of Comparative Psychology*, **105(3)**, 286–94.

Pepperberg, I. M. and Lynn, S. K. (2000). Possible levels of animal consciousness with reference to Grey parrots. *American Zoologist*, **40(6)**, 893–901.

Pepperberg, I. M. and McLaughlin, M. A. (1996). Effect of avian–human joint attention on vocal learning by Grey parrots (*Psittacus erithacus*). *Journal of Comparative Psychology*, **110(3)**, 286–97.

Pepperberg, I. M., Gardiner, L. I. and Luttrell, L. J. (1999). Limited contextual vocal learning in the Grey parrot (*Psittacus erithacus*): the effect of co-viewers on videotaped instruction. *Journal of Comparative Psychology*, **113(2)**, 158–72.

Pepperberg, I. M., Naughton, J. R. and Banta, P. A. (1998). Allospecific vocal learning by grey parrots (*Psittacus erithacus*): A failure of videotaped instruction under certain conditions. *Behavioural Processes*, **42(2–3)**, 139–158.

Pepperberg, I. M., Sandefer, R. M., Noel, D. A. and Ellsworth, C. P. (2000). Vocal learning in the Grey Parrot (*Psittacus erithacus*): effect of species identity and number of trainers. *Journal of Comparative Psychology*, **114(4)**, 371–80.

Pepperberg, I. M. and Sherman, D. V. (2000). Proposed use of two-part interactive modeling as a means to increase functional skills in children with a variety of disabilities. *Teaching and Learning in Medicine*, **12(4)**, 213–20.

Pepperberg, I. M. and Sherman, D. V. (2002). Use of two-part interactive modeling as a potential means to engender social behavior in children with various disabilities. *International Journal of Comparative Psychology*, **15**, 138–53.

Pepperberg, I. M. and Sherman, D. V. (2004). Use of two-part interactive modeling as a potential means to engender empathy in children within the autistic spectrum. *IMFAR conference, Sacramento, CA*.

Pepperberg, I. M. and Shive, H. R. (2001). Simultaneous development of vocal and physical object combinations by a Grey parrot (*Psittacus erithacus*): bottle caps, lids, and labels. *Journal of Comparative Psychology*, **115(4)**, 376–84.

Pierce, K. and Schreibman, L. (1995). Increasing complex social behaviors in children with autism: effects of peer-implemented pivotal response training. *Journal of Applied Behavior Analysis*, **28(3)**, 285–95.

Pierce, K. and Schreibman, L. (1997a). Multiple peer use of pivotal response training social behaviors of classmates with autism: results from trained and untrained peers. *Journal of Applied Behavior Analysis*, **30(1)**, 157–60.

Pierce, K. and Schreibman, L. (1997b). Using peer trainers to promote social behavior in autism: are they effective at enhancing multiple social modalities? *Focus on Autism and Other Developmental Disabilities*, **12(4)**, 207–18.

Pollard, I. (2001). A comparison of the model/rival approach and a standard approach for teaching children with autism to understand belief, emotion and pretence. MA thesis, Department of Psychology, University of New England, Armidale, New South Wales, Australia.

Premack, D. (1978). On the abstractness of human concepts: why it would be difficult to talk to a pigeon. In S. H. Hulse, H. Fowler and W. K. Honig (eds.), *Cognitive Processes in Animal Behavior*. Hillsdale, NJ: Erlbaum Associates, 421–51.

Premack, D. (1983). The codes of man and beasts. *Behavioral and Brain Sciences*, **6**, 125–67.

Rizzolatti, G., Fogassi, L. and Gallese, V. (2001). Neurophysiological mechanisms underlying the understanding and imitation of actions. *Nature Review Neurology*, **2**, 661–70.

Ruby, P. and Decety, J. (2001). Effect of subjective perspective taking during simulation of action: a PET investigation of agency. *Nature Neuroscience*, **4(5)**, 546–50.

Rumbaugh, D. M. and Pate, J. L. (1984). Primates learning by levels. In G. Greenberg and E. Tobach (eds.), *Behavioral Evolution and Integrative Levels*. Hillsdale. NJ: Erlbaum, 221–40.

Savage-Rumbaugh, S., Murphy, J., Sevcik, R. A., Brakke, K. E., Williams, S. L. and Rumbaugh, D. M. (1993). Language comprehension in ape and child. *Monographs of the Society for Research in Child Development*, **233**, 1–258.

Schlesinger, M. and Parisi, D. (2004). Beyond backprop: emerging trends in connectionist models of development: an introduction. *Developmental Science*, 7, 131–2.

Sherratt, D. (2002). Developing pretend play in children with autism: a case study. *Autism*, **6(2)**, 169–79.

Smith, I. M. and Bryson, S. E. (1994). Imitation and action in autism: a critical review. *Psychological Bulletin*, **116(2)**, 259–73.

Strain, P. S., Kerr, M. M. and Ragland, E. U. (1979). Effects of peer-mediated social initiations and prompting/reinforcement procedures on the social behavior of autistic children. *Journal of Autism and Developmental Disorders*, **9(1)**, 41–54.

Striedter, G. (1994). The vocal control pathways in budgerigars differ from those in songbirds. *Journal of Comparative Neurology*, **343**, 35–56.

Tager-Flusberg, H. (2000). Language and understanding minds: connections in autism. In S. Baron-Cohen, H. Tager-Flusberg and D. J. Cohen (eds.), *Understanding Other Minds: Perspectives from Developmental Cognitive Neuroscience*. Oxford, UK: Oxford University Press, 124–49.

Thorpe, W. N. (1974). *Animal and Human Nature*. New York: Doubleday.

Thorpe, W. N. and North, M. E. W. (1965). Origin and significance of the power of vocal imitation: with special reference to the antiphonal singing of birds. *Nature*, **208**, 19–222.

Todt, D. (1975). Social learning of vocal patterns and modes of their applications in Grey parrots. *Zeitschrift für Tierpsychologie*, **39**, 178–88.

Tomasello, M. (1999). *The Cultural Origins of Human Cognition*. Cambridge, MA: Harvard University Press.

Visalberghi, E. and Fragaszy, D. M. (2002). "Do monkeys ape?" Ten years after. In K. Dautenhahn and C. L. Nehaniv (eds.), *Imitation in Animals and Artifacts*. Cambridge MA: MIT Press, 471–99.

Wessberg, J., Stambaugh, C. R., Kralik, J. D., Beck, P. D., Laubach, M., Chapin, J. K., Kim, J., Biggs, S. J., Srinivasan, M. A. and Nicolelis, M. A. L. (2000). Real-time prediction of hand trajectory by ensembles of cortical neurons in primates. *Nature*, **408**, 361–5.

Whiten, A. (2002). Imitation of sequential and hierarchical structure in action: experimental studies with children and chimpanzees. In K. Dautenhahn and C. L. Nehaniv (eds.), *Imitation in Animals and Artifacts*. Cambridge, MA: MIT Press, 191–210.

Williams, J. H. G., Whiten, A., Suddendorf, T. and Perrett, D. I. (2001). Imitation, mirror neurons and autism. *Neuroscience and Biobehavioral Reviews*, **25**, 287–95.

Wolf, N. S., Gales, M. E., Shane, E. and Shane, M. (2001). The developmental trajectory from amodal perception to empathy and communication: the role of mirror neurons in this process. *Psychoanalytic Inquiry*, **21(1)**, 94–112.

Woodard, W. T. and Bitterman, M. E. (1972). Further studies of reversal learning with singly presented stimuli in pigeons and goldfish. *Psychonomic Science*, **28**, 170–2.

19 Task learning through imitation and human–robot interaction

Monica N. Nicolescu and Maja J. Matarić

19.1 Introduction

Human–robot interaction is a rapidly growing area of robotics. Environments that feature the interaction of humans and robots present a number of challenges involving robot *learning (imitative)* and *interactive* capabilities. The two problems are tightly related since, on the one hand, social interaction is often an important aspect of imitation learning and, on the other, imitative behavior enhances a robot's social and interactive capabilities. In this work we present a framework that unifies these issues, providing a natural means for robots to interact with people and to learn from interactive experiences.

We focus on two major challenges. The first is the design of robot social capabilities that allow for engagement in various types of interactions. Examples include robot teachers (David and Ball, 1986), workers, team members (Matsui *et al.*, 1997), museum tour-guides (Thrun *et al.*, 1999), toys (Michaud and Caron, 2002), and emotional companions (Breazeal, 2002; Cañamero and Fredslund, 2000). Designing control architectures for such robots presents various, often domain-specific, challenges.

The second challenge we address is endowing robots with the ability to learn through social interaction with humans or other robots, in order to improve their performance and expand their capabilities. Learning by imitation (Dautenhahn and Nehaniv, 2002; Hayes and Demiris, 1994; Schaal, 1997) provides a most natural approach to this problem; methods using gestures (Voyles and Khosla, 1998), natural language (Lauria *et al.*, 2002), and animal "clicker training" (Kaplan *et al.*, 2002) have also been successfully applied.

We present an approach that unifies the above two challenges, interaction and learning in human–robot environments, by unifying perception

Imitation and Social Learning in Robots, Humans and Animals, ed. Chrystopher L. Nehaniv and Kerstin Dautenhahn. Published by Cambridge University Press.
© Cambridge University Press 2007.

and action in the form of *action-based interaction*. Our approach uses an architecture that is based on a set of behaviors or skills consisting of *active* and *perceptual* components. The *perceptual* component of a behavior gives the robot the capability of creating a mapping between its observations and its own actions, enabling it to learn to perform a particular task from the experiences it had while interacting with humans. The *active* component of a robot behavior allows the use of implicit communication based on action whose outcomes are invariant of the specific body performing them. A robot can thus convey its intentions by suggesting them through actions, rather than communicating them through conventional signs, sounds, gestures or symbols with previously agreed-upon meanings. We employ these actions as a vocabulary that a robot uses to induce a human to assist it for parts of tasks that it is not able to perform on its own.

To illustrate our approach, we present experiments in which a human acts both as a collaborator and as a demonstrator for a mobile robot. The different aspects of the interaction demonstrate the robot's learning and social abilities.

19.2   Action-based representations

Perception and action are the essential means of interaction with the environment. A robot's capabilities are dependent on its available actions, and are thus an essential component of its design. The underlying control architecture we use is behavior-based (Matarić, 1997; Arkin, 1998). Behaviors are time-extended sequences of actions (e.g. *go-home, avoid-obstacles*) that achieve or maintain certain goals and are different than low-granularity single actions (e.g. *turn-left-by-10-degrees*).

Within our architecture, behaviors are built from two components, one related to perception (*abstract behavior*), the other to action (*primitive behavior*) (Figure 19.1). Abstract behaviors are explicit specifications of the activation conditions (pre-conditions) and effects (post-conditions). Primitive behaviors perform the work that achieves the effects specified by those conditions. Specifically, an abstract behavior takes sensory information from the environment and, when its pre-conditions are met, activates the corresponding primitive behavior(s) which achieve the effects specified in its post-conditions.

Using these types of behaviors, the architecture provides a natural way of representing robot tasks as hierarchical behavior networks (Nicolescu and Matarić, 2002) (Figure 19.2), and has the flexibility required for robust function in dynamically changing environments. This

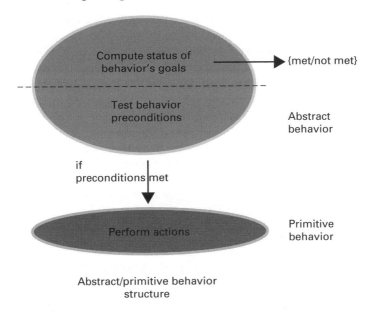

Abstract/primitive behavior
structure

Figure 19.1 Structure of the inputs/outputs of an abstract and primitive behavior.

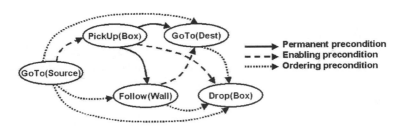

Figure 19.2 Example of a behavior network.

architecture is capable of computations required by more traditional symbolic architectures, but also uses behaviors continuously grounded in perception.

Abstract behaviors embed representations of goals in the form of abstracted environmental states. This is a key feature critical for learning from experience. To learn a task, the robot must create a mapping between its perception (observations) and its own behaviors that achieve the observed effects. This process is enabled by abstract behaviors, the perceptual component of a behavior, which activate each time the robot's observations match the goal(s) of a primitive behavior. This correlation enables the robot to identify its own behaviors that are relevant for the task being learned.

Primitive behaviors execute the robot's actions and achieve its goals. They are also used for communication and interaction. Acting in the environment is a form of implicit communication. By using evocative actions, people and other animals convey emotions, desires, interests and intentions. Action-based communication has the advantage that it need not be restricted to robots or agents with a humanoid body or face: structural similarities between interacting agents are not required for successful interaction. Even if there is no direct mapping between the physical characteristics of the robot and its user, the robot can still use communication through action to convey certain types of messages, drawing on human common sense (Dennett, 1987).

19.3   Communication by acting – a means for robot–human interaction

Consider a pre-linguistic child who wants an out-of-reach toy. The child will try to bring a grown-up to the toy and will then point and reach, indicating his desires. Similarly, a dog will run back and forth to induce its owner to come to a place where it has found something it desires. The ability of the child and the dog to demonstrate their desires and intentions by calling a helper and mock-executing actions is an expressive and natural way to communicate a problem and need for help. The human capacity to understand these intentions is also natural and inherent. We apply the same strategy in enabling robots to communicate their desires and intentions to people.

The action-based communication approach we propose is general and can be applied on a variety of tasks and physical bodies/platforms. The robot performs its task independently, but if it fails in a cognizant fashion, it searches for a human and attempts to induce him to follow it to the place where the failure occurred, and then demonstrates its intentions in hopes of obtaining help. Attracting a human to help is achieved through movement, using back-and-forth, cyclic actions. After capturing the human's attention, the robot leads the human helper to the site of the task and attempts to resume its work from the point where it failed. To communicate the nature of the problem, the robot repeatedly tries to execute the failed behavior in front of its helper. This is a general strategy that can be employed for a wide variety of failures but, notably, not for all. Executing the previously failed behavior will likely fail again, effectively expressing the robot's problem to the human observer.

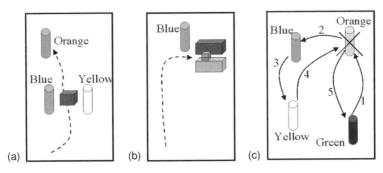

Figure 19.3 The human–robot interaction experiments setup.

19.3.1 Experiments in communication by acting

We implemented and tested our concepts on a Pioneer 2-DX mobile robot, equipped with two sonar rings (eight front and eight rear), a SICK laser range-finder, a pan-tilt-zoom color camera, a gripper and on-board computation on a PC104 stack. The robot had a behavior set that allowed it to track cylindrical colored targets (**Track** (*ColorOfTarget, GoalAngle, GoalDistance*)), to pick up (**PickUp**(*ColorOfObject*)) and to drop small colored objects **Drop**. These behaviors were implemented in AYLLU (Werger, 2000).

In the validation experiments, we asked a person that had not worked with the robot before to be near-by during task execution and to expect to be engaged in an interaction. There is no initial assumption that people will be helpful or motivated to assist the robot. The robot is able to deal with unhelpful or misleading humans by monitoring their presence along with its progress in the task. The following main categories of interactions emerged from the experiments:

- *Uninterested*: the human was not interested, did not react to, or did not understand the robot's need for help. As a result, the robot searched for another helper.
- *Interested but unhelpful*: the human was interested and followed the robot for a while, but then abandoned it. As above, the robot searched for another helper.
- *Helpful*: the human was interested, followed the robot to the location of the problem, and assisted the robot. In these cases, the robot was able to finish the task.

We purposefully constrained the environment used in the experiments to encourage human–robot interaction, as follows:

- *Traversing blocked gates*: the robot's task was to pass through a gate formed by two closely placed colored targets (Figure 19.3(a)), but its path was blocked by a large box. The robot expressed its intentions by executing the **Track** behavior, making its way around one of the targets. Trying to reach the desired distance and angle to the target while being hindered by the box resulted in its clear manifestation of the direction it wanted to pursue, blocked by the obstacle.
- *Moving inaccessible located objects*: the robot's task was to pick up a small object which was made inaccessible by being placed in a narrow space between two large boxes (Figure 19.3(b)). The robot expressed its intentions by attempting to execute the **PickUp** behavior, lowering and opening its gripper and tilting its camera downward while approaching the object, and then moving backwards to avoid the boxes.
- *Visiting non-existing targets*: the robot's task was to visit a number of targets in a specific order (green, orange, blue, yellow, orange, green), in an environment where one of the targets had been removed (Figure 19.3(c)). After some time, the robot gave up searching for the missing target and sought out a human helper. The robot expressed its intentions by searching for a target, which appeared as aimless wandering. This behavior was not conducive for the human to infer the robot's goal and problem. In this and similar situations, our framework would benefit from more explicit communication.

19.3.2   Discussion

From the experimental results (Nicolescu and Matarić, 2001b) and the interviews and report of the human subject who interacted with the robot, we derived the following conclusions about the robot's social behavior:

- Capturing a human's attention by approaching and then going back-and-forth is a behavior typically easily recognized and interpreted as soliciting help.
- Getting a human to follow by turning around and starting to go to the place where the problem occurred (after capturing the human's attention) requires multiple trials in order for the human to follow the robot the entire way. Even if interested and realizing that the robot wants something from him, the human may have trouble understanding that *following* is the desired behavior. Also, after choosing to follow the robot, if wandering in search of the place with the problem takes too long, the human gives up not knowing whether the robot still needs him.
- Conveying intentions by repeating a failing behavior in front of a helper is effective for tasks in which the task components requiring help are observable to the human (such as the blocked gate). However, if some

part of the task is not observable (such as the missing target), the human cannot infer it from the robot's behavior and thus is not able to help (at least not without trial and error).

19.4   Learning from imitation and additional cues

Learning by observation and imitation are especially effective means of human skill acquisition. As skill or task complexity increases, however, teaching typically involves increased concurrent use of multiple instructional modalities, including demonstration, verbal instruction, attentional cues and gestures. Students/learners are typically given one or a few demonstrations of the task, followed by a set of supervised practice trials. During those, the teacher provides *feedback cues* indicating needed corrections. The teacher may also provide additional demonstrations that could be used for *generalization*. While most of these learning and teaching tools are typically overlooked in the majority of robot teaching approaches, considering them collectively improves the imitation learning process considerably.

Toward this end, we developed a method for learning representations of high level tasks. Specifically, we augmented imitation learning by allowing the demonstrator to employ additional instructive activities (verbal commands and attentional cues) and by refining the learned representations through generalization from multiple learning experiences and through direct feedback from the teacher.

In our work, the robot is equipped with a set of skills in the form of behaviors (Matarić, 1997; Arkin, 1998); we focus on a strategy that enables it to use those behaviors to construct a high-level task representation of a novel, complex, sequentially structured task. We use *learning by experienced demonstrations* in which the robot actively participates in the demonstration provided by the teacher, experiencing the task through its own sensors, an essential characteristic of our approach. We assume that the teacher knows what behaviors the robot has, and also by what means (sensors) the robot can perceive demonstrations. The advantage of putting the robot through the task during the demonstration is that the robot is able to adjust its behaviors (via their parameters) using the information gathered through its own sensors: the values of all behaviors' parameters are learned directly from sensory information obtained from the environment. In addition, executing the task during the demonstration provides observations that contain temporal information for proper behavior sequencing (which would otherwise be tedious to design by hand).

During the demonstration the robot follows the teacher while all of its behaviors continuously monitor the status of their post-conditions

Nicolescu and Matarić

(without executing any of their actions). Whenever the robot's observations match the goals of one or more primitive behavior, this means the robot has observed something it is also able to perform, and the corresponding abstract behavior activates, allowing the robot to learn which of its own behaviors are relevant for the particular portion of the task being demonstrated. Feedback cues received from the teacher are used in conjunction with these observations, to eliminate any irrelevant observations.

The general idea of our task-learning algorithm is to add to the robot's behavior network an instance of all behaviors whose post-conditions have been detected as true during the demonstration, and during which there have been relevance signals from the teacher, in the order of their occurrence (on-line stage). At the end of the teaching experience, the intervals of time when the effects of each of the behaviors were true are known, and are used to determine if these effects were active in overlapping intervals or in sequence. Based on that information, the algorithm generates proper dependency links (*permanent, enabling* or *ordering*) between behaviors (off-line stage). This one-step learning process is described in detail in Nicolescu and Matarić (2001b).

Through this process, the robot may learn a correct, but over-specialized version of the task. Two types of errors can occur in the learning process: learning irrelevant steps (false positives) and omission of steps that are relevant (false negatives). It is thus important that the robot can generalize over multiple demonstrations and incorporate additional feedback from the demonstrator. To enable a robot to generalize from multiple demonstrations of the same task (presented in similar or different environments), we build a task representation that encodes the specifics of each of the given examples, and also incorporates their common components (Nicolescu and Matarić, 2003). However, repeated observations of irrelevant steps will also inadvertently lead the learner to include them in the learned representation. Also, limitations in robot sensing and challenging structures in the environment may prevent the robot from observing some relevant steps.

To address these issues, we allow the teacher to provide feedback to the robot while observing the robot's execution of the learned task, during practice experiments. The teacher signals any detected errors as they occur, through appropriate feedback cues (as spoken commands). The provided feedback allows the robot to eliminate irrelevant observations and, by re-demonstrating relevant steps that were previously missed, the demonstrator enables the robot to make its learned task representation more complete (Nicolescu and Matarić, 2003).

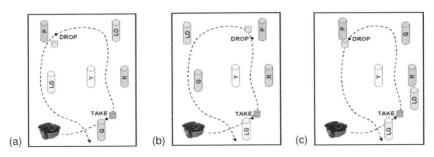

Figure 19.4 Structure of the environment and course of demonstration.

19.4.1 Experiments in learning from multiple cues

We implemented and tested our approach to learning with additional cues on the Pioneer 2-DX mobile robot described in Section 19.3.1 For the voice commands and feedback we used an off-the-shelf Logitech cordless headset, and the IBM ViaVoice software recognition engine. We performed two sets of robot teaching experiments to validate the key features of the proposed approach.

Generalization from a small number of examples

In the first experiment set, we demonstrated the robot's generalization capabilities by teaching it an object transport task in three consecutive demonstrations, performed in different environments (Figure 19.4), and designed to contain incorrect steps and inconsistencies.

The environment consisted of a set of colored cylindrical targets. The teacher lead the robot around those, instructing it when to pick up or drop a small orange box. The task to be learned was as follows: go to either the *green* (G) or the *light green* (LG) targets, pick up an *orange* (O) box, go between the *yellow* (Y) and *red* (R) targets, go to the *pink* (P) target, drop the box there, then go to the *light orange* (LO) target, and come back to the *light green* target.

The shown courses of the three demonstrations illustrate that none corresponded exactly to the intended task description. Some contained unnecessary steps (such as a final visit to a green target in the first trial), and some had inconsistencies (such as the visits to the light orange target at various demonstration stages). Figure 19.5 shows the task representations (their topological form) obtained after each learning demonstration, followed by generalization. The topological representation of a task network is obtained by applying a topological sort on the behavior network graph; this representation shows the succession of behavior execution for

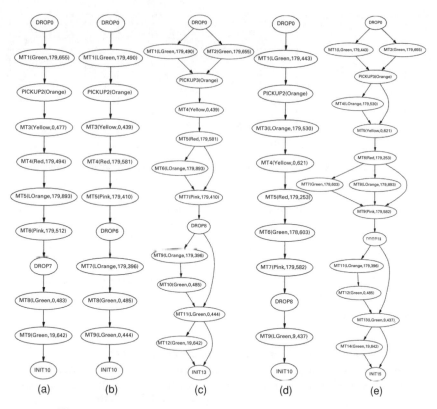

Figure 19.5 Evolution of the task representation over three successive demonstrations.

the task. With generalization, the following types of alternative paths can be obtained:
- Both paths contain actual behaviors. For example, Figure 19.5(c) encodes the fact that both going to the green or to the light green targets is acceptable for the task. Given such alternate paths, the robot chooses opportunistically, as induced by the state of the environment (e.g. go to the target seen first).
- One path is a direct link to the end of the other alternate sequence. In Figure 19.5(c), there is a direct link from MT5(Red, . . .) to MT7(Pink, . . .), bypassing the behavior MT6(LOrange, . . .). For such paths, the robot automatically chooses the direct path, short-cutting the alternate sequence.

The generalized representation captures the main structure of the task while correctly treating the irrelevant and inconsistent components: they are captured as parts of a by-passed alternate path that will never be

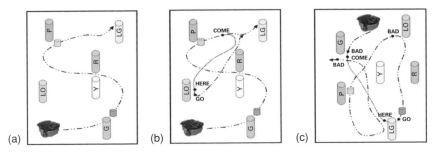

Figure 19.6 Structure of the environment and course of task execution during practice and feedback.

executed. While irrelevant actions are thus effectively pruned, any necessary but inconsistently demonstrated steps would have to be included by different means. This is to be expected; generalization alone, when provided with inconsistent examples, is not sufficient for learning a correct representation. The next section shows how practice and teacher feedback can be used for solving this problem.

Learning from practice and teacher feedback
We allowed the robot to refine the previously learned task representation through practice (Figure 19.5(e)) in a different environment (Figure 19.6(a)). Figure 19.6(b) shows the robot's trajectory and the teacher's intervention (dotted). After dropping the box at the destination pink target, the robot started moving toward the light green target. Observing this, the teacher intervened ("COME") and demonstrated to the robot the step it had missed (i.e. the visit to the light orange target). During this stage, the demonstrator also made use of informative feedback cues ("HERE") to prevent the robot from considering passing by irrelevant targets (pink and yellow in this case) as relevant visits. The teacher signaled that it finished demonstrating the missing step ("GO"), after which the robot continued with and finished the task by itself. Figure 19.7(a) shows the structure of the task after this practice run. The newly added steps are marked on the graph: they also include a **Drop** behavior, as the robot had nothing in the gripper at the point of the demonstration, and therefore the goals of this behavior were also detected as true. At execution time, the existence of this behavior had no influence, since the robot had already dropped the object.

We now consider an alternate approach for instruction, starting from the first demonstration in the previous section (Figure 19.4(a), 19.5(a)). Assume that, for a second object transport task, the teacher considered the initial visit to a green target wrong, and that the light green target

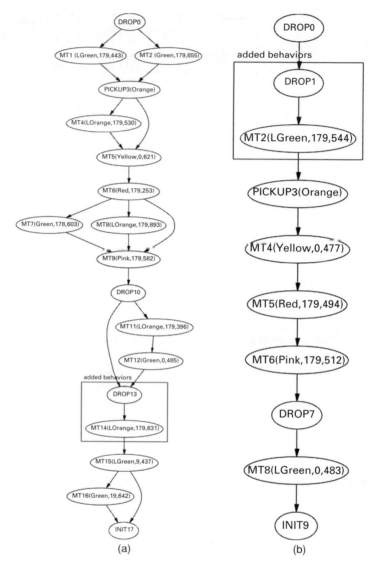

Figure 19.7 Topologies obtained after practice and feedback.

should have been visited instead. Furthermore, the visit to the light orange target was also wrong, and not a part of the task to be learned. Figure 19.6(c) shows the trajectory of the robot and the intervention (dotted) and messages of the teacher during the robot's practice run. The effects of the teacher feedback were that: the visit to the green target was replaced by a visit to the light green target, and the visits to the light orange and green were removed. Figure 19.7(b) presents the structure of the task after this practice run.

The robot correctly executed the tasks learned after both of the above practice runs. In each case, it successfully adapted its task representations according to the teacher's feedback, resulting in a graph structure that matched the user's target tasks.

19.4.2 Discussion

The spectrum of tasks learnable with our method includes all tasks achievable with the robot's basic set of behaviors. If the robot is shown actions for which it does not have any representation, it will not be able to observe or learn from those experiences. For the purposes of our research, it is reasonable to accept this constraint; we are not aiming at teaching a robot new behaviors, but at showing the robot how to use its existing capabilities to perform more complicated tasks.

An additional factor influencing the performance of the proposed learning approach is the level of robotics expertise of the trainer. In prior experiments we had two non-expert users (Nicolescu, 2003) serve as teachers to another robot. The results indicated that it is possible for these users to learn how to successfully teach the robot a task in a small number of trials, and with no other prior training. We have also demonstrated that the approach works for learning from robot teachers, which have significantly less expertise (Nicolescu and Matarić, 2001a).

The *practice–feedback* experiments described above are a fast and precise method for refining previously learned tasks, since errors can be naturally indicated by the teacher immediately upon being noticed. To give the robot appropriate feedback, the teacher does not need to know the structure of the task being learned or the details of the robot's control architecture.

19.5 Related work

The presented work is most related to human–robot interaction (HRI) and robot learning. Most HRI approaches so far rely on using predefined, common *vocabularies* of gestures (Kortenkamp et al., 1996), signs, or words. They can be said to be using *symbolic languages*, whose elements explicitly communicate specific meanings. One of the most important forms of implicit communication, on the other hand, is *body language*. It has been applied to humanoid robots (in particular

420   Nicolescu and Matarić

head-eye systems), for communicating emotional states through facial expressions (Breazeal and Scassellati, 1999) or body movements (Cañamero and Fredslund, 2000). Facial expressions cannot be readily applied to mobile robots whose platforms typically have non-anthropomorphic or non-biomimetic physical structure. The work we described demonstrates how the use of implicit, action-based methods for communication and expression of intention can be applied to the mobile robot domain, despite the structural differences between mobile robots and humans, and also how communication between robots and humans can be achieved without explicit prior vocabulary sharing.

Endowing robots with the ability to imitate is of growing interest in robotics (Billard and Dautenhahn, 1999; Gaussier and Quoy, 1998). In the mobile robot domain, Hayes and Demiris (1994) demonstrate learning to navigate a maze (learning forward, left, and right turning behaviors) by following another robot. In the humanoid robot domain, Schaal (1997) used model-based reinforcement learning to speed up learning for a system in which a seven DOF robot arm learned the task of balancing a pole from a brief human demonstration. Other work (Matarić, 2002; Jenkins et al., 2000), related to ours in philosophy, explored imitation based on mapping observed human demonstration onto a set of behavior primitives, implemented on a 20-DOF dynamic humanoid simulation. Drumwright et al. (2004) describes how the behavior primitives are learned and how they are recognized and classified in the imitation process. The key difference between that work and ours is at the level of learning: the above work focuses on learning at the level of action imitation (and thus usually results in acquiring reactive policies), while our approach enables learning of high-level, sequential tasks.

Ramesh and Matarić (2002a) have demonstrated a hierarchical architecture for learning by imitation, employing HMMs to learn sequences (and thus potentially tasks) of primitive behaviors which are themselves learned and clustered. Ramesh and Matarić (2002b) describe related work on learning by imitation using two levels of primitives, the higher level employing self-organizing maps to combine (but not sequence) the lower-level primitives.

The above techniques use demonstration as the sole means for teaching and the complexity of the learned tasks is limited to reactive policies or short sequences of sensory–motor primitives. Our approach allows for learning high-level tasks that involve arbitrarily long sequences of behaviors. Methods for robot task teaching that consider additional instructive modalities in addition to demonstration have also been proposed. Kaiser (1997) presents an approach in which *good/not good* feedback was given at the end of a run in which the robot performed the demonstrated skill. However, such delayed reward generates problems of credit assignment; our approach relies on immediate feedback. Friedrich and Dillmann (1995) consider fusing user intention with demonstration information as additional means for instruction. The approach enables the robot to successfully learn the correct task, but may become burdensome as the teacher is expected to provide, at each step, information on what goals he has in mind, and what actions and objects are relevant. In contrast, our approach relies solely on the teacher's observation of the robot's execution during practice.

19.6   Conclusions

We have presented an *action-based* approach to human–robot interaction and robot learning that addresses aspects of designing socially intelligent robots. The approach was shown to be effective in using implicit, action-based communication and learning by imitation to effectively interact with humans.

We argued that the means of communication and interaction for mobile robots, which do not have anthropomorphic, animal, or pet-like appearance and expressiveness, need not be limited to explicit types of interaction, such as speech or gestures. We demonstrated that simple *body language* could be used allowing the robot to successfully interact with humans and express its intentions and need for help. For a large class of intentions of the type: "I want to do 'this' – but I can't," the process of capturing a human's attention and then trying to execute the action and failing is expressive enough to effectively convey the message and obtain assistance.

Learning capabilities are essential for successful integration of robots in human–robot domains, in order to learn from human demonstrations and facilitate natural interaction with people. Due to inherent challenges of imitation learning, it is also important that robots be able to improve their capabilities by receiving additional training and feedback. Toward this end, we presented an approach that combines imitation learning with additional instructional modalities (relevant *cues*, *generalization*, *practice*), to enable a robot to learn and refine representations of complex tasks. This is made possible by the control architecture that has a perceptual component (*abstract behavior*) that creates the mapping between the observations gathered during demonstration and the robot's behaviors that achieve the same observed effects. We demonstrated these concepts on a Pioneer 2-DX mobile robot, learning various tasks from demonstration, generalization, and practice.

While we believe that robots should be endowed with as many interaction modalities as is possible and efficient, this work focuses on action-based interaction as a lesser studied, but powerful methodology for both learning and human–machine interaction in general.

Acknowledgments

This work was supported by DARPA Grant DABT63-99-1-0015 under the Mobile Autonomous Robot Software (MARS) program and by the ONR Defense University Research Instrumentation Program Grant N00014-00-1-0638.

REFERENCES

Arkin, R. C. (1998). *Behavior-Based Robotics*. Cambridge, MA: MIT Press.

Blllard, A. and Dautenhahn, K. (1999). Experiments in learning by imitation – grounding and use of communication in robotic agents. *Adaptive Behavior*, **7(3/4)**, 415–38.

Breazeal, C. (2002). *Designing Sociable Robots*. Cambridge, MA: MIT Press.

Breazeal, C. and Scassellati, B. (1999). How to build robots that make friends and influence people. *Proceedings of the IROS, Kyonju, Korea*, 858–63.

Cañamero, L. D. and Fredslund, J. (2000). How does it feel? Emotional interaction with a humanoid lego robot. Tech Report FS-00-04, AAAI Fall Symposium, Menlo Park, CA.

Dautenhahn, K. and Nehaniv, C. L. (eds.) (2002). *Imitation in Animals and Artifacts*. Cambridge, MA: MIT Press.

David, A. and Ball, M. P. (1986). The video game: a model for teacher-student collaboration. *Momentum*, **17(1)**, 24–6.

Kortenkamp, D., Hubet, E. and Bonasso, R. P. (1996). Recognizing and interpreting gestures on a mobile robot. *Proceedings of the AAAI*, 915–21.

Dennett, D. C. (1987). *The Intentional Stance*. Cambridge, MA: MIT Press.

Drumwright, E., Jenkins, O. C. and Matarić, M. J. (2004). Exemplar-based primitives for humanoid movement classification and control. In *IEEE International Conference on Robotics and Automation*, 140–5.

Kaplan, F., Oudeyer, P.-Y., Kubinyi, E. and Miklûsi, A. (2002). Robotic clicker training. *Robotics and Autonomous Systems*, **38**, 197–206.

Friedrich, H. and Dillmann, R. (1995). Robot programming based on a single demonstration and user intentions. *Proceedings of the 3rd European Workshop on Learning Robots (EWLR-3), Heraklion, Crete, Greece, April 1995*.

Hayes, G. and Demiris, J. (1994). A robot controller using learning by imitation. *Proceeding of the International Symposium on Intelligent Robotic Systems*, 198–204.

Kaiser, M. (1997). Transfer of elementary skills via human–robot interaction. *Adaptive Behavior*, **5(3–4)**, 249–80.

Matarić, M. J. (1997). Behavior-based control: examples from navigation, learning, and group behavior. *Journal of Experimental and Theoretical Artificial Intelligence*, **9(2–3)**, 323–36.

Matarić, M. J. (2002). Sensory-motor primitives as a basis for imitation: linking perception to action and biology to robotics. In Nehaniv, C. and Dautenhahn, K. (eds.), *Imitation in Animals and Artifacts*. Cambridge, MA: MIT Press, 392–422.

Matsui T., Asoh, H., Hara, I., Motomura, Y., Akaho, S., Kurita, T., Asano, F. and Yamaski, N. (1997). An office conversation mobile robot that learns by navigation and conversation. *Proceedings of the Real World Computing Symposium*, 59–62.

Michaud, F. and Caron, S. (2002). Roball, the rolling robot. *Autonomous Robots*, **12(2)**, 211–22.

Nicolescu, M. (2003). *A Framework for Learning from Demonstration, Generalization and Practice in Human-Robot Domains*. Ph.D. thesis, University of Southern California.

Nicolescu, M. N. and Matarić, M. J. (2001a). Experience-based representation construction: learning from human and robot teachers. In *Proceedings of the IEEE/RSJ International Conference on Intelligent Robots and Systems*, 740–5.

Nicolescu, M. N. and Matarić, M. J. (2001b). Learning and interacting in human–robot domain. *IEEE Transactions on Systems, Man, and Cybernetics, Part A: Systems and Humans, Special Issue on Socially Intelligent Agents – The Human in the Loop*, **31(5)**, 419–30.

Nicolescu, M. N. and Matarić, M. J. (2002). A hierarchical architecture for behavior-based robots. In *Proceedings of the First International Joint Conference on Autonomous Agents and Multi-Agent Systems*, 227–33.

Nicolescu, M. N. and Matarić, M. J. (2003). Natural methods for robot task learning: instructive demonstration, generalization and practice. *Proceedings of the 2nd International Joint Conference on Autonomous Agents and Multi-Agent Systems*, 241–8.

Jenkins, O. C., Matarić, M. J. and Weber, S. (2000). Primitive-based movement classification for humanoid imitation. *Proceedings of the First IEEE-RAS International Conference on Humanoid Robotics*, 858–63.

Gaussier, P., Moga, S., Banquet, J. and Quoy, M. (1998). From perception–action loops to imitation processes: a bottom-up approach of learning by imitation. *Applied Artificial Intelligence Journal*, **12(78)**, 701–29.

Ramesh, A. and Matarić, M. J. (2002a). Learning movement sequences from demonstration. In *Proceedings of the International Conference on Development and Learning*, 203–8.

Ramesh, A. and Matarić, M. J. (2002b). Parametric primitives for motor representation and control. In *IEEE International Conference on Robotics and Automation*, 863–8.

Schaal, S. (1997). Learning from demonstration. In M. C. Mozer, Jordan, M. I. and Petsche, T. (eds.), *Advances in Neural Information Processing Systems 9*. Cambridge, MA: MIT Press, 1040–6.

Lauria, S., Bugmann, G., Kyriacou, T. and Klein, E. (2002). Mobile robot programming using natural language. *Robotics and Autonomous Systems*, **38**, 171–81.

Thrun, S., Bennewitz, M., Burgard, W., Dellaert, F., Fox, D., Haehnel, D., Rosenberg, C., Roy, N., Schulte, J. and Schulz, D. (1999). A second generation mobile tour-guide robot. In *Proceeding of the IEEE International Conference on Robotics and Automation*, 14–26.

Voyles, R. and Khosla, P. (1998). A multi-agent system for programming robotic agents by human demonstration. *Proceedings of the AI and Manufacturing Research Planning Workshop*. Menlo Park, CA: AAAI Press, 184–90.

Werger, B. B. (2000). Ayllu: distributed port-arbitrated behavior-based control. *Proceeding of the The 5th International Symposium on Distributed Autonomous Robotic Systems*, 25–34.

Part VIII

The ecological context

The evolutionary history and ecological context of matching behaviour of various types plays an important role in shaping its character. In this section, two chapters show radically contrasting types of matching in the animal kingdom.

In the first by Ludwig Huber, the capacity of a highly socially intelligent species, the kea (*Nestor notabilis*) for emulation learning of object affordances is demonstrated by a series of ingenious experiments on the behaviour of this playful and curious bird that has not only survived, but thrived despite the invasion of its homeland, New Zealand, by humans and other troublesome mammals. When human-reared, 'enculturated' keas may exhibit even more of a propensity toward social learning by observing others (see the discussions of Tomasello and Call (1997) on the effects of enculturation on primate cognition). Combining their social learning capacity together with individual learning in a successful reconciliation of social and technical cognition, keas have benefited from and continue to employ social learning and curiosity to drive their success in their particular changing ecological context.

This kind of socially intelligent learning is in sharp contrast to the type of matching surveyed by Mark D. Norman and Tom Tregenza in the final chapter of this book. Mimicry here is a form of deceptive resemblance (see Cott, 1940; Wickler, 1968; Hanlon and Messenger, 1998), which in invertebrates is a type of matching generally unlikely to involve much intelligence or learning within individuals, but whose genesis generally operates on evolutionary timescales in particular ecological contexts rather than within the lifetime of single individuals. Mimicry involves the beneficial matching of the behaviour or appearance of another species. Unlike social learning, it might not even involve behaviour at all, although this does appear to be the case in the recently discovered mimic octopus and in other cephalopods such as the Caribbean reefsquid

Imitation and Social Learning in Robots, Humans and Animals, ed. Chrystopher L. Nehaniv and Kerstin Dautenhahn. Published by Cambridge University Press.
© Cambridge University Press 2007.

Sepioteuthis sepioidea (Moynihan and Rodaniche, 1982). The appearance and behaviours of the mimic octopus appear to allow this naked shell-less mollusk to survive in an environment with many dangerous predators (for whom it is essentially a tasty swimming ball of meat) by apparently selectively mimicking an array of dangerous sea creatures.

The vast range of the broad spectrum of types of matching, behavioural or otherwise, in organisms is illustrated by these two chapters which treat organisms at the extremes of this spectrum. In both cases, the evolutionary and ecological contexts have shaped the capacity to match aspects of other individuals' behavioural characteristics. At one end of the spectrum, keas illustrate the adaptive function of matching goals via social learning within a population of conspecifics. At the other end of the spectrum, the invertebrates illustrate the adaptive value of non-communication or deception via matching the appearance of non-conspecifics via evolved capacities for achieving resemblance, such as visual and behavioural camouflage.

REFERENCES

Cott, H. B. (1940). *Adaptive Coloration in Animals*. London: Methuen and Co.
Hanlon, R. T. and Messenger, J. B. (1998). *Cephalopod Behaviour*. Cambridge, UK: Cambridge University Press.
Moynihan, M. and Rodaniche, A. F. (1982). The behavior and natural history of the Caribbean reef squid *Sepioteuthis sepioidea*, with a consideration of social, signal and defensive patterns for difficult and dangerous environments. *Advances in Ethology*, 25, 1–151.
Tomasello, M. and Call, J. (1997). *Primate Cognition*. Oxford, UK: Oxford University Press.
Wickler, W. (1968). *Mimicry in Plants and Animals*. Translated from the German by R. D. Martin. New York: McGraw-Hill.

20 Emulation learning: the integration of technical and social cognition

Ludwig Huber

A decade ago, the term *emulation* had been used by Tomasello (1990) to describe the performance of chimpanzees that seemed to him neither imitative nor a result of simple motivational or attentional influences. However, some researchers have questioned if emulation has been sufficiently well established to be used as a valid alternative in attempts to discover *imitation*, and whether its definition is precise enough for reliable identification of its operation (Byrne, 1998). As is a common feature of the social learning literature, the term has different meanings in different domains (e.g. Wood, 1989; Whiten and Ham, 1992). Let me first recall what Tomasello and his colleagues (Tomasello *et al.*, 1987; Tomasello, 1990, 1996, 1998) have found and then add some recent evidence, including our findings, for this underestimated learning phenomenon. This endeavour will not only reveal that many findings reported in the literature support the emulation learning account if re-evaluated by recent methodological and theoretical developments (Huang *et al.*, 2002; Want and Harris, 2002; Horowitz, 2003; Whiten *et al.*, 2004; Zentall, 2004), but also that imitation has been dramatically overestimated in terms of occurrence and importance.

In a study by Tomasello *et al.* (1987) different groups of chimpanzees were presented with three experimental conditions. The first group observed a conspecific demonstrator using a T-bar to rake food items into reach. The second group observed a chimpanzee simply manipulating the tool without a food item being present. The third group did not observe any demonstrator. Observation of the model did not make the tool more desirable or salient, because all chimpanzees were equally interested in it and manipulated it. Nevertheless, chimpanzees from the first group clearly benefited from the opportunity to watch a skilful conspecific because they obtained the food faster than either of the two other groups of chimpanzees. Yet these successful chimpanzees

Imitation and Social Learning in Robots, Humans and Animals, ed. Chrystopher L. Nehaniv and Kerstin Dautenhahn. Published by Cambridge University Press.

used a different tool technique from the demonstrator, most probably one from their own repertoire. Therefore, those subjects who observed a conspecific using this sort of tool learned something about the task. The authors argued that by watching the stick touch and move the food in particular ways the chimpanzees learned about its function as a tool, and they then incorporated this knowledge into their own attempts at use. Local enhancement and observational conditioning (Heyes, 1994; Zentall, 2004) cannot account for this observational advantage because subjects learned something more specific than the context or the particular stimuli involved. Instead, Tomasello (1990, 1996) suggested that they learned to use the tool via emulation learning because as a result of observation they understand something of the causal structure of the task.

20.1   Distinguishing between imitation and emulation

As I argued some years ago (Huber, 1998), imitation should not be used as the default explanation for how an individual has learned to do something that we consider somewhat unlikely to have been discovered individually. Instead we should take into account the circumstances of, and the subject's experiences prior to, the social learning occasion. In cases where animals are confronted with a difficult object manipulation task, such as in the opening of secured food or the use of tools, it became crucial to determine whether insight into the causal structure of a task is involved. An understanding of either the causal relationships or the intention of the conspecific model's behaviour is likely to reduce what is learned about the finer details of an action. For example, the imitator may attend to the affordances of an object (affordance learning; Huang *et al.*, 2002; Zentall, 2004; Whiten *et al.*, 2004), the goal of the behaviour (goal emulation; Whiten and Ham, 1992; Hobson, 2002), the serial order of the actions involved (sequence learning; Whiten *et al.*, 1996), or the program structure (program-level imitation, Byrne and Russon, 1998). If, however, an understanding of the causal structure of the task is not available, or is beyond the cognitive capacity of an observer, then faithful (slavish) copying of the behaviour of a model, called *mimicry* (Tomasello *et al.*, 1993) or *mimicking* (Tomasello, 1996), is a valuable alternative (Huber, 1998; but see Byrne and Russon, 1998). Using marmosets, such low-level, action-specific imitation was clearly demonstrated (Bugnyar and Huber, 1997; Völkl and Huber, 2000).

Although emulation may be considered as a form of imitation with low copying fidelity (Whiten and Ham, 1992), it seems to me as if this would not capture the essence of this learning process. As stated by Whiten and Custance (1996), 'It is easy to appreciate that in the appropriate circumstances, emulation may represent the cognitively advanced option: an ability to select intelligently just those pieces of information which are useful, neglecting details of behavioural form judged to be redundant, perhaps because the requisite skills needed to bring about the observed result are already in place' (p. 306).

Call and Carpenter (2002) have presented a multi-dimensional frame-work for investigating social learning that is based on focusing on different types of information that a demonstrator produces simultaneously when performing the target action. A demonstrator's model releases at least three products: *goals*, i.e. the final state of affairs the demonstrator wants to bring about; *actions*, i.e. the motor patterns the demonstrator uses to bring about those results, and *results*, i.e. the changes in the environment that are a consequence of the demonstrator's actions. According to this scheme, imitation occurs only if all three types of information are acquired through observation, whereas emulation occurs if only the results are reproduced. Beside these two prominent mechanisms are a number of possibilities of combinations of the three sources of information. For instance, it is possible to reproduce the results, but not the target actions, of a demonstrator from an understanding of the demonstrator's goal (goal emulation). It is also possible to reproduce both actions and results, but fail to understand the demonstrator's goals (mimicking).[1]

The problem with this framework is that it underestimates or ignores other aspects of the model performance that also confer some advantage to the side of the observer. For instance, the observer may also attend to the motivational state of the model, thereby becoming 'energized' and thus being more persistent and willing to find a solution to a difficult task. Moreover, it seems that the demonstrator not only draws the observer's attention to the result of its actions, i.e. the change in the environment brought about by its behaviour, but also to the object or some parts of the object with respect to its function (Huang et al., 2002). By saying that the observer copies or reproduces the result one should emphasize that this may require a quite high level of sensorimotor intelligence and ample experience with similar tasks, leading to learning about the cause–effect relations between tool and goal, which are then incorporated into the observer's own attempts at tool use (Want and Harris, 2002). Indeed, observers might have understood something of the spatial–temporal–causal structure of the task, what Köhler (1921) and Thorpe (1956)

---

[1] See also Carpenter and Call, Chapter 7 this volume; Nehaniv, Chapter 2 this volume. –Ed.

called *insight*. In this sense, emulation learning might be thought of as the cognitivist's answer to local or stimulus enhancement (Tomasello, 1996).

20.2   Studying an unusual species: the kea

Keas (*Nestor notabilis*), the alpine parrots of New Zealand's south island, are a perfect choice for the investigation of non-human social learning abilities and their functional significance in technical problems. The general adaptive ability of this species has been manifested in the bird's outstanding intelligence, curiosity and mischievousness. All these attitudes occur in a highly social environment (Figure 20.1, Plate 1). Keas show a variety of social behaviour, including elaborate play and social manipulation of cooperation (Tebbich *et al.*, 1996). Also foraging is done primarily in groups. These birds remain in family groups and flocks until they are sexually mature.

It was mainly their unusual exploratory and manipulative behaviour that attracted me. I was fascinated by their overall curiosity and especially their interest in novel objects (neophilia) introduced into the aviary, which were immediately investigated, manipulated with great diligence and then oftly destroyed. This exploratory attitude has not manifested itself in the kea's conquering of new habitats, as is characteristic of other curious birds, like the ravens. Instead, it has obviously enabled the kea to have an extremely variable diet, feeding on more than 100 species of plants, complemented by insects, eggs, shearwater chicks and carcasses. Because their foraging is a wholly open and opportunistic process, their diet is the result of essentially trying everything and keeping what works. Perhaps this is the reason why keas survived the mass destruction wrought by human settlement, while a large number of species including ravens were forced into extinction. Even the devastating impact on New Zealand's flora and fauna by the introduction of huge numbers of sheep was turned into an advantage by keas by firstly feeding on sheep carcasses and eventually attacking live sheep to obtain highly nutritious parts from the fatty tissue and the kidney.

When we started to investigate the social learning ability of captive keas in Vienna, Diamond and Bond (1999) published the first complete survey of kea biology, integrating the findings of their several years field observation of keas at Arthur's Pass. From this research the authors developed a sort of evolutionary recipe to describe the factors that promoted the kea's extreme behavioural flexibility. The ingredients are: (1) a lineage predisposed to sociality; (2) low food abundance; (3) short-term limitations

Figure 20.1 (Plate 1) Snapshots showing curious keas (*Nestor notabilis*) in Mt. Cook National Park, New Zealand. Photos by D. Werdenich and B. Voelkl.

on food availability; and (4) delayed maturation and lenience by adults towards the young, so the young have time to play. Object exploration and play seemed to me the most important features of this species with regard to social learning, because the former points to the animal's orientation toward learning and the latter to the animal's orientation towards the social partner. However, whether these two pre-dispositions are actually combined to generate highly developed social learning mechanisms, and whether those are actually used in the wild were open questions at the time that we started our experiments.

20.3   The artificial fruit experiment

The aim of this experiment with captive young keas in Vienna was to examine broadly if keas are influenced by the activity of others in their exploration behaviour and, more specifically, if they also learn something from the skilful performance of conspecific models (Huber *et al.*, 2001). The keas' task was to open the lid of a large box that was fixed to its frame by numerous tricky locking devices. It was adapted from Whiten *et al.*'s (1996) 'artificial fruit' for chimpanzees by functionally mimicking a resource that needed various types of manipulations to open it and extract an edible or otherwise attractive core. The manipulations necessary to dismantle the devices involved twisting a screw, forcefully removing a metal stick and poking a bolt out of rings. We investigated how the opportunity to observe the skilled actions of a trained conspecific influenced the initial attempts to explore and open this 'artificial fruit'. We employed the 'two-action test' (Whiten and Ham, 1992) to enable testing for true imitation *sensu* Thorpe (1956), i.e. whether observers copied a novel or otherwise improbable act demonstrated by the model; two groups of observers with two and three individuals, respectively, were permitted to watch one of two conspecifics demonstrating one of two alternative opening techniques on each device. In addition, five non-observers were used to determine the amount of social effects on motivation, perception or learning in the observers.

The experiment was conducted in a big outdoor aviary at the Konrad Lorenz Institute of Ethology in Vienna. All keas were full siblings bred at the institute and kept with each other since fledging. Two males received training by the method of step-wise approximation to the task of opening the apparatus. These birds were used as models after they became proficient. We allowed the observers to watch the model for about 200 min within three consecutive days, thereby observing about 50 complete openings of the model. They were then tested individually on three consecutive days. Tests were also made with five non-observers, who were completely naive to the task.

What we found surpassed our expectations. The five keas that observed the skilled performances of a demonstrator showed in comparison with the naive birds: (1) faster approach to the locking devices, (2) extended persistence in their manipulative actions, (3) relatively more tactile exploration, and (4) greater success in opening the locking devices.

The highly significant effects of observing a model on manipulation persistence point to the operation of *social facilitation* (Zajonc, 1965). The models' extraordinarily repetitive and persistent activities at the empty box during model training appeared to depend on a very powerful, intrinsic motivation. This may reflect an innate preference for object play and exploration, which are both highly facilitative. We suggest that the combination of a highly active conspecific and a novel object increased the keas' curiosity.

Furthermore, the observers' performances indicated fine-tuned *stimulus enhancement* effects (Spence, 1937; Fritz and Kotrschal, 1999; Fritz *et al.*, 2000) by drawing the observers' attention to the specific parts of the object with which the model was interacting. While the non-observers – though immediately interested in the apparatus – explored the box first, the observers were instantly attending to the locking devices.

Finally, our results provide evidence that the keas learned something important during observation; we found a striking difference between observers and non-observers in their success at opening the three locking devices. Overall, observers opened five times as many devices as the non-observers. One of them opened all three devices within the first two minutes of the test. Given the fact that the observers did not copy the exact details of the opening technique shown by the demonstrator, why were they so extraordinarily efficient? We suggested that having seen the devices used in some way, the observer knows that this functional use is possible for this sort of object. Then, in contrast to imitative learning, observers used what they have learned in devising their own behavioural strategies. We suggested that the keas acquired very specific information about the function or the potential use of the locking devices. Rather than learning that the split pin, for instance, is a signal for food (observational conditioning), or is an attractive object (stimulus enhancement) or has an attractive loop end, the observers have learnt something of the operating characteristics of the locking objects, for instance that the split pin 'can be removed'. It is also possible that they learnt something of the causal relationship between pin and lid, for instance that the pin locks the lid.

One may also agree with Tomasello *et al.* (1987) that a futher plausible explanation of these findings is in terms of a cognitively sophisticated variant of stimulus enhancement. In this interpretation, it is not just the split pin as an object that is made more salient: what is made more salient is the split pin in its function as a locking device. Clearly, a combination of stimulus enhancement (directed to the functional areas of the apparatus) and of prior knowledge of how one object can limit the mobility of another (the split pin as a locking device) could account for this finding. However, as Tomasello (1996) emphasized, just looking in the direction of environmental changes is not enough to learn about and reproduce them; the cognitive capacities of the particular organism and its prior knowledge must always be considered.

In sum, our keas' performance is perfectly predicted by Diamond and Bond (1999), who concluded from detailed observation in the wild that the keas' 'interest in objects for demolition is related more to the objects' affordances than to its potential for providing food resources' (p. 79).

But are keas completely unable to imitate? Even if there were no evidence of imitation in this study, it would be too hasty to conclude that this means that keas do not have the capacity to imitate. It might be argued that the alternative directions of manipulation were too similar at the observers' distance to have such fine-grained effects, or that the differences between the alternatives had no special meaning for the observers in order to copy them. One further reason for the failure to find imitation is that the observers in this experiment saw too much too fast during demonstration sessions (Heyes, pers. comm.). That is, the demonstrated skill may have been too complex, and too swiftly executed, for the observers to learn the actions in the available time, and without prior experience of manipulating the apparatus themselves.

20.4   Technical intelligence in keas

If we restrict our discussion of emulation to those cases in which the reproduction of the results of the model's actions requires some understanding of the means–end relationship between the target action and its resulting change in the environment, it is useful to seek additional, independent evidence for the keas' causal understanding. The apprehension of a cause–effect relation between two or more physical objects determines how objects are manipulated, which of several alternative objects are used, and how the individual responses are assembled into a coherent whole.

In a recent study of keas not involved in the social learning experiments (Werdenich and Huber, 2006), the subjects were confronted with the string-pulling problem (Heinrich, 1995). It involved the presentation of food suspended by a string fixed on a perch, not accessible from the ground or from flight. In order to obtain the food, the birds had to co-ordinate their bill and foot movements involving a sequence of several different steps and repeating the sequence in the correct order several times. All individuals were born in captivity and no string-like objects had been presented to them prior to the onset of the experiment.

Before we started, about a dozen bird species had been tested with the string-pulling task. Our keas seemed to put them all to shame, including ravens (Heinrich, 1995) and Grey parrots (Pepperberg, in press). Within a few seconds of their first attempt, four of seven keas showed the most effective and intelligent solution to this problem. These keas immediately perched above the string with food, then reached down, grasped the string with their bill, and pulled the baited string up. The birds appeared to have achieved these effective solutions spontaneously, because the complete act was accomplished in a rapid and smooth manner, and with the entire absence of fumbling. More importantly, there was no steady improvement of the performance in the course of ten trials, confirming the absence of conditioning. The application of an innate string-pulling response is also very unlikely, because the birds used up to seven different techniques in this study.

Insight into the causal structure of the task enables generalization to variants of the original task. In subsequent tests we forced the keas to choose between two different strings, only one holding a reward. We altered the sessions in various ways, using different rewards and colours for the strings, varied the spatial relationship between the strings, used heavy weights or a string that almost reached the ground. Indeed, in most of the test trials their choice was spontaneous, confirming that they had a functional understanding of the problem. But in the final task, in which we presented a string that reached the ground, the keas seemed to follow a win-stay/lose-shift strategy. Only one female changed her strategy; she remained at some distance for a while, before flying down and obtaining the food directly. After seeing this shortcut her mate also adopted it.

These results confirm and extend the findings by Johnston (1999) investigating string pulling in wild keas. A total of 19 keas were tested and 6 of them solved the problem in their first trial. Although the presence of conspecifics and the vicinity of a ski field might have negatively affected their performance, the significantly better performance of the captive keas in the same task might be primarily a result of higher amounts of stimulation and experience during ontogeny. Extensive interactions with humans can potentiate some human-like social and cognitive skills in animals that their wild counterparts do not seem to possess (Tomasello et al., 1993). Our captive keas in Vienna are permanently confronted with tricky laboratory tasks and have explored dozens of toys and other human artefacts. A recent study, in which we compared the performance of our aviary group with wild keas on their performance at a tube-lifting apparatus (Gajdon *et al.*, 2004), proved this advantage. The superiority of the captive keas was striking.

20.5   Conclusion

Taking our results and the reports from the field together, we suggest that the keas' propensity for exploration, object play and demolition runs counter to the exact reproduction of movements demonstrated by others. Generally, it may be a chief characteristic of explorative and playful animals to employ their own, idiosyncratic methods to manipulate attractive objects. In our captive keas, which are released from an urge to feed, their extreme inclination to explore novel objects and then to play with or demolish them, limits their willingness to copy with high fidelity actions seen in conspecifics. In our experiments we found clear evidence that keas primarily focus on the change of state in the world produced by the manipulations of a demonstrator, thereby uncovering the functional properties of the objects involved. Additionally, the keas may acquire some understanding of the causal relationships among its parts or their role in the process (Tomasello, 1998). However, it would be misleading to say that the keas copied the movement trajectory of the split pin ('object movement re-enactment', Whiten *et al.*, 2004), because the models sometimes threw it away with a swift head movement, and sometimes dropped it immediately after pulling it out of the screw. It is much more plausible to argue that the observers learned that a certain end-state is possible, like 'getting the split pin out of the screw'. However, as Whiten *et al.* (2004) argued, further control experiments would be necessary to clarify this, like presenting the observers only the end-result or final configuration of the model's manipulated apparatus (Huang *et al.*, 2002).

Therefore, affordance learning as originally described by Tomasello *et al.* (1993) and recently addressed in a study by Horner and Whiten (2005) seems at present the most appropriate explanation of our keas' social learning performance. But even in this restricted sense of the label 'emulation' we are facing a range of possible strategies between learning quite simple affordances in the sense of pushing directions, as recently shown by pigeons (Klein and Zentall, 2003), and very intelligent and creative learning processes. This leads to an expectation different from the traditional one that imitation should be shown by particularly intelligent taxa of animals: (slavish) copying of the form of other's acts may be avoided by intelligent species – even if it is within their capability.

Under certain circumstances, even humans show a surprising reluctance to copy exactly the demonstrated (target) action. Children appeared to learn about the dynamic affordances of the objects rather than about the model's intentions or the modelled actions that are not consistent with the object affordances (Huang *et al.*, 2002). Likewise, the variation in adult performances on the same artificial fruit box as used in Whiten *et al.* (1996) for chimpanzees and children indicated the preference for other solutions. It seemed as if humans are able to determine, through observation or quick manipulation, what is actually required to open the artificial fruit. Although the adult behaviour was sometimes influenced by a demonstration, it often was not. Some other, more efficient way seemed to be too compelling for many of the subjects to ignore. Ultimately, functionality overwhelmed their strategy.

In terms of both inferential and representational complexity, this non-imitative social learning account has the appeal of parsimony (Heyes and Ray, 2002). The emulation-learning explanation is simpler than the intentional attribution explanation because it involves only first-order representation (of object properties), whereas the attributing of intentions involves both first-order representation (of body movements) and second-order representation (of the actor's intentions). Although reading adults' intentions may not be irrelevant to imitation of actions by infants, more developmental research is necessary to assess the effect of non-imitative social learning, in accordance to the situation in the animal literature (Want and Harris, 2002). Ultimately, the combined efforts of developmental and comparative psychologists may reveal that emulation is equally important and cognitively complex as imitation and that it should be investigated in its own right.

REFERENCES

Bugnyar, T. and Huber, L. (1997). Push or pull: an experimental study on imitation in marmosets. *Animal Behaviour*, **54**, 817–31.
Byrne, R. W. (1998). Comment on Boesch and Tomasello's 'chimpanzee and human cultures'. *Current Anthropology*, **39(5)**, 604–5.
Byrne, R. W. and Russon, A. E. (1998). Learning by imitation: a hierarchical approach. *Behavioral and Brain Sciences*, **21**, 667–721.
Call, J. and Carpenter, M. (2002). Three sources of information in social learning. In K. Dautenhahn and C. L. Nehaniv (eds.), *Imitation in Animals and Artifacts*. Cambridge, MA: MIT Press, 211–28.
Diamond, J. and Bond, A. B. (1999). *Kea, Bird of Paradox. The Evolution and Behavior of a New Zealand Parrot*. Berkeley: University of California Press.
Fritz, J., Bisenberger, A. and Kotrschal, K. (2000). Stimulus enhancement in greylag geese (*Anser anser*): socially mediated learning of an operant task. *Animal Behaviour*, **59**, 1119–25.

Fritz, J. and Kotrschal, K. (1999). Social learning in common ravens, *Corvus corax*. *Animal Behaviour*, **57(4)**, 785–93.

Gajdon, G. K., Fijn, N. and Huber, L. (2004). Testing social learning in a wild mountain parrot, the kea (*Nestor notabilis*). *Learning and Behavior*, **32**, 62–71.

Heinrich, B. (1995). An experimental investigation of insight in common ravens (*Corvus corax*). *Auk*, **112**, 994–1003.

Heyes, C. M. (1994). Social learning in animals: categories and mechanisms. *Biological Reviews*, **69**, 207–31.

Heyes, C. M. and Ray, E. D. (2002). Distinguishing intention-sensitive from outcome-sensitive imitation. *Developmental Science*, **5**, 34–6.

Hobson, P. (2002). *The cradle of thought. Exploring the origins of thinking*. London: Pan Macmillan.

Horner, V. and Whiten, A. (2005). Causal knowledge and imitation/emulation switching in chimpanzees (*Pan troglodytes*) and children (*Homo sapiens*). *Animal Cognition*, **8**, 164–81.

Horowitz, A. C. (2003). Do humans ape? Or do apes human? Imitation and intention in humans (*Homo sapiens*) and other animals. *Journal of Comparative Psychology*, **117**, 325–36.

Huang, C.-T., Heyes, C. M. and Charman, T. (2002). Infants' behavioral reen actment of 'failed attempts'. Exploring the roles of emulation learning, stimulus enhancement, and understanding of intentions. *Developmental Psychology*, **38(5)**, 840–55.

Huber, L. (1998). Movement imitation as faithful copying in the absence of insight. *Behavioral and Brain Sciences*, **22(5)**, 694.

Huber, L., Rechberger, S. and Taborsky, M. (2001). Social learning affects object exploration and manipulation in keas, *Nestor notabilis*. *Animal Behaviour*, **62**, 945–54.

Johnston, R. (1999). *The Kea (Nestor notabilis): A New Zealand Problem or Problem Solver?* Unpublished Master thesis, University of Canterbury, Christchurch, New Zealand.

Köhler, W. (1921). *The Mentality of Apes*. London: Methuen.

Klein, E. D. and Zentall, T. R. (2003). Imitation and affordance learning by pigeons (*Columba livia*). *Journal of Comparative Psychology*, **117**, 414–19.

Pepperberg, I. (2004). 'Insightful' string pulling in Grey parrots (*Psittacus erithacus*) is affected by vocal competence. *Animal Cognition*, **7**, 263–6.

Spence, K. W. (1937). Experimental studies of learning and higher mental processes in infra-human primates. *Psychological Bulletin*, **34**, 806–50.

Tebbich, S., Taborsky, M. and Winkler, H. (1996). Social manipulation causes cooperation in keas. *Animal Behaviour*, **52**, 1–10.

Thorpe, W. H. (1956). *Learning and Instinct in Animals*. London: Methuen.

Tomasello, M. (1990). Cultural transmission in the tool use and communicatory signaling of chimpanzees? In S. T. Parker and K. R. Gibson (eds.), *"Language" and Intelligence in Monkeys and Apes: Comparative Developmental Perspectives*. Cambridge, UK: Cambridge University Press, 274–311.

Tomasello, M. (1996). Do apes ape? In B. Galef and C. Heyes (eds.), *Social Learning in Animals: The Roots of Culture*. San Diego: Academic Press, 319–46.

Tomasello, M. (1998). Emulation learning and cultural learning. *Behavioral and Brain Sciences*, **21**, 703–4.

Tomasello, M., Davis-Dasilva, M., Camak, L. and Bard, K. (1987). Observational learning of tool-use by young chimpanzees. *Human Evolution*, **2(2)**, 175–83.

Tomasello, M., Kruger, A. C. and Ratner, H. H. (1993). Cultural learning. *Behavioral and Brain Sciences*, **16**, 495–552.

Völkl, B. and Huber, L. (2000). True imitation in marmosets. *Animal Behaviour*, **60**, 195–202.

Want, S. C. and Harris, P. L. (2002). How do children ape? Applying concepts from the study of non-human primates to the developmental study of 'imitation' in children. *Developmental Science*, **5**, 1–13.

Werdenich, D. and Huber, L. (2006). A case of quick problem solving in birds: string-pulling in keas (*Nestor notabilis*). *Animal Behaviour*, **71(4)**, 855–63.

Whiten, A., Custance, D. M., Gomez, J.-C., Teixidor, P. and Bard, K. A. (1996). Imitative learning of artificial fruit processing in children (*Homo sapiens*) and chimpanzees (*Pan troglodytes*). *Journal of Comparative Psychology*, **110**, 3–14.

Whiten, A. and Ham, R. (1992). On the nature and evolution of imitation in the animal kingdom: reappraisal of a century of research. In P. J. B. Slater, J. S. Rosenblatt, C. Beer and M. Milkinski (eds.), *Advances in the Study of Behavior*. New York: Academic Press, Vol. 21, 239–83.

Whiten, A., Horner, V., Litchfield, C. A. and Marshall-Pescini, S. (2004). How do apes ape? *Learning and Behavior*, **32**, 36–52.

Wood, D. (1989). Social interaction as tutoring. In M. H. Bornstein and J. S. Bruner (eds.), *Interaction in Human Development*. Hove, England: Erlbaum, 59–80.

Zajonc, R. B. (1965). Social facilitation. *Science*, **149**, 269–74.

Zentall, T. R. (2004). Action imitation in birds. *Learning and Behavior*, **32**, 15–23.

21 Mimicry as deceptive resemblance: beyond the one-trick ponies

Mark D. Norman and Tom Tregenza

21.1 Introduction

The primary aim of research into artificial intelligence is to replicate biological capabilities either through attempting to directly copy biological mechanisms or by engineering solutions from non-biological principles. Either way, the first hurdle is to replicate the behaviour of animals. The biological phenomenon of mimicry includes a range of behaviours that are of particular interest because they represent a signal–receiver relationship in which the interests of both signallers and receivers are much more clearly defined than in many communication systems. Unlike examples of communication such as mate attraction where it is far from clear what the best evolutionary interests of signaller and receiver are, in mimicry it is generally clear that the mimic aims to deceive the receiver and the receiver aims to avoid being deceived. A second interesting feature of mimicry is that it is possible for human observers to estimate how accurate particular examples of mimicry are through their own (albeit subjective) observations. It is striking that examples of mimicry vary substantially in their accuracy, providing information about the selection pressures acting on the evolution of the trait.

Mimicry is widespread in nature and the term encompasses diverse behaviours, morphologies and/or capacities involving three parties (of up to three species): the imitator (mimic), the imitated (model) and the recipient (signal receiver). These terms may refer to one organism resembling another in order to fool a third (as in the familiar butterfly mimics), in other situations they may refer to mechanisms that aid an individual's reproductive success (as in female impersonation by sneaker males), in others again it may refer to complex learned and acquired abilities used to pass skills from one generation to the next within a species (as in primate learning).

Imitation and Social Learning in Robots, Humans and Animals, ed. Chrystopher L. Nehaniv and Kerstin Dautenhahn. Published by Cambridge University Press.

To narrow the scope of this chapter, we will review the subset of imitation and mimicry that takes the form of 'deceptive resemblance'. This subset consists of adaptations and/or behaviours designed to deceive the senses of target individuals, species or groups. Our aim in this chapter is to provide a brief review of this field with an emphasis on the mimetic behaviours of cephalopods – octopuses, cuttlefish, squid and related free swimming marine invertebrates. Cephalopods are of particular interest in this field because although they lack the large brains of large vertebrates they display the most dramatic and complex examples of mimicry found in any animal group.

21.2   Forms of deceptive resemblance in nature

Deceptive resemblance occurs across many plant and animal groups (Wickler, 1968). Many organisms (from moths and leafy seadragons, to owlet nightjars) match their backgrounds as camouflage. The step beyond camouflage is to allow yourself to be seen, but not to be correctly identified, and thereby avoid rigid restrictions to a particular substrate or context.

The most obvious examples of deceptive resemblance in nature, and by far the best studied are visual. In its simplest form, the deception consists of static visual representations of the shape of an organism or object. Examples are found in both the plant and animal kingdoms. The flowers of many orchid species take the form of female bees or wasps to attract males in order to ensure pollination. Some praying mantises mimic orchid flowers to catch the pollinators. Many moths and butterflies have underwing designs in the perfect shape and markings of dead leaves. Many spiders of the family Araneidae, such as *Celaenia kinbergi*, take the form of bird droppings deposited on leaves. Shallow-water anglerfishes (family Antennariidae), take the form of sponges, complete with siphon-like markings. The juvenile Tinsel Fish (*Grammicolepis brachiusculus*) has greatly extended and branched anal fin rays that trail behind the body, giving this vulnerable open-ocean fish the appearance of a drifting deadly jellyfish colony (siphonophore).

Many mimics supplement their visual deceptions with body motions or behaviours that aid the disguise. Stick insects sway in the wind like a loose stick, taking a step at a time to enable them to move through vegetation without detection. When attacked, caterpillars of some moth species raise the abdomen with a pair of eye markings to resemble a striking snake. Harmless mimic butterflies have flight patterns that match their poisonous butterfly models. Flatworms such as *Pseudoceras imitatus* bunch up their body to move like the poisonous sea slug *Phyllidiella pustulosa*

(Newman and Cannon, 2003). Some juvenile batfish (e.g. *Platax pinnatus*) mimic poisonous flatfishes, swimming on their side in an undulating, very un batfish-like manner. The False Cleanerfish, *Aspidontus taeniatus*, is a blenny that looks and behaves just like the genuine Cleaner Wrasse, *Labroides dimidiatus*. These mimics establish cleaner stations complete with the welcoming dance that lures customers in to be cleaned, instead to have chunks bitten out of them.

Not all deceptive mimicry is restricted to visual forms. Chemical mimicry is also common. A plant known as the Dead-horse Arum impersonates the smell of rotting meat to attract insect pollinators (Stensmyr *et al.*, 2002). The spider *Cosmophasis bitaeniata* wears cuticular hydrocarbons that exactly match the pheromones of the ants on which this spider preys (Elgar and Allen, 2004). Wearing this chemical cloak, the spider is free to walk into the inner sanctums of the ant colony to feed on fat ant larvae. The chemical coatings of clownfishes mimic the taste of the tentacles of the host anemone, thus preventing discharge of the stinging cells and ensuring the fishes' protection. Pelagic octopuses such as the Blanket Octopus (genus *Tremoctopus*) and the argonauts (genus *Argonauta*) employ the same deception to commandeer the defences of open-ocean jellyfishes (Jones, 1963; Norman, 2000; Norman *et al.*, 2002).

Vocal or audio mimicry also occurs. Many birds such as bower birds, mynahs and parrots, employ mimicry of the calls and noises of other animals. The Superb Lyrebird, *Menura novaehollandiae*, is capable of a wide repertoire of mimicked calls and sounds primarily based on local bird species (Higgins *et al.*, 2001). Such capacities clearly have an environmental and ontological component. In regions adjacent to urban development, individuals intersperse their calls with impersonations of barking dogs, chainsaws, mobile phones and even crude parodies of human speech.

21.3 Fixed vs. dynamic mimicry

Mimicry of dead leaves   (Figure 21.1, Plate 2) provides an example of the increasing levels of complexity in mimicry found in nature. The Australian Leaf-wing Butterfly, *Dolleschallia bisaltide* (Figure 21.1a), has underwing patterns identical to a dead leaf. This static mimicry only occurs in the adult life-cycle stage. The Cockatoo Waspfish, *Ablabys taenianotus* (Figure 21.1b), resembles dead leaves for most of the fish's life cycle, supplementing the deception by swaying back and forth to resemble a light leaf moving in the seafloor currents or swell. The juvenile Round Batfish, *Platax orbicularis* (Figure 21.1c), drifts along in the current like

Figure 21.1   Leaf mimicry.
a. Australian Leaf-Wing Butterfly, *Dolleschallia bisaltide*; b. Cockatoo Waspfish, *Ablabys taenianotus*; c. Juvenile Round Batfish, *Platax orbicularis*; d. Broadclub Cuttlefish, *Sepia latimanus* 'impersonating' dead mangrove leaf; e. same individual in resting colour pattern. Photos: M. Norman.

a dead leaf with a heavy trailing stem. The most impressive 'dead leaf' is the temporary guise donned by the Broadclub Cuttlefish, *Sepia latimanus* (Figure 21.1d, Norman, 2000). It impersonates dead mangrove leaves when moving over open ground, bobbing along complete with stem, veins and leaf spot markings. Once back in the cover of protective coral, the guise is dropped and the animal returns to its more normal colour patterns (Figure 21.1e).

The vast majority of mimics that use deceptive resemblance are one-trick ponies. The deceptions tend to be fixed and place restrictions on the organism's ability to transfer to different contexts or strategies. Transformations between juvenile and adult forms occur in some groups, however the mimicry is typically restricted to either the juvenile or adult stages (i.e. juvenile fishes or adult insects). Very few animals are capable of switching their mimicry to different models.

Certain fishes and lizards (i.e. chameleons) can undergo gradual colour or marking changes. Anglerfishes can slowly transform their colours and markings to mimic different sponges or sea squirts. Ant Mimic Spiders can gradually switch ant colonies by modifying the identifying pheromones to match the new colonies. However, all these processes are slow. An Ant Mimic Spider taken from one colony and dropped into the centre of a distant new colony will immediately be attacked and killed.

Transient leaf mimicry by the Broadclub Cuttlefish shows the unique transformational capabilities of the cuttlefishes, squids and octopuses (the *cephalopods*). Of all the examples in nature, the cephalopods are the most dynamic, able to don the tool of mimicry as one of a suite of defensive, feeding and/or reproductive strategies. Certain species are also capable of mimicry of multiple models.

21.4   The cephalopods

Of all the forms of deceptive resemblance, it is those found in the octopuses and their relatives (the cephalopods) that are the most complex. Cephalopods have a number of unique morphological attributes that enable dramatic colour and shape transformations, and complex behaviours.[1] They have well-developed brains and neural networks, particularly in the cuttlefishes and octopuses (see Nixon *et al.*, 2003). The brain consists primarily of large optic lobes with the majority of the computing power being related to visual interpretation and representation. With the exception of the nautiluses, cephalopods lack external protection. In cuttlefishes, the gas-filled shell is reduced to the internal cuttlebone. In squids, the shell is further reduced to a chitinous and flexible gladius. Octopuses have lost the shell completely. For the vast majority of cephalopods, the entire body is muscular with the absence of rigid internal skeleton or external armour. As a result, the plastic/elastic body is not as restricted in shape as it is in groups such as the crustaceans. Octopuses are the most plastic in form and are able to extrude themselves

---

[1] See Hanlon and Messenger (1996) for a comprehensive introduction to these fascinating animals. –Ed.

through tiny openings that are almost as small as their eye diameter. Conversely muscle contractions enable limbs to be used as rigid structures for manipulating struggling prey, in predator deterrence or in construction of lairs.

Other than the nautiluses, the entire external surfaces of cephalopods are covered in soft skin. In many species this unique and complex organ is capable of colour, pattern and shape changes. Colour and pattern changes are effected by three types of structures in the skin (Mangold *et al.*, 1989): *chromatophores*, *leucophores* and *iridophores*. Chromatophores are tiny elastic pigment-filled sacs surrounded by spoked muscle fibres that enable these tiny dots to be rapidly expanded and contracted. Chromatophores come in up to five colours and in densities of up to 200–300 per square millimetre. These act in concert to produce markings, patterns and colour shifts. They are neurally controlled at numerous levels from individual chromatophores to subunits within set patterns, to half and whole body colour flushes. Leucophores are fixed structures that form the white components of markings and patterns. Iridophores are the reflective component of the skin, reflecting ambient light or, in certain species, selecting particular wavelengths (as in the spectacular blue rings of the blue-ringed octopuses).

The texture of the skin can also be modified in different species, particularly in the cuttlefishes and bottom-living octopuses. Rings or strips of circular muscle can be contracted to project spikes or flaps of skin. Secondary rings of muscle on the sides of raised papillae enable branched 'trees' of skin to be raised and lowered.

21.5   Mimicry in cephalopods

Figures 21.2 (Plate 3) and 21.3 (Plate 4) provide examples of the increasing levels of deceptive resemblance exhibited by cephalopods. It is important to note that the following examples are transient behaviours within diverse behavioural repertoires, not permanent guises.

Many cephalopod species are excellent at camouflage, employing the matching tones, pattern and skin sculpture to perfectly merge into their backgrounds (e.g. Figures 21.2a–b). Mimicry goes beyond camouflage when the model stands alone as a deception independent of the background. Static mimicry examples in cephalopods include rock impersonations and representations of seaweed, as in the Indo-Malayan Hairy Octopus (*Octopus* sp. 16, Norman, 2000, Figure 21.2c). Certain octopus species add motion to their algal impersonations. Octopuses such as the Southern Keeled Octopus, *Octopus berrima*, bob along like drifting seaweed, complete with raised and coiled tendril arms (M. Norman,

Figure 21.2 (Plate 3) Camouflage and deceptive resemblance in
cephalopods.
a. *Octopus* sp. 5 (Norman, 2000) active in rock pools; b. same individual moments later in camouflage; c. Hairy Octopus (*Octopus* sp. 16
(Norman, 2000)) showing branching skin sculpture; d. Snail Mimic
Octopus (*Octopus* sp. 6 (Gosliner *et al.*, 1996)); e. Giant Cuttlefish, *Sepia
apama* – sneaker male (centre) impersonating female amongst breeding
pair (male on right) Photos: a, b, e: M. Norman; c: Becca Saunders; d.
M. Severns.

pers. obs.). They time their forays across open sand to synchronize with
the pulses of the swell to give the appearance of tumbling loose seaweed.

As described above, the Broadclub Cuttlefish, *Sepia latimanus*, is capable of mangrove leaf mimicry, bobbing along in the current (Norman,

2000). Figure 21.1d shows the side view of the animal in this guise. As the head-on view may give away the fact that the animal has more bulk than a drifting mangrove leaf, the arms are held in a way that makes the animal look like a different perspective of a complete leaf.

Hanlon and Messenger (1996) reported parrotfish impersonation by the Caribbean Reef Squid, *Sepioteuthis sepioidea*. These squid produce black eye-like spots on either side of the body and draw their arms into a tail-like shape. The squid travel within moving schools of herbivorous parrotfish, waving their arms side-to-side to resemble the swimming motion of the fish. Hanlon and Messenger speculated that this behaviour provided both a defensive guise against predators and also enabled the squid to approach prey undetected. This squid species has also been reported to mimic drifting weed and even its own ink squirts as a last defence from pursuers (Moynihan, 1985).

The senior author has observed impersonation of garden eels (*Gorgasia japonica*) by a related squid species in Indonesia, the Bigfin Reef Squid, *Sepioteuthis lessoniana*. These eels form dense colonies on sand areas where they feed on passing plankton while retaining their tails within burrows. When approached by potential predators, these fishes rapidly retract into their burrows. On approaching such a bed of garden eels in Northern Sulawesi, an individual squid was observed and filmed in an extended, vertical, eel-like posture. The squid's posture was completed by the tentacles bent to one side to mimic the curved neck and head of the eel.

A small undescribed octopus in Indonesia (*Octopus* sp. 6, Gosliner *et al.*, 1996) mimics gliding gastropod snails as it forages over coral faces. Body markings match the small patches of algae that grow on the shells and the octopus moves by drawing the arm tips under the body and tiptoeing along on the tips of the suckers (Figure 21.2d). A variant on this theme has been observed in an undescribed species from the Great Barrier Reef (*Octopus* sp. 4, Norman, 2000). This species mimics rambling hermit crabs by holding the body in the same ovoid shape of a shell, bunching the arm tips up under the body and ambling along on the 'elbows' in a jerky erratic fashion that matches the behaviour of foraging hermit crabs found in the area (Japan Underwater Films, 2001).

The males of at least one cuttlefish species are capable of mimicking the opposite sex in order to enhance mating success. At large breeding aggregations, small males of the Giant Cuttlefish, *Sepia apama*, switch between the appearance of a female and that of a male in order to foil the guarding attempts of larger territorial males (Norman *et al.*, 1999). Mature male Giant Cuttlefish have long webbed arms and display zebra stripes along their body, while females have shorter arms and typically show a blotched colour pattern. Sneaker males in this species retract their arms and show the blotched colour pattern (Figure 21.2e). While the larger males are distracted in disputes with other males, these sneaker males rapidly display their maleness and attempt to mate with the egg-laying females, often with success.

The most impressive example of dynamic mimicry is the recently dis-covered Mimic Octopus (Norman and Hochberg, 2005) from the Indo-Malayan Archipelago (Norman *et al.*, 2001). This octopus forages over exposed sand and mud substrates during daylight hours, fully exposed to passing fish predators and protected solely by a diverse mimicry repertoire. The Mimic Octopus establishes lairs in the burrows of other animals, typically in the tops of Acorn Worm mounds (Figure 21.3a). When emerged, this species forages over sand in drab brown coloura-tion, probing arms into burrows (Figure 21.3b). When swimming by jet propulsion close to the sea floor, the octopus draws the arms around its body to form an elongate oval shape (Figure 21.3c). The markings and swimming motion match that of poisonous sole, *Zebrias* sp., common in the region (Figure 21.3d). At other times, this octopus swims above the seafloor with banded arms extended around the body (Figure 21.3e), taking on the form of a lionfish (*Pterois* sp.) with its long banded banner-like spines (Figure 21.3f). This octopus has also been observed to adopt a posture where six arms are threaded down a hole and two are raised in opposite directions, banded, curled and undulated (Figure 21.3g), in the form of a banded sea-snake (*Laticauda* sp.) (Figure 21.3h). This posture was most commonly adopted in response to attacks by small territo-rial damselfishes (*Amphiprion* spp.). All these models occur in the same exposed sand habitat and are either poisonous or are armed with other defences (such as stinging cells). Other mimicry has also been reported for this species including mimicry of solitary stinging anemones, the heads of buried Crocodile Snake Eels and stingrays (Steene, 1998).

21.6   Origins of dynamic mimicry

The Mimic Octopus lives in a specific habitat type: shallow-water soft substrates (sand, silt and mud) in clear tropical waters, typically adjacent to river mouths. This environment is rich in food with myriad small inver-tebrates and fishes living in or on the substrate, feeding on the rich organic nutrients that flow from the adjacent rivers. Despite this rich infauna, this is a dangerous environment for larger bottom-living animals. There is no hard cover or protection from the many passing visual predators such as schools of barracouta and giant trevally. Most bottom-living predators in this system emerge from the substrate or move into this habitat under the

Figure 21.3   Mimic Octopus (*Octopus* sp. 19 (Norman, 2000)) and models.
a. sentinel state in mouth of burrow; b. normal foraging colour pattern; c. flatfish mimicry; d. flatfish model, banded sole (*Zebrias* sp.); e. lionfish mimicry; f. lionfish model (*Pterois* sp.); g. sea snake mimicry; h. sea snake model, banded sea snake (*Laticauda* sp.). Photos: a, b, d-f: M. Norman; c, g, h: R. Steene.

cover of darkness. The primary animals able to emerge during daylight hours are those equipped with strong toxins or defences. In the midst of this is the Mimic Octopus. How did the mimicry skills of this animal evolve?

There are two possible evolutionary scenarios: repertoires are either learned or are hard-wired. In other words, does the complexity derive from sophisticated neural and learning capabilities that are rediscovered by each generation, or are the forms of mimicry innate and genetically based? To date, there are no reports of the behaviour of juvenile Mimic Octopuses. There is no evidence of learning in the Mimic Octopus, nor for any of the other cephalopod species cited. Studies of other octopus species (Boal et al., 2000) suggest that the learning capacities of these animals are limited. As cephalopods lack any form of parental care (all being independent from birth), there is no protective environment in which the first crude attempts at mimicry could be trialled, i.e. learning to mimic models present in the same habitat. With the high numbers of visual predators commonly passing over this exposed habitat, there would be limited room for error. It is far more likely, instead, that the observed repertoires are hard-wired from birth in the form of genetic memory, the product of millennia of selective pressures.

A scenario can be envisaged where an ancestor to this octopus resided in coral reef or rubble habitats adjacent to these food rich soft substrate habitats. Under pressure within this habitat or in order to access prey in the soft substrates, short forays from the refuge of the coral may have been made out onto the mud. Slight resemblance in form or motion to toxic models found in the area would convey slight advantage to individuals. This advantage could take the form of momentary hesitation by a predator or discounting it as a prey item from a distance. Under extreme predation pressure and over millennia, these slight advantages would be selected for until the mimicry became fixed and the animals no longer required the refuge of adjacent reefs.

The evolution of mimicry of multiple models is a more complex question than the evolution of mimicry per se. Multiple mimicry occurs through genetic polymorphism (individuals of different genotypes have different mimicry phenotypes) in a number of groups, notably papilionid butterflies and hoverflies (Mallet and Joron, 1999), but in general is much less common than might be expected (Joron and Mallet, 1998). One possible explanation for the rarity of polymorphic mimics is frequent selection towards the most noxious or abundant model (Turner, 1984; Speed, 1993). Alternatively, polymorphism may be rare because of the tight linkage between mimicry genes that is necessary to prevent recombination (the shuffling of lengths of DNA that occurs during the production of gametes) breaking up the co-adapted complex of the many genes needed to produce a convincing mimic.

The dynamic mimicry of the mimic octopus may escape this genetic constraint because it is not employed continuously: all individuals can carry alleles for all forms of mimicry simultaneously. This has been described as a 'neural polymorphism', whereby cephalopods gain the benefits of polymorphism, such as increased apparent rarity, without genetic polymorphism (Hanlon and Messenger, 1996). The potential for a lower frequency of specific predator–morph encounters may also allow the octopus to use mimicry that is less accurate than that seen in species where permanent mimicry is employed. It is the absence of a rigid skeleton and the transformational properties of the skin of cephalopods that make this dynamic mimicry possible.

Dynamic mimicry has the unique advantage that it can be employed facultatively, with the octopus adopting a form best suited to the perceived threat at any given time. Evidence for such sophisticated behaviour comes from the observation that on all occasions when sea-snake mimicry was observed it was exclusively a reaction to an attack by territorial damselfishes (Norman *et al.*, 2001). In discussions of these complex behaviours, human subjectivity tends to seek examples of apparent cleverness or learned capacities. However, there is no shortage of examples of animal groups with complex innate capacities.

Acknowledgments

The senior author wishes to thanks the AISB for support to attend the Symposium on Imitation in Animals and Artefacts in Aberystwyth, Wales in 2003. TT is funded by a Royal Society Fellowship. Both authors would like to thank the encouragement and support of Kerstin Dautenhahn and Chrystopher Nehaniv, and three reviewers for perceptive comments on an earlier version of this chapter.

REFERENCES

Boal, J. G., Wittenberg, K. M. and Hanlon, R. T. (2000). Observational learning does not explain improvement in predation tactics by cuttlefish (*Mollusca cephalopoda*). *Behavioural Processes*, **52**, 141–53.

Elgar, M. A. and Allan, R. A. (2004). Predatory spider mimics acquire colony-specific cuticular hydrocarbons from their ant model prey. *Naturwissenschaften*, **91(3)**, 143–7.

Gosliner, T. M., Behrens, D. W. and Williams, G. C. (1996). *Coral Reef Animals of the Indo-Pacific*. Monterey: Sea Challengers.

Higgins, P. J., Peter, J. M. and Steele, W. K., eds. (2001). *Handbook of Australian, New Zealand & Antarctic Birds*, Volume 5 (Tyrant-flycatchers to Chats). Oxford University Press, Melbourne.

Hanlon, R. T. and Messenger, J. B. (1996). *Cephalopod Behaviour.* Cambridge, UK: Cambridge University Press.

Japan Underwater Films (2001). *Amazing Creatures: Squid and Octopus.* Natural History Documentary Film.

Jones, E. C. (1963). *Tremoctopus violaceus* uses *Physalia* tentacles as weapons. *Science*, **139**, 764–6.

Joron, M. and Mallet, J. L. B. (1998). Diversity in mimicry: paradox or paradigm? *Trends in Ecology and Evolution*, **13**, 461–6.

Mallet, J. R. B and Joron, M. (1999). Evolution of diversity in warning color and mimicry: polymorphisms shifting balances, and speciation. *Annual Reviews of Ecological Systems*, **30**, 201–33.

Mangold, K., Bidder, A., Bidder, M. and Portmann, A. (1989). Structures cutanées. In Mangold, K. (ed.), *Traité de Zoologie, Tome V, Cephalopodes.* Paris: Masson, 121–62.

Moyniham, M. (1985). *Communication and Noncommunication by Cephalopods.* Bloomington: Indiana University Press.

Newman, L. and Cannon, L. (2003). *Marine Flatworms: The World of Polyclads.* Collingwood, Australia: CSIRO Publishing.

Nixon, M., Allen, R. E. and Young, J. Z. (2003). *The Brains and Lives of Cephalopods.* Oxford, UK: Oxford University Press.

Norman, M. D., Finn, J. and Tregenza, T. (1999). Female impersonation as an alternative reproductive strategy in giant cuttlefish. *Proceedings of the Royal Society, London*, **266**, 1347–9.

Norman, M. D. (2000). *Cephalopods: A World Guide.* IKAN Publishing, Frankfurt, 320.

Norman, M. D., Finn, J. and Tregenza, T. (2001). Dynamic mimicry in an Indo-Malayan octopus. *Proceedings of the Royal Society, London*, **268**, 1755–8.

Norman, M. D. and Hochberg, F. G. (2005). The "Mimic Octopus" (*Thaumoctopus mimicus* n. gen. et sp.), a new octopus from the tropical Indo-West Pacific (Cephalopoda Octopodidae). *Molluscan Research*, **25**, 57–70.

Norman, M. D., Paul, D., Finn, J. and Tregenza, T. (2002). First encounter with a live male blanket octopus: the worlds most sexually size-dimorphic large animal. *New Zealand Journal of Marine and Freshwater Research*, **36**, 733–6.

Speed, M. P. (1993). Muellerian mimicry and the psychology of predation. *Animal Behaviour*, **45**, 571–80.

Steene, R. (1998). *Coral Seas.* Bathurst: Crawford House Publishing.

Stensmyr, M. C., Urru, I., Collu, I., Celander, M., Hansson, B. S. and Angioy, A. (2002). Rotting smell of Dead-horse Arum florets. *Nature*, **420**, 625–6.

Turner, J. R. G. (1984). Mimicry, the palatability spectrum and its consequences. In Vane-Wright, R. I. and Ackery, P. R. eds. *The Biology of Butterflies.* London, Orlando: Published for The Royal Entomological Society by Academic Press, 141–61.

Wickler, W. (1968). *Mimicry in Plants and Animals.* Weidenfeld and Nicolson, London, 153.

Index

476   Index